# Income Property Valuation

# Income Property Valuation

## Principles and Techniques of Appraising Income-Producing Real Estate

William N. Kinnard, Jr.
Center for Real Estate and Urban
Economic Studies
University of Connecticut

**Heath Lexington Books**
D.C. Heath and Company
Lexington, Massachusetts

Published simultaneously in Canada

Printed in the United States of America

International Standard Book Number: 0-669-74245-7

Library of Congress Catalog Card Number: 74-153365


Year and number of this printing:

91   92   23

# Contents

# List of Exhibits

# Preface

Appraising income-producing real estate is a challenging, stimulating, and intellectually rewarding occupation. The problems posed by clients or employers who need help in making investment decisions are frequently complex. They are nearly always significant in community development as well. The skills required are exacting and the judgments nice. The standards of analysis and performance imposed on appraisers are being raised continually, as the demands of appraisal problems increase and the significance of the decisions on which appraisals are based expands.

This book is directed toward the student of appraisal, with or without experience in the residential property field, who has little or no background in income property valuation. It deals with basic principles and techniques. It introduces the income capitalization process as a fundamental but extremely powerful tool of analysis. It assumes an understanding and working knowledge of the principles of real estate, the nature of real property interests, and the structure and operations of real estate markets. It expects the reader to be able to work comfortably with simple algebra and elementary mathematical processes. Most importantly, it assumes prior exposure to the principles and techniques of real estate appraisal *other than* income capitalization, through either formal course work or meaningful applied experience in residential property appraising, or both.

Starting from this presumed base of working knowledge and/or experience, the present volume provides the means to develop and sharpen the analytical tools and skills required in income-property appraising. It offers the opportunity to acquire these skills from a combination of the best current thinking of valuation theorists and the cumulative experience of leading appraisal practitioners. The reader is given the benefit of this thinking and experience to develop a strong foundation of skill and knowledge. His own subsequent experience can be superimposed on that foundation, and combined with it to create ultimately the professional judgment sorely needed in making income property appraisals.

Many of the ideas and some of the terminology presented here are relatively new to appraisal literature. They represent carefully considered efforts to improve, expand, or clarify communication and understanding in the appraisal field. Much of the material in this volume is not new or different, but it is presented in a framework that is somewhat innovative. That framework treats appraisal analysis, especially income-property appraisal analysis, as a systematic effort in problem-solving directed at rational investor decision-making. It incorporates much of the modern approach to financial investment decision-making. It introduces elements of flexibility and adaptability that make the tools of income-property valuation analysis applicable to an almost infinite variety of appraisal problem situations. Moreover, the approach has been successfully tested and refined in appraisal classes over several years.

Although the actual organization of the materials and the writing of the book have been the work of one individual, the author has intellectual obligations to many previous contributors to the body of appraisal theory and literature. In particular, the late Dr. David T. Rowlands provided the initial stimulus to my entry into the field of real estate finance and valuation. The pioneering but incomprehensibly neglected work of Dr. Frederick A. Babcock has long been a source of excellent analysis and stimulating ideas. So, too, have been the writings of L.W. Ellwood and Dr. Alfred A. Ring. Over many years, I have benefited greatly from personal communications as well as the publications of Dr. Richard U. Ratcliff, Dr. James A. Graaskamp, James E. Gibbons, and M.B. Hodges, Jr.

I have received continuing support and the opportunity to test new ideas from my colleagues at the University of Connecticut: Dr. Byrl N. Boyce, Dr. Robert O. Harvey, and Dr. Sidney Turoff. In addition, Dr. Jerome J. Dasso at the University of Oregon has commented on several points that are presented in improved form as the result of his suggestions.

Many officials of the Society of Real Estate Appraisers have been particularly helpful in offering critical commentary to improve, correct, and encourage the production of the materials in this book. They include: Joseph A. Nowicki, E.B. Horton, Jr., William C. Coyle, Bernard Carmichael, Bruce A. Saunders, Wayne A. Hagood, and H. Grady Stebbins, Jr. Special thanks are due John J. Deisher, who reviewed the entire manuscript and made many useful suggestions and corrections. The Society of Real Estate Appraisers has generously released materials that I developed earlier, for incorporation in this volume.

Thanks are also due Mrs. Christina Concepcion for her typing skill and secretarial effort. It is impossible to express adequate appreciation to Mrs. Jean C. Alcorn for her untiring help in organizing and carrying out the production and editing schedule that resulted in the finished manuscript. Moreover, she unselfishly supervised and maintained the author's schedule so that this book actually materialized.

Finally, two colleagues require special recognition and thanks for their continuing help, support and commentary over the several years when this book was transformed from a series of ideas to scattered notes to a course syllabus to its present form. Dr. Stephen D. Messner, Director of the Center for Real Estate and Urban Economic Studies at the University of Connecticut, has always been available to react to an idea or to suggest a more effective way to present it. More importantly, he has consistently served as a reliable but critical sounding board. Donald E. Snyder, Staff Vice-President of the Society of Real Estate Appraisers, has worked closely with me since 1962 in the development, presentation, and evaluation of course materials from which most of this book is derived. To both of them goes my heartfelt appreciation for helping make it a reality.

Even with all this assistance and professional criticism, there may well be erroneous or contentious statements in the book. For these, and for all the opinions or judgments expressed, the author must of course remain solely responsible.

**William N. Kinnard, Jr.**

Storrs, Connecticut
February 1971

# Income Property Valuation

**Part I
Background
to Income Property
Valuation**

# 1 Introduction and Statement of Purpose

**Problem-Solving for Decision-Makers**

Real estate appraisals are made because someone has a problem. An investor is considering the purchase of a property and wants to know how much the interest in the real estate that he might acquire is "worth." A lending institution has been asked to make a loan on a property, and the loan officer (and his superiors) need to know how much they can "safely" or "prudently" lend. A property owner is considering selling, and wants to know how much his property is "worth." A tenant seeks to buy up the remaining term of his lease and wants to know how much he "should" pay. A public agency has condemned a property, and the court needs advice in deciding how much compensation should be awarded the property owner.

In these and countless other decision situations involving the use and transfer of real estate—some of them extremely complex as legal and financial issues—a decision-maker is confronted with a problem that requires an estimate of the value of specified rights in real estate in order to solve that problem. Such an estimate is an appraisal.[1] If it is professionally produced, the estimate of value will be economically and financially defensible in terms of a specified set of market conditions or decision criteria. It will be supportable in the courts if necessary. However it is produced, the estimate of value is a *measure* of value expressed in dollars: the answer to the question "How much?"

The structure of real estate appraisal analysis is predicated on a rational decision-making approach by informed decision-makers. That is to say, once presented with the best available information about the alternatives or decision choices confronting him, the decision-maker is presumed to apply impeccable logic in selecting the alternative course of action that promises to come closest to his stated objective. Real estate decision-makers, especially those dealing with income-producing properties, are generally seeking to maximize or optimize their economic well-being. This translates to selecting the alternative that appears to offer the most present wealth or highest current dollar value, usually based on a forecast future stream of benefits or dollar income to be received. The "best available information" on which the decision choice is made is (or should be) provided by an appraisal.

As noted above, real estate appraisal problems can arise from a wide variety of decision-choice situations confronting many different potential participants in a proposed real estate transaction. Decision-makers needing and seeking an appraisal are typically action-oriented, and usually want help to determine the best course of action for them in terms of their decision standards. One course of action that is frequently overlooked by potential decision-makers is to take

3

no action at all, and therefore not to go through with the proposed transaction. One of the most meaningful uses of a professionally competent real estate appraisal is to lead a potential participant in a transaction to the conclusion that he should *not* proceed as planned, but withdraw from that transaction.

Real estate appraisers must usually work under less than ideal conditions, particularly because of time pressures and/or the unavailability of data required or desired to complete their analysis. Yet the best possible judgment must be reached about how much (in dollars) the property interests being appraised are worth under the market conditions or decision standards specified in the appraisal problem. This is why different, alternative techniques for approaching a professionally acceptable and reliable valuation conclusion have arisen. There are different perspectives in looking at an appraisal problem, depending in part on the identity and point of view of the party whose actual or projected interests are to be valued. The perspectives also depend on the nature of those interests, which indicate what claim the party involved has on the future income or benefits anticipated to be produced by the real estate, and over what time period. They depend further on what value is to be estimated, which is considered in some detail in Chapter 2. Each perspective has different data requirements and calls for slightly varied techniques to produce a defensible value estimate that is appropriate to the standards set by the problem.

These different perspectives are significant because the appraiser, in applying the tools of analysis at his disposal to the problem at hand, seeks to simulate the thought processes and analytical approaches of one decision-maker or potential participant. It is often a purportedly typical or most probable decision-maker rather than a particular one with specified individual standards. The character of the decision-maker identifies the perspective from which the appraiser approaches his problem. He must therefore consider the alternative courses of action potentially available to the decision-maker or client to reach a value conclusion consistent with the decision-maker's objectives. The so-called approaches to valuation are merely simulations of these alternative courses of action potentially open to the decision-maker.[2]

The appraiser does not exercise judgment about what the decision-maker's objectives or choice criteria "ought" to be, or what market conditions "ought" to be considered in making the decision. These are given by the conditions of the problem. The appraiser's judgments concern the applicability of alternative tools of analysis to the facts of the case, the data and information needed to apply those tools, and the selection of the analytical approach and data most responsive to the problems at hand. One of these analytical tools which is peculiarly applicable to the valuation of interests in income-producing real estate is income capitalization. Because of its specific usefulness in income property appraisal, the development of the framework of income capitalization analysis occupies the bulk of this book and represents its primary focus.

## Objectives of the Book

The basic purpose of this book is to introduce the reader or student to the basic framework of analysis for income property valuation. It presents the tools of analysis available to appraise interests in income-producing real estate, and explains the principles on which they are based. It demonstrates the applicability of these tools to a variety of income property appraisal problems, and identifies the basis for selecting specific tools to cope with particular problems. It provides an opportunity to develop technical appraisal skills by offering periodic Review Exercises that call for application of the tools to representative appraisal problems. In brief, it seeks to equip the reader or student with the necessary skills and mastery of technique to begin appraising income property interests in a professionally acceptable and meaningful way.

This book is specifically designed to serve as a text in an intermediate or second-level course on Principles of Income Property Appraising. The progressive development of the materials reflects this design. The individual reader can use it as a reference source as well as a tool for learning, however. Because of its text characteristics, it seeks to complement the knowledge and skills acquired in previous course work in appraisal principles.

The analytical tools emphasized here are those which are most widely applicable and most flexibly adaptable to the many varieties of basic valuation problems that confront the professional income-property appraiser. Not all are universally accepted as current orthodoxy, but they do represent the best current (and past) thinking on the subject and have been gathered from several sources. Mastery of the basic principles emphasized in the earlier sections of the book, together with a good working knowledge of the techniques presented and illustrated later, should equip the student to cope effectively with all known current appraisal problems as well as those most likely to emerge in the foreseeable future. The framework of systematic analysis put forward here can be adapted to the specifics of any given appraisal problem. The mechanics and the underlying principles are constant; only the format of combinations in which they are used need change as individual appraisal circumstances dictate.

Finally, this volume seeks to explain *why* particular approaches and techniques are applicable in given problem situations by continually showing the workings of the basic underlying principles of economics, finance, mathematics, and investment decision-making that are involved. This emphasis on *why* is coupled with necessary presentations of *what* is to be done, and *how* to do it. Only when all three aspects are fully understood and the mechanical processes mastered will the student have the skills required for effective use in actual appraisal practice.

## Organization of the Book

This text is not organized along traditional lines. Because it presumes that the student or reader is already familiar with the fundamentals of real property valuation and the principles of real estate and urban land economics that underlie them, it places particular emphasis on the principles and techniques of income capitalization. It is purposely and consciously one-sided in topic coverage. Subjects that are necessarily introduced and learned in earlier course work or texts on appraisal fundamentals (such as Market Area Analysis, Direct Sales Comparison Analysis, or Cost Analysis) are included only to the extent required to show their applicability to the valuation of interests in *income* real estate.

There are four major sections in the book. The first includes three chapters that introduce the subject of income property valuation, review the principles of appraising and the appraisal framework, and discuss the peculiarities of income-producing real estate for appraisal purposes. This background section is followed by eight chapters on the rationale, mathematical foundations, principles, and mechanics of the process of income capitalization. These eight chapters of Part II constitute the real heart of the book. They provide the foundation for the applications of income capitalization techniques to real property valuation that are presented in Part III. Income forecasting is given particular attention in Part II, along with the processes for converting those income forecasts to present worth or value estimates.

Part III includes the generally applicable tools of analysis that can be used effectively in virtually every conceivable type of problem requiring the valuation of an interest in real estate based on an anticipated or forecast future income stream. The specific mechanics developed in Part II are combined into a framework of analytical technique that is widely accepted and used by professional appraisers. This framework is given a somewhat new and different perspective in Part III, with emphasis on its adaptability as a general tool of analysis. Throughout Parts II and III, the special concern is to develop the skills to value *any* future income stream with the same basic tools.

The fourth and final section of the book deals with the use of all elements of the entire appraisal framework, including income capitalization, in appraising income properties. It places Income Capitalization Analysis in its proper perspective with Sales-Comparison Analysis and Cost Analysis as possible alternative routes to effective valuation of interests in income property. The special but recurring problem of valuing Leased Fee and Leasehold interests created by a lease are given particular attention in Part IV. The final chapter considers how two or more value estimates which have been derived relatively independently are translated into a final value estimate for the interests being appraised.

*Chapter Organization*

Beginning with Chapter 2, each chapter is organized along similar lines. Following the text presentation, in which illustrative examples are given to demonstrate mechanics wherever appropriate, there are Review Exercises. These are provided to permit the student or reader to test himself on the principles and mechanical techniques presented in the body of the chapter. It is strongly suggested that the serious reader attempt to work out his own answers to each of these illustrative Review Exercises before turning to the suggested solutions that are given in Appendix A.

There are also lists of Supplementary Readings at the end of each chapter. These serve a twofold purpose. First, some provide basic information sources for readers whose personal familiarity with the background materials and fundamental principles of real estate or appraisal may have dimmed. Second, others offer the seriously interested student of appraisal more intensive discussions of each chapter's subject matter.

A few basic appraisal texts are referred to continually throughout this work. They are important components of any appraisal library. They include the fifth edition of *The Appraisal of Real Estate*, prepared and published by the American Institute of Real Estate Appraisers; the second edition of *Valuation of Real Estate*, by Alfred A. Ring; and Richard U. Ratcliff's *Modern Real Estate Valuation*. In addition, frequent reference is made to *Real Estate Appraisal and Investment*, by Kahn, Case, and Schimmel.[3]

Particular mention should be made of the third edition of L.W. Ellwood's monumental *Ellwood Tables for Real Estate Appraising and Financing*.[4] It offers a detailed exposition of, and precalculated tables of factors for, the Ellwood formulation of mortgage-equity analysis. Part II of Ellwood's book provides one source of the basic compound interest factor tables used in appraisal analysis, in a form that is particularly useful and adapted to appraising. The examples and Review Exercises in Parts II, III, and IV of this volume utilize compound interest factors continually. For purposes of exposition, references are provided to Ellwood's third edition, both to accompany this text and for use as a basic working reference in the future. However, any adequate set of compound interest tables can be used to derive the factors used here.

*Repetition and Review*

Because this is a text, it introduces many concepts and techniques that are new to the student or reader. Both the underlying principles and the techniques of estimating present worth or value through discounting (capitalization) are relatively involved and complex. Income forecasting is not always readily understood on one exposure. The idea of discounting future income to present worth requires time to be understood fully. The existence of more than one meaningful avenue to value, and the characteristics and significance of each, can be absorbed only after a period of mental adjustment.

As a result of these and similar considerations, periodic reviews of what has gone before are provided throughout this book. The materials presented here, which cannot usually be absorbed readily on one reading, are basic to good, professional practice. They therefore warrant periodic repetition and summary reviews. The ultimate objective, after all, is for the student to be able to apply the tools properly to solve appraisal problems.

*A Concluding Note to the Reader*

The student or reader who has successfully completed a course in the fundamental principles of real-property valuation already knows that the appraisal framework is composed of several interrelated parts. The framework in its entirety cannot be fully appreciated or properly applied in practice until each of these components has been studied in its turn. Then all the parts are combined into a meaningful whole.

The same is true of income capitalization analysis. Each of its component parts is interrelated and interconnected with the others. As the reader progresses through Part II of this book, he should keep firmly in mind that each successive chapter provides one more important element in the total framework. Only after the cycle is completed can the *what, how,* and *why* of income capitalization be mastered for application to income property appraisal problems in Parts III and IV.

## Notes

1. The nature, content, and definition of an appraisal are considered in more detail in Chapter 2. For a full discussion of this issue, see American Institute of Real Estate Appraisers, *The Appraisal of Real Estate*, fifth edition (Chicago: American Institute of Real Estate Appraisers, 1967), pp. 2-6; and W.N. Kinnard, Jr., *An Introduction to Appraising Real Property: Student Reference* (Chicago: Society of Real Estate Appraisers, 1968), pp. 1-2 through 1-4.

2. For detailed but opposing views on the existence and meaning of different "approaches" to real-property value estimation, consult AIREA, *Appraisal of Real Estate*, pp. 60-66; Kinnard, *Appraising Real Property*, pp. 7-7 through 7-14; R.U. Ratcliff, *Modern Real Estate Valuation: Theory and Application* (Madison, Wisconsin: Democrat Press, 1965), pp. 2-4; and R.U. Ratcliff, *A Restatement of Appraisal Theory* (Madison, Wisconsin: Bureau of Business Research and Service, University of Wisconsin, 1963), chapters I and IV.

3. AIREA, *Appraisal of Real Estate*; Ratcliff, *Modern Real Estate Valuation*; A.A. Ring, *The Valuation of Real Estate*, second edition (New York: Prentice-Hall, 1970); S.A. Kahn, F.E. Case, and A. Schimmel, *Real Estate Appraisal and Investment* (New York: Ronald Press, 1963).

4. L.W. Ellwood, *Ellwood Tables for Real Estate Appraising and Financing*, third edition (Chicago: American Institute of Real Estate Appraisers, 1970).

# 2

## Appraisal and Real Estate Fundamentals

### Nature of Appraisals and Appraising

The discussion in this chapter is essentially a review of materials to which the reader has previously been exposed. It should serve as a refresher for those who have been away from formal appraisal study for any appreciable time. Moreover, it provides a necessary common foundation of concepts and terminology on which the remainder of the book relies. Readers who require more detailed explanations of any points reviewed here should consult one or more of the several basic references cited as supplementary readings.

### Definition of an Appraisal

An appraisal is an estimate of value. A real estate appraisal is an estimate of the value of rights in realty, which is the technical, legal term for the physical thing called real estate.

But a real estate appraisal, at least in the sense that the term is used in the appraisal profession as well as throughout this book, is more than just an estimate. It is a professionally derived conclusion about the present worth or value of specified rights or interests in a particular parcel of real estate under stipulated market conditions or decision standards. Moreover, it is (or should be) based on the professional judgment and skill of a trained practitioner. Its conclusions should be presented in a thoroughly logical and convincing way to a client or an interested third party who requires the value estimate to help make a decision or solve a problem involving the real estate in question.

An appraisal opinion is usually delivered in written form. A professional appraisal report should contain as a minimum the essential ingredients of an appraisal identified above: (1) the identity and legal description of the real estate; (2) the type of value being estimated; (3) the interests being appraised; (4) the market conditions or decision standards in terms of which the value estimate is made (frequently identified by specifying an "as of" or effective date for the appraisal); and (5) the value estimate itself. Moreover, the report should indicate the data and reasoning employed by the appraiser in reaching his value conclusion, any special or limiting conditions that impinged on his analysis and conclusion, and the appraiser's certification and signature.[1] Each of these components requires separate consideration for full appreciation of the character of a real estate appraisal.

**The Importance of Forecasting.** The value of rights in real estate can be expressed as the present worth of the future benefits anticipated to be derived from the possession of those rights. Real estate is a long-term asset whose benefits, in the form of money income and/or ownership amenities, are produced over a considerable period of time. Estimating the present worth or value of those benefits requires the appraiser to forecast market and property conditions in order to reach a judgment about what and how much those benefits most likely will be. This is particularly true of income properties, which are valued primarily in terms of forecast future income.

**Appraising as Measurement.** In making value estimates, the basic task of the appraiser is to *measure* value, as defined, in money terms. All other considerations aside, important though they may be, the appraiser is essentially seeking to answer the question: "How much?" This must always be kept in mind. It is easy to lose sight of this fundamental objective among the myriad details and complexities of technique frequently associated with income property appraisals in particular.

However, to say that every appraisal is a problem in measurement of value does not necessarily mean that a single value figure is sought or is responsive to the client's problem in every case. Most Market Value appraisals do call for a single value figure. Decisions about mortgage loan amounts, about *ad valorem* property and capital gains taxation, about the amount of payment that represents just compensation in an eminent domain proceeding, and even many buy-sell decisions require that the value estimate be expressed as a single specific dollar amount. But in other instances, especially those involving the kinds of investment decisions often associated with the transfer of interests in income real estate, it is particularly helpful to identify the reasonable range of values within which Most Probable Selling Price or Investment Value will most likely be found.[2] Within this range, the appraiser can and should indicate the specific money figure that in his professional judgment most nearly represents the value being sought.

*Value to Be Estimated: The
Purpose of the Appraisal*

The purpose of any appraisal is to estimate value. Early in his analysis of any appraisal problem, the appraiser must identify *what* value is to be estimated. A specific interest in a parcel of real estate may have more than one value at any given time. Most significant of these for income property appraisals are Market Value and Investment Value. Estimated or forecast Market Value can also be regarded as a forecast of Most Probable Selling Price. A property interest has only one Market Value, and only one Investment Value to a specific investor, at any given time; but Market Value and Investment Value to a particular decision-maker can be quite different amounts. Thus, it is essential that the particular type of value sought by the client or required by the nature of the appraisal problem be carefully ascertained at the outset. The estimation of that value must then be clearly identified as the purpose of the appraisal.

**The Nature of Value.**[3] Value is a price. It is a price that would tend to prevail under specified market conditions as a result of the interaction of the forces of supply and demand. This price reflects the capacity of an economic good to command other goods in exchange. This is the basis for Value in Exchange, of which Market Value as used in appraising is one manifestation. Value is also the present worth of future benefits anticipated or forecast to be receivable from the ownership of an asset. This is the basis for Value in Use. Rights in real estate represent ownership of an asset. Their Value in Use is measured in appraisal analysis by Investment Value.

In the perfect market of economic theory, informed and rational buyers would pay no more, and informed and rational sellers would accept no less, than the present worth of the anticipated future benefits from ownership of an asset (discounted at market-determined rates). Thus, all transactions would take place at prices that reflected Value in Use, and represented Value in Exchange. Value in Use would equal Value in Exchange, and Price would be synonymous with Value.

The real estate market, or any real estate submarket, is imperfect by the standards of market perfection in economic theory.[4] As a result, Price and Value are not synonymous and are infrequently equal. *Price* is an historic fact: the sum of money actually paid for a property, or offered by a potential buyer, or asked by a would-be seller. *Value* is the price that would tend to prevail under specified conditions, which may or may not be realized. Appraising involves the estimation of value, not the prediction of price.

Every appraisal is a forecast. If Market Value is to be estimated, it is a forecast of a transaction price that would most probably occur provided specified market conditions are met. If Investment Value is to be estimated, it is a forecast of what a rational investor/decision-maker would pay for the right to recieve the benefits of ownership under specified investment decision criteria. When income property is appraised, whether to estimate Market Value or Investment Value, the appraiser must also forecast the amount and character of the income stream most likely to be received by the owner of the rights being appraised.

**Market Value.** The bulk of appraisal problems confronting the income-property appraiser require the estimation of Market Value. As already noted, this is the price that would tend to prevail under specified market conditions. Market Value is variously defined. Whatever the definition, there are several essential ingredients to Market Value that must be understood.

Market Value assumes competitive market conditions. There must be several buyers and sellers competing with one another to provide alternatives to other market participants. These buyers and sellers must be informed. They must have reasonable, readily available knowledge about the property being appraised, its probable future income-producing capacity under present use; the alternative uses to which it can be put and the most probable income streams associated with those uses; prevailing market conditions and market standards of investment acceptability; and the character and intensity of their competition. They must know what "the market" is. In brief, potential buyers and/or sellers are assumed to possess the typical knowledge about the property and the market that a prudent market participant can reasonably be expected to have.

Buyers and sellers are further presumed to act "rationally" on the basis of the information they possess. Each party to a transaction is expected to act in his own self-interest to maximize his economic or financial well-being: his profit, the rate of return on his investment, and/or the value of his interest in the real estate. Rational behavior consists of behaving logically to achieve the stated investment or market objective with the "typical" property and market information at hand. This maximizing rational behavior is exemplified by putting the property to its Highest and Best Use.[5] Market Value is necessarily estimated in terms of Highest and Best Use.

A reasonable turnover or marketing period must be allowed for the transaction to take place. There must be no undue time pressure on either buyer or seller. The type of property involved and existing market conditions determine what a "normal" marketing period is, or should be. Market Value reflects neither an immediate sale (especially for many types of special-purpose or specifically designed income properties) nor an extended waiting period for the seller or buyer to achieve a specific price objective.

It is also assumed that there is no fraud, collusion or misinformation on the part of either party.

Payment must be consistent with the prevailing standards of the market for the type of property, the type of property interest to be exchanged, and the type of transaction involved. Typical or normal financing and payment arrangements are presumed. For income-producing properties, this will usually mean some form of debt (mortgage) financing by the buyer, under prevailing mortgage market conditions for the type of property and the type of borrower involved. The seller may still receive full payment in cash, unless typical financing in the current market for the type of property being appraised includes a purchase-money mortgage. The terms of sale are also expected to be competitive with those on other similar properties in the same market.

Finally, Market Value is usually viewed from the perspective of the *buyer*. It is most frequently expressed as the maximum price that an informed buyer, acting rationally, would pay under the stipulated market conditions. Indeed, the character of the most probable type of purchaser tends to establish the limits and characteristics of "the market" in terms of which value is estimated.

In brief, Market Value can be regarded as the price that a willing buyer would pay, and a willing seller would accept, with each acting rationally on the basis of available market information, under no undue pressure or constraint, with no fraud or collusion present. It represents Value in Exchange for interests in real estate. There are two widely accepted formal definitions of Market Value with which every practicing appraiser should be thoroughly familiar. Each contains the essential elements included in the concept of Market Value, and each has professional recognition. They are:

1. The price which a property will bring in a competitive market under all conditions requisite to a fair sale, which would result from negotiations between a buyer and seller, each acting prudently, with knowledge, and without undue stimulus.[6]

2. The highest price in terms of money which a property will bring if exposed for sale on the open market, with a reasonable time to find a purchaser, buying with full knowledge of all the uses to which it is adapted and for which it is capable of being used.[7]

**Most Probable Selling Price.** Market Value is a rather rigidly defined concept. Frequently, not all of its conditions can be strictly met. Yet single-figure value estimates are widely sought and required by buyers, sellers, lenders, taxing authorities, and courts to serve as a basis for significant decisions about interests in realty. One alternative way of looking at such a figure is to consider it a forecast of Most Probable Selling Price (Vp).[8] This is the price at which a transaction is most likely to occur under actually existing market conditions and actually prevailing levels of information on the part of buyers and sellers. Vp is somewhat less rigid and idealistic a concept than Market Value. It has come into considerable acceptance and use among professional appraisers, especially in valuing interests for prospective buyers and sellers in private market transactions. Legal constraints still impose the standards of Market Value, as defined, on institutional lenders, taxing authorities, public agencies exercising the right of eminent domain, and the courts.

When Most Probable Selling Price is estimated, the use pattern in terms of which value is estimated (or selling price is forecast) should be Most Probable Use rather than Highest and Best Use. The buyer or user is expected to produce the best return he can under the conditions of existing market information, but not necessarily with the full knowledge stipulated as part of Market Value. The estimation of Vp does not require that the prospective buyer search out every possible alternative type and intensity of use for the property before rationally selecting the best one. As a result, the existing use pattern of improved properties producing a reasonably competitive and attractive rate of return usually turns out to be the Most Probable Use. This is the use most likely to be continued by the prospective purchaser, and the one in terms of which Vp is estimated.

**Investment Value.** The value of rights in real estate, especially that producing money income, can be expressed as the present worth of the anticipated future benefits (or forecast future income receipts) accruing to the owner. When the forecast income stream is "typical" of that produced by competitive properties in the market; when management and operating expenses are "typical;" when a

14

market-determined "typical" rate of return is used to discount the forecast income to a present worth estimated; and when the terms of financing and conditions of sale are "typical"–then this present worth estimate meets the conditions of Market Value. Indeed, *any* interest in real estate which is transferable and marketable can have a Market Value or a Most Probable Selling Price.

On the other hand, if the forecast income stream, the rate of discount, and the terms of financing and sale are all associated with a specific potential investor, the present worth estimate derived represents Investment Value. The data employed in the analysis and the decision standards used in reaching the appraisal conclusion are all specific to a particular purchaser-investor. They represent what that specific investor anticipates, is seeking, or will accept. In effect, they are obtained from the investor by the appraisers as givens, and then processed through exactly the same analytical framework to derive a present worth estimate.

Investment Value has particular significance in income-property appraising. It is used by potential investors as a basis for deciding whether to buy a given property, or whether to assume a specific investment position. Given the expectations or standards of the investor, the appraiser can indicate what the forecast income stream which is to be generated by the property is worth to that investor.

The forecast-income stream utilized in the analysis may be the stabilized Net Operating Income (NOI) employed in Market Value analysis, based on Market Rentals. It may be the actual NOI or Cash Flow being generated by the property, based on Contract Rents and actual observed Operating Expenses under present management. It may also be what the investor states he forecasts or expects. The investor's needs and expectations dictate which is used.

Similarly, the pattern of financing used in the analysis may be the typical, normal type found in the market for similar properties and similar types of investors; or it may be the financing most likely to be obtainable by the particular investor.

Most importantly, the rate of return (Discount Rate) used in Investment Value estimation is based on the Equity Yield Rate specific and peculiar to the particular purchaser-investor in question. The result of capitalizing the forecast-income stream at that rate is Investment Value: the present worth of a given income stream to a specific investor.

The mechanical techniques and tools of analysis used in estimating Investment Value are precisely the same as those employed to estimate Market Value. The applicable segments of the Appraisal Framework are identical. The basic difference lies in the standards of judgment or decision-making that apply. They are reflected in the data and figures that are inserted into the calculations to derive a final value estimate. Market Value is based on market-derived standards reflecting the expectations and aspirations of a typically informed, prudent, rational purchaser-investor. Investment Value is based on the specific standards and expectations of a particular investor, given the information he possesses. In the latter case, rational behavior consists of acting logically to achieve his own individual standards or goals, rather than those of the market.

**Value to Whom: Market Identification.** From the preceding discussion, it can be seen that the type of value to be estimated in an appraisal problem, and hence the purpose of the appraisal, depends primarily on *whose* viewpoint is to be taken in making the value or present worth estimate. Both Market Value and Investment Value (as well as Most Probable Selling Price) are expressed in terms of the standards and behavior of a potential buyer.

That buyer is a typically informed, prudent, rational purchaser-investor who puts the property to its Highest and Best Use when Market Value is to be estimated. He is also typically informed, prudent, and rational when Most Probable Selling Price is to be estimated, but he puts the property to its Most Probable Use. He derives a reasonable, competitive, acceptable rate of return on his investment by market standards, but not necessarily the maximum possible rate of return, as is required under the conditions of Market Value. The purchaser-investor is reasonably informed and rational in terms of his own stated investment objectives when Investment Value is to be estimated. The use to which he puts the property is one which will yield the rate of return that he seeks or anticipates.

The identification of the *type* of purchaser-investor who meets the standards of the definition of value to be estimated also identifies "the market" in terms of which value is to be estimated. This is not particularly significant in estimating Investment Value, since a specific investor is "the market" whose investment criteria set the standards for calculating present worth. In the case of Market Value, however, it can be critically important. The *type* of purchaser-investor (not a specific one) most likely to be typical of the market identifies the standards in terms of which Market Value is estimated. For example, prime shopping center investments may be peculiarly attractive to life insurance companies. If this is the case, then life insurance companies in the equity investment field represent "the market" whose standards establish the basis for estimating Market Value.

Similarly, the estimation of Most Probable Selling Price requires early identification of the most probable *type* of purchaser-investor. While other types of theoretically potential investors may be active in the same geographic area, the *type* of most probable purchaser of the type of property being appraised identifies what the "market" for that property realistically is.

*What Is to be Valued*

**Rights in Realty.**[9] Real estate is a physical asset. Its technical, legal term is *realty*. Because of its peculiar physical attribute of immobility (or fixity of location), it cannot be physically transferred from one owner to another. As a result, an entire body of law has grown up over the centuries relating to the ownership of *rights* in realty. These rights are technically termed *real property*, although the term "property" is commonly (if loosely) used to refer to the physical real estate.

In actuality, appraisers do not appraise real estate. They estimate the value of real property: rights or interests in realty. It is possible, and indeed common, for more than one party to have a legally enforceable interest or right in a particular parcel of real estate. Each such interest can have value as of the date of the appraisal. It may have a Market Value, since most interests in realty are transferable and may also be marketable, as well as an Investment Value. Moreover, the existence of one interest in a particular parcel of real estate will usually affect the value of any other interests in that same parcel. A lease on a property will influence the value of the lessor's (landlord's) interest. A right of way across the parcel may affect the value of the owner's interest (the fee) by limiting the uses to which the real estate can be put.

The appraiser, therefore, must carefully identify the precise rights that are to be valued in the particular realty involved. This requires identification of any other interests in the same realty, as well as any limitations such as zoning or deed restrictions that impair the free exercise of the rights being appraised. Value, after all, is partly determined by use. This is inherent in the definitions of value used in appraising. Anything that affects *what* is to be valued or *how* it may be used also affects its value.

*Bundle of Rights.* The several rights in realty that together constitute "ownership" of real estate are likened to bundle. They are both *separable* and *divisible*. That is, different parties may process different rights in the same parcel of real estate, and two or more parties may possess portions of the same right, at the same time. The possession of the full bundle of rights by a private party, with no other valid claimant to any portion of the rights of ownership and subject only to the limitations on the full and free exercise of those rights imposed by society, is known as the *unencumbered fee simple estate*. This circumstance is only infrequently realized because of claims by lenders (mortgagees), holders of rights of way, tenants under leases (leasehold estates), or other partial interests in the realty.

While the precise listing of ownership rights varies from one authority to another, one widely accepted classification identifies them as the rights of *use, exclusion*, and *disposition*. These rights are enforceable at law if necessary. The right of use includes the right to receive the benefits of use of the realty, either through occupancy by an owner or tenant, or through the receipt of rental payments by a landlord. The right of exclusion means that the legal occupant of the real estate may keep others off the premises, with the assistance of the legal system if necessary. The right of disposition gives the owner the options of selling or leasing the other rights, giving them away, or transferring them by will or descent after death. This provides legal transferability, and the basis for marketability.

Some or all of these rights, in full or in part, constitute what is actually transferred in real estate markets. The specific interest of a party to a real estate transaction consists of those rights which are to be disposed of or acquired. The appraiser's task is to estimate the value of this particular interest or package of rights.

**Identification of the Real Estate.** Rights in realty are valued by appraisers because rights are transferred on the market. So the appraiser must carefully identify the rights to be appraised. But he must also indicate "Rights in what?" The real estate in which rights are to be valued is identified in both physical and legal terms. The two together must constitute an unequivocal description of the realty.

*Physical Description.* Realty consists of land and all improvements on and to the land. The physical description includes its location (e.g., street address); the size, shape, and dimensions of the site; the type of improvement (e.g., apartment building); the size and dimensions of the building(s); and the quality and condition of the building(s). Any visitor to the property should be able to identify it immediately from the physical description provided by the appraiser.

*Legal Description.* The location of the realty being described can be identified unquestionably and unequivocally with a proper legal description. Methods of legally describing realty vary among different sections of the United States. Whatever the method employed—whether by U.S. Government Survey, by metes and bounds, or by monuments—the description is contained in deeds and other documents on public record in a governmental repository. This is the county clerk's office in most of the United States, but the town clerk's office throughout New England.

### Effective Date of the Appraisal

Every estimate of value is valid only under specified market conditions. This applies whether Market Value, Most Probable Selling Price, or Investment Value is to be estimated. Value is the result of the interaction of the forces of market supply and demand. When these conditions change, so will a value estimate based upon them. Therefore, every appraisal must be made as of a specific date to identify the prevailing market forces and conditions in terms of which value is estimated. This is the effective date of the appraisal, sometimes called the "as of" date.

### Uses and Functions of Appraisals

While it is true that the purpose of any appraisal is to estimate value, it is the *client's* purpose or objective that determines what value is to be sought. The decision-maker with a problem to solve or a decision to make establishes the nature of the appraisal problem. The appraiser must therefore clearly identify the client's or the decision-maker's purpose in seeking an appraisal before the purpose of that appraisal—the value to be estimated—can be established.

Once this appraisal purpose is ascertained, it makes no difference to the appraiser what use the client makes of the value conclusion. As long as the value to be estimated is carefully defined and the meaning of the final value estimate is clearly indicated in the appraisal report, the appraiser's professional function and responsibility have been met.

The use to which a client or decision-maker puts an appraisal is its function. A Market Value appraisal can be used in buy-sell decisions, in property tax and income tax cases, in mortgage lending decisions, in property exchanges, or in eminent domain cases. Whenever a Market Value estimate is needed to help solve a problem or make a decision, its use has no influence on the value conclusion reached. The same is true of estimates of Most Probable Selling Price or Investment Value. The client's or decision-maker's stated objective in seeking an appraisal influences the value estimate by determining what value is to be estimated; his subsequent use of the appraisal does not.

### Principles of Real Estate and Urban Land Economics

The appraiser estimates the value, as defined, of rights in realty or real estate. Whatever value is estimated, the appraiser must function with knowledge of the distinguishing characteristics of real estate as an asset or economic good. He must appreciate the impact of those characteristics on the structure and organization of real estate markets. Market forces determine value, so he must also recognize and account for the functioning of the real estate market segment pertinent to the appraisal problem at hand. Non-agricultural real estate at least can also be treated as urban space. The allocation of urban space among competing alternative uses is explained by the principles of urban-land economics. Since use is an important influence on value, a working knowledge of those principles is necessary for effective appraising.

### *The Nature of Real Estate*[10]

Real estate must be analyzed from three separate but interrelated points of view. It can be considered as a physical entity, a legal entity, and/or an economic good or asset.

**The Physical Viewpoint.** Real estate as a physical thing is technically known as *realty*. It consists of land and man-made improvements on and to the land. Land consists of the surface of the earth as well as sub-surface and supra-surface area.

It is fixed in location. This immobility means that it is critically dependent on its surrounding environment, including man-made off-site improvements and access, to determine feasible uses for which it is suited.

Land which has necessary on-site and off-site improvements available to enable it to be put to one or more urban uses is termed a *site*. For practical purposes, the total supply of land within a given area is fixed, but sites for specific uses can be created or destroyed by the actions of man.

Improvements are man-made and typically have a finite life. With the passage of time, they wear out or otherwise lose their capacity to perform their intended function(s) effectively. Improvements *on* the land or site consist of buildings and fixtures "permanently" attached to the land. Improvements *to* the land (site improvements) include drainage, utilities, grading, paving, or access roads.

Land or site and improvements together constitute urban space, which is characterized by the fact that its use and value are largely determined by its *location*. As with sites, urban space can be created and destroyed.

Real estate is fixed in location, and is extremely durable or long-lived. Since only one unit of matter can occupy the same space or location at any one time, every parcel of real estate or unit of urban space is unique; it is differentiated from every other parcel or unit. These three physical characteristics of real estate have a strong influence on its economic attributes, and on the organization and functioning of real estate markets.

**The Legal Viewpoint.** The fixed location of real estate means that it cannot physically be possessed or transferred. Rights in realty are therefore owned and marketed, and are termed *real property*. In the United States' legal system, property consists of enforceable rights in an asset. The private property system protects ownership rights under law.

As noted earlier in this chapter, private property rights in realty consist of a bundle that includes the rights of use, exclusion, and disposition. These rights are both separable and divisible. Equally important, they are transferable. They are also marketable when there is market demand for them. The possession of enforceable rights in realty is demonstrated by legal documents, giving evidence of what is termed *title*.

*Estates and Chattel Interests.* Ownership interests in realty consisting of any legitimate claim on any part of the bundle of rights are called *estates*. Possession of the full bundle of private property rights, without any legitimate claim to any part of the bundle by another party, is known as the *unencumbered fee simple estate*. A party may also be the holder of a fee simple estate "encumbered" by partial claims on the bundle of rights. A fee holder of a property with a lease or a mortgage has an encumbered fee. The fee holder is the "owner" of the real estate.

Non-ownership interests also represent enforceable rights in the realty. A tenant under a lease has a leasehold interest; a lender under a mortgage loan has a mortgagee's interest; the holder of an easement or a lien has a non-possessory chattel interest. In addition to being specifically enforceable against the real estate, which means that the holder of any such interest can force the sale of the property to satisfy his claim, these interests are usually transferable. Thus, they may have value independently of the fee estate. They also represent potential limitations on the transfer and value of the fee estate, which the appraiser must consider and evaluate if his assignment is to estimate the value of the fee.

*Limitations on the Exercise of Private Property Rights.* Private ownership of real-property rights is never complete or unrestricted. There are always public or governmental limitations to their free exercise, and there may be private limitations as well.

*Public limitations.* Government at all levels places restrictions and limitations on the free exercise of private property rights in realty "in the public interest." No private property owner is free from the actual or potential impact of such limitations. The appraiser must identify not only those limitations, but also their quantitative impact on the value of the private rights being appraised.

The first and most basic public limitation is *property taxation.* Property taxes increase the costs of ownership, reducing the net benefits or income to be derived from the use of the real estate. Property taxes represent a lien (enforceable claim) against the realty until they are paid. They are enforceable through the right of the taxing authority to force the sale of the property to satisfy the claim. A tax lien "goes with the land," which is to say that it is enforceable against a new owner if the property is transferred. This can seriously limit the marketability of the property.

Public bodies and some private organizations "affected with the public interest," such as public utility companies, may *acquire rights* in privately owned real estate through the exercise of the right of *eminent domain.* The acquisition must be for a public use or a public purpose, and "just compensation" must be paid. All or part of a private owner's bundle of rights may be acquired. Transfer of the rights may be forced through the legal process known as *condemnation.* The potential threat of eminent domain hangs over every private property owner. The appraiser must evaluate the prospects of any known or planned public improvement program affecting the enjoyment of rights in the property being appraised.

Government may also *limit* the free exercise of private property rights, especially the right of use, through application of the *police power.* The limitation may not be specific to a single parcel. No compensation need be paid, provided the limitation serves the interests of public health, public safety, public morals, and/or the general welfare. Zoning regulations, subdivision controls, and building codes are all based on the police power. These are three examples of public controls which the appraiser must study and evaluate carefully in every appraisal assignment. They strongly influence both the type and the intensity of use of the affected property, and use is a prime determinant of value.

A relatively unimportant governmental limitation on the right of disposition is called *escheat.* No property can be ownerless, so if a property owner dies leaving no will and no heirs, his property "escheats" to the state.

*Private limitations.* The exercise of private rights in realty can also be limited privately, either voluntarily or involuntarily. Voluntary limitations are contractual, and include leases, mortgages (or deeds of trust), easements, and deed restrictions. These all come about through voluntary acceptance by the holder of the fee or the purchaser of the property. Involuntary limitations are placed against the property by others, usually because of some action or inaction on the part of the owner. They include liens, encroachments, and prescriptive easements. The existence of any such limitations reduces the marketability of the property.

**The Economic-Financial Viewpoint.** Real estate is an asset. An asset is also termed an economic good. Economic goods have the characteristics of scarcity, transferability, and utility. Real estate (or rights in realty) possess these same characteristics. Utility is the capacity of a good, such as real estate, to satisfy human wants and desires. The worth or value of a good is indicated by its total utility. Unfortunately, utility cannot be measured directly. Money serves as a proxy measure. This is why dollar value is estimated in appraising: to measure and compare the utility of real properties with the standards of the market.

Apart from general attributes which it holds in common with all other economic goods, real estate has distinguishing economic characteristics which stem directly from the physical and legal characteristics discussed in the preceding sections. These economic attributes influence value primarily by affecting use and income-producing capacity.

*Fixed Location (Immobility).* Real estate produces its benefits at a fixed location. It cannot move or be moved to better or more favorable markets. It must be used or exploited where it is. The user or beneficiary of its services must come to the real estate to enjoy the benefits of those services.

*Dependence on Environment and Setting.* Because it is fixed in location and immobile, real estate is particularly sensitive to changes in the immediate vicinity. It is also dependent on external support services (utilities, access roads, protection) to allow it to be used effectively. The nature, stability, and functional adequacy of the surrounding environment and support facilities help determine the feasible use patterns of a property, and thereby influence its value.

*Highly Differentiated.* Each parcel or property is unique. It is different from all others. Comparisons among properties are often difficult, and require careful analysis and judgment. Market analysis is complicated by market imperfections stemming from this property differentiation. This is why there are appraisers. The high degree of differentiation also means that every appraisal problem is a separate research study requiring individual analysis.

*Durability.* Real estate is an especially long-term asset, whose benefits are receivable over a prolonged period of years. Decisions about real estate involve long-term commitments of funds and productive resources. Real estate is a relatively high-priced asset requiring commitments of large sums of money, based in part on long-term income expectations. As a result, debt financing is usually necessary to support property acquisition and ownership. Relatively large economic units are also associated with the large sums involved. This tends to narrow the base of the market, and constitutes a market imperfection. The necessity to make long-term income forecasts and to cope with a narrowed, imperfect market complicates the appraiser's task.

*Urban Land Economics*

Economics is the study of the allocation of scarce resources among competing alternative uses and desires in such a way as to maximize human satisfactions. These satisfactions are usually expressed and measured in dollar terms. Urban land economics concentrates on the allocation of urban space among competing alternative uses. Real estate (land and/or improvements) that is used primarily as a location for some human activity is termed urban space. The allocation and use of urban space or urban real estate involve decisions about both horizontal (extensive) and vertical (intensive) utilization of that space.

Price or value is the basic market mechanism for the allocation of urban real estate. Value is determined by the interaction of the market forces of supply and demand. Decision-makers are assumed to choose use patterns rationally on the basis of value or present worth estimates for competing alternative uses. The basic decision in urban land economics analysis is the use to which a parcel of urban real estate is to be put. Use decisions are made at two levels: type of use and density of use. The fundamental principle in terms of which use decisions and allocations are made is the principle of Highest and Best Use (Most Profitable Use): in the long run, urban space tends to be put to its Highest and Best (or Most Profitable) Use, with decision-makers acting rationally on the basis of full market information. It is this use that tends to produce maximum present worth: Market Value.

The value of urban space is based on the capitalized (discounted) net value of its services. This net value or income-producing capacity of these services is a measure of the productivity of the urban space. Productivity is a direct function of use. Use decisions, the heart of urban land economics, are thus important determinants of value.

**Hierarchy of Use Decisions.** Different categories of uses and use decisions are employed in urban-land economics analysis. They must be distinguished carefully by the appraiser in reaching his conclusion as to Highest and Best Use—or even Most Probable Use. They are presented here in increasing order of specificity: most general to most specific. The appraiser must consider each in turn, eliminating at each level proposed uses which do not qualify, before reaching his final conclusion. This process simulates the thought process of the rational and informed decision-maker through whose eyes the appraiser is viewing the real estate being appraised.

*Legal Use.* Is any of the proposed uses permitted at all? Some may be prohibited by zoning or deed restriction, or by law. If so, they are not realistic alternatives and must be discarded.

*Possible Use.* From among legally permissible uses, which ones are physically possible on the parcel in question? The size, shape, topography, subsoil conditions, or location of the site may preclude some of the remaining suggested uses.

*Appropriate Use.* Are the necessary supporting facilities—such as utilities, access, linked uses—available for any of the remaining proposed uses, regardless of whether it makes economic or financial sense to inaugurate those uses? The others proposed must be discarded.

*Feasible Use.* Is there economic or financial logic in pursuing any of the remaining proposed uses? Will any of them pay in the sense that they offer the prospect of producing a net return, especially a competitive net return? These uses represent the range of alternatives from which Highest and Best Use is selected.

*Highest and Best (Most Profitable) Use.* From among the proposed uses that have been found to be legally permissible, physically possible, appropriately supported and financially feasible, which one is expected to generate the highest rate of net return over a given income-forecast period *at the time the decision is made*? This is the Highest and Best Use. If none of the proposed uses is legal, possible, appropriate, *and* feasible, then under existing market conditions there is no Highest and Best Use.

**Economics of Location.** The distinguishing economic influence on the value of urban space or urban real estate is location.[11] Urban real estate produces services (amenities and/or dollar income) at a fixed location. In valuation analysis, "location" is an economic concept even though the location can also be identified and described in physical and legal terms. Location largely determines use and productivity. Because of its immobility, urban real estate is dependent on its external environment for the supporting facilities that make its use pattern possible. Access is particularly important to appropriate use, but the appraiser-analyst must clearly identify "access to what" in terms of the use pattern that constitutes the basis of the valuation approach. Urban activities tend to congregate at or near locations where maximum economy in movement to and from related locations and activities is anticipated.

*Real Estate Markets*

A real estate market provides for the exchange or transfer of rights in realty.[12] It represents a course of commercial activity for the purchase and sale of such rights.

Markets in real estate, and especially income-producing real estate, are not physically defined. Although the real estate itself is physically fixed and immobile, market participants (buyers, sellers, landlords, tenants, lenders) are not. The market is neither an identifiable meeting place for buyers and sellers of real property rights, nor the region in which a specific group of properties is located.

On the supply side, a real estate market can be defined in terms of parcels of real estate or units of urban space that are highly competitive with one another. This means that they represent realistic alternative substitutes for one another in the minds of typical or most probable buyers. When a prime determinant of the market attractiveness of real estate of a particular type is its location, as for example an apartment property in a particular neighborhood with a "good address," then the market may be delineated in specific geographic terms. In other instances, however, such as regional truck terminals or "prime" investment office buildings, the physical market area can be nationwide or even international.

On the demand side, a real estate market consists of competing potential buyers of rights with similar standards of acceptability with respect to use and/or investment. Potential purchasers or tenants of the same type, with similar perceptions of the use capabilities of the realty, will constitute "a market" in the sense that they represent the most probable buyers of rights. This point has already been noted in the discussion of *Value to Whom: Market Identification* earlier in this chapter.

**Characteristics of Real Estate Markets.** The peculiar and distinguishing characteristics of real estate as an asset influence the character of real estate markets. By the standards of economic theory, real estate markets are highly imperfect. The chief result of this imperfection is that value and price are rarely equal, and never synonymous. It is important for appraisers to appreciate the nature of real estate markets and their operation because value is determined through the interaction of the forces of supply and demand on the market.

*Relatively Uninformed Participants.* One of the basic requirements for the maximizing typical purchaser of the definition of Market Value is that he act rationally with "full knowledge." Moreover, the perfectly competitive market of economic theory, in which price and value are both equal and synonymous, requires full knowledge on the part of buyers and sellers. In real estate markets, full knowledge is rarely achieved by any participant. Many buyers and sellers are only occasionally in the market, and most are non-professionals. They rarely have the time or the training to acquire "full knowledge." Moreover, much necessary or useful information is often simply not available because it is restricted or confidential. Verification of apparent facts can be extremely time-consuming, but it is necessary because publicly available information is often only part of the entire story—or downright misleading. For all of these reasons, decision-makers in real estate markets frequently must act on the basis of incomplete knowledge of market facts, which inhibits truly rational behavior in terms of whatever decision standards are applied.

*Few Buyers and Sellers.* In a perfectly competitive market, there must be sufficient numbers of buyers and sellers so that no one can exert an appreciable influence on price or value. This is often not the case in real estate markets, especially when extremely high-priced or specialized properties are involved. Many real estate markets are "thin," with only a few potential participants on one or both sides of the market. Identification of who or what constitutes "the market" for a specific type of urban space is essential so that the relative influence of potential suppliers or users can be assessed and incorporated into valuation analysis.

*Stratified Supply and Demand.* It is impossible to speak 'in meaningful or realistic terms of "the" real estate market. There are actually large numbers of submarkets functioning semi-independently of one another, with only modest overlap. This is because both supply and demand are stratified or compartment-alized by type of space and use, by type of potential purchaser or tenant, by type of potential seller or landlord, by type of transaction and occupancy (sale or lease), and even by geographic area. Owner-occupancy housing cannot conceivably be regarded as competitive with rental space in a regional shopping center, except in the broadest possible (and essentially a meaningless) sense. Potential buyers and prospective tenants of even the same space are only partially competitive with one another. Thus, the appraiser must examine the competition on both the supply side and the demand side in relation to the property being appraised in order to identify "the market" in terms of which value is to be estimated. This is necessary because the pertinent submarket is the only appropriate source of most of the data required to carry out the appraisal assignment.

*Inelastic Supply.* The supply of space is not readily responsive to sales or rental price changes. The quantity of available space of a given type changes slowly in most real estate markets. Both new construction and conversion are time-consuming; there are physical and legal deterrents to speed. This means that under changing conditions of market demand, values can vary substantially.

*Volatile Demand.* Demand for urban space is derived from factors outside the real estate system. It stems from a combination of population, standards or tastes, and incomes. Because of population mobility, changes in employment and incomes, fluctuations in the availability and price of credit, and changing tastes and standards of use, demand for urban real estate can and does vary widely and rapidly. Coupled with the relative inelasticity of supply, this reinforces the potential for significant fluctuations in value over short periods of time. It also emphasizes further the importance of carefully identifying the market conditions in terms of which a value estimate is made, by specifying the effective date of the appraisal.

*Localized Area.* The fixed location and immobility of real estate tend to limit the geographic area within which properties of a similar type compete effectively with one another. This is less true of highly specialized types of properties or those which can provide service coverage for a large region, but it certainly applies to such ubiquitous uses as apartments, parking lots, or general-purpose retail space. The geographic limitation commonly exists in the minds of typical potential purchasers or tenants. When this occurs, the applicable market segment can be highly localized, and meaningful data for value estimation are concentrated within this area.

**Functions of the Real Estate Market.** Real estate markets or submarkets operate primarily to bring together buyers and sellers of rights in realty. This is accomplished through the interaction of the forces of supply and demand. To be able to evaluate the impact of these forces on the value of the property rights being appraised, the appraiser must have a good working knowledge of the several functions performed by a real estate market and the efficiency of its operating performance.

*Facilitate the Exchange of Rights in Realty.* By providing a mechanism by which buyers and sellers, landlords and tenants, or borrowers and lenders are brought together, real estate markets and submarkets make possible the transfers of rights in realty that constitute sale, exchange, leasing, or mortgage financing.

*Set Prices for Mutually Advantageous Exchanges.* Any *bona fide* market exchange is one that appears advantageous to the participating parties. Market activity by potential buyers and sellers of real property rights establishes the price(s) at which transfers of rights will occur. These prices represent the amount that at least one potential buyer is willing and able to pay, and at least one potential seller is willing to accept. Through bid-and-ask negotiations among buyers and sellers, market prices are set.

*Allocate Urban Space Among Competing Alternative Uses.* Price is the basic allocating mechanism provided by the market. Buyers and sellers are assumed to act rationally and logically in their own economic self-interest. This means that the buyer will offer and pay no more than the present worth to him of the future benefits anticipated to be derived from ownership of the real property rights in question. The seller, in turn, will accept the highest or best offer to him from among the bids made by potential buyers. Urban space is therefore allocated in the private market on the basis of the highest price offered for the ownership rights in that space. Since urban space must be put to its Highest and Best Use in order to support the highest price or present worth of those rights, it follows that urban real estate (urban space) is allocated according to its Highest and Best Use as perceived by potential users or buyers in the market. Price is the measure of the benefits anticipated from that use. Value, which is the appraiser's ultimate objective, is that price which would tend to prevail (by being offered and accepted) under prescribed market conditions.

*Determine the Pattern of Land and Space Use.* Market allocations of urban space through the price mechanism and the operation of the principle of Highest and Best Use are made individually on a parcel-by-parcel or unit-by-unit basis. Each allocation is a separate decision by a given investing or purchasing decision-maker. The sum of these individual use decisions in a given market area establishes the pattern of land and space use in that area. This pattern reflects the consensus of individual private and public decisions, influenced or limited by public or community controls such as zoning, development plans, and building codes. Real estate markets are "mixed" in the sense that they represent a combination of public or social influences and limitations superimposed on individual use and exchange decisions.

*Adjust Supply to Demand.* The potentially volatile demand for rights in realty is determined by factors external to the market: changes in the level and composition of population; changes in the levels and composition of incomes; changes in tastes and standards of use. It is a derived demand, based on needs for urban space to house and shelter human activities. In real estate markets, supply adjusts to demand. The market should provide the proper economic, financial, and legal environment for supply to respond effectively to changes in demand. Increased demand tends to be reflected first in increased prices (or rents or interest rates), thereby making it appear more attractive to potential suppliers to produce and provide more urban space.

**Operation of Real Estate Markets.** Because real estate markets are imperfect by the nature of the commodity traded, they perform their functions less than efficiently. Price and value are not equal. Not all use decisions are demonstrably rational. Existing land and space use patterns are frequently not responsive to current tastes, standards, or desires. Because of technical, legal, and financial considerations, supply adjusts quite slowly to changes in demand. In the short run, price changes reflect changing demand; construction, demolition, and/or conversions occur only after a considerable time lag. All exchanges are not mutually advantageous, in large part because of inadequate information flows and the uncertainty inherent in forecasting the future. The influence of government at all levels is strongly felt in markets for rights and urban real estate, particularly through the limitations imposed by taxation, the police power, and eminent domain.

28

These and other limitations on the ideal or efficient functioning of real estate markets explain why real estate appraisals are required to help solve problems or make decisions that involve the use and ownership of real estate.

**Analysis of Real Estate Markets.** Any appraisal requires both careful identification of the pertinent market(s) within which the rights being appraised will most probably be traded, and an analytical evaluation of the probable impact of current market forces on the value being estimated. Market identification results from ascertaining what the competition for the property involved will be, and who or what the most probable type of purchaser will be. Market analysis consists of segregating and estimating the effects of the applicable segments of demand and supply. Since the appraiser is estimating present worth, demand and supply analysis must be future-oriented. The appraiser must be able to forecast and predict trends in these markets forces, and to estimate the most probable perception and impact of those trends in present real estate decisions. This requires an appreciation of the composition of applicable demand and supply forces, and how they reached their present levels.

*Demand Analysis.* After identifying who or what the most probable purchaser(s) of the rights being valued most probably will be, the appraiser must both estimate the present levels and forecast probable future movements in the demand stemming from that type of potential buyer. Demand is desire or need backed up by purchasing power. Without money to support the desire, only potential demand exists; with supporting funds, *effective* demand exists.

The determinants of demand include population (both human and business or enterprise), income, and tastes and standards of functional adequacy. In addition, prices influence the extent to which demand can be made effective at any time. The appraiser must indicate the levels, composition, and trends in each of these components of demand. The estimate of demand is a statement of present and forecast future quantities of urban space of a given type that can be marketed at given price levels.

*Supply Analysis.* Supply represents the quantity of urban space of a given type that is currently available and is forecast to be made available on the market at given price levels. The existing stock of that type of urban space in the applicable market is the starting point in supply analysis. Changes in that stock can occur through new construction, demolitions, and/or conversions. Legal restrictions or constraints such as zoning, building codes, or financial regulations can inhibit or encourage changes in supply, as well as the timing of those changes. The appraiser's final judgment in supply analysis is the probable quantity, type, and speed of adjustment in the stock of urban space of a given type to an anticipated or forecast change in demand.

*Judgment Model.* Once the factors of supply and demand have been identified and analyzed for the particular type of property and the particular submarket in question, the appraiser is then in a position to judge what the most probable market conditions will be, in terms of which value is to be estimated. The conclusion of this "judgment model" specifies the market environment within which value is determined.

## Review Exercises

1. List the necessary components of any appraisal report, and explain why each is considered essential.
2. An appraiser has just concluded that a typically informed, prudent, and rational purchaser would be justified in paying $250,000 for a property. In his professional judgment, his client could pay only $235,000 and fulfill his (the client's) objectives. The property was sold three months ago for $260,000. What does each of these three figures represent?
3. An experienced real estate investor has stated that he never purchases a property unless he can buy it for less than it is worth. What concepts of value are involved in this statement?
4. The unencumbered fee simple estate in a property has an estimated Market Value of $125,000. There is an $80,000 mortgage and a $5,000 tax lien outstanding. What is the value of the fee holder's estate? What types of claim do the mortgage and the tax lien represent?
5. An influx of population is expected in Bigtown as a result of the expansion of a major manufacturing plant in the area. Existing apartment buildings have almost no vacancies, and there are none currently under construction. What will be the probable short-run effect on the apartment property market in the Bigtown area?

## Supplementary Readings

American Institute of Real Estate Appraisers, *The Appraisal of Real Estate*, fifth edition (Chicago: American Institute of Real Estate Appraisers, 1967), Chapters 1, 2, and 5.

Sanders A. Kahn, Frederick E. Case, and Alfred Schimmel, *Real Estate Appraisal and Investment* (New York: Ronald Press, 1963), Chapters 2-5.

William N. Kinnard, Jr., *An Introduction to Appraising Real Property: Student Reference* (Chicago: Society of Real Estate Appraisers, 1968), Sessions 1-6.

William N. Kinnard, Jr., "New Thinking in Appraisal Theory," *The Real Estate Appraiser*, Volume 32, Number 8, August 1966, Pages 1-12.

Richard U. Ratcliff, *A Restatement of Appraisal Theory* (Madison, Wisconsin:

Bureau of Business Research and Service, University of Wisconsin; 1963), Chapters 1 and 2.

Richard U. Ratcliff, *Modern Real Estate Valuation: Theory and Practice* (Madison, Wisconsin: Democrat Press, 1965), Chapters 1-3.

Alfred A. Ring, *The Valuation of Real Estate*, second edition (New York: Prentice-Hall, 1970), Chapters 1, 3-6.

Alfred A. Ring and Nelson L. North, *Real Estate Principles and Practices*, sixth edition (New York: Prentice-Hall, 1967), Chapters 1, 3, and 4.

Arthur M. Weimer and Homer Hoyt, *Real Estate*, fifth edition (New York: Ronald Press, 1966), Chapters 4-7.

## Notes

1. For a detailed presentation of what one professional real estate organization requires its members to include in every appraisal report, see Society of Real Estate Appraisers, *Standards of Professional Practice and Conduct* (Chicago: Society of Real Estate Appraisers, January 1971), Article II of "Standards of Professional Practice."

2. For a discussion of the importance and applicability of including a reasonable range within which estimated value will most probably be found, see R.U. Ratcliff, *Modern Real Estate Valuation: Theory and Practice* (Madison, Wisconsin: Democrat Press, 1965), pp. 60-61 and 138-140.

3. American Institute of Real Estate Appraisers, *The Appraisal of Real Estate*, fifth edition (Chicago: American Institute of Real Estate Appraisers, 1967), pages 12-22; William N. Kinnard, Jr., *An Introduction to Appraising Real Property: Student Reference* (Chicago: Society of Real Estate Appraisers, 1968), pages 5-8 through 5-10, and 6-1 through 6-12; and A.A. Ring, *The Valuation of Real Estate*, second edition (New York: Prentice-Hall, 1970), Chapter 1.

4. The implications of the imperfect character of real estate markets and submarkets are examined further in a subsequent section of this chapter, and in Kinnard, *Appraising Real Property*, pp. 5-1 through 5-8.

5. This concept is discussed in detail later in this chapter.

6. Society of Real Estate Appraisers, *Real Estate Appraisal Principles and Terminology* (Chicago: Society of Real Estate Appraisers, 1960), page 84.

7. This is the widely used, so-called California Definition enunciated by the Supreme Court of California in *Sacramento R.R. Co. et al., vs. Heilbron*, 156 Calif. 408.

8. The concept Most Probable Selling Price (Vp) was developed by Dr. R.U. Ratcliff. It is expounded at length in his *Modern Real Estate Valuation*, Chapter III.

9. For a fuller discussion of the topic of rights in realty, see A.A. Ring and N.L. North, *Real Estate Principles and Practices*, sixth edition (New York: Prentice-Hall, 1967), Chapter 4; or A.M. Weimer and H. Hoyt, *Real Estate*, fifth edition (New York: Ronald Press, 1966), Chapter 5.

10. More details on the physical, legal, and economic characteristics of real estate are provided in Ring and North, *Real Estate Principles and Practices*, Chapters 1, 3-9, 11, and 13-15; and Weimer and Hoyt, *Real Estate*, Chapters 4-6.

11. The economic meaning of location is explained at length in Weimer and Hoyt, *Real Estate*, Chapter 13; and R.U. Ratcliff, *Real Estate Analysis* (New York: McGraw-Hill, 1961), Chapter 4.

12. Fuller and more detailed coverage of the topic of real estate markets is provided in Ring and North, *Real Estate Principles and Practices*, Chapter 3; and Weimer and Hoyt, *Real Estate*, Chapters 6 and 12.

# 3

## Valuation Principles and the Appraisal Framework Applied to Income Properties

### Peculiarities of Income-Producing Properties for Appraisal Purposes

The physical, legal, and economic characteristics that distinguish real estate as an asset determine the structure and operation of real estate markets. They also influence the application of basic economic principles in the valuation process, as well as the structure of the analytical framework within which these principles are applied to estimate value.

The same basic principles of valuation and the same appraisal framework apply to every type of property, for every type of potential purchaser, and for every type of value estimate. Appraising income-producing real estate, however, requires the appraiser to emphasize certain of its distinguishing characteristics. To do so, he must first recognize those peculiarities.

As with all real estate, income property is a highly differentiated commodity that is fixed in location. Its immobility places a premium on location as a determinant of value. It is exchanged in imperfect markets characterized by relatively small numbers of relatively uninformed buyers and sellers of rights. Because it is relatively high-priced among all goods in the economy, its purchase typically requires some debt (mortgage) financing. Beyond all this, however, lie the peculiar features that set income properties apart and require particular consideration.

### Importance of Money Income as the Basis for Value, Valuation, and Financing

Income-producing real estate is urban space that commands a price for its use. It is commonly occupied or used by a tenant who pays for the locational and shelter services provided by the realty in periodic dollar payments called rentals.[a] If it is owner-occupied, the dollar saving experienced by the owner-occupant in not having to make rental payments is known as the "imputed rental." The underlying motivation for owning or acquiring income property is to receive the actual or imputed rental income generated by the use of the space.

---

[a]"Rent" is a technical term in economic theory and analysis that refers to an excess payment beyond what is necessary to bring or keep a productive resource in use on the market. To avoid confusion, the term applied to the periodic payment by a tenant for the use of urban space is called "rental" throughout this book. See the discussion of "market rental" as opposed to "economic rent" in Chapter 6 for further details.

33

Residential real estate is *amenity* property. The income received by the owner from his employment or from other property provides the basis for paying the purchase price. Mortgage financing of residences focuses on the income stability, income level, and credit history of the borrower rather than of the property.

In the case of income-producing real estate, on the other hand, the property itself provides the basis for its own purchase price and for mortgage financing, through the rental payments for its use. An investor-owner realizes a net income, or expects to, from which he will recover his purchase price. In the process, the property is expected to generate sufficient net income (more precisely, cash flow) to amortize any mortgage debt incurred in purchasing the property.

The imputed rental income produced by owner-occupied income properties represents rentals saved. From these savings, funds are generated to support purchase, ownership, and financing.

In both cases, value can be represented and measured by the discounted present worth of the forecast future income to be received by the owner, based on either actual or imputed rentals. Moreover, income capitalization or discounting is the appropriate valuation process to apply in deriving this present worth estimate.

*Investor Viewpoint*

In the valuation of income-producing real estate, the typical purchaser is frequently an investor, seeking benefits in the form of rental income rather than from his own use of the property. This reinforces the emphasis placed on the income-generating capabilities of the property. Value is typically viewed and measured as the present worth of the anticipated future income forecast to be derived from possession of ownership rights in the real estate.

As a corollary to this emphasis, attention is also focused on the profit or capital gain anticipated on resale or refinancing of the property at some future date. This consideration enters specifically into the investor's calculations of the investment attractiveness of the property, and is included among the future benefits whose present worth is estimated.

*Stratification of Investor Demand*

All real estate markets are stratified. The markets for income-producing real estate are specifically stratified according to the investment characteristics of the type of property, or the type of investor-purchaser, involved. It is no accident that sale-leaseback transactions involving high-credit tenants are particularly attractive to life insurance companies; while small office buildings or older apartment properties tend to be acquired by private, tax-liable individuals investing singly or in small groups.

Every property must be appraised in terms of "the market" in which it is competitive. The investment characteristics of the property help identify the most likely type of purchaser-investor, and hence the appropriate market for the property. Identification is made in terms of investment objectives of purchasers, as well as their broad income tax liability and financial status.

Specific tax status influences Investment Value. General tax status helps determine the market for a particular property or type of property, and hence Market Value.

## User Orientation

The valuation of income-producing properties requires identification of the most probable type of user as well as the most probable, or Highest and Best, use of the property. First, use is one determinant of value. Income-producing real estate is more likely to be user-designed and user-oriented, to the extent of being special-purpose or even single-use property. It is necessary to identify the most probable user or category of users before use can be ascertained.

Second, the character and credit rating of the user frequently influence the amount and terms of financing available to the owner, which in turn influence value. A highly rated tenant on a long-term lease considerably enhances marketability in most instances. This is one support for the Market Value of the leased fee or lessor's estate.

## Greater Emphasis on Use Analysis

Use is a direct determinant of value. Alternative uses frequently exist for both sites and improved income properties. As a result, much more emphasis must be placed on the analysis and conclusion of most probable or Highest and Best Use by the appraiser, More care and detail are required in applying this analysis to reach a conclusion as to Highest and Best Use.

## Emphasis on Functional Utility

Both user tastes or standards, and technological change, are important determinants of the changing economic life of income-producing buildings. Functional utility is a major component of their capacity to produce income, and hence of their present worth. Functional obsolescence is therefore much more significant in measuring both Diminished Utility (accrued depreciation) and the remaining economic life of improvements. The appraiser must be sensitively attuned to these changes in user tastes and standards of use when making income and use forecasts for income-producing properties, especially special-purpose and single-use properties.

*Mobility of User-Occupants*

Occupants of income properties who are not owners, and who are not committed to long-term leases, frequently exhibit considerable mobility. This stems from the changes in user standards, requirements, and tastes previously noted, as well as changes in building and space-use technology. Moreover, since a large proportion of income-property occupants are tenants, their opportunities for mobility are frequently greater than those of owner-occupants. The appraiser must take these phenomena into account in forecasting property income, and turn-over and vacancy rates. He must also consider conversion or renovation as an alternative use pattern in appraising existing income properties.

*Emphasis on Leasing*

Because a large proportion of income properties are leased, the appraiser must pay much greater attention to rental markets, as well as the mobility of occupants noted above. In addition, the appraiser of income-producing real estate must be skilled in leased fee and leasehold valuation. He must also be knowledgeable about leasing and lease terms, since they establish the future rental income whose present worth to the owner is being estimated.

*Influence of Financing*

Terms and conditions of mortgage financing (and sometimes equity financing as well) directly influence cash flows to the owner of income-producing real estate. Debt service is one determinant of cash throw-off to the owner's equity. Moreover, terms of financing are incorporated into the derivation of the rate(s) of return that a property must promise in order to be an attractive investment or purchase. Both income and rates of return influence the value of the property, whether Market Value or Investment Value is being sought.

In addition, financing terms determine the amount of financial leverage that a purchaser or investor is able to exercise. Leverage (which is explained in detail in Chapter 7) is one device to achieve the high rates of return anticipated on equity investment. This is important in identifying and understanding the rate(s) that a typically informed purchaser will seek on the market.

*Influence of Income Tax
Considerations*

It may be necessary to know the specific tax status of an individual investor in estimating Investment Value. After-tax cash flow represents the income that many investors use in making investment decisions.

More importantly, the income tax status of the most probable purchaser of a particular type of property influences required rates of return, and thus the most probable prices that such properties will command. It also helps identify the market in which the property being appraised is competing.

Income taxes tend to reduce net cash income. Since investors generally seek to maximize after-tax cash income, tax avoidance (which is legal, in contrast with illegal tax evasion) is a major motivating force for tax-liable investors. Tax avoidance includes deferring taxable income, treating income as long-term capital gain rather than ordinary income, and maximum exploitation of depreciation charges to reduce taxable income. The appraiser must understand how these considerations enter into real estate purchase and investment decisions, how they affect the terms of sale and terms of financing, and how they influence value. The graduated income tax is a fact of economic life which does in fact condition buyer behavior and the prices that buyers can and will pay for income property.

### Financing and Use as Determinants of Economic Life

As already noted, changing standards and requirements of use tend to place greater emphasis on the measurement of functional obsolescence of income-producing buildings. The use(s) to which an existing building are capable of being profitably put influence its remaining economic life. They also help determine the appropriate period of capital recapture for income properties.

Similarly, the amount and terms of financing available to a particular type of property or investor can influence the capital recapture period that is appropriate. They can lengthen or shorten economic life by affecting the period over which the property can be maintained in its present use and produce a competitive rate of return or profit to the owner. Income property investors are buying rights to money income flows rather than to real estate *per se*. Hence, the appraiser must be able to analyze and evaluate money and mortgage markets in relation to the property being appraised.

### Division of Income Property Into Analytical Components

Residential properties are typically appraised as a whole, or else divided into their physical components of site and improvements for appraisal analysis. Income-producing property can be and is divided into three sets of components for meaningful and useful analysis.

**Physical: Site and Improvements.** In applying Cost Analysis, and in the traditional land and building residual techniques of Income Capitalization necessary and appropriate to separate site and improvements for analytical purposes. The individual contribution of each physical component to total property value may be measured independently.

**Legal: Leased Fee and Leasehold.** Income-producing properties are frequently leased. A lease creates two or more marketable interests in the realty. The owner's (lessor's) interest is termed the Leased Fee; the tenant's (lessee's) interest is the Leasehold Estate. Both may have either Market Value or Investment Value, or both. Each is valued separately. The appraiser must be capable of dealing with this situation in appraising income properties.

**Financial or Investment: Mortgage and Equity.** Most income-producing real estate is acquired with mortgage financing. The interests of the lender (mortgagee) and the owner-borrower (mortgagor) are separable and individually marketable. One meaningful approach to valuation is to estimate the values of the mortgagee's and mortgagor's (equity investor's) interests separately. Indeed, much of Investment Value analysis focuses on estimating the value of the equity position. Each interest can also have a Market Value.

## Applicability of Valuation Principles to Income-Producing Properties

The basic principles of real estate valuation are universally applicable to all appraisal problems.[1] They therefore apply with equal force to the valuation of income-producing properties. Because of the distinguishing characteristics and peculiarities of income properties, however, different emphases are placed on these basic principles.

### Supply and Demand

Value, as defined, is determined by the interaction of the forces of supply and demand on the market.

Market Value is the result of the bids and offers of "typical" buyers, and the reactions of "typical" sellers, of rights in the type of realty being appraised. The market is defined in terms of the competition among buyers with similar characteristics, objectives, and market perceptions as investors. This competition among buyers represents the demand side. The supply side of the market is represented by competing properties that are similar and substitutable in the minds of competing buyer-investors. To understand the workings of supply and demand in a particular appraisal problem, the appraiser must analyze and evaluate their components as indicated in Chapter 2. This analysis should focus on those particular components that are pertinent to the impact of market forces on the value of the particular property being appraised.

The pertinent market for the estimation of Investment Value is easier to define. It is the specific potential purchaser-investor and the specific property being considered. Yet, it is still necessary to ascertain all the pertinent facts about each before a value estimate can be developed.

For income property valuation, demand analysis helps indicate the type, character, and objectives of the probable purchaser(s). Supply analysis indicates the amount, location, and character of the competition of the property being appraised, as well as the levels of prices and rentals most likely to occur.

## Highest and Best Use

As noted in Chapter 2, urban space tends to be put to its Highest and Best Use in a competitive market over the long run. Operating through the price mechanism of the market, urban real estate is generally allocated on the basis of user perceptions of that Highest and Best Use.

Highest and Best Use (or Most Profitable Use) is that reasonable and probable use that will support the highest present value, as defined, as of the effective date of the appraisal. Alternatively, it is the most profitable likely use to which a property can be put. It is usually *measured* by the present worth of the highest net return that a property can reasonably be forecast to produce over a stipulated long-run period.

The Highest and Best or Most Profitable Use of the land or site if vacant and available for use can be, and frequently is, different from that of the improved property. In each instance, the appraiser must make a selection from among those uses which are legally permissible, physically possible, appropriate, and financially or economically feasible. It may well be that a given site could be best used as a site for a shopping center if it were vacant, but is already improved with apartment buildings and is producing a competitive net return on the total investment in the property. In this case, the Highest and Best Use of the site would be for a shopping center, but the Highest and Best Use of the improved property (including site) would be its present use as an apartment complex.

For income properties, the appraiser must be much more specific and precise in his estimation of Highest and Best (or even most probable) Use. The variety of potential uses is much greater, and seemingly minor differences can have substantial effects on value. It is not enough to categorize Highest and Best Use as "Commercial," or even "Retail." The specific category must be identified and justified. Therefore, considerably more time and effort must go into Highest and Best Use analysis, and much more basic economic and financial analysis must support the conclusion.

In addition, particular care must be taken to identify the density or *intensity* of land use associated with a given *type* of use to ascertain Highest and Best Use. In many instances, the intensity of use (e.g., number of stories in an office building) can be more important than the selection of the most appropriate type of use.

Finally, alternative use programs must also be considered for existing buildings. Conversion, renovation, or even demolition frequently represent real possibilities. This is especially true when zoning and other land use controls permit broad categories of uses and wide ranges of densities. One has only to consider upper Park Avenue in New York City to recognize the significance of supersession of uses; or to examine the fate of mill-type industrial buildings in many cities and towns to see examples of conversion and renovation.

## Substitution (Opportunity Cost)

A prudent purchaser-investor would pay no more for a particular property than the cost (to him) of acquiring an equally desirable substitute property on the open market. Therefore, value tends to be set by the probable acquisition costs (prices) of such substitute properties that appear capable of providing the same utility to the owner as the property being appraised.

The application of this principle involves use of the economic concept of Opportunity Cost: the value or utility of a property is measured by the benefits of ownership foregone or given up by not selecting an alternative or competing property. For effective appraisal of income-producing real estate, it is necessary for the appraiser to identify the market alternatives that are realistically available to the most probable type of purchaser of the property in question. This indicates what he would be giving up to buy the subject property.

It is assumed that the decision-maker will act rationally and logically in selecting from among the alternative courses of action available to him. Three alternative means of acquiring a substitute property are potentially available to the purchaser-investor. First, he can buy an existing property with the same perceived utility as the one being appraised. This course of action provides the basis for Direct Sales Comparison Analysis. Second, he can produce or have produced a property with the same utility as the subject. This alternative is the basis for Cost Analysis, including the measurement of Diminished Utility of any improvements. Finally, the purchaser-investor can acquire an investment that provides a forecast future income stream of the same amount, duration, stability, quality, and risk as that forecast for the subject property. This is the basis for Income Capitalization Analysis.

In appraising income property, Substitution or Opportunity Cost provides a guide to value measurement. Value, as defined, can be measured by the amount that an informed and rational purchaser-investor would pay for competitive substitute property already in existence; the amount that he would pay to have a competitive substitute property produced; and/or the amount that he would pay for a competitive substitute income stream. In particular, consideration of Substitution helps identify the amount and other characteristics of income flow required for the property to be competitive. Equally importantly, Substitution is a major guide to the rate(s) of return that will be required by investors to make the subject property a competitively attractive purchase.

*Contribution (Marginal*
*Productivity)*

The value or present worth of any component of a property is measured by the amount it contributes to the value of the entire property. Alternatively, its value is measured by how much its absence does or would reduce the value of the whole. This means of net contribution is termed marginal productivity in economic analysis.

Contribution is the conceptual foundation for the estimation of the present worth of improvements in cost analysis (the so-called Cost Approach). In estimating the amount of Diminished Utility experienced by improvements in cost analysis, the appraiser is measuring how much the presence or absence of a particular characteristic either adds to or detracts from the value of the entire property. Similarly, the measurement of differences between the subject property and comparable sales (substitute) properties, to make adjustments in Direct Sales Comparison Analysis, is based on the Principle of Contribution.

The most important applications of the idea of Contribution or marginal productivity to income property appraisals occur in Income Capitalization Analysis. The residual techniques of traditional income capitalization are predicated on the appraiser's ability to identify the contribution of each physical component of the property (site and improvements) to the net income it is forecast to produce. Similarly, leased-fee and leasehold analysis values each legal component in terms of its respective income productivity or contribution. Mortgage-equity analysis permits the appraiser to estimate the present worth of the investor's equity by capitalizing its contribution to the investment. Indeed, the heart of capitalization analysis is to measure and value the present worth of the contribution, in money-income terms, of the investment or any of its major components.

*Anticipation*

Value is the present worth of *anticipated* future benefits or income forecast to be derived from ownership of the property rights being appraised. The expectations of buyers and sellers about future market conditions and future property benefits directly influence this estimate of worth. Real estate, it will be remembered, is a durable capital asset whose services are produced over a prolonged period of time.

The estimation of remaining economic life in Cost Analysis is based upon anticipations of the future. Entire market areas can feel the impact of anticipations of potential market participants. For example, a proposal to build a highway through a given area frequently dampens property values in the vicinity of the proposed right of way, and also reduces the level of market activity. At the same time, prices of properties which will remain in the vicinity of proposed interchanges are often bid up speculatively in anticipation of new use patterns and increased demand.

Income capitalization involves the conversion of anticipated future income or benefits to a present worth figure. The appraiser is continually forecasting or anticipating income flows in applying Income Capitalization Analysis. Discounting of future income, which is the mathematical and financial foundation of capitalization, is based on anticipation.

## Change

Value is subject to continual change, as the market conditions which determine value change. The dynamics of the market are such that the forces of demand and supply are constantly changing. This is why a value estimate is always expressed as of a specified effective date.

Changing user tastes, standards, and requirements are constantly being encountered in the appraisal of income-producing real estate. The same is true of changing technology, changing money-market conditions, and changing locational patterns. Change as a concept is no different in income-property appraisal. What is different is the critical importance of indicated and anticipated change as an influence on remaining economic life, required capital recapture periods, functional obsolescence, net incomes, and cash flows—all of which work directly to determine value.

## Conformity

Value is enhanced when the property being appraised is in conformity with the standards of acceptability applicable in the market(s) in which it is competing. Residential properties are enhanced in value when they tend to conform to one another in a given neighborhood or market area. In the case of income properties, however, physical conformity is not as significant as is conformity to the tastes, standards, and requirements of potential users. Moreover, anticipated income flows must conform to the standards of potential investors or purchasers with respect to stability, risk, and amount. It is, therefore, most important for the appraiser to know and understand the occupancy standards of potential users and the investment standards of potential purchasers when income-producing properties are being appraised.

## Variable Proportions

When successive increments of one or more factors of production are added to fixed amounts of the other factors, income tends first to increase at an increasing rate, then at a decreasing rate, and finally decreases absolutely. This is an important principle in comparing alternative use patterns and *intensities* of use to reach a conclusion as to Highest and Best Use. In real estate appraisal, the amount of land is typically the fixed factor and alternative improvement programs represent the variable factors. This phenomenon is sometimes referred to as Increasing and Decreasing Returns, and is the basis for the so-called economic principle of diminishing returns.

The point of maximum productivity, and therefore of maximum value, is achieved when all factors of production are in balance with one another. This principle applies to a development program for a parcel of land; it applies to maximizing the amenities of a neighborhood as well. The point of maximum productivity of "balance" is known in economic analysis as the point of diminishing returns. Beyond this point, successive increments of the variable factors of production result in a less than proportionate increase in productivity, and hence in value. The combination of factors resulting in maximum productivity represents the Highest and Best Use of the property.

Because alternative possible improvement and use programs usually exist for income properties, estimation of their Highest and Best Use requires special emphasis on varying patterns of intensity of use.

### The Appraisal Framework[2]

Every appraisal requires the appraiser to apply a systematic framework of analysis—a judgment model—to a set of data dictated by the nature of the problem. The objective is to reach a conclusion or estimate of value as defined. The same framework of systematic stages of data-gathering, analysis, and judgments is legitimately applied in every case. Only the data utilized will vary, according to the value sought, the rights appraised, the type of realty, and the type of most probable purchaser. The peculiar and distinguishing characteristics of income-producing real estate necessitate consideration of the application of this analytical framework to such properties.

#### *Value Estimation as a Forecast*

Value, however defined, is the present worth of anticipated future benefits to be received from possession of rights in realty. These anticipations are based on forecasts. In the case of income-producing real estate appraisals, the forecasts are of future dollar income receipts and of the market conditions that will influence the amount, timing, duration, and certainty of those income receipts. Based on these forecasts of the economic and financial factors related to the property and its market environment, the appraiser then must forecast the manner in which the most probable purchaser-investor will react to these anticipated future conditions. A real estate appraisal is always forward-looking from the effective date as of which the value estimate is made.

**Forecasting as Opposed to Prediction and Projection.** The appraiser makes forecasts. His estimates of the future are not predictions, however, and only infrequently are they based on projections.

*Forecasting.* A forecast is an estimate of a future happening or condition. It consists of estimating what will most probably happen in the future, based in part on analysis of trends of the recent past, but tempered in the analytical judgment. A forecast is also based on the existence of accrued or stipulated conditions of forces external to the factor(s) being forecast.

*Prediction.* A prediction is an attempt to foretell precisely a specific happening or condition. It contains an implied or expressed degree of accuracy or precision that is impossible in appraising. The best that an appraiser can hope to be expected to provide is a defensible estimate of what may or most probably can be anticipated to occur under specified conditions, not what will happen.

*Projection.* A projection is a forecast developed by the mechanical process of extrapolating or extending the experience of the recent past into the future with the use of a mathematical formula. It may be a simple straight-line projection, or it may be based on a more complex formula. In any event, it is founded on the presumption that the same conditions and rates of change that have been observed in the past will continue in precisely the same relationships to one another in the future. This position is at variance with the experience of real estate markets and of appraisers. An appraiser may well begin his market analysis with projections of past trends, but they must be tempered with judgment based on an appreciation of the workings of the forces making for different market conditions in the future.

*A Systematic Approach to
Problem-Solving*[3]

Real estate appraisals are sought and made because a decision-maker has a problem to solve, and an estimate of the present worth of rights in realty is expected to help in solving that problem. The potential purchasers of those rights wants to know how best to allocate his capital resources to uses that will best fulfill his objectives. The most rational and defensible approach is to apply a systematic process of analysis and judgment to available information in order to identify the course of action most responsive to the decision-maker's stated goals.

**What is a Problem?** A problem exists when there are resources available to the decision-maker to permit *alternative* approaches to attack a block in the path toward the realization of the decision-maker's objectives. The "problem" lies in choosing the best among the alternative possible solutions. No "problem" exists if there are no alternative solution strategies available, although the decision-maker may certainly experience difficulty or discomfort. Investment decisions, including those involving income-producing real estate, are always problems because there are always alternative uses of investment funds.

**What is Problem-Solving?** Problem-solving is decision-making. It involves making a selection from among alternative courses of action to remove or circumvent deterrents to the realization of the decision-maker's goals. The process of problem-solving can be regarded as a sequence of definitions and identifications, with each succeeding one more specific and precise than the one preceding it. The final definition or identification is the solution strategy (course of action) most consistent with the stated choice criteria or judgment standards of the decision-maker.

The "best" solution is the one with the optimal value measurement (highest present worth) in terms of the goals of the decision-maker. The value of a decision follows from the consequences of putting a strategy into action. Decision-making is action-oriented. It is meaningless without execution of the strategy, even when the best strategy is to do nothing.

**What is a Systematic Process?** The rational real estate investment decision-making model is a systematic process applied to choices among alternatives in the allocation of capital funds and in the uses of real estate. A systematic process is a consciously designed approach to solve a problem: to remove or circumvent blocks in the path toward realization of an investment decision-maker's objectives. The approach is a logical sequence of definitional steps in an analytical framework that can be applied in a variety of circumstances. It may be subject to quantification. The more valid and reliable the quantification, the less uncertainty there is about the results. The real objective of a systematic process of analysis is to reduce and identify the areas of uncertainty where judgment remain necessary.

The Appraisal Framework is a systematic process of analysis. So, too, is the logical, rational investment judgment model which the appraiser of rights in income-producing real estate seeks to simulate in making his value estimate.

**The Investment Decision Model.** The decision model that constitutes a simulation of a rational investment decision-maker's problem-solving approach is a systematic process of some eight successive steps of sequential definition and identification. Readers familiar with the Appraisal Framework will note a striking similarity between the two. Both represent a systematic process of problem-solving: the latter used by the appraiser in reaching his value conclusion; the former applied by the investor-client in reaching a decision based in part on the estimate of value provided by the appraiser.

*Define the Problem.* This is often the most important—and difficult—step in the entire process. What is the nature of the block that must be removed so that the decision-maker may achieve his objectives? Is there truly a problem, in the sense that potential alternative courses of action to remove the block actually exist?

*Identify the Decision-Maker's Goals or Objectives.* These must be stated as explicitly as possible. They represent the answer to the question "A block to *what*?" What are the standards or criteria of the decision-maker for reaching a decision?

*Develop Initial Hypotheses about the Directions of Investigation.* What types of actions, either by the decision-maker or by others, have been successful or responsive in solving similar problems in the past? What resources and alternative action strategies appear available?

*Identify Events.* These are actions and conditions from the outside environment over which the decision-maker can be expected to be able to exercise no appreciable control. What are the external, market-given forces which the decision-maker must accept as uncontrollable influences on the outcome of any actions he takes?

*Identify Strategies for Solution.* These are actions under the control of the decision-maker, given the resources available to remove the block that exists in the path toward realization of his objectives. What alternative courses of action are realistically open to the decision-maker?

*Identify the Probable Outcomes of Alternative Solution Strategies.* Each solution strategy involves a specific course of action with associated anticipated or forecast results. They are expressed in value measures of goal attainment. What is the forecast present worth to the decision-maker of each alternative possible course of action?

*Make Forecast Judgments.* Select, quantify, and rank the forecast outcomes of each alternative course of action in terms of the probability of the results. What are the implications of those results in each instance?

*Identify the "Best" Solution Strategy.* From among the forecast outcomes of alternative possible courses of actions, which comes closest to fulfilling the decision-maker's goals. This conclusion is reached in terms of the choice criteria or decision standards established in identifying the objectives of the decision process.

*Application of the Appraisal Framework*
*to Income Properties*

The Appraisal Framework is a systematic process of analysis applied by the appraiser to the solution of every appraisal problem. Every appraisal is a problem because the appraiser must identify and select from several potentially applicable routes to estimating a specifically defined value. Every appraisal is also a form of research project because the appraiser must identify and gather systematically the data required in the analysis.

As with any systematic process of problem-solving analysis, the steps in the Appraisal Framework move from the general to successively more specific considerations. The external market environment within which decisions will have to be made, and from which data on general forces influencing value must be derived, is identified and analyzed first. Then the characteristics of the subject property and those substitute properties that constitute its effective competition are identified and evaluated. Next, the alternative courses of action realistically available to the type of purchaser-investor involved are identified and their implications measured. Finally, a choice of most probable value, as defined, is made.

To be effective, the application of this systematic framework requires good, reliable data. The appraiser needs a good working knowledge of the best sources of needed information, and the ability to judge the validity, reliability, and representativeness of this information. The data must be not only reliable, but current as well. To conduct effective appraisal analysis, the appraiser has a continuing responsibility to establish and maintain current a bank of data files. Moreover, there must be an appreciation of what data are required, and how best they may be utilized in both market and property analysis.

As a research project, every appraisal involves four major steps:

1. prepare an outline: a plan or blueprint for action by the appraiser;
2. assemble materials for analysis: market and property data;
3. apply appropriate tools of analysis: analytical techniques and approaches; and
4. apply judgment to reach a conclusion: selection in terms of decision standards.

The successive definitions and identifications that constitute the Appraisal Framework simply represent amplifications and classifications of these four basic steps. The peculiar emphases required in income-property appraisals are noted under the consideration of each.

**Define the Problem.** For income properties, the problem usually involves a potential investor's decision whether to acquire rights in investment realty, and for how much. The appraiser's problem is to identify what is to be valued, what value is to be estimated, and the effective date of the appraisal.

*Identify the Decision-Maker's Problem.* This defines the performance expected of the appraiser. It is also important in defining what value(s) the appraiser is to estimate.

*Identify the Realty.* Both physical and legal identification are required to provide an unequivocal indication of the realty involved. The appraiser must know where and how to obtain this information.

*Identify the Property Rights to be Valued.* What portion of the bundle of rights in the realty is to be appraised? The appraiser should never *assume* that the unencumbered fee is to be valued. Income properties are often subject to leases and/or mortgages, and it is essential to ascertain what interest(s) the client wants appraised. In addition, both public and private limitations on the exercise of the rights being valued can affect the income receivable by the owner of these rights. This requires especially careful identification of property taxes, zoning, and other land-use controls, deed restrictions, and liens outstanding.

*Identify the Value to be Estimated.* This establishes the purpose of the appraisal. Market Value is commonly sought, but not necessarily. The value estimate must be responsive to the decision-maker's needs. The value to be estimated must be clearly elicited from the client, in part as a result of identifying his problem. The definition of the particular type of value being sought will dictate the kinds of data required and the analytical tools to be used in reaching the final value estimate.

*Identify the Effective Date of the Value Estimate.* This indicates the market conditions in terms of which the estimate of value is to be made. It also helps identify the data required to make the appraisal, and the appropriate sources of those data.

**Plan the Appraisal.** Once the problem is clearly defined, the appraiser must then carefully plan the approach to be used in solving the problem.

*Identify the Market.* For income property appraisals in particular, this requires an identification of the type of substitute properties most likely to represent the competition for the subject property, and their location. It also requires identification of the most probable type of purchaser-investor likely to represent potential and effective demand for the rights being appraised. This is the decision-maker's competition. It identifies the submarket in which he must function and compete. The appraiser must also be able to indicate the important characteristics of a property that will make it a reasonable, effective alternative to the subject, in the minds of this most probable type of purchaser. Market definition and delineation are important in specifying what data will be needed to estimate value as defined.

*Identify Pertinent Demand and Supply Factors.* Within the framework of the applicable submarket for the type of property being appraised, what components of demand and supply are particularly pertinent? Terms and availability of financing for properties of the type being appraised can be critical in demand analysis for investment real estate. The value, location, amenities offered, and rentals of new construction may be important components of supply analysis for an apartment property. The nature of the appraisal problem and the character of the market establish what demand and supply factors are pertinent. These factors in turn determine the data required for appropriate analysis by the appraiser.

*Identify the Appropriate Methods and Tools of Analysis to be Employed.* Given the nature of the appraisal problem, the type of value to be estimated, the characteristics of the property, and the character of the market, the appraiser can identify which analytical tools appear particularly appropriate to reaching the value estimate sought. There are several alternative analytical techniques and tools potentially available to the appraiser of income-producing real estate.[a] At this stage, his task is to identify those which appear to be responsive to the particular appraisal problem and should be applied as guides to the value to be estimated. Each has peculiar characteristics and data requirements. The selection of technique(s) and tool(s) to be used helps further in identifying the data required to complete the appraisal.

The nature of the problem and of the property may preclude the use of one or more of the available analytical tools. The estimation of Investment Value usually calls for income capitalization only. A value estimate for an existing functionally obsolescent industrial property may not rely on cost and diminished utility analysis. The valuation of a leasehold interest may not permit sales comparison or cost analysis.

*Identify Data Requirements.* These are established by the nature of the problem and the property, the type of value to be estimated, and the analytical tools previously determined as potentially applicable. At this point, both background market data and specific property data should be indicated. Full identification of all data needed will save time and effort when the appraiser actually gathers the data.

*Identify Sources and Probable Availability of Required Data.* Unless they are already available in the appraiser's files, which is rarely the case, data previously identified as necessary to complete the appraisal analysis have to be obtained from authoritative and reliable sources. The appraiser must be thoroughly familiar with those sources and have access to them. He must also be aware of the effective availability of required data. No matter how applicable a particular technique or tool of analysis may be to the appraisal problem, if data are not available or if they are questionable, then the technique cannot be defended for

---

[a]Most appraisal authorities currently refer to different "approaches" to value estimation. Three major "approaches" are usually identified: the Cost Approach, the Direct Sales Comparison Approach, and the Income (Capitalization) Approach. These are discussed more fully in a subsequent section of this chapter: A Note on the "Three Approaches."

use in the particular appraisal. The data sources should be identified clearly and fully, so as to avoid unnecessary delays in carrying out the appraisal assignment.

*Design the Research Program.* This involves setting out in detail the several steps to be taken in gathering and analyzing data. It also necessitates a systematic program of work activities, with time priorities established to identify the order in which the steps are to be completed.

*Outline the Appraisal Report.* This will help the appraiser check his previous work to make sure that no essential steps have been omitted, and that the work program is scheduled in the proper sequence. For income-property appraisals in particular, the myriad details required to complete the analysis necessitate careful identification of the format within which the data, analysis, and conclusions are to be presented.

**Gather the Data.** After the appraisal has been carefully planned, the first overt action by the appraiser is to gather the required data systematically.

*Sequence Data-Gathering in the Order of Use.* By doing this, the appraiser will identify earlier any difficulties that may emerge in obtaining required information. Backup sources can be identified and exploited as needed. Since appraisal analysis is sequential, the specific data build upon and are influenced by the more general market data.

*Verify the Data as They Are Gathered.* Data used in appraisal analysis must be valid and authoritative. "Indications" of apparent facts are insufficient. Continued verification of data as they are gathered eliminates the necessity to reject apparent factual information later, and avoids the development of improper conclusions. Moreover, the ability or inability to verify crucial data helps determine the actual applicability of techniques of analysis that previously seemed to be appropriate.

**Analyze the Data.** Once gathered, verified data must be subjected to further analysis to derive both findings and, ultimately, conclusions. While the final objective of any appraisal is to estimate value as defined, a large number of intermediate findings, judgments, and conclusions must be reached in the process. This is particularly true of income-property appraisals that include income capitalization analysis, as is clearly shown in Chapter 4.

*Evaluate Market Area and Neighborhood Influences.* Market trends in demand and supply forces, and their probable impact on the value of the property being appraised, must be identified. Forecasts of these environmental influences must be made, with a conclusion about their probable effect on current market decisions.

*Identify Highest and Best Use of the Property.* Both market and property data are employed in making this judgment. Market Value is estimated in terms of Highest and Best Use. For Investment Value estimates, Most Probable Use must be identified. In either case, the selection is based on available data about what uses are legal, possible, appropriate, *and* feasible.

*Identify Salient, Pertinent Property Characteristics.* It is necessary to discover features or units which form the basis of use of the type of property being appraised. Use is a major determinant of value. The desires and reactions of typical or most probable users and buyers indicate what features of the property actually do make a difference on the market. Room size may be significant in apartment or office building appraisals. Clear span area or ceiling height may be critical for industrial warehouse users. Parking area may be important to shopping center investors and tenants. These are the characteristics that make a difference to potential purchasers, and which must be subjected to comparative market analysis with competitive substitute properties.

*Ascertain Applicability of Analytical Methods and Tools.* Given the availability of reliable, verified data, the appraiser must identify which of the potentially and logically applicable techniques and tools of analysis can actually be employed in making the appraisal.

**Apply the Data and Analysis to the Alternative Methods of Valuation Identified as Applicable.** There are at least three alternative formats of analysis to simulate the alternative courses of action potentially available to the purchaser-investor of income-producing real estate. Within each of these, there are sub-structures which use different tools and data to achieve the same basic valuation objectives. The appraiser will have already identified which alternative tools and methods are applicable to the problem. This identification is based on (1) the nature of the appraisal problem; (2) the underlying logic of the several analytical methods available; and (3) the availability and verified reliability of required data. He then subjects each of these applicable alternatives to an analysis which results in a preliminary indication of value as defined.

*Direct Sales Comparison Analysis.* When the availability of data permit its use, this analytical method produces an indication of what the purchaser-investor would most probably have to pay for the same rights in existing substitute properties on the same market, as of the effective date of the appraisal.[4] It is most commonly applied to the valuation of income-producing real estate when there is an active market for substitute properties, especially those which are adaptable to more than one use or whose use has a broad-based demand. Value is frequently expressed as so many dollars per unit of use, or unit of comparison. Value for both sale and rental can be estimated through the application of this approach. It is equally applicable to site valuation and to the valuation of improved properties. It is most useful in developing an estimate of Market Value or Most Probable Sales Price.

*Cost and Diminished-Utility Analysis.* The appropriate and defensible application of this analytical method produces an indication of what the purchaser-investor would most probably have to pay to produce or have produced an improved property which is highly substitutable for the property being appraised.[5] This substitutability is typically expressed, but impossible to measure directly, in terms of equal utility. In income-property appraising, cost analysis is particularly helpful in estimating Market Value for new or proposed developments. It is also useful in providing a basis of comparison in making decisions about conversion or changes in use. It has little general applicability when either reliable comparative sales data or good comparative income and rate-of-return data are available to the appraiser.

*Income-Capitalization Analysis.* This is the major topic of the present book. It provides an indication of what the purchaser-investor would most probably have to pay to acquire the right to receive an income stream with the same characteristics (amount, timing, duration, stability, certainty) as those identified for the forecast-income stream of the property being appraised. It can be used to estimate the Market Value of an interest in income property. It is also the only usable method for estimating Investment Value.

**Identify Final Value Estimate.** The application of more than one analytical method or set of tools to the verified data gathered by the appraiser will frequently result in preliminary indications of value that are not identical. Market imperfections, especially less than full availability of all required and desired data, virtually guarantee this. Yet, appraisal assignments commonly require the appraiser to estimate a single dollar figure that in his professional judgment most nearly represents the value sought.

The next-to-last step in the Appraisal Framework, therefore, is to derive that single figure from the several indications of value developed in the analysis. It may often be appropriate to indicate the range within which the value being sought most probably can be found as well.

To reach his final value estimate, the appraiser must re-examine the nature of the problem, the probable applicability and responsiveness of the several analytical methods employed to that problem, the adequacy and reliability of the data used in applying those analytical methods, and the logic and validity of his own thought processes in conducting the analysis. From this "examination of professional conscience," the price that will tend to prevail under the specified market conditions will emerge. This figure is the final estimate of value as defined.[6]

**Write the Appraisal Report.** Income property valuation is not merely a stimulating mental exercise. Moreover, it is not enough for the appraiser to be convinced of the logical impeccability and defensibility of his value estimate. An appraisal is made for the use of a decision-maker with a problem to solve. The appraiser's findings and conclusions must therefore be communicated effectively and convincingly to the party or parties seeking to use the value estimate to make a decision.

These findings are almost always presented in a written report. The specific contents of the report may vary with the nature of the assignment and the client's (or employer's) instructions.[7] Yet, every appraisal report should always contain sufficient information for the reader or user to be able to follow the procedures and thinking employed by the appraiser. The data and analysis should be presented in such a way that the reader is led inexorably and inevitably to the same conclusion(s) reached by the appraiser.

### A Note on the "Three Approaches"

There is considerable controversy current in appraisal thinking and writing over whether there are or are not "three approaches" to value estimation. Traditionally, it has been argued and generally accepted that there are.[8] More recently, some leading writers have maintained there is only one "approach"— the market approach—and that the several alternative techniques and methods employed by appraisers are only different manifestations of market analysis and a single Market Approach.[9]

This argument is essentially one of semantics or terminology. Debate over labels is sterile, provided the tools of analysis are responsive to the needs of appraisers and the decision-makers they serve. What is really required is for neither side to be doctrinaire. If the labels are helpful in identifying tools and techniques that the appraiser should *consider* as potentially applicable in solving an appraisal problem, calling them "approaches" to value estimation may be appropriate. Certainly, all data used in appraisal analysis must be derived from the market identified as applicable to the problem. To this extent, every tool of analysis employed in an appraisal is part of a "market approach."

Much more importantly, every estimate of Market Value, at least, includes a presumption that the appraiser will consider and judge the applicability of each of the alternative courses of action potentially available to the decision-maker. What are these alternatives? He can purchase the rights in the realty being appraised. He can also decide not to go through with the transaction and do nothing. In deciding whether to acquire the rights in question, he is concerned with the utility of those rights as measured by their dollar value.

If he acts rationally to meet his objectives on the basis of available market information, he will pay no more for the property rights being appraised than the cost to him of acquiring property rights with the same perceived utility. The applicable submarket provides indications of what that acquisition cost most probably will be. The realistic alternative choices confronting the decision-maker (ignoring the alternative to do nothing) do happen to be three in number.

The purchaser-investor can acquire through purchase an existing substitute property with the same apparent utility. The value of the subject property is measured by the price(s) at which effective substitute properties can be or have been purchased, under similar market conditions. Analyzing sales data for competitive substitute properties constitutes what is called Direct Sales Comparison Analysis here, and what is widely termed the Market Data Approach.

Alternatively, the purchaser-investor may possibly produce or have produced a substitute property with the same perceived utility as the subject property has. The cost of production of this substitute property, provided it is market-determined, represents another measure of the value of the property being appraised. This cost-of-production figure is derived by what is termed Cost and Diminished Utility Analysis here, and what is generally known as the Cost Approach.

For income-producing real estate, the purchaser-investor has a third possible choice. He can acquire a substitute investment whose forecast income stream has the same size, duration, timing, stability, and certainty (or risk) as the income stream forecast for the subject property. The present worth or capitalized value of such an income stream represents the value of the right to receive that income stream. The cost of acquiring a competitive substitute income stream on the market measures the value of the property rights being appraised. This acquisition cost is calculated by what is called Income Capitalization Analysis here, and what is usually known as the Income Approach.

These three alternatives provide the conceptual foundation for approaching the valuation of property rights in income-producing real estate. They are interdependent and interrelated, and they all require data from the same market. Whatever labels are attached to them, they are applicable when (1) their underlying logic represents a realistic course of action for the decision-maker whose thinking is simulated in appraisal analysis; and (2) the market data required for their use are obtainable by the appraiser.

## Review Exercises

1. An appraiser has concluded that apartments of the same general type, size, and location as those in the property being appraised are typically renting for $45 per room per month in the current market. What principle of valuation is illustrated by this finding?
2. A new office building is being proposed on a vacant site. Market analysis has revealed that there is strong demand in the area for office space of the type planned. The developers are trying to decide whether the building should contain 14, 16, or 20 stories. What valuation principles would the appraiser apply in trying to help the developers make this decision?
3. After completing the analysis required in Question 2, the appraiser concludes that the property would be worth $1,400,000 with a 14-story building;

$1,700,000 with a 16-story building; and $1,900,000 with a 20-story building. Assuming constant site costs and constant unit construction costs, explain what valuation principles these different value estimates represent, and how.

## Supplementary Readings

American Institute of Real Estate Appraisers, *The Appraisal of Real Estate*, fifth edition (Chicago: American Institute of Real Estate Appraisers, 1967), Chapters 3-4.

Frederick M. Babcock, "Valuation Process and Appraisal Purpose," *The Real Estate Appraiser*, Volume 31, Number 4, April 1965, pp. 9-14.

Byron M. Church, "How Many Approaches?" *The Real Estate Appraiser*, Volume 33, Number 5, May 1967, pp. 26-30.

William N. Kinnard, Jr., *An Introduction to Appraising Real Property: Student Reference* (Chicago: Society of Real Estate Appraisers, 1968), Chapters 6 and 7.

Richard U. Ratcliff, *A Restatement of Appraisal Theory* (Madison, Wisconsin: Bureau of Business Research and Service, University of Wisconsin, 1963), Chapters 1 and 6.

Richard U. Ratcliff, *Modern Real Estate Valuation: Theory and Application* (Madison, Wisconsin: Democrat Press, 1965), Chapters 1, 4, and 8.

Alfred A. Ring, *The Valuation of Real Estate*, second edition (New York: Prentice-Hall, 1970), Chapter 3.

Halbert C. Smith and Ronald L. Racster, "Should the Traditional Appraisal Process Be Restructured?" *The Real Estate Appraiser*, Volume 36, Number 7, November-December 1970, pp. 6-11.

## Notes

1. Further classifications and discussions of the principles of real-property valuation may be found in American Institute of Real Estate Appraisers, *The Appraisal of Real Estate*, fifth edition (Chicago: American Institute of Real Estate Appraisers, 1967). Chapter 3; W.N. Kinnard, Jr., *An Introduction to Appraising Real Property: Student Reference* (Chicago: Society of Real Estate Appraisers, 1968), Session 6; and A.A. Ring, *The Valuation of Real Estate*,

second edition (New York: Prentice-Hall, 1970), pp. 31-42. Slight differences in terminology exist among these sources, but the basic principles themselves and the economic foundations on which they are based are the same.

2. While there may be variations in terminology and specific formulations of the structure of the Appraisal Framework, there is general agreement among appraisal authorities about the existence of a necessary systematic framework of analysis. Most authorities also agree on the basic steps and content of this network. See, for example, AIREA, *Appraisal of Real Estate*, Chapter 4; and Kinnard, *Appraising Real Property*, Session 7. See also R.U. Ratcliff, Modern Real Estate Valuation: *Theory and Application* (Madison, Wisconsin: Democrat Press, 1965), Chapters 1, 4, and 8.

3. For more detailed presentations of the scientific decision-making process, especially as it is applied to investment decisions, consult: E.C. Bursk and J.F. Chapman, eds., *New Decision-Making Tools for Managers* (New York: New American Library, 1965), Chapters 6 and 7; G.D. Quirin, *The Capital Expenditure Decision* (Homewood, Illinois: Irwin, 1967), especially Chapters 1, 2, and 9; and P.F. Wendt and A.R. Cerf, *Real Estate Investment Analysis and Taxation* (New York: McGraw-Hill, 1969), especially Chapters 1, 9, and 10.

4. The details of Direct Sales Comparison Analysis as it is applied to the valuation of income property are provided in Chapter 17. The basic framework of technique and data requirements is precisely the same as that presented in any introductory appraisal text or course. It is variously called the Direct Sales Comparison Approach, the Market Sales Comparison Approach, the Comparative Sales Approach, or the Market Data Approach. See, for example, AIREA, *Appraisal of Real Estate*, pp. 63-65, and Chapters 20 and 21; Kinnard, *Appraising Real Property*, pp. 7-9 and 7-10, and Session 13; and Ring, *Valuation of Real Estate*, Chapter 10.

5. The application of Cost and Diminished Utility Analysis to income-property appraisal is discussed in Chapter 16. Its structure, techniques, and data requirements are those of the so-called Cost Approach. Every basic appraisal text or course deals with it in detail. Examples are: AIREA, *Appraisal of Real Estate*, Chapters 9-14; Kinnard, *Appraising Real Property*, pp. 7-10 and 7-11, and Sessions 15-17; and Ring, *Valuation of Real Estate*, Chapters 11-13.

6. The process of deriving a final-value estimate from two or more preliminary indications of value is commonly referred to as "Correlation," although some authorities object to this terminology. See Chapter 20 for details. Correlation and Final Value Estimation are discussed in AIREA, *Appraisal of Real Estate*, Chapter 23; Kinnard, *Appraising Real Property*, Session 17; and Ring, *Valuation of Real Estate*, Chapter 23. An opposing view is contained in R.U. Ratcliff, *A Restatement of Appraisal Theory* (Madison, Wisconsin: Bureau of Business Research and Service, University of Wisconsin; 1963), Chapters 1 and 6.

7. The essential ingredients of an appraisal, and hence of an appraisal report, have already been noted in Chapter 1. The writing of appraisal reports for income properties is discussed further in Chapter 20. Professional appraisal societies have established standards of appraisal reports for their members. Those of the Society of Real Estate Appraisers may be found in Kinnard, *Appraising Real Property*, Session 18 and Appendix C; those of the American Institute of Real Estate Appraisers are presented in AIREA, *Appraisal of Real Estate*, Chapter 24 and Appendix A.

8. See, for example, AIREA, *Appraisal of Real Estate*, pp. 60-67. For a variation on this theme, see Kinnard, *Appraising Real Property*, pp. 6-15—6-17, and 7-11—7-14.

9. For further developments of this position, consult Ratcliff, *Restatement of Appraisal Theory*, Chapters 1 and 6; and H.C. Smith and R.L. Racster, "Should the Traditional Appraisal Process be Restructured?" *The Real Estate Appraiser*, Volume 36, Number 7, November-December 1970, pp. 6-11.

**Part II
Income Capitalization**

# 4

# The Framework of Income
# Capitalization Analysis

## An Introductory Note on Terminology

Real estate appraisal is a constantly changing, dynamic field. As a consequence, there is no universal agreement on all points of theory and practice, or of terminology. Yet, it is a technical field that requires precise thinking that should be reflected in clear and unequivocal technical language, at the least. It is based upon and derived from urban land economics and financial investment analysis. Its lexicon should include terms that are compatible with those of economics and finance, yet they should be sufficiently differentiated from them to avoid confusion and misunderstanding.

The finest appraisal analysis is useless unless its results and meaning can be communicated effectively to the appraiser's clients and employers. Moreover, appraisers must be able to communicate clearly and precisely with one another. Neither of these objectives is realized in every case at the present time because some widely used terms are not as precise or as clear as they might be. In addition, there are frequently several different variations of the same term in current use.

An effort has been made throughout this book, and especially with this introduction of Income Capitalization Analysis, to use terms that are accurate, widely accepted, descriptive, understandable, and unequivocal. These objectives have proved incompatible in several instances. Where necessary, technical precision and accuracy have been given preference over common usage in the interests of descriptive presentation and understanding. Wherever possible, and appropriate, generally accepted terms already in use have been retained. Only when it has appeared necessary to avoid confusion or misunderstanding—or inaccuracy—have new or different terms been introduced. Each is explained and related to the one(s) it has replaced.

Internal consistency in usage has been emphasized. Whenever more than one acceptable or descriptive term is in current use in the appraisal field, the preferred term is emphasized here. However, the others are noted for reference in case they are encountered in the reader's subsequent work.

## Rationale of Income-Capitalization Analysis

This presentation is an overview of the theory and mechanics of the entire process of income capitalization as applied to real estate valuation. It is also a preview of the several topics that are discussed in detail in the following seven chapters. It is also designed to serve as a review when those topics have been studied and absorbed in turn.

Income Capitalization Analysis depicts one alternative course of action potentially available to the decision-maker considering the acquisition of rights in income-producing real estate. It is the basis for the so-called "Income Approach" to value estimation. It results in an estimate of the amount that a decision-maker would be justified in paying to acquire the right to receive an income stream of a specified amount, with specified characteristics of timing, duration, stability, and certainty or risk—given the standards of acceptability provided by the market. This amount is the present worth of the income stream, and may represent either Market Value or Investment Value. The income-producing characteristics of income real estate make the use of Income Capitalization Analysis to estimate value particularly appropriate.

*Basic Premise: Present Worth of*
*Anticipated Future Benefits*

Real estate is a capital good. This means that the benefits from owning it—whether in the form of money income or amenities, or both—are received over a prolonged period of time. Operationally, this means more than one year; in fact, it is typically for 10, 20, 40 or more years.

In all economic and investment analysis, of which real estate appraisal is an integral part, the value of a capital good is established and measured by calculating the *present worth*, as of a particular valuation date, of the anticipated future benefits (income) to the owner over a specified time period. The process of converting an income stream into a single capital value is known as *capitalization*. The result of the capitalization process is a present worth estimate. This is the amount or capital sum that a prudent, typically informed purchaser-investor would pay as of the valuation date for the right to receive the forecast net income over the period specified.

The mathematical procedure of applying a specific rate (usually derived from the market) to the anticipated future income stream in order to develop a present worth estimate is known as *discounting*. Because of the uncertainty about the future—coupled with considerations of marketability, liquidity preference, and time preference,—future income or benefits are worth less than present funds or benefits. To derive a present worth figure, future income is *discounted* to the present at the appropriate rate. This is necessary to overcome liquidity preference, time preference, and the risks associated with uncertainty about the future. Discounting is the mathematical foundation for capitalization when present worth is to be measured.

When market rates of discount or rates of capitalization are appropriately applied to anticipated future income over the proper market-derived period of capitalization or discounting, the resulting present worth figure is an estimate of Market Value.

*Valuation Principles Involved*

As already noted in Chapter 3, all the basic principles of real estate valuation presented in introductory appraisal courses are applicable in the valuation of income-producing properties. These principles have particular applicability to Income Capitalization Analysis.

**Highest and Best Use.** Under informed ownership, income-producing real estate will be put to the use that will, over the appropriate investment period, produce the highest net money income. Thus, the anticipated future benefits capitalized to a present worth figure which represents Market Value are those net income receipts anticipated from putting the property to its Highest and Best Use. Under given market conditions, this is its most probable use.

**Supply and Demand.** Analysis of demand defines the market for the property being appraised in terms of the most probable type of purchaser. This in turn guides the appraiser to the data sources and the market standards that must be employed in developing the proper rates of discount or capitalization to apply to the net income to derive a Market Value estimate. Supply analysis offers data and standards for identifying appropriate rates of discount by indicating what sales and loan terms are being accepted on the market at the time of the appraisal.

**Substitution (Opportunity Cost).** Rates of return on alternative, competing investment outlets set the limits for the appropriate rate(s) to apply to the income forecast for the subject property. The analysis involves comparisons of risks, money interest rates, financing terms, and terms of sale. These factors combine to determine the rate(s) of return necessary to attract investment capital to an investment with the same income and risk characteristics as those of the property being appraised.

**Contribution (Marginal Productivity).** Present worth estimation is a measure of the contribution of a property or any of its component to the financial well-being of the investor-purchaser. Thus, income capitalization may be regarded as measuring a property's market contribution.

**Anticipation.** All income to be generated by the property is anticipated in the future. The income stream capitalized represents the market's or the investor's best judgment of the future, taking into account the risks and uncertainty involved in forecasting. The rate of discount or capitalization is an expression of the market's or the investor's anticipations of that uncertain future.

**Change.** While change itself is virtually certain, the character, direction, and quantity of that change is quite uncertain. In the absence of any hard evidence of the direction or amount of any changes, income projections are frequently "stabilized" or level at the time of the appraisal. Thus, the rate of discount frequently reflects compensation for this uncertainty. The tight money market conditions of the late 1960s illustrate the risks involved in changing financing terms, and the uncertainties associated with making long-term financial commitments.

## Nature of Capitalization

Capitalization is the process of converting an income stream to a lump-sum capital value. In real estate appraising, it usually takes the form of discounting.

### Conversion of Future Income to Present Worth

The value estimate developed in income capitalization is a present worth figure based on discounting forecast future income. By convention, annual incomes and annual rates of discount are used.

**Rates of Capitalization.** Present worth is calculated by dividing forecast future annual income by the appropriate annual rate. The formula is simple.

The following symbols are universally employed:

$V$: value or present worth
$I$: annual income to be capitalized
$R$: annual rate of capitalization (rate of discount)

Then
$$V = I/R.$$
If any two of the three components are given, or can be derived from the market, the third can be calculated:
$$I = V \times R$$
$$R = I/V$$
As used throughout appraisal and investment analysis, a *rate* is a ratio between income and value expressed as a decimal or a percentage on an annual basis. All calculations require that rates be expressed as decimals. An annual rate of 8% must be converted to .08 before it can be used in income and present worth calculations.

An $80,000 annual income on an investment of $1,000,000 represents a rate of return of 8% ($80,000/$1,000,000 = .08); this illustrates $R = I/V$. An investment of $1,000,000 at an 8% annual rate will yield an annual income of $80,000 ($I = V \times R$; $1,000,000 \times .08 = $80,000). Finally, a property producing $80,000 per year capitalized at 8% has a present worth or value of $1,000,000 ($V = I/R$; $80,000/.08 = $1,000,000).

In appraisal analysis, the term "rate" is applied to several different types of returns. It is necessary for the appraiser to distinguish among them carefully and use them properly. As used in this course, and in appraisal-investment analysis, the following terms apply:

*Nominal Rate.* This is the contract rate on a mortgage or the apparent rate on an investment. It is the annual payment of interest or income divided by the original amount of a loan or investment. For example, a straight, non-amortized loan of $50,000 at 8% would carry annual interest charges of $4,000 ($50,000 × .08 = $4,000).

*Effective Rate.* This is the actual rate paid on a loan or produced by an investment. It is actual payments divided by actual investment or loan outstanding. For example, assume a $50,000 loan discounted for a year at 8%. Interest charges are $4,000 (.08 × $50,000). However, the $4,000 is deducted or discounted at the beginning of the period, so that only $46,000 is actually advanced to the borrower. The *effective* rate is thus 8.69% ($4,000/$46,000 = .0869).

*Rate of Interest.* This is the rate on borrowed money. It must be distinguished from the term "interest rate" used by many appraisers. It is the loan or borrowing rate.

*Interest Rate or Rate of Return.* This is the rate earned *on* an investment, irrespective of and independent of any capital recovery received or demanded by the investor. It is used in capitalizing net income in perpetuity, as in the case of land valuation. "Interest rate" is not recommended terminology.

*Discount Rate.* This means the same as "interest rate" in appraisal analysis. It is preferable to "interest rate" because it is consistent with terminology in other types of investment analysis, of which appraisal is a part. It also emphasizes the fact that future income receipts are being capitalized into a present worth figure. It is also synonymous with "rate of discount." It does *not* include provision for capital recovery or the expiration of the income stream at the end of any finite period of time. This is the rate that reflects the compensation necessary to attract an investor or lender to give up liquidity, to wait or defer consumption, and to assume the risks of investing. It is the rate of return *on* an investment.

*Capital Recapture Rate; Capital Recovery Rate.* This is the annual return *of* invested capital, expressed as an annual rate. It is applied only to improvements or wasting assets with a finite economic life. It is also synonymous with "amortization rate" to express an investor's desire or expectation to recover his equity investment over a specified period of time.

As a simple example, assume an equity investment of $60,000 and a planned holding period of 12 years. The average annual capital recovery rate would be 8.33% (100%/12). Similarly, a building with an estimated remaining economic life of 20 years would require annual capital recovery at a rate of 5% (100%/20). In mortgage lending, the rate at which principal is repaid over the nominal term of the loan is the "amortization rate." This is the lender's "capital recovery rate."

*Capitalization Rate.* This term has very specific meaning in appraisal analysis. A Capitalization Rate is the sum of a discount rate and a capital recovery rate. It is applied to any income stream with a finite term over which the invested principal is to be returned to the investor or lender. In income property appraising, it is applied to the income attributable to improvements (buildings) in physical residual techniques, and to the income produced for the equity investment over a specified holding period in mortgage-equity analysis.

*Mortgage Constant.* This is the total annual payments of principal and interest (annual debt service) on a level-payment amortized mortgage, expressed as a percentage of the initial principal amount of the loan. It is analogous to a "capitalization rate" on a mortgage loan. It is used in mortgage-equity analysis, as well as in estimating cash flows generated by income-producing real estate. For example, assume a $100,000 mortgage at 8.5% for 20 years, with equal monthly payments of principal and interest. The monthly payments would be $867.80.[a] Annual debt service would be $10,413.60 (12 X $867.80). The *mortgage constant* is therefore 10.41% ($10,413.60/$100,000). The *nominal*rate of interest is still 8.5%.

*Overall Rate.* This is the direct ratio between forecast annual Net Operating Income and value or sales price. NOI/SP = Overall Rate. It incorporates a weighted average between Discount Rate (on land) and Capitalization Rate (on improvements) in the physical residual techniques. It is used when feasible in Direct Capitalization.

In Mortgage-Equity analysis, an Overall Rate is also used to capitalize Net Operating Income directly. In this instance, it is the weighted average of the mortgage constant and the equity yield rate, including an average annual adjustment for forecast capital appreciation or depreciation.

*Equity Dividend Rate.* This is derived by expressing annual before-tax cash flow to the equity investment as a percentage of that equity investment. It is used in

---

[a]This figure is obtained by applying the monthly Installment to Amortize One factor at 8.5% for 20 years (.008678) to the principal sum of $100,000. The factor is taken from L.W. Ellwood, *Ellwood Tables for Real Estate and Appraising and Financing*, third edition (Chicago: American Institute of Real Estate Appraisers, 1970), Part II, Page 89, Column 6. All subsequent references in this book to compound interest factors taken from "Ellwood" refer to the work cited here.

Mortgage-Equity analysis to estimate the present worth of the forecast annual-income stream receivable by the holder of the equity position, without regard to proration of any forecast decline or increase in property value on resale. When no appreciation or depreciation is forecast on resale, the Equity Dividend Rate is numerically equal to the Equity Yield Rate; it is different in concept, however. The Equity Dividend Rate is the "equity rate" used in deriving a Discount Rate via the simple Band of Investment method (explained in Chapter 9).

*Equity Yield Rate.* This is the rate of return on equity investments. It is used in mortgage-equity analysis, including the Ellwood formulation. It is derived by expressing annual before-tax cash flow plus prorated annual depreciation or appreciation in the reversion on resale of the property, as a percentage of equity investment. It is the rate of discount at which the present worth of the total income forecast to be received on the equity investment is equal to the cost of that investment. It is also called the Investment Yield in some variants of mortgage-equity analysis. The Equity Yield Rate is represented by $y$ in the Ellwood Formulation.

**Capitalization Factors.** Present worth can also be calculated by multiplying forecast annual net income by a *factor*. This is frequently necessary because some factors are available in published tables whereas their related rates are not. Thus,

$$V = I \times F.$$

Also,

$$I = V/F \text{ and } F = V/I.$$

Arithmetically, a factor is simply the *reciprocal of a rate*: $F = 1/R$. It is a *ratio* between value or sales price and annual net income: $F = V/I$.

Many factors incorporate capital recovery over a specified time period, together with a specified rate of return on the investment. They are thus the reciprocals of Capitalization Rates. All are based on the premise of money at compound interest. All may be termed Discount Factors.

Among the most widely employed compound interest factors in appraisal analysis are:

*Reversion Factor (Present Worth of One).* This is used to discount a *single* future payment to a present worth figure, given the appropriate discount rate and discount period.

*Level Annuity Factor (Inwood Factor).* This is used to discount a *series* of level future payments to a present worth figure, given the appropriate discount rate and discount period. This is also called the Present Worth of One per Annum.

*Sinking Fund Factor.* This indicates the periodic amount that must be set aside at a specified compound interest rate over a specified period to provide for recovery of a given investment amount.

*Amortization Factor.* This is the reciprocal of the level annuity or Inwood Factor. It is used to identify the periodic level payment required to amortize a given investment at a specified discount rate over a specified period of time. Both investment return *on* and return *of* the investment are provided over the period specified. One form of the amortization factor, when expressed on an annual basis, is the Mortgage Constant.

*Gross-Income Multiplier (GIM).* This is also a factor. It is the ratio of sales price (*SP*) or value (*V*) to annual *gross* income (*GI*): $GIM = SP/GI$; and $V = GI \times GIM$.

**Capitalization in Perpetuity vs. Capitalization over a Finite Period.** Capitalization in perpetuity is mechanically very simple. Because the capital value of the investment (property) is assumed to continue undiminished and unchanged indefinitely, the entire annual net income is a return *on* the investment. Income is simply divided by the discount rate to develop a present worth estimate. This is particularly applicable in land or site valuation. For example, a site returning $10,000 net per year at a rate of 9.5% has a present worth of $105,263.16 ($10,000/.095 = $105,263.16).

Capitalization over a finite period is a reflection of the investor's or the market's expectation that the investment will produce the specified net income for only a specified period of time. All improvements are treated this way, as are all real estate investments in the mortgage-equity and property residual methods of capitalization. So, too, are all lease interests. This is why appropriate capitalization rates or discount factors are widely employed in appraising income-producing properties. The rate(s) or factor(s) applied to net income include both a competitive market rate of return *on* the investment and systematic return *of* the investment over the period specified.

### The Concept of Present Worth

The present worth of forecast future income receipts is the amount that a prudent, typically informed investor would pay, as of the valuation date, for the right to receive that income, given the discount rate and the time period over which the income is expected to be received. Present worth is always less than the sum of the anticipated future net income receipts. These future receipts must be discounted to the present because of:

**Time Preference.** One always prefers a given sum of money in hand to the promise (no matter how nearly certain) of that same sum at some time in the future. A bird in the hand may not be worth precisely *two* in the bush, but $1 today is worth the promise of $1.23 three years from today if the appropriate discount rate is 9%. This phenomenon reflects the "price" of the alternative opportunity to invest that is foregone or given up. It represents an application of the basic economic principle of Opportunity Cost.

**Liquidity Preference.** One typically prefers assets that are readily convertible into cash at face value to those which take time to liquidate or which may have to be sold at a discount to realize cash quickly. Giving up liquidity for a specified period requires compensation, which may be reflected in the discount rate. Income-producing real estate is moderately to highly illiquid, depending on how specialized it is and how active the market for it is. This is partially reflected as a measure of marketability.

**Uncertainty and Risks.** Any projection into the future involves uncertainty. In dealing with this uncertainty, the investor is assuming risks for which he must be compensated. Compensation for this risk-bearing must also be incorporated in the discount rate applied to anticipated future net income.

## The Nature of Income Produced by Real Estate

Real estate is a mixed asset composed of non-depreciating land or site, and depreciating improvements. The income analytically attributable or assignable to the land consists of only a return *on* the investment, while that portion assignable to the improvements must include both return *on* and return *of* the investment. Moreover, except in the very special case of income capitalization in perpetuity for land, the income stream is projected for a finite time period. At the expiration of that period, there is always something of value left: the land, the reversionary fee interest of the lessor, the resaleable property as an entirety. This "something of value" is termed the Reversion. It is a single sum or payment that must be discounted to the present or valuation date. Its present worth is added to that of the annual income stream.

The Reversion may be equal to, less than, or greater than the original investment or sale price. Each alternative can be treated readily in appraisal analysis.

The complex character of future income(s) generated by income-producing real estate makes the mechanical process of discounting more complicated, but no more difficult. Systematic step-by-step handling of any real estate income capitalization problem will yield a defensible solution if good data are available. Without good, reliable market data, however, the mechanical processes are sterile.

## Steps in the Income Capitalization Process

This presentation summarizes the outline of income capitalization methodology, the terminology involved, and the data required. Each of the steps and decisions noted here is considered in detail in subsequent chapters. This outline can also serve as a periodic reminder of the place of each step in the complete capitalization process. Because different items must be estimated, obtained, and assembled, the precise order is not critical. Rather, any systematic approach that includes all of these items and their processing into a present-worth estimate is both acceptable and defensible.

### Estimate Future Annual-Income Flow

All of the annual "income" figures used in appraising income-producing properties are *cash flows* rather than accrual accounting incomes. That is, they represent forecast cash receipts during the year. The investor is typically interested in how much money income he has available to meet operating expenses, to pay debt service, to pay taxes, and to spend. In estimating annual income produced by the property, the appraiser must specify carefully *which* income he is using, and relate it to the proper investment base or discount rate to develop a meaningful value estimate.

**Net Operating Income.** This has traditionally been termed "Net Income Before Recapture," or sometimes "Net Income." These are confusing terms to the non-appraiser, and to many appraisers as well. Simple "Net Income" is too easy to be mistaken for accounting income, and the term also raises the question: "Net of what?" It is frequently not clear to many clients that Net Income Before Recapture means before *deducting* a provision for capital recapture.

On the other hand, "Net Operating Income" (NOI) describes just what the figure is: the net receipts from operating the property as an investment. Moreover, NOI is a term used in other branches of investment analysis, including real estate investment. Usage consistent with this closely related field is a distinct advantage.

*Estimate Potential Gross Receipts.* This is the rent roll or market rental for all rentable space at 100% occupancy in Market Value appraisals. It is the contract rent stipulated in the lease(s) for valuation of a leased fee or lessor's interest.

*Estimate Rate of Vacancy and Rent Loss.* This is the most probable rate based on the market experience of competitive substitute properties. The annual dollar amount is deducted from Potential Gross Receipts.

*Add Estimated "Other Income."* This is net income from concessions (coin-operated laundry equipment in apartment properties), from sale of utilities (retailing electricity in industrial loft buildings), from parking, and the like.

*Derive Estimate of Effective Gross Receipts.* This is a forecast of rent collections plus "other income." It is the gross cash flow anticipated to be available to cover operating expenses, debt service, capital recovery, income taxes, and profit or return on the investment.

*Deduct Operating Expenses.* These are the expenses typically borne by the owner-investor in properties of the type involved in the current, local market. They are expressed on an annual basis.

Operating Expenses include:

(1) *Fixed charges*, such as property taxes and owner's property insurance, which do not vary with occupancy.
(2) *Variable charges* (variable expenses), which tend to vary with occupancy, such as utilities, management fees, heating and cooling expense.
(3) *Repairs and maintenance*, which are prorated or "stabilized" on an annual basis.
(4) *Replacements* of equipment provided by the owner, such as air conditioners.

These expenses are also prorated or "stabilized" on an annual basis.

Operating expenses do *not* include:

(1) Income taxes or business taxes borne by the owner.
(2) Capital improvements which enhance the value of the property or prolong its economic life.
(3) Capital recovery charges or accounting depreciation deductions.
(4) Business expenses of the owner other than those directly associated with the operation of the property being appraised.
(5) Debt service on the property.

These items must be covered by Net Operating Income or Cash Flow.

*Estimate Net Operating Income.* NOI equals Potential Gross Receipts *less* allowance for vacancy and rent loss *plus* other property income *less* Operating Expenses. All are expressed as annual figures.

NOI is the basic annual income figure used in discounting future income to a present worth estimate. When divided by an Overall Rate, it can be used directly to estimate the value, as defined, of the property.

**Before-Tax Cash Flow (Cash Throw-off).** This is Net Operating Income *less* Annual Debt Service. It is the cash flow available to the owner-investor after necessary Operating Expenses and contractual Debt Service are covered, but before deducting income tax liability. Before-tax cash flow is generated by the property under *any* ownership, assuming normal competent management, and available as a return on the owner's equity. In mortgage-equity analysis, it is useful in calculating an equity yield.

**After-Tax Cash Flow (Net Spendable Income).** This is Cash Throw-Off *less* Income Tax Liability. It is the amount the specific investor or category of investor will have available net of all expenses and taxes. Taxable Income will vary from year to year as mortgage interest payments and depreciation charges vary. These are deductions from Cash Throw-Off to obtain Taxable Income.

Income taxes themselves will vary accordingly. Thus, After-Tax Cash Flow will be different each year by at least the tax differential caused by constantly declining interest deductions.

After-Tax Cash Flow is used in estimating Investment Value by means of discounted cash flow analysis. With the growth of computer programs to carry out the many and complex calculations, this technique has become increasingly useful to appraisers.

*Estimate Necessary Rate of*
*Return on Investment*

The rate of return *on* the investment required by the market or by a specific investor is the Discount Rate derived from market data and analysis.

The Discount Rate must include appropriate compensation to the purchaser-investor for:

(1) *Time preference*: This is the basis for the riskless or "pure" rate of interest.
(2) *Illiquidity*: The investor in real estate gives up considerable liquidity in his asset holdings.
(3) *Investment management*: This is *not* management of the property, which is an operating expense, but of the investment: e.g., tax accounting, making mortgage payments, managing money flows, and the like.
(4) *Risk assumption*: These risks vary by type of property and investment position. They are influenced by the forecast timing, stability, and certainty of the forecast annual income flow.

The Discount Rate may be estimated or derived by one or more of several methods, depending in large part on the availability of necessary data. It may be estimated directly from market-sales data on competitive properties. It may be abstracted from the Gross Income Multiplier. It may be, and commonly is, developed by construction through the Band of Investment method. This method recognizes the Discount Rate as the weighted average of mortgage interest rate(s), based on typical financing patterns; and the equity yield rate, derived from market data.

*Estimate the Type and Amount*
*of the Reversion*

This is the second basic component of income expected by an owner-investor from a real estate investment. It must be estimated in all cases involving a finite time period over which income is to be received and capital recovery is to occur. Investors' market expectations are the best guide to the future amount of the reversion, either in dollars or as a percentage of the original investment.

The form and source of the reversion must be identified. It may consist of site only, at the expiration of the economic life of the improvements. This is the case when physical residual techniques of income capitalization are employed. It may be the entire property at the expiration of a lease. Especially in mortgage-equity and property residual analysis, the reversion is indicated by the resale price of the property at the end of the indicated investment-holding period.

The amount and character of the reversion indicate the amount and type of capital recovery anticipated by the typically-informed, prudent investor.

*Estimate the Capital Recovery Period*

This is derived from market evidence about typical investor behavior, as well as the previous estimate of the form the reversion will take. The several periods which may be appropriate are:

1. *Economic life of the improvements*, when physical residual techniques of analysis are employed and the reversion is the site;
2. *Investment holding period*, especially when mortgage-equity analysis is employed and the reversion is the entire property for resale or refinancing;
3. *Mortgage amortization period*, when market evidence indicates this to be the appropriate investment period;
4. *Lease term*, when a leased fee (lessor's interest) is being valued and the reversion is the entire property.

*Establish the Method of*
*Capital Recovery*

This has a substantial influence on the final estimate of value. It is determined by the character or quality of the forecast income stream, the capital recovery period, the form of the reversion, and typical investor market behavior. There are several methods of capital recovery from which the appropriate one must be selected.

**Straight Line.** By this method, a capital recapture *rate* can be derived directly. This method is highly questionable in concept, but is still widely used. It is simple and its results appear to be easily understood.

**Sinking Fund.** With the Sinking Fund method, a capital recovery *rate* can also be derived directly, or incorporated into a *Factor* which includes both discount rate and capital recovery rate. While mathematically and conceptually valid, this method has extremely limited applicability in real estate appraisal.

**Annuity (Level Annuity).** This method treats the forecast income stream as a level annuity which covers both discount rate and capital recovery rate. It is usually applied with a Factor (e.g., the Inwood Factor). The level annuity method of providing for capital recovery is widely used in mortgage-equity analysis and in the appraisal of leased fee interests.

**Overall Rate.** An Overall Rate includes provision for both return on the entire investment and recovery of the wasting or depreciating portion over the capital recovery period, in one market-derived rate. This method really avoids direct and separate estimation of capital recovery. It requires particularly reliable (and frequently unobtainable) market transactions data before it can be applied appropriately.

**Mortgage Amortization.** In mortgage-equity analysis, at least part of capital recovery is provided through debt service by systematic reduction of the outstanding mortgage loan balance. The effectiveness of mortgage amortization as a method of capital recovery depends on the relationship between mortgage loan principal and the amount of capital recovery required.

**Resale of the Property.** Whenever the capital recovery period is less than the remaining economic life of the improvements, traditional capital recovery methods (straight line, sinking fund, annuity) can lead to inappropriate results. In such a situation, the proceeds of the resale of the property represent one, if not the only, source of capital recovery. This is the case in mortgage-equity analysis, where the results of mortgage amortization are actually realized in cash on resale of the property.

**Refinancing.** This is essentially an alternative to resale as a means of realizing equity build-up through mortgage amortization. The same applications and limitations apply to refinancing as to resale, as a method of providing for capital recovery.

*Establish the Capitalization Technique
to Employ; Identify the Residual*

Every capitalization technique available to the appraiser save one requires that one component of the property be somehow valued independently for analytical purposes. Then, the remaining or residual component(s) is capitalized to derive a value estimation for the entire property. The one exception is Direct Capitalization using a market-derived Overall Rate.

The appraiser really does not have a *choice* of techniques to apply. Rather he must *select* the alternative technique which best suits the available data, the character of the property, the income stream that it is anticipated to produce, and the capitalization method or type of capital recovery dictated by the market.

**Direct Capitalization.** In this case, Overall Rate is applied directly to forecast NOI to develop a present worth estimate. No residual is involved, but particularly reliable market transactions data on properties closely competitive with the subject are required.

**Building Residual.** This technique separates an improved property into its physical components for purposes of analysis. When site value can be reliably estimated independently, the residual income available to cover the investment in the improvements or buildings is capitalized by the appropriate capitalization rate or discount factor to a present worth figure for the improvements.

**Land Residual.** This technique also separates an improved property (existing or proposed) into its physical components for purposes of analysis. Given the verified cost new of new improvements that represent the Highest and Best Use of the site, the income necessary to provide a competitive return *on* and appropriate capital recovery *of* that cost new is derived. The residual income available to cover the investment in the site is then capitalized at the discount rate to a present worth figure for the site.

**Property Residual.** This technique involves capitalization of the entire NOI at a *capitalization rate* over a specified period. The time period is frequently the remaining term of a lease. Then the present worth of the reversion is added to the present worth of the income stream. The reversion is the forecast value of the entire property remaining at the end of the income period. Thus, the entire property is the residual.

**Mortgage-Equity (Equity Residual).** In this form of analysis, the equity interest is the residual. Either the principal amount or the loan-value ratio of the mortgage is given. Annual debt service—the amount necessary to cover the mortgage constant—is deducted from NOI to derive Cash Throw-off. This in turn is capitalized at the appropriate equity yield rate (including prorated capital appreciation or depreciation on resale) to derive the present worth of the equity interest. The latter is added to the mortgage principal to estimate present worth of the property.

*Estimate Present Worth of Anticipated*
*Annual-Income Flow*

The appraiser has already derived the following: Net Operating Income; Discount Rate; Capital Recovery Period; Method of Capital Recovery; Capital Recovery Rate or Factor; and Residual Technique to be Employed.

The calculation is then simple: $PW = NOI/R$; or $PW = NOI \times F$.

*Estimate Present Worth of Anticipated*
*Future Reversion*

The estimated future worth of the reversion (FW) is discounted at the discount.

76

rate over the indicated discount period: $PW = FW \times F$. The Factor used here is the Present Worth of One.

*Estimate Value (Present Worth) of the Property*

The present worth of the forecast annual income stream is added to the present worth of the reversion to derive the present worth of the property. This is the value being estimated.

## Summary of Estimates and Conclusions to be Reached by the Appraiser in Capitalizing Net Income to a Value Estimate

In applying income capitalization analysis to property value estimation, the appraiser must rely on and obtain market data at every step. These required data must be verified and authoritative. However, the nature of the problem and of the property, together with the availability of reliable and usable data, determine which processes, methods, and techniques the appraiser must select and apply. The judgment of the appraiser comes into play in analyzing the market, the property, and the income stream to reach these conclusions. The following list summarizes these required judgments, which represent successive definitions and identifications to reach a final value estimate. This reflects the character of income capitalization analysis as a systematic process, as discussed in Chapter 3.

*Identify Gross Annual Income to be Projected*

1. Select unit rentals to be used: market rentals; actual rentals on the subject property; contract rentals under a lease.
2. Identify vacancy and rent loss allowance to deduct: market experience of competitive properties; general market standards; actual experience of the subject property.
3. Identify and justify type and amount of "other income": market experience of competitive properties; actual experience of the subject property.

*Identify and Stabilize Amount and Type of Annual Operating Expenses to be Projected*

1. Identify items typically paid by owners of this type of property: market

experience and standards; actual experience of the subject property; terms of a lease.
2. Establish relative quality of subject property management.
3. Identify time period for stabilizing the operating expense experience of the subject property: e.g., 3-5 years. Identify any trends in expense items for making a projection.
4. Develop itemized estimates of applicable operating expenses under typical competent management: market experience of competitive properties; general market standards; actual experience of the subject property; terms of a lease.

## Identify Risks Inherent in Type of Investment Involved

1. Evaluate probable certainty of projected income flow and reversion.
2. Evaluate probable stability of forecast income flow.
3. Estimate probable timing of forecast income receipts.

## Identify Most Probable Type of Purchaser-Investor

1. Identify investment and income objectives: market experience; interviews.
2. Identify most probable tax status.
3. Identify the competitive market for the subject property: geographic area; type of property and/or income stream; demand from purchaser-investors.

## Identify Most Probable Financing Pattern and Terms

1. Mortgage rate of interest: market standards; terms available to specific investors.
2. Loan-to-value ratio: market standards; leverage sought and allowed.
3. Term of mortgage: amortization period; due date.
4. Amortization provisions: full or partial amortization; timing of payments (monthly, semi-annually, etc.); pattern of amortization (level payments, equal amortization payments, etc.).
5. Calculate mortgage constant and annual debt service.
6. Identify lender objectives and policies: most probable terms from the most likely sources (lenders) for this type of property and investor, in this market at this time.

## Identify Equity-Yield Requirements

1. Identify components of yield: return on equity position; return on cash investment; prorated property appreciation or depreciation.

2. Identify yields required by investors on competitive properties: market experience.

*Identify Discount Rate to Use; Select*
*Method of Rate Estimation*

1. Discount Rate: market experience of competitive properties; expectations of investors.
2. Selection of Method: availability of data; market experience of competitive properties and investors.
3. Overall Rate: market experience of competitive properties; applicability of mortgage-equity analysis; availability of data.

*Identify Applicable Income-Projection Period*

1. Duration of forecast income: standards set by market; experience of competitive properties; identified objectives of most probable purchaser-investor.

*Identify Method of Providing*
*for Capital Recovery*

1. Identify character, risk, stability of anticipated income flow.
2. Identify form of capital recovery: straight-line, sinking fund, annuity; resale, refinancing; mortgage amortization. Market standards of the most probable type of purchaser-investor help establish the form.

*Identify Type of Residual*
*Analysis to be Employed*

The nature of the problem and the appropriate method of separating the property into analytical components determine the outcome of this judgment.

1. Physical components: building residual; land residual; property residual.
2. Legal components: leased fee and leasehold; property residual.
3. Financial components: mortgage-equity (equity residual).

*Identify Type and Amount of Reversion*

1. Form of Reversion: this is determined from prior judgments about the method and period of capital recovery to be selected.

79

a. Site: physical residual techniques (building, land, and property residuals).
b. Property: legal and financial residual techniques (lease reversion; resale or refinancing; mortgage amortization).
2. Amount of Reversion: market indications of purchaser-investor expectations; evidence from experience of competitive properties or investments.


## Review Exercises

1. An investment is producing $12,000 per year at a 14% annual rate of return. What is its present worth?
2. A purchaser paid $70,000 for an investment property. How much annual income must it produce to yield an 11% rate of return?
3. What annual capitalization factor is represented by an 8.5% annual rate of return?
4. If an investment property costing $90,000 is producing $7,500 annual net income, what is the indicated Overall Rate of return?
5. An income property has just been purchased for $200,000, which represented its estimated Market Value. A mortgage of $150,000 was obtained by the purchaser, at a loan rate of interest of 8.5%. Annual debt service is $15,620. Net operating income is $24,000, leaving before-tax cash flow (cash throw-off) of $8,380. The indicated Equity-Yield Rate is 18%.
   a. What does the 8.5% rate represent?
   b. What is the mortgage constant?
   c. What is the indicated equity dividend rate?
   d. What is the indicated overall rate on the investment?
   e. What does the 18% rate represent?


## Supplementary Readings

American Institute of Real Estate Appraisers, *The Appraisal of Real Estate*, fifth edition (Chicago: American Institute of Real Estate Appraisers, 1967), pp. 259-268.

L.W. Ellwood, *Ellwood Tables for Real Estate Appraising and Financing*, third edition (Chicago: American Institute of Real Estate Appraisers, 1970), pp. 1-7.

Sanders A. Kahn, Frederick E. Case and Alfred Schimmel, *Real Estate Appraisal and Investment* (New York: Ronald Press, 1963), pp. 99-103 and Chapter 24.

William N. Kinnard, Jr., "The Financial Logic of Income-Property Appraising," *The Real Estate Appraiser*, Volume 35, Number 4, May-June 1969, pp. 13-21.

Richard U. Ratcliff, *Modern Real Estate Valuation: Theory and Application* (Madison, Wisconsin: Democrat Press, 1965), Chapter 10.

Alfred A. Ring, *The Valuation of Real Estate*, second edition (New York: Prentice-Hall, 1970), Chapter 18.

Paul F. Wendt, "Recent Developments in Appraisal Theory," *The Appraisal Journal*, Volume 37, Number 4, October 1969, pp. 485-500.

# 5 Discounting and Compound Interest

## Nature of the Discounting Process

As noted in Chapter 4, discounting is the process of converting forecast future income receipts to a present worth estimate. The mathematical foundation of this process is the basic formula for compound interest. Discounting is the mechanical basis for all income capitalization analysis in income property appraising.

### Present Worth of Anticipated Future Income

Value as of a given valuation date is the discounted present worth of the anticipated future income(s) reasonably expected to be generated by an income-producing property over a specified period of time. The appraiser is called upon to identify the value, as defined, of the future income receipts forecast to be receivable by the holder of a specific interest (rights) in the income-producing realty being appraised. This has already been pointed out in preceding chapters. The process by which future income receipts are converted to a present capital-value estimate is termed *discounting*.

*Capitalization* is the process of converting periodic income payments into an appropriate lump-sum capital value. It may be used to estimate either present worth or future worth. Discounting is that form of capitalization specifically concerned with the calculation of present worth of future receipts. Appraisals nearly always involve discounting because the final objective is usually a present-worth estimate.

Many different capitalization methods and techniques are available to process anticipated future income into a present-worth estimate. The method used depends primarily on the characteristics of the forecast income stream itself. Each technique incorporates specific assumptions about the character of that income stream, the form of the appropriate rate of return, or discount rate, and the time period involved. The appraiser cannot properly select the appropriate technique without being fully aware of these underlying assumptions. He must assure himself that they correspond to and describe the income, rate, and time characteristics of the appraisal problem represented by the subject property. Only then can the appraisal reflect the appraiser's best analytical judgment applied to pertinent and relevant facts of the market.

Every capitalization method or technique therefore requires inputs of amount of income, time of receipt, and rate or yield. The role of discounting and compound interest is to develop the proper factor(s) in terms of rate and time, which are then used in processing income to a present-worth estimate.

The basic valuation formula for all appraisals is, as presented in Chapter 4, $V = I/R$. This formula is a simple representation of the discounting process. $I$ represents the forecast future income receipts. $R$ is the rate incorporating compensation to the investor for waiting a specified time, for giving up alternative investment income opportunities, and for assuming the risks of the investment position. Finally, $V$ is the present worth of the forecast future income ($I$) discounted at the applicable rate of discount ($R$).

Similarly, the basic valuation formula can also be expressed at $V = I \times F$. $V$ and $I$ are the same, while $F$ is the discount *factor* represented by the reciprocal of the appropriate $R$.

If a parcel of realty is forecast to produce an annual net return ($I$) of $12,000 and the applicable rate of discount is 15% ($R = 0.15$)[a], then the present worth ($V$) would be $80,000. $V = I/R$; $12,000/0.15 = $80,000.

In this case, the discount factor ($F$) would be the reciprocal of 0.15, or 6.6667. (1/0.15 = 6.6667.) Then, $V$ would still be $80,000 (as a rounded figure): $V = I \times F$; $12,000 \times 6.6667 = $80,000.

**Discounting as a Mechanical Process.** Discounting is based on rigidly defined mathematical relationships. It is *not* appraising. Merely processing an income stream by an undisputably correct mathematical formula does not in itself produce supportable present worth or Market-Value estimates. Discounting *is* necessary to *measure* value correctly, which is the appraiser's task. The mathematical or arithmetic manipulation of figures is sterile, however, without good, reliable, and appropriate market data. Moreover, the appraiser's judgment—based on his informed, trained observations and analysis of the market—is essential to select the most applicable technique for the given appraisal problem. It is also necessary to identify and obtain the data required to put into the formula.

Discounting is based on the concept of Time Preference. This means that present money is always worth more than future money; conversely, money (income) due and receivable in the future is worth less today. This is because the investor is foregoing alternative income opportunities or alternative uses of the money, while it is committed to the investment in question. The anticipated future income receipts must be discounted at the appropriate rate and time period to *measure* that present worth, by *measuring* how much future income receipts are to be discounted. A rate of discount that reflects compensation for overcoming time preference only is termed a "riskless money rate," and represents the opportunity cost of making a particular investment.

**Future Income.** It has already been pointed out in Chapter 4 that the future income receipts receivable from ownership of rights in income-producing real estate can be categorized in two ways: an annual stream of net cash income and

[a]Percentage rates of discount are always expressed in decimal form in all present-worth and capitalization calculations.

a lump-sum reversion at some specified future date. In fact, the total flow of future income receipts is really a *series* of individual payments, and can be treated as such in the discounting process. When the annual stream of future income is forecast to behave in a *systematic* way (level, increasing, or decreasing), it is convenient to discount it with a single factor or rate. This saves time and reduces the risk of making mechanical errors.

Assuming no errors in calculation, however, any income flow can be discounted as a series of individual payments (reversions), using the appropriate Present Worth of One factors. This point is developed more fully in subsequent chapters, especially Chapters 6 and 11. It is noted here because it is basic to an appreciation of the applicability of discounting to appraisal analysis.

## Rate of Discount

The Discount Rate, also called the "Interest Rate" or "Rate of Return on Investment" in appraisal literature, is the basic building block in the capitalization process. It is determined by the forces of market supply and demand for investment funds. Thus, the appraiser must evaluate the market environment in terms of which the subject property is being appraised. There are in fact many sub-markets in "the money market," just as there are in "the real estate market." The appraiser must identify the sub-market in which an investor in the property in question would be competing in order to identify the prevailing rate that must apply to the subject property.

A Discount Rate is a *ratio* between annual net income and value or sales price. It is expressed as a percentage on an annual basis, or as a related decimal figure. It represents one basis for comparing alternative investments: what is the rate of return on alternative investment A as compared with that on alternative investment B?

A rate of return is paid or offered on an investment in order to attract investment capital. The rate offered or anticipated must be competitively attractive in terms of similar alternative investments with the same risks and income streams. This represents the operation of the Principle of Substitution or Opportunity Cost. A rate of return *must* be paid or offered to compensate the investor for:

(1) overcoming time preference;
(2) giving up liquidity;
(3) assuming investment management burdens; and
(4) assuming the risks of investment and ownership.

The Principle of Substitution or Opportunity Cost dictates that a rate of return must be offered or paid to meet the competition of alternative investment outlets for the investor's funds. This is the basis for the "pure" or riskless rate of discount. Even with no change in the purchasing power of the dollar and absolute certainty of receipt of the income in the future, a rate of return must be anticipated to overcome the opportunity cost of waiting and for giving up liquidity. Discount factors found in compound interest tables represent this opportunity cost of time only. Mathematically, they ignore changes in purchasing power and are based on certain receipt of the future income.

*Differential* rates of return must be offered or paid by different properties to compensate the investor for:

(1) differences in liquidity or marketability;
(2) differences in investment management or administrative costs; and
(3) differences in investment risks. These investment risks include the risk of loss or diminution of principal; the risk of non-payment or decline of anticipated net income; the risk of instability or variability of anticipated net income; and the risk of a decrease in the time period over which net income is actually generated.

## Influence of Time Period for Capitalization

The second important ingredient in developing an appropriate discount factor is the time period (usually called the income projection period or capital recovery period) over which net income is forecast or expected to be received. Generally speaking, the longer the period, the greater the deviation of the discount factor from 1.

**Capitalization in Perpetuity.** As noted in Chapter 4, non-wasting assets such as land or site are capitalized in perpetuity simply by dividing the anticipated annual net income by the discount rate. The capital value of the investment is expected to continue undiminished indefinitely, and, therefore, no provision for capital recovery is required. For example, the present worth of a site returning $12,000 net cash flow per year at 8% is $150,000 ($12,000/.08 = $150,000).

Another way of viewing an income stream in perpetuity is to identify the amount that would have to be invested to produce a forecast income stream that never changes or ends. In the example given here, $150,000 could earn $12,000 per year forever at 8%. A perpetual annuity (income stream) is the longest income stream that can be created, and results in a higher present worth at any given rate of discount than is produced with *any* finite income stream. As the time period (n) of a finite income stream increases, present worth approaches but never reaches the present worth produced by a perpetual income stream of the same amount.

**Capitalization for a Finite Period.** In all other income-capitalization situations, capital recovery is included along with return on the investment. Thus, a discount factor must be employed. An income stream for a finite time period has built into it the requirement that the investor recover his capital investment along with receiving a return on that investment for the time period specified.

*Future Income Stream.* The longer the time period involved, the larger will be the capitalization or discount factor at any given rate of discount. For example, the annual ordinary annuity factor for 15 years at 8% is 8.559479: the factor for 20 years at 8% is 9.818147 (Ellwood, page 84, column 5). The factor *increases* continually at a mathematically definable decreasing rate as the time period is extended.

*Future Single Payment.* The longer the time period involved, the smaller will be the discount factor (for the reversionary interest) at any given rate of discount. For example, the reversionary factor for 15 years discounted annually at 8% is 0.315242; the factor for 20 years at 8% is 0.214548 (Ellwood, page 84, column 4). The factor *decreases* continually at a mathematically definable decreasing rate as the time period is extended.

## Compound Interest

If one dollar is deposited to earn interest periodically, and the interest payments added to the original deposit are also left on deposit to earn interest in successive periods, the principal sum grows or accumulates at a compound rate. This is the basic fact of compound interest: interest payments left on deposit earn interest themselves in subsequent periods. All variations of compound interest factors and discount factors are derived from this fundamental relationship.

The principles and techniques of deriving compound interest factors are described in detail in many mathematics and appraisal texts.[1] The presentation here is confined to an indication of the several basic compound interest factors of concern and use to income-property appraisers, together with their meaning and application in deriving present worth estimates of forecast future income receipts.

### The Nature of Compounding

The compound interest concept provides the theoretical mathematical basis for discounting, and hence the entire process of income capitalization. Compounding consists of continuous and systematic additions to a principal sum (or discounted deductions from principal) over a series of successive time periods. The *rate* of interest (or discount) is constant throughout the process, and the time periods are all of equal length (year, month, etc.) over a specified finite number of periods.

Compounding refers to successive accumulations from the present to a specified future date. Discounting, as previously noted, involves successive deductions from a future sum or sums receivable at specified future dates to the present. Discounting is therefore simply the obverse of compounding, in mathematical terms. Since compounding is usually more readily understood, it is treated first.

Both compounding and discounting are applied over specified finite time periods. Thus, the recovery or retention of invested principal is always provided, along with the rate of return on that invested principal represented by the compound interest rate or the rate of discount. The mechanical process of compounding or discounting provides compensation to overcome time preference only. Risk of non-payment, irregularity in payment, or changes in purchasing power are reflected in the rate itself. This latter point is developed more fully in Chapters 8 and 9.

## Formula Notations and Terminology

Even in an area as conceptually standardized and rigid as compound interest and discounting, there are variations in notations, symbols, and specific terminology. Throughout the remainder of this book, a standard set of symbols and terms is employed. Every effort has been made to reconcile minor differences among published authorities, especially appraisal texts and tables. The notations and terms used here are widely (but unfortunately not universally) accepted. The important point to remember, however, is that the concepts, the principles, the mathematics, and the relationships between discount rate or compound interest rate and time, are exactly and necessarily the same.

The basic notations and symbols used in compound interest formulas are:

$1$: the number "one"

$P$: the principal sum of the original investment in the present

$p$: the periodic amount of a series of investments over a specified number of time periods

$i$: the discount rate (rate of interest) applied to overcome time preference in each successive period

$n$: the number of time periods (years, months, etc.) over which compounding or discounting occurs

$S^n$: the future worth (compound amount, accumulated sum) of a single investment ($P$) made at the present, or in time period zero, compounded at a specified rate of interest ($i$) over a specified number of successive time periods of equal length ($n$)

$s_n$: the future worth (compound amount, accumulated sum) of series of level income payments ($p$) at the end of each period after time-period zero, compounded at a specified rate of interest ($i$) over a specified number of successive time periods of equal length ($n$)

$a_n$: the present worth or discounted amount of a series of level income payments ($p$) receivable at the end of each period after time period zero, discounted at a specified rate of discount ($i$) over a specified number of successive time periods of equal length ($n$)

With these symbols and terms, any significant compound interest formula can be derived. Each of the six compound interest or discount factors most widely employed in income capitalization analysis depends on the interrelationships among these items.

## Nature and Use of Compound Interest Factors

There are two basic sets of compound interest factors. The first are used to derive a future sum or value from the present by means of compounding. The second, which are generally more important operationally to the appraiser, are used to derive a present worth figure from the future by discounting. Because present worth factors have their origins in future worth factors, however, it is useful to consider future worth factors first.

**Future Worth Factors.** When the objective of the calculation is to show the relationship between some future capital sum and payments in the present or intervening periods, future worth factors are used.

*Future Worth of One.* This is the basic compound interest factor from which all others are derived. It is variously termed the "Compound Amount of One," the "Future Worth of One Dollar with Interest," or the "Amount of One at Compound Interest." The Future Worth of One indicates the amount ($V$) to which a single lump-sum investment ($P$) made in the present or at time period zero will grow at compound interest, given the rate of interest ($i$) and the number of time periods of equal length ($n$) over which compounding is to occur.

The formula for the Future Worth of One (FW) factor is: $S^n = (1+i)^n$. Future worth or value is represented by: $FW = PS^n = P(1+i)^n$.

For example, suppose that $5,000 is deposited today to earn interest at 7%, compounded annually at the end of each year for 15 years. The Future Worth of One factor at 7% for 15 years, with annual compounding, is 2.759032 (Ellwood, page 68, column 1).

At the end of 15 years, the original deposit of $5,000 will have accumulated to $13,795.16. Since $FW = PS^n$, and $P$ is $5,000 and $S^n$ is 2.759032, then $FW = $5,000 \times 2.759032$, or $13,795.16.

To illustrate how this comes about, the individual annual interest receipts are compounded in the manner illustrated in Exhibit 5-1. The difference of *two cents* in the laboriously calculated figure is the result of rounding to two decimal places, since interest payments are expressed in dollars and cents.

Exhibit 5-1 shows that the precalculated Future Worth of One factors do indeed work. Every compounding problem *can* be solved on a step-by-step, period-by-period basis, but the calculations are laborious and time-consuming. At the least, an electronic calculator is virtually a necessity. But the need to carry out these lengthy calculations is eliminated when tables of precalculated factors, such as those contained on pages 1-166 in Part II of Ellwood, are available. Since the Future Worth of One is so basic to all other compound

**Exhibit 5-1**

**Composition of Annual Compound Interest Accumulation**

| Year | Principal Amount at Beginning of Year | Interest on Principal at 7% (End of Year) | Accumulated Principal Amount at End of Year | Ratio of End-of-Year Principal to Initial Investment |
|---|---|---|---|---|
| 1 | $ 5,000.00 | $350.00 | $ 5,350.00 | 1.070000 |
| 2 | $ 5,350.00 | $374.50 | $ 5,724.50 | 1.144900 |
| 3 | $ 5,724.50 | $400.72 | $ 6,125.22 | 1.225044 |
| 4 | $ 6,125.22 | $428.77 | $ 6,553.99 | 1.310798 |
| 5 | $ 6,553.99 | $458.78 | $ 7,012.77 | 1.402554 |
| 14 | $12,049.24 | $843.45 | $12,892.69 | 2.578538 |
| 15 | $12,892.69 | $902.49 | $13,795.18 | 2.759036 |

interest factors, it is provided in Column 1 of Ellwood's compound-interest tables.

While this factor has limited applicability in appraisal analysis, it does have occasional uses in decision problems involving value. The example already given can be phrased as a valuation issue by supposing that an investor had paid $5,000 for a parcel of real estate 15 years ago. Considering *only* compensation for his waiting 15 years, how much must he sell it for today in order to have earned 7% at an annual compound rate of return on his investment? The answer is $13,795: the original investment of $5,000 times the 15-year, 7% annual compound-interest factor of 2.759032.

*Future Worth of One per Annum.* This is also called the "Future Worth of an Annuity of One," the "Compound Amount of One per Annum," and the "Accumulation of One per Period." It is the factor which is applied to an ordinary level annuity (a series of equal periodic payments made at the *end* of each period) to derive the total sum to which all the payments will accumulate if they are left on deposit to earn compound interest (also at the end of each period), at a specified rate of interest over a specified number of time periods of equal length. The symbol for this factor is $s_n$.

The formula is:
$$s_n = \frac{S^n - 1}{i} = \frac{(1+i)^n - 1}{i}.$$

Then,
$$FW = ps_n = p\left[\frac{(1+i)^n - 1}{i}\right].$$

To illustrate the applicability of the Future Worth of One per Annum, suppose $3,000 is deposited annually at the end of each year for 17 years. The deposits are left to accumulate at 8.5%, compounded annually at the end of each year. At the end of 17 years, the total sum accumulated would be $105,962.20.

The Future Worth of One per Annum factor for 8.5%, compounded annually for 17 years, is 35.320733 (Ellwood, page 92, column 2). Then $3,000 × 35.320733 = $105,962.20.

The derivation of the 35.320733 factor can be demonstrated by adding together the Present Worth of One factors for 8.5% at annual compounding, for 16 years. This is because the deposits are made at the *end* of each year. Then, 1.000000 is added to that sum because the final payment earns nothing. A *series* of deposits or income payments can always be treated as individual payments whose values are then summed to indicate the value or worth of the series. In this case, one deposit of $3,000 earns compound interest annually for 16 years, the next for 15 years, and so forth. The precalculated Future Worth of One per Annum factors simply save the analyst time and effort, as well as reducing the opportunities to make a mechanical calculating error.

*Sinking-Fund Factor.* This factor is the mathematical reciprocal of the Future Worth of One per Annum. It is presented as Column 3 in Ellwood's compound interest tables. It is used to indicate the periodic (usually annual) payment or deposit required to accumulate a specified principal sum, if the payments are left to accumulate at compound interest at the end of each period, at a specified rate of interest for a specified number of time periods of equal length.

The Future Worth of One per Annum is used when the amount of each periodic end-of-period payment ($p$) is known, the rate of interest ($i$) is given, and the number of periods ($n$) is specified. When the principal sum ($FW$), rate of interest ($i$), and number of payment periods ($n$) are all given, the Sinking Fund factor is used to derive the level end-of-period payment ($p$) required. This has considerable applicability in income capitalization, especially when the Ellwood formulation of mortgage-equity analysis is being employed.

The symbol for the Sinking Fund factor is $1/s_n$. This reflects the fact that it is the reciprocal of the Future Worth of One per Annum factor.

The formula is:
$$\frac{1}{s_n} = \frac{i}{(1+i)^n - 1} .$$

To illustrate its applicability, suppose that an investor had paid $100,000 for a building with an anticipated remaining economic life of 17 years. He wants to recover his investment over that remaining economic life. What amount must be set aside from income annually if it can accumulate at 8.5%, compounded annually at the end of each year, in order to have $100,000 accumulated at the end of 17 years?

Since $p = (FW)\, 1/s_n$, the solution of this problem would be:
$$p = \$100,000 \times 0.028312 \ (\text{Ellwood, page 92, column 3})$$

Then $100,000 \times 0.028312 = \$2,831.20$. The investor should set aside $2,831.20 to recover his $100,000 in 17 years, with annual end-of-year compounding at 8.5%.

The calculation of capital-recovery requirements for level annuity income streams, and for proration of changes in value on resale in Ellwood analysis, employs Sinking Fund factors. These applications are discussed in detail in Chapters 10 and 13, respectively.

**Present-Worth Factors.** The Future Worth of One is basic to all compound-interest factors, and therefore should be thoroughly familiar to income-property appraisers. All future worth factors have occasional applicability in appraisal problems. However, since value (however defined) is a present worth figure based on discounting forecast future income receipts, present worth factors have special and continuous significance for the appraiser.

*Present Worth of One.* This is the so-called Reversion factor, also known as the "Present Value of a Reversion of One." It is applied to a lump-sum payment to be received at a specified future date, to indicate the single amount that would have to be invested at time period zero in order to accumulate to the specified lump sum, if interest is compounded at the end of each period at the specified rate of interest. The Present Worth of One factor is the *reciprocal* of the Future Worth of One factor for the same number of periods at the same rate.

Whereas the Future Worth of One factor is used in solving for $FW$ in the equation represented as $FW = P(1+i)^n$, the Present Worth of One factor is used to solve for $P$. The symbol for the Present Worth of One factor is $V^n$.

The formula is:
$$V^n = \frac{1}{S_n} = \frac{1}{(1+i)^n} \cdot$$

It can be derived, however, by solving for $P$, as follows:

$$FW = P(1+i)^n$$

$$P = \frac{FW}{(1+i)^n} = FW \times \frac{1}{(1+i)^n}$$

Therefore, the present worth of one (the reversion) is obtained by multiplying the forecast amount of the reversion ($FW$) by the Present Worth of One factor ($V^n$).

For example, suppose the owner of an income property anticipates being able to sell it for $14,000 in 15 years. The appropriate rate of discount to compensate him for waiting is 7%, on an annual end-of-year compound basis. What amount should he accept today for the right to receive the expected $14,000 15 years hence?

The Present Worth of One factor at 7% for 15 years, discounted annually on a compound basis at the end of each year, is 0.362446 (Ellwood, page 68, column 4). This is the reciprocal of the 2.759032 Future Worth of One factor for 15 years at 7% used in the preceding discussion of the future worth of one $(1/2.759032 = 0.362446)$.

Since $P = FW \times V^n$, then the present worth of the $14,000 payment 15 years in the future is $5,074.24 ($14,000 $\times$ 0.362446). This is the amount that an informed purchaser would be justified in paying for the right to receive $14,000 15 years hence, discounted annually at 7%.

Every future income payment can be valued in terms of the Present Worth of One factor. This factor is essential in calculating the present worth of any reversionary interest in income property. It is widely employed in the physical residual techniques, in mortgage-equity analysis, and in the valuation of leased fee interests. Moreover, it is the foundation of the level annuity factors used in estimating the present worth of a level-payment income stream, and of the mortgage constant used in mortgage debt service estimates.

*Present Worth of One per Annum.* This is variously termed the "Level Annuity factor," the "Inwood factor," and the "Present Value of an Ordinary Annuity of One per Period." While every periodic income stream is technically an annuity, an *ordinary* or *level annuity* is frequently given the label "annuity" in much appraisal literature. A level annuity is a stream of payments of equal amounts over a series of time periods of equal length. Payments are always assumed to be made or received at the *end* of each time period. Since the income period most commonly used by appraisers in income capitalization analysis is the year, the level annuity compound-interest factor is called the Present Worth of One per Annum here.

This factor is used to discount a level annuity to a present worth figure, given the rate of discount ($i$) and the number of time periods ($n$) of equal length over which the level annuity is forecast to be received. The symbol for the Present Worth of One per Annum is $a_n$.

The formula is:
$$a_n = \frac{1-V^n}{i} = \frac{(1+i)^n - 1}{i(1+i)^n} .$$

In the absence of precalculated Present Worth of One per Annum factor tables (which are in fact available as column 5 in Ellwood's compound interest tables), calculating the basic compound interest component of $(1+i)^n$ for the discount rate and number of time periods involved will enable the appraiser to develop $a_n$ relatively easily with the formula given above. For example, the Present Worth of One per Annum for a 20-year level annuity discounted annually at 8% is 9.818147 (Ellwood, page 84, column 5). The value of $(1+i)^n$ or $S^n$ for 20 years at 8% compounded annually is 4.660957 (Ellwood, page 84, column 1, or by calculation). In this case, $i = .08$ and $n = 20$. Then:

$$a_n = \frac{(1+i)^n - 1}{i(+n)^n} = \frac{4.660957 - 1}{.08(4.660957)} = \frac{3.660957}{0.3728766} = 9.818146$$

Much more important to the appraiser and income-property analyst is the fact that *any* Present Worth of One per Annum factor is equal to the *sum* of the Present Worth of One factors for the same number of time periods, discounted at the same rate. Before this is demonstrated arithmetically, it is useful to consider why. Assume that an investor has an opportunity to acquire a property which has a highly rated tenant under a 20-year lease that produces $26,000 absolute net income per year, payable at the end of each year. What is the present worth of this 20-year level annuity of $26,000 per year, discounted annually at 8%?

The right to receive $26,000 per year net at the end of each year for 20 years can be broken down to 20 "rights": the right to receive $26,000 at the end of year 1, the right to receive $26,000 at the end of year 2, the right to receive $26,000 at the end of year 3, and so on until the right to receive $26,000 at the end of year 20. This income stream can therefore be treated mechanically or arithmetically as a series of separate, individual reversions of $26,000 each. The 8% annual Present Worth of One factors are provided in Ellwood, page 84, column 4. This can be depicted as shown in Exhibit 5-2.

This example illustrates clearly the fact that the Present Worth of One per Annum factor at a given rate and over a given number of time periods is equal to the sum of the Present Worth of One factors for the same discount rate and the same number of time periods. The present worth of a level annuity discounted at a given rate over a given number of time periods is also equal to the sum of the present worths of the individual payments, discounted at the same rate over the same number of time periods. Since the Present Worth of One per Annum factor ($F$) is 9.818147 and the annual net income receipts ($I$) are $26,000, then the present worth ($V$) of this level annuity is: $V = I \times F = \$26,000 \times 9.818147 = \$255,271.82$. The difference of *six cents* between this figure and the sum of the present worths of the individual annual payments is the result of rounding.

No appraiser with the applicable Present Worth of One per Annum table available would logically use the longer method of summing the present worths of the individual payments. The relationship is important to grasp and understand, however, because it points the way to cope with valuation problems involving forecast future income streams that are *variable*. This issue is considered in detail in subsequent chapters.

Many appraisal problems do require discounting a forecast level annuity to a present-worth estimate. These are discussed in Chapters 11, 12, 13, 18, and 19. It is essential, therefore, to be able to work with the Present Worth of One per Annum factor and apply it properly as the facts of the problem warrant it.

*Installment to Amortize One.* This is the reciprocal of the Present Worth of One per Annum factor. It is also called the "Ordinary Annuity which has a Present Worth of One" and the "Amount whose Present Value is One." In some contexts, it represents the *mortgage constant* which was discussed in Chapter 4, and whose use in appraisal analysis is demonstrated in Chapters 7 and 13.

The symbol for the Installment to Amortize One factor is $1/a_n$. Its formula is:

**Exhibit 5-2**

**Representation of Level Income Stream as a Series of Periodic Reversions**

| Year | End-of-Year Payment | Present Worth of One Factor at 8% | Present Worth of End-of-Year Payment |
|------|------|------|------|
| 1 | $26,000 | 0.925926 | $ 24,074.08 |
| 2 | $26,000 | 0.857339 | $ 22,290.81 |
| 3 | $26,000 | 0.793832 | $ 20,639.63 |
| 4 | $26,000 | 0.735030 | $ 19,110.78 |
| 5 | $26,000 | 0.680583 | $ 17,695.16 |
| 6 | $26,000 | 0.630170 | $ 16,384.42 |
| 7 | $26,000 | 0.583490 | $ 15,170.74 |
| 8 | $26,000 | 0.540269 | $ 14,046.99 |
| 9 | $26,000 | 0.500249 | $ 13,006.47 |
| 10 | $26,000 | 0.463193 | $ 12,043.02 |
| 11 | $26,000 | 0.428883 | $ 11,150.96 |
| 12 | $26,000 | 0.397114 | $ 10,324.96 |
| 13 | $26,000 | 0.367698 | $  9,560.15 |
| 14 | $26,000 | 0.340461 | $  8,851.99 |
| 15 | $26,000 | 0.315242 | $  8,196.26 |
| 16 | $26,000 | 0.291890 | $  7,589.14 |
| 17 | $26,000 | 0.270269 | $  7,026.99 |
| 18 | $26,000 | 0.250249 | $  6,506.47 |
| 19 | $26,000 | 0.231712 | $  6,024.51 |
| 20 | $26,000 | 0.214548 | $  5,578.25 |
|  |  | 9.818147 | $255,271.88 |

$$\frac{1}{a_n} = \frac{i(1+i)^n}{(1+i)^n - 1}.$$

In the expression, $V = p(a_n)$, the appraiser estimates present worth by solving for $V$. The annual amount of the level annuity payable at the end of each period is represented by $p$, and $a_n$ is the Present Worth of One per Annum factor. When using the Installment to Amortize One factor, the appraiser is solving for $p$. The principal sum to be amortized is known, as is the discount rate and the number of time periods over which payments are to be made. The issue is to identify the level periodic payment that will provide a specified rate of return on a given investment principal over a specified number of time periods, and return the full amount of the principal to the investor by the end of the final time period.

This factor has wide applicability in appraisal analysis. It is used to identify the capitalization rate applied to an investment with a finite forecast-income stream. It is particularly useful in identifying the mortgage constant for a specified loan amount over a specified number of years at the given mortgage-interest rate. As previously noted in Chapter 4, a mortgage constant is always expressed as an *annual* percentage of the initial principal of a mortgage loan. It can be applied to this principal amount to indicate the annual debt service (principal and interest payments) that will provide interest on the outstanding balance of the loan at the stipulated rate of interest and also pay back the full amount of the loan by the end of the contract term of the loan.

Because many mortgage loans require monthly, quarterly, or semi-annual payments of principal and interest, the Installment to Amortize One factor must be converted to an annual basis to derive the applicable mortgage constant. For example, suppose an investor borrows $250,000 at 9% interest. Monthly payments are to be made over 25 years to amortize the loan fully. The *monthly* Installment to Amortize One factor (Ellwood, page 97, column 6) is 0.008391. Applying this factor to the $250,000 loan principal yields a monthly payment of $2,097.75. Annual debt service would then be 12 × $2,097.75 = $25,173.

The mortgage constant can be developed in two ways. It is equal to twelve times the monthly Installment to Amortize One: 12 × 0.008391 = 0.100692, or 10.07%. It is also equal to annual debt service divided by mortgage principal: $25,173/$250,000 = 0.100692, or 10.07%.

## Use of Compound-Interest and Discount-Factor Tables

Compound-interest and discount factors can be calculated for any rate of compound interest, for any number of time periods of any length. The key building block in any such calculations is the derivation of a value for $(1+i)^n$. These calculations are usually laborious and time-consuming, even with an electronic calculator, and offer numerous opportunities for mechanical errors. Precalculated tables of factors for different rates of interest (or discount) and different numbers of time periods of different lengths are widely available in published form, however. The appraiser or valuation analyst should be familiar with and able to use such tables.

As previously noted in earlier chapters, one very useful set of compound interest tables particularly designed for appraisal analysis is provided on pages 1-166 of Part II in the third edition of Ellwood's *Tables for Real Estate Appraising and Financing*. Because the examples throughout this book are keyed to Ellwood's tables, their format deserves special mention.

Monthly, quarterly, semi-annual and annual factor tables are available in Ellwood for rates of interest in 0.25% increments from 3% through 12%. Annual factor tables are available in one-percentage-point increments from 13% through 30%. Each table contains all six of the basic compound interest and discount factors discussed in this chapter, arranged in columns as follows:

Column 1: Future Worth of One factor
Column 2: Future Worth of One per Annum factor
Column 3: Sinking Fund factor
Column 4: Present Worth of One factor
Column 5: Present Worth of One per Annum factor
Column 6: Installment to Amortize One factor

*General Rules of Compound-Interest and Discount Factors*

**Influence of Rate.** The lower the rate of discount used in deriving its associated discount factor, the higher the present worth of the future income payment(s) will be. Conversely, the lower the rate, the lower a future worth estimate based on the associated compound interest factor will be.

**Influence of Time.** The greater the number of time periods employed at any given rate to derive the associated compound interest or discount factor, the more that factor will deviate from 1.000000. The impact of this derivation on the value or worth estimate depends on whether the factor is greater than or less than 1.000000. If it is greater, the worth estimate will be higher; if it is less than 1.000000, the worth estimate will be lower.

**Exponents.** In the expression $(1 + i)^n$, $n$ is an exponent. It is the *power* to which $(1 + i)$ is raised: the number of times it is multiplied by itself. Exponents are capable of arithmetic processing in accordance with strict mathematical rules. The ability to manipulate exponents properly greatly enhances the usefulness of precalculated compound-interest and discount factor tables such as are provided in Ellwood. A review of these rules, with illustrative applications to compound interest factors, is provided in the Appendix to this chapter. The Chapter 5 Appendix also contains a brief discussion of logarithms, which are a special form of exponents potentially useful in calculations with complex numbers.

**Rounding and Significant Digits.** Many figures used in income capitalization in particular are *rounded*. They are necessarily approximations reflecting less than perfect accuracy or precision. This is true, for example, of nearly all compound interest and discount factors, even though they are usually provided to six decimal places.

In dealing with rounded numbers, appraisers should be aware of the mathematical rules of rounding and significant digits. A brief review of these rules, together with a summary of rules for working with decimal figures, may be found in the Appendix to this chapter.

---

96

*Varying Payment Patterns*

Compound-interest and discount factors are constructed on the assumption that income or interest payments are made and received at the *end* of each time period. In addition, many published tables provide factors based on *annual* compounding or discounting only (as in the case of the 13% through 30% tables in Ellwood). The income streams assumed in the construction of factors relating to the capitalization of income flows are always *level annuities*.

None of these assumptions necessary for the mathematical integrity of the factors is *always* valid in actual appraisal and valuation problems. Leases frequently require the payment of rentals at the beginning of each period. Mortgages and leases often call for monthly, quarterly, or semi-annual payments. Variable income streams are frequently forecast and require discounting to a present worth estimate. Each of these kinds of deviations from the basic mathematical assumptions of compound interest and discount factors can be handled easily by making relatively simple, though sometimes complicated, mechanical adjustments.

**Payments in Advance.** An income stream calling for payments at the beginning of each period can be handled simply. Mechanically, the appraiser merely identifies the factor for *one period less* than the number of actual payment periods, and adds 1.000000 to it. The logic of this adjustment is that the first payment is received immediately and therefore is not subject to discounting. Its present worth is 100% of itself. The factor by which it is multiplied is 1.000000. The payment at the beginning of time period 2 is the same as a payment at the end of time period 1, and is discounted as such. Each successive beginning-of-period payment is the same as an end-of-period payment for the preceding period. The payment at the beginning of the last period $(n)$ is the same as a payment at the end of the next-to-last period $(n-1)$.

For example, suppose that a lease calls for 18 annual rental payments of $3,600, payable at the beginning of each year. The appropriate rate of discount is 10%. The 18-year annual Present Worth of One per Annum factor at 10% is 8.201412 (Ellwood, page 116, column 5). However, this factor is based on end-of-year payments. The rental income stream in this case is actually an immediate payment of $3,600 with a present worth of $3,600 (and hence a Present Worth of One per Annum factor of 1.000000), *plus* a series of 17 more payments receivable annually.

The Present Worth of One per Annum factor for 17 years at 10%, discounted annually, is 8.021553. The present worth of the 17-year income stream of $3,600 per year is therefore $28,877.59 ($3,600 × 8.021553). To this must be added $3,600, the present worth of $3,600 receivable immediately. The present worth of the 18-year rental stream of $3,600 per year, payable in advance is thus $32,477.59.

The Present Worth of One per Annum factor for 18 annual payments in advance, discounted at 10%, is 8.021553 *plus* 1.000000, or 9.021553. Then, the present worth of this income stream at $3,600 per year is calculated as $3,600 × 9.021553 = $32,477.59.

**Periods of Less than One Year.** When the income payment period is less than a year, adjustments may have to be made to derive an accurate discount factor. Annual factors cannot legitimately be used, except as rough approximations. For example, assume a forecast income stream of $12,000 per year for 30 years, discounted at 11%. The income could be $1,000 per month, $3,000 per quarter, or $6,000 semi-annually—as well as $12,000 annually. The time period of payment would influence the Present Worth of One per Annum factors, and hence the calculated present worth estimates, as follows:

Annual Payments:          $12,000 ×     8.693793 (p. 132, col. 5) = $104,325.52
Semi-annual Payments: $  6,000 ×   17.449854 (p. 131, col. 5) = $104,699.12
Quarterly Payments:     $  3,000 ×   34.961315 (p. 130, col. 5) = $104,883.95
Monthly Payments:       $  1,000 × 105.006345 (p. 129, col. 5) = $105,006.35

It should be noted that the *amount* of the periodic income payment must be adjusted to conform to the amount to be received during the period in question. The present worth estimates vary somewhat, because the factors are not *arithmetically* related. Their relationship is based on exponential factors. The semi-annual factor is more than half the annual factor; the monthly factor is more than one-twelfth the annual factor; and so forth. Using the annual factor to capitalize the monthly income stream would result in a conceptually incorrect present-worth estimate, even though it is a close approximation in this example.

Precalculated factor tables for periods of less than one year are available in Ellwood for rates of interest from 3% through 12%, in 0.25% increments. But suppose they were not. A quarterly income stream of $7,500 per quarter for 10 years, discounted at 12% per year can be treated as an income stream for 40 quarters (periods) at an *effective* rate of 3% per quarter (period). The 40-period 3% Present Worth of One per Annum factor is 23.114772 (Ellwood, page 4, column 5). The present worth of the income stream would then be $7,500 × 23.114772 = $173,360.79. If the appraiser were forced to use the 10-year 12% annual factor of 5.650223 (Ellwood, page 148, column 5), the present worth approximation would be $169,506.69.

In point of fact, the 10-year *quarterly* factor at 12% is exactly 23.114772 (Ellwood, page 146, column 5). The appraiser would use the published 12% quarterly table to derive the proper factor in this case. The point is that he *could* derive it from the 3% annual table if he were forced to do so.

**Non-Level Annuities.** Appraisers frequently encounter problems in which the forecast future income stream is not a level annuity. In such cases, the Present Worth of One per Annum factor cannot be applied. Future income may be forecast to decline periodically in a systematic way, in which case it is a "declining annuity." Alternatively, it may be an "increasing annuity" which is forecast to increase systematically over each period. Both of these situations can be handled with special formulas which are discussed in some detail in Chapter 9. The widely used straight-line method of providing for capital recovery, for example, is a special case of a declining annuity in which annual income payments are forecast to decrease in accordance with a specific mathematical formula.

Yet another possibility is that the forecast future income stream will vary from year to year, increasing and/or decreasing in a way that cannot be reduced to a mathematical formulation. This is a "variable annuity."

All these categories of non-level annuities can be capitalized by treating each individual payment as a separate reversion and discounting each to a present-worth estimate with the proper Present Worth of One factor for the rate of discount ($i$) and time period ($n$) involved. These present worth estimates are then simply added together to derive the present worth estimate for the entire forecast future income stream. This is exactly the same technique that was illustrated in the discussion of the derivation and meaning of the Present Worth of One per Annum factor in a preceding section of this chapter.

For example, assume a five-year income stream should be discounted on an annual basis at 14%. The forecast annual income receipts at the end of each year are:

| Year | Income |
|------|--------|
| 1 | $10,000 |
| 2 | $ 8,000 |
| 3 | $12,000 |
| 4 | − $ 4,000 |
| 5 | $ 3,000 |

The present worth of this highly variable income stream is the sum of the present worths of the forecast individual payments, as shown in Exhibit 5-3. The Present Worth of One factors are found on page 150, column 4 in Ellwood.

The present worth of this variable income stream is $22,217.10. Negative income (losses, net cash outflows) can be handled as readily as positive income or cash inflows.

This procedure is admittedly lengthy and somewhat time-consuming when a long income stream is being discounted. With an electronic calculator, however, the preceding illustration took less than a minute to calculate. Moreover, this approach is totally supportable and defensible in both mathematical and appraisal terms. Indeed, it is *the* basic technique for estimating the present worth of *any* future income stream. All other methods, formulas and factors are simply short-cut variations applicable to special cases.

**Deferred Factors.** One special case that deserves mention here because it is frequently encountered in the valuation of leased-fee interests in particular is the

**Exhibit 5-3**

**Illustrative Calculation of Present Worth of a Variable Annuity**

| Year | Income | Present Worth of One Factor | Present Worth |
|---|---|---|---|
| 1 | $10,000 | 0.877193 | $ 8,771.93 |
| 2 | $ 8,000 | 0.769468 | $ 6,155.74 |
| 3 | $12,000 | 0.674971 | $ 8,099.65 |
| 4 | − $ 4,000 | 0.592080 | − $ 2,368.32 |
| 5 | $ 3,000 | 0.519368 | $ 1,558.10 |
| Present Worth of 5-Year Income Stream | | | $22,217.10 |

use of so-called "deferred factors." Appraisers often encounter "step-up" or "step-down" leases that are actually a series of level annuities that start at a specified future date. Deferred factors are used whenever a level annuity starts at some time *after* time period one.

For example, suppose a property is leased for 15 years. The lease calls for net rentals of $3,600 per year payable at the end of the year for the first 5 years, $4,800 per year for the next five years, and $5,400 per year for the last 5 years. This actually represents three separate income streams of five years each. The appraiser has several alternative mechanical approaches available to help solve this problem. Each will produce the same result, and each is equally acceptable.

The rental-income stream can be treated as a 5-year level annuity of $3,600 per year; a 5-year level annuity of $4,800 per year, *deferred* 5 years; and a 5-year level annuity of $5,400 per year, *deferred* 10 years. Alternatively, it can be regarded as a 15-year level annuity of $3,600 per year; plus a 10-year level annuity of $1,200 per year, *deferred* 5 years; plus a 5-year level annuity of $600 per year, *deferred* 10 years. Both alternatives are depicted in Figure 5-1.

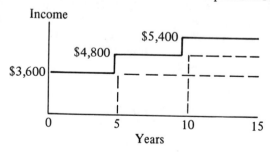

**Figure 5-1** Alternative Income Flows Represented by Step-Up Lease

If the discount rate is 9.5%, the Present Worth of One per Annum factors (from Ellwood, page 108, column 5) would be: 5 years, 3.839709; 10 years, 6.278798; and 15 years, 7.828175.

Treating the income stream as three successive 5-year flows of $3,600, $4,800, and $5,400, respectively, involves applying the 5-year Present Worth of One per Annum factor to each, *but* the $4,800 from years 6 through 10 and the $5,400 from years 11 through 15 have to be discounted further. Since the $4,800 5-year flow does not start for five years, its capitalized value must be discounted to the present by applying the 5-year Present Worth of One factor at 9.5% to it. Similarly, the 5-year flow of $5,400 per year is first capitalized at 9.5%, and then discounted to the present through the 10-year Present Worth of One factor (Ellwood, page 108, column 4).

The derivation of the present worth of the entire income stream is shown in Exhibit 5-4.

**Exhibit 5-4**

**Estimation of Present Worth of Step-Up Lease Income Stream**

| Years | Annual Income | P.W. One per Annum | Capitalized Value | P.W. One Factor | Present Worth |
|-------|---------------|--------------------|-------------------|-----------------|---------------|
| 1-5   | $3,600 | 3.839709 | $13,822.95 | – | $13,822.95 |
| 6-10  | $4,800 | 3.839709 | $18,430.60 | 0.635228 | $11,707.63 |
| 11-15 | $5,400 | 3.839709 | $20,734.43 | 0.403514 | $ 8,366.63 |
| Present Worth of Income Stream | | | | | $33,957.21 |

The net effect of applying both the Present Worth of One per Annum factor and the appropriate Present Worth of One factor to the deferred segments of the income stream can be duplicated by using the *difference* between the Present Worth of One per Annum factors for the periods at the beginning and the end of the deferred income stream. Take, for example, the $4,800 per year receivable in years 6 through 10. The *deferred factor* applicable to it is the difference between the 10-year and the 5-year factors at 9.5%:

$$
\begin{array}{ll}
\text{10-year factor} & : 6.278798 \\
less\ \text{5-year factor} & : \underline{3.839709} \\
\text{Deferred factor} & : 2.439089
\end{array}
$$

The present worth of $4,800 per year for five years, *deferred* for five years, is, therefore, $4,800 × 2.439089 = $11,707.63. This is exactly the same as the present worth figure derived above by combining the Present Worth of One per Annum factor and the Present Worth of One factor.

Similarly, the present worth of $5,400 in years 11 through 15 is $8,366.63. The *deferred factor* is 1.549377: the difference between 7.828175 and 6.278798.

If the breakdown of the income stream were: $3,600 per year for 15 years; $1,200 per year for 10 years, deferred 5 years; and $600 per year for 5 years, deferred 10 years—then its present worth could be calculated as:

| | |
|---|---|
| $3,600 X 7.828175 (15-year factor) | = $28,181.43 |
| $1,200 X 2.988466 (15-year factor *less* 5-year factor) | = $ 4,786.16 |
| $ 600 X 1.549377 (15-year factor *less* 10-year factor) | = $  929.63 |
| | $33,897.22 |

Whichever mechanical technique is used, the resulting present worth estimate is $34,000. The important point for the appraiser to recognize is that the deferred or postponed start of some portion of the income stream requires that a deferred factor be applied to derive a proper present worth estimate.

The same technique can also be used in valuing a step-down lease. In either case, the deferred-factor technique is simply a short-cut method of duplicating the results that treating the income stream as a series of individual reversions would produce.

## Review Exercises

1. A client purchased a parcel of land twelve years ago for $8,800.
   a. How much must he sell it for today in order to have earned 10.5% per year on his investment? (Ignore all holding costs over the twelve-year period.)
   b. If he is actually able to sell it for $26,875, what rate of return (on an annual compounding basis) will he have earned over the twelve years?
   c. What compound interest factor is illustrated here?
2. An investor has agreed to buy a property on the installment plan, paying $1,000 per month for 120 months. Assuming the appropriate rate of interest is 11%, compounded monthly, what will be the total value of the 120 monthly payments when the last payment is made? What compound interest factor is illustrated in this case?
3. A tenant has just purchased a sub-leasehold interest enabling him to occupy certain premises for 7 years. The applicable rate of interest is 13%. What annual rental saving would accumulate to the purchase price of $75,000 in 7 years? What compound interest factor is represented here?
4. A property owner leases his realty for 20 years at $6,000 per year net rental, payable quarterly at the end of each quarter. At the end of the 20-year lease term, the tenant has an option to buy the property for $50,000. The indicated discount rate applicable to this transaction is 9.25%.

a. What is the present worth of the 20-year rental income stream?

b. What is the present worth to the lessor (owner) of the property 20 years hence, assuming the lessee (tenant) exercises the option to buy?

c. What is the present worth of the leased fee interest (income stream plus reversion)?

d. What discount factors are illustrated here?

e. What would be the present worth of the rental income stream if rental payments were made *annually in advance*?

5. A mortgage loan has just been made for $300,000. It has a 15-year maturity, an 8.75% rate of interest, and full amortization in equal monthly payments over the full 15-year maturity.

a. What annual debt service is indicated?

b. What is the indicated mortgage constant?

c. What discount factor is used in answering the above questions?

d. At the end of 10 years, what is the outstanding balance of the loan?

6. An appraiser is called upon to estimate the present worth of a leased fee on a parcel of land. The lease payments are made annually, in advance, and should be discounted at 14%. The schedule of ground rent payments (in advance) is:

| Year | Ground Rent |
|------|-------------|
| 1 | $2,000 |
| 2 | $3,000 |
| 3 | $4,000 |
| 4 | $5,000 |
| 5 and to perpetuity | $5,500 |

What is the present worth of this income stream?

7. A lease has 17 years remaining. Rental payments are made semi-annually, and should be discounted at a 11.5% rate. The schedule of annual rentals is:

| Years | Annual Rental |
|-------|---------------|
| 1-6 | $4,200 per year |
| 7-12 | $4,000 per year |
| 13-17 | $3,750 per year |

What is the present worth of this rental income stream?

# Appendix to Chapter 5

The use of compound interest factors and tables requires modest mathematical and arithmetic skills. Many of these skills are also required throughout other portions of appraisal analysis, especially in income capitalization.

The income property appraiser needs to be able to work comfortably with relatively simple linear algebraic equations. He must be thoroughly familiar with the rules and techniques of addition, subtraction, multiplication, and division of directed numbers. Further, he is continually required to deal with both constants and variables in algebraic equations, and to simplify equations through the removal of brackets and parentheses. Finally, he must be able to apply the fundamental rules of manipulation of components in an equation through addition, subtraction, multiplication, division, and transposition.

These basic skills in arithmetic and simple algebra may have dimmed with the passage of time. The student or reader with any uncertainty about his skills should consult a basic refresher reference prior to proceeding beyond this point in the study of income capitalization.[a]

Beyond these fundamental considerations, there are two areas that have specific and peculiar applicability in work with compound-interest factors and tables. The first is the rule of exponents, including manipulations with exponents and the use of logarithms. The second involves guidelines in working with decimals. This is required throughout all of income capitalization analysis, and, therefore, deserves special emphasis here.

## Exponents

An exponent is a mathematical notation used to indicate the *power* to which a number or expression is to be raised. That is, it represents the number of times a number or expression is to be *multiplied by itself*. In the basic compound interest expression $(1 + i)^n$, the $n$ is the exponent. In this case, it is presented symbolically. For calculations, it must be given a numerical value.

Exponents can be expressed as positive, negative, fractional-decimal, or

---

[a]There are excellent references now available which are designed specifically to refresh or sharpen the basic skills referred to here. One is *Basic Mathematics* by C.H. Springer, R.E. Herlihy, and R.I. Beggs. This is Volume One of the Mathematics for Management Series, published by Richard D. Irwin, Inc. in 1965. Chapter 4 of this volume contains an especially useful review of algebra. A most comprehensive treatment of the material is available in programmed learning form for self-instruction and self-testing in E.W. Martin, Jr., *Mathematics for Decision-Making; Volume 1: Linear Mathematics* (Homewood, Illinois: Richard D. Irwin, 1969).

compound numbers. The same rules of manipulation apply to the base number being multiplied by itself as apply to any operations with numbers.

The expression $5^6$ means "5 multiplied by itself 6 times." It is a shorthand way of writing $5 \times 5 \times 5 \times 5 \times 5 \times 5$. It can also be written $5^3 \times 5^3$: $(5 \times 5 \times 5) \times (5 \times 5 \times 5)$; or $5^2 \times 5^4$: $(5 \times 5) \times (5 \times 5 \times 5 \times 5)$.

When *negative* figures are used, even-numbered exponents result in *positive* values of the expression, while odd-numbered exponents result in *negative* values of the expression. For example, $-5^3$ is $-5 \times -5 = +25 \times -5 = -125$. On the other hand, $-5^4 = -5 \times -5 = +25 \times -5 = -125 \times -5 = +625$.

A fractional exponent indicates taking the *root* of a number. The expression $27^{1/3}$ means "27 to its third or cube root." Thus $27^{1/3}$ is equal to 3.

By mathematical convention, any number raised to the *zero* power is equal to *one*. Thus, $5^\circ = 1$; $250^\circ = 1$; $0.25^\circ = 1$.

**Rules of Exponents.** Exponents are additive. This means that when the number being raised to a power is multiplied further by itself, the exponents are added. It has already been seen that $5^6 = 5^2 \times 5^4$. The exponents (2 and 4) are added to reach the correct expression $5^6$. The *expressions* ($5^2$ and $5^4$) are multiplied to reach the correct result.

When division of expressions is to take place, the exponents are subtracted. Thus, $5^6 \div 5^4 = 5^2$ (6 − 4 = 2). This expression could also be written $5^{6-4}$; $5^{-4}$ is the same as $1/5^4$

This rule is very useful in deriving compound interest factors applied to income capitalization analysis. When tables such as those on pages 1-166 in Part II of Ellwood are not available, successive simple calculations can be used to avoid the drudgery of lengthy manipulations. For example, suppose the appraiser needs the value of $(1 + 0.10)^{80}$ in deriving $(1 + i)^n$. Eighty successive multiplications are time-consuming and offer many opportunities for error. Since $n = 80$, the value can be derived by using $n = 20 + 60$, or $n = 40 + 40$. The problem can be broken down into fewer steps and solved as follows, using factors from Column 1 on page 116 in Ellwood:

$$\begin{array}{rl} (1.10)^{20} = & 6.727500 \\ \times(1.10)^{60} = & \underline{304.481600} \\ (1.10)^{80} = & 2048.400233 \end{array}$$

This could also be written as:

$$\begin{array}{rl} (1.10)^{40} = & 45.259256 \\ \times(1.10)^{40} = & \underline{45.259256} \\ (1.10)^{80} = & 2048.400254 \end{array}$$

The slight difference in the two calculated compound interest factors is the result of *rounding* to six decimal places. Rounding and significant digits are discussed in a later section of this Appendix.

**Logarithms.** A logarithm is an exponent. In common logarithmic tables most useful to appraisers, the logarithms are expressed as exponents of base 10. That is, they represent the exponent or power to which 10 must be raised to equal the number being manipulated.

The rule of exponents applies to logarithms. They can be multiplied by adding their logarithms, and divided by subtracting their logarithms. They can be raised to powers by multiplying their logarithms, and their roots derived by dividing logarithms. Their use helps simplify complex operations with large compound numbers in particular.[b]

## Working with Decimals

A decimal figure is greater than zero but less than one, expressed on a base of 10, 100, 1000, etc. Numbers to the left of a decimal point are whole numbers; those to the right of a decimal point are decimal figures. Thus, the number 4.1723 means four whole units *plus* 1,723 *ten thousandths* of one whole unit.

When a decimal figure is entirely a fraction of one, a zero is usually written to the left of the decimal point to indicate this fact. For example, 0.008678 is preferred to .008678.

**Decimal Places.** When decimal figures are added or subtracted, the sum or difference contains the same number of decimal places as the figure in the addition or subtraction with the largest number of decimal places. Zeros are usually added to the other figures to avoid confusion and possible misplacement of the decimal point in the sum or difference.

For example, if 4.1723 and 0.008678 were to be added, the preferable form of presentation would be:

$$\begin{array}{r} 4.172300 \\ +0.008678 \\ \hline 4.180978 \end{array}$$

Multiplication of decimal figures results in a product that contains the same number of decimal places as the *sum* of the decimal places in the two figures being multiplied. If the multiplier contains three decimal places and the multiplicand contains five, then the product must contain eight decimal places (3 + 5). This is particularly important to remember in multiplying decimal figures containing zeros to the right of the decimal point preceding the first significant figure.

For example, suppose two Present Worth of One discount factors are to be multiplied to derive a factor beyond the limits of a printed table available to the

---

[b]The uses and rules of logarithms are discussed in detail in Springer, Herlihy, and Beggs, *Basic Mathematics*, Chapter 4.

appraiser. He needs to derive the Present Worth of One factor at 11%, discounted on an annual basis for 60 years, but his tables go only to 50 years. (In point of fact, the 11% annual tables on page 132 of Ellwood, Part II, go to 60 years. This illustration is used to enable the reader to check his work.)

From the rule of exponents, the appraiser knows that the Present Worth of One factor for 11% discounted annually for 60 years is the *product* of the Present Worth of One factor for 30 years *times* the factor for 30 years. He could also use the factor for 20 years *times* the factor for 40 years; or any other combination adding to 60 years. Turning to the Present Worth of One table for 11% discounted annually (Ellwood, Part II, page 132, column 4), he finds the following:

> 20-year factor: 0.124034
> 30-year factor: 0.043683
> 40-year factor: 0.015384

The appropriate factor for 60 years can then be readily calculated:

| 0.124034 | (20-year factor) | 0.043683 (30-year factor) |
|---|---|---|
| | or | |
| X0.015384 | (40-year factor) | X0.043683 (30-year factor) |
| 0.001908639056 | (60-year factor) | 0.001908704489 (60-year factor) |

In each case, the product contains 12 decimal places. The factor actually used for 60 years would then be *rounded* to six decimal places, according to the rules of rounding and significant digits presented below. The important point here is that the appraiser must insert zeros to the right of the decimal point and preceding the first significant digit, so that the product contains 12 decimal places. (The reader will also note that the six-place decimal factor for 60 years produced by this multiplication is the same as that provided on page 132 in Ellwood.)

In division, when the divisor (denominator) is a decimal figure, the decimal point in both divisor and dividend (numerator) is moved to the right a sufficient number of places to make the divisor a whole number. Then division is carried out as if the divisor were a whole number.

For example, if 0.0076 were to be divided by 4.13, the problem could be expressed as: $0.0076 \div 4.13$, or as $\frac{0.0076}{4.13}$. In either case, the divisor (denominator) would be converted to 413, and the dividend (numerator) would become 0.76, for purposes of division. The answer (quotient) would contain two decimal places, at least:

$$\begin{array}{r} .001840 \\ 413 \overline{)0.760000} \end{array}$$

This rule is particularly important in income-capitalization analysis because *rates* of capitalization are always decimal figures, although they are usually expressed as percentages. To apply the basic capitalization formula ($V = I/R$), the rate ($R$) must first be converted to a decimal figure, and then the rule of division by decimals applied.

Suppose that a 20-year level-payment mortgage has annual debt service of $18,000 per year, payable in monthly installments at 9.5% interest. The installment to amortize one factor (Ellwood, page 105, column 6) is 0.009321. The annual mortgage constant would then be 12 X 0.009321 = 0.111852, or 11.1852%. To find the principal amount of the mortgage, the appraiser would divide $18,000 by 0.111852, as follows:

$$\begin{array}{r} 160\ 926.939 \\ 111852 \overline{)\ 18\ 000\ 000\ 000.000} \end{array} \text{, or } \$160,926.94$$

This could be rounded to $161,000 if an estimate rather than a precise amount were called for.

**Rounding and Significant Digits.** Value or present worth estimates are precisely that: estimates. While it is possible to calculate figures with impeccable mathematical precision to many decimal places (as in the example of 12 decimal places for the 60-year Present Worth of One factor provided above), this can give a false impression of a level of accuracy that is not justified. Therefore, most figures used in income capitalization analysis are *rounded*. In part, rounding is dictated by the behavior of market participants and the reliability or quality of the data employed. There are also mathematical rules for rounding with which the appraiser should be familiar.[c]

Rounding is required whenever calculations are made with numbers or data that are not completely accurate. The results of arithmetic calculations, no matter how correctly the figures are manipulated, can be no more accurate than the component figures that are inserted into the calculations. Rounded numbers are approximations. Whenever rounded numbers are used in addition or subtraction, which is almost always the case in appraisal analysis, the resulting sum or difference is no more accurate than the *least* accurate (or most rounded) component.

For example, suppose that the value of a vacant site is estimated at $55,000, and that the cost of a new building on the site is verified at $278,869.50. The sum must be rounded to the nearest $5,000, because this is the degree of accuracy of the site value estimate.

The use of rounded figures requires the appraiser to recognize the *significant digits* in those figures. As a broad generalization, those digits in a rounded number that indicate its degree of accuracy are significant digits, as opposed to digits that simply indicate its order of magnitude. In the example above, the

---

[c]The discussion here is a brief overview of the rules relating to rounding and significant digits. For a more thorough treatment, see J. Neter and W. Wasserman, *Fundamental Statistics for Business and Economics* (Boston: Allyn and Bacon, 1961), pages 60-62.

building cost would be rounded to $280,000. The first three digits (280) are significant digits in this case, since they indicate the degree of accuracy to the nearest $5,000. If rounding were to the nearest $1,000, then the cost figure would be $279,000, and the significant digits would be 279. The three additional zeros merely indicate the fact that the figure is expressed in thousands of dollars, which is the order of magnitude. Zeros that indicate the order of magnitude are *not* significant digits, whether they appear to the left or to the right of the decimal point.

In multiplication or division with rounded numbers, the appraiser should retain no more significant digits in the product or quotient than there are in the component of the calculation with the least number of significant digits. The derivation of the 60-year Present Worth of One factor presented earlier in this Appendix illustrates this point. Each of the components contained six decimal places and six significant digits. The product necessarily contained twelve decimal places, but for further use should be rounded to six significant digits.

As a further example, suppose that an apartment containing 1042 square feet rents for $375 per month. By calculation, the rental per square foot per month is $0.359884. Since the component with the least number of significant digits ($375) contains three significant digits, the rental per square foot per month should be expressed as $0.360. In this case, the final zero is a significant digit.

One final point should be noted. In *intermediate steps* of calculations, more digits are usually retained than are warranted. This avoids the possibility of compounding errors if successive rounding occurs in the same direction. It is for this reason that most compound interest factors are expressed and used to six decimal places, even though the final value estimate will be rounded to the nearest thousand or ten thousand dollars.

### Supplementary Readings

American Institute of Real Estate Appraisers, *The Appraisal of Real Estate*, fifth edition (Chicago: American Institute of Real Estate Appraisers, 1967), pp. 296-301 and 317.

L.W. Ellwood, *Ellwood Tables for Real Estate Appraising and Financing*, third edition (Chicago: American Institute of Real Estate Appraisers, 1970), Part I, pp. 17-50; Part II, pp. 1-166.

Sanders A. Kahn, Frederick E. Case, and Alfred Schimmel, *Real Estate Appraisal and Investment* (New York: Ronald Press, 1963), Chapter 11.

E. Wainwright Martin, Jr., *Mathematics for Decision Making: Volume I: Linear Mathematics* (Homewood, Illinois: Irwin, 1969).

Alfred A. Ring, *The Valuation of Real Estate*, second edition (Englewood Cliffs, New Jersey: Prentice-Hall, 1970), Chapter 17.

Clifford H. Springer, Robert E. Herlihy, and Robert I. Beggs, *Basic Mathematics: Volume One of the Mathematics for Management Series* (Homewood, Illinois: Irwin, 1965), Chapters 1–4.

## Notes

1. See, for example, L.W. Ellwood, *Ellwood Tables for Real Estate Appraising and Financing*, third edition (Chicago: American Institute of Real Estate Appraisers, 1970), Part I, Pages 17-50; and A.A. Ring, *The Valuation of Real Estate*, second edition (Englewood Cliffs, New Jersey: Prentice-Hall, 1970), Chapter 17.

# 6

# Income Estimation and Forecasting

Discounting is the mechanical, mathematical process by which forecast future income receipts are capitalized to present-worth estimates. Once the future income forecasts have been made and the appropriate rate(s) at which those income receipts are to be discounted is established, the results are produced by inexorable mathematical logic. It is therefore essential for the income-property appraiser to have a thorough working command over the several compound-interest and discount factors described and illustrated in Chapter 5. He must understand their meaning, their derivation, and their interrelationships with one another. Most importantly, he must recognize their individual applicability to specific income-capitalization situations.

But discounting is only a mathematical process; it is not appraising. It merely provides the *how* of capitalization. In the basic capitalization equation $V = I/R$, the appraiser must extract $I$ and $R$ from the applicable market to produce the $V$ being sought, by applying the proper discount or compound-interest factors to the forecast future-income receipts $(I)$. $I$ is the *what* in the capitalization process. $R$ (or its reciprocal $F$) indicates *by what* $I$ is capitalized.

There is no absolute necessity for the income estimate or forecast to precede the identification of the rate(s) of discount that the applicable market dictates should be applied to that income forecast. There are logical reasons for it to come first, however. The characteristics of the forecast income other than its size or quantity do condition the market's response to it, and hence the rate(s) of return that should be employed in capitalizing it to a present-worth estimate. For these reasons, the discussion here and in the next several chapters follows the sequence of the systematic outline of the capitalization process presented in Chapter 4.

## Basic Guidelines to Income Forecasting

*Forecasting*

Every income estimate for income-producing realty is necessarily oriented to the future. The appraiser must *forecast* the most probable future benefits most likely to be receivable or anticipated by the holder of the rights being appraised. As previously noted, this forecast must be based on the most probable influence of a specified set of market conditions, and hence on careful analysis of the most probable market conditions that will prevail.

Forecasting deals in probabilities. In appraising, these probabilities are rarely rigidly defined in objective mathematical terms that permit the use of statistical forecasting devices. Rather, they are *subjective* probabilities.[1] They are derived from the experience and judgments of market participants, as evidenced by their stated expectations and their market behavior. The probabilities are also conditioned by the appraiser's past experience and knowledge of market responses to similar conditions and trends.

The important point is that an income forecast is neither a mechanical projection of past performance nor a precise prediction of what will in fact occur. The income forecast represents the amount, timing, duration, and stability of cash flows most likely to be received by the holder of the property rights being appraised. The appraiser must therefore estimate *how much* is likely to be received, *when*, over *how many periods of what length*. He must finally evaluate the degree of certainty in these estimates. This identifies the compensation for risk-taking that must be incorporated into the rate of discount applied to the forecast future income stream.

### Basic Guidelines

Whatever the characteristics of the future income receipts forecast by the appraiser (which are considered in the following section), there are several general conventions followed in income forecasting for income-property valuation.

**Cash Flows.** The income receipts (as well as operating expenses and debt service) used in appraisal analysis are cash flows. They represent amounts of dollars received (or expended) during the income reporting period. They differ from the "incomes" derived from accrual accounting methods. The latter are measurements of an asset's periodic contribution to the increase (or decrease, in the case of a "loss") in the net worth of a firm. As a result, periodic increases or decreases in asset values, such as depreciation, are included in accounting income estimates.

Cash flows, on the other hand, count all cash receipts and payments in the period when they are actually received (or forecast to be received) and expended. In income-property appraising, the basic cash-flow concept is adjusted slightly so that the "net" income figures used are commonly *stabilized* or *typical* cash flow estimates for a *typical* income period.

The emphasis on cash flow forecasts means that the appraiser must be able to analyze an accrual income statement provided by a property owner on his account and adjust it to the cash flow figures necessary for capitalization to a present worth estimate.

**Annual Forecasts.** Although cash payments may be made and received on several other time bases (monthly, quarterly, semi-annually), all "incomes" used in appraisal analysis are conventionally expressed as *annual* flows. The rates of discount applied to them are always expressed as percentages on an *annual* basis.

**Market Rental vs. Contract Rental.** The nature of the value to be estimated, given by the statement of the appraisal problem, determines the nature of the income that is to be capitalized to a present worth estimate that represents that value. When a Market Value estimate is the objective of the analysis, Market Rental must be used. This is the rental that the space would most probably command if it were vacant and available for rent on the open market as of the effective date of the appraisal. It is the going market rate of rental for competitive space as of that date. Market Value represents the most probable selling price of the property under specified market conditions. For a present worth estimate to reflect Market Value, it must be based on rentals that reflect those same market conditions.

Contract Rental is the rental actually being paid, or contracted to be paid, by a tenant for the use of the space. It may or may not be specified under a written lease, although as the term implies it often is. A lease is a contract between the lessor (landlord) and the lessee (tenant). Contract rental is used primarily as the basis for estimating Investment Value because it represents what a specific investor-purchaser will most probably receive under current or specified tenancy. However, when Contract Rental falls within the reasonable range of Market Rental forecast for the property being appraised, it can be used to derive net income forecasts that are capitalized to a Market Value estimate.

*Market Rental.* Throughout the remainder of this book, the term "market rental" is used to refer to the rental income that the space in question would most probably command on the open market, as of the effective date of the appraisal. It has been traditional in appraisal literature to call this "economic rent." Unfortunately, "economic rent" has quite a different longstanding meaning in economics. It is the *surplus* payment in excess of that necessary to bring the property on the market (or to attract any factor of production into production). It is important to avoid confusion and conflict between appraisal analysis on the one hand, and economics and finance on the other. Thus, "market rental" is recommended in preference to "economic rent" in income-capitalization analysis.

*Imputed Rental Income.* Although the income estimates used in appraising are cash-flow forecasts, it is probable to impute or assign a rental to owner-occupied income property, *provided* there is an active market for similar, competitive space. An imputed rental will reflect what the space would most probably command if it were made available on the open market. This means that Market Rental can be imputed to owner-occupied income properties.

**Typically Competent Management.** In making rental and net income forecasts, the appraiser normally assumes that the property will be managed according to the standards of typically competent management. This means that the level of management is what a professional management firm would reasonably be expected to provide (for a fee) to an absentee owner-investor. Neither extremely productive nor particularly bad management is forecast, except in the case of an

Investment-Value estimate that is defined in terms of existing management. Tenant selection, rent collection, property maintenance, and maintenance of tenant services are all otherwise presumed to conform to the standards of acceptable professional performance established by the market.

**Categories of Income to be Forecast.** As many as five categories or levels of future income may be forecast by the appraiser in estimating present worth. These levels represent successive steps from longest or most "gross" to most "net" from the investor's point of view. Each of these estimates is expressed as an annual income flow before it is processed further.

The outline presented in Chapter 4 indicated that the successive estimates that may be required are: Potential Gross Income, Effective Gross Income, Net Operating Income, Cash Throw-Off (Before-Tax Cash Flow), and After-Tax Cash Flow. The techniques for estimating and forecasting each are considered in turn in subsequent sections of this chapter. It is important for the appraiser to recognize the meaning and uses of each, because each has specific applicability in responding to particular types of appraisal problems.

*Income Characteristics*

The discussions in Chapters 4 and 5 have already pointed out that in most appraisal problems the appraiser must forecast both a periodic future income stream and a lump-sum reversion to be received at a specified future date. In either case, the appraiser must forecast several characteristics of the future income to be received: its dollar amount, when it is to be received, the length of the periods over which it is to be discounted, the number of periods over which it is to be discounted, its stability or variability, and the degree of certainty (or risk) associated with the forecasts of the other characteristics. Each of these considerations has an impact on the present worth estimate.

**Amount.** The basic question to be answered in making any income forecast is, of course, "How much?" The dollar amount receivable per period or at the end of a specified number of periods is the quantitative value of $I$ in the basic value formula $V = I/R$ or $V = I \times F$.

**Pattern.** The time and variability components of forecast future income constitute its pattern. They help determine which discount factor should be used to derive the present worth estimate.

*Timing.* When income is forecast to be received is critical to the present worth of its future amount(s). The illustrations in Chapter 5 demonstrated that an income stream with payments in advance is worth more than one with the same number of payments of the same size, but payable at the end of each period. It also makes a considerable difference whether an income stream starts immediately, or is deferred to start at a future date. The terms of the lease contract will specify the timing of contract rental. Market standards and the expectations of informal investors provide the basis for forecasting the timing of market rentals.

*Periodicity.* The length of the income periods used in the discounting process will also affect the present-worth estimate by causing the discount factor to vary somewhat. It was shown in Chapter 5 that the same rate of discount and over the same total span of time, a monthly payment pattern has a higher present worth than a quarterly pattern of the same annual income. Similarly, the present worth of a quarterly pattern is higher than that of a semi-annual pattern, and a semi-annual factor is greater than an annual factor. The period of discounting for contract rental is specified in the lease contract. It is determined once again by market standards and the expectations of informed investors when market rental is being forecast.

*Duration.* The number of time periods ($n$) over which future income receipts are discounted has a twofold effect on the present worth of an income stream. First, the longer its duration, the more payments there are, and hence the greater its present worth. Second, the further into the future a payment is forecast to be received, the more it is discounted, and therefore the less its present worth. But no matter how little an additional future payment adds to present worth, it always adds *something*. At the same rate of discount, no matter what the length of discount periods, a 50-year income stream always has a higher present worth than a 49-year income stream of the same annual amount. Lease terms set the duration of contract rental. Market standards and informed investor expectations establish it for market rental forecasts. The forecast duration of an income stream is the capital recovery period for the investor.

The reverse is true for a single lump-sum reversion. The longer the period over which a given future sum is discounted at the same rate, the less its present worth will be. This has been demonstrated in the several examples of the use of the Present Worth of One factor provided in Chapter 5.

*Variability.* In some traditional but now outmoded income capitalization techniques, it was considered acceptable and defensible to estimate first-year income and then simply project it over the remaining economic life of the improvements, or whatever the appropriate capital recovery period was estimated to be. This "level" income stream was then capitalized with either straight-line or annuity-like capital recovery; the former was employed unless the property was under a long-term lease to a high-credit tenant.

This simplistic approach has been replaced by a recognition of the potential and even probable variability of future income streams. One possibility is still a level, constant income flow with the characteristics of a level annuity. When this pattern of future income payments is found to be most probable, the proper Present Worth of One per Annum factor can be applied directly to the annual income figure to produce the estimate of present worth.

As already pointed out in Chapters 4 and 5, however, income streams can increase, decrease, or vary irregularly—as well as remain constant or level. All of these patterns can be handled by converting the forecast income stream to a series of individual reversions, and discounting each to a present worth estimate via the appropriate Present Worth of One factor. Increasing and decreasing flows of contract rental are forecast in accordance with the terms of a lease. Declining market rental forecasts are based on forecasts of declines in competitive attractiveness of the subject property, a declining market or neighborhood, increased competition, or increased operating expenses. Similarly, increasing market rentals are based on forecasts of expanding market conditions, increasing rates of occupancy, improved competitive attractiveness, or decreased operating expenses. Either pattern must be justified by the evidence of market expectations and behavior on the part of informed investors. Variable annuities are most commonly encountered with after-tax cash flows.

A forecast income stream must be based on careful examination and evaluation of market evidence and property or lease data. It is important to recognize that a future income stream will not necessarily be level or vary according to a set mathematical formula. Unless the assumptions of systematic variation according to formula can be supported variability in the forecast income is justified.

**Risks.** The risks, or conversely the degree of certainty, inherent and evident in the particular income stream deemed most probable for the property being appraised must be identified and evaluated by the appraiser. These risks are reflected in the rate of discount on which the applicable discount factors are based.

There is always uncertainty about the future. There is necessarily uncertainty about each of the component characteristics of forecast future income receipts: the amount, the timing, the periodicity, the duration, and the variability. The degree of uncertainty over whether each of these components will be realized as forecast is measured in part by the subjective probabilities assigned them by market participants, and by the appraiser. The risks borne by the income-property investor combine to form the *quality* of the income stream. The perceived levels of these risks help establish the rate of discount used in capitalizing the forecast future income.

*Income Risk.* This is the risk that the future income receipts will not be as great as the forecast amounts, or that their timing will be other than that forecast. It is based on the possibility that gross income or rental receipts will be lower, or that operating expenses will be higher, or both. It is also derived from the risk that rent will not be paid on time, or may not be paid at all by some tenants. Moreover, the property may be vacant for a time. This risk is more evident in Market Rental estimates. When a well-rated tenant occupies the property under a long-term lease with fixed rentals, contract rental generally has a low Income Risk.

*Principal Risk.* This is the risk that capital investment, especially that represented by the reversion, will be less than forecast. Unless the amount is specified in an option to purchase in a long-term lease contract and there is high probability that the purchase option will be exercised by the tenant, this risk is always present. It depends largely on the future operation of market and neighborhood forces that must be forecast at the time the appraisal is made. In the case of a highly leveraged equity investment (which is discussed in Chapter 7), the risk of total loss of principal exists as a corollary to the income risk. Generally speaking, the further into the future that a reversionary payment is forecast, the greater is the Principal Risk.

*Interest Or Money Market Risk.* This is the risk that future rates of discount will be higher than those applicable at the time the appraisal and the investment decision is made. If this occurs, then the income stream being produced by the property will have a lower present worth because it must be discounted at a higher rate. Money market and investment market conditions totally beyond the control of the investor determine what are acceptable market rates of return, so the evaluation of the Interest Risk depends primarily on forecasts of money market conditions. This risk is particularly significant for fixed-level income streams, such as level rentals under a lease or fixed debt service on mortgage loans. The rapid rise in rates of interest during the late 1960s illustrates the degree of Interest Risk that a long-term investor faces. Once again, the longer the income forecast period, the greater the Interest Risk will be.

*Market Rental Risk.* This is the risk that market rentals for competitive properties will rise markedly while the property is subject to fixed rentals under a long-term lease. It is peculiarly applicable to leased properties, and represents a trade-off against the reduced Income Risk under a fixed-rental, long-term lease. It increases as the term of the lease increases. It is greater the more "gross" a lease is. That is, the longer the lessor's (landlord's) commitment to pay operating expenses which are not fixed in amount, the greater is the risk that net income expectations or forecasts will not be realized. Some effort to affect this Market Rental Risk is found in "escalation clauses" in long-term leases. The impact and use of such clauses is discussed in more detail in Chapter 19.

*Purchasing Power Risk.* This is the risk that dollars received in the future will have less purchasing power as the result of inflation. It is encountered in every long-term investment, whether in real property or other assets. Purchasing Power Risk is not usually taken into account overtly in appraisal analysis. Neither the mathematics of the discounting process nor rates of discount specifically include compensation for the assumption of this risk by the investor. Because it is universal in the economy, its influence is felt primarily in basic long-term rates of interest on which discount rates for real estate investments are based.

The several risks of long-term investments in real property are beyond the control of the individual investor. He must recognize and usually accept them, hopefully providing compensation for assuming these risks through the discount rate at which forecast future income receipts are capitalized. In providing sound information on which the investor-decision-maker bases his judgments, the appraiser must develop the most supportable income forecasts and risk evaluations possible.

The risks enumerated here are not mutually compatible. Trying to affect the Income Risk by contracting for fixed-income receipts can render the income stream more liable to greater Interest and Market Rental Risks, for example. Leases with escalation clauses and participation mortgage loans represent attempts by long-term investors to protect themselves from conflicting groups of risks. These mechanisms are considered more fully in Chapters 7 and 19.

### Gross Income Estimation

With the foregoing considerations and guidelines in mind, the appraiser's first task in applied income forecasting is to estimate gross income. There are actually two "gross incomes" to forecast in most income-property appraisals: Potential Gross Income and Effective Gross Income. The former estimate necessarily precedes the latter. Each is considered in turn here.

Gross income is always converted to annual terms for further processing and analysis. It is a forecast of the number of dollars that a property can reasonably be expected to produce annually, under typically competent management, irrespective of the costs or expenses necessarily incurred to produce those receipts.

**Emphasis on Market Rental.** Throughout the remainder of the consideration of income estimation and forecasting in this chapter, the illustrations and examples focus on the derivation and use of Market Rentals. Precisely the same techniques and mechanical processes are applicable when income forecasts based on Contract Rental are to be developed. The difference is that Contract Rental is nearly always provided in the appraisal problem itself. The lease contract is the source of the data employed. As is noted in Chapter 19, the appraiser's primary task in identifying Contract Rental is to *read the lease*, and have it interpreted by an expert if necessary.

When Market Rental is to be derived and used as the starting point for income forecasting, on the other hand, a considerable amount of market and property analysis is required of the appraiser. These requirements and the techniques for meeting them effectively are emphasized here. Once the gross income estimate is produced, whether it is based on Market Rental or Contract Rental, the steps in processing it to net income(s) are identical.

### *Influences on Gross Income*

**Market Competition.** The number, quality, and rentals charged of similar properties competing with the subject in its market area influences the levels of rentals it can reasonably be expected to command. This market competition, in relation to the demand for the type of space provided by the subject property, influences how much vacancy can be expected. In addition to existing competition, buildings under construction or definitely planned also affect the rentability or marketability of the space in the subject. New construction frequently has a negative impact on existing space as leases expire and tenants seek the attractions and amenities of new facilities.

**Location and Neighborhood Influence.** Because real estate is fixed in location, its marketability and rentability are strongly influenced by the economic and social trends in its immediate environment. The continuing attractiveness of this neighborhood environment to potential users and tenants, and its competitive relation to those of substitute properties, must therefore be evaluated and forecast by the appraiser. In particular, perceived neighborhood trends affect both the quantity and the quality of the revenues the subject property can reasonably be expected to generate.

**Quality of Management.** Good management can help keep an income property competitive for a longer period through good maintenance and tenant services. This makes it easier to keep the space in the property rented at competitive rentals. Efficient rent collection systems help maintain the stability of property revenues, in part by reducing expenses. Effective tenant selection can reduce the problems of rent collection, vacancy, and turnover. Together, these procedures can help increase and maintain the level of revenues produced by the property.

Income forecasting based on Market Rentals presumes that the property will have typically competent management. The standards of acceptability and competence are set by the behavior of property owners and managers in the competitive market.

*Potential Gross Income*

The annual amount of cash rental receipts that the property could generate if it were 100% occupied is its Potential Gross Income. It is based on Market Rentals when Market Value is to be estimated, and Contract Rental when Investment Value or the Market Value of the leased fee is being estimated. The Potential Gross based on Contract Rental is also called the Rent Roll for multi-tenant properties (apartment houses, office buildings, etc.).

**Services Included.** The type and quality of services normally provided a tenant must be identified and specified before market comparisons can be made with competitive properties and their rentals. A Market Rental estimate must be based on the same pattern of services provided by the landlord as those of competing properties. For example, suppose that competing apartments are renting for $45 per room per month, with heat provided by the landlord (i.e., included in the rental). Suppose that it costs an average of $5 per room per month to provide heat. Apartments in an otherwise similar and competitive apartment property in which tenants paid for their own heat would therefore have a Market Rental of approximately $40 per room per month. The *tenants* would be paying an average of $45 per room per month for comparable occupancy: $40 rental plus $5 for heat. The landlord would be receiving $5 less per room per month in rental income, but his operating expenses would also be reduced $5 per room per month.

In every instance of Market Rental estimation, the appraiser must identify what services the landlord is providing tenants in comparable, competing properties for the rentals being charged. These and only these services must be included in the Market Rental estimated for the subject property. If necessary, adjustments must be made as in the example above to bring the Market Rental estimated and forecast for the space in the subject property into line with the standards of the competitive market. The kinds of services and facilities that may be included in going rentals for competitive space include utilities, parking space, and kitchen, laundry, or air-conditioning equipment.

**Unit of Rental.** The appraiser must identify the unit in terms of which competitive properties are used and rented on the market. These units will vary from one market area to another, and from one property type to another. The Potential Gross Income of the subject property is then the *annual* unit rental times the number of units of space in the subject property. Since rentals are frequently quoted and paid on a monthly, weekly, or other fraction-of-a year basis, it is important to make sure that these estimates are converted to an annual basis before proceeding to derive net income figures.

The appraiser may also discover units that represent a common denominator for the type of space being appraised, even though it may not be rented on those terms in the market. For example, one useful unit of comparison or measurement for apartment rentals in some market areas is the rental per square foot of living area per month. Apartments may not actually be rented in these terms, but if this measure permits real comparison among competing properties to establish a unit Market Rental, it is both useful and usable.

*Apartment property* rentals may be measured at so much per apartment (dwelling unit) per month, per room per month, or per square foot of living area per month—or per year. In specific market circumstances, the rental unit may be so much per year—or even per week. Whatever the unit used, it must be carefully defined. For example, what is a "room"? Are bathrooms counted as rooms or not? What is a "half room"? Absolute consistency in definition is necessary if true comparability and meaningful market pattern are to be developed by the appraiser.

More than one unit of comparison can be used in many cases, both to check the validity of an apparently useful unit rental and to identify which unit(s) form a consistent pattern on which to base the Market Rental estimate. For example, suppose the following rental information has been obtained for three apartment properties judged to be comparable and competitive with an apartment property being appraised. There is no implication that three comparable properties are enough to establish a market pattern. All that is illustrated here is the technique that would normally be applied to a larger sample of data.

The subject property contains 200 apartment units: 160 two-bedroom, 4-room units with 850 square feet of living area; and 40 one-bedroom, 3-room units with 675 square feet of living area.

Comparable Property A has 180 units. There are 90 two-bedroom, 4-room units with 825 square feet of living area, renting for $175 per month. The remaining 90 units contain one bedroom, 3-rooms, and 645 square feet of living area; and rent for $135 per month. There are currently 4 two-bedroom and 4 one-bedroom units vacant.

Comparable Property B has 190 two-bedroom units. All have 4 rooms and contain 900 square feet of living area. They rent for $185 per month. There are 11 vacancies at present.

Comparable Property C has 120 units, of which 80 are two-bedroom units and 40 have one bedroom. The two-bedroom units contain 4 rooms each, with 855 square feet of living area, and rent for $180 per month. The one-bedroom units contain 3 rooms each, with 675 square feet of living area, and rent for $140 per month. There are currently 3 two-bedroom and 2 one-bedroom units vacant.

In all other respects, the three comparable properties are judged to be highly competitive with the subject. Services provided and neighborhood influence are essentially the same. With this rental information in hand, the Market Rentals for the units in the subject property can be estimated as illustrated in Exhibit 6-1 (p. 122).

From this information, it is clear that in this instance the most sensitive and consistent measure of unit rental is the rental per square foot per month. For both one-bedroom and two-bedroom units, the range of rental per room per month is also relatively narrow. It serves to reinforce the conclusion that the Market Rental for one-bedroom units is most probably $140 per month. The indicated figure for two-bedroom units is $180 per month. This example also illustrates the point that when properties and unit characteristics are extremely similar, the units closest in size to the subject property's represent the best comparables.

Units of rental for *commercial properties* are commonly so much per square foot of gross floor area per year, per square foot of usable floor area (e.g., selling space) per year, per square foot of gross leasable floor area per year, or per front foot of building per year. Occasionally, the rental for commercial space is expressed on a monthly basis. *Office space* is typically rented annually, at so much per square foot of net rentable floor area, per room, or even "per suite." Generally speaking, the higher the rental, the smaller the rental unit. *Industrial* and *warehouse space* is most commonly rented at so much per square foot of floor area—per year or per month.

Other types of income-property space are usually rented in terms of the unit

**Exhibit 6-1**

**Derivation of Unit Market Rentals for Apartment Property**

A. Two-Bedroom Units

|  | Subject Property | Comparable A | Comparable B | Comparable C |
|---|---|---|---|---|
| Monthly Rental | – | $175 | $185 | $180 |
| Number Rooms | 4 | 4 | 4 | 4 |
| Rental per Room per Month | – | $ 43.75 | $ 46.25 | $ 45.00 |
| Square Feet | 850 | 825 | 900 | 855 |
| Rental per Square Foot per Month | – | $ 0.21 | $ 0.21 | $ 0.21 |

B. One-Bedroom Units

|  | Subject Property | Comparable A | Comparable C |
|---|---|---|---|
| Monthly Rental | – | $135 | $140 |
| Number Rooms | 3 | 3 | 3 |
| Rental per Room per Month | – | $ 45.00 | $ 46.67 |
| Square Feet | 675 | 645 | 675 |
| Rental per Square Foot per Month | – | $ 0.21 | $ 0.21 |

of use and income production, without particular regard to physical size. For example, parking lots and garages are often rented at so much per parking stall per year. Nursing homes may be rented at so much per bed (or per bed licensed) per year. The rental unit for motels is usually the bed, and for theaters the seat. All of these are the units of use in terms of which revenues are produced.

**Number of Units.** Whenever Market Rental is expressed on a unit basis, it is critically important for the appraiser to obtain an accurate count or measurement of the *number* of such units in the subject property. The number of units times the unit rental, expressed on an annual basis, is the Potential Gross Income.

In addition to accuracy in count, the appraiser must make sure the units are defined consistently in the subject property and in all the comparable properties used in the analysis. A "room" must mean the same thing in every property, and the same definition of "net rentable floor area" must apply in every case.

*Estimation of Potential Gross Income*

While alternative methods of estimating Market Rentals used to produce Potential Gross Income forecasts are available to the appraiser, by far the most widely used and commonly accepted method is market comparison. This was illustrated in a simplified way in the example summarized as Exhibit 6-1. The appraiser must search the market for comparable, competitive properties that provide tenants the same services as are offered by the subject property. Locational influences and other market conditions should be the same as for the subject. The unit rentals commanded by such properties serve as a guide for estimating the current Market Rental(s) for this type of space. Through the identification of the most nearly consistent pattern of unit rentals, the appropriate unit Market Rental for the subject property emerges.

Within the limits established by time pressures to complete the appraisal and the availability of reliable, verified rental data for truly comparable competitive properties, as many rental comparison properties should be used as possible. Normally at least half a dozen (and preferably more) are required to establish a meaningful and supportable measure of the market. The example on which Exhibit 6-1 is based employed only three comparable properties. This was done solely in the interests of conserving space and focusing on the technique of analysis that is employed. Ordinarily, such a limited number of comparable data will not yield particularly reliable unit rental figures.

**Derivation and Adjustment of Comparable Rental Data.** The method of deriving a Market Rental Estimate illustrated in Exhibit 6-1 and described in the preceding section is an application of Direct Sales Comparison Analysis. This is the same approach to value estimation presented in my introductory course or text in real property valuation. Its application to income property valuation is the subject of Chapter 17. In the present case, the "value" being estimated is the rental value of the space in the subject, usually expressed on a unit basis.

The example of unit rental estimation given earlier *assumed* that the comparable rental properties were virtually identical competitors of the subject property, with only size and mix of apartments different from the subject's and one another's. This was done in part to focus attention on technique of analysis, but also in part to emphasize the importance of keeping necessary property adjustments to a minimum. When such a high degree of competitive similarity among the comparable rental properties and the subject does not exist, the appraiser must adjust unit rentals in the comparable properties to reflect the market's reaction to the meaningful, salient observed differences between each comparable property and the subject. The mechanical process of measuring and adjusting for property differences that are meaningful on the market is exactly the same as that illustrated in Chapter 17. The only difference is that the "value" derived from the combination of adjustments and correlation of net adjusted figures is unit rental instead of unit sales price.

No list of adjustment factors can be comprehensive enough to include all those considerations that *might* be appropriate in deriving rental per unit in any given case. However, there are categories of property characteristics which should be considered as possibly significant determinants of differences in unit rentals. The significance of any such differences between the comparable and the subject property should be studied carefully by the appraiser to identify whether an adjustment in indicated rental is required. The categories of factors include:

size (physical units, units of use);
age and condition of improvements;
estimated remaining economic life;
services provided by the landlord;
facilities and equipment available and provided by the landlord;
services available but paid for by the tenant;
facilities and equipment available but paid for by the tenant;
location: access to and from required and desired area facilities;
characteristics of tenants: uses, stability, compatibility; and
quality of management.

The relevance or significance of any of these factors to a specific appraisal problem varies with the type of property and the character of the market involved. It should be noted that an adjustment for size is actually made when rentals are reduced to a per-unit basis—provided the units are identical in definition between the comparable property and the subject.

It is still best to base unit Market Rentals on comparisons with competitive substitute properties that require as few adjustments as possible to remove differences between themselves and the subject property.

**Estimation of Contract Rental.** When there is a long-term lease on the property being appraised, the reasonable expectation is that the tenant will remain in occupancy and pay rent until the lease expires. All the appraiser has to do to derive Contract Rental is read the lease. Moreover, if the actual rent roll of a multi-tenant property is to be used, the estimate of Contract Rental is simply the forecast of the timing and stability of that rent roll. Both estimates can be used as a starting point to forecast Potential Gross Income in estimating Investment Value.

Sometimes, the objective of an appraisal analysis is to indicate the annual rental revenues necessary to support a given total investment, rather than to estimate the amount of investment that an annual income will support. An analog of this alternative way of posing an appraisal problem is the indication of the annual debt service necessary to pay off a given loan amount at a specified mortgage rate of interest, over a specified period of time. As demonstrated in Chapter 5, the solution is found by applying the proper Installment to Amortize One factor, converted to an annual basis, to the principal amount of the mortgage loan.

The same mechanical technique is applied in deriving an appropriate and required annual rental when the original amount of the investment is known or given. Suppose an investor is planning to acquire an income property for $500,000. He is looking for a *rental* (not net operating income or cash throw-off to equity) that will produce an annual rate of return of 16% over the next 20 years, and also provide full capital recovery of his investment over that same period. This is not necessarily what the market will pay to rent this type of space. It is simply what the investor is seeking.

If capital recovery over the 20-year income projection period were *not* required, the problem would be very simple indeed. The appraiser would merely calculate 16% of $500,000 and get an answer of $80,000 per year (.16 X $500,000 = $80,000). However, in this case the problem is to calculate the annual rental receipts in dollars, receivable for 20 years and discounted annually at 16%, whose present worth is $500,000. This requires using the 20-year, annual Installment to Amortize One factor at 16%, which is found in Column 6 on page 152 of Ellwood to be 0.168667. The annual rental required is then calculated to be $84,333.50 (0.168667 X $500,000).

The estimated annual rental receipts of $84,333,50 is based on the assumption that annual rentals are receivable at the end of each year. If they are in fact payable in advance at the beginning of each year, the Installment to Amortize One factor must be calculated. Since it is the reciprocal of the Present Worth of One per Annum factor, as demonstrated in Chapter 5, the first step is to find the value of the Present Worth of One per Annum factor for a 20-year annual income stream payable in advance, discounted at 16%. Based on the reasoning and technique explained in Chapter 5, the appropriate factor is the 19-year factor of 5.877454 (Ellwood, page 152, Column 5) plus 1.000000. This sum is 6.877454. Its reciprocal 0.145403 (1/6.877454) is the 20-year annual Installment to Amortize One factor with rental payments in advance, discounted at 16%. The annual rental requirement for the investment in question is therefore $72,701.50 (0.145403 X $500,000).

**Mechanics of Estimating Potential Gross Income.** Potential Gross Income is the number of dollars of rental income that the property could generate annually at 100% occupancy. When Potential Gross is to reflect Market Rental, it is the unit Market Rental times the number of units in the property being appraised, expressed as an annual flow. In the 200-unit apartment property example given earlier in this chapter, the property contained 160 two-bedroom units with an estimated Market Rental of $180 per unit per month, and 40 one-bedroom units with an estimated Market Rental of $140 per unit per month. The Potential Gross Income of this property would then be calculated as follows:

| | | |
|---|---|---|
| Two-bedroom units: | 160 X $180 = $28,800 X 12 | = $345,600 |
| One-bedroom units: | 40 X $140 = $ 5,600 X 12 | = $ 67,200 |
| Potential Gross Income (annual) | | = $412,800 |

In this example, the 160 two-bedroom units could generate $28,800 in monthly rentals, and the 40 one-bedroom units could produce $5,600 monthly. These monthly totals are multiplied by 12 to provide required annual rental forecasts.

When Potential Gross Income reflects Contract Rental, it is calculated by multiplying the unit Contract Rental by the number of units in the subject property, expressed on an annual basis. Thus, a 150,000 square foot warehouse rental at $1.35 per square foot per year has a Potential Gross Income of $202,500 (150,000 X $1.35).

*Allowance for Vacancy and Income Loss*

Both the investor and the appraiser are primarily interested in the cash revenues that an income property is *likely* to produce annually over a specified period of time, rather than what it *could* produce if it were always 100% occupied and all the tenants were actually paying their rent in full and on time. Except in the case of a property fully occupied by a high-rated tenant or tenants under a long-term lease, some income loss is normally expected. It may result from vacancy and turnover, or from non-payment or slow payment of rent by tenants. Because stabilized or level income flows are forecast in most income capitalization techniques employed in income property appraising, an annual allowance or deduction from Potential Gross Income for this income loss must be made. The allowance is estimated for a "typical" year, and deducted to derive a "stabilized" level forecast of annual rent collections. When no "Other Income" is forecast for the property, these forecast annual rent collections represent the Effective Gross Income of the property.

The allowance for vacancy and income loss is commonly expressed as a percentage of Potential Gross Income and then converted to a dollar figure. By convention, the estimated allowance for vacancy and income loss is usually rounded to the nearest dollar, regardless of the rules of rounding and significant digits discussed in the appendix to Chapter 5. The percentage of vacancy and income loss is the complement of the occupancy ratio for a multi-tenant income property.

For example, if the typical occupancy ratio for properties of the type being appraised is 93% in the current market, then the allowance for vacancy and income loss would be 7%. Sometimes, the appraiser is able to obtain data on collections ratios for competitive properties in the same market. The allowance for vacancy and income loss applicable to the subject property would then be the complement of this market collections ratio.

These measures of vacancy and income loss are particularly applicable to multi-tenant properties. The going current ratio of vacancy and income loss for competitive properties can be derived from their vacancy experience. For example, in the illustration of Market Rental estimation provided earlier in this chapter, the number of vacant units, by type, was given for each comparable rental property. The appropriate percentages of vacancy can be calculated for this type of property as shown in Exhibit 6-2.

**Exhibit 6-2**

**Calculation of Vacancy Ratios**

|  | Comparable A | Comparable B | Comparable C | Total "Market" |
|---|---|---|---|---|
| **Two-Bedroom Units** | | | | |
| Number | 90 | 180 | 80 | 350 |
| Vacancies | 4 | 10 | 4 | 18 |
| Percent Vacant | 4.4% | 5.6% | 5.0% | 5.1% |
| **One-Bedroom Units** | | | | |
| Number | 90 | — | 40 | 130 |
| Vacancies | 4 | — | 3 | 7 |
| Percent Vacant | 4.4% | — | 7.5% | 5.4% |

The figures in Exhibit 6-2 indicate that the current market vacancy ratios are approximately 5% for two-bedroom units and 5.5% for one-bedroom units. There are really insufficient data to provide a definitive set of estimates, but these percentages appear to be representative to the extent that the three comparable rental properties reflect the market. What the appraiser does *not* do is average the percentages for each of the properties. This is both statistically invalid because of the small numbers of properties involved, and illogical because there is no evidence that each property is equally "typical" of the market.

Applying these percentages to the Potential Gross Income forecasts developed earlier for the 200-unit apartment property being appraised yields the following forecasts of stabilized annual rent collections in a "typical" year:

| | |
|---|---:|
| Two-bedroom units | |
| Potential Gross Income | $345,600 |
| *Less* 5% Vacancy and Income Loss Allowance | – 17,280 |
| Rent Collections | $328,320 |
| One-bedroom units | |
| Potential Gross Income | $ 67,200 |
| *Less* 5.5% Vacancy and Income Loss Allowance | – 3,696 |
| Rent Collections | $ 63,504 |
| Forecast Annual Rent Collections, Total Property | $391,824 |

It should be noted that all apartment "units" were not lumped together and a single vacancy and income loss percentage applied to the total Potential Gross Income. This is because one-bedroom and two-bedroom apartments appeal to different groups of potential tenants, and are really competing in different sub-markets, even though the properties in which they are located are treated as being in the same "market."

Single-tenant properties pose a different sort of problem. By definition, they are not partially occupied or partially vacant; a single-tenant industrial plant is either 100% occupied and rented, or it is 100% vacant and producing zero rental income. The appraiser is usually reluctant to forecast 100% occupancy over the income forecasting period in the absence of a long-term lease with a well-rated tenant, however. Indeed, he would usually not be justified in doing so. Industrial plants are periodically vacant. To find an appropriate vacancy and income loss factor to apply to his Potential Gross Income forecast in such a case, therefore, he would have to survey the market to discover current vacancy rates.

Suppose that he found 1,080,000 square feet of rental industrial floor space that was competitive in the same market with the property he was appraising. Suppose further that he found that plants totaling 63,200 square feet of floor space were currently vacant. Assuming that all the plants in the survey were truly competitive with one another and with the subject property, the current market vacancy ratio for industrial floor space of the type being appraised is 5.85% (63,200/1,080,000). The appraiser might then use 5.85%, 5.9%, or 6.0% as his allowance for vacancy and income loss.

**Sources and Standards for Estimating the Vacancy and Income Loss Allowance.** The percentage or dollar amount deducted from Potential Gross Income for vacancy and income loss allowance must be supported by reliable data. There are basically three sources of such information, which will provide the appraiser with the appropriate standards and guidelines to make the estimate.

*Experience of the Subject Property.* Even when the estimates are based on Market Rentals aimed at estimating Market Value, and therefore must be consistent with the standards of the market as represented by the observed experience of competing substitute properties, the past 3-5 years' operating experience of the subject property itself can be a useful guide and starting point. There must be evidence available, however, to support the proposition that that experience is representative or typical of competitive properties in the same market, and that the subject property has been under typically competent management over the period in question. If it appears that these conditions can be met, then the appraiser can and should use the average annual rate experienced by the subject property in the recent past. If the experience of the subject property deviates from the market norm, however, it must be adjusted to conform with market standards, no matter how well-documented that experience may be. In particular, less-than-market vacancy and income loss rates must be adjusted upward despite any objections of the present owner or manager.

*Market Experience of Comparable Properties.* These are essential in making deductions from Potential Gross Income based on Market Rentals, if only as a check against the representatives of the actual experience of the subject property. At least half a dozen (and preferably more) vacancy and income loss figures should be obtained for similar competing properties, and correlated to a single market figure. Such information can be obtained from property managers, owners, other appraisers and brokers, lenders (sometimes), and occasional market surveys by professional research groups.

*Published Studies.* Occasionally surveys are published by professional trade or research groups that indicate typical occupancy or vacancy and income loss experiences of different types of properties. These surveys must be used with care because they often cover larger market areas (e.g., the nation) than the appraiser wants or needs. They can be helpful in establishing general standards of performance, however, and can serve as guides to how reasonable it is to use the subject property's experience. Such surveys are generally available annually for apartment properties of different types, hotels and motels, and office buildings. Some of the more widely available and useful surveys are cited at the end of this and subsequent chapters.

**Elements of Vacancy and Income Loss.** The appraiser should consider (but not necessarily include unless they are found to be present and pertinent) at least the following items when he is seeking to identify the amount of vacancy and income loss appropriate for the type of property being appraised, under current market standards and conditions:

1. vacancy rate by type of unit (or occupancy rate subtracted from 100%);
2. delinquencies (non-payment or partial payment of rent by tenants);
3. rent concessions (usually made in a tenant's market); and
4. pilferage.

*Other Income*

Many income-producing properties generate gross revenues for the owner-investor other than space rentals. Although rental income is typically the major source of gross revenues, it is not necessarily the only source. The other sources should be identified and investigated by the appraiser, and their net amount measured by the appraiser when they are found to be present. These are additional revenues that the owner-investor would normally anticipate receiving as a result of ownership and operation of the property as a revenue-producing investment. They are added to forecast annual rent collections (Potential Gross less Allowance for Vacancy and Income Loss) to derive the forecast of Effective Gross Income.

**Parking Space Rental.** Especially in apartment developments and office buildings, parking space rental can represent a significant proportion of total forecast revenues. When a parking space or stall is not included in the base rental for the space being rented in the property, and the tenants have an option whether to rent a parting space or how many to rent, the revenues from parking space rentals are included as "other income."

**Equipment Rental.** In some cases, equipment and the services it provides (air conditioning, for example) is optional in the rental space. If it is rented for a fee by the landlord to the tenant, the rental income it produces is also part of "other income."

**Concessions Income.** Coin-operated laundry equipment in apartment buildings and food dispensing equipment machines in office buildings often provide the property owner with additional income. The right to install and maintain the equipment is leased to a concessionnaire, with the landlord participating in the revenues produced by the machines. The net receipts from concessions receivable by the owner-investor should also be included as part of "other income."

**Sale of Utilities.** Particularly in older apartment, office and industrial loft buildings in center city areas—and in increasing numbers of shopping centers—landlords may buy electricity, water, or other utilities services at wholesale and then retail them to their tenants either at flat rates or by metering. In some industrial loft buildings in at least one major city, the income from retailing electricity to tenants actually exceeds gross rentals for the space in the buildings.

*Effective Gross Income*

Both the investor-owner and the appraiser of income-producing property are primarily interested in the forecast of the annual dollar amount of receipts the owner of a particular property or type of property most probably will actually receive. This is the Effective Gross Income: Potential Gross Income *less* Allowance for Vacancy and Income Loss *plus* Other Income. This is the figure from which forecast Operating Expenses are deducted to arrive at the forecast of annual Net Operating Income. It is also the figure most logically and appropriately used in Gross Income Multiplier analysis to estimate value as defined, provided Effective Gross Income can be obtained for comparable sales properties used in deriving the Gross Income Multiplier.

For purposes of illustration, suppose that the apartment property whose Potential Gross Income and Allowance for Vacancy and Income Loss have already been derived earlier in this chapter also produces "Other Income" for the owner-investor. One parking stall is provided in the apartment rental for each of the 200 units, but additional spaces are available for rent at $8 per month. The past experience of the subject property, substantiated by that of competing properties in the same market, is that 50% of the tenants will have two cars and will rent one additional parking space. This represents 100 parking stalls at $8 per month, or $9,600 per year. In addition, the coin-operated laundry equipment is currently producing 50 cents per unit per month revenue to the owner, and is forecast to continue to do so. The vacancy rates indicate that 190 units are forecast to be occupied annually. Vacant units do not have residents who will use the laundry equipment. The revenues from the coin-operated laundry equipment are therefore forecast at $95 per month, or $1,140 per year.

The forecast Effective Gross Income for the apartment property being appraised is thus estimated at $402,564, as follows:

| | | |
|---|---|---|
| Potential Gross Income (annual) | | $412,800 |
| *Less* Allowance for Vacancy and Income Loss | | − 20,976 |
| Annual Rent Collections | | $391,824 |
| *Plus* Other Income: | | |
| Parking Stall Rentals | $9,600 | |
| Concession Income | 1,140 | 10,740 |
| Effective Gross Income (annual) | | $402,564 |

## Net Income(s)

Most valuation analyses in appraising seek to estimate the present worth of some form of net annual cash flow forecast to be available to the purchaser-investor. In descending order of size, these are: Net Operating Income, Cash Throw-Off (or Before-Tax Cash Flow to the equity investment), and After-Tax Cash Flow to the equity investment. In nearly every appraisal problem, the appraiser must first identify the annual amount of gross income forecast to be produced by the property. The meaning of and techniques for estimating Potential Gross Income, Rent Collections, and Effective Gross Income have now been considered. The next step in the process is to identify and measure the annual expenses that the owner-investor most probably will have to incur in order to produce the gross income(s) that the property is capable of generating. These are called Operating Expenses.

### Operating Expenses

Operating Expenses are the annual expenses or annual cash outflows borne by the owner-investor of income-producing property as the necessary cost of generating the gross income(s) it is forecast to be capable of producing. They represent what the owner of the type of property being appraised pays for according to custom or market standards, when Market Value is to be estimated and the Net Operating Income forecast is to be based on Market Rentals. They represent what the owner-investor has contracted to pay for under a lease contract when Contract Rental is being used to derive a Net Operating Income forecast. The figures used are typical or "stabilized" annual cash expenses forecast to be payable by the owner of the property over the income projection period.

**Categories of Operating Expenses.** Operating expenses are not "costs" in the accounting sense. Rather, they are forecast cash outlays, stabilized on the basis of a typical year's operation of the property. All the expenditures, and only the expenditures, necessary for the production of gross income are included.

To assist the appraiser in identifying what items to include and what to exclude in developing an estimate of Operating Expenses, as well as to help in making sure that everything that might be included is at least considered, Operating Expenses can be grouped into categories. The precise labeling of these categories and the items included within some of them varies slightly from one published source to another.[2] The important point is not how items are labeled or their precise positioning under established labels, but rather that they be identified and classified in a checklist somewhere so that the appraiser will consider them for possible inclusion as Operating Expenses.

*Fixed Expenses.* These are expenses that tend not to vary with occupancy. They usually have to be paid whether the property is occupied or vacant. They also tend to vary over time, but in a relatively predictable way. Current or very recent levels are usually used to indicate most probable first-year Fixed Expenses, just as current rentals are used as the starting point for forecasting Gross Income flows. Fixed Expenses are generally of two types: Property Taxes and Property Insurance.

*Property taxes.* These include all levies on real property. The most recent figures are the best guide to the forecast estimate, tempered by recent local trends. Informed purchaser-investors do buy in recognition and anticipation of definable trends; the recent experience of many localities supports the view that most investors will anticipate an increase in property tax levies over time that exceeds the rate of decline in the purchasing power of the dollar.

The amount of property taxes is different from the tax rate. Frequently, the appraiser must first ascertain the *assessment* of the property, taking care to include all elements because land, buildings, and "other" elements of the property are frequently assessed separately. The combined assessment of the property is the "value" assigned it by the taxing authority for purposes of taxation. It is most frequently calculated as a percentage of Market Value (or "Fair Market Value"), and often called "assessed value."

The tax rate is usually expressed as so many dollars per hundred dollars of assessment (assessed valuation), or as so many *mils*. A mil is one-tenth of a cent, or one-thousandth of a dollar. Thus, a tax rate of 54 mils means that the tax bill will be 5.4 cents per dollar of assessment, $5.40 per hundred dollars of assessment, or (very commonly) $54 per one thousand dollars of assessment.

An alternative and frequently useful method of estimating and providing for property tax liability is to calculate the rate of taxation as a *percentage of property value*. In many jurisdictions, the dollars of taxes may vary, but the percentage of current Market Value of the property represented by the tax bill is surprisingly constant. In this method, the property tax is not deducted from Effective Gross Income as an Operating Expense; instead, its ratio to Market Value is added to the Discount Rate as another return to be covered by Net Operating Income. This method is particularly useful in assessment valuation problems, in valuing proposed developments, and in dealing with anticipated increasing taxes of uncertain amounts. It is recommended by the International Association of Assessing Officers, and is illustrated in examples in subsequent chapters of this book.

In estimating property taxes as part of Operating Expenses, no matter what method is used, the appraiser must be careful to include only that portion of the tax bill that will normally or by lease contract be expected to be paid by the owner-investor.

*Property insurance.* Only that normally paid by a landlord in his capacity as landlord is included. It may vary with the *type* of use or occupancy, but not with percentage of occupancy. Because premiums are frequently paid on a three-year basis in advance, stabilization to annual figures is usually required. The most common forms of insurance expenses borne by the landlord include: (1) fire and extended coverage; (2) landlord's liability; (3) workmen's compensation; and (4) boiler insurance. Insurance coverage for the landlord's business apart from the maintenance of the property is not part of Operating Expenses of the property.

*Variable Expenses.* This second major category of Operating Expenses includes items that are usually paid annually, tend to vary somewhat with the percentage of occupancy, and must be stabilized and forecast from market experience of the same type of property. The specific items to be included in any given appraisal problem depend on the type of property, the climate (e.g., snow-plowing), and the terms of the landlord-tenant relationship. These are only those items that the landlord normally or by lease contract provides to the tenant and pays for himself.

*Management fee.* This must be included even in an owner-managed property. It is usually a percentage of *rent collections.* While 3-5% is a common range for most multi-tenant properties, the appraiser must ascertain the going rate for typically competent professional management of the type of property involved, in the current local market.

*Payroll and personnel.* This includes all maintenance and support staff (e.g., doorman) salaries, plus Social Security, unemployment insurance, and all fringe benefits. If a free apartment is made available to an apartment superintendent, the market rental of the apartment should be deducted as an operating expense—assuming it has been included in gross income. The personnel include both landlord's staff and contractors.

*Supplies and materials.* These are items actually used in the operation of the property.

*Utilities.* This includes electricity, gas, water, and sewerage service paid for by the landlord. This may be expressed as a percentage of Effective Gross Income, or possibly as so much per occupied unit of space, if the standards are available. Air conditioning service is usually included as a subitem of electricity; the equipment cost is included under Replacements.

*Heat.* The fuel expense borne by the landlord is included here, either as a percentage of Effective Gross Income at a given level of occupancy, or so much per occupied unit of space.

*Grounds care.* This includes parking lot maintenance, snow removal, and maintenance of lawn and plantings.

*Other items.* Depending on the type of property, this might include swimming pool maintenance, sign maintenance, and so forth.

*Repairs and Maintenance.* Although these expenses also tend to vary at least in part with occupancy, they also tend to be concentrated in some years. They therefore must be stabilized to average annual figures. For some types of buildings (especially apartments, office buildings, and hotels-motels), published figures are available indicating national average annual maintenance costs per square foot of building area. Maintenance and repair activity must be compatible with typically competent management.

*Replacements.* Short-lived items of equipment and building parts will normally have to be replaced before the expiration of the income projection period. These must first be identified (e.g., air conditioners, elevators, lighting fixtures), their replacement costs estimated, and their useful lives projected. Dividing the replacement cost for each category by the forecast useful life yields an annual payment to cover replacement.

**Excluded Items.** Certain items included in a typical owner's operating statement are not operating expenses *of the property.* They must be eliminated in reconstructing the Operating Expense Statement. Otherwise, Net Operating Income will be understated, and double counting of expenses can occur.

*Income Taxes, Corporation Taxes and Personal Property Taxes.* These are expenses of the owner, not of the property.

*Capital Recovery (Depreciation).* Capital recovery is not an operating expense; it is not required to produce gross income. Neither is it an annual expenditure of funds. Rather, it is a provision for recovery of a capital expenditure already made. Net Operating Income incorporates a provision for capital recovery for the owner-investor, which is reflected in the rate or factor used to capitalize NOI into a present worth estimate.

*Debt Service (Financing Costs).* This annual payment is an expense to the investor, but is not necessary to produce the forecast gross income.

*Business Expenses of the Owner.* These must be carefully separated from the expenses of operating the property, particularly in the case of owner-occupied income-producing properties.

*Capital Improvements (Capital Outlays).* These are expenditures that *increase* (or are designed to increase) the property's income-producing potential and/or its economic life. They are not operating expenses, which are necessary to *maintain* the forecast gross income and economic life of the property.

**Sources of Data.** Rental income, "other" income, vacancy and income loss allowance, and operating expense data may be derived from three basic sources: operating experience of the subject property; market data on competitive, comparable properties; and published studies of property experience and standards. Ideally, all three should be used in estimating the quantities involved in working from Potential Gross Income, through Effective Gross Income and Operating Expenses, to Net Operating Income.

*Experience of the Subject Property.* A minimum of three years' operating experience, and preferably five years; is required to make the data from the subject property itself meaningful and usable. Annual averages and modest trends can be discerned over five years. These figures can be used directly if they are consistent with figures developed from the market of competitive properties and/or published standards for the type of property in question.

*Market Experience and Standards.* The market for the subject property is identified in terms of properties competitive and comparable with it. Rental, occupancy, and operating expense data can be obtained from competitive, comparable properties, both to help establish the stabilized quantities to be used, and to develop standards by which to judge the experience of the subject property. This necessary information on operating statements can usually be obtained from among (1) leasing agents, brokers, or principals in competitive properties; (2) other appraisers; (3) financial institutions, mortgage brokers, mortgage bankers, mortgage correspondents; (4) the appraiser's own files; and (5) public agencies and public records.

*Published Income Statement Standards.* Surveys and studies of various types of income properties are frequently carried out (some annually) which provide rental, occupancy, and operating expense standards—usually on a national or regional basis. All but rental standards are usually expressed as percentages, either of the gross income or of the gross receipts of the business occupying the space.

Studies by local chapters of professional real estate associations are frequently available. National real estate associations also publish periodic studies.

Local development groups and research units of colleges and universities often carry out market studies.

Specific references to the most commonly available and useful continuing surveys of operating experiences of different types of properties are provided in later sections and chapters. Excellent citations and critical evaluations of some of these sources may be found in A.A. Ring's text.[3] Apartment operating standards are periodically analyzed by regional offices of the Federal Housing Administration, by the Institute of Real Estate Management in their *Apartment Building Experience Exchange*, by the National Apartment Owners' Association, and by the National Association of Building Owners and Managers (BOMA).

Office building operations are analyzed periodically by BOMA, and in *Skyscraper Management* and the *National Real Estate Investor*. Hotel and motel operations are reviewed annually by two national accounting firms: Laventhol Krackstein, Horwath and Horwath; and Harris, Kerr, Foster and Co. Shopping centers and retail stores operating data are published periodically by the Urban Land Institute, the Supermarket Institute of America, and Dun and Bradstreet.

Industrial park and industrial property operations are reviewed occasionally by the Society of Industrial Realtors and the Urban Land Institute. Finally, there are occasional reviews and analyses of operations of different types of income properties in *The Real Estate Analyst*, published by Roy Wenzlick and Co.

**Stabilization of Operating Statements through Market Standards.** Operating Expense estimates used in the estimation of Market Value must reflect the standards and behavior of typical, competitive properties in the market. Aside from inclusion of all items that are pertinent to the type of property and owner-tenant relationship involved, and exclusion of all nonproperty expenses incurred by the owner, the statement must be "stabilized" to reflect the typical year's experience under competitive market conditions. Many outlays tend to be concentrated in individual years. They must be averaged out on an annual basis to reflect the "stabilized" typical annual cash outlay necessary for the owner to make in order to generate the forecast level of gross revenues.

*Use of Owner's Income Statement.* The owner's income statement is typically prepared for accounting and income tax purposes, and is based on different concepts of "income" and "costs" from those used in the stabilized cash-flow of appraisal analysis. The necessary data for estimating Operating Expenses can usually be extracted from the Income Statement, however, if the appraiser keeps firmly in mind the items to be included (and excluded) as Operating Expenses, and the fact that he must stabilize the figures to an annual, typical-year basis. Usually, at least three years' statements are required to indicate variations and trends in expenditures.

The actual experience of the property being appraised is one guide, but only one guide, to the Operating Expense figures most appropriately used. When these actual figures, stabilized to a typical annual basis, are consistent with the standards and patterns of behavior of the market, the figures derived for the subject property can be used. The appraiser must be able to defend the proposition that they are in fact representative, however. There is an excellent illustration of extracting Operating Expense figures from an owner's Income Statement in Chapter 15 of the Ring text.[4]

*Stabilization from Market Standards.* The process of stabilization is almost but not quite averaging. The end figures are supposed to represent a typical current and forecast year's expenditures for the item in question, ignoring the impact of inflation or changes in purchasing power. The most important basis for making stabilizing adjustments is the experience of similar, competing properties in the same market. Next in usefulness are standards for similar types of properties derived from published studies covering larger areas.

Component items are stabilized from the experience of competitive properties and/or market standards either as a percentage of Effective Gross Income, or as a fixed dollar amount per unit of space. For example, suppose that market standards indicate that personnel expenses for a given type of property should be approximately 14% of Effective Gross. This serves as a check against the actual experience of the subject property, and can be the basis for adjusting actual expenditures to conform to the standards of typically competent management. In an example of Market Rental estimation used earlier this chapter, it was revealed that some units were rented without heat and some with heat provided by the landlord. It was also indicated that market experience showed a heat cost averaging $5 per room per month. This figure could be taken as the market standard against which the heating expenses of the subject property would be compared, and it would be adjusted if it were found to be significantly out of line.

An alternative method of estimating annual expenses for long-lived items such as equipment is to take the estimated total expenditures on the item for the entire income forecasting period (say 10 years), and then take an average annual figure to represent typical annual expenses. Thus, if $21,500 were forecast to be spent on elevator repairs over a 10-year period, the annual operating expense figure would be $2,150.

*Lease Contract Stipulations.* When a property is subject to a long-term lease which can reasonably be expected to remain in force until it expires, the contract terms of the lease largely determine which items should be included as Operating Expenses. They also determine what basis should be used in estimating their annual amounts. In such cases, the appraiser must read the lease carefully, and have its terms explained by the leasing broker or an attorney if necessary.

*Reconstruction of Operating Statement.* Once the component items that should be included in the typical Operating Expense statement for the type of property involved have been identified and stabilized on an annual basis by the appraiser, he can reconstruct the operating statement using those stabilized figures for the appropriate items.

As an example, consider the 200-unit apartment property whose gross income has previously been estimated. Suppose the owner's income statement looks something like Exhibit 6-3.

The concept of "income" illustrated in Exhibit 6-3 is at variance with the stabilized annual cash flow which represents "income" in appraisal analysis. Armed with necessary additional information, the appraiser can work from this income statement, however, and derive a stabilized operating statement for the property.

The information needed represents the standards and behavior of the market, and their application to the Effective Gross Income forecast already developed for the property. Management fees are normally 4% of rent collections for apartments in this market. Resident managers receive $5 per occupied unit per month, plus one two-bedroom apartment rent-free. Insurance premiums must be stabilized to an annual basis. Property taxes are forecast to be based on an assessment of $1,100,000 and a 50-mil tax rate. Water service costs landlords of comparable properties an average of $5 per unit per month, regardless of the level of occupancy (within reasonable limits, at least). Only $4,000 of the $12,000 fee for legal services was for work related to the subject property. Tenants furnish their own gas (heat) and electricity, but electricity for common and public areas costs an average of $50 per month. Repairs and maintenance are forecast to average $30,000 per year. Pool and grounds maintenance and advertising charges listed in the owner's income statement are in line with forecast amounts. So is the charge for supplies.

The owner furnishes four items of equipment in each apartment: a $150 dishwasher; a $102 disposal; a $210 refrigerator; and a $270 range and oven. The prices indicated are estimated replacement prices, installed. It is estimated that each of these items has a useful life of 12 years, so 1/12 of total estimated replacement costs must be charged each year to stabilize the annual expense statement.

Neither debt service (which is a cash outlay) nor depreciation (which is not) are Operating Expenses.

Given this information and the figures for the apartment property being

**Exhibit 6-3**

**Apartment Property Owner's Income Statement**

Total Receipts:

| | | |
|---|---|---|
| Rent Collections | $395,400 | |
| Parking and Concession Receipts | 10,600 | $406,000.00 |

Expenses:

| | | |
|---|---|---|
| Property Taxes | $ 54,652.00 | |
| Mortgage Payments | 219,517.20 | |
| Management Fee (4%) | 15,816.00 | |
| Resident Manager—Salary | 11,400.00 | |
| Water | 11,898.77 | |
| Electricity | 611.43 | |
| Legal Fees | 12,000.00 | |
| Insurance Premium (3 years) | 8,550.00 | |
| Supplies | 1,000.00 | |
| Pool and grounds maintenance | 4,500.00 | |
| Advertising | 1,500.00 | |
| Repairs and maintenance—building | 27,865.00 | |
| Replace two range-oven combinations | 540.00 | |
| Replace three refrigerators | 630.00 | |
| Depreciation | 84,000.00 | |
| | | −454,480.40 |
| Income for the year (loss) | | −$48,480.40 |

appraised, the appraiser would reconstruct the operating statement as illustrated in Exhibit 6-4.

*Net Operating Income*

The difference between Effective Gross Income and Operating Expenses is Net Operating Income. This is the annual dollar amount that the property is forecast to generate under typically competent management. It is based on Market Rentals and market-determined Operating Expenses when the objective of the appraisal is to estimate Market Value. It represents the impact of lease terms or

**Exhibit 6-4**

**Reconstruction of Income Property Operating Statement**

Potential Gross Income:

| | | |
|---|---|---|
| 160 2-bedroom units, $180 per month | | $345,600 |
| 40 1-bedroom units, $140 per month | | 67,200 |
| | | $412,800 |
| *Less* Allowance for Vacancy and Income Loss: | | −20,976 |
| Rent Collections: | | $391,824 |
| *Plus* Other Income: | | |
| Parking Space Rentals | $ 9,600 | |
| Concession Income | 1,140 | 10,740 |
| Effective Gross Income: | | $402,564 |
| LESS Operating Expenses: | | |
| Property Tax (.05 x $1,100,000) | $55,000 | |
| Insurance (1/3 x $8550) | 2,850 | |
| Management (.04 x $391,824) | 15,816 | |
| Resident Manager ($5 x 12 x 190) | 11,400 | |
| Resident Manager—Apartment | 2,160 | |
| Water ($5 x 200 x 12) | 12,000 | |
| Electricity ($50 x 12) | 600 | |
| Supplies | 1,000 | |
| Advertising and Legal Fees | 5,500 | |
| Pool and Grounds Maintenance | 3,500 | |
| Repairs and Maintenance | 30,000 | |
| Replacements: | | |
| Dishwashers ($150/12 x 200) | 2,500 | |
| Refrigerators ($210/12 x 200) | 3,500 | |
| Disposals ($102/12 x 200) | 1,700 | |
| Stoves ($270/12 x 200) | 4,500 | −152,026 |
| Net Operating Income (annual forecast): | | $250,538 |

investor expectations when the end result is to be an estimate of Investment Value.

In either case, Net Operating Income (NOI) is the basic building block in income capitalization analysis. It is the $I$ in virtually every variant form of income capitalization seeking property value as the final result. It is equal to $d$ in the Ellwood formulation. It is a modified or "stabilized" cash flow forecast of what the property is capable of generating for its ownership, before deducting mortgage debt service if cash flow to the investor is needed, and before deducting any charge for capital recovery if the total return *on* the investment in the property is required.

NOI incorporates both a stipulated return *on* the investment in the property over the income forecast period, and a proportional annual return *of* that portion of the investment which is to be recovered by the end of the income projection period. Because it incorporates both the return *on* and a portion of return *of* the investment, it has been called Net Income Before Recapture (NIBR) for many years. However, there has always been some confusion among non-appraisers (and some appraisers as well) over the fact that the "before" in Net Income Before Recapture meant "before making a *deduction* for capital recapture." Moreover, NOI is a term with wide acceptance in the investment and financing fields, which are closely allied with appraising. Therefore, NOI is used throughout this book.

### Cash Throw-Off (Before-Tax Cash Flow)

NOI represents the stabilized typical year's cash flow to the investment in the entire property. When the valuation problem is approached particularly from the viewpoint of the purchaser-investor, as is the case in mortgage-equity analysis for example, the cash flow available to the equity investor to provide a return on (and of) his equity investment takes on significance. Starting with the NOI generated by the property, a deduction must be made for any other property-investment-related cash outflows for which the investor-owner is responsible. There is one such outlay annually: debt service on any mortgage loan(s) outstanding. If there is no mortgage loan on the property, then the equity investor has a 100% equity in the property, and all of NOI is a return to the equity investment. This is rarely the case, however, for reasons developed in detail in Chapter 7.

Therefore, before a cash flow forecast to the equity investment can be derived, the annual cash outlay necessary to pay off any mortgage debt outstanding must be deducted from NOI. NOI *minus* annual debt service is called Cash Throw-Off or Before Tax Cash Flow. This is the cash flow to the equity investment before any further deduction for income tax liability is made. Cash Throw-Off expressed as a percentage of the equity investment is the Equity Dividend Rate, identified in Chapter 4.

For example, suppose the apartment property used as a continuing illustration in this chapter were financed with a $2,100,000 mortgage with a 22-year maturity and interest at 9%. Full amortization of the debt will be realized in 22 years through equal monthly payments of principal and interest.

To find the amount of annual debt service, the mortgage constant (defined and illustrated in Chapters 4 and 5) must first be derived. The monthly Installment to Amortize One factor for 22 years at 9% is 0.008711 (Ellwood, page 97, column 6). The mortgage constant is 12 X 0.008711, or 0.104532. It could also be expressed as 10.45%. Annual debt service is then found by multiplying the mortgage constant times the principal amount of the mortgage loan: 0.104532 X $2,100,000 = $219,517.20. In most cases, this would be rounded to the nearest whole dollar.

Cash Throw-Off to the Equity Investment is then NOI minus Annual Debt Service, or $31,021 ($250,538 − $219,517). If the amount of equity investment were known, Cash Throw-Off could then be used to calculate the Equity Dividend Rate. If the Equity Dividend Rate were known, it could be combined to develop an indication of the present worth of the equity investment. In both instances, the appraiser would be back to application of the basic valuation formula: $V = I'R$.

Assuming original equity investment to remain intact, Cash Throw-Off is basically a return *on* equity investment. Capital recovery of the amount of borrowed capital is provided through mortgage amortization.

### After-Tax Cash Flow

Particularly in Investment Value analysis, the investor frequently wants to know how much cash return he is going to have left and available to put to use (for whatever purposes he sees fit). In the era of the income tax, Before-Tax Cash Flow as represented by Cash Throw-Off simply does not represent such a figure. Income Tax Liability must be deducted from Cash Throw-Off to obtain forecast annual After-Tax Cash Flow. Because the interest component in annual debt service surely, and capital recovery charges possibly, will vary from year to year, deductions from NOI to derive Taxable Net Income will also vary annually. As a result, After-Tax Cash Flow will be different in each year of the income projection period, even when NOI and annual debt service are forecast to remain constant throughout the period. Thus, the only way to develop present worth estimate for a series of After-Tax Cash Flow estimates is to treat each as a separate lump-sum payment, discount each to the present, and sum the present worths to a present worth estimate for the entire income stream. This is the technique illustrated and explained in Chapter 5 as applicable to any income stream.

Income Tax Liability estimation requires several calculations. These are illustrated in Chapter 18 when After-Tax Cash Flows are considered as part of the valuation of investment interests in real property. After-Tax Cash Flow is also a return *on* equity investment; capital recovery is provided through mortgage amortization.

**Review Exercises**

1. A 10-story office building contains 12,000 square feet of total area on each floor. Net rentable area is 80%. First floor space of a comparable type is renting at $8.00 per square foot per year; and top floor space of a comparable type is renting for $7.50 per square foot per year. The space on the intervening floors is competitive with space renting at $6.00 per square foot on the market. Market vacancies are running at 3% for top-floor space, 5% for "middle" floor space, and 2% for ground floor space. Lobby concessions are forecast to produce $1.00 per year for every square foot of occupied rental space.
   a. Develop a forecast of Effective Gross Income.
   b. What would the annual management fee be if professional management firms are currently receiving 3% of annual rent collections?
   c. If the entire building were fully rented on 15-year leases to well-rated tenants at the rentals specified above, and the income projection period in your appraisal were 10 years, what would the estimated Effective Gross Income be?
2. You are appraising a 200-unit apartment property and want to develop an appropriate vacancy and income loss allowance. A recent survey of 1,200 similar apartment units reveals that 67 units are vacant, and there is a total of 6 "no-pay" tenants in the process of being evicted.
   a. What vacancy and income loss allowance factor does this survey indicate?
   b. If the subject property currently has 14 vacancies and 3 delinquent tenants, what would you conclude?
3. In the office building in Problem 1, the following operating expense standards are found to be applicable:
   Management: 3% of rent collections
   Personnel: $200 per 1,000 square feet of total building area per year
   Maintenance: 25 cents per square foot of total building area per year
   Insurance: $24,000 every three years
   Taxes: 40 mils on an assessment of 50% of 7 times Potential Gross Income
   Utilities (including heat and air conditioning): 1.5% of Effective Gross
   Replacements: 2.0% of Effective Gross
   Other Expenses: $6,000 per year
   Using the gross income estimates based on Market Rentals, develop a stabilized Operating Expense statement, and derive forecast Net Operating Income.
4. An income property is forecast to produce an Effective Gross Income of $28,000 per year. Stabilized Operating Expenses are $12,000. Annual debt service is based on an 8.75%, fully amortized, level payment, monthly payment, 25-year mortgage in the amount of $120,000.
   a. What is the mortgage constant?

b. What is the indicated annual debt service?

c. What is the forecast amount of Net Operating Income?

d. What is the forecast amount of annual Cash Throw-Off?

e. If the mortgage represents 75% of the amount of an investment that has just been made, what is the indicated Equity Dividend Rate?

## Supplementary Readings

American Institute of Real Estate Appraisers, *The Appraisal of Real Estate* (Chicago: American Institute of Real Estate Appraisers, 1967). Chapters 15 and 16.

Sanders A. Kahn, Frederick E. Case, and Alfred Schimmel, *Real Estate Appraisal and Investment* (New York: Ronald Press, 1963), pp. 103-120.

William N. Kinnard, Jr., *A Guide to Appraising Apartments,* third edition (Chicago: Society of Real Estate Appraisers, 1973), pp. 17-20 and 32-35.

Alfred A. Ring, *The Valuation of Real Estate*, second edition (Englewood Cliffs, N.J.: Prentice-Hall, 1970), Chapters 14 and 15.

William M. Shenkel, *A Guide to Appraising Industrial Property* (Chicago: Society of Real Estate Appraisers, 1967), pp. 95-97.

## Notes

1. A formal and detailed discussion of the use and limitations of subjective probabilities in forecasting is beyond the scope of this book. It involves a consideration of so-called Bayesian statistical inference. One presentation of the topic in relatively simple terms, with illustrations from business decision-making, is found on pages 15-31 of Volume Four of the Mathematics for Management Series: C.H. Springer, R.E. Herlihy, R.T. Mall, and R.I. Beggs, *Probabilistic Models* (Homewood, Illinois: Irwin, 1968).

2. See, for example, the discussions in American Institute of Real Estate Appraisers, *The Appraisal of Real Estate*, fifth edition (Chicago: American Institute of Real Estate Appraisers, 1967), Chapter 16; and A.A. Ring, *The Valuation of Real Estate*, second edition (Englewood Cliffs, N.J.: Prentice-Hall, 1970), Chapter 15.

3. Ring, *Valuation of Real Estate*, Chapter 15.

4. *Ibid.*, pp. 226-228.

# 7

# Debt Financing and Its Influence on Income Property Valuation

It has long been taught and accepted that Market Value estimation requires the valuation of the fee simple interest "free and clear of all encumbrances." These "encumbrances" include mortgages. This position is expounded in the AIREA text, and supported in the Ring text.[1] There is much appeal in the argument, and it has the weight of tradition behind it. It states that Market Value is Market Value regardless of the mortgage financing the purchaser-investor can obtain. Therefore, to include mortgage financing as part of valuation analysis is to introduce specific individual investor considerations rather than those of the market.

The strict "free and clear" position has been modified somewhat over time. From an original argument that Market Value was a *cash value* figure, it evolved to a concept of *cash to the seller*. How the buyer raised the necessary funds was immaterial, and not an influence on Market Value. However, the definition of Market Value most widely accepted and used in appraising, and presented in Chapter 2, takes the viewpoint of the typically informed buyer; a typically informed buyer knows that he can usually obtain debt financing.

Moreover, a typically informed purchaser-investor of an income property knows that by using mortgage financing he can take advantage of leverage. In this way, he hopes to increase the rate of return on his equity investment. Since the typically informed buyer-investor is also presumed to act rationally to maximize (or at least optimize) his investment returns, it follows that he will take full advantage of any mortgage financing typically available on properties of the type in question in the current local market, to realize that maximum or optimum rate of return on his equity investment.

There has been growing recognition in appraisal literature that at least the *typical* pattern of financing available to the most probable type of investor (in this type of property in the current local market) should be taken into account in estimating the Market Value of the fee simple estate in the property. This recognition is represented by the Supplementary Readings at the end of this Chapter. Rational investors do take advantage of mortgage financing and the leverage it offers. The appraiser is supposed to view the property through the eyes of the typically informed, rational purchaser-investor. If the buyer seeks and obtains available financing, the appraiser as a recorder of market behavior cannot ignore it just to remain loyal to a "free and clear" concept of Market Value.

Typically available mortgage financing and its terms can and do influence *value*, not just the price a specific purchaser-investor is willing or believes he can afford to pay. The "free and clear" argument thus fails to depict what the *market* is doing. Moreover, appraisal theory has for years used available financing

145

terms to develop an appropriate market discount rate via the Band of Investment approach discussed in Chapter 8. In using market sales data that necessarily reflect the financing obtained by purchasers, the derivation of Overall Rates of Capitalization at least tacitly recognizes the influence of debt financing on value. Finally, mortgage-equity analysis can use a Cash Throw-Off forecast in estimating value.

Thus, the terms and conditions of debt financing typically available to the most probable type of investor in the current local market represent a significant part of the market environment that surrounds and influences the income-producing property sales transaction. Appraisers must understand the influence of each of these loan terms and recognize the most probable combination that an informed, rational purchaser would choose. Moreover, the stratification of both demand and sources of loan funds into many sub-markets requires the appraiser to identify the most probable sub-market(s) for the property in question as of the valuation date. The loan terms and types of loans typically available from the most probable sources in the applicable sub-market(s) then become an integral part of the appraisal analysis.

## Importance of Debt Financing to
## Income-Producing Property Transactions

Nearly all real estate sales, and especially those of income-producing properties, involve the use of mortgage (debt) financing. The most probable purchaser-investor will seek mortgage financing for two basic reasons: he needs to supplement his available cash or equity funds with borrowed funds in order to complete the purchase; and it is usually to his advantage to trade on equity through the use of leverage.

Mortgage financing is a fact of the market. The typical income-producing property sales transaction is accomplished with mortgage financing. The appraiser must recognize this fact and include the most probable pattern of financing in his analysis leading to a present worth or Market Value estimate.

### Conserve or Extend Investor's
### Available Cash

For many types of income property transactions, typical or most probable investors do not usually have sufficient cash to purchase the properties on a 100% equity basis. Private individuals or groups formed to purchase the properties as investments commonly fall into this category, especially on small apartment, retail and office building investments. In these cases, mortgage financing is absolutely essential; otherwise the transaction will not take place. This extends the effectiveness of the purchaser-investor's available cash.

Both commercial and industrial business firms that acquire income-type properties for their own use frequently do not have the necessary cash to buy their properties outright. They, too, require mortgage financing to acquire the needed or desired property. Moreover, most business firms that do have sufficient funds available to pay cash in full do not choose to do so. They can (or expect to) earn more on the money as working capital in the business that they can save by not paying mortgage interest. Therefore, they typically seek the maximum (or optimum, as discussed below) amount of mortgage loan available, to enable them to conserve on their available cash and put as much as possible into more productive use in the business.

Knowledgeable investors recognize that mortgage interest rates are typically lower than the overall rate of return on income-producing real estate. By borrowing as much as possible (or the optimum amount dictated by the pattern of all mortgage loan terms), they serve two important related investment objectives. First, through leverage they expect to earn a higher rate of return on their equity investment. Second, their available funds can be extended into more investments, also leveraged, to produce expected higher equity yields.

*Enhance the Investor's Rate of*
*Return through Leverage*

Leverage is the use of borrowed funds to complete an investment transaction. The larger the proportion of borrowed funds used to make the investment, the higher the leverage is. Also, the lower the proportion of equity funds will be.

Trading on the equity (the use of leverage) is the use of borrowed funds to acquire an income-producing asset in the *expectation* of producing a higher rate of return on the equity investment. The idea is that money can be borrowed at a lower rate than that produced by the property. To the extent that the property does in fact produce return *on* investment at a rate higher than the contractual mortgage interest rate, the portion of the investment covered by mortgage loan funds produces a "surplus" that is available to the equity investor. This increases the yield on the equity investment.

For example, assume a property priced at $200,000 produced $20,000 per year *after* deducting an allowance for capital recovery. This is a 10% rate of return. If an investor pays 100% cash for the property, his equity dividend rate is 10% and his return is $20,000.

If, on the other hand, he can borrow 70% of the purchase price ($140,000) at 8.5% interest, then $11,900 of the annual return of $20,000 is required to cover his annual interest payments. (For purposes of simplification in this example, amortization is ignored; the mortgage is a "straight" loan with a 100% "balloon" at maturity.) This means that the property must earn 5.95% on the total investment to cover mortgage interest. The remaining $8,100 is left as a return on the 30% equity investment of $60,000. This is an equity dividend rate of 13.5%.

The foregoing situation can be expressed entirely in percentages, as follows:

| | | |
|---|---|---|
| Total Investment: | 100% × .10 | = 10.00% |
| Mortgage Interest: | 70% × .085 | = 5.95% |
| Return to Equity (30%) | | 4.05% ÷ .30 = 13.5% |

The higher the proportion of total investment financed by borrowed funds, the greater the leverage. Also, as property income varies, the greater the variability in equity returns and equity dividend rates will be. The equity investor is assuming the contractual obligation to pay mortgage interest in exchange for the expectation (or chance) of earning a higher equity return, but he is also assuming the risk that it may be lower.

For example, if an 80% loan at 8.5% can be obtained on the $200,000 property earning 10% net of capital recover, then the equity yield becomes:

| | | |
|---|---|---|
| Total Property: | 100% × .10 | = 10.00% |
| Mortgage Interest: | 80% × .085 | = 6.80% |
| Return to Equity (20%) | | 3.20% ÷ .20 = 16.0% |

If property income declines to a 9% return on investment (a 10% decline in rate), the equity yield rate declines by over 31% to 11.0%.

| | | |
|---|---|---|
| Total Property: | 100% × .09 | = 9.00% |
| Mortgage Interest: | 80% × .085 | = 6.80% |
| Return to Equity (20%) | | 2.20% ÷ .20 = 11.0% |

The foregoing examples illustrate one way in which equity yield rates can be derived via the Band of Investment approach, as discussed in Chapter 8.

Trading on equity need not be successful. If the rate of return on the entire investment falls below the mortgage interest rate, the impact is entirely on the equity investor. The greater the leverage (the higher the percentage of total investment represented by borrowed funds), the greater this negative impact on the equity dividend rate can be. This is the risk assumed by the equity investor in contracting to pay fixed interest on borrowed funds and trading on equity.

For example, if the rate of return on the $200,000 property with an 80% mortgage at 8.5% interest falls to 8%, the impact on the equity returns is:

| | | |
|---|---|---|
| Total Investment: | 100% × .08 | = 8.00% |
| Mortgage Interest: | 80% × .085 | = 6.80% |
| Return to Equity (20%) | | 1.20% ÷ .20 = 6.0% |

## Nature of Mortgage Loans

A mortgage loan is a loan secured by a pledge of real estate as collateral. It is a contract between the lender (mortgagee) and the borrower (mortgagor). In the event of default (non-payment by the mortgagor in accordance with the terms of the contract), the mortgagee in most states can force the sale of the pledged real estate to satisfy his claim.

The loan contract takes the form of a *mortgage note*. The pledge of the securing property takes the form of a mortgage deed, a mortgage lien or a deed of trust, depending on state law. For consistency in this discussion, the term "mortgage" is used, whatever legal form the pledge of the property may take.

Both interest and principal payments (amortization) are fixed by contract. Interest is a fixed rate throughout the term of the loan. All terms of the loan, which are discussed in the following section, are stipulated in writing in the mortgage note.

The mortgage note is a negotiable instrument, and as such may be bought and sold on the open market. It can have a Market Value of its own, as well as an Investment Value. Its present worth is estimated by treating annual debt service as a level annuity, which it is.

The contractual and legal characteristics of mortgage instruments permit fiduciary financial institutions to lend on real estate. Protection of the funds of depositors or policy holders is provided on such long-term loans through these contractual documents and the rights they give to mortgagees. Limitations on loan terms are set both by law and by institutional policy.

## Mortgage Loan Terms

The terms of a mortgage loan comprise a package that determines the cost of loan funds to the borrower, the amount of money he may borrow, the period over which he may have use of the funds, the method and timing of repayment, and the annual amount of debt service (repayment). This package is a reflection of money market conditions, alternative lending outlets available to lenders, institutional policy standards and limitations, and limitations set by state and local law. No one lending term is exclusively significant to the appraiser. All must be considered and evaluated in order to forecast the most probable financing *pattern* available on the type of property being appraised, given the most probable type of purchaser-borrower, and current local market conditions. In the process, the most probable source(s) of mortgage loan funds for the type of property involved must also be identified.

Since the most common type of mortgage loan is the fully amortized, level monthly payment loan, the following discussion of mortgage loan terms uses this form as the standard. Other types are also considered, however.

### *Interest Rate*

This is by far the most obvious and most commonly recognized term of lending.

It is the annual cost to the borrower per dollar of loan. It is not necessarily the most significant loan term, however.

**Fixed Character.** Mortgage interest rates are almost always fixed by loan contract for the full maturity of the loan. Although variable rate mortgages have been proposed and even experimented with from time to time, they are as yet rarely employed.

**Impact of Changes in Mortgage Interest Rates.** A change in mortgage interest rates has a direct impact in the same direction on financing costs for the mortgagor. If property income remains the same, then a mortgage interest rate change also has a direct impact in the same direction on the equity return. Generally speaking, if other loan terms remain the same, the lower the interest rate, the higher the equity dividend rate will be, and the higher the value of both the equity investment and the entire property will be.

Ignoring amortization for the moment, recall the $200,000 investment producing a 10% return on investment, or $20,000 per year. Assume a 70% mortgage at 8.5% interest. The mortgage principal would be $140,000.

As noted earlier, mortgage interest would be $11,900, leaving $8,100 as equity return. It is also necessary for the investment to earn 5.95% to cover mortgage interest payments. As a result of trading on equity, the equity dividend rate is 13.5%

Now suppose mortgage interest rates rise to 9%, with no other change. The situation then becomes:

| | | | |
|---|---|---|---|
| Total Investment: | 100% X .10 | = 10.00% | ($20,000) |
| Mortgage Interest: | 70% X .09 | = 6.30% | ($12,600) |
| Return to Equity: | 30% X $y$ | = 3.70% | ($ 7,400) |

$$y = 3.70\% \div .30 = 12.33\% \ (\$7,400/\$60,000 = 0.1233)$$

Thus, a one-half point increase in mortgage interest rates results in a decrease in equity dividend rate of 1.17 percentage points. The increase in mortgage interest rate is less than 6%; the decrease in equity dividend rate is in excess of 12.3%.

A similar result in the opposite direction occurs when interest rates decline.

If amortization is included (which is usually the case), the Net Operating Income is the point of departure. Mortgage amortization gives a close approximation to capital recovery over the maturity of the loan. Assume that the 70% ($140,000) loan at 8.5% interest is a fully amortized loan with constant monthly payments (including both principal and interest) over a 20-year term. Net Operating Income on the $200,000 property investment is $23,000 per year, for an 11.5% overall rate of return.

The monthly payments on the 20-year, 8.5%, $140,000 loan are $1,214.92. ($140,000 X .008678: Ellwood, page 89, column 6). Annual debt service is $14,579.04 (12 X $1,214.92). The mortgage constant is 10.41% (12 X .008678).

Thus:

| | | | |
|---|---|---|---|
| Total Investment: | 100% X .115 | = 11.50% | ($23,000) |
| Debt Service: | 70% X .1041 | = 7.29% | ($14,579) |
| Return on Equity: | 30% X $e$ | = 4.21% | ($ 8,421) |

$e = 4.21\% \div .30 = 14.03\%$ ($8,421/$60,000 = 0.1403)

If all else remains the same, but mortgage interest rates rise to 9%, then monthly payments become $1,259.58 ($140,000 X .008997: Ellwood, page 97, column 6). Annual debt service is $15,114.96 (12 X $1,259.58). The mortgage constant is 10.80% (12 X .008997).
Thus:

| | | | |
|---|---|---|---|
| Total Investment: | 100% X .115 | = 11.50% | ($23,000) |
| Debt Service: | 70% X .108 | = 7.56% | ($15,115) |
| Return on Equity: | 30% X $e$ | = 3.94% | ($ 7,885) |

$e = 3.94\% \div .30 = 13.13\%$ ($7,885/$60,000 = 0.1313)

With a one-half point increase in mortgage rate (less than 6%) the equity dividend rate declines 0.9 points (over 7%). The same result occurs in the opposite direction when mortgage interest rates decline.

**Effective vs. Nominal Rates: Mortgage "Points".** Because contract mortgage interest rates tend to be "sticky" or relatively insensitive to short-term money market changes (at least they did until the late 1960s), lenders sometime discount mortgage loans to increase the *effective* mortgage rate over the *nominal* or *contract* rate. This is known as charging "points."

Ignoring amortization, assume the 70% ($140,000) mortgage loan at 8.5%. Annual interest charges are $11,900. Assume further that the lender insists on a 3% discount (a charge of 3 points). This means that the borrower receives only 97% of the face amount of the loan, or $135,800, although he signs a note for $140,000 and must pay $11,900 annual interest. The *nominal* or *contract* rate is 8.5%; the *effective* mortgage interest rate is 8.75% ($11,900/$135,800).

Discounting a mortgage loan or charging "points" results in a twofold reduction of value of the equity investment. First, it increases the effective mortgage interest rate. Second, it increases the amount of equity investment and the percentage of total investment represented by equity that are required. The return on equity remains the same, but since the amount of equity required is increased, the equity dividend rate declines.

**Interest Rate Terminology.** The *nominal* rate of interest is the contract rate in the mortgage note. It is periodic interest payments divided by the face amount of loan outstanding, expressed as an annual rate.

The *effective* rate of interest is periodic interest payments divided by the amount of loan actually advanced and outstanding, expressed as an annual rate.

A *point* is one percentage point. The difference between an 8.5% rate and a 9.5% rate is one point; the difference between an 8.5% rate and a 9.0% rate is one-half point.

A *basis point* is one-hundredth of one percentage point. The difference between a 10.41% constant and a 10.73% constant is 32 basis points.

A *mortgage constant* is annual debt service (interest and amortization of principal) divided by the original principal amount of the loan (contract or actual), expressed as an annual percentage rate.

*Loan-to-Value Ratio*

This is the percentage of property value represented by the initial principal amount of the mortgage loan. Based on a combination of limits set by state or federal law and lender policy, it indicates the amount or percentage of mortgage loan that can or will be granted by the lender. The complement to the loan-to-value ratio is the percentage of equity investment required. In dollar terms, this is the down payment (usually but not always in cash) required of the borrower.

Loan-to-value ratios, and hence equity investment or down-payment ratios, are expressed as percentages of *value*, not of actual or contract sales price.

The higher the loan-to-value ratio, the lower the down payment requirement and the higher the leverage. A mortgage loan with a 70% loan-to-value ratio is one on which 70% of value will be loaned by the lender; 30% is required as a down payment. If the loan-to-value ratio is 80%, then the required equity investment or down payment is 20%. A 70% loan has a *leverage factor* of 3.3 (100%/30%); an 80% loan has a leverage factor of 5.0 (100%/20%).

All other factors remaining the same, a higher loan-to-value ratio means a higher equity dividend rate. This assumes that the rate of return on total investment is higher than the mortgage interest rate, and that trading on equity is therefore successful. Given the $200,000 property producing a $20,000 (10%) return and an 8.5% mortgage interest rate, the equity dividend rate is 13.5% for a mortgage with a 70% loan-to-value ratio. If the loan-to-value ratio is 80%, the equity dividend rate becomes:

| | | | |
|---|---|---|---|
| Total Investment: | 100% X .10 | = 10.00% | ($20,000) |
| Mortgage Interest: | 80% X .085 | = 6.80% | ($13,600) |
| Return on Equity: | 20% X $y$ | = 3.20% | ($ 6,400) |

$y = 3.20\% \div .20 = 16.0\%$ ($6,400/$40,000 = 0.16)

Equity return in dollars is lower but so is equity investment. What matters to the equity investor is the *rate of return* on his investment.

A higher loan-to-value ratio means higher leverage; it also means that the equity position is more vulnerable to a decline in property income. Equity return rates are susceptible to wider fluctuations as rate of return on total property investment varies.

A higher loan-to-value ratio means further that the total amount paid for and on the property over the term of the loan is greater, because the total amount of interest is greater. Annual debt service is also higher, thereby reducing cash throw-off to the (smaller) equity investment. The loan-to-value ratio does not affect the mortgage constant, however.

As a simplified example, consider the 70% and 80% non-amortized loans at 8.5% on the $200,000 property investment used earlier in this chapter, assuming a 20-year loan maturity. Annual mortgage interest at a 70% loan-to-value ratio is $11,900; over 20 years it totals $238,000. On an 80% loan, annual mortgage interest is $13,600, a total of $272,000 over 20 years. The borrower thus receives a higher rate of equity return on his investment, but pays a total of $34,000 for the privilege. It is not quite this simple, because of discounting future payments, but the basic point remains valid.

Similar results are obtained if a comparison of total debt service over 20 years is made between a 70% and an 80% amortized loan at 8.5%.

*Loan Maturity*

The maturity of a mortgage loan is the length of time over which it is to run, i.e., its term to maturity. A 15-year loan is one which is to be fully repaid at the end of 15 years, regardless of the method of repayment. Loan maturities are set by a combination of the limitations established by state or federal law and lender policy.

All other loan terms remaining the same, the longer the loan maturity is, the greater the total amount of mortgage interest the borrower will pay, regardless of the method of repayment or amortization. Assuming that the economic life of the property extends beyond the maturity of the loan (and lenders typically seek to protect themselves by granting loan maturities comfortably less than expected remaining economic life), then the longer the loan maturity, the greater the period over which trading on the equity can occur. Hence, the greater the present worth or value of the equity position will be.

Lengthening the maturity of amortized mortgages reduces annual debt service, and thus increases cash throw-off. This enhances the present worth of the equity position, even though a greater total amount of mortgage interest must be paid. For example:

If a $200,000 property with NOI of $23,000 (11.5%) has a 70% mortgage for 20 years at 8.5%, annual debt service is $14,579 and the mortgage constant is 10.41%. The Cash Throw-Off is $8,421 or an equity yield rate of 14.03%. This has been demonstrated in an earlier section.

If the loan term is extended to 25 years, monthly payments are $1,127.28 ($140,000 X .008052: Ellwood, page 89, column 6). Annual debt service is $13,527.36 (12 X $1,127.28) leaving a Cash Throw-Off of $9,472.64 ($23,000 − $13,527.36). This represents an equity dividend rate of 15.79% (9,473/$60,000).

The same process of equity yield rate calculation can be accomplished without using dollar figures, when the loan-to-value ratio is known but the principal amount of the mortgage is not. Here, the mortgage constant is 9.66% (12 × .008052).

| | | |
|---|---|---|
| Total Investment: | 100% × .115 | = 11.50% |
| Debt Service: | 70% × .0966 | = 6.76% |
| Return on Equity: | 30% × $y$ | = 4.74% |

$$y = 4.74\% \div .30 = 15.80\%$$

*Amortization*

Amortization is the periodic repayment or return of a principal sum over a specified period. All mortgage loans have *some* form of amortization because the debt is a contractual obligation that must be repaid. Even a "straight" loan on which only interest is paid until maturity has one lump-sum amortization payment at maturity, equal to the full principal amount of the loan (a 100% "balloon" payment). Basically amortization provisions divide mortgage loans into two types: fully amortized and partially amortized over the term of the loan.

**Fully Amortized Mortgage Loans.** These are by far the most common in the United States. Loans on income-producing properties sometimes call for annual, semi-annual, or quarterly payments over the life of the loan sufficient to amortize it fully at maturity, often on a straight-line basis. The most typical amortization pattern, however, is monthly.

*Level Payment Direct Reduction Amortization.* This is the usual amortization feature of fully amortized loans, most often on a monthly basis. Equal monthly dollar payments including both interest on the outstanding balance of the loan and a payment of principal are made over the term of the loan. The proportion of the monthly payment represented by interest declines regularly as principal is reduced, and the proportion represented by principal increases correspondingly.

The annual debt service is in effect a level ordinary annuity representing return on the investment (loan principal) at the mortgage interest rate and a sinking fund build-up of principal compounded at the same rate. The periodic payments required for any size loan can be calculated from a mortgage payment table or from a table of the Installment to Amortize One (Column 6 in Ellwood is compound interest tables).

Annual debt service is found by multiplying the monthly mortgage payment by 12. This is illustrated in previous examples in this chapter. The mortgage constant is derived from published mortgage constant tables, or by converting the Installment to Amortize One Factor (Column 6 in Ellwood's compound interest tables) to an annual figure: multiply the monthly factor by 12, the quarterly factor by 4, the semi-annual factor by 2.

**Partially Amortized Mortgage Loans.** When the loan is not fully amortized over its maturity, the portion of the loan principal outstanding at maturity must be repaid as one lump sum. Since this payment is larger than the periodic debt service payments, it is called a "balloon payment."

Partial amortization is often achieved by writing a loan for one maturity (say 20 years) but calculating debt service payments on the basis of a longer amortization period (say 25 years). This reduces annual debt service over the term of the loan, thereby increasing cash throw-off; the examples in the preceding section on Loan Maturity phenomenon. Since present or near-term dollars are worth more than long-term future dollars to the investor-borrower, partial amortization and higher cash throw-off may be attractive to him even though his total interest charges and "balloon" payment will also be higher. The income tax deductibility of interest charges is a further inducement; this is discussed in Chapter 18.

Investor-borrowers typically seek to maximize their cash throw-off to equity, in part by minimizing debt service. Partial amortization provisions in the mortgage loan help in this effort, and they also reduce the amount of capital "tied up" in the equity investment. The less equity investment the owner has in the property, the greater the leverage and the greater the opportunity for successful trading on equity.

Lenders, on the other hand, typically prefer full amortization loans because they provide a known, predictable flow of funds for reinvestment. They also offer greater protection by increasing the borrower's equity, and thereby reducing the lender's commitment, in the property more rapidly.

*Estimating the Balloon Payment.*[a] When a mortgage loan is only partially amortized over its contract term, the borrower-investor is frequently interested in knowing in advance how much the outstanding balance of the loan will be at contract maturity. This represents the "balloon payment" he will have to make.

Either the dollar amount of the balloon payment, or the percentage of original loan principal still outstanding, or both, can be calculated easily if the necessary data are available. The data for at least one must always be available, or the entire appraisal problem cannot be solved. The only real analytical requirement of the appraiser is to remember that the Installment to Amortize One factor is the reciprocal of the Present Worth of One per Annum factor at the same rate of discount, over the same number of payments. Then it is easily recognized that debt service is simply a level annuity whose present worth is the principal amount of the loan. This has already been demonstrated in Chapter 5, and reiterated earlier in this chapter.

---

[a]The author is deeply indebted to his colleague, Dr. Stephen D. Messner for making available the analytical techniques used in this section. To the author's knowledge, this is the first time that this simple but highly effective approach has appeared in print. Dr. Messner is Associate Professor of Finance and Real Estate and Director of the Center for Real Estate and Urban Economic Studies, in the School of Business Administration at the University of Connecticut.

Thus, the 25-year, level-monthly-payment mortgage loan of $140,000 at 8.5% interest has a mortgage constant of 0.096624 (12 × 0.008052). Annual debt service is $13,527.36, based on level monthly payments of $1,127.28.

This can be regarded as a 300-month level annuity of $1,127.28 per month, discounted at 8.5%. The Present Worth of One per Annum factor is 124.188570 (Ellwood, page 89, column 5). The present worth of $1,127.28 per month for 300 months, discounted at 8.5%, is $139,995.29 ($1,127.28 × 124.188570). The difference from $140,000 is the result of arithmetic rounding.

So far, the appraiser has not been told anything he doesn't already know. The important point has been the demonstration of the principle. Now, suppose the loan has a 20-year contract maturity. This means that there will still be five years' worth of payments left to amortize the loan fully when the balloon payment is due. The *amount* of the balloon payment, and the outstanding balance of the loan 20 years hence, is the present worth of 60 monthly payments (5 years' worth) of $1,127.28 discounted by the monthly Present Worth of One per Annum factor for 60 months at an 8.5% annual rate of discount. That factor is 48.741183 (Ellwood, page 89, column 5). The outstanding balance of the loan is therefore $54,944.96 ($1,127.28 × 48.741183).

Suppose, however, the appraiser does not have dollar figures to work with. The *percentage* of loan outstanding is the *ratio* of the 5-year monthly Present Worth of One per Annum factor at 8.5%, to the 25-year factor: 48.741183/124.188570 = 0.392477 or 39.25%. As a check against this result, $54,944.96/$140,000 = .0392464 or 39.25%. Thus, at the end of 20 years, 39.25% of the mortgage principal remains unpaid, and represents the "balloon payment."

A corollary problem frequently encountered, especially in mortgage-equity analysis, is to estimate the amount or percentage of mortgage loan that has been paid off during a specified period shorter than the full amortization period of the loan. This represents equity build-up, and is particularly important in solving for the Mortgage Coefficient in the Ellwood formulation. This, in turn, is essential in deriving both overall rates of return ($r$ and $R$) in the Ellwood analysis.

This percentage of loan paid off over a specified period (called $P$ in the Ellwood formula) is simply the *complement* of the percentage of principal still unpaid. In this example, it is 60.75% (100.00% − 39.25%), or 0.6075. The complement of the ratio of applicable Present Worth of One per Annum factors is easy to calculate, and this approach emphasizes the underlying appraisal and mathematical logic of the calculations the appraiser is making. This point is explored and illustrated further in Chapter 13.

*The Pattern of Loan Terms*

Every mortgage loan involves all four of the loan terms discussed above: interest rate, loan-to-value ratio, maturity, and amortization provisions. The entire package of these loan terms controls or determines the impact of the loan on the investment, and on the debt service or mortgage constant. Income-property mortgage loans are frequently the result of negotiations between borrower and lender, subject to the competitive influence of prevailing general money market and mortgage market conditions. The informed, prudent, and rational investor-borrower must know which terms are negotiable and which are not; which terms are variable and which are not; and how his cash flow from the property is affected by his conceding on one term to gain an apparent advantage on another. The appraiser needs this same knowledge to estimate the value or present worth of that cash flow through the eyes of the informed, prudent, rational investor.

Prevailing mortgage terms tend to vary by type of lender. The appraiser must identify the pattern of terms appropriate to the appraisal problem at hand. The more favorable these terms are to the borrower, the greater the opportunity for successful trading on equity. They represent one factor in the changing market environment surrounding the property that can be measured with reasonable accuracy. As with other market factors, a change in loan terms available influences the value of the property.

## Influence of Market Conditions and
## Operations on Mortgage Loan Terms

In addition to the limitations set by statutes and by lender policies, mortgage loan terms are influenced by three sets of market forces: money market, mortgage market, and real estate market. To be able to understand and interpret trends, and to be able to evaluate just what prevailing mortgage loan terms are, the appraiser must appreciate how supply and demand in each of these interrelated and often overlapping markets operate.

### Money Market

Because money is a universally desired and used good, the demand for it comes from an almost limitless variety of sources. Consumers, businesses, investors, and governments all compete for the available supply for short-term, intermediate, and long-term uses. Real estate purchaser-investors are therefore competing not only with one another for funds; but also with house buyers, securities buyers, business firms, and governments, and buyers of consumer goods.

Interest rates represent the price of borrowed money and serve to allocate the available supply among competing borrowers. Mortgage loan rates are part of the entire pattern of interest rates. If one form of lending becomes more attractive because it offers an increased rate, loan funds are mobile enough to move from other forms of lending (say mortgage loans) to the more lucrative one. Thus, mortgage loan rates must compete with other rates, or else the supply and the market becomes "tight." In the late 1960s, increasing demand and willingness to pay high rates on the part of government and business firms forced mortgage loan rates to record high levels. Even then mortgage loan funds became difficult to obtain.

Loanable funds come primarily from private savings accumulated in lending institutions (banks, life insurance companies) and in endowment and trust funds (union pension funds). Most of these lenders have latitude in placing their investment funds; only a few are limited in the outlets for their loans or equity investments. As a result, they tend to gravitate to the loans or investments that offer the greatest return commensurate with the risks they are willing to assume.

Many lenders are also empowered to make equity investments: in securities, in business, in real estate. When the competitive attractions of equity investing outweigh those of lending on long-term, fixed rate mortgages, their funds flow to equity outlets. Moreover, private savers may be attracted to direct investing (especially in securities, as happened in the mid and late 1960s) rather than saving, cutting down the supply of loanable funds from institutional lenders.

The appraiser therefore has to be informed about current money market conditions and trends. They have a direct impact on the availability of mortgage loan funds and the terms on which those funds are available. It does make a difference to real estate values what the United States government had to pay on its most recent issue of notes; it does make a difference what the prime rate is, and in which direction it is moving; it does make a difference how AT & T decides to raise $300 million, and what terms it has to pay; it does make a difference what proportion of mutual savings bank funds is going into securities or consumer loans, or what proportion of life insurance funds is going into equity investment.

*Mortgage Market*

A mortgage market is a loosely defined, relatively unorganized operation in which borrowers and lenders on the same general type(s) of property come together. It is not a definable place. Rather, it represents the sets of available alternatives that exist in the minds of potential borrowers and lenders at any given time. There is no such thing as *the* mortgage market. Instead, there are many interrelated and frequently overlapping sub-markets in which borrowers are competing for the same funds with one another, and with non-mortgage loan outlets.

The mortgage markets for income-producing properties tend to be broader in geographic scope than either residential mortgage markets or real estate markets. Many institutional lenders operate nationally. Generally speaking, the geographic area of the mortgage market increases as the credit rating of the borrower increases (and tender risk declines), as the amount of the loan increases, and as the collateral property is more specialized.

**Mortgage Market Intermediaries.** Although mortgage markets are not highly organized, there are organizations that act as intermediaries to bring borrower and lender together, and thereby facilitate the flow of funds from one area to another.

*Mortgage brokers* place mortgages by finding appropriate borrowers or willing lenders for a fee, which is usually a percentage (e.g., 0.5%) of the amount of the loan.

*Mortgage correspondents* act as agents for national lenders (usually life insurance companies) and make loan commitments for them in accordance with standards of acceptability established by the lender. They also frequently service the loans for the lender for an additional fee (e.g., 0.25-0.50% of principal amount per year).

*Mortgage bankers* place mortgage loans on their own behalf with their own funds, usually in the expectation of reselling the loans to national lenders at a profit. This sale of existing mortgages is termed "secondary market activity"; the original placement of a mortgage by a lender is "primary market activity." For a fee, the mortgage banker usually retains the servicing of the mortgages sold. Mortgage bankers frequently finance their mortgage originations with short-term loans from commercial banks in a process known as "mortgage warehousing."

**Functions of Mortgage Markets.** Mortgage markets function to allocate available loan funds among competing potential borrowers. They do this by setting interest rates and other loan terms in response to the forces of supply and demand.

Mortgage demand is essentially a derived demand; it is derived from the demand for real estate for use or as an investment. To analyze mortgage demand, it is necessary to study the forces that make up the demand for the type of property being appraised.

The supply of mortgage funds comes from institutional lenders, public agencies, and private (non-institutional) lenders. The key elements in this supply are the amount of money available to be loaned, competition from alternative mortgage and non-mortgage outlets, and lender policy.

**Sources of Mortgage Loan Funds: Characteristics and Policies.** A great variety of lenders and lending institutions participate in the financing of some or all types of income-producing properties. Some of the more important, and their general policies and scope of activities, are as follows:

*Commercial Banks.* These institutions lend on income-producing real estate of all types: apartments, retail stores, shopping centers, warehouses, industrial properties. They sometimes "participate" or share in loans between two or more institutions. Their loan terms are generally among the more conservative for institutional lenders: relatively low loan-to-value ratios and relatively short maturities. They tend to favor high-credit borrowers, not necessarily local. They are restricted in their geographic lending areas in many states. Competition for their loanable funds from short-term and intermediate-term business ("commercial") loans, and from highly lucrative consumer loans, is severe. Commercial banks often participate in secondary market activities as both buyers and sellers.

*Savings and Loan Associations.* The major source of residential mortgage lending in the United States, these institutions (known as "savings associations" or "cooperative banks" in some states) tend to concentrate on apartment loans among income-producing properties. They are usually local-market oriented in their lending, both by law and by policy. They occasionally make retail or commercial property loans, and sometimes participate with other lenders on especially large loans or loans on distant properties. Savings and loans are real estate-oriented, and there is only modest competition from non-mortgage lending outlets. Their loan terms are generally liberal: relatively high loan-to-value ratios and relatively long maturities.

*Mutual Savings Banks.* Although concentrated primarily in some eleven states in the northeastern and east north central United States, these institutions are a powerful force in income-property mortgage lending, especially on apartment and commercial properties. While limited by state laws in their area of primary lending, they are active both as participants with other lenders on more distant properties and as buyers on the secondary market. Their loan terms are relatively liberal, although loan-to-value ratios are usually not as generous as those of savings and loan associations. They have historically been major lenders on FHA-insured apartment property loans. In recent years, many mutual savings banks have made equity participation loans to guard against the risks of inflation. Non-real estate loans and investments became increasingly competitive for savings bank funds in the mid-1960s.

*Life Insurance Companies.* These are *the* source of income-producing property loans for many types of properties and borrowers. Large loans (over $500,000); high-credit, low-risk-property loans; and equity participation loans are their particular interests. They frequently engage in sale-lease back transactions as purchaser-lessors, and they have become deeply involved as equity investors in major developments: regional shopping centers, resort centers, industrial parks, new towns. They lend nationally, often through local mortgage companies or correspondents. Their terms are usually less liberal than those of savings and loans or mutual savings banks, but they have wide latitude in this respect. They can lend and invest in many different types of activities so that mortgage loans are constantly under competitive pressure to attract life insurance company funds.

*Trusts and Funds.* Pension, retirement, and endowment funds, together with trusts of various types, offer a good opportunity for high-credit, low-risk income property financing. These organizations need virtual assurance of steady income to meet their financial and legal obligations. Because they are income-tax exempt, they can and do concede slightly on interest rates to attract the highest quality borrowers and property loans. Their mortgages are typically "credit" loans. They lend nationally, and offer generally favorable terms to borrowers who can meet their standards. In many states, they may now make equity investments in real estate, which offers competition for mortgage lending.

*Mortgage Intermediaries.* Mortgage bankers and mortgage companies, as described above, initiate loans on all types of properties locally. However, they are influenced by the loan standards of life insurance companies, mutual savings banks and commercial banks, in particular. Such institutions are the most likely secondary market purchasers of mortgage company and mortgage banker originations. These firms are in the business of mortgage lending. Their loan terms will vary widely, depending on the type of property, location, borrower, and institution to which a secondary market sale is anticipated.

*Public Agencies.* This is a disparate group whose lending policies and loan terms vary considerably. It is possible here to note only a few to indicate their scope and range. The U.S. Small Business Administration makes real estate loans to qualified "small" businesses; the Federal Housing Administration, although primarily a residential mortgage insurer, may lend directly on apartment developments of specific types. State agencies frequently finance industrial properties on terms favorable to the lender in order to stimulate industrial development, as do many local industrial development groups and agencies.

*Other Lenders.* Small Business Investment Companies will make loans on "small" business properties of all types, usually confined to a local area, and typically including some form of equity participation, stock option, or convertible note for the SBIC. Some Real Estate Investment Trusts make mortgage loans, including hard-to-obtain land development loans. When they do, their geographic scope is broad, their terms of lending are flexible, and the type of property on which they lend is varied. Private individuals and groups of individuals (often organized in "syndicate" form) are a major but scattered and disorganized source of income-property mortgage loans. They frequently make high-risk loans at "appropriately" higher rates with other terms favorable to the lender. The loan terms usually depend on how anxious the seller is to dispose of the property, in the case of purchase-money mortgages.

## Real Estate Market

As noted in Chapter 2, the typical real estate sub-market for a particular type of property tends to be localized, narrow and somewhat uninformed. The market is stratified into sub-markets by type of property and by type of most probable purchaser-investor. These three characteristics—property type, most probable type of purchaser-investor, and geographic market area—influence the terms of lending by identifying the competition for loan funds, and the most probable type of lender.

**Type of Borrower or Investor.** Generally speaking, the better the credit rating of the most probable type of borrower-investor, the more favorable the loan terms to that borrower will be. In addition, the high-credit borrower or loan generally has access to a broader range of potential lenders. There are usually more alternative loan "packages" from which to choose as well.

*"Real Estate" Loans.* When the credit of the borrower or tenant is not particularly high, or the borrower is a corporation whose only significant asset is the real estate itself, then the property securing the loan becomes the chief consideration of the lender in making the loan decision, and in setting loan terms. Generally speaking, "real estate" loans are not available from life insurance companies, or pension funds and trusts, unless the property is especially marketable or rentable and located in a strong, well-established or growing area. The terms on "real estate" loans tend to be more favorable to the lender.

*"Credit" Loans.* These are also termed "paper transactions." When the credit of the borrower is high and actually backs the loan along with the real estate, or (more frequently) when the property is under long-term lease to a highly rated tenant or tenants and the rents are assigned to the mortgagee, the lender tends to look more to the credit aspects of the loan (the "paper") for security of payment than to the real estate itself. Such loans are particularly attractive to life insurance companies, pension funds, and trusts. They tend to carry loan terms more favorable to the borrower.

Mortgage insurance and lease insurance may sometimes increase the credit status of a loan, and thereby make it more attractive to lenders. This may make the difference in inducing them to consider it at all. The idea of both types of insurance or guarantee is to superimpose the higher credit rating of the insuror or guarantor on that of the borrower and/or tenant, and thereby gain more favorable loan terms for the borrower. FHA offers mortgage insurance on many types of apartment properties, as well as nursing homes. Private mortgage insurance is available on commercial and industrial as well as apartment properties from a few national and regional insurors, most notably the Commercial Loan Insurance Corporation of Milwaukee (a subsidiary of MGIC). The Small Business Administration has inaugurated a program of lease guarantee insurance for "small" business tenants to provide, among other things, better financing terms for lessor-borrowers, which are presumably shared with the tenants in the form of lower rentals. CLIC also has a private program of lease guarantee insurance with essentially the same objective: converting a "real estate" loan to a "credit" loan. The responsibility for payment of insurance premiums can have an impact on NOI.

**Type of Property.** Generally speaking, more favorable loan terms are available on well-located properties in well-established or growing areas; highly marketable or highly rentable properties; new, well-designed properties; properties in markets with strong demand and relatively little local market competition; properties with broad national or regional market appeal; and properties with a high degree of adaptability to alternative uses. Few properties have all of these characteristics, but the list can serve as a guide to the appraiser in identifying the most probable source(s) of mortgage loan funds and the most probable terms of lending.

**Geographic Location and Character of Market.** Major national lenders prefer to lend on properties in markets with strong and growing demand for the type of space involved. Some life insurance companies will not consider a "real estate" loan outside a major metropolitan market area, fearing difficulty in sale or rental in the case of default. These locational strictures are less severe for "credit" loans.

*Source of Information about Money*
*Markets and Mortgage Markets*

In order to appreciate the impact of money market conditions on mortgage financing trends and terms, and hence on income-producing property values, the appraiser should keep current with those market conditions. Reading one or more publications that present both data (current and historic) and analysis of market conditions will help. There is a wide variety to choose from. Some of the best and most commonly available are:

**Money Market Conditions.**
*Federal Reserve Bulletin* (monthly), Board of Governors, Federal Reserve System
*Real Estate Analyst* (occasional surveys), Roy Wenzlick and Co.
*Survey of Current Business* (monthly), U.S. Department of Commerce
*Wall Street Journal* (daily)
*Commercial and Financial Chronicle* (weekly)

**Mortgage Market Conditions.**
*Housing and Urban Development Trends* (bimonthly), U.S. Department of Housing and Urban Development
*Real Estate Analyst* (occasional studies), Roy Wenzlick and Co.
*Commercial and Financial Chronicle* (weekly)
*Banking* (monthly), American Bankers Association
*The Mortgage Banker* (monthly), Mortgage Bankers Association
*The Savings Banks Journal* (monthly), National Association of Mutual Savings Banks

*Savings and Loan News* (monthly), U.S. Savings and Loan League
*Mortgage Market Survey* (quarterly), National Association of Real Estate Boards
*National Real Estate Investor* (monthly)
*Architectural Forum*
*House and Home*

## Types of Real Estate Debt
## Financing Instruments

Although all mortgage loans are contracts that have many fundamental elements in common, there are several variations on the basic form that can affect the impact of financing on cash flow, and on rates of capitalization or discount, for income-producing properties. The appraiser should be familiar with the characteristics of each. He should be able to identify the type of mortgages most likely to be made in the given case—given the type of property, the most probable type of purchaser-borrower and lender, and current market conditions.

### Conventional Mortgage

This term applies to the usual, typical mortgage loan. It is a first lien, non-insured (or non-guaranteed), and a direct loan of funds from mortgagee to mortgagor. All other types of mortgages are variations or deviations from the conventional mortgage.

### Insured or Guaranteed Mortgages

FHA insures some types of apartment property loans, as well as some loans on other types of income properties such as nursing homes. In exchange for insurance of principal to the lender in the event of default by the borrower, FHA imposes underwriting standards on borrowers, and on properties offered as loan security, before the loan can qualify for insurance. Interest rate limitations as well as mortgagee performance standards are also imposed on lenders. The fee for FHA insurance is 0.5% of the outstanding principal balance on the loan, over and above the mortgage interest rate charged.

Private mortgage insurance or guarantees are also available on qualified income-producing properties that meet insurors' risk and underwriting standards. A premium similar to that of FHA is charged, but without FHA's accompanying limitations on loan terms. In both cases, the effort is to reduce the risk of lending on otherwise unattractive or even unacceptable transactions, borrowers, or properties. The result is designed to be greater availability of mortgage loan funds on the insured transactions, and on terms more attractive to the borrower, by substituting or superimposing the credit of the insuror for that of the borrower.

## Purchase-Money Mortgage

The usual mortgage loan is an advance of funds by a third party (the lender) to the purchaser-borrower. With a purchase-money mortgage, however, no money changes hands. The seller accepts the buyer's promise to pay, backed by a pledge of the transferred property, as part of the purchase price. Such mortgages are usually extended to enable the seller to obtain his asking price, or to dispose of a hard-to-move property. Because of this motivation, there is no regular pattern to purchase-money mortgage loan terms. Frequently, the seller will take back a second (junior lien) purchase-money mortgage to make up any difference between available first-mortgage financing and the purchaser's available equity funds.

## Junior Liens

Whatever its precise legal form, a mortgage represents a specific lien against the real estate securing the loan. This means that the lender can force the sale of the property in the event of default by the borrower, and use the sale proceeds to satisfy its accumulated claim under the note, plus costs of collection and foreclosure. More than one lien, and therefore more than one mortgage, can be placed against a property. However, liens are satisfied in the event of foreclosure and forced sale in strict order of their priority; the first lien is fully paid off before anything is paid on the second lien, and so forth. The same priority of claim relates to property income available to meet debt service.

Mortgage liens subordinate to the first mortgage are junior liens, commonly called "junior mortgages." The number attached to the title of a mortgage describes the priority of the lien it represents: First mortgage, second mortgage, third mortgage, etc. Junior mortgages inherently require the mortgagee to assume more risk and logically call for more demanding terms, especially higher interest rates and shorter maturities. This is usually the case when junior mortgage funds are *borrowed* from third-party lenders. However, as noted above, purchase-money mortgages are frequently junior liens. Their terms tend to reflect the relative anxieties of buyer and seller to complete the sale transaction.

Nearly all mortgage loans from financial institutions are first mortgages. High-quality, low-risk loans, whether "real estate" or "credit," rarely require or involve junior mortgage financing. The low-credit-rated, high-risk, even marginal transaction usually includes junior mortgage financing, frequently because the first-mortgage lender seeks protection in a low loan-to-value ratio loan. Aside from junior lien purchase-money mortgages, most junior mortgages are made by noninstitutional lenders: private individuals or groups, risk-taking syndicates, and some public or quasipublic agencies in special cases (e.g., a local industrial development agency loan to attract a new industry).

## Equity Participation Loans

Since the mid-1960s, certain institutional lenders have increasingly required some form of "participation" in the anticipated future income of the mortgaged property, over and above all other normal loan terms, as part of the price of granting a loan. The ostensible objective is to protect the lender against the purchasing power risk represented by the impact of inflation on fixed interest returns. Life insurance companies, mutual savings banks, and commercial banks in particular have insisted on so-called "income participations" whenever their relative bargaining power vis-a-vis the borrower has permitted them to do so.

Income participations usually last for the contract maturity of the loan, regardless of prepayment by the borrower. Indeed, prepayment under such loans is either forbidden or severely penalized by a prepayment premium.

Income participation arrangements usually take one of three basic forms, each of which influences (by decreasing) the NOI produced by the property and the Cash Throw-Off available to cover the equity investment.

**Participation in Gross Receipts.** Some participations take the form of a percentage of gross receipts, usually a fixed percentage (e.g., 5-10%) of the *excess* of effective gross income over the stabilized forecast amount or the current level of actual collections. In this way, the lender is participating in the additional income generated by the property, whether through inflation or any other cause. This form of participation typically lasts for the maturity of the mortgage loan.

**Participation in Net Operating Income.** A second form of income participation is for the lender to share in a fixed percentage (e.g., 25-50%) of Net Operating Income. The rationale here is that inflationary gains in receipts may be somewhat offset by increased operating expenses. The net income participation may be on the entire NOI, or sometimes on the excess of actual NOI over the stabilized forecast amount. This form of participation also usually remains in effect over the maturity of the loan.

**Participation in Equity.** Sometimes, the lender receives a fixed percentage of the equity in the property, with or without an additional investment of funds beyond the amount of the mortgage loan. In this case, the lender receives a percentage of NOI or Cash Throw-Off *beyond* the maturity of the loan, and also participates in a fixed proportion on the proceeds of any resale or refinancing of the property.

*Leasing as a Financing Device*

Although it does not involve a loan of funds, a long-term lease can have the effect for the tenant-occupant of 100% financing of the property over the term of the lease. The tenant (lessee) gains by having fixed, known occupancy costs, except under a net lease. The lessee's funds are available for use in the business, and rental payments are fully deductible for income tax purposes. The lessee loses participation in any long-term capital gain that might be realized on resale. He loses occupancy and title to any leasehold improvements that might be made at the expiration of the lease. Finally, he usually pays somewhat higher annual occupancy costs than are represented by operating expenses plus debt service.

The landlord (lessor) has the advantage of a generally higher rate of return than is associated with mortgage interest rates. He has the prospect of capital gain on resale, and title to the property and any leasehold improvements at the expiration of the lease. The lessor has the disadvantage of bearing fully any decline in value experienced by the property. He risks a loss of potential income because of a contractual commitment in a rising rental market, and potentially declining NOI with rising operating expenses, unless the lease is "net" or fully escalated.

### Refinancing

It is frequently possible for a borrower to renegotiate a mortgage loan, either on the expiration of an existing loan, or by using part of the proceeds of the new loan to pay off the outstanding balance on an existing loan. The existing mortgage must permit prepayment in order to make refinancing possible.

When mortgage loan terms on the current market become more favorable to the borrower, refinancing can have the effect of reducing annual debt service and thus increasing cash throw-off. Refinancing also allows the borrower to recover some of his equity build-up in the property from prior amortization payments, without immediate income tax liability. Even in tight mortgage market conditions, this has attractions for equity investors.

**Wrap-Around Mortgage.** One refinancing device employed during the late 1960s involved the use of a second mortgage from the original mortgagee; or the assumption of an existing mortgage by a new mortgagee when the existing mortgage could not or would not be paid off, and the writing of a new mortgage on the entire property. In either case, this device was used in a period of increasing interest rates and tight money, when existing mortgages carried lower-than-current-market interest rates. The mortgagor paid the *current* rate (e.g., 8.5%) on the full amount of the new financing while the existing mortgage assumed by the new mortgagee carried a lower rate (e.g., 6%). The *effective* rate earned by the new mortgagee on the amount of cash actually advanced was thus in excess of the nominal rate on the larger mortgage debt outstanding. The borrower was frequently willing to pay this higher interest rate and accompanying higher debt service in order to extract "tax-free" dollars from the property immediately. The new mortgage was "wrapped around" the existing mortgage; hence the term.

### Influence of Mortgage Financing on Value and Valuation

Mortgage loan terms and mortgage loan availability on the market do affect and influence value: both Investment Value and Market Value. They influence the present worth of the forecast future-income stream in several ways, and enter into the appraiser's judgments and conclusions at several stages of the income-capitalization process.

## Market Conditions

Value is a function of the interaction of the existing forces of market supply and demand as of the valuation date. The availability of mortgage loan funds and the terms on which they are available for the most probable type of purchaser-borrower and from the most probable type of lender, for the type of property being appraised, are an integral part of the market environment surrounding and influencing value. As market facts, mortgage lending and its terms must be included in value estimation.

## Impact on Cash Throw-Off
## and Cash Flow

Cash Throw-Off is Net Operating Income *less* Annual Debt Service. The terms of the mortgage loan directly influence the size of annual debt service, and therefore directly influence the size of forecast Cash Throw-Off to be capitalized into present worth of the equity position.

## Impact on Amount of Equity Investment

The loan-to-value ratio of the mortgage dictates the amount of initial equity investment required. Amortization provisions in the loan influence the amount and pattern of equity build-up during the income-projection period.

## Impact on Rate of Return
## on the Investment

**Discount Rate.** Mortgage financing terms are critical to the estimation of a discount rate via the Band of Investment Approach, as demonstrated in Chapter 9. Discount rate estimation via Market Comparisons uses the actual experience of similar, competitive properties in the current local market. Since the vast majority of these transactions also include mortgage financing, there is an implicit and direct influence of mortgage financing terms on the indicated discount rate developed.

**Overall Rate.** When overall rates are developed and used, as also discussed in

Chapter 9, the analysis requires the use of actual market transactions. The bulk of these will also reflect typical patterns of mortgage financing.

*Impact on Equity Returns*

Both cash throw-off to equity and the amount of equity involved ($I$ and $V$, respectively, in the formula $R = I/V$) are directly influenced by mortgage loan terms. The equity dividend rate derived by dividing cash throw-off by equity investment is therefore a function (in part) of mortgage loan terms. Equity dividend rates are part of the entire pattern of investment rates of return in the money and mortgage markets. The acceptable and competitive level of equity yields necessary to attract investment funds is influenced in part by mortgage interest rates.

The equity dividend rate is also a function of leverage or trading on equity. The loan-to-value ratio and amortization provisions in the mortgage loan influence the extent to which the leverage can be exercised by the investor. The mortgage interest rate is one determinant of whether the use of leverage or trading on equity will be successful and profitable to the investor.

**Review Exercises**

1. What is the leverage factor in an 80% mortgage loan?
2. How many basis points are represented by a 5.25% discount of a mortgage loan? How many points?
3. A mortgage loan of $75,000 has just been made on a property valued at $125,000. The interest rate is 7.75%, and the maturity is 15 years. Monthly amortization payments are based on a 22-year maturity.
   a. What is the indicated loan-to-value ratio?
   b. What is the mortgage constant?
   c. What is the annual debt service?
   d. What will be the dollar amount of the balloon payment 15 years hence?
   e. What percentage of the original principal will have been paid off when the loan matures in 15 years?
4. In the example used in question 3, what would happen to annual debt service if the loan were fully amortized in 15 years?
5. How much total interest is paid on a 75% loan on a $100,000 property if level monthly payments are made at 8% interest for 17 years?
   a. How much total interest would be paid if the maturity were reduced to 14 years? What would happen to annual debt service in this event?
   b. How much total interest would be paid if the maturity remained at 17 years, but the loan-to-value ratio became 80%? What would happen to annual debt service in this event?
6. An income property is producing a net return *on* the total investment of 11%.

The purchaser has several alternative financing patterns from which to choose. They are:
   a 70% loan-to-value at 8%;
   a 75% loan-to-value ratio at 8.25%; or
   an 80% loan-to-value ratio at 9%.
Ignoring amortization and loan maturity, which would he choose? Why?


## Supplementary Readings

Henry A. Babcock, "The Appraiser and Mortgage Lending," *The Real Estate Appraiser*, Volume 33, Number 2, February 1967.

E. Norman Bailey, "Real Estate Investment Trusts: An Appraisal," *The Appraisal Journal*, Volume 34, Number 4, October 1966.

Jerome J. Dasso, William N. Kinnard, Jr., and Stephen D. Messner, "Participation Loan Financing: Part I," *The Real Estate Appraiser*, Volume 37, Number 2, March-April 1971.

T.C. Hitchings, Jr., "Fluctuating Terms May Affect Values," *The Real Estate Appraiser*, Volume 35, Number 3, May-June 1969.

Sanders A. Kahn, Frederick E. Case, and Alfred Schimmel, *Real Estate Appraisal and Investment* (New York: Ronald Press, 1963), Chapters 19 and 24, Appendix L.

William N. Kinnard, Jr., *A Guide to Appraising Apartments,* third edition (Chicago: Society of Real Estate Appraisers, 1973), pp. 41-49.

William N. Kinnard, Jr., "The Financial Logic of Investment Property Appraising," The Real Estate Appraiser, Volume 35, Number 3, May-June 1969.

William N. Kinnard, Jr. and Stephen D. Messner, *Industrial Real Estate,* second edition (Washington: Society of Industrial Realtors, 1971), Chapters 8 and 9.

George Molinari, "Capitalization Rates and Incentive Financing," *The Appraisal Journal*, Volume 37, Number 3, July 1969.

E.W. Stunard, "Capitalization Approach and Financing," *The Real Estate Appraiser*, Volume 33, Number 5, May 1967.

**Notes**

1. See the discussions in American Institute of Real Estate Appraisers, *The Appraisal of Real Estate*, fifth edition (Chicago: American Institute of Real Estate Appraisers, 1967), especially Chapters 16-18; and in A.A. Ring, *The Valuation of Real Estate*, second edition (Englewood Cliffs, N.J.: Prentice-Hall, 1970), Chapter 21.

# 8

# Rates of Capitalization and Rates of Return

## Nature of Rates of Capitalization

Rates of capitalization are *ratios* expressing a relationship between annual *net* income and present worth (value) or sales price. They are usually expressed as annual percentage rates, but they are expressed as decimal figures in all present-worth calculations. Because the income generated by income-producing real estate can take different forms and may be measured at different levels of "net-ness," there are different rates of capitalization which are peculiarly applicable to these different components of net income. Each has specific applicability to a particular income component, and each is identified by a different label. Indeed, several labels or terms are in current usage to refer to each, adding to some of the confusion in appraisal literature and analysis.

### *Importance of Rates in the Capitalization Process*

Chapter 4 explained the rationale of the income capitalization or discounting process, and outlined the steps to be followed applying it to the valuation of an income-producing property. Since the value derived through capitalization is the present worth of a forecast future stream divided by a rate of discount or multiplied by a distant factor $(V = I/R)$, the appraiser must identify the amount and character of that income stream, as well as the rate(s) or factor(s) at which it is to be discounted. He must also understand the discounting process, so as to be able to identify the appropriate compound-interest or discount factor to use. Chapter 5 presented the mathematical and financial logic of compound interest and discounting, and explained the mechanics of capitalization and discounting.

Income estimation and forecasting produce one major category of inputs required to put discounting to work in present worth estimation. The underlying principles and techniques of income forecasting for income-producing real estate were the topic of Chapter 6. Pointing out the important fact that in every income-property appraisal there is both a periodic future income stream and a future reversion to forecast and then discount to present worth; Chapter 6 then proceeded to identify the considerations of timing, duration, and variability that must be combined with quantity to make appropriate income forecasts. The different types of income flows and their respective roles in appraisal analysis were also considered.

The second category of inputs necessary to apply discounting in appraisal analysis has to do with rates of return: *on* and *of* the capital investment. Chapter 5 introduced the notion of mortgage debt financing terms and their influence on real estate investment decisions. It was noted that they have a peculiar impact on both required and anticipated rates of return on income-property investments, as well as on the cash flows produced by those investments. That presentation was a necessary background to the topic of this chapter and the three that follow it: the derivation and uses of rates of capitalization and rates of discount in appraisal analysis.

This topic concentrates on the identification and measurement of the appropriate $R$ to use in the valuation of the property being appraised. In point of fact, $R$ is frequently developed as a composite of several component rates, weighted by the relative significance of the components of the forecast future income receipts to which they apply. Many different rates of return or discount are potentially useful to the income-property appraiser. Overall Rates and Discount Rates are considered in Chapter 9. Capital Recovery Rates are the topic of Chapter 10, while the discussion in Chapter 11 focuses on Capitalization Rates and Factors. After the meaning, derivation, and uses of each of these is considered in turn, the whole capitalization process is put together and the several alternative techniques available to process future income receipts to value estimates for income properties are illustrated in Part III.

So much time and space are devoted to rate derivation because there are several different rates and applications of those rates that are essential for the appraiser to understand. Present worth or value estimates cannot be supported unless the appraiser can justify the answer to "By what?", as well as "How much?" and "How?"

**Basis for Comparisons.** Rates of capitalization represent one basis for comparing and valuing comparable, competitive properties. They represent the rate of return *on* the investment. It should be carefully borne in mind that income-producing properties most probably attract purchaser-investors who compare returns and risks on competing investments in deciding whether and where to invest their money. Money is being invested and must earn a competitive rate of return (or at least promise to do so) in order to attract investors. This is why a rate of return must be paid. It is necessary to overcome the Opportunity Cost of foregoing alternative investments and of giving up liquidity.

A rate of return can be paid because the investment offers the prospect of *net* income in excess of operating and/or holding costs. Gross income estimates can also be used as a basis for comparisons, as in the use of the Gross Income Multiplier. Gross income forecasts are not used in income capitalization, however.

**Descriptions of Purchaser-Investor Behavior.** Appraisal analysis is supposed to reflect the behavior and thinking of the most probable, typically informed, prudent, and rational purchaser-investor. For analytical purposes, however, it is frequently both desirable and necessary to use measures, such as rates of capitalization, that do not correspond exactly and directly with measures or concepts used by participants in the income-producing real estate market. The important point is that the tools and concepts used by the appraiser should *describe* adequately the behavior of purchaser-investors and serve as a basis for measuring present worth or value defensibly.

**Impact on Present Worth and Value.** Rates of capitalization are important determinants of the final value estimate. It has been demonstrated in Chapter 5 and 7 that the lower the rate applied to a given income flow, the higher will be the present worth estimate; the higher the rate, the lower the present worth. Thus, it is critical to derive rates of capitalization that are accurate representations of the hazards and advantages of the forecast income flow, as perceived by the most probable type of purchaser-investor. To carry out this important task, the appraiser continually turns to the appropriate current sub-market for information and guidance.

*Rate Terminology*

As noted in Chapter 4, there is both confusion and variety in the use of rate terminology in appraising. This presentation is a review of the terms introduced in Chapter 4. In some instances, the usage here represents new or different terms and labels. The basic objective of technical terminology is to be descriptive of the phenomenon it identifies, unequivocal, and unique (in the sense that a term is not confused with or a duplicate of another). The suggested use of "market rental" in place of the more traditional but potentially misleading "economic rent" in Chapter 6 is an example of one attempt to meet these standards. Throughout the remainder of this book, the terms applied to different rates of capitalization are intended to meet these standards. Following are the terms used here.

*Rate of capitalization:* any annual percentage rate applied to an annual income flow or reversion to convert it into a present worth or value estimate.

*Rate of discount:* any annual percentage rate applied at compound interest to a future income payment (flow or lump sum) to convert it to a present worth estimate.

*Overall rate (Overall rate of capitalization):* an annual percentage rate that expresses the relationship between Net Operating Income and present worth or value for the entire investment or property. In mortgage-equity analysis (especially the Ellwood formulation), this is also termed the Composite Rate or Composite Overall Rate. This label reflects the fact that it incorporates prorated capital appreciation or depreciation along with Net Operating Income.

*Discount rate:* the annual percentage rate that reflects the competitive market rate of return on an investment. This is what traditional appraisal writing calls the "interest rate." "Discount rate" is used to distinguish a rate of return on an investment from the rate of interest on borrowed funds, most especially the mortgage interest rate or mortgage rate of interest. The Discount Rate is the rate at which the net income representing the return *on* the investment in real estate (both land and improvements) is discounted to derive a present worth estimate. It is also the base rate at which future lump-sum reversions are discounted to present worth estimates.

*Capital recovery rate:* the annual percentage rate at which invested capital is recovered at compound interest over a specified income projection period. This represents the rate at which the investor receives a return *of* a portion of his investment in the real estate.

*Capitalization rate:* the annual percentage rate at which income attributable to, or available to cover, the investment in the recoverable portion of income-producing real estate is discounted or capitalized into a present worth estimate for that portion of the entire investment. This rate is frequently applied to income available to cover the investment in improvements, especially in the traditional residual techniques of capitalization. The Capitalization Rate is the sum of the Discount Rate and the Capital Recovery Rate. Its reciprocal is a discount *Factor*; examples are the Inwood (Level Annuity) Factor, the Hoskold Factor, and the Ring Factor. A mortgage constant is a Capitalization Rate. A Present Worth of One per Annum Factor is a Capitalization Factor.

*Rate of interest:* the annual percentage rate charged on borrowed funds. Because of possible confusion with traditional appraisal terminology, it is wise to avoid use of the unmodified term "interest rate." Thus, the annual interest charge on a mortgage might be referred to as the "mortgage rate of interest" or the "mortgage interest rate" to avoid ambiguity.

## General Characteristics of Rates Used in Appraising Income Properties

### Overall Rates

The application of an Overall Rate to Net Operating Income is known as Direct Capitalization. Since NOI includes both return *on* the entire property or investment at the appropriate Discount Rate, and return *of* the recoverable portion of the investment at the Capital Recovery Rate, Direct Capitalization via the Overall Rate is feasible *provided* the specifications for estimation of a supportable Overall Rate are met.

**Direct Capitalization Requirements.** The Overall Rate must represent what informed, prudent, and rational investors are requiring and obtaining for similar, competitive property investments in the current market. "Similar" refers to similarity with respect to *risk* and *duration* of income or investment return.

The market transactions data used to derive the Overall Rate must be open-market sales of similar, competitive properties with similar income streams representing the same types and levels of risks as the subject property. Moreover, the income projection period and the amount and character of the forecast reversion must be essentially the same as those forecast for the subject. The less similar to the subject's the comparable properties' income stream and reversion characteristics are, the less applicable Direct Capitalization via an Overall Rate will be. This point is developed further in the discussion of estimating Overall Rates in Chapter 9.

The Composite Rate, which is a variant of an Overall Rate, is particularly applicable in mortgage-equity analysis, and most especially in the Ellwood formulation. It provides for both a competitive rate of return *on* the investment over the income projection period, and capital recovery through a combination of mortgage amortization and capital appreciation or depreciation in the reversion on resale. Ellwood's *R* is divided directly into Net Operating Income (*d*) to derive a present worth estimate; this is Direct Capitalization.

**Weighted Averages.** Overall Rates are weighted averages. In traditional *physical* residual techniques of capitalization, the Overall Rate is the weighted average of the Discount Rate on the investment in site (non-depreciable and hence non-recoverable except as a reversion), and the Capitalization Rate on the investment in the improvements (including capital recovery over the remaining economic life of the improvements). The weights are the relative percentages of the entire investment represented by the site and the improvements. In mortgage-equity analysis, the Overall Rate is the weighted average of the Equity Yield Rate and the Mortgage Constant (which presumably includes capital recovery through amortization). The weights are the percentages of the total investment represented by the mortgage principal and the equity investment. In both instances, there is an implicit assumption that there will be no change in the value of the reversion.

**Income Multipliers.** The reciprocals of Overall Rates are Factors which might be called "net income multipliers." This is a potentially misleading term and is not recommended for appraisal usage. Nevertheless, it is mechanically possible to multiply by the reciprocal of an Overall Rate and obtain the same result. For example, assume a property is producing an annual Net Operating Income of $15,000, and the market-derived Overall Rate for this type of property is 12.5%. The reciprocal factor to apply to NOI would then be 8.0 (100%/12.5% = 8.0). Thus:

$$\$15,000/.125 = \$120,000$$
$$\$15,000 \times 8.0 = \$120,000$$

*Gross Income Multipliers.* One unit of comparison or measurement in the Direct Sales Comparison analysis for value estimation is the Gross Income Multiplier. The GIM and its use are discussed in detail in Chapter 16. By analyzing recent sales of similar, competitive properties producing gross incomes at competitive rentals and with similar flows and proportions of "other" income, the appraiser may derive a ratio between annual gross income (potential or effective) and sales price. This ratio can be multiplied by the forecast gross income for the property being appraised to develop one indication of value. This GIM is a factor, and, mathematically, it can be converted into a rate by taking its reciprocal. It is sometimes erroneously called a "gross capitalization rate" and considered usable in income capitalization. Net income forecasts are required for capitalization in appraisal analysis, however.

## Discount Rates

As a rate of return *on* investment ("investment rate of return"), the Discount Rate is applied to that portion of the investment return which does *not* include capital recovery or amortization. It is the base rate of return on invested capital in the property, and other rates of capitalization (e.g., Overall Rate, Capitalization Rate) build upon it.

The Discount Rate is applied directly to income attributable to, or available to cover, the investment in land or site. Land does not depreciate systematically, although obviously its value can increase or decrease over time, and no provision for capital recovery of an investment in land is provided. Thus, if a site has an annual rental value of $3,400 and the market-derived Discount Rate is 8.5%, then the present worth of that income stream (and hence the value of the site) is $40,000 (3,400/.085 = $40,000). This is capitalization in perpetuity. It carries the assumption that the forecast income stream will remain level indefinitely, as will the market price of the site.

The Discount Rate applied to both site and improvements in the same property will necessarily be the same. The investment in the property cannot be separated except for analytical purposes by the appraiser, and the dollars of net income assigned to the site or to the improvements must represent the same rate of return on the investment. The Discount Rate is labeled $i$ in the Ellwood formulation.

## Capital Recovery Rates

Required information for the appraiser before the applicable Capital Recovery Rate can be estimated include (1) amount (dollars) or proportion (percentage) of total investment represented by the portion of the total property investment to be recovered; (2) the time period ($n$) over which capital recovery is to occur; and (3) the method of providing the capital recovery.

The Capital Recovery Rate is the annual amount of capital recovery to be provided, expressed as an annual percentage of the total amount of investment to be recovered. For example, if annual capital recovery installments (the amount of net income receipts allocated to capital recovery) are $3,500 and the amount to be recovered over the capital recovery period is $70,000, then the Capital Recovery Rate on a straight-line basis is 5% ($3,500/$70,000 = 0.05).

**Amount to be Recovered.** Capital recovery is required whenever the most probable expectation of the typically informed, prudent, and rational purchaser-investor is that the amount of the reversion in dollars (usually as the proceeds of resale) will be *less than* the original amount of the investment in the property. This is not necessarily an accurate representation of investor expectations. It must be recalled that much of appraisal analysis evolved during the declining markets of the 1930s, when capital appreciation at resale was virtually unthinkable. Capital recovery, then, is a periodic payment included as part of NOI to compensate the investor for an anticipated decline in property value at the end of the income projection period.

In phsyical residual techniques of capitalization, Capital Recovery Rates are applied to that portion of the investment in the property represented by the improvements. These are supposed to depreciate, lose utility, and lose their capacity to produce net income at a competitive rate with the passage of time. The time period over which capital recovery of the investment in the improvements occurs is their Remaining Economic Life. At the end of that period, they are anticipated to have a net value of zero, since they are forecast to add nothing to the value of the site if it were vacant and available to be put to its Highest and Best Use.

In mortgage-equity analysis, Capital Recovery Rates are applied to the forecast difference between present worth or value of the property, and the anticipated or forecast amount of the proceeds of resale at the end of the income projection period. Capital recovery occurs only when the value of the property is forecast to be less on resale than its present worth.

It should be noted that mortgage amortization is also a form of capital recovery. The periodic, usually increasing, portions of debt service that repayment of the principal in a form of capital recovery. By the end of the mortgage maturity term, the lender will have recovered 100% of his original capital (loan funds) under a fully amortized loan. This is necessary because on maturity of the loan the lender's interests in the mortgaged property are extinguished.

**Mathematics of Capital Recovery Rates.** Capital recovery payments need not be level amounts. Indeed, mortgage amortization payments follow a schedule of continually increasing amounts with each monthly or annual payment. Similarly, level annuity income flows capitalized via the Present Worth of One per Annum factor also provide for non-level, continually increasing repayments of capital over the income projection period. With access to, and a working understanding of, the compound interest factor tables discussed in detail in Chapter 5, the appraiser can treat any form of capital recovery stream with an appropriate *rate*.

All Capital Recovery Rates can be treated mathematically as Sinking Fund rates. It will be recalled from the discussion in Chapter 5 that a Sinking Fund Rate is a factor which enables the analyst to identify the periodic level deposits required to be made and left on deposit to accumulate at compound interest for a specified time period in order to accumulate to a specified capital sum. In the case of capital recovery payments, the specified capital sum is the amount of

\

forecast decline in property value to be recovered over the income projection period. The rate of interest at which periodic compounding is to occur is specified in the identification of the capital recovery method to be employed: it is the Discount Rate in Level Annuity (Inwood) capitalization; it is the "safe rate" in Sinking Fund capitalization; and it is *zero* in Straight-Line capitalization.

*Straight-Line Capital Recovery.* This method produces the same numerical results as a sinking fund compounded at a *zero* rate of interest. For example, suppose that the $70,000 to be recovered in the illustration above is to be recovered on a straight-line basis. The indicated rate of capital recovery as shown above is 5% when the capital recovery period is 20 years, or when the annual capital recovery payments are $3,500. If $3,500 were deposited in a safe deposit box each year for 20 years, the accumulated sum would be $70,000, which is the sum to be recovered. This is not to say that the investor will actually do this. What he does with the $3,500 portion of NOI representing capital recovery is a matter of indifference to the appraiser. The important point is that straight-line capital recovery can be represented mathematically as a sterile income stream earning zero interest.

*Sinking Fund Capital Recovery.* In this method of providing for capital recovery, it is assumed that the portion of NOI represented by capital recovery payment *is* deposited in a sinking fund to earn compound interest at the "safe rate" over the income projection period. Then, at the end of the period, the total accumulation of principal deposits and compound interest will equal the amount of capital loss to be recovered by the investor.

For example, assume that the $70,000 to be recovered over 20 years in the illustration above was to be recovered through a sinking fund accumulating annually (at the end of the period) at 5%. The annual sinking fund factor at 5% for 20 years (Ellwood, page 36, column 3) is 0.030243. Multiplying this factor by $70,000, the amount of capital to be recovered over 20 years, yields an annual capital recovery payment of $2,117.01. If this amount were deposited annually at the end of each year and left to earn compound interest at an annual rate of 5%, it would total $70,000 at the end of 20 years. The Capital Recovery Rate in this example is 3.02%, as opposed to the 5% required in straight-line capital recovery. If compounding at the same rate is assumed, then it takes fewer dollars from NOI each year to provide for full recovery of the $70,000 in 20 years. As a result, more of NOI is available as a return *on* investment, and its present worth is therefore higher. It does make a difference how capital recovery is treated, and it therefore does make a difference what the relationship between present worth of the property and the forecast amount of the reversion is forecast to be.

*Level Annuity Capital Recovery.* Practically speaking, there really is no Capital Recovery Rate as such in level annuity capitalization. As previously demonstrated in earlier chapters, the present worth of an ordinary level annuity is found by multiplying the annual amount of the annuity by the appropriate Present Worth of One per Annum Factor for the given rate of discount, over the specified number of periods. The Present Worth of One per Annum Factor, and its reciprocal the Installment to Amortize One Factor, have built into them the full recovery of the principal sum invested over the income projection period.

Mathematically, it can be demonstrated that the Installment to Amortize One, which is the Capitalization Rate for a level annuity, is a composite of the Discount Rate and the Sinking Fund Factor at that rate, over the specified income projection period. For example, suppose that the $70,000 in forecast capital loss referred to in preceding sections were to be recovered in annual installments over 20 years, and the Discount Rate were 9%. The Present Worth of One per Annum Factor at 9% annually for 20 years is 9.128546 (Ellwood, page 100, column 5). Its reciprocal, found in column 6 on the same page in Ellwood, is the Installment to Amortize One: 0.109546. This could be regarded as the Capitalization Rate for a level annual income stream, discounted at 9% for 20 years. The 20-year Sinking Fund Factor at 9% is 0.019546 (Ellwood, page 100, column 3). If this Sinking Fund Factor is added to the Discount Rate, the sum is the Installment to Amortize One Factor: 0.019546 + 0.09000 = 0.109546.

If the appraiser's problem were to identify the level annual payment which, if deposited to earn compound interest at 9% per year for 20 years, would accumulate to $70,000 at the end of 20 years, then the answer would be found by multiplying $70,000 times 0.019546: $1,368.22. Note that this is lower than the installment required to recover the $70,000 in 20 years under either straight-line capital recovery or sinking-fund capital recovery with a "safe rate." As a result, more dollars in any given NOI are available to provide a return *on* investment when level-annuity capital recovery is used than with any other method of capital recovery. Capitalized at the same Discount Rate, this larger return on investment has a higher present worth.

Investors rarely think or behave in this fashion. They certainly do not deposit the proceeds of capital recovery at the Discount Rate, unless, of course, they are investment portfolio managers placing inflows of funds into new investments at going market rates. It does not matter what the investor does with the proceeds. The point is that he has the opportunity to behave in this way, and the mathematical formulation of the Present Worth of One per Annum presumes that time-discounting at the Discount Rate accounts for this. Capital recovery is not time-discounted. If $100,000 is invested today and is forecast to be recoverable over the income projection period, only $100,000 in capital recovery is provided—not the future sum whose present worth is $100,000. The level annuity discount factors provide for exactly that. The only reason for considering their sinking fund equivalents is to demonstrate further the intricate and useful interrelationships among the several compound interest and discount factors that should be familiar working tools for any appraiser of income-producing real estate.

*Distinction between Capital Recovery and Depreciation.* Capital Recovery Rates must be distinguished from depreciation rates. The former are used in real estate appraisal analysis to represent a portion of the investment to be recovered as part of annual NOI, through mortgage amortization, through resale of the property, and/or through refinancing. The latter are accounting entries to identify recovery of a portion of initial cost of an asset, primarily to calculate taxable net income.

## Capitalization Rates

Capitalization Rates are the sum of the Discount Rate and the Capital Recovery Rate, both identified from market evidence for the type of property involved, in the applicable current sub-market. Capitalization Rates can be (and frequently are) expressed as reciprocal Capitalization Factors.

A Capitalization Rate or Capitalization Factor is applied to net income attributable to that portion of the total investment on which recovery of investment is expected by the investor over the capital recovery period. It therefore represents both a return *on* and a return *of* the amount of investment involved. The present worth of the portion of investment to be recovered is obtained by dividing the appropriate portion of NOI by the Capitalization Rate $(V = 1/R)$; or by multiplying the appropriate portion of NOI by the Discount Factor $(V = 1 \times F)$.

Capitalization Rates can be obtained by taking the reciprocals of published discount Factors. This is usually not necessary, but it is possible. The Ring Factor is a representation of Capitalization Rates on the straight-line capital recovery premise. The Hoskold Factor is a representation of Capitalization Rates on the sinking-fund capital recovery premise with compounding at the "safe" rate of interest (usually 3% in published Hoskold Tables). The Inwood Factor is a representation of Capitalization Rates on the level-annuity capital recovery premise. It is simply the Present Worth of One per Annum Factor, named after the early nineteenth century English mathematician, William Inwood.

Capitalization Rates are applied to the portion of NOI attributable to, or available to cover, the investment in improvements in the traditional residual techniques of capitalization. These techniques separate the property into land and buildings for purposes of analysis.

The mortgage constant can be regarded as a Capitalization Rate for a mortgage loan. Indeed, the annual Installment to Amortize One Factor *is* the Capitalization Rate for any level annuity, of which mortgage debt service is one example.

## Review Exercises

1. An investor has just paid $200,000 for an income property producing

$50,000 per year in Effective Gross Income. Annual Operating Expenses are stabilized at $20,000. A 25-year, 8.5%, level monthly payment mortgage in the amount of $160,000 has just been obtained. The investor plans to hold the property for 15 years, and then sell it at 70% of his purchase price. Assume the income stream will remain constant over the 15 years.
  a. What is the indicated Overall Rate on this investment?
  b. What is the indicated operating expense ratio for this property?
  c. What is the indicated Cash Throw-Off?
  d. What is the indicated Equity Dividend Rate?
  e. What amount of capital recovery over the 15-year period is indicated?
  f. What is the indicated level annuity Capital Recovery Rate?
  g. What is the indicated Discount Rate?
  h. What would be the indicated Capital Recovery Rate and Discount Rate if straight-line capital recovery were employed in this case?
2. A level annuity income stream of $10,000 per year is forecast for a property. It is expected to run for 35 years. The indicated Discount Rate is 13%. Annual discounting is specified.
  a. What is the present worth of this income stream?
  b. Demonstrate that the applicable Capitalization Rate in this situation is the sum of the Capital Recovery Rate and the Discount Rate.
3. A 5-year lease with a well-rated tenant provides net rentals of $24,000 per year. The Annual Discount Rate is 12%.
  Show the distribution of each annual $24,000 payment between return on investment and capital recovery.


## Supplementary Readings

American Institute of Real Estate Appraisers, *The Appraisal of Real Estate*, fifth edition (Chicago: American Institute of Real Estate Appraisers, 1967), Chapter 17.

L.W. Ellwood, *Ellwood Tables for Real Estate and Financing; Part I: Explanatory Text*, third edition (Chicago: American Institute of Real Estate Appraisers, 1970), pp. 51-53.

Sanders, A. Kahn, Frederick E. Case, and Alfred Schimmel, *Real Estate Appraisal and Investment* (New York: Ronald Press, 1963), pp. 121-132.

Alfred A. Ring, *The Valuation of Real Estate*, second edition (Englewood Cliffs, N.J.: Prentice-Hall, 1970), Chapter 16.

# Derivation of Overall Rates and Discount Rates

Understanding the nature and characteristics of the several rates of capitalization used in the valuation of income-producing real estate is quite important, but it is not sufficient to carry out appraisal assignments. It is also necessary to know how to derive these rates, and when to use them.

For virtually every type of rate of capitalization or rate of discount, there are alternative methods and techniques available to the appraiser for use in assigning a number value to that rate. One reason for this diversity of techniques is that most parts of income-property appraisal problems can be approached from different viewpoints or directions. Each is logically valid and technically acceptable. A second and more pressing reason stems from the unavailability of needed data that is frequently encountered in appraisal practice. The techniques are useless without reliable, verified, appropriate data to apply to them. Much of income-property appraisal technique has developed because the most direct and simplest method of approaching a problem is foreclosed by the lack of needed data. In rate estimation, as in many other aspects of the capitalization process, technique and method are frequently dictated by what data are available, and which of these are most reliable.

Since the appraiser can never foresee what data will actually be available to him, he needs to be able to approach income capitalization problems armed with as many workable tools of analysis as possible. This is the chief reason that alternative methods of estimating and measuring Overall Rates and Discount Rates are presented here.

## Estimation of Overall Rates

Income-producing real estate must produce sufficient Net Operating Income annually to cover three sets of requirements at rates of return that are competitive in terms of applicable current market standards and alternatives. These three sets of requirements are:

1. mortgage interest payments on borrowed funds, payable to the lender (mortgagee) at the mortgage rate of interest;
2. return on the equity investment, at the Equity Yield Rate or Equity Dividend Rate applicable to the type of equity investor involved; and
3. return of the recoverable portion of the investment in the property, at the mortgage interest rate for mortgage principal amortization, and at the Equity Yield Rate for proration of any forecast capital loss in the property investment on resale; or recovery of forecast loss of capital at the Capital Recovery Rate.

185

Alternatively, Net Operating Income may be regarded as a series of annual payments to cover (1) return on the entire investment at the Discount Rate; and (2) return of the recoverable portion of the investment forecast to represent capital loss on resale, at the Capital Recovery Rate.

This second formulation of the coverage provided by NOI is sometimes expressed as a return on the portion of the investment represented by site (land) at the Discount Rate; and a return *on* and *of* the portion of the total investment represented by the improvements (buildings) at the Capitalization Rate.

No matter how the items to be covered by returns at competitive market rates are identified and expressed, the coverage is provided by Net Operating Income. This is the cash flow the property is forecast to be able to produce under typically competent management. NOI is the $I$ in the basic valuation equation. The several rates of return to be covered combine to make up the $R$.

As a simple illustration (perhaps unrealistically oversimplified for purposes of illustration), take a property that has just been sold at a market price of $50,000. It is producing a NOI of $7,000 per year. This represents an Overall Rate of 14%. But what elements of return does this $7,000 cover?

Assume that the recoverable portion of the property—the improvements—have a present worth of $40,000, and that the income projection period is 20 years. Thus, the capital recovery period is also 20 years. Just to make the illustration easy to follow, assume further that straight-line capital recovery is to be provided over 20 years. This is not a recommended method of providing for capital recovery except under very special circumstances, as is demonstrated in Chapter 10. The point of this illustration, however, is to indicate the allocation of portions of NOI to cover different requirements of investors. Straight-line capital recovery is easier to demonstrate mathematically, and enables the reader to focus attention on the point of the example.

Suppose now that a non-amortized $30,000 mortgage loan at 8% interest has been obtained. This is an unrealistic assumption, but it makes it easier to focus on the allocation process. From this information, it appears that the equity investment is 40% or $20,000 ($50,000 − $30,000 = $20,000). Also, the straight-line Capital Recovery Rate is 5% (100% / 20 = 5%).

The $7,000 Net Operating Income could be allocated among the several patterns of requirements as follows:

1.  NOI = $7,000; Overall Rate = 14% ($7,000/$50,000 = 0.14)
    Mortgage Interest = .08 × $30,000 = $2,400
    Capital Recovery = .05 × $40,000 = $2,000
    Equity Return = $7,000 − $2,400 − $2,000 = $2,600
    Equity Dividend Rate = $2,600/$20,000 = 0.13 or 13%
    Discount Rate =  Mortgage Coverage:  .60 × .08 = 0.048
                     Equity Coverage:  .40 × .13 = 0.052
                     Discount Rate:  0.100 = 10.0%

The derivation of the Discount Rate in this example illustrates the use of the simple Band of Investment method described later in this chapter. The distribution of NOI among mortgage interest, equity dividend, and capital recovery identifies both the dollar amounts and the rates of return associated with each. They can be combined back to the Overall Rate by making them effective rates on the entire investment. This is done by weighting each rate of return by the percentage that its component represents of the entire investment. This also illustrates the fact that any Overall Rate is a weighted average of rates of return on component parts of the investment, as is pointed out in more detail in the following section. In this case, the indicated Overall Rate can be derived as follows:

| | |
|---|---|
| Mortgage Rate: | $.08 \times .60 = 0.048$ |
| Equity Rate: | $.13 \times .40 = 0.052$ |
| Capital Recovery Rate: | $.05 \times .80 = \underline{0.040}$ |
| Overall Rate: | $0.140$ or 14% |

2. With the Discount Rate established at 10% and the Capital Recovery Rate at 5%, the distribution of coverage among the physical components of the investment would be:

| | |
|---|---|
| Return on Property: | $.10 \times \$50,000 = \$5,000$ |
| Return of Capital: | $.05 \times \$40,000 = \underline{\$2,000}$ |
| Total Return (NOI) | $\$7,000$ |

3. The Capitalization Rate is 15%. It is the sum of the Discount Rate (10%) and the Capital Recovery Rate (5%), applied to the position of the total property investment represented by the improvements. The alternative distribution of coverage between the physical components of the property would then be:

| | |
|---|---|
| Land: | $.10 \times \$10,000 = \$1,000$ |
| Improvements: | $.15 \times \$40,000 = \underline{\$6,000}$ |
| Total Return (NOI) | $\$7,000$ |

## Weighted Averages

The foregoing examples illustrate emphatically that an Overall Rate is a weighted average of the component claims or requirements on the NOI produced by an income property. The rate of return required by each claimant is weighted by the proportion of the total property investment represented by that claim. The result of each calculation indicates the rate of return on the entire property investment required to meet the claim of that component. The individual weighted rates are then summed to obtain the Overall Rate which the entire property must earn to cover the individual claims on annual NOI.

This process is the Band of Investment method of rate derivation, applied to

Overall Rate estimation. The term "Band of Investment" is usually reserved for the process when it is used to derive a Discount Rate. However, it is exactly the same procedure in each case.

In the first example given above, the weight assigned to the mortgage interest rate was .6, because the mortgage represented 60% of the total investment. If 8% is required to be earned on 60% of the investment to cover mortgage interest payments, then 4.8% (.08 × .6) must be produced by the property to provide these interest payments. Similarly, the 13% equity return was weighted by .4 because it represented 40% of the total investment. The property had to produce 5.2% on the total investment to cover the 13% return requirement on the 40% equity investment. Finally, the weight for the Capital Recapture Rate was .8 because the recoverable investment in the improvements represented 80% of the total investment in the property.

The same weighting process applies to whatever distribution of claims on income is used in the analysis. If the proper components and the proper weights are used, the resulting sum is always the Overall Rate required to provide the stipulated rates of return for each of the components.

As a further example of the process of building an indicated Overall Rate under different capital recovery premises, assume a property is producing a NOI of $15,000. Mortgage funds are available at 8.5% on a 70% loan-value ratio, payable monthly over 20 years. The equity yield rate is concluded from market analysis to be 11%. Capital recovery is forecast to occur over 25 years, and the best estimate of the proportion of total investment represented by site is 20%. Depending on the *method* of capital recovery ascertained to be most appropriate for the type of income stream produced by the property in question, indicated Overall rates would be as follows:

Discount Rate (Band of Investment):
        Mortgage Rate Coverage:      .70 × .085 = .0595
        Equity Yield Coverage:        .30 × .110 = .0330
        Indicated Discount Rate:            .0925 = 9.25%

Capital Recovery:
    Straight-Line Premise: 1.00/25 = .04 = 4.00%
    Level Annuity Factor (9.25%, 25 years): 9.626891(Ellwood, page 104, column 5)

Capitalization Rate:
    Straight-Line Premise: 9.25% + 4.00% = 13.25%
    Inwood Factor (Reciprocal): 1.000000/9.626891 = .103876 = 10.39%
        (also page 104, column 6)

Sinking Fund Factor (9.25%, 25 years): .011387 (page 104, column 3)

Mortgage Constant (8.5%, 20 years, monthly payments): 10.4136%
      (12 × .008678 = .104136; (page 89, column 6)

Thus:

| | | |
|---|---|---|
| 80% Improvements: | .80 X .1325 = | .10600 (Straight-Line premise) |
| 20% Site: | .20 X .0925 = | .01850 |
| Indicated Overall Rate: | | .12450 = 12.45% |

| | | |
|---|---|---|
| 80% Improvements: | .80 X .1038 = | .08304 (Annuity Premise) |
| 20% Site: | .20 X .0925 = | .01850 |
| Indicated Overall Rate: | | .10154 = 10.15% |

| | | |
|---|---|---|
| 70% Mortgage: | .70 X .1041 = | .0729 (Mortgage Constant) |
| 30% Equity: | .30 X .1100 = | .0330 (Equity Rate) |
| Indicated Overall Rate: | | .1059 = 10.59% |

| | | |
|---|---|---|
| 100% Property: | 1.00 X .0925 = | .0925 |
| 80% Improvements: | .80 X .0400 = | .0320 (Straight-Line premise) |
| Indicated Overall Rate: | | .1245 = 12.45% |

| | | |
|---|---|---|
| 100% Property: | 1.00 X .0925 = | .0925 |
| 80% Improvements: | .80 X .0114 = | .0089 (Sinking Fund Rate, Annuity premise) |
| Indicated Overall Rate: | | .1014 = 10.14% |

These are the mechanical techniques for deriving an estimated Overall Rate from given market information, *and* the character of the forecast income stream. Not all are valid or correct in this instance. It depends partly on the character of the income stream, which determines which form of capital recovery is to be used. It also depends on the relationship between the loan-to-value ratio of the mortgage and the proportion of the total property investment to be recovered. Unless mortgage amortization is an accurate proxy for capital recovery, the mortgage-equity formulation cannot be used without further adjustment.

In the foregoing examples, the estimated Overall Rate can be divided into NOI to derive an estimate of present worth or value via Direct Capitalization:

| | |
|---|---|
| Straight-Line Recovery: | $15,000/.1245 = $120,482 (say $120,000) |
| Level Annuity: | $15,000/.1015 = $147,783 (say $148,000) |
| Mortgage-Equity: | $15,000/.1059 = $141,643 (say $142,000) |

## Direct Market Comparisons

Overall Rates can theoretically be derived directly from evidence of recent sales transactions of similar, competitive properties sold under market conditions similar to those applicable to the property being appraised. "All" that is necessary is to obtain the verified sales price and Net Operating Income for each such comparable sale property. *If* the properties are truly similar and competitive, both with one another and with the subject property, then the Overall Rate for each can be derived simply by dividing NOI by sales price ($I/V = R$). Truly similar and competitive properties will produce a pattern of Overall Rates that fall into a narrow range, and from these indicators the appropriate Overall Rate for the subject property can be estimated.

Provided good, reliable market data are available, this direct method of Overall Rate estimation is both defensible and valid. It also enables the appraiser to process Direct Capitalization of the subject property's NOI to a present worth or value estimate.

This method of Overall Rate estimation is sometimes regarded as part of Direct Sales Comparison analysis, rather than Income Capitalization. The argument is essentially a semantic one. Net Operating Income is the basis for capitalization, and the Overall Rate is applied directly to it. *All* rate estimations are ultimately derived from market data if they are to be defensible at all. It happens in this method that the market data are sales prices and NOI figures on similar, competitive properties that have sold recently under market conditions similar to those applicable to the subject property.

The real drawback in attempting to derive Overall Rates from market sales transactions data is that the necessary data and comparability of properties are infrequently available. If any significant adjustments must be made, then the method loses validity and applicability. The requirements for similarity include:

(1) similar types of property, with essentially the same remaining economic lives, physical condition, and ratios of site-to-improvements as proportions of total property value or investment;
(2) similar income streams with the same characteristics of risk, timing, stability, and income projection period;
(3) similar terms of financing;
(4) similar types of investor-purchasers with buying motivations the same as those of the most probable type of purchaser-investor likely to be attracted to the subject property;
(5) similar terms of sale; and
(6) similar market conditions prevailing at the time of sale.

If these conditions cannot be met (and they are demanding), then in all probability the Overall Rate cannot legitimately be estimated directly from market sales transactions data. If they *are* met, however, the complexities and opportunities for both mechanical and judgmental error inherent in other methods of rate estimation can be avoided.

*Abstraction from Gross*
*Income Multiplier*

It is frequently possible to estimate reliably the Gross Income Multiplier in the current local market for the type of property being appraised. *If* the properties used in developing the GIM are truly similar to and competitive with the subject property, and further *if* they exhibit operating ratios similar to that of the subject property, then an Overall Rate can be estimated by abstraction.

**Operating Ratios.** The Operating Ratio is the percentage of Effective Gross Income represented by Operating Expenses. If this is subtracted from 100%, the result is the income ratio for this type of property in the current market.

For example, assume an income-producing property with Effective Gross Income of $15,000 and stabilized Operating Expenses of $6,000. The Operating Ratio is 40% ($6,000/$15,000 = .40). NOI is then $9,000, and the income ratio is 60%. From closely similar and competitive property sales, a reliable GIM of 7.2 is derived. This is convertible into a rate of 13.88% (100%/7.2 = 13.88%). Applying the income ratio of 60% to this rate, an Overall Rate of 8.328% (possibly rounded to 8.33%) is derived: .1388 X .60 − .08328.

To be applicable, this method of Overall Rate estimation must be based on reliable, verified sales and income data for truly similar, competitive properties which exhibit the same operating ratios as does the subject property.

*Composite Overall Rate*

In the Ellwood formulation of mortgage-equity analysis, the $R$ in the basic formula $V = d/R$ is an Overall Rate. Ellwood calls it a Composite Capitalization Rate, as well as an Overall Capitalization Rate. In fact, the terms are synonymous.[1] This Overall Rate is estimated by weighting in a conceptual manner similar to the Band of Investment presentation in a preceding section of this chapter. The mechanics are much more involved and complex, however, primarily because they take into account the phenomenon of equity build-up through amortization payments in a direct-reduction level-payment mortgage.

Because of its complexity, as well as its peculiar applicability in mortgage equity analysis, detailed consideration of the Ellwood formula to derive $R$ is deferred until Chapter 13. For the interest of the reader, the formula for $R$ is:[2]

$$R = y - mc + \text{dep. } 1/s_n; \text{ or } R = y - mc - \text{app. } 1/s_n$$

The components in solving for $R$, the Overall Rate, are:

$y$: equity yield rate
$m$: mortgage loan-to-value ratio
$c$: mortgage coefficient, reflecting periodic equity build-up through mortgage amortization at the mortgage interest rate
dep.: percentage decline forecast in property value on resale
app: percentage increase forecast in property value on resale
$1/s_n$: sinking fund factor at the equity yield rate

## *Influence of Financing*

The discussion in Chapter 7 has already demonstrated that the terms and availability of mortgage financing influence value and value estimates in several ways. Overall Rates derived from direct sales transaction comparisons must be predicted (among other requirements) on similar patterns of financing for all properties involved in the analysis, including the subject property. The same requirement applies to Overall Rate estimation by abstraction from the Gross Income Multiplier.

The examples in the preceding sections also illustrate the influence of mortgage loan terms on the Discount Rate in developing an Overall Rate as a weighted average between Discount Rate and Capitalization Rate, or between Discount Rate and Capital Recovery Rate. Developing an Overall Rate as the weighted average of Mortgage Constant and Equity Yield Rate exhibits perhaps the most obvious influence of financing terms, since they directly determine the Mortgage Constant.

## Estimation of Discount Rates

The Discount Rate is the rate of return on the entire investment, ignoring capital recovery in whatever form it appears. It is the investment rate of return. It is also the base on which Overall Rates are built, especially in traditional residual techniques of capitalization which separate the property investment into physical components (site and improvements) for purposes of analysis. The Discount Rate as such is not employed directly in Mortgage-Equity analysis. However, it is an influence on the base rates and overall rates developed to derive a Composite Rate, which are then applied to NOI in estimating present worth or value.

All estimates of Discount Rates must be based on reliable, verified market data. However constructed, a Discount Rate incorporates sufficient return to cover interest payments on a mortgage, plus an equity dividend rate on the equity investment which is competitive with alternative similar investments in the current market.

## *Components of a Discount Rate*

Every Discount Rate must incorporate a return for four elements of compensation any investor is seeking. These have already been noted in Chapter 5. While the amount for each may vary from case to case, the components are always present. It is helpful to the appraiser to recognize and understand these elements, although it is a practical impossibility to attempt to measure each separately and "build up" a Discount Rate.

**Compensation for Giving up Control over Money.** This is the compensation required to overcome time preference. It is represented by the "riskless" rate of interest on long-term United States government bonds or notes. Such securities are highly liquid, involve virtually no investment management, and carry virtually no risk of principal loss or non-payment of income. Interest rates on savings deposits are another proxy measure of the "pure" or "riskless" rate of interest. As noted earlier, time preference represents the Opportunity Cost of putting money into a particular investment.

**Compensation for Giving up Liquidity.** This is necessary to overcome liquidity preference. The less readily an asset can be converted quickly into cash at face value, the less liquid it is. Real estate represents a relatively illiquid asset, and investors seek compensation for non-liquidity to overcome their basic liquidity preference. The less liquid the asset, the greater the compensation required in the form of a higher rate of return.

**Compensation for Investment Management.** The more time and effort an investment requires of the investor, the greater the compensation he requires in the form of a higher rate of return. This is not the management of the property, for which an element of Operating Expense is already included in the stabilized operating statement or income statement for the property. Rather, it is the activity required of the absentee owner-investor in keeping accounts, recording receipts, making mortgage payments, and other duties related to being an investor.

**Compensation for Investment Risks Assumed.** The discussion in Chapter 6 indicated the several risks assumed by an investor. The greater these risks, the greater the compensation he will require for assuming them. The most significant risks in income-producing real estate are the risks of principal loss or decline, income decline, and income instability: in other words, the risk that income forecasts will not be realized.

**Illustrative Example.** To indicate the several components of any Discount Rate, the following example provides numbers for illustrative purposes only. It is rarely possible to quantify liquidity preference or risk compensation separately. It is not possible to "build up" a Discount Rate by identifying the rates required for each of its components.

| | |
|---|---|
| Riskless or Pure Rate (time preference): | 5.0% |
| Management: | 0.25% |
| Nonliquidity (liquidity preference): | 0.50% |
| Risk: | 4.00% |
| Required Rate of Return (Discount Rate): | 9.75% |

*Direct Market Comparison*

While conceptually attractive, direct estimation of Discount Rates from market sales transaction data is a virtual impossibility. It is even more stringently demanding of comparable data than is estimation of an Overall Rate from market sales transactions data.

*If* data are available, the following requirements must be met:

(1) sales prices of similar, competitive properties sold to the same type of purchaser-investor in arm's-length open market transactions under market conditions similar to those affecting the subject property;
(2) properties with essentially the same physical and locational characteristics as the subject's (age, condition, site-improvements ratio, etc.);
(3) similar terms of financing;
(4) similar terms of sale;
(5) income streams with the same risk and stability characteristics, with the same income projection periods; and
(6) similar capital recovery periods and methods of capital recovery, based on the same ratio of improvements-to-site in the total property investment.

In the unlikely event all this information is in fact available, then the indicated Discount Rates for the several comparable sales properties should fit a pattern within a narrow range, from which the Discount Rate for the subject property is derived. Even if all the necessary information required to derive a Discount Rate through direct market comparisons is available, the appraiser will rarely choose to do so. If the objective of the analysis is to estimate value, it can be done more readily and as defensibly by using the same market transactions data to derive an Overall Rate instead, and then applying this Overall Rate directly to NOI to estimate value.

*Band of Investment Analysis*

This is a widely used and conceptually defensible approach to estimating an appropriate Discount Rate. It is based on the premise that investments in income-producing properties are typically financed with a mortgage, and that the equity investor will seek to obtain the best available loan terms in order to maximize the potential benefits of leverage.

The estimation of a Discount Rate by Band of Investment analysis develops a weighted average between the return on investment that is required to cover mortgage interest and the return on investment that is required to provide a competitive equity dividend rate. The weights are the percentages of total investment represented by the initial principal of the mortgage loan(s) and the initial equity investment. The mechanics are precisely the same as those used in developing an indicated Overall Rate by Band of Investment analysis (see the examples provided in earlier sections of this chapter).

Although the procedures involved in the Band of Investment method of rate estimation have already been illustrated earlier in this chapter as part of the discussion of Overall Rate estimation, as well as in Chapter 7 in the section on leverage, it seems appropriate to provide two further examples. The first demonstrates the capability of the method to deal with more than one mortgage on which interest must be paid. So long as the component weights total 100%, virtually any combination of claims against the return on investment in the property can be handled.

Assume a property is financed with a 60% first mortgage at 8.25% interest and a 15% second mortgage at 12%. Equity investors are seeking a 13% return on this type of investment in the current local market. The indicated Discount Rate would be developed via Band of Investment analysis as follows:

| First Mortgage: | $.0825 \times .60 = 0.0495$ |
|---|---|
| Second Mortgage: | $.1200 \times .15 = 0.0180$ |
| Equity Investment: | $.1300 \times .25 = \underline{0.0325}$ |
| Indicated Discount Rate: | $0.1000 = 10.0\%$ |

The second supplementary example involves the use of dollar figures, which are sometimes available, instead of percentage loan-to-value ratios. The result of the analysis is the required annual dollar return on total investment in the property necessary to cover the claims of lenders and the equity investor.

Suppose the same rates of return are required by the participating parties, and the total investment in the property is $80,000. The principal amount of the first mortgage loan is $48,000, and the principal of the second mortgage is $12,000. This leaves an equity investment of $20,000. The dollar return on investment required by these claimants would then be:

| First Mortgage: | $\$48,000 \times .0825 = \$3,960$ |
|---|---|
| Second Mortgage: | $\$12,000 \times .1200 = \$1,440$ |
| Equity Investment: | $\$20,000 \times .1300 = \underline{\$2,600}$ |
| Total Required Return on Investment: | $\$8,000$ |

This $8,000 required return on the investment of $80,000 is 10%, which is the Discount Rate.

**Limitations.** One major difficulty with traditional Band of Investment analysis is that it does not include provision for continual increase of equity investment over the term of an amortized mortgage. To this extent, the estimated Discount Rate is an approximation, or is a first-period rate only. It is possible to account for mortgage amortization in Band of Investment analysis. This technique does not provide for capital recovery through mortgage amortization, but it accounts for the fact that equity investment is continually increasing with each amortization payment.[3] The equity investor, after all, is seeking the same Equity Dividend Rate on this increasing equity.

Despite this serious limitation, Band of Investment analysis is widely used in capitalization methods that require the Discount Rate as a starting point.

**Market Data Required.** Band of Investment analysis should be based on the most probable, typical pattern of mortgage financing available to the most probable type of investor in the type of property represented by the subject property. Even in the physical residual techniques of capitalization, when value is purportedly estimated "free and clear of any encumbrances" (which includes mortgages), the Discount Rate used is most commonly developed through Band of Investment analysis. The data required for Band of Investment analysis are few, and they are usually readily available in the market:

1. most probable or typical mortgage loan terms: most especially the loan-to-value ratio and the mortgage interest rate; and
2. Equity Yield Rate required to attract investors into this type of equity investment.

*Abstraction from the Gross
Income Multiplier*

An indicated Discount Rate can be abstracted from a GIM in essentially the same fashion demonstrated earlier for deriving an Overall Rate, except that a further step is required. It is necessary to deduct the portion of NOI, as an *effective* rate of capital recovery, represented by annual capital recovery payments. This *effective* rate of capital recovery is the Capital Recovery Rate times the proportion of total investment represented by the recoverable investment in the improvements.

For example, using the information used earlier in abstracting an Overall Rate, a Discount Rate can be abstracted as follows:

GIM: 7.2  1/GIM: .1388  Operating Ratio: 40%  Improvements ratio: 80%
Capital Recapture Rate: 4%
Thus:

| | | |
|---|---|---|
| Reciprocal of GIM: | 13.88% | |
| *Less* Operating Ratio: | 5.55% | (.40 × .1388 = .0555) |
| Overall Rate: | 8.33% | (NOI/V) |
| *Less* Effective CRR: | 3.20% | (.80 × .04 = .0320) |
| Indicated Discount Rate: | 5.13% | |

While possible and occasionally feasible, this method also suffers from the limitation that a high degree of comparability is required among properties used to derive the GIM. It also requires market evidence of a standardized operating expense ratio and improvements-site ratio. Moreover, if the objective is to estimate value and really reliable market data are available, then an intermediate step in this analysis is the Overall Rate. It can be used directly in capitalizing NOI to a present worth or value estimate, without all the complications that are associated with less direct capitalization methods.

## Selection of Method(s) of
## Rate Estimation

While the appraiser theoretically has a choice among several methods of estimating either the Overall Rate or the Discount Rate, or both, the apparent choice is illusory. The method to be employed in any given appraisal problem is influenced and often determined by two sets of considerations.

The first consideration is the applicability of the method to the specific appraisal problem at hand. The appraiser is essentially attempting to analyze the property and the income stream it is forecast to produce through the eyes of the most probable, typically informed, prudent, rational purchaser-investor. The way in which this most probable type of purchaser-investor will react to the forecast income stream is a strong influence on the identity of the rate(s) that should be used to capitalize it, and the most appropriate way to derive or estimate them.

Second, every method of rate estimation requires reliable, verified market data. No matter how logical or attractive a given method of rate estimation may be for the appraisal problem at hand, if the required data are not obtainable, the method cannot be employed.

## Review Exercises

1. A property has just been purchased for $130,000. It is producing an annual Net Operating Income of $15,600. $100,000 of the purchase price was allocated to improvements, which have an estimated remaining economic life of 25 years.
   a. What is the indicated Overall Rate?
   b. What is the indicated straight-line Capital Recovery Rate?
   c. What is the *effective* straight-line Capital Recovery Rate?
   d. What is the indicated Discount Rate?
2. A property can be financed with a 65% mortgage at 8.5% interest, with a 20-year maturity, and level monthly-payment amortization. Equity investors in this type of property are currently requiring an 11.5% Equity Yield Rate. What is the indicated Overall Rate for this property investment?
3. An office building just sold at a price reflecting a Gross Income Multiplier of 4.5. The Operating Ratio is 35%. The building itself represents an estimated 75% of the total purchase price and has an estimated remaining economic life of 40 years.
   By abstraction, derive the indicated Overall Rate and Discount Rate for this property.

4. A purchaser is able to obtain an $80,000 first mortgage at 7.75% on a property he has just acquired. The seller has taken back a $12,000 second purchase-money mortgage at 11.5% interest. The investor put up $8,000 cash to complete the transaction, on which he expects a return of 15%.

   a. What Net Operating Income is necessary to meet these requirements?

   b. What is the indicated Discount Rate?

   c. What principle of finance does the equity investor's return illustrate?

## Supplementary Readings

American Institute of Real Estate Appraisers, *The Appraisal of Real Estate*, fifth edition (Chicago: American Institute of Real Estate Appraisers, 1967), Chapter 17.

Sanders A. Kahn, Frederick E. Case, and Alfred Schimmel, *Real Estate Appraisal and Investment* (New York: Ronald Press, 1963), Chapter 10.

William N. Kinnard, Jr., *A Guide to Appraising Apartments,* third edition, (Chicago: Society of Real Estate Appraisers, 1973), pp. 35-36.

D.S. Moss, "Equity Yields on Real Estate Investments," *The Appraisal Journal,* Volume 37, Number 3, July 1969.

Roland D. Nelson, "Overall Rate—Band of Investment Style," *The Appraisal Journal,* Volume 37, Number 1, January 1969.

Alfred A. Ring, *The Valuation of Real Estate*, second edition (Englewood Cliffs, N.J.: Prentice-Hall, 1970), Chapter 16.

William M. Shenkel, A. *Guide to Appraising Industrial Property* (Chicago: Society of Real Estate Appraisers, 1967), pp. 99-102.

## Notes

1. L.W. Ellwood, *Ellwood Tables for Real Estate Appraising and Financing; Part I: Explanatory Text*, third edition (Chicago: American Institute of Real Estate Appraisers, 1970), pp. 7, 10, and 11.

2. *Ibid.*, p. 11.

3. *Ibid.*, pp. 63-66.

# 10 Finite Income Streams: Providing for Capital Recovery

## Rationale of Capital Recovery

Capital Recovery Rates and capital recovery payments are rarely estimated or sought for their own sake in income-property appraising. They are essential building blocks in the derivation of Capitalization Rates, however, and Capitalization Rates *are* important factors in the income capitalization process. Especially in physical residual techniques of income capitalization, Capitalization Rates represents the $R$ by which the appraiser capitalizes the income from an asset whose value is forecast to decline by the end of the income projection period.

It has been noted previously in Chapters 4 and 6 that the income forecast for income-producing properties is typically projected for a finite period of time. Only the special case of site income involves income projection into perpetuity. The value of the site or land is forecast to remain intact (at least) in perpetuity. All other income streams produced by income properties have specific, finite ending dates. At the end of that time, something of value will remain. If the value of that something (the reversion) is forecast to be less than the original investment or present worth of the property as of the effective valuation date, then some capital loss is forecast. The investor will want to recover that capital loss out of periodic annual net income over the income projection period. The rate at which that recovery of anticipated capital loss occurs is the Capital Recovery Rate.

The length of the income projection period has a direct bearing on the annual rate at which the anticipated capital loss (if any) is to be recovered. In the traditional physical residual techniques of analysis, that capital recovery period is represented by the estimated remaining economic life of the improvements. In mortgage-equity analysis, it is the typical investment holding or turnover period for the type of property and the type of purchaser-investor involved. In the valuation of leased fee and leasehold interests, it is the remaining term of the lease. In some instances, it may be the remaining term of a mortgage. The income projection period and the capital recovery period in any appraisal problem are the same length; the terms simply reflect different viewpoints toward the same time span.

Whatever the appropriate income projection period for the appraisal problem at hand, the forecast future income receipts (both NOI and the reversion) are forecast to cease at some future date. Indeed, this is built into all discount factors used in appraising: a specific time period $n$. Income produced by or allocated to (1) the improvements in physical residual techniques; (2) the entire property in mortgage-equity analysis; (3) the lease position in leased fee or leasehold analysis, and (4) the lender on a mortgage loan—in each case includes a provision for return of a portion of a declining or wasting asset which will not or cannot provide the forecast income stream payments beyond a specified date.

Fully amortized loans and leasehold interests represent "pure" capital recovery situations. The forecast value of the reversion in these leases is zero, so if the investor is to have his capital intact by the end of the income projection period, he must receive it in full through periodic capital recovery payments included in the forecast income stream. In all other situations, the reversion is forecast to have *some* value. The amount of capital recovery required is therefore the difference between the present worth of the property and the forecast future amount or value of the reversion.

To estimate the annual *rate* at which capital recovery is to occur in order to provide full money of the capital loss over the income projection period, the appraiser must identify (1) the duration of the income projection or capital recovery period; and (2) the applicable sinking fund rate at which capital recovery payments could accumulate at compound interest over that period. The appraiser has little or no *choice* in the selection of the applicable income projection and the appropriate method of capital recovery to use in any appraisal problems. These are determined by the facts of the market, the characteristics of the forecast income stream, and the nature of the appraisal problem itself. The different alternative measures available to the appraiser represent the appropriate measures and techniques associated with the different types of income streams he may encounter. For any given appraisal, he must *identify* the salient characteristics of the forecast income stream; and then apply the capital recovery period, the capital recovery method, and the Capital Recovery Rate that best represent that income stream and its characteristics.

## Investment and Investor Considerations

The typically informed, prudent, rational purchaser-investor is seeking to maximize the net cash return (before or after income taxes) on his investment. This means receiving the highest possible competitive rate of return on that investment. He considers both return on the total property investment, and more especially, the return on his equity investment. This is why financing and leverage are important considerations in income-property appraisal.

The typical purchaser-investor is also seeking to maintain his investment capital intact, at least at its original level. If any decline in the reversion is forecast at the end of the income projection period, then the investor will want that amount returned periodically as part of his annual net income receipts (NOI). To the extent that NOI includes a return *of* capital investment to compensate for the forecast decline in the amount of the reversion from the initial amount of the total property investment, the return *on* the investment is reduced.

Capital recovery payments are the annual amount to cover the forecast decline from initial investment to reversion. They represent only the amount necessary to maintain the original investment. The larger the annual capital recovery payments are, the lower the residual net income remaining as a return *on* the investment will be. Hence, the lower the present worth or value of the income stream (NOI) will be. Conversely, the lower the amount of annual capital recovery payments, the higher the present worth or value of the NOI will be. It is therefore critical to estimate accurately and properly the amount of annual capital recovery payments.

As already noted in the introduction to this chapter, the size of annual capital recovery payments depends on (1) the amount of capital investment to be recovered; (2) the time period over which capital recovery is to occur; and (3) the rate at which capital recovery payments are compounded or discounted. This rate of discount is determined by the character of the forecast income stream and the method of capital recovery selected, which in turn depends on the most probable expectation of the investor with respect to the certainty of his annual receipts. The appraiser must reach conclusions about each of these determining influences before a Capital Recovery Rate or factor appropriate to the appraisal problem at hand can be derived.

**Nature of Capital Recovery.** The forecast or anticipated decline in the reversion from initial total property investment is the amount to be provided or returned through capital recovery. It stems from reduced capacity of the property to produce a competitive, forecast annual net return—either because of physical deterioration and/or obsolescence of the improvements, or because of a reduced resale price of the property, or both. The appraiser must estimate its amount from available market evidence.

The wearing out and/or obsolescence of the improvements is reflected in the traditional physical residual techniques of capitalization, in which the reversion is the value of the site. Capital recovery is provided for the investment in the improvements, usually over the estimated remaining economic life of the improvements.

A forecast decline in resale price of the entire property (if any) is most commonly reflected in mortgage-equity analysis, and frequently in leased fee valuation. The period of capital recovery is typically the investment turnover period or the term of the lease, respectively. If an increase in resale price (capital appreciation) is forecast or anticipated, then the Capital Recovery Rate will be negative, and present worth accordingly enhanced.

**Terminology in Capital Recovery.** There is potential confusion among three different types of diminution of property value, each of which has on occasion been termed "depreciation." Since each has some impact and use in income property appraising, they should be carefully distinguished and used by appraisers.

(1) *Depreciation* refers to annual accounting charges deducted from the original cost of a "wasting" asset. It is a deductible charge before taxable net

income is derived, designed to account for recovery by the investor of the original investment cost or outlay. Depreciation is allowable against improvements only, and must be allocated over the established *useful life* of the improvements. Depreciation is not allowed against land.

(2) *Accrued depreciation* in appraising refers to the difference between the reproduction cost new of improvements and the present worth of those improvements, both measured as of the valuation date. It is a measure of the proportion of total *economic life* of new improvements lost through physical deterioration and/or obsolescence. Accrued depreciation is a lump-sum measure of value decline or decrease as of the valuation date, and is applied to improvements only; site or land does not incur accrued depreciation.[a]

(3) *Capital recovery*, as already defined above, is the return to the investor of a portion of his property investment expected to be lost over the *income projection period*. This period may be but need not be the remaining economic life of the improvements. It is frequently but not necessarily applied to the portion of the total property investment represented by the improvements. Capital recovery is future-oriented, identifying future payments required to return the portion of the investment to be recovered by the investor over the income projection period.

**Capital Recovery Period (Income Projection Period).** Since the income forecast to be produced by an income property is expected to last for only a specified, finite time period, it is critical in any income capitalization analysis to identify the period that applies to the type of property and investor involved in the appraisal at hand. There are several different income projection periods applicable to any given property and its forecast income stream. Each depends on the nature of the income being forecast and on the perception of that income stream by the most probable type of purchaser-investor. It is essential for the appraiser first to identify *which* income projection period is appropriate for the income capitalization analysis he is undertaking, and then to estimate its *length* on the basis of available market evidence.

*Physical Life.* This is the period over which an improved property may be expected to remain in existence and to be capable of generating *any gross income* through services produced. This period is irrelevant in appraising. It is noted here simply to distinguish it from the other income projection periods which do have relevance and use in appraising. Remaining physical life is the physical life projected as of the valuation date.

*Useful Life.* This is the period over which an improved property may be

---

[a] A preferred term is "diminished utility," referring to the amount of total utility inherent in new improvements which has been lost through the effects of physical deterioration and/or obsolescence. See *An Introduction to Appraising Real Property* William N. Kinnard, Jr., (Chicago: Society of Real Estate Appraisers, 1968), Chapter 16.

expected to produce *some net* operating income. This period is most significant as the base for calculating accounting depreciation charges for income tax purposes. The U.S. Internal Revenue Service has published a *Table of Useful Lives* (Bulletin F). Remaining useful life is the useful life of an existing asset as of the valuation date; it is the difference between original useful life and the amount of useful life already expired.

*Economic Life.* This is the period over which an improved property may be expected to produce net income at a competitive rate of return (the Discount Rate). This period is widely used and useful in income-property appraising, especially when expressed as remaining economic life as of the valuation date. It sets the capital recovery period for improvements in the traditional physical residual techniques of income capitalization. It is also used in the estimation of accrued depreciation (or "diminished utility") in the Cost Approach to value estimation. Remaining economic life must be expressed in the terms of the market's or the most probable purchaser-investor's expectations of the period over which the improved property will produce a competitive net return.

*Lease Term.* This is the contract period over which a tenant (lessee) has a contractual obligation to pay the contract rental specified in the lease. It is used in leased fee and leasehold valuations, and is also useful as a guide to remaining economic life and/or investment holding period. The amount of capital to be recovered over the remaining lease term is usually the difference between the present worth or value of the entire property, and the forecast amount of the reversion at the expiration of the lease. Remaining lease term is the period from the valuation date to the lease expiration date stipulated in the lease contract..

*Mortgage Amortization Period.* This is the contract period over which mortgage amortization payments are made, and at the end of which the original amount of the mortgage loan is to be fully repaid to the lender (mortgagee). It is one determinant of the Mortgage Constant, and hence of Cash Throw-Off in mortgage-equity analysis. The remaining mortgage amortization period is rarely a meaningful period in appraisal analysis. Mortgage financing and loan terms are typically incorporated into the analysis on the basis of market conditions prevailing as of the valuation date. Thus, new mortgage financing is almost always assumed.

*Investment Holding or Turnover Period.* This is the period over which the most probable type of purchaser-investor of the type of property being appraised will expect to hold the property, and at the end of which he expects to resell it. It is used primarily in mortgage-equity analysis. Some equity capital recovery is provided by mortgage amortization over the investment holding period, through continuing equity build-up. The appropriate turnover (holding) period to use in any appraisal is determined by investor behavior in the market, conditioned in part by income tax capital gains provisions. The investment holding period is always future-oriented from the valuation date.

*Methods of Providing for*
*Capital Recovery*

This is not yet a discussion of methods of *measuring* or *estimating* Capital Recovery Rates or Factors. Before the mechanics can be explained and illustrated, it is necessary to understand the theory and the principles that underlie them. Every method of providing for capital recovery can be expressed in the form of a sinking fund. A specific sum is to be recovered over a specified period of time. Periodic annual payments are made as part of NOI to cumulate to the full amount of capital to be recovered by the end of the capital recovery period. Depending on the assumptions made about the disposition of periodic capital recovery payments, the sum total of the annual capital recovery payments themselves need not necessarily equal the amount of capital loss to be recovered.

There are basically three alternative methods of providing for capital recovery, with accompanying sinking fund or compound interest assumptions. Each is based on a different character (risk, timing, stability) of the net income stream represented by the return *on* the investment, and by a different presumed pattern of that income stream.

**Straight-Line Capital Recovery.** This can be measured in terms of equal annual payments which cumulate at *zero* compound interest. Since each successive capital recovery payment reduces the principal amount of outstanding investment remaining, each successive income payment also declines. A declining dollar return on remaining investment is therefore forecast at a determinable rate of decline. Capital recovery payments are largest under this method, since no reinvestment return is presumed on the annual payments. As a result, total dollar return *on* investment is lowest with straight-line Capital Recovery among the three basic methods.

**Sinking Fund (Safe Rate) Capital Recovery.** This represents equal annual payments which are reinvested by the investor (or a trustee) to cumulate at compound interest at the *safe rate* (e.g., the rate on savings accounts). The "deposits" of capital recovery payments earn compound interest annually at the end of each year; thus, smaller annual payments are required than under straight-line capital recovery to cumulate to the total amount to be recovered by the end of the capital recovery period. As a result, larger dollar amounts are available each year to cover return *on* investment. This return also declines annually, but at a lower rate.

**Level Annuity Capital Recovery.** This can be measured in terms of equal annual payments which are reinvested by the investor to cumulate at compound interest at the *Discount Rate*. This is Column 3 of the compound interest tables in Ellwood, at the Discount Rate. Because the Discount Rate is higher than the "safe rate" (and also greater than zero), the amount of annual capital recovery payments necessary to cumulate to the total loss to be recovered is smallest among the three methods. Annual dollar return *on* investment is therefore higher at the outset than in the other two methods, and declines annually at a lower rate.

Mortgage debt service is analogous to annuity capital recovery, since amortization payments in effect cumulate on an annual compound interest basis at the mortgage rate of interest.

**Return on Investment as a Residual.** NOI includes both return *on* investment at the Discount Rate and return *of* a portion of the amount of investment capital to be recovered at the Capital Recovery Rate. No prudent investor will acquire a property on which sufficient capital recovery is not provided to cover full return on the anticipated decline in capital value over the income projection period. The return *on* investment is a residual, available to the equity after capital recovery and mortgage interest. Thus, as capital recovery payments vary with different methods of capital recovery, the return on equity is directly affected in the same amount. The greater the leverage, the greater the impact of this variation in return on equity on present worth or value.

The same multiplier impact is felt on Cash Throw-Off in mortgage-equity analysis as capital recovery amounts vary. The only difference is that at least part of capital recovery is provided through mortgage amortization, which is determined by the pattern of mortgage loan terms.

## Market Considerations

Market alternatives tend to set the standards for appropriate capital recovery rates, as well as for Discount Rates and other rates of capitalization applicable to the type of property being appraised. Recovery of the anticipated loss in capital value is both necessary to meet competition from other properties and investors, and permissible because of income tax laws. Market influences, set by the patterns of similar, competing investment properties, largely determine the characteristics of capital recovery for the property being appraised. The applicable capital recovery period is influenced by what investors are seeking and obtaining on competitive properties. The method of capital recovery is a function of what is generated by competing properties and accepted by investors.

The method and period of capital recovery identified by the appraiser from market evidence as applicable to the subject property directly influence the estimated value of the appropriate income stream by helping determine (1) the amount of return on investment; and especially on equity; (2) the pattern and timing of return on investment, and on equity; and (3) the indicated *rate* of return on investment, and on equity.

**Methods of Deriving Capital Recovery**
**Rates and Amounts**

The identification of the appropriate capital recovery period and the applicable method of providing for capital recovery through NOI results from the appraiser's judgment. It is based on evidence about the existing market environment, periods, and methods applicable to similar competing properties, the type of property and most probable type of investor involved, and the character of the forecast future income flow for the property being appraised. Once these judgments are made and the method and period of capital recovery established, the appraiser has no further decisions to make. The *rate* of capital recovery is mathematically determined by the length of the capital recovery period and the rate at which capital recovery payments are discounted. The derivation of the rate is a mechanical computation using the Sinking Fund Factor Formula (Ellwood, pages 1-166, column 3):

$$\frac{1}{s_n} = \frac{i}{(1+i)^n - 1}$$

where:

| | |
|---|---|
| 1 | = the number one |
| $i$ | = the rate at which capital recovery payments are compounded |
| $n$ | = the number of compounding periods (usually years) during the capital recovery period |
| $1/s_n$ | = the capital recovery rate (CRR) |

*Mechanics of Calculating Capital*
*Recovery Rates*

For purposes of illustration in the remainder of this chapter, assume the following income characteristics for an income-producing property:

| | | |
|---|---|---|
| Effective Gross Income: | $25,000 | GIM: 5.00 |
| Net Operating Income: | $15,000 | (Operating Ratio: 40%) |
| Discount Rate: | 9% | Safe (Savings Deposit) Rate: 5% |
| Remaining Economic Life of Improvements: | | 25 years |
| Improvements: | | 75% of value (estimated) |
| Mortgage: | | 70% at 8.5% interest for 20 years (level monthly payments) |

*Annuity Recovery* uses the Discount Rate (9%) as $i$. Thus, from Ellwood, page 100, column 3, $1/s_n$ = .011806 = *1.18%*.

*Sinking Fund (Safe Rate) Recovery* uses the "safe rate" (5%) as $i$. Thus, from Ellwood, page 36, column 3, $1/s_n$ = .020952 = *2.10%*.

*Straight-Line Recovery* is a special case, since $i$ = 0. The formula for $1/s_n$ must be recognized as representing the *sum* of $n-1$ compound interest cumulations ($S_n$).

Thus,

$$s_n = (1 + i)^{n - n} + (1 + i)^{n - (n - 1)} + (1 + i)^{n - (n - 2)} + \dots + (1 + i)^{n - 1},$$

where

$$i = 0.$$

Then

$$s_n = n, \text{ and } 1/s_n = 1/n.$$

Thus, with

$$n = 25, 1/n = .04 \text{ or } 4.0\%.$$

In other words, the straight-line Capital Recovery Rate is obtained by dividing the amount of capital loss to be recovered (100%) by the number of years in the income projection period ($n$).

## Inclusion in Overall Rates

NOI includes both return *on* investment at the Discount Rate, and return *of* investment at the Capital Recovery Rate. The Overall Rate represents $NOI/V$. Thus, if Direct Capitalization is employed by dividing *NOI* by the Overall Rate, capital recovery is implicitly included, compounded at the Discount Rate. This is legitimate when the Capital Recovery Period is the Remaining Economic Life of the improvements.

In mortgage-equity analysis, the Composite Rate ($R$) developed includes capital recovery from two sources: (1) mortgage amortization; and (2) prorated annual recovery of any forecast decline in resale price, discounted at the Equity Yield Rate.[1] In this analysis, the Capital Recovery Period is the Income Projection Period or Investment Holding Period. Thus, capitalizing NOI by the appropriate Composite Rate includes provision for full recovery of forecast capital loss over the Income Projection Period.

## Application of Straight-Line
## Capital Recovery

The principles and underlying rationale of Straight-Line Capital Recovery, together with the mechanical process for calculating a Straight-Line Capital Recovery Rate, have already been presented in earlier sections of this chapter. Straight-Line Capital Recovery, when it is applicable at all, may be applied to improvements only, over the Remaining Economic Life of the Improvements. The *effective* rate of capital recovery is the annual capital recovery payment as a percentage of total property investment. It is the Capital Recovery Rate weighted by the percentage of total property investment represented by improvements. In the general example given earlier, the Capital Recovery Rate was 4.0%, and improvements represented an estimated 75% of total property value. The effective Capital Recovery Rate is thus .04 × .75 = .03 or 3.00%.

The forecast loss in capital value (100% of the improvements) is fully recovered over the Remaining Economic Life of the improvements. Annual return *on* investment is forecast to decline at a predictable rate, represented by the formula:

$$\frac{r \times d}{r + d}$$

$r$ is the discount rate (.09)
$d$ is the capital recapture rate (.04)

In the general example given earlier, the annual rate of decline in return *on* investment is thus

$$\frac{.09 \times .04}{.09 + .04} = \frac{.0036}{.13} = .0277 \text{ or } 2.77\%.$$

This is because the remaining investment on which net income is earned declines by 4% per year as capital recovery payments are received. In other words, the use of Straight-Line Capital Recovery involves a forecast of NOI as a *declining annuity*. It declines systematically in terms of the formula $r \times d/r + d$. Straight-Line Capital Recovery is not valid or applicable unless the forecast NOI is in fact a declining annuity with these characteristics.

**Alternative Methods of Calculating Straight-Line Capital Recovery.** By using the same principles described above, it is possible to utilize different mechanical techniques in applying straight-line capital recovery to an estimate of the present worth of a finite income stream (e.g., income from improvements over their remaining economic life). In each instance, the procedure involves identifying the level return *on* investment and subjecting it to annuity capitalization at the Discount Rate. Whichever technique of calculation is employed, the mathematical result is the same. These alternatives are rarely used in practice. They do emphasize the declining annuity character of the income stream forecast when Straight-Line Capital Recovery is used, however.

*Declining Annuity Treatment.* Ellwood[2] presents one technique of treating the investment return assumed in straight-line capital recovery as a *series* of annuities, each of which is discounted at the Discount Rate. While this technique would be used only in very special cases, it does demonstrate clearly the declining-annuity character of the income stream forecast when straight-line capital recovery is used.

The total investment to be recovered over the income projection period, while earning a return at the Discount Rate over that period, is the sum of the present worth of two income streams. One is the amount of capital recovery per year; the other is a series of individual annuities extending in length from one year to $n$ years. The amount of each of these individual annuities is given by the formula $\frac{r \times d}{r + d}$, applied to the total amount of present worth of the capital to be recovered.

In the general example given above, $n$ is 25; the Discount Rate is .09; the Capital Recovery Rate is .04; and the rate of decline, which gives the amount of each of 25 level annuities, is .0036. Using an Overall Rate of 12% (.09 + .03, the *effective* Capital Recovery Rate), the present worth of the NOI of $15,000 is $125,000. Since improvements represent an estimated 75% of property value, the amount to be recovered in 25 years, while earning 9% over that period, is $93,750 (.75 × $125,000).
Then:

.04 × $93,750 = $3,750 annual capital recovery amount
.0036 × $93,750 = $337.50 individual level annuity amount

The amount of annual capital recovery is multiplied by the Present Worth of One per Annum annual factor for 25 years at 9%: 9.822580 (Ellwood, page 100, column 5). This gives the present worth of the annual capital recovery payments.

The factor for capitalizing the series of level annuities of $337.50 each, ranging in length from one to 25 years, is:

$$\frac{n - \text{P.W. 1 per Annum Factor}}{\text{Discount Rate}} = \frac{25 - 9.822580}{.09}$$

The resulting factor is 168.638 in this case. Then, the present worth of the capital investment to be recovered is proved as follows:

$3,750 × 9.822580 = $36,834.675
*plus* $337.50 × 168.638 = $56,915.325
$93,750.00

This demonstrates that straight-line capital recovery does indeed presume a systematic annual decline in NOI.

*Effective Capital Recovery Rates to Derive an Overall Rate.* The Ring text[3] presents another alternative technique which uses the *effective* rate of capital recovery as a constant percentage return of capital to be recovered. It further treats NOI as a level rather than declining annual payment. After deducting the effective rate of capital recovery from NOI generated by the improvements, the residual return *on* investment is capitalized at the Discount Rate. This method can also be used to derive the applicable Overall Rate.

In the general example given earlier, the Discount Rate is .09; the Capital Recovery Rate is .04; and the recoverable improvements are estimated at 75% of property. The *effective* Capital Recovery Rate is thus .03 (.75 × .04).

Then:

| | |
|---|---|
| Effective Capital Recovery Rate: | .03 |
| Discount Rate: | .09 |
| Overall Rate: | .12 |

*Stabilization of Income.* Ring[4] also presents a variant of the Ellwood alternative in developing a "stabilized" income and capitalizing it via annuity capitalization at the Discount Rate. The "stabilized" income rate is the annuity *rate* at the Discount Rate (provided by the Installment to Amortize One Factor) *divided by* the straight-line capitalization rate.

In the general example earlier:

Annuity rate is $1/9.82258 = .1018 = 10.18\%$
Straight-Line Capitalization Rate is .13 (.09 + .04)
Stabilized income as a percentage of NOI is:
$$\frac{.1018}{.13} = .7831 = 78.31\%$$

This means that 78.13% of the annual income produced by or attributable to the improvements can be treated as a "stabilized" level annuity over the 25-year income projection period, discounted at 9%. It will be recalled that the 25-year annual Present Worth of One per Annum factor at 9% is 9.822580. The annual income attributable to the improvements is found by multiplying their present worth ($93,750) by the Capitalization Rate (.13). Then, .13 × $93,750 = $12,187.50. This is "stabilized" to a level annual flow over 25 years of $9,544.03 (.7831 × $12,187.50).

The present worth of $9,544.03 for 25 years, discounted at 9%, is:

$$9.822580 \times \$9,544.03 = \$93,747.$$

The slight difference is the result of rounding.

*Treatment as a Series of Reversions.* Finally, it is possible to treat the forecast declining net income stream assumed under straight-line capital recovery as a series of reversions, each of which is discounted by the Present Worth of One Factor (Ellwood, compound interest tables, column 4) at the Discount Rate. This is exactly the same method as was demonstrated in Chapters 5, 6, and 7.

**Uses of Straight-Line Capital Recovery.** This method of providing for capital recovery has perhaps the widest use and acceptance among practicing appraisers, the legal profession, and much of the investing public (especially the less sophisticated segment). It is certainly the most commonly used method in appraising income properties via the traditional physical residual techniques. In large part, this widespread usage is the result of the mechanical attractions of straight-line capital recovery. Actually, most of these attractions and purported advantages are either illusory or invalid. Nevertheless, the appraiser should be aware of the claims made for straight-line capital recovery, in order to guard against its improper use.

Straight-line capital recovery appears easy to understand. In its simplest form, the mechanics are easy to explain to others. The fact that its theoretical and logical foundation is questionable at best is either overlooked or simply not realized. There is an attraction in thinking of capital recovery as a constant amount which is multiplied by the number of payments $(n)$ to total the amount of forecast capital loss to be recovered.

Straight-line capital recovery rates and payments are simple to calculate, especially when 100% of capital loss to be recovered over the capital recovery period is merely divided by $n$. The fact that this simplicity hides several typically unrealistic assumptions about the character and shape of the forecast income stream is also frequently ignored or not understood.

A myth has grown up and been generally accepted that level annuity capitalization using the Present Worth of One Per Annum Factor is limited to almost certain, level income streams. As a result, straight-line capital recovery is widely held to be applicable to nearly all income flows that are not based on a long-term lease with a highly rated (AAA) tenant. The writings of Ellwood[5] in particular have reinforced earlier attempts by Babcock to demonstrate that *any* income stream can be subjected to annuity capitalization, provided proper adjustments are made in the income forecasts and in the capitalization factors or rates applied to them: level annuity, declining annuity, increasing annuity, and even variable annuity.

Straight-line capital recovery always results in a lower estimate of present worth or value than does any other method because the rate at which annual payments are compounded is zero. This is frequently regarded as applicable in making a "conservative" value estimate, ignoring the fact that there is only *one* value as defined for any given income stream as of a specified valuation date.

**Limitations of Straight-Line Capital Recovery.** The questionable rationale for using straight-line capital recovery at all has already been alluded to above. Despite the attractions of its simplicity, straight-line capital recovery is not defensible and really should not be used. Effective alternatives which are more logical and valid do exist for capitalizing a declining income stream. The same value estimate will or should result, but in a way which can be justified and convincingly supported.

It is argued that straight-line capital recovery accounts for uncertainty about the income forecast and compensates for this uncertainty or risk by assuming a constantly declining return on investment over time. It is entirely illogical and unjustifiable to compensate for uncertainty about forecast income (the numerator in the valuation formula) by using a capital recovery method that effectively increases the denominator in the formula.

It is possible to "stabilize" forecast return on investment, which effectively lowers $I$ rather than raising $R$, as noted above. If income is expected to decline systematically, or to vary, this type of income stream can be capitalized with annuity capitalization factors. Taking this approach makes *explicit* the assumptions about the character of the income stream. It also forces the appraiser to justify and support his income forecast with market evidence, rather than allowing him to bury these assumptions in the capital recovery rate. Finally, if there is risk that the forecast income stream will not be realized as projected, this risk should be reflected in the Discount Rate rather than the Capital Recovery Rate.

### Applications of Sinking Fund ("Safe Rate") Capital Recovery

The principles and rationale underlying Sinking Fund Capital Recovery, together with the mechanical process for calculating a Sinking Fund Capital Recovery Rate, have already been presented earlier in this chapter.

Sinking Fund Capital Recovery at the "safe rate" is applicable to improvements only, and is used over the Remaining Economic Life of the improvements. The *effective* rate of capital recovery is the annual capital recovery payment as a percentage of total property investment. It is the Sinking Fund Capital Recovery Rate weighted by the percentage of total property investment represented by the improvements. In the general example used throughout this chapter, it is thus .021 (actually .020952) X .75 = .01575 or 1.575%.

The Sinking Fund Capital Recovery Rate can be expressed as a percentage rate taken from column 3 in Ellwood's compound interest tables, or as a factor: the reciprocal of the rate. As such, it is incorporated into the Sinking Fund Capitalization Rate (Discount Rate plus Sinking Fund Capital Recovery Rate) or the Sinking Fund Capitalization Factor. In the general example used throughout this chapter, the Sinking Fund Capitalization Rate would be 11.10% (.09 + .021 = .111). The reciprocal factor is 9.0129.

The Hoskold Factor frequently discussed in appraisal literature is simply the reciprocal of a Sinking Fund Capitalization Rate at a *3%* "safe rate" for capital recovery payments, given the appropriate Discount Rate and Capital Recovery Period. It has extremely limited applicability, since the "safe rate" used in sinking fund capital recovery must be derived from the current market. In the general example used here, for instance, the "safe rate" is 5%.

The forecast loss in capital value (100% of the improvements) is fully recovered as a lump sum at the end of the Remaining Economic Life of the improvements. Annual return *on* investment is forecast to remain constant over the capital recovery period. Because sinking fund capital recovery payments are assumed to earn compound interest at the "safe rate" over the capital recovery period, the annual capital recovery payment required to provide full recovery of the forecast capital loss is less than that required in straight-line capital recovery, but greater than that required in level annuity capital recovery at the Discount Rate. The proportion of NOI generated by the improvements that represent return *on* investment is therefore greater than that in straight-line capital recovery, but less than that in annuity capital recovery.

**Uses of Sinking Fund Capital Recovery.** If the investment and the most probable purchaser-investor are such that a sinking fund is most likely to be established to provide for recovery of capital loss, compounding capital recovery at the "safe rate" *may* be applicable. It must be a "one-shot" investment with the investor not likely to reinvest capital recovery proceeds at the Discount Rate. Some depletion cases are adaptable to sinking fund capital recovery; so, too, might be a non-profit cemetery with a perpetual care fund.

**Limitations of Sinking Fund Capital Recovery.** The chief limitation of this method is that it is rarely descriptive of purchaser-investor market behavior. Therefore, it has extremely limited practical applicability. The logic on which it is based is impeccable, however.

Sinking fund capital recovery is sometimes employed very improperly to develop an "intermediate" value estimate. This is wholly indefensible. Its use can be justified only when it represents typical behavior of the most probable purchaser-investor.

*Applications of Level Annuity*
*Capital Recovery*

The principles and rationale of Annuity Capital Recovery, together with the mechanical process of estimating or deriving the Annuity Capital Recovery Rate, were discussed earlier in this chapter. Annuity Capital Recovery involves the return of increasing annual amounts of capital recovery which are sufficient to total to the amount of forecast capital loss by the end of the capital recovery period. They are the equivalent of level annual deposits left to accumulate at compound interest at the Discount Rate. Annuity capital recovery can be applied to *any* type of forecast future income stream. All that is required is that the income forecast represent risks and other investment rate of return components that are fully and appropriately covered by the Discount Rate employed.

Mortgage amortization is a special case of annuity capital recovery. The mortgage amortization rate is the annuity capital recovery rate or sinking fund factor given in column 3 of Ellwood's compound interest tables, compounded at the mortgage interest rate over the mortgage maturity. In the general example used in this chapter, mortgage amortization payments are made monthly. The mortgage interest rate is 8.5%; the maturity is 20 years. The average annual rate of mortgage amortization to maturity (Ellwood, page 89, column 3) is 12 X .001595 = .01914 = 1.914%. Thus, the mortgage amortization factor or Mortgage Constant given as Column 6 is the *sum* of the mortgage interest rate, plus the sinking fund factor at that rate.

The amount of capital loss is fully recovered over the appropriate capital recovery period in level annuity capital recovery. In traditional physical residual techniques of capitalization, the capital loss to be recovered is the investment in the improvements, recovered over their remaining economic life. In mortgage-equity analysis, the capital loss to be recovered is the difference between property investment as of the valuation date and forecast resale price or reversion, recovered over the income projection period. In leased fee valuation, the capital loss to be recovered is the difference between present worth as of the valuation date and the forecast amount of the reversion, recovered over the remaining term of the lease.

Whatever the form of the future income stream forecast, the annuity capital recovery *rate* is derived from the Discount Rate and the Capital Recovery Period. This rate is the sinking fund factor, expressed as a percentage, found in Column 3 of Ellwood's compound interest tables. To find the applicable sinking fund factor, the appraiser must have the appropriate Discount Rate, Capital Recovery Period, and frequency of capital recovery payments—annual, monthly, etc.

In the general example used throughout this chapter, the Annuity Capital Recovery Rate is 1.18% (Ellwood, page 100, Column 3). It means that 1.18% of the investment to be recovered is received annually as part of NOI. This is based on a 9% Discount Rate, a 25-year Capital Recovery Period, and annual compounding.

The income stream produced by the property and available to cover the investment which is to be recovered over the capital recovery period can be a level annuity, a declining annuity, an increasing annuity, or a variable annuity. The mechanics of estimating the present worth of that income stream will differ according to its characteristics. The Annuity Capital Recovery Rate, however, is the same as long as the Discount Rate, Capital Recovery Period, and frequency of capital recovery payments remain the same.

**Uses of Level Annuity Capital Recovery.** Whenever the Discount Rate realistically reflects the risks and components of investment return represented by forecast NOI, and discounting of capital recovery payments at compound interest at the Discount Rate can be justified by market evidence of investor behavior and investment alternatives, Annuity Capital Recovery can be applied to *any* forecast future income stream of finite length. This means that there must be a *market* of alternative, competing investments available to the investor. If one-time investment or an isolated, unique property is postulated, annuity capital recovery cannot be justified unless the property is subject to a long-term lease. In such special circumstances, however, it is also difficult to visualize Market Value as being applicable as a concept. Annuity Capital Recovery is *not* limited in its applicability to long-term leases with highly rated tenants.

Because capital recovery payments are discounted at the Discount Rate, the periodic capital recovery payment required under Annuity Capital Recovery is less than those required under either Straight-Line or Sinking Fund Capital

Recovery. As a result, the proportion of NOI available each year as a return *on* the investment is larger. When capitalized at the Discount Rate, the larger return *on* investment produces a higher present worth estimate.

Annuity Capital Recovery is a realistic representation of the way most investors behave in the market. As a result, it is considerably more applicable to the valuation of the vast proportion of income-producing real estate than is any alternative method of providing for capital recovery. It is also most consistent with the assumption of a typically informed, prudent, rational, purchaser-investor who seeks to maximize or optimize his investment returns.

Finally, because Annuity Capital Recovery is applicable to all forms of forecast future income flows, the appraiser may adjust for income variations in the numerator of the valuation equation (which is both logical and proper), rather than in the denominator.

**Limitations of Level Annuity Capital Recovery.** Annuity Capital Recovery is more complex as a concept and more complicated mechanically than is Straight-Line Capital Recovery, but it is no more so than is Sinking Fund Capital Recovery. However, its conceptual and logical validity are the critical attractions that determine its use. They more than offset the small amount of extra calculation time or the additional effort required to explain the method to a client or an interested third party. Moreover, the availability of precomputed tables covering a large range of Discount Rates, capital recovery periods, and frequencies of payment significantly reduces the mechanical complications of Annuity Capital Recovery.

Annuity Capital Recovery should not be applied to an income stream with characteristics that require Sinking Fund Capital Recovery at the "safe rate."

**Review Exercises**

1. Assume a property has a forecast first-year NOI of $27,000. The income projection period is 20 years. A mortgage can be obtained for 60% of appraised value at 7.5% interest. Equity investors in this type of property are currently seeking a 12.5% return on their equity investments. It is estimated that the improvements (building) represent 80% of the present worth of the property, and that they have a remaining economic life of 20 years.
   a. What is the indicated Discount Rate?
   b. What is the indicated Straight-Line Capital Recovery Rate?
   c. What is the *effective* Straight-Line Capital Recovery Rate?
   d. What is the indicated Overall Rate?
   e. What is the indicated present worth of the property, using the Overall Rate via Direct Capitalization?
   f. What is the indicated amount of capital loss or decline to be recovered over the capital recovery period?
   g. What is the dollar amount of annual straight-line capital recovery?

2. Using the figures from Problem 1 above, calculate and tabulate the annual dollar amount of NOI, return on investment, capital recovery, and end-of-year total investment in the property for each of the first five years of the income projection period.
3. In Problem 1 above, assume that NOI is forecast as a level annuity over the income projection period. Assume further that the forecast amount of the reversion (through resale) is $40,000, and that the initial amount of the investment in the property is $200,000. Use the Discount Rate derived in Problem 1.
   a. What is the total amount of capital loss to be recovered over the income projection period?
   b. What is the Level Annuity Capital Recovery Rate?
   c. What is the annual amount which, if deposited to earn compound interest at the Discount Rate annually at the end of each year, would cumulate to the full amount of capital recovery required by the end of the income projection period?
4. Assume a property investment calls for $160,000 in capital recovery in 20 years. The indicated Discount Rate is 9.5%. Savings accounts in the market are currently earning 5% compound interest.
   a. With annual end-of-year compounding, what is the indicated Sinking Fund Capital Recovery Rate?
   b. What dollar amount would have to be deposited annually to cumulate to $160,000 at the Sinking Fund rate at the end of 20 years?
5. A mortgage loan has been granted in the amount of $120,000. It calls for level monthly payments for 25 years at 7.5% interest on the outstanding balance of the loan.
   a. What is the dollar amount of each monthly payment? (Round to the nearest cent.)
   b. Show in a table the distribution of the first five monthly payments between interest and principal amortization. Show the outstanding balance of the loan at the end of each of the first five months. (Round to the nearest cent.)

**Supplementary Readings**

American Institute of Real Estate Appraisers, *The Appraisal of Real Estate*, fifth edition (Chicago: American Institute of Real Estate Appraisers, 1967), pp. 278-287, 301-310, and 325-326.

L.W. Ellwood, *Ellwood Tables for Real Estate Appraising and Financing; Part I: Explanatory Text*, third edition (Chicago: American Institute of Real Estate Appraisers, 1970), pp. 28-45 and 75-78.

Sanders A. Kan, Frederick E. Case, and Alfred Schimmel, *Real Estate Appraisal and Investment* (New York: Ronald Press, 1963), Chapter 10.

Alfred A. Ring, *The Valuation of Real Estate*, second edition (Engelwood Cliffs, N.J.: Prentice-Hall, 1970), Chapter 18.

## Notes

1. L.W. Ellwood, *Ellwood Tables for Real Estate Appraising and Financing; Part I: Explanatory Text*, third edition (Chicago: American Institute of Real Estate Appraisers, 1970), pp. 2-10.

2. *Ibid.*, pp. 75-77.

3. Alfred A. Ring, *The Valuation of Real Estate*, second edition (Englewood Cliffs, N.J.: Prentice-Hall, 1970), Chapter 18.

4. *Ibid.*, p. 272.

5. Ellwood, *Ellwood Tables; Part I*.

6. Frederick M. Babcock, *The Valuation of Real Estate* (New York: McGraw-Hill, 1932).

# 11 Finite Income Streams: Capitalization Rates and Factors

In most instances, Capital Recovery Rates are estimated not for themselves but to provide the appraiser with one necessary component of Capitalization Rates and Capitalization Factors. As indicated in both Chapters 5 and 9, a Capitalization Rate can be derived arithmetically by adding together the Discount Rate and the Capital Recovery Rate appropriate to the method of capital recovery. This is essential when and if either the straight-line or sinking fund (safe rate) capital recovery is to be used, since the two components (Discount Rate and Capital Recovery Rate) represent different rates of discount. It is unnecessary whenever level annuity capital recovery is postulated. This is because the Installment to Amortize One factor, which *is* the Level Annuity Capitalization Rate, incorporates within it a provision for capital recovery, discounted at the Discount Rate. It can usually be taken directly from published precalculated tables such as those found in column 6 of the tables on pages 1-166 of Ellwood.[1] If it must be calculated, the mechanics involved are less complex than they are for calculating the Level Annuity Capital Recovery Rate and then adding it to the Discount Rate.

Only in the Ellwood formulation of mortgage-equity analysis is a Capital Recovery Rate, expressed as the Sinking Fund factor discounted at the Equity Yield Rate, used directly as a separate rate in income-property appraising. Otherwise, Capitalization Rates are used in valuation analysis whenever a finite income stream is to be valued. When they can be estimated directly, the intermediate step of estimating the Capital Recovery Rate separately is unnecessary.

It should be remembered throughout this discussion that the central issue or objective for the appraiser is the valuation of a *finite income stream*. This is accomplished by discounting the forecast future income stream to a present worth estimate. The discount factor used in this process is the appropriate Capitalization Rate, or its reciprocal, the Capitalization Factor. In valuing a finite income stream, the Capitalization Rate is thus the $R$ in the basic valuation formula $V = I/R$; the Capitalization Factor is $F$ in the formula $V = I \times F$.

## Review of the Nature of Capitalization Rates and Factors

A Capitalization Rate is a *ratio* between the portion of NOI that is produced by or attributable to that segment of the total property investment forecast to represent capital loss at the end of the income projection period, and the principal sum represented by that forecast capital loss. It is usually expressed as an annual percentage rate. It provides for both periodic return *on* the portion of the investment representing forecast capital loss over the income projection period at the Discount Rate, and periodic return *of* that portion of the investment at a Capital Recovery Rate in such amounts that the full capital loss forecast will have been recovered by the end of the income projection period. In this way, the investor has his investment capital intact at the end of the income projection period, and he has earned a competitive return on the outstanding balance of his investment at the Discount Rate over that period.

Any finite income stream has a forecast reversionary value of zero, by definition. Thus, a Capitalization Rate may also be regarded as the annual percentage ratio between the annual dollar amount of a finite income stream, and the present worth of that finite income stream. When a Capitalization Rate is applied to the income attributable or assignable to improvements in physical residual techniques of capitalization, it reflects the fact that the improvements are forecast to make no contribution to the value of the property above the value of the site (if vacant and available to be put to its Highest and Best Use) at the end of the estimated remaining economic life of the improvements. Indeed, this is what the estimate of remaining economic life means.

Similarly, when the present worth of the income stream to be produced under a lease is estimated, the use of a Capitalization Rate reflects the fact that the lessor's (landlord's) rights to rental income have no further value when the lease expires. The present worth of the lessee's (tenant's) rental advantage under a lease is discounted by a Capitalization Rate to indicate that the lessee has no further claims to this advantage when the lease expires. A mortgagee (lender) has no further right to interest income when the mortgage loan matures and is fully paid off in full. This is why a Mortgage Constant, which is simply the Capitalization Rate for a mortgage loan, is applied to the principal amount of the loan to indicate annual debt service payments that will both amortize the loan over its maturity and provide interest income at the contract rate on the outstanding balance of the loan.

It must be remembered that income-property appraising is the valuation of *rights* in income-producing real estate. In any finite income stream, the right of the affected party to receive that income is limited to a finite time period; i.e., the income projection period, however it may be identified in the particular appraisal problem. At the end of that period, he has no further right or expectation of income from that source; his reversionary interest in that specific source of rights to income is zero. Thus, the present worth of that source (improvements, lease, mortgage loan) must be fully recovered over the income projection period to realize the investment objective of keeping his capital intact. This is why Capitalization Rates must provide for both return *on* and return *of* the present worth of that source of income.

**Direct Derivation from Income and Value Estimates**. Recalling the general example used throughout Chapter 10, the appraiser was given the following information:

Net Operating Income: $15,000
Discount Rate: 9%
Remaining Economic Life of Improvements: 25 years
Present Worth of Improvements: $93,750
Value of Site: $31,250

The remaining economic life of the improvements of 25 years also represents both the income projection period and the capital recovery period. Since the site is assumed to have the capacity to generate income at the Discount Rate indefinitely (in perpetuity), the finite income stream is the 25-year flow forecast to be produced by and attributable to the improvements. At the end of that period, the net contribution of the improvements to total property value will be zero. The portion of capital investment to be recovered over the 25-year income projection period, therefore, is $93,750.

The dollar amount of forecast annual income produced by or attributable to the $93,750 investment in the improvements can be obtained by abstraction. The Capitalization Rate is as yet unknown, but it is known that the investment in the site must equal 9% per year to be competitive. The annual dollar income that must be generated by the site is therefore .09 × $31,250 = $2,812.50. Subtracting this amount from NOI leaves $12,187.50 annual income from the portion of the investment represented by the improvements ($15,000.00 − $2,812.50 = $12,187.50). This is the annual income available to provide a 9% return on the $93,750 investment in the improvements, plus recovery of the entire $93,750 by the end of the 25-year income projection period.

Using the basic valuation formula $V = I/R$, it is now possible to calculate the indicated Capitalization Rate in this example. $R = I/V$, so $R = \$12,187.50/\$93,750.00 = 0.13$ or 13%.

Of course, the problems confronting the income-property appraiser are only infrequently presented in this fashion. Only rarely is the issue to estimate how much the annual amount of a finite income stream must be to provide return on a given investment at a specified rate, plus full amortization of that investment capital over a specific income projection period. It is a very pertinent question in mortgage financing and in investment decision-making about forecast cash flows, however, where both the Mortgage Constant and Annual Debt Service can be critical factors. Moreover, it is useful in identifying what rate of return to the lessor is indicated under a long-term lease. But the usual appraisal problem has value or present worth as its end-product, rather than its starting point. This example has been presented to illustrate graphically the relationships involved in Capitalization Rates.

**Construction of Capitalization Rates.** Most commonly, the appraiser must construct Capitalization Rates without benefit of estimates of the amount of capital to be recovered. Indeed, the estimation of this figure is part of the purpose of the appraisal: to estimate the value of specified rights in income property. The appraiser must therefore be able to develop Capitalization Rates from data on Discount Rate, income projection period, and method of capital recovery (based on the character of the forecast future income stream) only.

If the Capital Recovery Rate has been estimated in accordance with the techniques presented in Chapter 10, the Capitalization Rate can be constructed by adding the Discount Rate and the Capital Recovery Rate. In the general example provided in Chapter 10 and repeated in the preceding section of this chapter, the Discount Rate is 9%. The Straight-Line Capital Recovery Rate was found to be 4%; the Sinking Fund Capital Recovery Rate was 2.095%; and the Level Annuity Capital Recovery Rate was 1.181%. From these figures, the Capitalization Rates associated with each of the theoretically possible methods of capital recovery are:

Straight-Line Capitalization Rate:    $0.09 + 0.04 = 0.13 = 13.00\%$
Sinking Fund Capitalization Rate:    $0.09 + 0.02095 = 0.11095 = 11.10\%$
Level Annuity Capitalization Rate:    $0.09 + 0.01181 = 0.10181 = 10.18\%$

**Mechanics of Present Worth Estimation with Capitalization Rates**. Capitalization Rates are applied to estimate the present worth of only that portion of total property investment which is to be recovered over the capital recovery period or income projection period. They are thus used only in estimating the present worth of a finite income stream. The present worth of that portion of the investment, or of that income stream, is calculated by *dividing* the annual amount of net income forecast to be produced by the recoverable portion of total property investment *by* the Capitalization Rate, expressed as a decimal. In the general example in Chapter 10 and this chapter, the investment in the improvements is forecast to produce $12,187.50 per year for 25 years. Applying the Capitalization Rates derived in the preceding section to this finite annual income flow results in the following present worth estimates for the improvements under each of the theoretically possible methods of providing for capital recovery:

Straight-Line Capital Recovery:    $12,187.50/.13 = $93,750
Sinking Fund Capital Recovery:    $12,187.50/.1110 = $109,797
Level Annuity Capital Recovery:    $12,187.50/.1018 = $119,720

These figures have not been rounded as final value estimates would be, in part because they are intermediate estimates that would normally be used in conjunction with site value estimates to produce a property value estimate, and in part because they are presented here to illustrate the principles involved. Actually, the Capitalization Rates are already rounded to four decimal places. They were taken from percentage rates which are conventionally rounded to the nearest basis point. As observed in Chapter 7, a basis point is one one-hundredth of a percentage point. Capitalization Rates are frequently provided to six decimal places, especially when they or their components are taken from published tables such as those provided in Ellwood.

The three different answers developed above do not mean that there are three different present worths of the improvements, or that the appraiser has a choice of which to use in his final value estimate. Since this is an illustrative example, the three figures were calculated to show the present worth estimate that would result under each of the three potentially or theoretically applicable methods of providing for capital recovery. Each capital recovery premise produces a different Capital Recovery Rate consistent with its assumptions, and each results in a different Capitalization Rate. Only one premise meets the conditions and describes the characteristics of the forecast future income stream in the appraisal problem at hand, however. The appraiser's responsibility is to identify those income characteristics and then select that method of capital recovery, with its associated Capitalization Rate, that most closely responds to the characteristics of the forecast finite income flow. Because different types of income streams are encountered in income-property appraising, he must have working familiarity with all the possible alternative methods.

Because its income stream is forecast to continue indefinitely, and therefore no capital recovery is required, site is valued by *dividing* the portion of NOI produced by the investment in the site. In this case it is $2,812.50; dividing it by the Discount Rate produces a present worth estimate for the site of $31,250 ($2,812.50/.09 = $31,250).

## Capitalization Factors

Capitalization Factors are simply the reciprocals of Capitalization Rates ($F = 1/R$). The annual amount of the finite income stream is *multiplied* by the Capitalization Factor instead of being divided by the Capitalization Rate to produce a present worth estimate for that income stream. Capitalization Factors are widely used by appraisers in part because they are available in published form, and in part because division by mechanical calculator was a cumbersome process fraught with opportunities for error or misplacement of decimal points. The Present Worth of One per Annum factor (Column 5 in Ellwood's compound interest tables) *is* the Level Annuity Capitalization Factor. It is also widely available in appraisal texts labeled as the "Inwood Factor."[2] Ring has published "Direct-Ring" Capitalization Factors which are the reciprocals of Straight-Line Capitalization Rates at selected Discount Rates and for selected income projection periods.[3] Finally, the "Hoskold Factor Tables" are precalculated Sinking Fund Capitalization Factors for selected Discount Rates and selected income projection periods, with capital recovery at a 3% "safe rate."[4]

With the availability of electronic desk calculators and an understanding of the composition and use of the six basic compound interest factor tables discussed in Chapter 5 (and published on pages 1-166 in Part II of Ellwood), the appraiser can now divide as easily as he can multiply. These compound interest factors are more readily available and generally are published in more variations that permit greater flexibility in calculations, than are Inwood Factors, Hoskold Factors, or Ring Factors.

As reciprocals of Capitalization Rates, Capitalization Factors also provide for return *on* the investment at the Discount Rate, and return *of* the investment over the income projection period at the Capital Recovery Rate. Any Capitalization Rate can be converted into a Capitalization Factor by dividing the rate into 1.0000. The present worth of any finite income stream is obtained by *multiplying* the annual income payment by the appropriate Capitalization Factor.

Once again, it must be emphasized that the appraiser does *not* have a choice of Capitalization Factors to use in any given appraisal. The factor to be used is dictated by the method of capital recovery most descriptive of the character and duration of the forecast future income stream.

### Derivation of Appropriate Capitalization
### Rate or Capitalization Factor

The Capitalization Rate or Factor applicable in any appraisal is determined by the appropriate Discount Rate, income projection period, and method of capital recovery. The latter in turn depends on the character of the forecast future income stream and the market-determined reaction of the most probable purchaser-investor to that income stream.

*Annuity Capitalization*

Far from being restricted in applicability to level income streams with low risk of non-payment or variability (i.e., income streams with the characteristics of a level annuity contract, such as is provided under a long-term lease to a highly rated tenant), annuity capitalization can be used in estimating the present worth of *any* type of income stream, with two notable exceptions. One is the case in which capital recovery takes the form of a sinking fund compounded at the "safe rate." The second involves an income stream produced by a unique, non-market property for which there are no investment alternatives available to the purchaser-investor.

**Level Annuity**. This is the simplest mechanical form of an income stream. The annual income produced by or available to cover the portion of total property investment to be recovered over the income projection period is forecast to be a constant amount. It is available to cover a return *on* the investment at the Discount Rate plus the necessary return *of* the investment at the Capital Recovery Rate. These capital recovery payments are discounted at the Discount Rate under the Annuity Capital Recovery premise.

Thus, in the general example used throughout this chapter, with a Discount Rate of 9% and a 25-year income projection period, the Annuity Capital Recovery Rate is 1.181%. The Annuity Capitalization Rate is 10.18%, and the

Annuity Capitalization Factor is 9.822580. The Annuity Capital Recovery Rate is the 25-year annual Sinking Fund Factor at 9%, found in column 3 on page 100 in Ellwood. The Annuity Capitalization Rate is the 25-year annual Installment to Amortize One Factor at 9% (column 6). The Annuity Capitalization Factor is the 25-year annual Present Worth of One per Annum Factor at 9% (column 5).

If annual income of $12,187.50 is forecast to remain constant over the 25-year income projection period, then the present worth of this income stream (and of the improvements producing it) is $119,700 (rounded).

$$(\$12,187.50/.1018 = \$119,720)$$
$$(\$12,187.50 \times 9.822580 = \$119,713)$$

**Declining Annuity.** The Straight-Line Capital Recovery premise postulates a steadily declining annual income on the portion of total property investment to be recovered (e.g., improvements). The *rate* of decline forecast, as noted in Chapter 10, is provided by the formula:

$$\frac{r \times d}{r + d},$$

where $r$ is the Discount Rate and $d$ is the Straight-Line Capital Recovery Rate.

In the case of the general example used throughout Chapter 10 and this chapter, the forecast rate of decline under the Straight-Line Capital Recovery premise is 2.77% (.09 × .04/.09 + .04). This means an annual dollar decline of $337.50. (.0277 × $12,187.50). Annual capital recovery payments are .04/.13 × $12,187.50 = $3,750. This declining annuity can be handled in either of the ways illustrated in Chapter 10.

The first method treats the income stream as a series of 25 separate annuities of $337.50 each, but with different durations from one to 25 years. To the present worth of this series is added the present worth of the $3,750 in capital recovery, discounted over 25 years at 9%. The factors to use in this example were derived in Chapter 10.
Thus:

$3,750 × 9.82258 = $36,834.68
$337.50 × 168.638 = $56,915.32
Present worth of investment to be recovered: $93,750.00

This is the same dollar figure ($93,750) as that derived via Straight-Line Capital Recovery. However, its derivation is more logical and consistent. It makes the necessary adjustment for a forecast declining income in the income stream itself, rather than in the Capitalization Rate or in the Capital Recovery Rate on which it is based.

The declining annuity implicitly assumed in the Straight-Line Capital

Recovery premise can also be "stabilized" to a level or constant annuity, as demonstrated in Chapter 10. The "stabilized" annual income assignable to the portion of total property investment to be recovered (improvements) in the example used in Chapter 10 has been shown to be 78.31% of first-year income attributable to the improvements (.1018/.13 = .7831). This amounts to $9,544.03.
Thus:

$$\$9,544.03 \times 9.82258 = \$93,747 \text{ (rounded to } \$93,750)$$

This method produces the same dollar amount of present worth of the portion of total property investment to be recovered (improvements). It is a preferable approach to Straight-Line Capitalization because it treats capital recovery more logically and consistently.

Finally, a declining annuity can always be treated as a series of individual reversions. The Present Worth of One Factor at the Discount Rate is applied to each successive annual income payment over the appropriate discount period (one year for the first year's payment, two years for the second, five years for the fifth, etc.). The series of present worth estimates is summed to derive the present worth estimate for the entire income stream. This technique is exactly the same as that illustrated in Chapter 5 and in a following section of this chapter for a variable annuity.

A "step down" lease is also a form of declining annuity. As illustrated in Chapter 5 in the section on "Deferred Factors," the several steps or levels of income can be treated as separate income streams. A separate level Annuity Capitalization Factor (Present Worth of One per Annum) is applied to each "step"; the factor for the second and successive "steps" is called a "deferred factor."

**Increasing Annuity.** An increasing annuity is an income stream in which NOI is forecast to increase, either annually or in periodic "steps" (as under a "step-up" lease). The procedures for capitalizing an increasing income stream are exactly the same as those for capitalizing a declining annuity. Only the annual dollar income figures are different. An increasing annuity can best be capitalized as either a series of individual annual reversions, or a series of "steps." In either case, the present worth estimates of the individual components are summed to derive the present worth of the entire income stream.

**Variable Annuity.** A forecast income stream may vary from year to year in either direction—up or down. This can be handled in a simple and straightforward fashion by treating each year's forecast income as separate reversion. Then the appropriate Present Worth of One Factor at the Discount Rate is applied to each year's income forecast to derive its present worth. The present worth of the income stream is simply the sum of the individual years' present worth estimates.

For example, if the Discount Rate is 9%, the present worth of a 5-year variable income stream might be as follows. The Present Worth of One Factors are found in column 4 on page 100 in Ellwood.

| Year | Income | P.W. of One Factor | Present Worth |
|------|--------|--------------------|---------------|
| 1 | $10,000 | .917431 | $ 9,174 |
| 2 | $12,000 | .841680 | $10,100 |
| 3 | $13,000 | .772183 | $10,038 |
| 4 | $11,000 | .708425 | $ 7,793 |
| 5 | $ 9,000 | .649931 | $ 5,849 |
| Present Worth of Income Stream: | | | $42,954 |

## Sinking Fund Capitalization

As noted in Chapter 10, Sinking Fund Capitalization is applicable in those rare circumstances when the conditions of Sinking Fund Capital Recovery at the "safe rate" are met. If the income stream is such that the typical purchaser-investor would in fact deposit capital recovery payments in a sinking fund to accumulate at annual compound interest at the "safe rate" (e.g., bank savings account rate), then Sinking Fund Capitalization is appropriate.

The Sinking Fund Capitalization Rate (or its reciprocal factor) is the *sum* of the Discount Rate plus the Sinking Fund Capital Recovery Rate. A Sinking Fund Capitalization Rate must always be derived by this summation process.

## Straight-Line Capitalization

This is rarely defensible or logical, despite the attractions of its simple and easy application. The income stream predicated under Straight-Line Capitalization is constantly declining annuity, decreasing at a predictable rate. This can better be treated as a declining annuity, even though the mechanics are somewhat more complex. Exactly the same present worth estimate is derived, whichever method of providing for capital recovery is employed, but the logic of Straight-Line Capital Recovery is much more difficult (if not impossible) to defend in most instances.

At the same time, the professional appraiser should be familiar with the mechanics as well as the rationale of Straight-Line Capitalization. Because it is still widely used, he should both understand its limitations in use by others and be prepared to explain why he does not use it, even when he derives essentially the same result by a more complex form of analysis and a more complicated mechanical process.

The Straight-Line Capitalization Rate is the sum of the Discount Rate and the Straight-Line Capital Recovery Rate. It must always be developed by this summation process.

## Applications of Capitalization Rates and
## Capitalization Factors in Appraisal Analysis

In physical residual techniques of capitalization, Capitalization Rates and Factors are applicable to that portion of NOI produced by or available to cover the investment in improvements. These techniques are the Building Residual and Land Residual Techniques discussed in Chapter 12. The capital recovery period in these techniques is usually the Remaining Economic Life of the improvements.

In the Property Residual Technique presented in Chapter 12, Capitalization Rates and Factors are applied to the total NOI produced by or available to cover the total property investment. The capital recovery period is also usually the Remaining Economic Life of the improvements. Capitalization Rates and Factors are also applied to the NOI produced by or available to cover the lessor's interest in Leased Fee Valuation. The Capital Recovery Period is the remaining lease term in this case, which is discussed in detail in Chapter 19. Leased Fee valuation is actually a special case of Property Residual Analysis.

Although rates of capitalization to provide both return *on* investment and return *of* forecast capital loss are employed in mortgage-equity analysis, they are not the same as Capitalization Rates and Factors developed here. This difference and the derivation of appropriate rates of capitalization for use in mortgage-equity analysis are considered in detail in Chapter 13.

## Summary and Review of Selection of
## Appropriate Rates of Capitalization

The materials in Chapters 7 through 11 have concentrated on one major topic: the estimation of appropriate rates of discount to incorporate as $R$ in the basic valuation formula $V=I/R$. This amount of space and discussion has been necessary because it is not always possible or appropriate to approach income property value estimation via Direct Capitalization by dividing Net Operating Income by the proper Overall Rate. This is by far the simplest and most direct method of capitalization, and it is most defensible when property value is to be estimated and the necessary data of the required quality are available. Unfortunately, these necessary data are infrequently available to the appraiser. Moreover, there are interests in income properties other than the fee simple estate that the appraiser is often required to value.

To approach present worth estimates by means other than Direct Capitalization, it has been necessary to devise methods that separate the property being appraised into analytical components (physical, legal, and investment-financial) and estimate the present worth of each component individually. Their sum is the indicated present worth or value of the property. In some instances, the present worth of one of these components is the objective of the appraisal.

Net Operating Income is the stabilized annual cash flow forecast to be produced by the total investment in the entire property. Each of the analytical components of the property has a portion of NOI associated with it. Each of these component flows has different characteristics. Each has a separate and distinctive rate of discount or capitalization peculiarly responsive to its characteristics. Thus, there are several different $R$s tied in with the several $I$s that an income property is capable of producing. It is necessary for the appraiser to understand the nature, derivation, uses, and limitations of each if he is to be equipped adequately to cope with the variety of income property appraisal problems that exists. Only then can he apply them with arithmetic accuracy and logical propriety.

## Present Worth Estimation
## via Capitalization

Value or present worth is income either divided by an appropriate rate or rates, or income times an appropriate factor or factors. In this context, a "factor" is simply the reciprocal of a "rate." Net Operating Income, which is capitalized to a present worth estimate, provides both a return *on* the entire property investment at a competitive market rate and a return *of* that portion of the total property investment which is forecast to experience capital loss over the income projection period. The amount, timing, stability, and duration of NOI must be estimated by the appraiser from market evidence before the proper rate(s) of capitalization can be selected.

The selection of the appropriate rate(s) of capitalization to apply in a given appraisal is dictated by the character of the forecast income stream and the market behavior of the most probable type of purchaser-investor for the type of property involved. It is *not* a matter of choice for the appraiser.

## Rates Used by the Appraiser

**Discount Rate.** The Discount Rate is the competitive rate of return *on* the property investment. It must cover both mortgage interest charges on any borrowed funds, plus a competitive equity return on the equity investment. Discount Rates are commonly estimated through Band of Investment analysis, which produces a weighted average of rates of return necessary to make the investment competitive on the market as of the valuation date. Discount Rates may occasionally be estimated directly from market sales data. Discount Rates are applied directly to annual income when capitalization in perpetuity is used to estimate the present worth of site or land.

**Capital Recovery Rate.** A Capital Recovery Rate is the annual rate of return *of* any forecast capital loss. The length of the capital recovery period is a determinant of the Capital Recovery Rate: the longer the period, the lower the rate, and vice versa. The length of the period is determined by the character of the income flow, the estimated remaining economic life of the improvements or the remaining term of a lease; and market reactions to the type of income flow involved.

The method of providing for capital recovery is also a determinant of the Capital Recovery Rate. It establishes the rate at which annual capital recovery payments may accumulate at compound interest over the Capital Recovery Period.

Except in rare cases when Sinking Fund Capital Recovery at the "safe rate" is applicable, Level Annuity Capital Recovery is the most logical and defensible method of providing for capital recovery. It can be applied to any type of forecast future income stream, including the special form of declining annuity assumed in Straight-Line Capital Recovery. Although still widely used, Straight-Line Capital Recovery is almost always a non-descriptive method of providing for capital recovery.

**Capitalization Rates and Factors.** These represent the combined rate of return *on* the portion of total property investment forecast to experience capital loss and the rate of return *of* that capital loss, over the capital recovery period. A Capitalization Rate is the sum of the Discount Rate and the Capital Recovery Rate. A Capitalization Factor is simply the reciprocal of a Capitalization Rate.

Except in rare cases, Level Annuity Capitalization Rates and Factors should be used in capitalizing to a present worth estimate the income produced by the portion of total property investment forecast to experience capital loss. Any systematically varying income stream (increasing or decreasing annuity) can be capitalized with Level Annuity Capitalization Rates, as can all level income streams. Capitalization Rates and Factors are typically employed in estimating the present worth of improvements in traditional residual techniques of capitalization and in estimating the present worth of the lessor's interest in leased fee valuation.

**Overall Rates of Capitalization.** An Overall Rate is the ratio of NOI to present worth of the entire investment in the property, expressed as an annual percentage rate.

In the absence of an appropriate Capitalization Rate or conversion formula, *any* income stream can be converted to a present worth estimate by treating each annual payment as a separate reversion. The present worth of the income stream is the *sum* of the present worth estimates for the individual payments.

It is the weighted average between the Discount Rate on site and the Capitalization Rate on improvements in physical residual techniques, or between the Capitalization Rate and the reversion discount factor (Present Worth of One) in leased fee and property residual analysis. Overall Rates may be estimated directly from market sales data if they are available. Otherwise, they may be constructed as weighted averages as noted above.

A form of Overall Rate termed the Composite Capitalization Rate is used in mortgage-equity analysis. It is a weighted average of the equity yield rate on the equity investment, the mortgage constant, and the rate of recovery of forecast capital loss on resale at the end of the income projection period.

However they are developed, Overall Rates are divided directly into NOI to produce a present worth estimate for the entire property. This process is called Direct Capitalization.

## A Concluding Note

The discussion thus far in the book has concentrated on presenting, developing, and explaining the basic tools of analysis available to the appraiser for capitalizing net income to a present worth estimate. The same tools can be used in the valuation of fee simple interests in income properties, or in the valuation of partial interests. The following sections deal with the selection and application of those tools to the major categories of valuation problems that periodically confront the income-property appraiser.

These tools are mathematical formulas and mechanical processes. Without a good command over their use, the appraiser is lost. But simply manipulating figures properly and accurately is not appraising, nor is it truly income capitalization. The tools are necessary, but the real role of the appraiser and the real challenge of income-property appraising are in identifying and quantifying in a defensible fashion in the character of the appropriate income to be capitalized, the appropriate Discount Rate, and the appropriate income projection period.

## Review Exercises

1. An 40,000 square foot industrial building is subject to a lease with an 18-year remaining term. It calls for annual rentals of $1.25 per square foot. Forecast annual Operating Expenses have been stabilized at $15,000. The estimated value of the site as of the valuation date is $55,000. Financing on the property is available at 9.25% on an 80%, 25-year mortgage with annual amortization. The mortgage was based on an appraised value of $300,000. Equity investors in this type of property are seeking a 13% return on their investment. It is estimated that the remaining life of the improvements is 40 years. The reversionary value of the property at the expiration of the lease is forecast to be $235,000. When the lease expires, it is estimated that the building can be rented at $1.10 per square foot for the remainder of its economic life, with Operating Expenses remaining level.
   a. What is the annual amount of forecast NOI over the term of the lease?
   b. What is the indicated Cash Throw-Off over the remaining term of the lease?
   c. What is the indicated Discount Rate?

232

   d. What is the indicated Equity Dividend Rate over the remaining term of the lease?

   e. What is the present worth of the NOI receivable over the remaining term of the lease?

   f. What is the present worth of the reversion at the end of the lease?

   g. What is the present worth of the leased fee interest (lessor's interest): i.e., the present worth of NOI under the lease plus present worth of reversion?

   h. What is the total amount of forecast capital loss to be recovered over the term of the lease?

   i. What is the mortgage constant?

   j. What is the amount of annual debt service?

   k. What is the amount of forecast capital loss forecast over the remaining economic life of the improvements?

   l. What is the annual amount of NOI forecast for years 19-40?

   m. What is the Capitalization Rate applied to the income stream in years 19-40:

     (1) with level-annuity capital recovery?

     (2) with straight-line capital recovery?

   n. What is the present worth of the income stream in years 19-40:

     (1) with level-annuity capital recovery?

     (2) with declining-annuity (straight-line) capital recovery?

   o. What will be the present worth of the property when the lease expires, assuming level-annuity capitalization?

2. A property is forecast to have the following NOI income stream for 10 years:

| Years | Net Operating Income |
|-------|----------------------|
| 1-5 | $23,000 |
| 6 | $22,000 |
| 7 | $21,000 |
| 8 | $20,000 |
| 9 | $19,000 |
| 10 | $17,500 |

The appropriate Discount Rate is found to be 11.5%. What is the present worth of this income stream?

**Supplementary Readings**

American Institute of Real Estate Appraisers, *The Appraisal of Real Estate*, fifth edition (Chicago: American Institute of Real Estate Appraisers, 1967), pp. 278-287, 301-310, and 325-326.

Frederick M. Babcock, *The Valuation of Real Estate* (New York: McGraw-Hill, 1932), Chapter 12.

L.W. Ellwood, *Ellwood Tables for Real Estate Appraising and Financing; Part I: Explanatory Text*, third edition (Chicago: American Institute of Real Estate Appraisers, 1970), pp. 75-78.

Sanders A. Kahn, Frederick E. Case, and Alfred Schimmel, *Real Estate Appraisal and Investment* (New York: Ronald Press, 1963), Chapter 10.

Alfred A. Ring, *The Valuation of Real Estate*, second edition (Englewood Cliffs, N.J.: Prentice-Hall, 1970), Chapter 18.

## Notes

1. L.W. Ellwood, *Ellwood Tables for Real Estate Appraising and Financing; Part II: Tables*, third edition (Chicago: American Institute of Real Estate Appraisers, 1970).

2. See, for example, American Institute of Real Estate Appraisers, *The Appraisal of Real Estate*, fifth edition (Chicago: American Institute of Real Estate Appraisers, 1967), Appendix B; and Alfred A. Ring, *The Valuation of Real Estate*, second edition (Englewood Cliffs, N.J.: Prentice-Hall, 1970), pp. 590-614.

3. Ring, *Valuation of Real Estate*, pp. 614-615.

4. AIREA, *Appraisal of Real Estate*, Appendix B; Ring, *Valuation of Real Estate*, pp. 616-617.

**Part III:**
**Income Capitalization Applications**

# 12

**Physical Residual Techniques of Income Capitalization**

## Property Valuation Through Income Capitalization

Up to this point, most of the discussion in this book has focused on the tools and mechanics of income capitalization. It is now time to recall that the purpose of an appraisal is to estimate some value, as defined, in terms of given market conditions as of a specific valuation date. Most commonly, the appraiser is seeking to estimate Market Value. Thus, the emphasis in Part III is primarily on Market Value estimation.

Income-producing real estate is valued in terms of the future net income stream it is forecast to be capable of producing, and most likely to produce, under typically competent management. Therefore, the best *measure* of Market Value, or of any other value sought, is the discounted present worth or that forecast future net income stream. Because real estate is a long-term capital asset with "mixed" components (i.e., depreciating improvements and non-depreciating site), the net income it produces takes two forms that must provide three types of returns. It generates annual Net Operating Income over a finite time period to cover both a competitive return *on* the entire investment and a return *of* the amount of capital loss to be recovered, both forecast over the income projection period. It also provides a lump sum of value at the expiration of the income projection period. This lump sum payment is what will be "left over" and available to the purchaser-investor to realize through resale, refinancing, and/or reinvestment for further use in producing a new income stream. It is called a reversion.

Thus far, there has been little actual appraisal analysis, except in almost casual discussions of Direct Capitalization which illustrated site valuation through the Discount Rate and property valuation through the Overall Rate. In Part III of this book, the concern for the first time is with property valuation.

## Rationale of Residual Analysis

It was pointed out in Chapter 3 that income properties can be divided into separate analytical components in three different ways. The *legal* components are created under a lease contract, and are the separate interests of the lessor (landlord) and lessee (tenant). This frequent but specialized set of relationships is given detailed consideration in Chapter 19. The *financial* or *investment* components are those of the mortgagee (lender) and the equity investor. Their interests are valued in mortgage-equity analysis, which is the topic of Chapter 13.

237

The traditional approach has been to recognize the *physical* components of site (land) and improvements (buildings), and to separate the property into these analytical components for valuation purposes when Direct Capitalization of Net Operating Income through the Overall Rate has proved infeasible. The logic and attraction of this analytical approach are obvious. Real Estate is composed of site and improvements. Each contributes, but only in combination with the other, to the production of Net Operating Income. The remaining economic life of the improvements sets an effective finite limit to income projection. The investment in the improvements requires capital recovery, while the investment in the site does not and cannot.

### Meaning of a Residual

Stemming from the foregoing considerations, residual techniques of income capitalization evolved. It operates from the supposition that the present worth of *one* of the physical components of the property (the site, the improvements, or the reversion at the end of the income projection period) can be estimated separately. Given the applicable rates of capitalization previously developed in the analysis of the property and its market, it is then possible to identify the dollar amount of net income necessary to support that investment. This "necessary" income will produce a competitive rate of return, which is the least that an informed and rational purchaser-investor will accept. Since value is expressed as the highest price that an informed purchaser-investor would pay, it follows that market competition will force the income and the rate of return it represents to the minimum acceptable market levels for informed investors. Whatever amount of NOI remains after providing this minimum acceptable coverage of the component whose present worth is known, is available to support the investment in the component whose present worth is unknown. This remaining annual income is the "residual income." It is the amount left over after providing income coverage of the known investment component at competitive market rates.

This residual income is then capitalized at the appropriate market rate(s) of discount to provide a present worth estimate of the "residual" component of the property. The two present worth estimates are then summed to produce a present worth or value estimate for the entire property. The present worth of the "residual" portion is a measure of its *contribution* to total property: what its presence adds to the value of the component is already known.

Throughout this residual analysis, it must be emphasized that both site and improvements *together*, in their particular and peculiar combination in the property being appraised, produce the estimated future net income flow that is forecast. A given dollar of income cannot be identified as having been generated or produced by the site or by the improvements, except under the very special circumstance of a separate ground lease, which is discussed in Chapter 19. Site and improvements together form an economic entity that normally produces a single, unified income stream.

**Real Property Income as a Residual.** The income to real estate itself, especially land, is held to be a residual in the sense that it has a low-priority claim on the income that it produces. For example, the gross income produced by an income property is subject to a series of claims. From the point of view of economic analysis, the productive factors of labor, capital (money), and entrepreneurship all are mobile; they can move readily to another source of income. Real estate, on the other hand, is fixed in location. Moreover, much income-producing real estate is operationally immobile in the sense that it cannot readily be adapted to an alternative use or uses. As a result, to attract and maintain the other productive resources to work in the property in question, they must be assured and receive at least a competitive rate of return for their services. Their claims must be paid first or they will move elsewhere. What is left after paying their claims is a *residual* income available to pay for the use of investment funds in the real estate. In this sense, NOI is a residual.

In estimation NOI, certain deductions are made from gross receipts. These are for operating expenses that must be paid in order to produce the gross income. Similarly, cash throw-off is the residual return to the equity investment, since debt service must be paid first or the investor loses his right to receive future income.

## Selection of the Residual Technique

In the selection of rates of capitalization and methods of capital recovery, the appraiser really has no "choice" but must merely select the method and approach dictated by the nature of the appraisal problem and the character of the forecast income stream. The appraiser *does* have some discretion in choosing whether to use a residual technique, however. He must still be sensitive to the influence of typical market behavior of most probable types of purchaser-investors, but it is a matter of professional judgment which technique is most descriptive of and responsive to the particular appraisal problem at hand.

Physical residual analysis can be justified if the availability of necessary data and the behavior of purchaser-investors in the market indicate that this will be a fruitful analytical approach. *Which* physical residual technique (Building Residual, Land Residual, or Property Residual) should be used is determined by the nature of the property and the appraisal problem, however, and is not within the appraiser's discretion. Mortgage-equity analysis may be selected in lieu of a physical residual technique. Properly applied, it will produce the same estimate of present worth of value for the property. When a property is subject to a long-term lease, market value can also be ascertained by leased fee-leasehold residual analysis. Once again, the results should be the same if the technique is properly applied.

If adequate data are available to permit the appraiser to apply Direct Capitalization, he may still utilize a residual technique in estimating value, sometimes as a check against the Direct Capitalization result.

**Identification of a Residual.** The identification of what the residual component is to be both depends on and influences the residual technique of capitalization selected.

1. In the Building Residual (physical) technique, the present worth of the site is "given," and the present worth or contribution of the improvements is the residual which is unknown.
2. In the Land Residual (physical) technique, the present worth of the improvements is "given," and the present worth or contribution of the site is the residual which is unknown.
3. In the Property Residual (physical) technique, the present worth of the reversion (usually but not necessarily the site only) is "given," and the present worth of the income from the entire property is the residual which is unknown.
4. In mortgage-equity analysis, the present worth or principal of the mortgage is "given," and the present worth or contribution of the equity investment is the residual which is unknown.
5. In leased fee-leasehold analysis, the present worth of the leased fee is "given" by calculation, and the present worth of the leasehold is the residual which is unknown. This is really a special case of the Property Residual technique.

**Determinants of Residual Technique Selection.** The selection of a specific residual technique by the appraiser is determined by several considerations:

1. the applicability of the prescribed conditions of the particular technique to the appraisal problem at hand;
2. the availability of sufficient amounts of reliable data of the type required to apply the particular technique; and
3. the responsiveness of the particular technique as a realistic description of purchaser-investor market behavior and thinking for the type of property being appraised.

*Identification of the Reversion and
Estimation of Its Present Worth*

Except in the special case of site valuation, when net income is capitalized in perpetuity, all income-producing real estate is assumed to have a finite income projection period. Capitalization is based on that assumption. At the end of the income projection period, something of value will invariably remain for the purchaser-investor. That "something of value" is the *reversion*.

**Income Projection Period.** A reversion is a lump sum which is available or payable to the investor at a specified date in the future. That date is the expiration of the income projection period identified as applicable to the particular appraisal problem.

1. The income projection period is typically the remaining economic life of the improvements in physical residual techniques of analysis.
2. The income projection period is typically the investment holding period for the entire property in mortgage-equity analysis.
3. The income projection period is typically the remaining term of the lease in leased fee-leasehold analysis.

**Form of the Reversion.** The reversion may take several forms, depending on the nature of the income projection period and on the residual technique employed.

1. The reversion is typically the site only in physical residual techniques when the income projection period is the remaining economic life of the improvements.
2. The reversion is the entire property in mortgage-equity analysis when the income projection period is the investment holding period.
3. The reversion is the entire property, which reverts to the lessor at the expiration of the lease in leased fee-leasehold analysis.

**Method of Realizing the Reversion.** Realization of the value of the reversion at the specified future date can take one of several forms. The method of converting the reversion into cash proceeds is not critical to the estimation of its present worth, but it is frequently of considerable interest to the investor.

The reversion may be realized by resale of the property at the specified future date; by refinancing the property, which provides cash proceeds to the investor; or by continued holding and use of the reversion to produce a new income stream starting at the specified future date.

**Amount of the Reversion.** The amount of the reversion may be:

1. The estimated value or future worth of the site as of the reversion date.
2. The estimated value or future worth of the entire property "as is" on the reversion date. This includes any estimated decrease or increase in forecast resale price from present worth or original investment as of the valuation date.
3. The net proceeds of any refinancing as of the date of refinancing.

**Estimating the Present Worth of the Reversion.** The present worth of the reversion is obtained by applying the Present Worth of One Factor at the applicable Discount Rate to the estimated amount of the reversion as of the reversion date, over the income projection period. The longer the income projection period, the lower the factor will be because the discount to the present will be greater. This will reduce the present worth of the future lump sum payment. Also, the higher the Discount Rate, the lower the factor will be, and the greater the discount to the present will be. This will also reduce the present worth of the future lump sum payment. Conversely, the shorter the income projection period or the lower the Discount Rate, the higher the present worth of the reversion will be.

Future income payments are uncertain. By discounting, the effect of variations or "errors" in estimating the amount of the reversion is substantially reduced. The longer the income projection period or the higher the rate of discount, the less the effect of such variations will be on the present worth estimate of the entire property.

For physical residual and leased fee-leasehold reversions, the appropriate rate of discount is the Discount Rate. In mortgage-equity analysis, the rate of discount applied to the reversion is the Equity Yield Rate. The reasons for this difference are explained in Chapter 13.

**Site as the Reversion.** Site is reversion in Building Residual or Land Residual analysis, as well as in Property Residual analysis when the income projection period is the remaining economic life of the improvements. In such cases, capitalizing the income available or necessary to cover the investment in site in perpetuity produces exactly the same result as assuming that site will produce a competitive return at the Discount Rate over the income projection period, and then will be a reversion equal to its present worth. This is because capitalization in perpetuity assumes that the capital value of the investment (site) will not depreciate or suffer capital loss over time, and will in fact remain unchanged indefinitely.

For example, assume that income attributable to site is $2,812.50 per year and that the Discount Rate is 9%. Capitalization of this income in perpetuity ($2,812.50/.09) results in a present worth or value estimate for the site of $31,250.

If the income is projected over 25 years at 9% and the reversion of $31,250 (100% of present worth) is discounted over 25 years at 9%, the result would be:

| | | |
|---|---|---|
| $2,812.50 X 9.82258 | (Ellwood, page 100, Column 5) = | $27,626 |
| $31,250 X 0.115968 | (Ellwood, page 100, Column 4) = | $ 3,624 |
| Present worth of site: | | $31,250 |

*Assumptions and Implications of*
*Residual Analysis*

1. Investment returns on income-producing real estate, and hence on any of its components, will satisfy typical purchaser-investors if they are produced at competitive market rates.
2. Capital recovery rates are applicable to broad categories of income-producing properties on the basis of the same method of capital recovery.
3. The amount of future reversions can be estimated.
4. The present worth of the reversion can be estimated by discounting the future lump sum payment at the appropriate Present Worth of One factor, based on the applicable Discount Rate over the applicable income projection period.
5. All components of the real estate produce a return *on* investment at the same rate, which is represented by the Discount Rate.

6. Residual analysis can be used to estimate Investment Value by substituting the rates of capitalization and discount acceptable to a specific investor in place of a market-derived and market-determined Discount Rate and Capital Recovery Rate.

*Information Required to Apply*
*Residual Analysis*

In order to apply any residual technique properly to estimate the present worth or value of an income-producing property, the appraisal must have at least the following information:

1. the estimated present worth of one component of the property (site, building, reversion, mortgage, leased fee);
2. the forecast amount and characteristics of Net Operating Income;
3. the length and periodicity of the income projection period (capital recovery period);
4. the applicable Discount Rate;
5. the applicable method of providing for capital recovery, and hence the Capital Recovery Rate; and
6. the forecast form and amount of the reversion.

With this information, the appraiser can calculate any other rates or factors required in the analysis. Then he can derive a present worth estimate for both the residual and the total property. Without all of this information, residual techniques of valuation cannot legitimately be applied.

## Direct Capitalization

Direct Capitalization is *not* true residual analysis. The Overall Rate discussed in Chapter 9 is simply divided directly into Net Operating Income to derive a present worth estimate for the entire property.

As noted earlier in this chapter, however, Direct Capitalization can be applied by using the Level Annuity Capitalization Rate based on the Discount Rate to estimate the present worth of a site. The future income receipts forecast can be broken down into a finite income stream capitalized at the Level Annuity Capitalization Rate and a reversion discounted to the present at the Discount Rate. Moreover, capitalization in perpetuity at the Discount Rate is a form of Direct Capitalization.

Direct Capitalization of NOI at the Overall Rate also implicitly includes a reversion. It is simply incorporated directly into the Overall Rate. The typical and most logical assumption is that the Overall Rate includes return *on* the total property investment at the Discount Rate, return *of* the investment in the improvements, and a reversion in the form of the site—all capitalized or discounted over the remaining economic life of the improvements.

*Data Required*

Only two items of information are necessary to apply Direct Capitalization: Net Operating Income and the Overall Rate. The Overall Rate, when it can be derived from reliable market sales data, is simply a composite weighted average of the three rates or returns itemized above. The best source from which to derive the Overall Rate is the ratio NOI/Sales Price for truly comparable, competitive properties that have recently sold under similar market conditions to those applicable on the valuation date.

As demonstrated in Chapter 9, the Overall Rate can also be derived by taking a weighted average of the Discount Rate weighted by the proportion of total property investment represented by the investment in the site, and the Capitalization Rate weighted by the proportion of total property investment represented by the investment in the improvements. The reversion is covered by applying the Discount Rate to the proportion of investment in the site, as indicated above.

For example, applying information from the general example used in previous chapters under Annuity Capital Recovery, the Overall Rate would be developed as follows:

NOI = $15,000
Discount Rate = 9%
Annuity Capitalization Rate = 10.18%
Site is 25% of Total Property Value
Improvements are therefore 75% of Total Property Value

Then:

$$.25 \times .09 = .0225$$
$$.75 \times .1018 = \underline{.0764}$$
Overall Rate: $\quad .0989 = 9.89\%$

## Building Residual Analysis

*Independent Estimate of Present*
*Worth of Site*

This analysis starts with the assumption that it is possible and feasible to estimate the present worth of the site independently. Most frequently, it involves a Direct Sales Comparison analysis, using recent sales of similar, competitive vacant sites as the basis for value estimation. This method of site valuation is demonstrated in Chapter 15.

Site is always valued as if vacant and available to be put to its Highest and Best Use. Further, it is valued on the assumption that the typically informed, prudent, rational purchaser-investor will in fact put it to its Highest and Best Use. These assumptions are explored further in Chapter 15.

Given the Discount Rate appropriate and necessary to produce a competitive return on the site, the amount of annual income necessary to provide this competitive return can be derived. This is accomplished simply by multiplying the estimated present worth of the site by the Discount Rate. This annual income necessary to produce a competitive rate of return on the investment in the site, and therefore to attract an investor who would purchase it for that price and put it to that use, is then deducted from Net Operating Income. The difference is the annual amount of NOI forecast to be available to support the investment in the improvements.

## Improvements (Buildings) are the Residual

With the present worth of the site estimated independently, the unknown value is the present worth of the improvements. The improvements are thus the residual. The question is how much they contribute to the present worth or value of the entire property, over and above the value of the site. This contribution is measured by dividing the residual income available to support the investment in the improvements by the appropriate Capitalization Rate, or by multiplying the residual income by the appropriate Capitalization Factor. The result is an estimate of the present worth of the improvements.

The present worth of the improvements thus estimated represents the amount of investment that a prudent and rational purchaser-investor would be warranted in paying for the right to receive the residual income available to support the investment in the improvements.

The Capitalization Rate or Capitalization Factor applied to the residual income is determined by (1) the Discount Rate; (2) the income projection period; (3) the method of providing for capital recovery; and, (4) by implication at least, the character of the forecast NOI.

## Estimate of Property Value

The estimated value of the property is the capitalized present worth of the forecast NOI. The reversion is the site, and the capital recovery period is the remaining economic life of the improvements. Present worth or value is derived by adding the previously estimated present worth of the site to the calculated present worth of the residual income flow available to support the investment in the improvements. For appraisal purposes, this calculated total present worth figure for the property is rounded to an appropriate value estimate. This rounded figure is the estimate of using the Building Residual technique of analysis.

## Uses and Limitations of Building
## Residual Analysis

Some residual technique must be employed when it is either impossible or inappropriate to utilize Direct Capitalization via the Overall Rate. Building Residual analysis requires that it be possible and feasible to estimate independently the value of the site, as if it were vacant and available to be put to its Highest and Best Use.

Building Residual analysis is probably the most widely accepted and used physical residual technique. It is certainly the most generally understood by appraisers and their clients, as well as the courts. This is in part because it is applicable to situations in which the improvements on a property may or may not represent the Highest and Best Use of the site. This makes it particularly useful in the appraisal of income properties containing older buildings. Site is valued first and independently in terms of its Highest and Best Use. The residual income is available to the improvements. If NOI is lower than it might otherwise be because the improvements are inappropriate or do not represent Highest and Best Use of the site, this is reflected directly and entirely in the present worth or estimated contribution of the improvements.

Building Residual analysis suffers from the limitation applicable to all *physical* residual techniques: it is not necessarily a realistic reflection of the way purchaser-investors behave toward investment real estate. Moreover, it is extremely difficult to apply when the income projection is less than the remaining economic life of the improvements, and the reversion therefore represents more than simply the site.

## Application of the Building Residual Technique[1]

To demonstrate the Building Residual Technique and its application, an illustrative example is provided here.

In this illustration and those that follow in subsequent sections of this chapter, only Annuity Capitalization is shown. This is done for two reasons. First, it has been pointed out emphatically in Chapters 10 and 11 that Straight-Line Capitalization is rarely an appropriate representation of the income flows of the handling of capital recovery payments produced by income properties. The same results can be obtained through Annuity Capitalization by treating the income flow as either a declining annuity or a "stabilized" level income stream. Moreover, Sinking Fund Capitalization is an exceptional case that does not warrant particular coverage.

Second, the purpose of these illustrations is to indicate the application of physical residual *techniques* of capitalization. The variability in present worth or value estimates that can result when different methods of providing for capital recovery are applied to the same income stream is irrelevant to this purpose. Since a real choice is not available to the appraiser, it seems most inappropriate to perpetuate potential confusion by continually providing examples of what difference the method of providing for capital recovery can make in the final value estimate.

The following illustration and the others presented later in this chapter are based on the property information provided in the general example used throughout Chapters 10 and 11. It will therefore not be necessary to refer to "new" discount factors in Ellwood. The emphasis here is the application of the *technique*.

The significant data are:

| | |
|---|---|
| NOI = $15,000 | Discount Rate = 9% |
| Site Value = $31,250 | Capital Recovery Period = 25 years |

Thus:

| | |
|---|---|
| Annuity Capital Recovery Rate | = .01181 = 1.181% |
| Annuity Capitalization Rate | = .10181 = 10.181% (.09 + .01181) |
| Annuity Capitalization Factor | = 9.82258 |

Then, the Building Residual technique is applied to estimate property value as follows:

| | |
|---|---|
| Net Operating Income | $15,000.00 |
| *Less* annual income necessary to cover investment in site at competitive return (Discount Rate) $31,250 X .09 = | $-2,812.50 |
| *Equals* residual annual income available to support investment in improvements | $12,187.50 |

Present Worth of improvements equals annual income available to support investment in improvements *divided by* Annuity Capitalization Rate:

| | |
|---|---|
| $\dfrac{\$12,187.50}{.10181}$ = | $119,708[a] |
| *Plus* Estimated Present Worth of Site | +$ 31,250 |
| Indicated Present Worth of Property | $150,958 |
| Estimated Value of Property via Income Capitalization, Building Residual Technique | $151,000 |

**Land Residual Analysis**

*Present Worth of Improvements*
*Estimated Independently*

This technique starts off with the assumption that it is both possible and feasible

---

[a]Also, $12,187.50 x 9.82258 = $119,713. The difference of $5 is the result of rounding.

to estimate the present worth of the improvements (building) separately. Since neither capitalization of income nor direct sales comparison analysis is logical or possible as a basis for estimating the present worth of the improvements alone, the basis for this present worth estimate must be reproduction cost. Moreover, it must be reproduction cost *new*. Otherwise, the appraiser must estimate accrued depreciation (diminished utility). Then, another basic assumption of this technique, that the improvements represent the Highest and Best Use of the site, would then be violated. The improvements must indeed represent the Highest and Best Use of the site. They may be either existing new improvements that fulfill this requirement, or proposed improvements that will.

The Net Operating Income estimate used is either that produced by the property with new improvements representing the Highest and Best Use of the site, or hypothecated NOI forecast to be produced by the property with proposed new improvements that do represent the Highest and Best Use of the site. The annual income necessary to cover the investment in new improvements representing the Highest and Best Use of the site, measured by their reproduction cost new, is derived by multiplying the estimated reproduction cost new by the Capitalization Rate, or by dividing it by the Capitalization Factor. This annual income assignable to the improvements is subtracted from NOI. The difference is the residual income available to support the investment in the site.

### Site (Land) Is the Residual

Since the reproduction cost new of appropriate improvements is estimated independently and known, the present worth of the site is the unknown residual. The residual income is available to support the investment in the site when put to its Highest and Best Use. The present worth of the site is estimated by dividing this residual income by the Discount Rate. This results in capitalizing site income in perpetuity. The Discount Rate is used because it is the competitive market rate of return that represents the return on the investment in the site when the site is put to its Highest and Best Use.

By capitalizing the income available to cover the investment in the site in perpetuity, it is implicitly assumed that the site is the reversion, and that the reversionary amount will be equal to the present worth of the site.

### Estimate of Property Value

The value of the property represented by the present worth of the forecast NOI is derived by adding the calculated present worth of the site to the estimated reproduction cost *new* of improvements that represent the Highest and Best Use of the site. For appraisal purposes, the calculated present worth figure is rounded to an appropriate value estimate. This rounded figure is the estimate of value (as defined) of the property via Capitalization Income, using the Land Residual technique of analysis.

## Uses and Limitations of Land Residual Analysis

When the key problem in the appraisal is the valuation of site, and it cannot be accomplished through any of the alternative methods presented in Chapter 15, the Land Residual Technique can be a useful device. *If* the preconditions of new improvements on site that represent the Highest and Best Use of that site are met, then the Land Residual Technique can legitimately be applied. These requirements are rarely met, however. As a result, it is often necessary to develop a reproduction cost new estimate for hypothetical improvements. Aside from the hazards inherent in making such estimates, there are also serious problems in justifying the gross income, operating expense, and NOI estimates that must be made in terms of a hypothetical improvement. There is often little market evidence to support these estimates, and certainly none from the past experience of the property being appraised. Generally speaking, then, because of the restrictive nature of its necessary preconditions, Land Residual analysis has very limited applicability or usefulness in income property appraising.

Because site frequently represents the smaller portion of total property value or investment, any variation in the estimated reproduction cost new of improvements will translate into a variation in the annual income necessary to cover that investment. This will usually have a magnified effect on the residual income available to support the investment in the site, and hence on the estimated present worth of the site.

## Application of the Land Residual Technique[2]

To illustrate the application of the Land Residual Technique in practice, the property data employed in exemplifying the Building Residual Technique will be used here. In this example, assume a new building representing the Highest and Best Use of the site is on the site, and that the verified reproduction cost new is $120,000.

Then, the estimate of property value via the Land Residual Technique would be as follows:

| | |
|---|---|
| Net Operating Income | $15,000.00 |
| *Less* annual income necessary to cover the investment in the improvements by providing a competitive rate of return on the investment, and appropriate capital recovery over their remaining economic life: | |
| $120,000 \times .10181 =$ | $-$12,217.20[b] |

[b]Also, $\dfrac{$120,000}{9.82258} = $12,216.75.$

| | |
|---|---|
| *Equals* residual annual income available to support investment in site | $ 2,782.80 |

— — — —

Present Worth of Site equals annual income available to support investment in site *divided by* Discount Rate:
$2,782.80/.09 =          $ 30,920

*Plus* estimated Reproduction Cost New of
    Improvements          $120,000

Estimated Value of Property via Income Capitalization, Land Residual Technique      $151,000

## Property Residual Analysis

### Amount of Reversion Estimated Independently

This technique starts with the assumption that it is possible and feasible to estimate the amount of the reversion as of the reversion date. The reversion is the site when Property Residual analysis utilizes the remaining economic life of the improvements as the income projection period. It is usually assumed further that the amount of reversion is equal to the present worth of the site.

The reversion may be the entire property when leased fee valuation is undertaken. As is explained in detail in Chapter 19, the valuation of the income stream under a long-term lease involves the same concept and the same mechanical process as the Property Residual Technique. In this instance, the income projection or capital recovery period is the remaining term of the lease.

The present worth of the reversion is estimated by discounting it at the Discount Rate, using the Present Worth of One over the income projection period.

### Entire Property Is the Residual

The present worth of the entire income stream (NOI) is unknown, and therefore the present worth of the entire property is the residual. NOI is capitalized to a present worth estimate by dividing it by the Capitalization Rate, or by multiplying it by the Capitalization Factor.

This present worth estimate provides for recovery of the entire investment in the property over the income projection period, as well as a competitive market rate of return on the total investment over that same period. This means that the investment in the site is also recovered, which is neither permissible nor reflective of the usual expectations of purchaser-investors. Thus, to reach an appropriate estimate of present worth for the property, the present worth of the reversion must be *added* to the present worth of the income stream represented by the NOI. This sum is the estimated value of the property via Capitalization of Income, using the Property Residual Technique.

*Uses and Limitations of Property
Residual Analysis*

The Property Residual technique has its widest applicability in valuing the leased fee interest under a long-term lease. The assumptions of the technique are both fulfilled by and descriptive of the character of the forecast future income flow produced by a property under a long-term lease: annual income from the entire property for a specified period, and then a lump-sum reversion to the lessor.

It is sometimes claimed that the Property Residual technique can be used in cases where *neither* the present worth of the site *nor* the present worth of the improvements can be estimated effectively from the available market evidence. The pragmatic argument is that, especially when the income projection period is "long enough" and/or the Discount Rate is "high enough," any variation or "error" in the estimated amount of the reversion is minimized when it is discounted to a present worth estimate. While arithmetically this may be correct, it is hardly calculated to convince either appraisers or their clients of the accuracy of the technique.

*Application of the Property
Residual Technique*[3]

The property data employed in illustrating the Building Residual and Land Residual techniques will also be used in this example. To show the minimal impact of varying the estimated amount of the reversion if there is uncertainty about it, assume alternative estimates of $20,000, $30,000, and $40,000—each receivable 25 years hence, discounted at 9%. The most probable amount is taken to be $30,000.

Then, the estimation of property value via the Property Residual technique would be as follows:

| | |
|---|---|
| Net Operating Income | $ 15,000 |
| Present Worth of Income Stream: NOI divided by Capitalization Rate: | |
| $\frac{\$15,000}{.10181} =$ | $147,333[c] |

---
[c]Also, $15,000 X 9.82258 = $147,339.

*Plus* Present Worth of Reversion:

| | |
|---|---|
| $30,000 X .115968 = | +$ 3,479 |
| ($20,000 X .115968 = $2,319) | |
| ($40,000 X .115968 = $4,639) | |
| Present Worth of Property | $150,812 |

Estimated Value of Property via Income Capitalization, Property Residual Technique     $151,000

Note that varying the forecast amount of the reversion from $20,000 to $40,000 results in a difference in estimated total property value of only $2,300, or about 1.3%.

## Review Exercises

1. A motel has 120 rooms that rent for $20 per night. Annual occupancy for this type of operation, with no restaurant or bar, is 82%. The rental is 35% of annual gross receipts. The site is estimated to be worth $200,000. The estimated remaining economic life of the improvements is 25 years. It is expected that revenues will decline over time as competition moves into the area. The operating expense ratio for this type of property (as opposed to the business itself) is 45%. Financing can be arranged for only 50% of value, at 9.5% for 20 years, with level monthly payments. Equity investors in this type of property are demanding a prospective return of 18.5%.
   a. What is the indicated Net Operating Income (in the first year)?
   b. What is the indicated Discount Rate?
   c. What is the "stabilized" amount of Net Operating Income over the income projection period?
   d. What "stabilized" annual income is necessary to support the investment in the site?
   e. What "stabilized" annual income is available to support the investment in the improvements?
   f. What is the indicated Capitalization Rate (or Factor) for the "stabilized" annual income available to support the investment in the improvements?
   g. What is the present worth of the improvements?
   h. What is the indicated value of the property, using the Building Residual technique?
   i. What is the mortgage constant?
   j. What is the amount of annual debt service?
   k. What is the indicated cash throw-off, based on "stabilized" NOI?
   l. What is the indicated equity dividend rate?
2. An office building has just been constructed at a cost of $2,800,000. It is judged to represent the Highest and Best Use of its site. It provides highly

functional space in a prime location and is expected to retain its rental attractiveness over its entire forecast 40-year economic life. The indicated Discount Rate is 11%. Net Operating Income is estimated at $475,000.

What is the indicated value of the property, using the Land Residual technique?

3. An apartment property is producing "stabilized" Net Operating Income of $80,000. The remaining economic life of the improvements is 22 years and the Discount Rate is 10.5%. The improvements represent an estimated 85% of total property value.

   a. What is the indicated Overall Rate?
   b. What is the indicated value of the property, using Direct Capitalization?
   c. If the resale price of the property in 22 years is forecast to be $225,000, what is the indicated value of the property, using the Property Residual technique?

4. An industrial property is under a lease with 17 years remaining until it expires. It calls for gross rentals of $72,000 per year. The indicated operating expense ratio for this type of property is 35%. It is anticipated that the property will be worth $200,000 when the lease expires. The rentals are in line with going market rentals on similar, competitive properties. The indicated Discount Rate is 9.75%.

   What is the indicated value of the lessor's interest (leased fee)?

5. An apartment property is producing annual NOI of $44,500. The Discount Rate for this property has been estimated at 10.25%, and the remaining economic life of the improvements is forecast to be 25 years. Three highly similar and competitive apartment properties within two blocks of the subject property, offering essentially the same amenities and the same services as the subject, have sold in the past month. All were open-market transactions with similar financing and terms of sale. Their sale prices and Net Operating Incomes were:

   Sale A: Sales Price $350,000; Net Operating Income $48,500
   Sale B: Sales Price $405,000; Net Operating Income $58,000
   Sale C: Sales Price $287,500; Net Operating Income $40,250

   a. What is the indicated Overall Rate for this property?
   b. What is the indicated Market Value of this property, based on Direct Capitalization?

## Supplementary Readings

American Institute of Real Estate Appraisers, *The Appraisal of Real Estate*, fifth edition (Chicago: American Institute of Real Estate Appraisers, 1967), pp. 287-295 and 310-316.

Sanders A. Kahn, Frederick E. Case, and Alfred Schimmel, *Real Estate Appraisal and Investment* (New York: Ronald Press, 1963), Chapter 12.

William N. Kinnard, Jr. and Stephen D. Messner, *Industrial Real Estate*, second edition (Washington: Society of Industrial Realtors, 1971), pp. 429-431.

Alfred A. Ring, *The Valuation of Real Estate*, second edition (Englewood Cliffs, N.J.: Prentice-Hall, 1970), Chapter 19.

William M. Shenkel, *A Guide to Appraising Industrial Property* (Chicago: Society of Real Estate Appraisers, 1967), pp. 102-105.

Norbert F. Wall, "A Case Study—Land Residual Technique," *The Real Estate Appraiser*, Volume 33, Number 2, February 1967.

**Notes**

1. Further illustrations of the application of Building Residual analysis may be found in American Institute of Real Estate Appraisers, *The Appraisal of Real Estate*, fifth edition (Chicago: American Institute of Real Estate Appraisers, 1967), Chapters 18 and 19; and in Alfred A. Ring, *The Valuation of Real Estate*, second edition (Englewood Cliffs, N.J.: Prentice-Hall, 1970), pp. 288-291.

2. For additional illustrations of applications of Land Residual Analysis, see AIREA, *Appraisal of Real Estate*, Chapters 18 and 19; and Ring, *Valuation of Real Estate*, pp. 284-288.

3. Further illustrations of the applications of Real Residual Analysis are contained in AIREA, *Appraisal of Real Estate*, Chapters 18 and 19; and Ring, *Valuation of Real Estate*, pp. 291-295.

# 13 Mortgage-Equity Analysis

No other aspect of real estate valuation theory and practice has received as much recent attention or caused as much shift in traditional thinking as mortgage-equity analysis in income capitalization. Although the basic analytical framework has been available for decades and had actually been in use by financial investors, the near-revolution in appraisal thinking was triggered by the publication of the first edition of the *Ellwood Tables*[1] in 1957. In this monumental work, Ellwood made at least two major contributions to income-property appraising.

First, he provided a formula for developing an Overall Rate (called variously the "Overall Capitalization Rate" or the "Composite Capitalization Rate") which has rightly come to be known as the Ellwood Formula. Its components and its meaning are discussed in detail later in this chapter. For now, the important points to note are that for the first time in appraisal literature explicit recognition of the phenomenon of equity build-up through mortgage amortization was incorporated into the rates of discount used to capitalize Net Operating Income to a present worth estimate; and that specific emphasis was placed on the treatment of income flows over income projection periods significantly shorter than the remaining economic life of improvements.

Second, to remove the drudgery (and reluctance) associated with lengthy and involved calculations before the advent of the electronic-calculator and the desk computer, Ellwood provided tables of precalculated factors to be inserted into his Overall Rate formula. Based on commonly used loan-to-value ratios, mortgage interest rates, equity yield rates, and income projection periods, these tables of precalculated factors made it feasible for the mathematically uninitiated or uncertain appraiser to apply the Ellwood Formula to derive market-responsive Overall Rates. As a result, it has become increasingly appropriate to value income properties through Direct Capitalization.[a]

Evidence of the relative newness of mortgage-equity analysis (of which the Ellwood formulation is an integral part) in appraisal thinking, and the continuing concerns in many quarters over its applicability and even acceptability, is provided by the fact that most of the numerous Supplementary Readings listed at the end of this chapter are journal articles. They represent only a selective sampling of the near-flood of explanations, "simplifications," justifications and

---

[a]The range and scope of these precalculated factors have been increased in subsequent editions of the *Ellwood Tables*. The appraiser now has a considerably more flexible tool in the Ellwood Formula with a minimum of calculation. In addition, Ellwood has provided a signal service to income-property appraisers by including increasingly detailed tables of the six basic compound interest factors in a format peculiarly useful to appraisers. Similar precalculated mortgage-equity factors are provided in Irvin Johnson's *The Instant Mortgage-Equity Technique*.

criticisms of mortgage-equity analysis in general, and the Ellwood formulation in particular, that have appeared since the mid-1960s. Few texts deal with this tool of analysis as yet.

The fact is that mortgage-equity analysis is one more tool available to the income-property appraiser. It is responsive to many income-property appraisal problems and sensitive to the market behavior of purchasers who are investors. When its conditions are justified by the facts of the market and of the appraisal problem, it is a highly useful tool for capitalizing forecast net income to a present worth estimate.

## Background to Mortgage-Equity Analysis

The discussion of physical residual techniques of income capitalization in Chapter 11 followed essentially traditional lines. In these techniques, income-producing real estate is analyzed and valued in terms of its *physical* components of site and improvements. Inseparable as site and improvements are as sources or generators of property income, they nevertheless must be separated for analytical purposes under relatively rigid rules (i.e., site is always valued as if vacant and available to be put to its Highest and Best Use). One of the physical components represents the unknown residual amount whose present worth must be derived.

It was noted in Chapter 11 that the investment in income properties can also be separated into its *financial* or *investment* components: mortgage and equity position. Since income-producing real estate is most likely to be acquired and owned by a purchaser-investor who regards the property as an investment, this analytical division of the property into its component mortgage and equity interests is held to be descriptive of market behavior. Investors typically utilize debt (mortgage) financing to extend their equity funds and to take advantage of the anticipated benefits of leverage, as explained in Chapter 7. Mortgage financing is therefore an integral part of the typical income property transaction. Acting prudently and rationally on available market information, the most probable purchaser-investor is presumed to seek to maximize or optimize his *cash* position: both income flows and cash equity.

The value of an income property, treated as an investment, can therefore be obtained by summing the present worth (principal amount) of the mortgage and the present worth (principal amount) of the mortgage and the present worth of the equity investment position. Since any transferable interest in real estate can have a Market Value—if indeed there is a market for such an interest—mortgage-equity analysis can be used to estimate Market Value. It is also an especially useful tool in investment analysis that produces Investment Value estimates. Throughout this chapter, as in preceding ones, the emphasis is on Market Value estimation. Exactly the same techniques and mechanical processes are used to estimate Investment Value. Only the data used in the analysis are different.

## Rationale of Mortgage-Equity Analysis

*Financial Investment Approach to*
*Residual Analysis*

Mortgage-equity analysis is another form of residual analysis, with the property divided into its financial-investment components of mortgage and equity investment position. The principal amount of the mortgage is known, while the present worth of the equity is the unknown residual.

**Mortgage Amount or Terms Identifiable in the Market.** At any given time and in any given market, it is possible to identify the most probable or "going" mortgage loan terms that the typical purchaser-investor can obtain for the type of property being appraised. *All* mortgage loan terms are included and must be identified. These include the mortgage interest rate, the loan-value ratio, the maturity or length of the loan, and the amortization provisions. The loan-value ratio is especially significant in establishing the amount or percentage of loan that most probably can be obtained. If the total amount of investment is given, the loan amount can be identified in dollars. Otherwise, the percentage of total property value represented by the loan is used. Also, the amortization provisions include the mortgage payment periods (e.g., monthly, semi-annually, etc.).

Once the pattern of mortgage loan terms is established from market evidence, it is then possible to derive the Mortgage Constant. For example, in the general example used throughout Chapters 10-12, it was established that a 70% mortgage at 8.5% interest could be obtained. If it is a 20-year, fully amortized, level monthly payment loan, the Mortgage Constant is 10.41%. (From Ellwood, page 89, column 6, the monthly Installment Amortize One is .008678. Then 12 X .008678 = .104136.)

This means that annual debt service, which includes both interest and principal amortization, is equal to 10.4136% of the original principal of the mortgage. Since this is 70% of total property value, then annual payments equal to 7.29% of total property value are necessary to cover annual debt service (.70 X .104136 = .0728952 = 7.29%).

**Equity Investment Is the Residual.** Since either the dollar amount of mortgage loan or the proportion of total investment represented by the mortgage loan is given, the amount or percentage of NOI required to cover the annual debt service can be ascertained. The *residual* income, which in this case is Cash Throw-Off, is available to support the equity investment. The present worth of the equity position is therefore the residual value to be derived through capitalization of the Cash Throw-Off.

*Cash Throw-Off.* As an illustration, use NOI of $15,000 from the general example in Chapters 10-12 and assume that a mortgage loan in the amount of $102,000 can most probably be obtained. With a Mortgage Constant of 10.41%, annual debt service (rounded to the nearest $5) is $10,620.

Thus:

| | |
|---|---|
| Net Operating Income | $15,000 |
| *Less* Annual Debt Service | – 10,620 |
| Cash Throw-Off to Equity | $ 4,380 |

In this instance, Cash Throw-Off (the residual income available to support the investment in the equity position) is the amount forecast to be produced by the property under typical or most probable investor-ownership. It is based on market standards and market evidence. It is *not* specific to a particular investor, with his particular financing arrangements or equity yield requirements.

*Present Worth of Equity Position.* The present worth of the equity position is derived by capitalizing the cash throw-off. This is accomplished by dividing it by the equity dividend rate. For example, if the equity dividend rate in the above illustration is 10%, then the present worth of the equity position is $43,800 ($4,380/.10).

*Equity Yield Rate.* The equity yield rate differs from the equity dividend rate in that it explicitly includes a provision for capital recovery. It is assumed in simple mortgage-equity analysis that mortgage amortization provides for capital recovery by building up the equity investment as an offset to any decline in total property value. The value of the equity investment remains the same and is fully recovered on resale of the property. In this case, the equity dividend rate is equal to (but not the same as) the equity yield rate.

Capital recovery can be provided for explicitly by making a forecast of depreciation in capital value on resale, and by incorporating a prorated annual return of capital loss into the equity return (cash throw-off). This is done in the Ellwood formulation, as explained later in this chapter. Capital recovery can also be provided by using a Present Worth of One per Annum factor at the equity yield rate to estimate the present worth of cash throw-off, and then adding the present worth of the net proceeds of property resale as a reversion.

To summarize, Net Operating Income is available to cover two required investment flows: debt service on the mortgage and equity return on the equity investment.

### Appraisal Principles Involved

As with other income capitalization techniques, mortgage-equity analysis involves the application of basic appraisal principles discussed in Chapter 3.

**Anticipation.** Value is still the present worth of anticipated future income receipts. These receipts take the form of an annual income flow (NOI), plus a lump-sum reversion at a specified date in the future.

**Substitution (Opportunity Cost).** The income, mortgage loan terms, and rates of return applied in mortgage-equity analysis are market-derived. They represent what other similar, competitive properties are producing or receiving in the competitive market of the subject property, as of the valuation date.

**Contribution (Marginal Productivity).** The essence of mortgage-equity analysis is to estimate the present worth of the equity position, which is the residual after the amount of debt service or required return on the mortgage loan is derived. This present worth is the measure of the contribution of the equity position to the value of the entire property.

## Description of Investor Market Behavior

Because income-producing real estate represents an investment to the most probable type of purchaser-investor, mortgage-equity analysis concentrates on the typical or most probable market behavior of that purchaser-investor.

**Maximize Cash Position.** The purchaser-investor is assumed to act prudently and rationally on the basis of typically available market behavior to maximize the cash value or present worth of his equity investment position. Before-tax cash flow (cash throw-off) is maximized through the use of leverage. The value of the equity investment position is maintained and enhanced through equity build-up from mortgage amortization.

**Short-Term Income Projections.** Relatively short-term income projections are used to reflect the fact that equity investors in income-producing real estate tend to turn over their properties to take maximum advantage of income tax laws. This tends to enhance the cash flows to the purchaser-investor, both as annual income flows and as cash reversions. The specific income tax status of the individual purchaser-investor is *not* considered or included. However, it *is* recognized that informed, prudent, and rational investors will act to minimize their income tax liability. Tax *avoidance* is legal and rational behavior; tax *evasion* is illegal and therefore not considered here.

*Income Tax Considerations.*[2] Through maximum use of depreciation charges allowable, the purchaser-investor minimizes present tax liability, enhances present cash flows, and *defers* tax liability to the future. Since present dollars are worth more than future dollars, increased cash flows in near-term years tend to increase the present worth of the investment. The Revenue Act of 1969 has significantly altered the ability of investors in income-producing real estate to enjoy the advantages of accelerated depreciation charges. Mortgage-equity analysis can still handle the projected income flows under the new tax laws and regulations. The most probable turnover or investment holding period, which is the income projection period for investment real estate, is simply lengthened.

By deferring income tax liability through depreciation charges, the purchaser-investor can convert much income to long-term capital gain status, which means it is taxed at a lower rate. The Revenue Act of 1969 has also severely limited the ability of investors in nonresidential income-producing real estate to take advantage of capital gains treatment of income. To the extent that it is still possible, however, the prudent and rational purchaser-investor will take advantage of capital gains treatment. The specific rate of taxation is immaterial here. The important point is that the availability of *any* capital gains treatment induces investors to seek such treatment to the maximum extent possible in order to maximize the cash receipts from their investments by minimizing taxes.

*Investment Holding Period.* The income projection period in mortgage-equity analysis is therefore the most probable investment holding period for the type of purchaser-investor identified for the type of property being appraised. This is also the period over which any forecast capital loss is to be recovered. Shorter income projection periods imply a higher degree of confidence about the amount and stability of income forecasts. As a result, level annuity capitalization is used throughout mortgage-equity analysis.

**Entire Property is the Reversion.** The reversion is the entire property in mortgage-equity analysis. The reversion may be realized in one or both of two different ways:

1. *Resale of the property* at the end of the income projection period. This enables the purchaser-investor to take advantage of capital gains treatment of at least part of the reversion, and enables him to reinvest his funds in the most attractive alternative at the time. Exchanges of property can also be handled through mortgage-equity analysis.
2. *Refinancing of the investment* at the end of the income projection period. This provides a non-taxable recovery of equity build-up at the time of refinancing; defers tax liability to a future, more heavily discounted date; and enables the owner-investor to continue to receive his cash flow at the existing rate of return on his investment.

**Capital Recovery.** Capital recovery is provided in large part through periodic mortgage amortization. This results in equity build-up, which is realized in cash by the owner-investor at the end of the income projection period through either resale, refinancing, or an exchange. To the extent that mortgage amortization is expected *not* to cover any forecast capital loss, the difference between original investment or value and forecast resale price or value for refinancing is recovered on a prorated annual basis through cash throw-off to equity.

Without specifically evaluating the impact of inflation or including the expectations of particular individual investors, mortgage-equity analysis makes it possible to account for forecast *appreciation* in capital value at the end of the income projection period. Since many investors, especially in growing market areas, do in fact purchase in anticipation of increasing values over time, this capability makes mortgage-equity analysis more adaptable to the realities of market behavior of the most probable purchaser-investor in the type of property being appraised.

**Available Mortgage Loan Terms.** The importance of the availability and terms of mortgage financing is specifically recognized in mortgage-equity analysis. As noted earlier, all terms of financing are included. Together, they comprise a package that the borrower "buys." The purchase-investor is assumed to select the optimum pattern of mortgage loan terms that will provide him with the largest cash throw-off in relation to his equity investment. He maximizes the effect of leverage by minimizing the mortgage constant.

Mortgage loan terms influence the rate of return on the entire property investment: the Overall Rate or Composite Rate. An exactly parallel influence is felt on the Discount Rate in traditional physical residual analysis, even when the estimate of value is purportedly "free and clear of encumbrances."

**Form of Organization of Most Probable Purchaser-Investor.** The purchaser-investor can take one of several different legal or organizational forms. The characteristics of the most probable *type* of purchaser-investor influence its behavior with respect to taxes, investment holding period, and type of income flow sought.

Space does not permit detailed consideration of the several alternative organizational forms that equity investors in income-producing real estate may take. The possibilities include:

1. *Single proprietorship*: an individual, ordinarily tax-liable investor.
2. *Partnership*: two or more individuals, ordinarily tax-liable.
3. *Corporation*: two or more parties joined in a single, separate legal entity with its own tax status. Non-profit corporations receive quite different income tax treatment. Syndicates, as well as investment holding companies and business corporations, may take the corporate form.
4. *Joint venture*: two or more parties joined for the specific purpose of acquiring, holding and operating a specific property or group of properties. A joint venture may be a partnership or a corporation.
5. *Syndicate*: typically a large number of investors joined together for the specific purpose of acquiring, holding, and operating a specific property or group of properties. It is usually in corporate or partnership form. Commonly, a few general partners or officers operate the syndicate and the remainder of the participants are passive investors.
6. *Investment Trust (REIT)*: a specialized legal form of corporation organized to acquire, hold, and operate investment real estate, with large numbers of passive investors and a few active operating officers. The Real Estate Investment Trust has particular income tax advantages provided it meets specified operating and investment requirements.
7. *Cooperative*: especially but not necessarily in the apartment field, a group of

owner-occupants holding income-producing real estate in common, each having an undivided interest in the ownership of the property.
8. *Condominium*: a group of owner-occupants holding income-producing real estate. Each participant owns his (its) particular space independently of the others, together with an undivided prorata share in the common space and land.

*Same Basic Valuation Formula*

Mortgage-equity analysis does not differ from any other form of capitalization technique in the basic valuation formula. It is still $V = I/R$. Ellwood does use $d$ in place of $I$, so that $V = d/R$.

**R is a Composite or Overall Rate.** The major focus of mortgage-equity analysis is the development of an appropriate Overall Rate to apply to NOI. The Overall Rate includes an appropriate return *on* investment plus a return *of* the portion of the total property investment forecast to represent capital loss over the income projection period.

The rates used in mortgage-equity analysis include:

1. return *on* and *of* the portion of total property investment represented by mortgage principal at the Mortgage Constant;
2. return *on* equity investment at the equity yield rate; and
3. return *of* that portion of forecast capital loss not covered by mortgage amortization, at the equity yield rate.

**Residual Income Is Capitalized at the Equity Yield Rate.** The residual income is that portion of NOI available to support the investment in the equity position after annual mortgage debt service has been deducted. The equity yield rate is the rate of return on similar, competitive equity investments currently being required and received by investors on the same market, as of the valuation date. The present worth of that income flow to equity is cash throw-off divided by equity dividend rate ($e$), which may be regarded as the *equity constant.*

**Income Capitalized Is Net Operating Income.** Because of the short-term income projections, NOI is typically treated as a level annuity. It is also possible to handle declining, increasing, or variable annuities in mortgage-equity analysis, however. The methods for dealing with these types of income flows are the same as those indicated in Chapters 5, 9, and 11. The critical income estimate is cash throw-off to equity. This is derived by deducting annual debt service from NOI. The Overall or Composite Rate is applied to NOI, while the equity dividend rate is applied to cash throw-off to equity.

*Summary of Specific Considerations in*
*Mortgage-Equity Analysis*

1. Purchaser-investors are assumed to take maximum advantage of the benefits

of leverage through the pattern of typically available mortgage loan terms for the type of property being appraised, as of the valuation date.

2. The amount and terms of most probable mortgage financing establish either annual debt service or the mortgage constant. Thus, the portion of NOI required to cover annual debt service is "given."

3. The residual income is cash throw-off to equity (NOI minus annual debt service). This is capitalized at the equity dividend rate to derive the present worth of the equity investment position, which is the residual.

4. Because the mortgage loan is a fixed contract, any capital loss or appreciation realized through the reversion is entirely attributable to the equity investment position, and directly influences its present worth.

5. The present worth of the reversion is estimated by discounting at the equity yield rate.

6. The income projection period is a relatively short-term investment holding period. It is equal to or less than the mortgage amortization period.

7. NOI forecasts are typically capitalized as level annuities.

8. Capital recovery is achieved through a combination of mortgage amortization and prorated annual payments to cover any forecast capital loss through the reversion. The former is a sinking fund accumulated at compound interest at the mortgage interest rate. The latter is discounted at the equity yield rate.

9. The reversion is the value of the entire property at the end of the income projection period.

10. The reversion is realized in cash through either resale, exchange, or refinancing of the property at the end of the income projection period.

11. NOI is capitalized at the Overall or Composite Rate to derive a present worth estimate for the entire property.

12. Capital appreciation as well as capital loss through the reversion may be handled in mortgage-equity analysis.

13. Income Tax consideration influence investor behavior, and hence the patterns of financing and length of investment holding periods, to maximize cash flows from the equity investment.

14. When market rentals, typical mortgage financing terms, and market-derived equity yield rates are employed in mortgage-equity analysis, the present worth estimate is Market Value. When contract rentals, specific mortgage financing terms, and an equity yield rate required by a specific investor are employed in mortgage-equity analysis, the present worth estimate is either Investment Value for a specific potential investor, or Value in Use for a specific owner.

*Property Value as the Sum of Mortgage Principal*
*and Present Worth of Equity Position*

Algebraically expressed, mortgage-equity analysis also approaches property value as the sum of the present worth of the mortgage investment position (the principal amount of the mortgage loan) and the present worth of the equity investment position: $V = V_m + V_e$. The entire framework of mortgage-equity analysis can be expressed in a few simple algebraic equations, for those who find this form of expression easier to understand.

The symbols used are:

$V$ = present worth or value of the property
$I$ = net operating income
$R$ = overall or composite rate
$V_m$ = present worth of the mortgage investment position (mortgage principal)
$I_m$ = annual mortgage debt service
$R_m$ = mortgage constant
$V_e$ = present worth of the equity investment position
$I_e$ = income available to support the equity investment (cash throw-off)
$R_e$ = equity dividend rate

Then:

$$V = I/R$$
$$V = V_m + V_e$$
$$V_m = I_m/R_m$$
$$V_e = I_e/R_e$$
$$I = I_m + I_e$$
$$R = (R_m \times V_m/V) + (R_e \times V_e/V)$$

So:

$$V = (I_m + I_e)/[(R_m \times V_m/V) + (R_e \times V_e/V)]$$

The last two equations require some brief explanation. The Overall or Composite Rate is a weighted average of the mortgage constant and the equity dividend rate, weighted by the proportion of total property value that mortgage principal and equity investment represent, respectively. If the loan-to-value ratio of the mortgage is 75%, then $R_m$ is weighted by 0.75, because $V_m/V$ is given as 0.75. Since $V_e = V - V_m$, and $V$ is 100% of itself, the weight for the equity investment is 0.25 (1.00 − 0.75 = 0.25).

The final complex equation is simply $V = I/R$ with $I$ and $R$ represented by their component parts.

This series of equations demonstrates that property value or present worth can be estimated in two ways with mortgage-equity analysis. First, an Overall or Composite Rate can be developed as a weighted average of appropriate mortgage and equity rates, and then divided directly into NOI. Second, the mortgage and equity investment positions can be valued separately, with mortgage principal given (as either a dollar amount or a percentage of value), and the equity investment position valued as a residual. The present worth estimates of the two investment positions are then summed to derive the present worth or value estimate for the property.

**Applications of Mortgage-Equity Analysis**

The most widely recognized and accepted form of mortgage-equity analysis is the Ellwood formulation. Because of its special significance, it is considered separately in a subsequent section of this chapter. There are alternative ways to express and apply mortgage-equity analysis, however. Both Direct Capitalization with an Overall Rate and treatment of the equity investment position as a residual can be used.

*Simple Mortgage-Equity Analysis:*
*No Equity Build-Up*

Both the Building Residual and Land Residual techniques of physical residual analysis operate on the assumption that the reversion is the site at precisely its present value. Similarly, mortgage-equity analysis can be applied on the assumption that no capital loss in *equity* will occur: the amount of the reversion will be 100% of present equity value. Theoretically, this could occur when mortgage amortization with its consequent build-up of equity over the income projection period exactly equals any decline in the value of the equity position. The equity investor then recovers his initial investment through resale or refinancing and the mortgage is paid off. Mechanically, mortgage amortization is ignored and the value of the equity position is forecast to remain constant. This is accomplished by capitalizing the income to the equity (cash throw-off) at the equity dividend rate, which is *equal to* the equity yield rate when the reversion is 100% of present equity value. $y = e - dep.\ 1/s_n$; $y = e + app.\ 1/s_n$. Therefore, when *dep.* or *app.* $= 0$, $y = e$.

**Simple Mortgage-Equity Analysis Using Overall Rates.** The Overall Rate is developed through a Band of Investment technique in simple mortgage-equity analysis. It is a weighted average of the mortgage constant and the equity dividend rate, weighted by *first-period* percentages of total property value represented by the mortgage and equity investment positions. The constantly changing ratios resulting from mortgage amortization and consequent equity build-up are ignored. This is unrealistic, but it forms a foundation for understanding the more complex rate development process required when mortgage amortization and equity build-up are incorporated into the analysis.

   For purposes of comparison, the same basic property information used in the examples throughout Chapters 10-12 are employed in the illustrations of mortgage-equity applications in this chapter. It will be recalled that:

   NOI = $15,000
   Mortgage Loan-to-Value Ratio = 70% (.70)
   Mortgage Interest Rate = 8.5%
   Mortgage Maturity = 20 years

Mortgage Amortization = 100% amortization, level monthly payments
Equity Dividend Rate = 10% (.10) [Also Equity Yield Rate]
Equity Investment = 30% of value (.30)

Then, the calculation of the Overall Rate with the Band of Investment technique under the assumptions of simple mortgage-equity analysis becomes:

| Mortgage: | .70 × .1041 = .0729 |
|---|---|
| Equity: | .30 × .1000 = .0300 |
| Overall Rate: | .1029 = 10.29% |

The estimation of value involves simple Direct Capitalization: $V = I/R$. In this instance, $I$ = $15,000 and $R$ = 0.1029, so value is estimated as $15,000/0.1029 = $145,772.59. This would be rounded to $146,000, since the most rounded figure ($15,000) is expressed to the nearest one thousand dollars.

It should be noted that the data used in this calculation and estimate of property value are all market-derived figures. NOI is based on market rentals and operating expenses stabilized in accordance with market standards. The mortgage constant is derived from the most probable pattern of financing terms available to the most probable type of purchaser-investor in the type of property involved, in the current competitive market. The equity dividend rate is the rate of return *to* equity investments required to attract equity funds into the type of investment represented by the type of property involved, as of the valuation date. As a result, the present worth figure of $146,000 is a Market Value estimate.

The same technique may be used to estimate Investment Value when the data employed are specific to a particular investor and property.

**Simple Mortgage-Equity Analysis with an Equity Residual.** When the *amount* of a mortgage loan is known, as well as the other mortgage loan terms or the mortgage constant, it is possible to estimate the cash throw-off to equity. This is a residual income flow. The present worth of the equity investment position is then derived by capitalizing the cash throw-off at the equity dividend rate.

With the same property income and rate data, and the same mortgage loan terms used in the foregoing example, assume that the principal amount of mortgage loan that can be obtained is $102,000. The valuation of the property, with the equity position as the residual, becomes:

| | |
|---|---|
| Net Operating Income | $ 15,000 |
| *Less* Annual Debt Service | |
| ($102,000 × 0.1041) | −$ 10,618 |
| *Equals* Cash Throw-Off | $  4,382 |
| | |
| Present Worth of Equity | |
| ($4,382/0.10) | $ 43,820 |

| | |
|---|---|
| *Plus* Mortgage Principal | +$102,000 |
| *Equals* Present Worth of Property | $145,820 |
| Estimated Value of Property | $146,000 |

This method also assumes that the value of the equity investment position remains unchanged over time. Equity build-up is ignored, or exactly offset by capital loss forecast on resale.

Alternatively, the cash throw-off could be capitalized as a level annuity at the equity yield rate for a finite income projection period. The forecast amount of the reversion would have to be estimated, and then discounted to a present worth estimate at the equity yield rate. The two present worth estimates would then be summed to derive the estimated present worth of the equity investment position.

Using the same figures as in the foregoing example, assume that a 15-year income projection period is applicable and that the forecast amount of the reversion is $44,000. The 15-year annual Present Worth of One per Annum factor at 10% is 7.606080, while the 15-year Present Worth of One factor with annual discounting at 10% is 0.239392 (Ellwood, page 116, columns 5 and 4). Then property value is estimated as follows:

| | |
|---|---|
| Net Operating Income | $ 15,000 |
| *Less* Annual Debt Service | − 10,618 |
| *Equals* Cash Throw-Off | $ 4,382 |
| | |
| Present Worth of Cash Throw-Off | |
| (7.606080 × $4,283) | $ 33,330 |
| *Plus* Present Worth of Reversion | |
| (0.239392 × $44,000) | + 10,533 |
| *Equals* Present Worth of Equity | |
| Position | $ 43,863 |
| *Plus* Mortgage Principal | + 102,000 |
| *Equals* Present Worth of Property | $145,863 |
| Estimated Value of Property | $146,000 |

In each of the three illustrative applications of simple mortgage-equity analysis, the same present worth estimate was produced. This is not surprising, since the same property income, rate, and mortgage financing data were used in each example. The similarity of results does emphasize the interrelations of the alternative methods of applying simple mortgage-equity analysis. They are merely different sides of the same coin.

Finally, the finite-term variation of treating the equity position as a residual points up graphically the implications of ignoring equity build-up through mortgage amortization in simple mortgage-equity analysis. The $44,000 reversion is the amount of the present worth of the equity position. This means that implicitly the capital loss forecast is the amount of the mortgage ($102,000 or 70%)!

*Mortgage-Equity Analysis with Equity Build-Up*

For purposes of presentation and discussion, mortgage-equity analysis that *does* take into account equity build-up through mortgage amortization will be considered as "regular" (as opposed to "simple") mortgage-equity analysis. Throughout the remainder of this book, it will merely be labeled "mortgage-equity analysis." Whenever the variant that ignores equity build-up is referred to, it will continue to be called "simple mortgage-equity analysis."

The income receipts forecast in mortgage-equity analysis consist of the two components forecast in any capitalization process: NOI over a finite period of time, and a lump-sum reversion receivable at the end of that period. The reversion, which is the remaining value of the entire property, may be expressed either as a dollar amount or as a percentage of present worth (the original amount of total property investment).

In "regular" mortgage-equity analysis, an *explicit* forecast of the amount or percentage of the reversion is required. This is different from the "simple" form in which the *implicit* reversion is the amount as the present worth of the equity position. Moreover, and this is quite important, mortgage-equity analysis is concerned with *cash* flows and *cash* receipts. Whenever the income projection period (or investment holding period) is less than the mortgage maturity, there will be some outstanding mortgage balance remaining unpaid when the reversion is realized through resale, refinancing, or an exchange. This must be deducted from the proceeds of resale to derive the *net cash proceeds* to the equity investment position.

**Use of an Overall Rate with Equity Build-Up.**[3] A weighted-average Overall Rate developed by the Band of Investment technique with the mortgage constant and the equity dividend rate suffers from the critical limitation that, in ignoring equity build-up through mortgage amortization, it tends to overstate forecast capital loss. That loss is necessarily the amount of the mortgage loan. It is usually an excessively gloomy forecast, particularly for relatively short-term income projections.

One way to compensate for this lack is to make a specific adjustment in the "simple" mortgage-equity Overall Rate. This adjustment reflects the sinking fund factor for mortgage principal amortization payments over the loan maturity, at the equity yield rate. This "credit for equity growth"[4] reflects the fact that a position of NOI must be allocated to capital recovery in order to keep the investor's *total* investment intact. If the income projection period is the same length as the mortgage maturity or longer, the sinking fund factor at the equity yield rate is taken for the length of the mortgage maturity. By the end of the mortgage maturity period, the total equity investment will be equal to the total original investment in the property (original mortgage principal plus original equity investment).

However, the equity yield rate is usually greater than the mortgage interest rate. Otherwise, the investor will have negative leverage results. It therefore requires a smaller annual amount to accumulate to the principal amount of the mortgage with compounding at the equity yield rate than it does with compounding at the mortgage interest rate. Thus, the Overall Rate developed by the Band of Investment technique includes the *difference* between the amortization (sinking fund) factor at the mortgage interest rate and the factor for the same number of periods at the equity yield rate.

Since equity build-up occurs on only that portion of the investment represented by the mortgage principal, the sinking fund factor at the equity yield rate, which identifies the rate of annual income required for capital recovery, must be weighted by the percentage loan-to-value ratio. This is the same weight given to the mortgage constant. The result is the "credit for equity build-up," which is deducted from the weighted average of mortgage constant and equity yield rate to derive the appropriate overall rate.

To illustrate this technique in practice, assume the same property income, rates, and financing terms that have been used in previous examples in this chapter. The only additional information required is the sinking fund factor for 20 years (the mortgage maturity) with annual compounding at 10% (the equity yield rate). That factor is 0.017460 (Ellwood, page 116, column 3). It will be recalled that the mortgage constant is 0.1041, and the loan-to-value ratio is 0.70. To be consistent, the 10% sinking fund factor is rounded to 0.0175 in this example. The calculation of the mortgage-equity Overall Rate would then be:

$$
\begin{array}{lll}
& \text{Mortgage:} & 0.70 \times 0.1041 = 0.0729 \\
plus & \text{Equity:} & 0.30 \times 0.1000 = \underline{0.0300} \\
& \text{Weighted Average} & \phantom{0.30 \times 0.1000 = }0.1029 \\
less & \text{Credit for Equity} & \\
& \text{Build-Up} & .070 \times 0.0175 = \underline{0.0123} \\
& \text{Overall Rate} & \phantom{.070 \times 0.0175 = }0.0906
\end{array}
$$

Applying this Overall Rate to Net Operating Income in Direct Capitalization results in a present worth estimate of the property of $165,563 ($15,000/.0906). This is the present worth of the property based on the assumptions of no capital loss in the property reversion, and an income projection period at least as long as the mortgage maturity.

*Income Projection Periods Less than Mortgage Maturity.* Since the income projection period (or investment holding period) for many income properties is less than the mortgage maturity, it is necessary to make one further adjustment in the Overall Rate calculation to compensate for this fact. The adjustment consists of weighting the (already weighted) "credit for equity build-up" by the percentage of mortgage loan paid off at the end of the income projection period. Equity build-up occurs only to the extent that mortgage amortization occurs. When the mortgage is only partially amortized at the time of resale (or refinancing or exchange), then only the percentage of the loan actually paid off at that time constitutes equity build-up.

It was shown in Chapter 7 that the percentage of a loan paid off can be calculated as the *complement* of the ratio of the Present Worth of One per Annum factors at the mortgage interest rate for (1) the remaining term of the loan at the end of the income projection period; and (2) the total loan maturity.

To continue the example used in the preceding section, assume an income projection period of 15 years. The 15-year sinking fund factor at 10% is 0.0315 (Ellwood, page 116, column 3). The other ingredients in the analysis remain the same, but it is necessary to calculate the percentage of the 20-year, 8.5% level monthly payment loan amortized at the end of 15 years. The Present Worth of One per Annum factors are found in column 5 on page 89 in Ellwood. The percentage of loan paid off is:

P.W. One per Annum, 5 years, 8.5% (monthly):     48.741183
P.W. One per Annum, 20 years, 8.5% (monthly):   115.230840

$$1 - \frac{48.741183}{115.230840} = 1 - 0.422987 = 0.577013 = 57.7\%^b$$

The calculation of the Overall Rate is then as follows:

|  |  |  |  |
|---|---|---|---|
|  | Mortagee: | .70 × .1041 = | 0.0729 |
| *plus* | Equity: | .30 × .1000 = | 0.0300 |
|  | Weighted Average |  | 0.1029 |
| *less* | Credit for Equity |  |  |
|  | Build-Up: | .577 × .70 × .0315 = | −0.0127 |
|  | Overall Rate: |  | 0.0902 = 9.02% |

On the basis of this Overall Rate, the value of the property is $166,000 ($15,000/.0902 = $166,297). This still forecasts no capital loss or gain on resale.

*Inclusion of Capital Loss (or Gain).* The successive examples of Overall Rate derivation that have been presented in this section have been based on one particular assumption which, while not necessarily unrealistic, does represent a special case. That assumption is that there will be no capital loss (or gain) in the proceeds of sale of the reversion at the end of the income projection period. With this assumption intact, the analysis is unnecessarily restrictive and excessively limited in its applicability.

The Overall Rate $(R)$ developed when there is no change in capital value between present worth or original investment in the property and proceeds of resale of the reversion is *equal to* Ellwood's Basic Capitalization Rate or "Basic Rate" $(r)$.[5] To produce a truly flexible Overall Rate concept and formulation, it is also necessary to include an adjustment for the prorated annual amount that must be deducted from NOI to provide for forecast capital loss—or added to NOI to reflect forecast capital appreciation (gain).

---

[b]Using Ellwood's formula $P = (\frac{f}{i} - 1) \ (S_p - 1)$, the calculated percentage is 57.6%. See *Ellwood Tables*, third edition, Part I, page 11.

Since the mortgage loan is a contract which specifies the interest return and the capital recovery (mortgage amortization) to be received by the mortgagee,[c] all capital loss or gain through the reversion is borne entirely by the equity investment position. To convert this forecast lump-sum reversionary loss or gain to a prorated annual amount, the amount or percentage of capital loss or gain is discounted at the sinking fund rate over the income projection period, with annual discounting at the equity yield rate. This is based on exactly the same principle that requires the use of the sinking fund factor at the equity rate to identify the "credit for equity build-up."

The unadjusted sinking fund factor at the equity yield rate over the income projection period identifies the annual amount that would provide for capital recovery of the entire property investment over that period. Since only a portion of total property value is represented by capital loss (or gain), the sinking fund factor at the equity yield rate must be *weighted* by the percentage of total property value represented by forecast capital loss (or gain). The notations for this percentage are those developed by Ellwood:[6] *dep.* is the percentage of total capital loss or "depreciation" forecast; *app.* is the percentage of total capital gain or "appreciation" forecast.

When capital loss is forecast, this weighted adjustment is *added* to the Basic Rate to produce the applicable Overall Rate. Conversely, when capital gain is forecast, the weighted adjustment is *subtracted* from the Basic Rate to produce the applicable Overall Rate.

To illustrate the inclusion of prorated annual capital recovery or capital appreciation payments in mortgage-equity Overall Rates, consider the property data and rate figures previously used in this chapter. Assume that a 30% decline in property value is forecast on resale in 15 years.

The annual 10% sinking fund factor for 15 years (Ellwood, page 116, column 3) is 0.031474. Since factors have been rounded to four decimal places in the preceding examples, 0.0315 is used here. Capital loss is forecast at 30%, so *dep.* = 0.30. The calculation of the Overall Rate then becomes:

|      |                   |                                     |          |
|------|-------------------|-------------------------------------|----------|
|      | Mortgage:         | $.70 \times .1041 =$                | 0.0729   |
| *plus* | Equity:         | $.30 \times .1000 =$                | 0.0300   |
|      | Weighted Average: |                                     | 0.1029   |
| *less* | Equity Build-Up: | $.577 \times .70 \times 0315 =$    | 0.0127   |
|      | Basic Rate:       |                                     | 0.0902   |
| *plus* | Capital Recovery: | $.30 \times .0315 =$              | 0.0095   |
|      | Overall Rate:     |                                     | 0.0997   |
|      |                   |                                     | (9.97%)  |

With capital gain or appreciation forecast at 20%, *app.* = 0.20. Then the Overall Rate would be:

---

[c]Variable-rate mortgages present a complicating but solvable problem that is beyond the scope of this book. The treatment of mortgagee participations in property income and/or equity is discussed in Chapters 18 and 19.

|          | Basic Rate:           |                | 0.0902   |
| -------- | --------------------- | -------------- | -------- |
| *less*   | Capital Appreciation: | .20 × .0315 =  | −0.0063  |
|          | Overall Rate:         |                | 0.0839   |
|          |                       |                | (8.39%)  |

Applying the Overall Rate to Net Operating Income of $15,000 through Direct Capitalization yields the following results:

Present Worth with 30% Capital Loss: $15,000/.0997 = $150,451
Present Worth with 20% Capital Gain: $15,000/.0839 = $178,784

*Summary of Overall Rate Results.* A property can have only one Market Value as of any given date. Only one set of assumptions and conditions will fit the facts of the market and of the appraisal problem. But different assumptions and conditions do produce markedly different results. The discussion thus far in this chapter has identified and demonstrated the derivation of mortgage-equity Overall Rates under varying assumptions and conditions. The appraiser must select the process that most nearly and accurately depicts the facts of the appraisal at hand. At the same time, he should be familiar with the several methods of rate derivation potentially applicable to the appraisal problem confronting him, and aware of the implications and impact of the assumptions of each. Only then can he justify the selection of method used.

The calculated Overall Rates and present worth indications through Direct Capitalization developed under these different sets of assumptions with the same property income, rates, and terms of financing were:

1. No equity build-up, simple Band of Investment: $R = 10.29\%$; $V = \$146,000$.
2. Equity build-up, income projection period equal to mortgage maturity, 100% reversion: $R = 9.06\%$; $V = \$165,500$.
3. Equity build-up, income projection period less than mortgage maturity, 100% reversion: $R = 9.02\%$; $V = \$166,000$.
4. Equity build-up, income projection period less than mortgage maturity, capital loss forecast: $R = 9.97\%$; $V = \$150,000$.
5. Equity build-up, income projection period less than mortgage maturity, capital gain forecast: $R = 8.39\%$; $V = \$179,000$.

The last three deserve a final note. The differences among the Overall Rate and the value estimates are entirely the results of different forecasts of the amount of the reversion on resale (or refinancing or an exchange). It is logical to conclude that an investment that offers the expectation of a capital gain is worth more than one that is anticipated merely to keep the investment capital intact, or to produce a capital loss—given the same level and characteristics of the forecast income stream. These relationships are reflected in the respective Overall Rates developed for each reversion forecast.

*Data Requirements and Applicability of Method.* The discussion of Overall Rates in Chapter 9 pointed out that market sales transactions data for similar, competitive properties provide the best and simplest basis for deriving an Overall Rate. It also pointed out that the required sales price and NOI data are only infrequently available to permit the appraiser to develop an Overall Rate appropriately.

The derivation of Overall Rates through mortgage-equity analysis, using a Band of Investment technique, is more involved and complex. However, it does utilize data that are usually available and verifiable from the market. The required information is:

1. terms of lending of typical mortgage financing available to the type of property being appraised;
2. rate of return on equity investments of the type involved being sought or demanded by typical purchaser-investors;
3. typical income projection period or investment holding period for property investments of this type; and
4. capital loss or gain anticipations of typical purchaser-investor over the income projection period specified. Since dollar amounts can rarely be forecast, the loss or gain is expressed as a percentage of original total investment.

If this information can be obtained from the market (and it usually can), then the Overall Rate developed is a *market* rate. It can be applied to a market-derived NOI to produce an estimate of Market Value through Direct Capitalization. Similarly, the expectations and requirements of a specific investor can be used as the basis for deriving an Overall Rate that will produce an Investment Value estimate.

**Mortgage-Equity Analysis in Property Residual Form.** Since the income receipts forecast for a property investment in mortgage-equity analysis consist of a level NOI over a specified income projection period and a reversion of the entire property at the end of that period, value estimation can be accomplished in property residual form. The principles and format for property residual valuation analysis were presented in Chapter 12. While it is possible to estimate the present worth of a reversion forecast as a dollar amount, as is required when the property residual technique is applied to the physical components of the property, reliable dollar forecasts are available to the appraiser. The mortgage-equity approach has the advantage of being able to deal with reversion forecasts expressed as percentages of the original investment.

As in ordinary residual analysis, NOI is treated as a finite income stream that provides for full recovery of the total investment over the income projection period. Since the two claims on this finite income stream are those of the mortgage lender and the equity investor, the mortgage-equity "capitalization rate" applied to NOI is the weighted average of the mortgage constant and the level annuity factor at the equity yield rate. The weights are the initial loan-to-value ratio and the initial percentage of equity investment. The present worth of the finite income stream is thus NOI divided by this mortgage-equity "capitalization rate."

The reversion is payable to the equity investor. Therefore, its present worth is its amount (or percentage) discounted by the Present Worth of One factor over the income projection period, with annual discounting at the equity yield rate. *However*, mortgage equity analysis deals with cash flows. When the income projection period is less than the mortgage maturity, as it frequently is, there will still be an outstanding unpaid balance on the mortgage. This mortgage balance (dollars or percentage) must be *deducted* from the forecast reversion (dollars or percentage) to derive the forecast *net cash reversion to the equity investor*. The present worth of this net cash reversion is added to the present worth of the finite income stream (NOI) to produce the present worth estimate of the property.

To illustrate this method with percentages rather than dollar amounts (which are much simpler to handle), assume the same property investment figures used in the examples throughout this chapter. This will make possible a comparison of results under the different methods. Also, discount factors and rates are again rounded to four decimal places in the interests of consistency.

In this example, *NOI* = $15,000. The mortgage is a 70% loan at 8.5%, with level monthly amortization over 20 years. The mortgage constant is 10.41%. The equity investment is therefore 30%, and the equity yield rate is 10%. The income projection period is 15 years, so the level annuity capitalization rate is 13.15% (Ellwood, page 116, column 6). The Present Worth of One factor for 15 years with annual discounting at 10% is 0.2394 (Ellwood, page 116, column 4).

Take first a forecast reversion of 70% of original investment, which represents a 30% capital loss in 15 years. The percentage outstanding balance of this mortgage at the end of 15 years has previously been calculated as 42.3%.

With this information in hand, the estimation of value via mortgage-equity analysis in Property Residual form proceeds as shown in Exhibit 13-1.

**Exhibit 13-1**
**Mortgage-Equity Analysis in Property Residual Form**

1. Derivation of Mortgage-Equity "Capitalization Rate"
   Mortgage: .70 × .1041 =        0.0729
   Equity: .30 × .1315 =          0.0395
   "Capitalization Rate":         0.1124

2. Derivation of Net Cash Reversion as a Percentage of Value
   Reversion = $.70V$
   Outstanding Balance of Mortgage = $.4230\ (.70V) = .2961V$
   Net Cash Proceeds (Percentage) = $.7000V - .2961V = .4039V$

3. Calculation of Present Worth of Property

$$V = \frac{NOI}{\text{``Cap. Rate''}} + (\text{Net Cash Proceeds} \times \text{P.W. One factor})$$

$$V = \frac{\$15,000}{.1124} + (.4039 \, V \times .2394)$$

$V = \$133,451.95 + .0967V$

$V - .0967V = \$133,451.95$

$.9033V = \$133,451.95$

$V = \$133,451.95/.9033 = \$147,738.24$, say $148,000

In the case of a forecast 20% increase in reversion on resale, the only difference is in the valuation of the net cash reversion to the equity investor. The present worth of the 15-year NOI stream is precisely the same. The estimation of the net cash reversion as a percentage of original investment is: $1.200V - 0.2961V = 0.9039V$. The present worth is $.2164V$ ($.9039V \times .2394$). The valuation equation then becomes:

$V = \$133,451.95 + 0.2164V$

$V - .2164V = .7836V = \$133,451.95$

$$V = \frac{\$133,451.95}{.7836V} = \$170,306.21, \text{ say } \$170,000$$

**Mortgage-Equity Analysis with an Equity Residual.** If the *amount* of mortgage principal is given instead of the loan-to-value ratio, it is possible to identify the annual debt service. Deducting this from *NOI* gives annual cash throw-off, which is capitalized at the equity dividend rate to derive to present worth of the equity investment.

In the example used throughout this chapter, the equity dividend rate is the Cash Throw-off divided by Present Worth of the Equity Investment. Assume the mortgage principal is $102,000, rather than 70% of value. Thus:

| | |
|---|---:|
| Net Operating Income | $ 15,000 |
| *Less* Annual Debt Service | |
| (.1041 × $102,000) | −10,618 |
| Cash Throw-Off | $ 4,382 |

$V = \$102,000 + (\$4,382 \times 7.606080) + .23932 (.70V - \$43,146)$

$V = \$102,000 + \$33,330 + .1676V - \$10,329$

$.8324V = \$125,001$

$V = \$150,169$

Present Worth of Equity = $150,169 − $102,000 = $48,169

Equity Dividend Rate = $4,382/$8,169 = .0910

There is no particular advantage to this method over Direct Capitalization with a mortgage-equity Overall Rate. The same data are required in each instance, except for the mortgage loan-to-value ratio, which is generally available market information. Approaching the appraisal as an equity residual problem *is* useful when the present worth of the equity position is the point at issue. It is also helpful as a means to understand and explain the composition of an equity dividend rate.

For purposes of comparison, the equity dividend rate when the reversion is forecast to represent 20% appreciation is:

$V = \$102,000 + (\$4,382 \times 7.606080) + ,239392 (1.2V - \$43,146)$
$V = \$102,000 + \$33,330 \$ ,2873V - \$10,329$
$.7127V = \$125,001$
$V = \$175,391$
Present Worth of Equity = $\$175,391 - \$102,000 = \$73,391$
Equity Dividend Rate = $\$4,382/\$73,391 = .0597$

### An Introduction to the Ellwood Formulation

The presentation is necessarily limited to introducing the composition, meaning, and applications of the Ellwood variant of mortgage-equity analysis. The implications and ramifications of this sensitive analytical tool are seemingly limitless, and are still being discovered and published.[d] Because this book is essentially an intermediate text on income property valuation, the discussion in this introductory presentation is restricted to those more commonly encountered problems relating to the valuation of income-producing real estate and equity investments in it.

**Ellwood Analysis as a Variant of Mortgage-Equity Analysis.** All of the principles, concepts, and tools required to understand and to apply Ellwood analysis (and the Ellwood formula) have already been explained and demonstrated in earlier chapters, or in the preceding sections of this chapter. Without in any way minimizing the significance or usefulness of the powerful tool that L.W. Ellwood has developed, it can be said that a working command

---

[d]See, in particular, Ellwood, *Ellwood Tables*, third edition, Part I, pages 51-134. The myriad examples in these pages clearly illustrate many of the uses of the Ellwood formula in appraisal and investment decision-making. The discussion also explains in detail the uses of the several precalculated factor tables provided in Part II of the two-volume third edition. The scope and purpose of this book preclude an in-depth exposition of appraisal and investment analysis with Ellwood's formula and tables. For that, the reader is referred to the source.

over compound interest factors, mortgage financing terms, the investor viewpoint, and the principles and techniques of mortgage-equity analysis is all the preparation that is needed to comprehend and apply the Ellwood formula effectively.

In brief, the Ellwood formulation is simply a logical extension of basic mortgage-equity analysis with some more realistic and descriptive assumptions about property income flows and the nature of the claims of those income flows. Everything is viewed from the vantage point of the equity investor. The arithmetic seems complicated at first, but the most complex mathematical concept involved is accumulation or discounting at compound interest.

The valuation concepts are really simple and straightforward. Direct Capitalization is used, and Net Operating Income is the forecast annual income flow that is capitalized to a present worth or value estimate. The whole analysis focuses on the development of an appropriate Overall Composite Rate $(R)$ as a weighted average of the several claims against NOI that must be met in order to make the investment competitively attractive. Either Market Value or Investment Value can be estimated through the Ellwood formula, depending on the data used in the analysis.

### Basic Principles of the Ellwood Formulation

**Viewpoint of the Investor.** As in general mortgage-equity analysis, Ellwood assumes that the most probable purchaser of income-producing real estate will be an investor. Moreover, this purchaser-investor will be typically informed about investment and financing opportunities in the market, and will act prudently and rationally on that information to maximize his cash position. He is interested in the cash income that the property will produce to support his equity investment.

Annual cash throw-off must produce a return on his equity investment at the equity yield rate. The proceeds of resale or refinancing of the property at the end of the income projection period provide further cash returns to recover the equity investment.

To the extent that mortgage amortization, and hence equity build-up, over the income projection period do not cover forecast capital loss on resale, Net Operating Income must include a prorated annual return to provide for capital recovery.

The purchaser-investor is sensitive to income taxes, and will behave in a way that allows for maximum tax avoidance. To the extent possible, present income will be covered by allowable income tax depreciation charges to provide a larger present cash flow to the investor; income tax liability will be deferred to the future, enhancing the amount of present and near-term cash flow; and the reversion will be given capital gains treatment rather than ordinary income treatment on resale.

The investor seeks to take maximum possible advantage of leverage to enhance his equity return. This equity return is expressed as the "Equity Income Dividend," which explains his use of $d$ rather than $I$ in the basic valuation equation.

The investor will typically retain the investment only so long as there is a cash income advantage in doing so. This is influenced in part by income tax considerations. The income projection period is therefore the normal investment holding period for the most probable type of purchaser-investor. This income projection period for most types of purchaser-investors is less than either the remaining economic life of the improvements or the maturity of the mortgage. The applicable income projection period for the type of investor and the type or property involved in any given appraisal is determined by market behavior of investors in similar, competing properties.

The investor typically will anticipate a level income flow over the relatively short income projection period. He will also have discoverable expectations about the most probable resale price of the property at the end of the income projection period. This forecast is based on market evidence relating to similar, competing properties, as well as market trends as of the valuation date.

**Components of Ellwood Analysis.** Based on this pattern of behavior assumed for informed, prudent, and rational purchaser-investors, the Ellwood analysis builds upon the basic framework of mortgage-equity analysis.

Net Operating Income is treated as a level annuity over the income projection period. It is capitalized at an Overall Rate or Composite Rate which incorporated:

1. return on the outstanding balance of the mortgage at the mortgage interest rate;
2. return of the principal amount of the mortgage through mortgage amortization, which is compounded at the mortgage interest rate;
3. return on the amount of equity investment, which is continually increasing as mortgage amortization payments contribute to equity build-up, discounted at the equity yield rate; and
4. return of the forecast amount of capital loss at resale, discounted at the equity yield rate; OR deduction of the amount of capital appreciation forecast at resale, discounted at the equity yield rate.

Equity build-up through mortgage amortization means that the amount of equity investment on which a return at the equity yield rate is required is constantly increasing. This phenomenon is accounted for in Ellwood's Mortgage Coefficient $(C)$. It was also considered in the earlier discussion of equity build-up as part of mortgage-equity analysis.

The present worth of the equity investment position is a residual. Mortgage debt service must be paid first before any cash flow is available to support the equity investment position. Cash flow to the equity is capitalized at the equity yield rate. Cash flow to the equity includes recovery of any forecast capital loss on the reversion.

The reversion is the entire property at the end of the income projection period, realized either through resale, refinancing, or exchange of the property. Either the dollar amount of the reversion as anticipated by the investor, or (more probably) the percentage decline or increase from the original investment in the property on resale, is used as the measure of capital loss or appreciation to be prorated over the income projection period.

**Information Required by the Appraiser.** Several items of information must be obtained by the appraiser before the Ellwood analysis can be applied to a valuation problem. These are typically available in the market, and little or no judgment on the part of the appraiser is required. The required information includes:

1. Mortgage loan terms most probable for the type of property being appraised:
   a. mortgage interest rate
   b. loan-to-value ratio
   c. mortgage loan maturity
   d. amortization provisions and period (monthly, semi-annually, etc.)
2. Amount of Net Operating Income
3. Equity Yield Rate required and/or being sought by investors on similar, competing investment properties
4. Income projection period (investment holding period) for the type of property being appraised and the most probable type of purchaser-investor
5. Forecast or anticipated percentage decrease or increase in the reversion from original property investment.

*Technique of the Ellwood Analysis*

The basic valuation equation discussed in preceding chapters is used to estimate value through Direct Capitalization. Ellwood expresses it as $V = \dfrac{d}{R}$, where

d is Net Operating Income, and
R is the Overall Rate or Composite Rate.

**Components of the Ellwood Formula.**[7] The essence of Ellwood Analysis is to estimate $R$. The "Ellwood formula" is the formula for $R$, which can be expressed in two ways:

$$R = y - mc + dep. \, 1/s_n$$
$$R = y - mc - app. \, 1/s_n$$

*r is the basic rate*. It is equal to the Overall Rate when neither capital loss nor capital appreciation is forecast from the reversion. It is also the weighted average of the mortgage constant and the equity yield rate, taking into account equity build-up through mortgage amortization, as was demonstrated in the section on "Use of an Overall Rate with Equity Build-Up" in the discussion of mortgage-equity analysis earlier in this chapter.

The formula is: $r = y - mc$, where

> $y$ is the Equity Yield Rate
> $m$ is the initial Loan-to-Value Ratio of the Mortgage
> $c$ is the Mortgage Coefficient

*Capital loss or appreciation* is prorated annually through the sinking fund factor at the equity yield rate, weighted by the percentage decline or increase in value forecast for the reversion. Ellwood calls capital loss "depreciation," and capital gain "appreciation."

When capital loss is forecast, the expression is "*dep.* $1/s_n$"; for capital appreciation, it is "*app.* $1/s_n$," where:

> *dep.* is the percentage decline forecast in the reversion
> *app.* is the percentage increase forecast in the reversion
> $1/s_n$ is the sinking fund factor over the income projection
> period at the equity yield rate

*Estimation of the Basic Rate* r

Since *dep.* $1/s_n$ or *app.* $1/s_n$ can be estimated independently—given the forecast percentage decrease or increase in the reversion, the equity yield rate, and the income projection period—the major focus of the Ellwood analysis in developing an appropriate Composite Rate $(R)$ is to estimate the Basic Rate $r$. The Basic Rate Formula is $r = y - mc$. Since $y$ and $m$ are already given, the problem in developing $r$ becomes the derivation of a value for $c$: the Mortgage Coefficient.

The derivation and meaning of $c$ are most easily explained by taking first a simple illustration with a non-amortized mortgage. The use of the Mortgage Coefficient is simply an alternative way of deriving an appropriate rate of discount by working from known components derived from the market.

The equity yield rate, loan-to-value ratio and mortgage interest rate are all derived from market evidence. Assume the income and financing information used in the general example used throughout this chapter.
Then:

> $y = .10$ or $10\%$
> $m = .70$ or $70\%$
> $i = .085$ or $8.5\%$

With no amortization, the Mortgage Coefficient is the *difference* between the equity yield rate and the mortgage interest rate $(c = y - i)$.
Thus:

$$c = .10 - 0.85 = .015$$

Then

$$r = y - mc = .10 - (.70 \times .015) = .10 - .0105 = .0895$$

As proof, treat this same information as a simple band of investment:

| | | |
|---|---|---|
| Mortgage: | .70 × .085 = | .0595 |
| Equity: | .30 × .10  = | .0300 |
| Discount Rate: | | .0895 |

It can therefore be seen that $r$, the Basic Rate in the Ellwood formula, is the same as the Discount Rate when mortgage amortization is ignored. Ellwood's formulation simply works from known components derived from the market, and derives $r$ as a Band of Investment rate. It starts from the equity yield rate, which would be applicable under 100% equity financing, and adjusts downward for mortgage financing. The traditional Band of Investment technique weights both equity yield rate and mortgage interest rate by the respective percentages of total property investment represented by equity investment and mortgage principal. The Ellwood formulation deducts the *difference* between equity yield rate and the mortgage interest rate, weighted by the loan-to-value ratio, from the equity yield rate.

*Incorporation of Mortgage Amortization and Equity Build-Up.* The significant contribution of the Ellwood analysis is that it enables the appraiser to incorporate mortgage amortization into the derivation of the basic rate $r$. This is a complicated process mechanically because each mortgage payment increases the amount of equity, but by a different amount. The amount of each level mortgage payment represented by principal amortization is continually increasing. These additions also continually increase the amount of equity on which the investor wishes to earn a return at the equity yield rate.

To minimize the required calculations in many cases, Ellwood includes in his book precalculated tables which provide $C$ factors for standardized loan-value ratios, mortgage interest rates, and mortgage maturities. In addition, there are subsidiary tables for components of the Mortgage Coefficient, labeled $Ca$, and $Cy$, and $r$.[8] Any combination of mortgage loan terms, equity yield rate, and income projection period that falls within the limits in these tables enables the appraiser to find the Basic Rate $r$ or the Mortgage Coefficient $c$ directly without further calculation.

*Calculation of the Mortgage Coefficient.* When the necessary components of $c$ fall outside the limits set in Ellwood's precalculated $c$ or $r$ tables, it is possible with relative ease to calculate $c$.

The formula is:

$$c = y + P \, 1/s_n - f$$

282

$P$ is the fraction of mortgage principal paid off over the income projection period, expressed as a decimal figure

$1/s_n$ is the sinking fund factor over the income projection period at the equity yield rate (Ellwood compound interest tables, column 3)

$f$ is the mortgage constant (Ellwood compound interest tables, column 6)

Ellwood has further precalculated factors in auxiliary tables that provide the $P$ and $f$ factors for a specified range of mortgage interest rates, mortgage amortization terms, equity yield rates, and income projection periods.[9] If the factors required cannot be found in the auxiliary tables because one of the basic components of information falls outside the range specified, it is possible to calculate $P$ through the formula:

$$P = (f/i - 1)(Sp - 1)$$

The only new factor to find here is $Sp$. This is the Future Worth of One, which is found in column 1 of Ellwood's compound interest tables. Care must be taken to use the table for the *mortgage interest rate* over the income projection period, and for the period of mortgage payments (e.g., monthly table for monthly mortgage payments).

The Mortgage Coefficient $c$ can be calculated, therefore, from information already obtained to apply both Ellwood and mortgage-equity analysis, together with compound interest tables such as are found in Ellwood. As an illustration, take the figures from the general example used throughout this chapter:

| | | | |
|---|---|---|---|
| $y$ | = | .10 | Income projection period = 15 years |
| $i$ | = | .085 | Mortgage amortization period = 20 years |
| $m$ | = | .70 | Mortgage payments are made monthly |
| $f$ | = | .1041 | (Ellwood, page 89, column 6: .008678 × 12 = .1041) |
| $Sp$ | = | 3.5627 | (Ellwood, page 89, column 1: 15-year projection) |

Therefore,

$P = (.1041/.085 - 1)(3.5627 - 1)$
$P = (1.2247 - 1)(2.5627) = (.2247)(2.5627)$
$P = .5757^e$

$1/s_n = .0315$ (10%, 15 years: Ellwood, page 116, column 3)
Thus:

$c = .10 + (.5757 \times .0315) - .1041 = .10 + .0181 - .1041$
$c = .1181 - .1041 = .0140$

To summarize and solve for $r$:

---

[e]The value of $P$ may also be derived as the complement of the ratio of Present Worth of One per Annum factors at the mortgage interest rate, for the remaining term of the loan and the mortgage maturity. This procedure was demonstrated in Chapter 7, and used in mortgage-equity illustrations earlier in this chapter. The results are virtually the same.

$$r = .10 - (.70 \times .0140) = .10 - .0098 = .0902$$
$$r = 9.02\%^{\text{f}}$$

*Inclusion of Forecast Depreciation or Appreciation.* Both capital loss (depreciation) and capital gain (appreciation) in the reversion on resale can be treated effectively in the Ellwood analysis. If $r$ is used without further adjustment for depreciation or appreciation, it means that the reversion is forecast to be 100% of the original investment amount. While this is possible, it is only one possibility. Others are for the reversion to be greater than or less than 100% of the original investment amount.

If no capital depreciation or appreciation in the reversion is forecast, then $R = r$.

*Capital loss.* If capital loss (depreciation) is forecast, this means that Composite Rate $R$ must cover both the basic rate $r$ and the prorated rate of annual capital recovery. Thus, NOI is discounted to a present worth estimate by the sum of the basic rate and the capital recovery rate.

When capital loss is forecast, the Composite Rate $R$ must be greater than the basic rate $r$. Since *NOI* is divided by $R$ to derive a present worth estimate for the property, the larger $R$ is, the lower the present worth of any given *NOI* will be. The capital recovery rate applies to the entire *NOI* because the forecast capital loss (depreciation) is experienced by the entire property, not merely one of its constitutent physical components. The *impact* of forecast capital loss (depreciation) is felt entirely by the equity investment position because the amount of mortgage principal to be recovered is fixed by contract.

The capital recovery rate is represented by the symbol *dep.* $1/s_n$. As noted previously, *dep.* is the forecast *percentage* decline in the value of the reversion from the original investment amount on resale at the end of the income projection period; $1/s_n$ is the sinking fund factor at the equity yield rate over the income projection period. It is found in column 3 of the Ellwood compound interest tables.

In the continuing example used throughout this chapter, assume that the reversion is forecast to be 70% of the original investment at the end of the 15-year income projection period. This means that *dep.* = 30% or .30; $1/s_n$ at 10% over a 15-year projection = .0315.

Thus, the indicated annual rate of capital recovery over 15 years of a forecast 30% decline in resale price, discounted at 10% is:

$$dep.\ 1/s_n = .30 \times .0315 = .00945 = 0.95\%$$

*Capital gain.* If capital gain (appreciation) is forecast, this means that the total income flow forecast to be received from the property is *NOI plus* a prorated annual return representing capital gain. The *rate* at which *NOI* is capitalized is the Composite Rate $R$. This Composite Rate is *less* than the base rate $r$, by a rate that represents the annual prorated forecast capital gain. Since *NOI* is divided by $R$ to derive a present worth estimate for the property, the smaller $R$ is, the larger the present worth of any given *NOI* will be.

---

[f]It will be recalled that the Basic Rate with equity build-up but no provision for capital loss or gain, calculated earlier in the discussion of mortgage-equity analysis, was also 9.02%.

The annual capital gain rate applies to the entire *NOI* because the forecast capital gain (appreciation) is experienced by the entire property. The *impact* of forecast capital gain (appreciation) is felt entirely by the equity investment position because the amount of mortgage principal to be recovered is fixed by contract.

The capital gain rate is represented by the symbol *app.* $1/s_n$; *app.* is the forecast *percentage* increase in the value of the reversion over the original investment amount, on resale at the end of the income projection period. The symbol $1/s_n$ represents the sinking fund factor at the equity yield rate over the income projection period. It is found in column 3 of the Ellwood compound interest tables.

In the continuing example used throughout this chapter, assume that the reversion is forecast to be 120% of the original investment at the end of the 15-year income projection period. This means that *app.* = 20% or .20. Thus, the indicated annual rate of capital gain over 15 years of a forecast 20% increase in resale price, discounted at 10%, is:

$$app. \; 1/s_n = .20 \times .0315 = .0063 = 0.63\%$$

**Derivation of a Composite Rate R.** If the basic rate $r$ = .0902 (as derived above), then the indicated Composite Rate $R$ with a forecast 30% decline in resale price would be:

$$R = r + dep. \; 1/s_n = .0902 + .0095 = .0997 = 9.97\%[g]$$

If the base rate $r$ is .0902, then the indicated Composite Rate $R$ with a forecast 20% increase in resale price would be:

$$R = r - app. \; 1/s_n = .0902 - .0063 = .0839 = 8.39\%[g]$$

The logic of the formula is that if a capital loss is forecast, then *NOI* must cover both return *on* the investment and return *of* the forecast capital loss over the income projection period. On the other hand, if capital gain is forecast, then income will come from two sources: *NOI* and prorated annual capital gain. The annual *rate* at which capital gain is forecast to be received reduces the amount of *NOI* necessary to produce the required base rate $r$ on the total investment. Since the *amount* of *NOI* is given, deducting the *rate* of capital gain from the base rate $r$ gives appropriate weight to the forecast capital gain.

---

[g]These are the same rates derived in the preceding section on "Mortgage-Equity Analysis with Equity Build-Up."

*Uses and Applications of Ellwood Analysis*

**Market Value Estimation.** The Ellwood formula develops an Overall or Composite Rate which can be applied to forecast *NOI* to derive a present worth estimate for the property. This is accomplished by Direct Capitalization: $V = d/R$.

The present worth estimate derived via Ellwood analysis represents market value when (1) the *NOI* is based on market rentals and stabilized operating expenses; (2) the mortgage loan terms used to estimate *mc* represent typical financing available to the most probable type of purchaser-investor for the type of property being appraised on the applicable market, as of the valuation date; (3) the equity yield rate represents what typical purchaser-investors in the type of property being appraised are requiring and seeking on similar, competing property investments; and (4) the income projection period represents the investment behavior of typical purchase-investors in similar, competing properties in the same market. While these conditions may appear stringent and limiting, they are precisely the same as those applied to any other income capitalization process or residual technique before the present worth estimate derived can be regarded as Market Value.

For example, take the property and income information in the continuing example used throughout this chapter:

$$NOI\ (d) = \$15,000$$
$$y = .10$$
$$m = .70$$
$$i = .085$$
$$n = 15\ \text{(income projection period)}$$
$$\text{Mortgage maturity} = 20\ \text{years}$$

Then:

$$C = .0140$$
$$1/s_n = .0315$$

If *dep.* = .30, then $R = .0902 + .0095 = .099$

$$V = d/R = \$15,000/.0997 = \$150,451, \text{rounded to } \$150,500$$

If *app.* = .20, then $R = .0902 - .0063 = .0839$

$$V = d/R = \$15,000/.0839 = \$178,784, \text{rounded to } \$179,000$$

**Investment Analysis.** The Ellwood formulation can be used effectively as an aid in investment decision-making. Ellwood analysis is much more susceptible to this type of application than is analysis through the traditional physical residuals. Because of this capability, there is a tendency to emphasize Ellwood analysis as a basis of investment analysis and the estimation of Investment Value. It is certainly not limited to these applications, however.

*Equity Yield Achievement.* One potential application of the Ellwood analysis is to identify the range of permissible or acceptable variation in the amount of the reversion associated with a given level or range of equity yield. This can be accomplished either algebraically or with the use of specially constructed analysis graphs.

The technique for yield calculation and for estimating the range of variation permissible for yield achievement are illustrated on pages 58-63 and 82-91 in Part I of the third edition of Ellwood.

*Impact of Varying Financing Terms.* Because mortgage financing is an integral and often major part of any real estate investment, the impact on income flows and values of varying the package of mortgage loan terms can be considerable. In terms of investment decision-making, variations in financing terms can make the difference between investing and not investing. Financing terms influence the level of cash throw-off and the indicated equity yield rate, both of which are of prime importance to the purchaser-investor.

It is possible to calculate laboriously the impact of financing terms on income flows and yield. It is also possible to reduce the time and effort required by using the Ellwood formulas. This is also illustrated in Part I of Ellwood on pages 58-63, and noted in Chapter 21 of the Ring text.

*Testing of Alternate Financing or Investment Programs.* It is possible and feasible to use the Ellwood formulas to calculate indicated equity yields; to estimate the range of variation in the reversion allowable to achieve a given level or range of equity yields; and to identify and measure the impact of alternative financing packages on the present worth of the equity investment position. Therefore, Ellwood analysis is most helpful in evaluating alternative investment plans and selecting the alternative that most nearly meets the investment criteria of the potential purchaser-investor. One alternative is always *not* to invest, and the Ellwood analysis can also be extremely valuable in identifying situations when this course of not investing is best.

**Limitations of Ellwood Analysis.** Despite its many applications and its high degree of adaptability to a variety of valuation problems, Ellwood analysis does have some limitations that should be recognized and accepted by the appraiser.

In common with other techniques of income capitalization, the Ellwood analysis requires reliable market data on several critical points. If the required information is not available in the market, then the appraiser is injecting his judgment and opinion in using nonmarket data, and the results are not justifiable Market Value.

Ellwood analysis is not easily understood by nonappraisers (especially many clients and the courts). Moreover, it cannot be readily explained in a brief presentation to a person lacking the necessary background in the mathematics of finance. This occasionally makes its use difficult to justify to a client or a court. It requires several calculations, some of which may appear rather complex if required factors are not readily available in precalculated tables. The results more than offset the possible additional time and effort required, however.

Not all investors in income-producing real estate are tax-liable or planning to turn over their investments after relatively short periods. If the assumptions about the income projection period and financing to take advantage of leverage are not applicable in a given type of situation, there is some question about the applicability of the Ellwood analysis.

## Review Exercises

1. An investment property producing $50,000 annual NOI is being appraised. The equity return is estimated at 14%, with an income projection period of 12 years. Mortgage financing at 65% of value can be obtained, with interest at 9.5% for a 17-year maturity. Full amortization is provided in level monthly payments. It is forecast that the property will be resold at the end of 12 years at 85% of its present value.
   a. What is the "simple" mortgage-equity Overall Rate with no equity build-up?
   b. What is the mortgage-equity Basic Rate, including a credit for equity build-up?
   c. What is the mortgage-equity Overall Rate, including a credit for equity build-up?
   d. What is the present worth of the investment, using Direct Capitalization with a mortgage-equity Overall Rate that includes a credit for equity build-up?
   e. If the forecast resale price at the end of the income projection period is 110% of present value, what is the present worth of the investment?
2. Using the property investment information provided in Problem 1 and a mortgage-equity property residual analysis:
   a. What is the percentage of mortgage loan still outstanding at the end of the income projection period?
   b. What is the present worth of the investment if the resale price at the end of the income projection period is 85% of present value?
   c. What is the present worth of the investment if the resale price at the end of the income projection period is 110% of present value?
3. With the property investment information provided in Problem 1, assume that the resale price of the reversion is 85% of the total original investment. A mortgage loan in the amount of $250,000 with the same loan terms as those noted in Problem 1 can be obtained.
   a. What is the amount of annual debt service?
   b. What is the amount of annual cash throw-off?
   c. What is the present worth of the equity investment?
   d. What is the indicated equity dividend rate?
4. Using the property investment information provided in Problem 1 and a

forecast resale price of the property at the end of the income projection period at 110% of present value, apply Ellwood analysis to provide the following:

    a. percentage of mortgage loan principal paid off by the end of the income projection period;

    b. Mortgage Coefficient $c$;

    c. the Basic Rate $r$;

    d. Composite Rate $R$; and

    e. present worth of the property.

5. In Problem 4, if the property were purchased for $350,000, what is the forecast amount of capital loss or appreciation in the reversion required to produce a 17% return on equity?

## Supplementary Readings

Charles B. Akerson, "Ellwood Without Algebra," *The Appraisal Journal*, Volume 38, Number 3, July 1970.

American Institute of Real Estate Appraisers, *The Appraisal of Real Estate*, fifth edition (Chicago: American Institute of Real Estate Appraisers, 1967), pp. 318-325.

Jerome J. Dasso, "Understanding the Mortgage-Equity Capitalization Technique," *The Real Estate Appraiser*, Volume 34, Number 5, September-October 1968.

L.W. Ellwood, *Ellwood Tables for Real Estate Appraising and Financing; Part I: Explanatory Text* (Chicago: American Institute of Real Estate Appraisers, 1970), pp. 1-16, and 51-119.

L.W. Ellwood, *Ellwood Tables for Real Estate Appraising and Financing; Part II: Tables* (Chicago: American Institute of Real Estate Appraisers, 1970), *passim*.

James E. Gibbons, "Mortgage-Equity Capitalization: Ellwood Method," *The Appraisal Journal*, Volume 34, Number 2, April 1966.

Irvin E. Johnson, *The Instant Mortgage-Equity Technique* (Lexington, Mass.: Heath-Lexington Books, 1972).

William N. Kinnard, Jr., "The Ellwood Analysis in Valuation: A Return to Fundamentals," *The Real Estate Appraiser*, Volume 32, Number 5, May 1966.

William N. Kinnard, Jr., "The Financial Logic of Investment Property Appraising," *The Real Estate Appraiser*, Volume 35, Number 3, May-June 1969.

Alfred A. Ring, *The Valuation of Real Estate*, second edition (Englewood Cliffs, N.J.: Prentice-Hall, 1970), Chapter 21.

Halbert C. Smith, "Investment Analysis in Appraising," *The Real Estate Appraiser*, Volume 33, Number 9, September 1967.

Paul F. Wendt, "Ellwood, Inwood and the Internal Rate of Return," *The Appraisal Journal*, Volume 35, Number 4, October 1967.

**Notes**

1. L.W. Ellwood, *Ellwood Tables for Real Estate Appraising and Financing*, first edition (Ridgewood, N.J.: L.W. Ellwood, 1957). The second (1967) and third (1970) editions were published by the American Institute of Real Estate Appraisers, Chicago, Illinois.

2. For a more detailed and authoritative discussion of the impact of the provisions in the Revenue Act of 1969 on income flows and investment decisions related to income-producing real estate, see J. Warren Higgins, *Impact of Federal Taxation on Real Estate Decisions* (Storrs, Conn.: Center for Real Estate and Urban Economic Studies, University of Connecticut, 1971).

3. The technique for deriving a mortgage-equity Overall Rate that incorporates a provision for equity build-up illustrated in this section is derived from an excellent article on the Ellwood analysis by Charles B. Akerson: "Ellwood Without Algebra," *The Appraisal Journal*, Volume 38, Number 3, July 1970, especially pages 328-332. It is believed that this article represents the first published explanation of the components of a mortgage-equity Overall Rate in this fashion.

4. *Ibid.*, page 332.

5. Ellwood, *Ellwood Tables*, third edition, Part I, pages 9, 11. This is also clearly indicated in Akerson, "Ellwood with Algebra," page 334.

6. Ellwood, *Ellwood Tables*, Part I, pages 3, 10 and 11.

7. For further details, see *Ibid.*, pages 2-15.

8. Ellwood, *Ellwood Tables*, Part II, pages 167-400.

9. *Ibid.*, pages 231-274.

# Part IV
# Appraising Income Properties

*Thus far, the items presented and explained in this book have not been directed at* appraising *income properties. Everything that has gone before has been related to this activity, and indeed represents a necessary background of principles, techniques and tools of analysis essential for the appraiser before he can appraise interests in income-producing real estate.*

*The principles of real estate, urban land economics and valuation reviewed in Part I, together with the summary discussions of investment decision-making and the appraisal framework, provided the necessary theoretical and analytical format for approaching solutions to appraisal problems. Part II concentrated on the income capitalization process, developing the several basic analytical tools available for use by the appraiser, and explaining the rationale underlying each. The mechanics of developing these tools for use in appraising were demonstrated with examples illustrating their derivation in commonly encountered appraisal situations. The several alternative processes and techniques of income capitalization were shown at work in Part III, using the principles and tools developed in Part II. The presentation in Part III was still not representative of income-property appraising, however, because it assumed the availability of required data and focused on how they can be processed appropriately to present worth or value estimates, through the capitalization of net income. Alternative approaches or focus of analysis to estimate income property value were largely ignored.*

*The following chapters seek to correct this omission, and to put income capitalization in its proper context in income property appraising.*

# 14 Market and Area Analysis for Income Property Appraising

Any appraisal requires data. A Market Value appraisal must use reliable, verified market data. Thus, any appraisal must start with an identification of the market forces that influence value, and an evaluation of their impact on the value of the property being appraised. Particularly but not exclusively because of its fixed location, income-producing real estate is significantly influenced by its market environment. To a large extent, this external influence determines both the use(s) to which real estate can and will be put; and its value.

The identification and evaluation of external market forces which influence the value of the subject property constitute area and neighborhood analysis. The materials on area and neighborhood analysis in this chapter are presented on the assumption that only a brief review is required to refresh readers' memories from previous exposure to the general principles, techniques and data sources.[1] The emphasis here is on their applicability in income-property appraising, with illustrations for different types of income-producing properties.

## Review of Basic Principles and Techniques

As noted in Chapter 2, income-producing real estate, in common with all other forms of real estate, is fixed in location. Its services must be produced and consumed at a given location. It is therefore a creature of its environment. Both its use and its value are significantly influenced by the operation of external market forces which the purchaser-investor can do little if anything to alter. Since this market framework or environment is one major determinant of value, the appraiser must identify the external forces at work on the property being appraised as of the valuation date, and evaluate their impact on the value of the subject property.

In the appraisal of income-producing properties, market analysis may well consume the major portion of time and effort expended by the appraiser. These market forces influence his identification and selection of data to use in making income forecasts, in estimating appropriate rates of capitalization, in identifying the most probable type of purchaser-investor and his investment or purchase motivation, and in characterizing the competitive framework that constitutes "the market" for the property being appraised.

To conduct market analysis at all levels, the appraiser must act no less prudently or rationally than the most probable purchaser-investor through whose eyes the appraiser views the appraisal problem. This means that he must analyze and evaluate the data he gathers, and not merely accumulate and list them.

*Similarity to Residential Property Market Analysis*

The basic principles and techniques of market area analysis are the same for all types of real estate. Those presented and discussed in any basic text or course on residential property appraisal are equally applicable to income properties.[2]

The major differences in income-property market area analysis lie in the *types of data* that are pertinent and significant to the analysis. A major part of the professional contribution of the appraiser consists of identifying and selecting those market factors and data that are necessary, significant and pertinent to the solution of the particular appraisal problem at hand.

*Fundamentals of Market Area Analysis*

For purposes of real estate appraisal, a market is an area within which properties are competing with the subject property. It represents the range of alternatives that confront the typical purchaser-investor, lender, or tenant. It is also the area within which data are to be gathered to apply to the solution of the appraisal problem.

Although a market area is usually defined in geographic terms, this is not necessarily the case. Investment markets and money markets often transcend geographic boundaries. Moreover, within a geographic area such as a metropolitan region or a city, the pertinent market for a particular type of property will not necessarily consist of contiguous areas. Economic functions and relationships are at least as important as physical boundaries in defining and delineating pertinent market areas for different types of income properties.

**Levels of Markets and Market Influence.** There is a hierarchy of markets which influence the value of income properties. They range from international markets through national and regional markets to metropolitan areas and local community markets, and finally to neighborhoods.

Generally speaking, the broader the market area is, the less direct and specific the influence of market forces will be on the value of the property being appraised. Broad market influences can be very significant, however, even though their impact may not be specific. For example, international gold flows do have an ultimate influence on the availability and terms of mortgage loan funds. Domestic inflation can and does have an impact on local construction costs and rentals. State budgets and taxing programs can and do have an impact on economic development in that state, and hence on the demand for income property space.

The professional appraiser must keep current with broad economic, financial, political, and social developments beyond a specific, local market area. Systematic reading of the current financial press is one way to maintain currency with market developments that influence income property values. Such publications as *Business Weeks, The Wall Street Journal, Fortune,* the *Federal*

*Reserve Bulletin*, and the *National Real Estate Investor* (to cite only a few) should be as much a part of the professional appraiser's regular reading as are professional appraisal journals.

As the level of market area becomes lower and the market area itself becomes smaller, the impact of market forces tends to be more direct and specific to the type of property being appraised, as well as to the subject property itself. When the neighborhood level is reached, virtually anything that occurs within the area has a direct and immediate impact on the value of the subject property. Because of the immediacy of market forces at the metropolitan area, community and neighborhood levels, the professional appraisal office should have a working file of both current and historic market data for use in income property appraisals.

**Categories of Market Forces Influencing Income Property Value.** For purposes of analysis and identification, the market forces that have an impact on the value of the property being appraised can be categorized under five major headings. These categories are not mutually exclusive in many instances, however. Their real significance lies in serving as a reminder to the appraiser of the factors to be *considered* in making a market area analysis.[3]

The important point for the appraiser to bear in mind is that each type of income property is responsive to somewhat different market forces, in addition to those that influence all income properties. Therefore, the analysis must be *specific* to the type of property being appraised, based on intensive investigation of purchaser-investor behavior with respect to this type of property.

The categories of market forces influencing value, and thus subject to analysis and evaluation by the appraiser, are summarized briefly below. Their components may be found in the works cited in the Supplementary Readings at the end of this chapter.

*Physical Forces.* These typically operate at the neighborhood level only, although such considerations as climate, area size, or topography may be significant at the community level as well.

*Social Forces.* These operate at all market levels at least up to the national level. Human attitudes, life styles, and population mobility or migration can have significant impacts on the value of income properties locally. So, too, can population characteristics and the reputation of the area.

*Political-Governmental Forces.* Government at all levels influences income property values through taxation and expenditure policy, through market controls (e.g., pollution controls, planning and zoning), and through the provision or encouragement of utilities and transporation services. The issue for the appraiser to resolve is which of these activities and influences are pertinent to the appraisal of the subject property. Then the quantities required and available must be measured in relation to each other.

*Economic-Financial Factors.*[4] Employment, income, interest rates, construction costs, and myriad other economic or financial influences can have a significant impact on the value of the property being appraised. They represent the basic quantities of market demand and supply that interact to determine prices, rentals, construction costs, interest rates—and value. They operate at all market levels. Once again, the task confronting the appraiser is first to identify the pertinent factors for the appraisal problem at hand, and then to evaluate their impact on value.

*Locational Forces.* These influences could well be included under one or more of the foregoing categories. Since location and its accompanying feature "access" are so critical to the utility and hence the value of most income properties, however, it is usually useful to analyze them separately. It is especially important for the appraiser to be able to identify "access to what?" and "access from what?" for the property being appraised. The answers to these questions must be quite specific in terms of a particular use.

**Supply and Demand Factors.** Value (however defined) is the result of the interaction of the forces of demand and supply. In estimating the value of an income property, the appraiser must identify and measure carefully the particular factors of market demand and supply that influence the value of the particular type of property being appraised. He must also be able to measure that influence under market conditions prevailing as of the valuation date.

Space does not permit an exhaustive listing and consideration of the demand and supply factors operating on each type of income-producing property.[5] However, some of the major items to be considered in any market area analysis, and measured as they are found to be applicable in the appraisal at hand, include the following:[6]

1. *Demand factors*
   a. population: size, rate of change, composition;
   b. incomes: size, distribution, rate of change, distribution;
   c. labor force: size, skills, composition, rate of change;
   d. employment: total, composition, unemployment, rate of change;
   e. industrial activity: market, diversity, stability, sales;
   f. economic base: activity, stability, diversity, trends;
   g. trade: retail and wholesale sales, trends, consumption;
   h. finance: savings, mortgage lending, interest rates, trends;
   i. prices: consumer, industrial, real estate: levels and trends;
   j. transportation: types, costs, services;
   k. real estate market: volume of sales, prices, trends;
   l. land use: existing, planned, trends;
   m. city (area) growth: land absorption rate, types of uses;
   n. tax and assessment structure: tax levels, trends; and
   o. investor activity: levels, types, trends.

2. *Supply factors*
    a. construction: volume, type, costs, location, trends;
    b. rentals: levels by type, trends, services included;
    c. tenancy: owner-occupancy vs. rental type, trends;
    d. vacancy: rates by type, location, trends;
    e. competition: number, location, rentals, prices, trends;
    f. standing stock: number, type, location, rentals, trends;
    g. geography: climate, topography, soil, barriers to growth;
    h. cultural facilities: type, location, services provided; and
    i. utilities: type, size, location, rates, trends.

Identifying the significant factors helps the appraiser to establish a meaningful and efficient data-collection program. It also helps him develop his presentation in the written appraisal report. The test in every instance is: what is the impact of this factor on the value of the property being appraised? Moreover, both the current status of the factor being analyzed and its past and projected future trends must be identified for analysis. The appraiser must remember that income property appraisal in particular is future-oriented; trend analysis is critical to forecasting anticipated future income whose present worth is the value estimate.

*Income Property Demand.* The demand for income-producing real estate or for space in income properties is a derived demand. That is, the user must have some space to carry out an activity that will produce income or save cost for him. Except in the case of residential income properties (i.e., apartments), the anticipated benefits from occupying the real estate are influenced by the estimated demand for the product or service to be produced in that space.

It is not enough to identify general categories of factors that comprise income-property demand: e.g., population, employment, income levels. The factors must be detailed and specific to the particular use anticipated for the property.

*Income Property Supply.* The combination of existing space readily adaptable to the proposed use and anticipated new construction in the competitive market area constitutes the stock of competing space. The prices, rentals and costs required to bring that space into use on the market, plus the competitive stock, constitute the supply available to meet the forecast demand. In analyzing supply, the appraiser should pay particular attention to the ease and cost of adapting space to the use in question, as well as the costs of adapting it from that use.

*Guidelines for Market Analysis*

**The Data and the Type of Analysis Employed Must Be Pertinent to the Specific aisal Problem at Hand.** "Regional, neighborhood and local information, therefore, should be presented only to the extent that they affect value . . . The type of valuation problem, experience of the appraiser and his general competence will largely determine the content of regional analysis. Generally the more experienced and the more competent the appraiser, the more likely that regional analysis will cover points essential to the valuation; the higher the probability that needless trivia will be eliminated; the greater the possibility that each fact will be related to market value."[7]

This quotation brings out the point emphatically that the indiscriminate accumulation and processing of masses of *potentially* useful and pertinent data can be extremely wasteful. Moreover, mere listing of data, facts, or factors influencing value is simply not enough. The job of the appraiser is to show *how* and *why* these items do influence the value of the subject property. There is a difference in the applicability of each factor, depending on the type and level of market area being analyzed, and on the type of property being appraised.

**The Analysis Must Be Objective and Unbiased.** Regardless of his personal feelings or professional judgment, the appraiser must record and report *all* market facts that have a bearing on the appraisal assignment. "The real job is to present information objectively; showing both favorable and unfavorable trends and proving disinterest of the appraiser by his unbiased interpretation of economic trends."[8]

**The Data Must Be Analyzed and Interpreted, Not Simply Listed.** Reinforcing the statement on this point given above is the following: "Regional analysis must be more than descriptive. It must emphasize trends . . . By this means the appraiser may lead the client to the same logical conclusion reached by the appraiser—and reasons supporting the market value opinion become much clearer."[9]

**The Market Data Employed in Area and Neighborhood Analysis Must Be Both Thoroughly Reliable and Current.** To achieve this objective, the appraiser must be fully conversant with appropriate sources of data at all market levels. Further, he should maintain a good working file of current information on the physical, social, governmental-political, and financial-economic forces at work in the market area(s) in which he is operating.

### Market Area Analysis Applied to Income Properties

*Real Estate-Related Markets to Be Identified and Analyzed*

In carrying out his market area analysis, the appraiser has several different "markets" to identify, delineate, measure and analyze. Each impinges on the value of the subject property.

**Sales Market.** The identification and measurement of this market area depends on the answers to the following questions:

1. What are the types of properties directly competing with the subject property as potential investment outlets, and as locations to provide space for some economic activity?
2. Who or what are the most probable types of purchaser-investors most likely to be attracted to this type of investment? What are their investment objectives and requirements?
3. Who or what are the most probable types of users or occupants of the type of space represented by the subject property? What are their desires, requirements, ability-to-pay, and space alternatives?

**Rental Market.** To delineate and measure a rental market, the appraiser must be able to answer:

1. Who or what are the most probable types of tenants for this type of property? What are their space requirements, ability-to-pay, and market alternatives?
2. What and where are the properties most directly competitive with the subject property? What is their operating experience, ability to attract tenants, rental level? What services do they provide?

**Investment and Money Market.** The character of these markets is identified by answering the following:

1. What and where are alternative investments competing directly with the subject property? What are their investment characteristics and their ability to attract investors?
2. What and where are the most probable sources of financing for investments of the type characterized by the subject property? What terms of financing are available? What competition is there for loan funds for investments of the type represented by the subject property?

### Markets for Goods or Services Produced by Proposed or Actual Occupants

It has already been noted that the demand for much income-producing real estate is a derived demand. It is derived from the demand for goods or services produced by the occupants or users of the space in income properties. To do a professional job of income-property appraising, the appraiser must satisfy himself that the property is responsive to the operational requirements, needs and desires of users for whom the property is suited or adaptable. He must also investigate whether the proposed use is feasible as measured by probable profitability at that location.

Feasibility and anticipated profitability of *operations* are determinants of use. Use in turn is a determinant of value. The feasibility of a proposed *use* depends on the marketability by sale or rental of the space provided by the subject property. The marketability of that space in turn depends on the marketability of the goods or services to be produced by the users of that space.

The feasibility of a proposed use can therefore be estimated through market analysis for the goods or services to be produced by the most probable type(s) of occupant. The appraiser must be familiar with the space, locational and rental requirements of different types of commercial, industrial, and other non-residential users of space.[10] Only by matching their needs and requirements with the facilities and services provided by the subject property can a probable, and ultimately "most probable," use pattern be forecast.

### Distinguishing Features of Market Analysis for Income Properties

Income-producing real estate is distinguished from residential or amenity real estate on several counts, as noted in Chapter 3. These distinguishing characteristics influence the cost, composition and specific character of market area analyses undertaken in appraising income properties.

**More Market Stratification.** Markets for income-producing real estate tend to be more highly stratified, compartmentalized, and specialized than are residential real estate markets. There are many more sub-markets. Since transferability from one sub-market to another depends largely on adaptability to other uses at a reasonable cost, there are fewer alternative uses and therefore narrower markets as properties become more specialized.

Income properties, and especially non-residential income properties, tend to be use- and user-oriented. The space provided in non-residential structures tends to be specific to a particular category of uses or users, and often is not readily adaptable to alternative uses. Market constraints tend to reinforce the non-transferability or limited adaptability of income properties to alternative uses. Zoning restrictions and other land use controls are one example.

**Geographically Broader Market Areas.** While the range of competing properties tends to narrow as income properties become more specialized or custom-designed for particular uses or users, the geographic spread of the market area of competing properties frequently tends to become broader. This makes "market area analysis" more complex and demanding, and forces the analyst to focus more on property and locational characteristics. The competitive market area for alternative locations or properties also tends to broaden as the market area for the product of the most probable type of use or user broadens.

**More Emphasis on Use and User Requirements.** Much income property is designed for a specific type of use or user. Function often determines design. As a result, there is greater sensitivity to functional obsolescense in income properties. The more specialized the space for a particular use or user, the greater the hazard or probability of functional obsolescence, especially if the original user leaves the property.

User standards are much more important as determinants of the marketability of the space than are investor standards. The marketability of the *property* depends on investor acceptance, but that acceptance is heavily influenced by the investor's judgment about the competitive marketability or rentability of the space. User standards and requirements can be highly volatile. They are influenced by technological change, locational preferences, and changing tastes. This reinforces the susceptibility of income properties to functional obsolescence.

**Financial Markets also Stratified.** There are many different markets and sub-markets for both lending on and investing in income properties. Although there may be general market standards for financing given types of income properties, these "markets" tend to be narrow and specialized. Some types of lenders concentrate on industrial properties or sale-leaseback transactions, for example; others avoid them entirely. Actual loan terms frequently tend to be the result of bargaining and negotiation between borrower and lender. In analyzing financial or investment markets for income properties, therefore, the appraiser must exercise special care in identifying precisely which "market" is involved.

**Confidentiality of Data.** Operating income data are frequently very difficult to obtain, particularly for specialized types of properties in "thin" markets. Investors and their representatives are often loath to reveal what they regard as confidential information. As a result, data sources tend to be specialized and limited. More care must be taken in verifying data, and little reliance can usually be placed on information available in public records beyond that which is readily verifiable, e.g., building permits, mortgage recordings, assessments, and the like.

**More Specific and Detailed Analysis of Market Components Required.** The result of all the distinguishing characteristics of income-property market analysis is that the appraiser must be quite specific and detailed in his analysis. This means that use and/or user must be specified clearly, space requirements for that use or user must be carefully identified, and a very specific data program must be developed. Particular data sources must be identified and exploited effectively. Special attention must be paid to what the competition for the subject property is, and where it is. The particular type of purchaser-investor most likely to invest in this type of property must be identified and the identification substantiated.

Only when all these specifications have been met can the appraiser embark on meaningful market area analysis. Only then can he study the pertinent trends most likely to influence the marketability of the subject property as of the valuation date.

*Objectives of Market Area Analysis
for Income Properties*

In applying the foregoing elements of market area analysis for income-producing properties to a specific appraisal problem, the appraiser is essentially seeking to answer two questions:

1. What are the forces that have been, are, and are expected to be at work within this competitive area influencing the value of properties similar to and competitive with the subject property?
2. How are these forces operating, and how are they expected to operate in the future?

## Neighborhood Analysis Applied to
## Income Properties

A neighborhood of income-producing properties is a geographic area characterized by similarity of uses and/or users, within which any change has a direct and immediate effect on the subject property and its value. The essence of neighborhood analysis for income properties is to identify and forecast trends in that neighborhood that will influence the capacity of the subject property to generate net income, at least over the income projection period.

*Delineation of Income-Property
Neighborhoods*

The first step in any income property neighborhood analysis is to identify the boundaries of that neighborhood. This may be accomplished in terms of one or more sets of characteristics.

**Physical Barriers or Boundaries.** Both natural and man-made barriers frequently serve as boundaries for income property neighborhoods. Rivers, lakes, ravines, swamps, and the like are effective barriers. So, too, are major arterial highways, especially if they are well above or below grade, railroads ("the other side of the tracks"), or other man-made dividers.

**Legal Boundaries.** Town lines, taxing district lines, and especially the boundaries of zoning districts serve as effective lines of demarcation for income property neighborhoods.

**Use Patterns.** Clusterings of similar, compatible, and supporting or complementary uses tend to identify income property neighborhoods. Even when there are other uses scattered throughout the area, it is often possible to identify rather precisely an apartment neighborhood, an industrial district, the Central Business District, a strip commercial district ("automobile row"), an office district, a medical service district, "motel row," and so forth. This is by far the most meaningful type of delineation, although legal and physical barriers can be helpful in setting precise limits.

**Availability of Services and Utilities.** Certain types of uses (e.g., manufacturing plants) absolutely require certain types and capacities of utilities or services. The end of the utilities lines or a bus route or a major highway connector can be an effective limit to an income-property neighborhood.

### Distinguishing Features of Neighborhood Analysis for Income Properties

Once the income property neighborhood applicable to the property being appraised has been identified, the appraiser's next task is to indicate the forces at work within that neighborhood which influence both property values and changes in those values. The basic approach and framework of analysis is the same as that applicable to residential neighborhoods.[11] The peculiarities of income-producing properties and their markets call for some variation, however.

**Accessibility More Important.** Location is a major determinant of value, and access is a major ingredient of location for income-producing real estate. As noted earlier, access is not an abstract concept. The appraiser, looking through the eyes of the most probable purchase-investor and sensitive to the reactions of the most probable user, must answer the two questions: "access to what?" and "access from what?"

The form of access that is significant varies among different types of income properties, depending on the most probable type of use or user of the property. In general, however, access to and/or from the following must be considered in any income-property neighborhood analysis:

a. customers;
b. workers;
c. suppliers, sources of materials;
d. utilities and transportation; and
e. supporting services (e.g., banks, equipment servicing firms, shopping facilities for residents or employees, etc.).

**Mixed Uses More Prevalent.** An income-property neighborhood is not necessarily a single-use neighborhood. In estimating future trends of the neighborhood, the issue is not whether the uses and occupants are all the same, but whether they are compatible and mutually supportive of long-run neighborhood growth stability.

**More Volatility in Patterns of Use**. Income-property neighborhoods are frequently more susceptible to rapid changes in use patterns than are residential neighborhoods. The appraiser must take special care to estimate the probable stability of use patterns at least over the indicated income projection period for the subject property. Indeed, the forecast stability of the neighborhood is one determinant of that income projection period.

Changing tastes, preferences, technology, and user requirements can seriously alter the pattern of use in an income-property neighborhood. The appraiser must investigate and evaluate the pattern of change in space requirements of the prevalent type of use or user in the income-property neighborhood when he forecasts its probable future trends.

Since proportionately more occupants of income properties are tenants, they have greater mobility over any given period of time. This greater mobility tends to reinforce the impact of changing tastes, preferences, and requirements on the long-run stability of the neighborhood and on property values within it.

The two characteristics of volatile space standards and more tenant-occupant mobility tend to mean a greater propensity for conversion and alteration of properties for new uses in an income-property neighborhood. The adaptability of the properties in the neighborhood to other uses and the identity of those possible new uses is a further point to be analyzed in forecasting use and value trends for the income-property neighborhood.

**More Detailed and Specific Data Required**. As in the case of market area analysis for income properties, so the analysis of income-property neighborhoods requires very specific and detailed data. The appraiser must be aware of these data needs, and know the best sources of the needed data.

*Objectives of Neighborhood Analysis for Income Properties*

Income-property neighborhood analysis serves several important purposes in income-property appraisal:

1. It provides one basis for forecasting the income projection period.
2. It frequently identifies price and rental trends among properties most directly competitive with the subject property.
3. It provides the basis for identifying and measuring locational or environmental obsolescence in the Cost Analysis in value estimation, which is discussed in Chapter 16.

**Sources of Data for Area and Neighborhood Analysis**[1,2]

Market area and neighborhood analysis cannot be carried out without good, reliable, accurate data which have been verified at the source whenever possible. The appraiser must be able to identify what data are required in a given market or neighborhood analysis. He should also be thoroughly familiar with the sources of required, basic data, both published and unpublished. He should further be aware of sources from which advice and guidance may be obtained for gathering less frequently needed or more elusive data. He should keep informed of current studies that he can utilize in his market area and neighborhood analysis. Finally, he should develop the skills and techniques necessary to gather market data in the field as the occasion demands.

Illustrative examples of some of the more basic and accessible data sources are enumerated here.

### Appraiser's Own Files

The first and most obvious source to which the appraiser should turn for obtaining neighborhood, local, regional, and even national data pertinent to the problem at hand is his own files. Once these are developed and organized systematically, a tremendous saving in time and effort can be effected by keeping them current. In building up these files in the first place, the appraiser should turn to other sources listed below. Moreover, he should have a regular, systematic arrangement for obtaining new information to bring his files up to date.

### Publications

A great deal of the material that the appraiser requires for market area analysis is available in published form. Some of the leading sources of information are enumerated here.

1. *Census of Population*, Bureau of the Census, U.S. Department of Commerce.
2. *Census of Housing*, Bureau of the Census, U.S. Department of Commerce.
3. *Survey of Current Business* (monthly), U.S. Department of Commerce.
4. *Economic Indicators* (monthly), Council of Economic Advisors, Office of the President.
5. *Building Permits Issued* (monthly), U.S. Department of Commerce.
6. *Value of Construction Put in Place* (monthly), U.S. Department of Commerce.
7. *Statistical Abstract of the United States* (annual) U.S. Department of Commerce.
8. *Housing and Urban Development Trends* (monthly), U.S. Department of Housing and Urban Development.
9. *Mortgage Recordings under $35,000* (monthly), Federal Savings and Loan Insurance Corporation.
10. *Urban Housing Market Analysis*, Federal Housing Administration.

11. *Economic Development* (monthly), Economic Development Administration, U.S. Department of Commerce.
12. *Construction Review* (monthly), Office of Business Economics, U.S. Department of Commerce.
13. *Census of Manufacturing*, Bureau of the Census, U.S. Department of Commerce.
14. *Census of Business: Retail Trade; Selected Services; Wholesale Trade* (Area Statistics), Bureau of the Census, U.S. Department of Commerce.
15. *City and County Data Book*, Bureau of the Census, U.S. Department of Commerce.
16. *Mortgage Recording Letter* (monthly), Federal Home Loan Bank Board.
17. *Real Estate Market* (quarterly), National Association of Real Estate Boards.
18. *Mortgage Market* (quarterly), National Association of Real Estate Boards.
19. *Federal Reserve Bulletin* (monthly), Board of Governors, Federal Reserve System.

**Regional and Local Data.** Many of the sources of national market data (e.g., Census publications, Department of Commerce publications) also provide regional and local community information. The sources listed here are in addition to those already noted above.

1. *Personal Income: A Key to Small Area Market Analysis*, U.S. Department Commerce.
2. *Sanborn Buying Power Maps*, Sanborn Map Company.
3. *Sales Management Survey of Buying Power* (annual), Sales Management, Inc.
4. *Rent Levels in Various Cities: Real Estate Analyst*, Roy Wenzlick and Company.
5. *Midwest Housing Markets*, Advance Mortgage Corporation, Detroit.
6. *The Community Builders Handbook*, Urban Land Institute.
7. *Census Data for Local Communities: Population, Housing, Manufacturing, Business*, Bureau of the Census, U.S. Department of Commerce.
8. *Boeckh's Building Cost Manual* (monthly supplements), American Appraisal Company.
9. *Dow Building Cost Calculator and Valuation Guide*, F.W. Dodge Corporation.
10. *Wenzlick Residential Cost Service*, Roy Wenzlick and Company.
11. *Residential Cost Handbook*, Marshall and Stevens Company.
12. Regional and Local Surveys of Vacancies, U.S. Post Office Department.
13. Regional and Local Housing Market Analyses, Federal Housing Administration.
14. Published economic base studies and research reports from universities, consulting firms, and local agencies.
15. Planning, Redevelopment, and Zoning Studies published by local agencies.

**Neighborhood Data.** There are fewer published studies of specific neighborhood data than are available for market areas or local communities. The appraiser can utilize most of the same information sources listed for Regional and Local Data. Potential additional sources of neighborhood data include:

1. *Census of Population*: Area, tract, and block statistics (where available). Data by enumeration district are also available for less densely populated areas.
2. *Census of Housing*: Area, tract and block statistics. Enumeration district data are also available for less densely populated areas.
3. *Neighborhood Standards* (by state), Federal Housing Administration.
4. *Small Area Market Analysis*: U.S. Department of Commerce.
5. *Private Surveys*: Universities and colleges, as well as consulting groups, often make studies of neighborhood areas for a variety of purposes. When these are published, they provide invaluable aids to the appraiser.

## Public Records

Information available either from public records or from the files of public agencies would include the following:

1. deed recordings: market volume, range of prices;
2. mortgage recordings (or Deeds of Trusts): volume, terms;
3. foreclosures: volume, type;
4. buildings permits: volume, type of property, estimated costs;
5. local regulations: planning, zoning, and subdivision regulations; housing codes, fire codes, building codes, pollution controls; and
6. taxes, assessments, tax rates.

## Private Sources

Much information can often be obtained from private sources, although occasionally this may be regarded as privileged or confidential information. These sources should be exploited, however, for studies which produce data that are not published, but are available for use by the appraiser. These would include:

1. Chamber of Commerce *data*;
2. research studies at local or area colleges and universities;
3. other brokers and appraisers;
4. private consultant studies for public and private development groups;
5. banks and savings institutions;
6. title insurance companies and title companies;
7. public utility companies;
8. National Association of Home Builders; Local Home Builders' Association; and

9. studies by local chapters of professional appraisal societies or other real estate groups.

*Field Interviews*

The appraiser often must obtain some of his information directly from participants in real estate transactions. This is particularly true when he is attempting to develop information about attitudes, and about differentials in sales prices resulting from the presence or absence of pertinent area factors. Interviews with the following would be included:

1. buyers and sellers of non-residential real estate;
2. tenants and owners of rental real estate;
3. real estate brokers (especially Realtors);
4. other real estate appraisers; and
5. banks and lending institutions.

### A Note on Review Exercises

The character of market area and neighborhood analysis does not lend itself to relatively short and specific review exercises of the type provided at the conclusion of the text presentation in the other chapters of this book. The kinds of illustrative problems required to bring out the techniques involved would be too long and involved to warrant inclusion in a text of this sort. There are therefore no review exercises for this topic.

The reader seeking illustrations of some aspects of area and neighborhood analysis applied to income-property appraisal problems is referred to the Ring and Shenkel texts cited throughout this chapter.[13]

### Supplementary Readings

American Institute of Real Estate Appraisers, *The Appraisal of Real Estate*, fifth edition (Chicago: American Institute of Real Estate Appraisers, 1967), Chapters 5 and 6, especially pp. 93-100.

Watson A. Bowes, "What is Market Analysis?" *The Real Estate Appraiser*, Volume 34, Number 4, July-August 1968.

Anthony Downs, "Characteristics of Various Economic Studies," *The Appraisal Journal*, Volume 34, Number 3, July 1966.

Sanders A. Kahn, Frederick E. Case, and Alfred Schimmel, *Real Estate Appraisal and Investment* (New York: Ronald Press, 1963) Chapters 5 and 6, especially pp. 63-73.

William N. Kinnard, Jr., *A Guide to Appraising Apartments*, second edition (Chicago: Society of Real Estate Appraisers, 1966), pp. 8-16.

William N. Kinnard, Jr., *Industrial Real Estate* (Washington, D.C.: Society of Industrial Realtors, 1967), pp. 399-404, 482-486, and 515-517.

William N. Kinnard, Jr., *An Introduction to Appraising Real Property* (Chicago: Society of Real Estate Appraisers, 1968), Chapters 8 and 9.

Jack Lessenger, "Econometrics and Appraisal," *The Appraisal Journal*, Volume 37, Number 4, October 1969.

Alfred A. Ring, *The Valuation of Real Estate*, second edition (Englewood Cliffs, N.J.: Prentice-Hall, 1970), Chapters 5-7.

William M. Shenkel, *A Guide to Appraising Industrial Property* (Chicago: Society of Real Estate Appraisers, 1967), pp. 11-23 and 38-44.

## Notes

1. Those readers unfamiliar with these general principles, techniques and data sources should refer to one or more of the Supplementary Readings at the end of this chapter. In particular, a good basic foundation is provided in the American Institute of Real Estate Appraisers text; the Kahn, Case, and Schimmel book; Kinnard's *Introduction to Appraising Real Property*; and the Ring text.

2. See in particular William N. Kinnard, Jr., *An Introduction to Appraising Real Property*, (Chicago: Society of Real Estate Appraisers, 1968), Chapters 8 and 9.

3. For more details, see *Ibid.*, Chapters 8 and 9; Alfred A. Ring, *Real Estate Valuation*, second edition (Englewood Cliffs, N.J.: Prentice-Hall, 1970), Chapters 5-7; and William M. Shenkel, *A Guide to Appraising Industrial Property* (Chicago: Society of Real Estate Appraisers, 1967), pp. 11-23. Shenkel also provides an illustrative example of regional analysis on pp. 16-19.

4. Comprehensive listings and discussions of economic-financial market forces in particular may be found in Kinnard, *Appraising Real Property*, Chapter 8; and Shenkel, *Appraising Industrial Property*, pp. 11-23.

5. See especially Kinnard, *Appraising Real Property*, Chapter 8.

6. This list is adapted from William N. Kinnard, Jr., *A Guide to Appraising Apartments* second edition (Chicago: Society of Real Estate Appraisers, 1966), pp. 14-16.

7. Shenkel, *Appraising Industrial Property*, p. 11.

8. *Ibid.*

9. *Ibid.*, p. 12.

10. Examples of the kinds of user space requirements data that must be developed and applied in the analysis of the feasibility of a specific use, using industrial property as a property as the basis, may be found in William N. Kinnard, Jr., *Industrial Real Estate* (Washington, D.C.: Society of Industrial Realtors, 1967), Chapters 2 and 3.

11. For detailed discussions of this approach and its technique, see American Institute of Real Estate Appraisers, *The Appraisal of Real Estate*, fifth edition (Chicago: American Institute of Real Estate Appraisers, 1967), Chapter 6; Kinnard, *Appraising Real Property*, Chapter 9; Kinnard, *Appraising Apartments*, pp. 10-12; and Shenkel, *Appraising Industrial Property*, pp. 20-23.

12. The materials presented in this section are adapted from those provided in Kinnard, *Appraising Real Property*, Chapters 8 and 9. Similar lists oriented to market area and neighborhood analysis for specific types of income properties may be found in Kinnard, *Appraising Apartments*, pp. 12-16; and Shenkel, *Appraising Industrial Property*, pp. 38-44.

13. Ring, *Valuation of Real Estate*, pp. 58-64, 72-73, 391-398, and 500-515; and Shenkel, *Appraising Industrial Property*, pp. 12-19.

# 15 Site Analysis and Site Valuation for Income Properties

The basic *principles* of site analysis and site valuation for income properties are the same as those used in *any* type of property appraisal, including residential properties.[1] The task here is to concentrate on their peculiar applicability to income-property appraisal, and on the techniques specifically designed to value future income flows produced by or attributable to income-property sites. Special emphasis should be placed on the fact that what is being analyzed and valued is *site* and not raw land. To be sure, the cost-of-development method of valuation is generally limited to the appraisal of raw or undeveloped land, usually in large parcels. Otherwise, however, the focus is on land served with necessary supporting facilities and improved to the point that it is ready for its intended use.

In the analysis and valuation of income-property sites, considerable attention must be paid to market acceptance of the site for its intended use, and on the economics of that use. The site is usually intended to be an integral part of a proposed use pattern that typically includes improvements in the form of building(s). The new material to most readers will be the techniques of site valuation other than Direct Sales Comparison. Of course, the Land Residual Technique has already been discussed in Chapter 12, and Direct Capitalization of ground rent is simply a variant of the Property Residual Technique.

## Review of Basic Principles of Site Analysis

### Site Rather than Land is Analyzed and Valued

*Land* consists of the surface of the earth, suprasurface air space, and subsurface area. It is essentially unimproved by man. To make this point clear, it is usually referred to as "raw land" or "unimproved land."

Site, on the other hand, is a parcel of land which is improved to the extent that it is ready and suitable for use for the purpose for which it is intended. This means typically that a site is a parcel of land that has been cleared, graded, and landscaped; that is has necessary improvements for drainage, water service, sewer service, electric service, gas service, access (streets, driveways, parking areas); and that it is not legally constrained from being put to its intended use.

Site analysis[2] is undertaken to establish the basis of comparison in making the estimate of site value, and to ascertain the degree of its suitability for the existing or proposed use.

311

## Components of Site Analysis

Site analysis includes identifying anticipated needs and requirements of proposed users, and matching these needs and requirements with the characteristics of the site in terms of:

1. *Physical attributes:* size, shape, dimensions, topography, soil and subsoil conditions, drainage, utilities, access, man-made improvements, proximity of hazards and/or nuisances.
2. *Economic factors:* prices of comparable sites, units of comparison or marketability, market competition, tax burden, costs of utilities and services, availability of financing, rentals.
3. *Legal-governmental factors:* legal description, title data, restrictions or easements, zoning and other public land and space use controls, deed restrictions, taxation and assessment policy, municipal services.
4. *Locational attributes:* relation to surrounding land use pattern, access to and from desired and needed facilities or groups, transportation facilities, compatibility with surrounding uses (including hazards and/or nuisances), orientation.

## Analysis and Evaluation of Site
### Data Required

As in the case of market area and neighborhood analysis, mere accumulation and listing of facts does not constitute site analysis. The appraiser must gather site data pertinent to the requirements of both the proposed use and the appraisal problem. Then he must evaluate the findings in terms of site characteristics required for the proposed use and forecast type of user. Finally, he must estimate the functional utility, competitiveness, and marketability of the site.

## Identification of Technique(s)

The basic principles and techniques of site analysis and site valuation are the same for all types of properties and/or uses. Differences emerge in terms of the specific factors pertinent to a particular type of use or user. The technique(s) of site valuation applied in any given income-property appraisal depend on:

1. the logic and defensibility of the technique as a reflection of prudent and rational behavior on the part of the most probable, typically informed purchaser-investor; and
2. the availability of reliable, verified data necessary to apply the site valuation technique(s) in question.

## Special Requirements of Income Property Site Analysis

While the basic principles and techniques of general site analysis are indeed applicable to all types of properties, there are some distinguishing characteristics of income-property site analysis with which the appraiser should be familiar.

### Careful and Accurate Measurement

Income-property sites typically are relatively valuable, not only in total but also on a per-unit basis. A seemingly minor error in measurement can have a substantial impact on the value estimate for the entire site.

**Identification of Appropriate Unit(s) of Measurement and Comparison.** Income-property sites are typically bought, sold, rented, and valued on a per-unit basis. The appraiser must identify the appropriate unit or units in terms of which value is to be estimated. These will vary from one use to another, as well as from one market area to another. It is important to use units which reflect the behavior of market participants wherever possible.

**Plans as an Aid in Physical Measurement.** Professionally prepared plot or site plans are most helpful to appraisers in measuring and estimating the number of physical units (square feet, front feet, etc.) in the site being valued. Once again, however, extreme care in measurement from plans is essential.

**Units of Use.** Units of use rather than physical units are frequently most appropriate for income-property site analysis and valuation. Zoning restrictions may limit the number of apartment units on a given site, or the number of square feet in an industrial plant. The appropriate unit of site valuation will frequently be the unit in terms of which income is produced in the improved property; e.g., apartment unit or room or square foot of living area for apartment properties; square foot of floor area for an industrial plant or warehouse; bed for a hospital or home for the aged. The number of such units of income production that the site can legally, physically, and economically support is often the best measure of the "size" of the site, regardless of its physical dimensions.

**Avoiding "Rules of Thumb".** Mechanical "rules of thumb" or tables should be avoided in measuring income-property sites unless there is strong market evidence that such mechanical devices actually reflect market behavior and reactions of the most probable purchaser-investors and users. Extreme caution must be exercised in attempting to apply depth tables and corner influence rules, for example.

*Adaptability to Alternative Uses*

The appraiser must consider carefully alternative uses to which an income-property site can be put, in addition to its proposed or existing use. This is more than Highest and Best Use analysis; it involves a consideration of the feasibility of different or alternative uses. Consideration of adaptability is important because of the dynamic, volatile nature of income-property markets and neighborhoods noted in Chapter 14.

In analyzing the adaptability of the site to alternative uses, the appraiser must consider all groups of factors applicable in site analysis: physical, economic, governmental-political, and locational. Without an understanding of site details and adaptability, comparisons with other properties for valuation purposes are seriously handicapped. Moreover, the principle of Substitution or Opportunity Cost indicates that the value of any site is influenced by its value in its next best alternative use.

*Consideration of Existing and
Planned Competition*

Highest and Best Use is much more volatile and susceptible to rapid change for income-property sites than it is for residential sites. The feasibility of a proposed or existing use can be seriously affected by the introduction of new competition. The capacity of the market area to sustain the type of use proposed is critical to the proper identification of Highest and Best Use, in terms of which site is always valued. This requires forecasts of market area and neighborhood development, and especially of market rates of absorption of the type of space to be provided in the proposed use.

*Suitability of the Site for the
Proposed or Existing Use*

Income-property sites must be evaluated in terms of their adequacy and suitability to support the proposed use pattern. This includes both *type* of use and *intensity* of use.

Evaluation of the suitability of both the type and intensity of the proposed use provides one basis for identifying functional obsolescence or inutility to be measured in Cost Analysis for income-property valuation. It is also important in establishing the basis of comparability with purportedly similar and competing properties in applying the adjustment process in Direct Sales Comparison analysis.

Because the site requirements of income-property uses are frequently quite specific, as well as subject to rapid change, it is important to match carefully those requirements of the proposed use as of the valuation date with the attributes of the site. The closer the match, the greater the functional utility of the site for the proposed use pattern.

## Compatibility of Proposed or Existing Use with Neighborhood Use Pattern

Income-property neighborhoods frequently are characterized by mixed use patterns, as noted in Chapter 14. Thus, the compatibility of the proposed or existing use of the site being valued with those surrounding it is a more overt issue in income-property site analysis. The identification of elements of incompatibility or inharmoniousness provides one basis for the estimation of Locational or Environmental Obsolescence in Cost Analysis.

## More Demanding Highest and Best Use Analysis

The process for estimating Highest and Best Use of an income-property site is exactly the same as that for residential sites.[3] Much more care must be exercised in reaching the conclusion, however, in part because there are many more alternatives to be considered for most income-property sites.

The appraiser still follows the progression of answering a series of questions. If the appraiser can justify his answers, he produces a supportable conclusion of Highest and Best Use of the site.

1. Is the proposed use legal or likely to be permitted?
2. Is the proposed use physically possible on the site?
3. Is the proposed use economically and financially feasible under current and projected market conditions?
4. Is the proposed use estimated to be most profitable among the alternatives that are legally permissible, physically possible, and economically feasible?

The question of economic and financial feasibility is particularly important in income-property site analysis. This is because of the volatility of income-property markets and neighborhoods, and the thinness of many local market areas in their ability to support the same type of use at more than one location. Changing tastes and standards, locational preferences, and technology all work to accelerate functional inutility among existing income properties, particularly special-purpose or single-purpose properties. As a result, site analysis and valuation for income properties, particularly with existing improvements, require consideration of alternatives use patterns. Existing use is not necessarily Highest and Best Use, as to either type or intensity. Moreover, surrounding land uses are not necessarily a good guide to the Highest and Best Use of the site being appraised, even though compatibility with the neighborhood use pattern is usually one essential component of Highest and Best Use.

Currently permitted uses under existing zoning may not necessarily be the optimum or Highest and Best Use of the subject site. This can be a consideration in income-property site valuation when there is evidence that zoning changes are likely.

## Use Densities Often as Significant as Types of Use

In analyzing an income-property site, it is not enough simply to identify the *type* of use, no matter how precisely, that appears to represent the Highest and Best Use. The intensity or density of the use pattern can be at least as significant. Highest and Best Use, therefore, includes both type and intensity of use.

When use restrictions such as zoning limit the intensity of use by specifying setbacks, building heights, floor area ratios, and/or the number of units permissible in a given area (e.g., one apartment unit per 1,000 square feet of land area), the capacity of the site to support income-producing space is limited. This also sets a limit on the value of that site, irrespective of its physical dimensions. Broadly speaking, the more productive units of space of a specific type possible on a given site, the greater the value of that site will be.

## More Specificity in Site Service Requirements

The site requirements of income-property uses are typically highly specific, and vary from one type and/or intensity of use to another. The appraiser must incorporate very specific itemization of site characteristics, available utilities and services, and site improvements (e.g., parking area) in his income-property site analysis. This is necessary to match site characteristics with the site requirements of the proposed use(s) in order to evaluate the ability of the site to serve the needs of the proposed use(s). For example, the *capacity* as well as the type of utilities service available is critical to many uses and users.

## Income Property Site Valuation

### General Rules

The valuation of income-property site follows the same general principles as those applicable to residential site valuation.[4] The techniques may differ because a wider range of alternative techniques is potentially available to the appraiser.

**Vacant and Available to Be Put to Highest and Best Use.** Site is always valued for Market Value purposes as if vacant and available to be put to its Highest and

Best Use. This is because site (land) is always the residual factor of production. It is therefore imperative to substantiate fully and convincingly the conclusion as to Highest and Best Use, as of the valuation date.

**Non-depreciable.** Site is held not to depreciate. It is also not depreciable for income-tax accounting purposes. There should therefore be no provision for systematic capital recovery of the investment in the site over the income projection period.

**Site Improvements Included.** Site improvements are included in the site value estimate. Site rather than raw or unimproved land is valued unless the appraisal problem specified the valuation of unimproved land.

**Units of Use.** Site is valued in terms of units of use. These are not necessarily physical units.

**Selection of Method.** The selection of the method of site valuation to be employed in any given appraisal depends on two sets of considerations. First, the logic and assumptions of the site valuation method must apply to the type of site being appraised and the nature of the appraisal problem. Second, reliable, verified market data of the type required for the application of the site valuation method specified must be available in usable quantities.

## Methods of Site Valuation

Several alternative methods of valuing income-property sites are potentially available to the appraiser. Rarely will more than one or two be appropriate in any given appraisal problem. However, the appraiser should be able to handle each, recognizing its limitations as well as its applications.

**Direct Sales Comparison.** Site as well as entire properties can be valued via the Direct Sales Comparison approach. The rationale and logic of this approach are presented in full detail in Chapter 16. It will be recalled that this is used in residential site valuation.[5] At this point it is sufficient to note that the informed, prudent purchaser-investor will pay no more (either *in toto* or per unit) for a given site than the cost to him of acquiring an alternative site with the same utility. The prices at which similar, competing sites have sold in the recent past on the same market provide a guide to that cost of acquisition.

*Selection of Units of Comparison or Measurement.* In applying the Direct Sales Comparison Approach to income-property site valuation, the appraiser must identify the appropriate unit in terms of which the type of site being appraised is typically bought and sold or rented on the market. This unit of comparison or measurement is not determined by the appraiser solely on the basis of arithmetic, or mechanical ease or convenience. Rather, it is provided by the market from the way investors in particular behave.

*Physical units.* The unit of comparison may be a square foot, a front foot, or an acre.

*Economic units.* For income-property sites, it is more likely that the unit of comparison is related to the unit of income production by the entire property. Some examples are:

1. apartment sites: site value per apartment unit, per room, per square foot of building area, per square foot of livable area;
2. retail sites: site value per square foot of building area, per square foot of selling area;
3. industrial sites: site value per square foot of building area, per employee;
4. hotels, motels, hospitals, etc.: site value per bed;
5. office sites: site value per square foot of building area, per square foot of net rentable area;
6. theater sites: site value per seat; and
7. parking lots: site value per stall or parking space.

The foregoing examples are suggestive and illustrative only. However, they do provide a basis for investigation by the appraiser to discover what the appropriate unit(s) happen to be for the type of site being appraised.

*Adjustments.* Sales information on similar, competing sites must usually be adjusted to reflect what each comparable sale would have sold for if it had possessed identical characteristics with those of the subject site, at the time of sale. Adjustments are made for time (market conditions), location, physical characteristics, permitted use densities, and terms of sale and financing.

All adjustments are made *from* the comparable sale site *to* the subject site. In the analysis, the subject site is the norm or standard in terms of which the comparables are measured. It is 100%.

Either dollar amount or percentage plus-and-minus adjustments may be made. Whichever is used, the adjustments must be supported by market evidence that they do reflect the indicated difference between the comparable sale site and the subject site. They must represent a market-supported measure of how much difference is sales price or value the absence or presence of the indicated characteristic would make. Cumulative percentage adjustments are not recommended. This procedure carries implications and assumptions that are rarely supported by market evidence.

Wherever possible, adjustments should be made for the entire site, and then an adjusted unit price developed for purposes of valuation of the subject site.

*Estimate of Value.* The several adjusted sales prices per unit are analyzed and correlated, as demonstrated in Chapter 16, to an indicated value per unit for the subject site. Then the indicated value per unit is multiplied by the number of units to derive an estimated value for the subject site. This final step reinforces the critical importance of accurate measurement of the number of units in the site.

*Direct Sales Comparison Analysis Illustrated.* To show the use of Direct Sales Comparison analysis in valuing income-property sites, take as an example a site on which an existing apartment building is located. The total area is 16,200 square feet, with 100 feet of frontage and an average depth of 162 feet. The building contains 54 apartment units with 202 rooms, and 80,850 square feet of total building area. At the time this six-year-old building was constructed, the zoning permitted a maximum density of one living unit per 300 square feet of site area. Two years ago, the zoning was changed to allow no more than one unit per 600 square feet of site area.

The market for land and sites in the subject neighborhood has been increasing approximately 10% per year for the past 10 years. An investigation of market activity for apartment sites in the area reveals that four such sites have been sold within the past three years and that apartment buildings similar to the subject were built upon them: two before the change in zoning, and two afterward.

*Sale number one* occurred less than a month ago. The site dimensions are 195 by 220, for a total area of 42,900 square feet. A building containing 72 units with 288 rooms is being built on the site. The verified sale price was $60,000.

*Sale number two* took place a year ago. It has an area of 51,100 square feet, with dimensions of 150 by 320. The building erected on the site has 350 rooms in 88 apartment units. The sale price of $66,000 has been verified with the seller.

*Sale number three* was completed three years ago. The verified sale price was $45,000. The site has an area of 21,600 square feet, with dimensions of 108 by 200. The building contains 72 units with 245 rooms.

*Sale number four* also occurred three years ago at a price of $50,000. That site contains 23,100 square feet, with 150 feet of frontage and 154 feet average depth. A building with 77 units and 270 rooms was built on the site.

From this information, it is possible to derive adjusted sales prices per unit of comparison for each comparable site sale, and then to develop an indication of value for the subject site. This is illustrated in Exhibit 15-1.

From the evidence in Exhibit 15-1, it is clear that the market does not react to or deal in *physical* units in the role of apartment sites. No clear pattern emerges in adjusted sales price per front foot; this reflects the varying shapes and dimensions of otherwise competitive sites suitable for apartment development. The change in land use density permitted by zoning is sharply reflected in the different adjusted sales price per square foot figures. Indeed, reducing the adjusted sales price figures to a unit of comparison is actually an adjustment for those differences in density of use which are permitted under the different zoning regulations.

The only adjustment necessary in sales prices in this example is for time, in order to account for the increasing market levels over the past several years. The

## Exhibit 15-1

**Sales Adjustment Analysis for Apartment Property Site**

|  | Subject Property | Sale No. 1 | Sale No. 2 | Sale No. 3 | Sale No. 4 |
|---|---|---|---|---|---|
| Sales Price | — | $60,000 | $66,000 | $45,000 | $50,000 |
| Date of Sale | Today | 1 Month ago | 1 Year ago | 3 Years ago | 3 Years ago |
| Time Adjustment | — | 0 | +10% | +30% | +30% |
| Adjusted Sale Price | — | $60,000 | $72,600 | $58,500 | $65,000 |
| Frontage (feet) | 100 | 195 | 150 | 108 | 150 |
| Area (Square feet) | 16,200 | 42,900 | 51,100 | 21,600 | 23,100 |
| Dwelling Units | 54 | 72 | 88 | 72 | 77 |
| Rooms | 202 | 288 | 350 | 245 | 270 |
| Rooms per D.U. | 3.74 | 4.00 | 3.98 | 3.40 | 3.51 |
| Square Feet Land per D.U. | 300 | 596 | 581 | 300 | 300 |
| Adjusted Sales Price per: |  |  |  |  |  |
|   Front Foot (Site) | -- | $307.69 | $485.33 | $541.67 | $433.33 |
|   Square Foot (Site) | — | $ 1.40 | $ 1.42 | $ 2.71 | $ 2.81 |
|   Dwelling Unit | — | $833.33 | $827.27 | $812.50 | $844.16 |
|   Room | — | $208.33 | $208.00 | $238.78 | $240.74 |

sales prices of the comparable sites are adjusted upward 10% per year to the present, indicating the estimated amounts they would have sold for if they had been sold under current market conditions. The subject site is being valued in terms of these current market conditions. Thus, the adjustment for time is made *from* the comparable site sale *to* the subject site and the market conditions that surround its sale in the present.

The adjusted sales prices per dwelling (apartment) unit and per room fall into a closer pattern. It is apparent that the market transfers apartment sites in terms of the unit of rental income production: the dwelling (apartment) unit or the room. Some judgment is still involved in selecting the unit value for the subject site, but an estimate of $830 per apartment unit and perhaps $220 per room appears justified by the analysis. The adjusted sales price per room is somewhat less responsive because of the variation in average rooms per unit among the five properties, with the subject falling approximately in the middle of the range.

The indicated value of the subject site could be estimated as:

$$\begin{array}{ll} \text{54 apartment units @ \$830} & = \$44,820 \\ \text{202 rooms @ \$220} & = \$44,440 \end{array}$$

If \$825 per apartment unit were used, the value estimate becomes \$44,550. If \$225 per room were used, the value estimate would be \$45,450.

The appraiser would be justified in concluding that the indicated Market Value of the subject site is between \$44,500 and \$45,500, with \$45,000 the most likely or probable figure.

*Applicability.* Estimation of site value via Direct Sales Comparison analysis is recommended whenever sufficient data on sales of truly comparable, competitive sites are available to allow the appraiser to develop a defensible unit value for the subject site. Only in cases of limited market activity should greater reliance be placed on a value estimate developed through an alternative method.

**Cost-of-Development Method.** When undeveloped acreage (usually in large tracts) is to be valued, one useful method is to derive an estimate of the maximum amount an investor-developer would be warranted in paying for the land, given the cost of developing it and the probable proceeds from the sale of the developed sites.

This method assumes that the most probable purchaser of the land will be a developer-investor who plans to dispose of the developed sites at a profit. It is applicable to large acreage tracts to be developed for a variety of uses, including single-family residential lots as well as apartments, industrial sites, and the like. Mechanically, the appraiser first develops a forecast of the future net income stream anticipated to be produced by the sale of the prepared sites. It usually will take the form of a variable annuity whose annual amount represents sales receipts *less* development costs expended during the year and *less* sales expenses during the year. The resulting net proceeds are discounted to the present by the Present Worth of One factor at the rate of return (discount) discovered from the market to be applicable to equity investments of this type. The result is the indicated Market Value of the land, if market prices, market costs, and market discount rates are used. When the prices, costs and equity discount rate are specific to a particular development plan and investor, the resulting present worth estimate represents Investment Value.

The mechanics of the technique are based on the income estimation and forecasting procedures developed in Chapter 6, and on the calculation of the present worth of a variable annuity demonstrated in Chapters 5 and 11. In applying the technique, the appraiser must first identify carefully the most probable sales prices of developed sites, as well as all costs of developing, holding and disposing of the developed sites on the market. Since land development and site sale are time-consuming processes, the *timing* as well as the amount of sales and costs must be forecast as accurately and as convincingly as possible. For sales forecasts, one important ingredient is the estimate of the rate of market absorption of sites of the type to be developed. For development cost estimates, the timing of the development process is a significant determinant.

One major fact of the land development process is that expenditures for development typically are made in advance of sales. The market will not normally buy sites from plans. Thus, development costs tend to be concentrated in the early years of the development-sales process, while site sales are usually heavier in the middle and later years. Moreover, especially in large developments, the unit prices of developed sites frequently vary from year to year. At first, this often takes the form of lower prices in order to attract buyers to the development. As market acceptance occurs, sales prices tend to rise. At the end of the sales program, the leftover "odds and ends" may have to be sold at reduced prices.[6]

*Cost-of-Development Method Illustrated.* To demonstrate the use of the cost-of-development method of land valuation, assume a 100-acre tract of land to be developed as residential sites. It will cost an estimated $1500 per acre of total land area to clear the land, prepare sites, and install utilities and streets. Streets and rights-of-way will absorb an estimated 20% of total land area, leaving a total of 80 one-acre sites available to be sold. It is forecast that developed sites will sell for $5,000 each. Total disposition and holding costs, including developer's profit (as opposed to investor's equity return), are forecast at $1,500 per developed site sold.

Market analysis reveals that a five-year development and sales schedule is most appropriate. Development costs will be incurred over 3 years: 40% the first year, and 30% in each of the two following years. The sales program most responsive to current and forecast market rates of return is 10 sites in each of the first two years, and 20 sites in each of the last three years. The appropriate rate of discount for investments of this type is 13%. To simplify the illustration, no debt financing is assumed.

The income stream forecast for this proposed development and its discounting to a present worth estimate are shown in Exhibit 15-2. Each annual forecast of net proceeds to the investor-developer is treated as a separate reversion, receivable at the end of each year. It is discounted to a present worth estimate by the Present Worth of One factor for the appropriate time period at 13% (Ellwood, page 149, column 4). The sum of these individual present worth estimates is the present worth of the forecast income stream, and represents the amount that an informed investor-developer would be justified in paying for the 100-acre tract of raw land. In this case, this sum is its Market Value. It is also the maximum amount or upper limit of what the investor could afford to pay, if his rate-of-return expectations are to be realized.

**Land Residual Technique.** Site value can be estimated by treating the net income available to support the investment in the site as a residual, after the income required to cover the investment in new improvements that represent the Highest and Best Use of that site has been deducted from Net Operating Income. This technique, its uses, and its limitations have been described and illustrated in Chapter 12.

**Exhibit 15-2**

**Land Valuation via Cost-of-Development Method**

A. Forecast Net Income Stream

| | | |
|---|---|---:|
| Year 1: | Site Sales (10 @ $5,000) | $ 50,000 |
| | *Less* Selling Costs @ $1,500 | −15,000 |
| | | $ 35,000 |
| | *Less* Development Costs | |
| | (.40 × $150,000) | −60,000 |
| | Net Proceeds, Year 1 | −$ 25,000 |
| Year 2: | Site Sales (10 @ $5,000) | $ 50,000 |
| | *Less* Selling Costs @ $1,500 | −15,000 |
| | | $ 35,000 |
| | *Less* Development Costs | |
| | (.30 × $150,000) | −45,000 |
| | Net Proceeds, Year 2 | −$ 10,000 |
| Year 3: | Site Sales (20 @ $5,000) | $100,000 |
| | *Less* Selling Costs @ $1,500 | −30,000 |
| | | $ 70,000 |
| | *Less* Development Costs | |
| | (.30 × $150,000) | −45,000 |
| | Net Proceeds, Year 3 | $ 25,000 |
| Year 4: | Site Sales (20 @ $5,000) | $100,000 |
| | *Less* Selling Costs @ $1,500 | −30,000 |
| | Net Proceeds, Year 4 | $ 70,000 |
| Year 5: | Site Sales (20 @ $5,000) | $100,000 |
| | *Less* Selling Costs @ $1,500 | −30,000 |
| | Net Proceeds, Year 5 | $ 70,000 |

B. Estimate of Present Worth

| | | |
|---|---|---:|
| Year 1: | −$25,000 × 0.884956 = | − $22,124 |
| Year 2: | −$10,000 × 0.783147 = | − $ 7,831 |
| Year 3: | $25,000 × 0.693050 = | $17,326 |
| Year 4: | $70,000 × 0.613319 = | $42,932 |
| Year 5: | $70,000 × 0.542760 = | $37,993 |
| Total Present Worth | | $68,296 |
| Indicated Value of 100-Acre Tract | | $68,300 |

The residual income available to support the investment in the site is capitalized to a present worth estimate by dividing it by the Discount Rate. The income necessary to provide adequate coverage of the investment in the improvements is derived by applying the appropriate Capitalization Rate or Factor to the reproduction cost new of the improvements.

Because the technique frequently requires a cost and income estimate based on a hypothetical building, it has limited applicability and must be used with extreme care. Moreover, the residual income to site varies exactly with minor differences in reproduction cost new estimates, thereby making the site value estimate highly volatile.

**Direct Capitalization of Net Ground Rent.** When a site is leased independently of the improvements (building) on it, or when a vacant site is leased, it is possible to estimate its value simply by capitalizing its annual net rental to a present worth estimate. If the ground rent (contract rent) is different from the Market Rental of the site as of the valuation date, present worth is estimated by treating the NOI with a Property Residual technique. The NOI based on contract rental is capitalized at the appropriate Level Annuity Capitalization Rate (or Factor) over the remaining term of the lease, and then the present worth of the reversion is added to it.

For example, assume that a site containing 20,000 square feet has a Market Rental of 12¢ per square foot per year. Assume further that the appropriate Discount Rate is 11%. Operating expenses are $4,000 or 2¢ per square foot per year.

If the site is actually rented for 12¢ per square foot per year, NOI is 10¢ per square foot per year. Then its present worth is:

$$.10 \times 20,000 = \$2,000/.11 = \$18,182 \text{ or } \$18,200$$

Alternatively, it could be valued at $.10/.11 = $.909 or 91¢ per square foot. Then 20,000 × $0.91 = $18,200.

Assume now that the site is actually rented for 11¢ per square foot per year with 20 years remaining on the lease. It is also estimated that 20 years hence the site will be worth $18,200. The Discount Rate is still 11%, and operating expenses are 2¢ per square foot per year.

The present worth of the rental income under the lease is:
.09 × 20,000 = $1,800 NOI × 7.963328 (Ellwood, page 132, column 5) = $14,333.99

The present worth of the reversion is:
$18,200 × .124034 (Ellwood, page 132, column 4) = $2,257.42

The present worth of the site is:    $14,334
+ 2,257
$16,591 *or* $16,600

**Abstraction Method.** This is also called the "Ratio of Improvement Value to Value of Site" method. It is highly subjective and questionable, and rarely is defensibly applicable to income-property site valuation. It is difficult to imagine a situation in which the ratio of site value to building "value" or total property value is known from market evidence, but yet none of the information necessary for any of the other methods of site valuation is available.

## Uses and Applications of Site Valuation

Separate value estimates are frequently required for income property sites. These estimates may be needed for a variety of uses, including the following:

1. valuation of vacant sites;
2. valuation of sites under separate ground leases;
3. application of the Building Residual Technique of income-property valuation;
4. application of the Cost analysis to income-property valuation;
5. estimation of the Highest and Best Use of a site, and evaluation of the investment attractiveness of alternative use programs; and
6. valuation of site for property tax (assessment) purposes.

## Review Exercises

1. A vacant site is currently leased for 15 years at 20¢ per square foot per year. The site contains 10,000 square feet. Operating expenses to the owner are 2¢ per square foot. The indicated Discount Rate is 12%. It is forecast that the site will be worth $15,000 when the lease expires.
   a. Calculate the value per square foot of site.
   b. Based on the calculated value per square foot, what is the indicated value of the site?
   c. If there were no lease on the site, and Market Rental were 17¢ per square foot per year, what would be the indicated Market Value of the site?
2. A new building representing the estimated Highest and Best Use of a site has just been constructed at a verified cost of $100,000. The forecast Net Operating Income for the property is $20,000, with an income projection period of 40 years representing the forecast economic life of the improvements. The indicated Discount Rate is 10%.
   a. If NOI is forecast to be level over the income projection period, what is the indicated present worth (value) of the site? Of the property?
   b. If NOI is forecast to decline systematically over the income projection period, what is the indicated present worth of the site? Of the property?
3. An investor-developer plans to acquire a 50-acre tract of land to develop as an industrial park. He plans to sell sites only. His anticipated rate of return on his investment in the land is 14%. The forecast sales price for developed sites is $10,000 per acre. Land development costs are estimated at $2,000 per acre

for the entire tract. Streets and rights of way will absorb an estimated 20% of total land area. Selling and holding, plus developer's profit, are estimated at $2,000 per acre of developed site. The development program is forecast to take four years, with 25% of development costs incurred each year. The projected sales program, based on current market absorption rates, calls for sales of 20% of developed site acreage in each of five years.
a. What is the forecast net income stream for the developer-investor?
b. What amount would the developer-investor be justified in paying for the 50-acre tract of land?
4. A vacant site can be used to support a 10-story apartment building or a 20-story office building. The apartment building has a forecast economic life of 50 years, while that of the office building is 40 years. The forecast reversion under apartment use is $1,000,000; under office building use it is $1,300,000. Net Operating Income for the property as an apartment development is $100,000 per year. For the office building development, NOI is forecast at $60,000 per year for the first 5 years, and $140,000 per year thereafter. The indicated Discount Rate for either investment is 11%.
a. If these are the only two feasible alternatives, what is the Highest and Best Use of the site?

## Supplementary Readings

American Institute of Real Estate Appraisers, *The Appraisal of Real Estate*, fifth edition (Chicago: American Institute of Real Estate Appraisers, 1967), Chapters 7b and 8.

William R. Benton, "Appraisal Analysis of Land Allocation for Industrial Use," *Valuation*, Volume 15, Number 4, December 1967.

Robert P. Boblett, "Factors in Industrial Location," The *Appraisal Journal*, Volume 35, Number 4, October 1967.

S.W. Brener, "Factors Involved in a Motel's Site Survey," *Valuation*, Volume 16, Number 4, December 1968.

Sanders A. Kahn, "Land: Does it Depreciate?", *The Real Estate Appraiser*, Volume 35, Number 1, January-February 1969.

Sanders A. Kahn, Frederick E. Case, and Alfred Schimmel, *Real Estate Appraisal and Investment* (New York: Ronald Press, 1963), pp. 73-75; Chapters 16, 23, and 30; Appendix F.

W.H. Kam, "Investment Analysis of Leased Commercial Land," *The Real Estate Appraiser*, Volume 33, Number 2, February 1967.

William N. Kinnard, Jr., *A Guide to Appraising Apartments*, second edition (Chicago: Society of Real Estate Appraisers, 1966), pp. 10-16 and 27-29.

William N. Kinnard, Jr., *Industrial Real Estate* (Washington, D.C.: Society of Industrial Realtors, 1967), pp. 417-419 and 448-455.

William N. Kinnard, Jr., *An Introduction to Appraising Real Property* (Chicago: Society of Real Estate Appraisers, 1968), Chapters 10 and 11.

Dexter D. MacBride, "The Value of Land," *The Real Estate Appraiser*, Volume 34, Number 3, March 1968.

Alfred A. Ring, *The Valuation of Real Estate*, second edition (Englewood Cliffs, N.J.: Prentice-Hall, 1970), Chapters 8 and 9.

William M. Shenkel, *A Guide to Appraising Industrial Property* (Chicago: Society of Real Estate Appraisers, 1967), pp. 24-44.

## Notes

1. For the reader who requires more detailed discussions of these principles and the general techniques of site valuation, see American Institute of Real Estate Appraisers, *The Appraisal of Real Estate*, fifth edition (Chicago: American Institute of Real Estate Appraisers, 1967), Chapters 7 and 8; or William N. Kinnard, Jr., *An Introduction to Appraising Real Property* (Chicago: Society of Real Estate Appraisers, 1968), Chapters 10 and 11.

2. For further details and explanations of these principles, see Kinnard, *Appraising Real Property*, Chapter 10.

3. More background discussion of Highest and Best Use analysis is provided in *ibid*.

4. See Kinnard, *Appraising Real Property*, Chapter 11.

5. *Ibid*.

6. A detailed discussion of this analytical procedure applied to industrial district development may be found in William N. Kinnard, Jr., *Industrial Real Estate* (Washington: D.C.: Society of Industrial Realtors, 1967), Chapter 15.

# 16 Direct Sales Comparison Analysis for Income Properties

There is widespread agreement among students, writers and practitioners in the appraisal field that Direct Sales Comparison analysis is probably the most defensible and generally applicable approach to valuation.[1] It certainly is descriptive of purchaser thinking and behavior. It postulates the view that an informed, prudent and rational purchaser-investor will pay no more for a property than the cost to him of acquiring a substitute property with the same utility. In this sense, "utility" means attractiveness and ability to satisfy the needs and desires of the purchaser. For income properties, those needs and desires are represented by net cash flows, so money is taken as the measure of utility.

Direct Sales Comparison analysis has the appeal of simplicity and descriptiveness. The concept is readily understood and accepted by clients and courts, as well as by appraisers. It utilizes market information exclusively, and always results in an estimate of market value.

Curiously, however, Direct Sales Comparison analysis, which is variously labeled the "Market Data Approach" or "Market Sales Approach," receives little real attention in appraisal texts, journals or courses. Its very simplicity and understandability tends to deceive writers and appraisers alike into thinking that little emphasis or time need be allotted to it. It is quite important not to gloss over the approach because of its seeming ease of understanding and application. There *are* complications that must be recognized and understood. There *are* judgments that have to be made and defended by the appraiser. There *are* differences of professional opinion about the handling of certain aspects of the technique.

Indeed, because relatively little attention has been paid to the structure and mechanics of Direct Sales Comparison analysis, there is probably less agreement on specific elements of technique than there is in the more complex Cost and Income Capitalization analyses. One important purpose of this chapter, therefore, is to attempt to bring some order and agreement into this analysis, as well as to examine some of the differences that currently exist in appraisal thinking.

Because of their probable exposure to some introductory appraisal course or text, most readers will have a reasonably good basic background in Direct Sales Comparison analysis. Moreover, it was alluded to in the discussion of Site Valuation in Chapter 15. Some of its components, notably the Gross Income Multiplier, have been considered in earlier chapters as well. The specific emphasis here is on the peculiarities of applying the approach to income properties.

A final introductory comment on terminology may be in order. The term "Direct Sales Comparison Analysis" (or approach) is used here rather than the

329

more widely applied "Market Data Approach" for two reasons. First, *all* methods of estimating value (especially Market Value) use market data; this particular format does not have an exclusive claim on market data usage. Second, "Direct Sales Comparison" describes what the appraiser does in applying this analysis, just as "Income Capitalization" is descriptive of the appraiser's activities in capitalizing net income to a value estimate. In Direct Sales Comparison analysis, the appraiser compares sales data and the properties involved in the transactions directly with one another, and with the subject property, to reach a value estimate for the subject.

## Review of Basic Principles and Techniques of Direct Sales Comparison Analysis

The underlying theory and the framework of technique for Direct Sales Comparison analysis are the same for any type of property. The distinguishing characteristics of the application of the analysis to income properties depend primarily on the data used and the units of comparison employed.

### Principles and Rationale

Applying the Principle of Substitution (Opportunity Cost), the Direct Sales Comparison approach[2] to real property valuation is based on the premise that the informed, prudent and rational purchaser (investor) will pay no more for a property than the cost to him of acquiring a similar, competitive property with the same utility, as of the valuation date. The approach is predicated on the assumption that there is, in fact, an active market for the type of property being appraised; and that data on recent sales prices of similar, competitive properties on the same market, representing *bona fide* arm's length transactions, are an appropriate guide to the most probable sale price that the subject property will command, as of the valuation date.

As used in this context, "utility" refers to the capacity of the property to satisfy the needs and desires of the purchaser. In the case of income properties, the functional utility of the property is particularly significant. That is, does it perform effectively the function for which it is intended, and does it do so on a comparable basis with similar, competing properties in the same market?

Money is held to be an effective proxy for and measure of utility. Therefore, properties that sell for the same price under the same market conditions in the same market are presumed to have the same utility. Utility is not measured directly and "objectively" by the appraiser. Rather, it is inferred from the market behavior of presumably informed and rational purchasers. This behavior is a reflection of the subjective perceptions of property utility by the purchasers.

*Techniques of Analysis*

The Direct Sales Comparison approach is a relatively straightforward procedure. The salient characteristics of the subject property (locational, physical and financial) are identified through detailed analysis of site and improvements, as well as market area and neighborhood. These transaction characteristics include terms of financing and conditions of sale most typical or probable on the current market.

Sales data for similar, competitive properties are then gathered from appropriate sources. The appraiser must be careful to obtain information about each of the several salient points about the subject property identified as pertinent in the current market to the most probable type of purchaser-investor. The comparable sales properties and the transactions involving them are then compared item by item with the subject property. Where meaningful or measurable (by market standards) differences are observed, adjustments must be made in the comparable sale transactions data.

**Adjustment Process.** The adjustment process essentially involves attempting to answer the following rather involved questions:

1. What would the comparable sale property have sold for if it had possessed identical characteristics with the subject property, instead of the characteristics it possessed at the time of the sale? In this sense, "characteristics" include market conditions, terms of financing and conditions of sale, as well as physical characteristics of the property.
2. How much difference in sale price did these differences in characteristics make? The answer to this question indicates the amount of adjustment to make for each difference, and must be based on market evidence—*not* the appraiser's opinion.

The subject property is taken as the base or norm in the adjustment process. Differences between the comparable sales property and the subject are adjusted *from* the comparable sales property *to* the subject. If the comparable sales property is superior to the subject in some characteristic, the adjustment is downward. In other words, because of this superior characteristic, the comparable sales property sold for more than it would have if it had been identical to the subject with respect to this characteristic. Therefore, its sales price must be adjusted downward by the appropriate amount indicated by market evidence for this difference. Similarly, if the comparable sales property is inferior to the subject in some characteristic, the adjustment in the sales price of the comparable sales property is upward in the appropriate market-derived amount.

A series of adjusted sales prices for the several comparable sales properties is developed. These adjusted sales prices (one for each comparable sales property) are then correlated to an indication of value for the subject property. The adjusted sales prices of the comparable sales properties are simply that: adjusted sales prices. They are not individual indicators of the value of the subject. Rather, the *pattern* of adjusted sales prices of the comparables serves as the basis for developing an indication of value for the subject property.

Appropriate units of comparison or analysis may be (and frequently should be) used in Direct Sales Comparison analysis, especially for income properties. Thus, the adjusted sales prices of the comparable sales properties are reduced to a *per-unit* adjusted sales price. The pattern of these adjusted unit prices serves as the indicator of the appropriate unit value for the subject. In Direct Sales Comparison analysis for income properties, *one* of the useful and meaningful units of comparison or analysis is the Gross Income Multiplier.

### Data Requirements and Data Sources[3]

**Subject Property Data.** Detailed property analysis of the subject property is the first requirement. This includes identifying the characteristics of the site, the improvements, the location, and the market as of the valuation date. It also includes discovering the most probable pattern of financing terms and conditions of sale.

**Comparable Sales Data.** Detailed transactions data on market sales of similar, competitive properties are also required. These must be at least as detailed as the itemization of salient features of the subject property. The required information includes:

1. date of transaction, to identify market conditions prevailing;
2. verified sales price;
3. location, land use controls, and environmental influences;
4. physical characteristics and condition;
5. income and expense information (at least potential and effective gross income);
6. terms of financing;
7. conditions of sale (only arm's length market transactions used); and
8. number of units in property: physical, and economic or operational.

**Sources of Data.** Much the same sources used in market area analysis can usually be exploited for comparable sales data as well. As discussed in detail in Chapters 12 and 15, these sources include:

1. published sales and financing information;
2. local land records (deeds and mortgages recorded);
3. assessors' records;
4. public agencies: planning commissions, development commissions, redevelopment agencies, FHA regional offices, etc.;

5. financial institutions and lenders;
6. interviews with investors, brokers, property managers;
7. other appraisers' files; and
8. the appraiser's own files.

*Uses and Limitations of Direct*
*Sales Comparison Analysis*

When the requirements and conditions of the approach are met, Direct Sales Comparison analysis is a direct reflection of the market behavior of purchasers (investors) on the current local market. As such, it is responsive to the requirements of the definition of Market Value. It will be recalled that Market Value stipulates an informed, prudent purchaser acting rationally to pay no more than the cost of acquiring a substitute property with the same utility.

Direct Sales Comparison analysis is based entirely on market evidence, so that little intrusion of the appraiser's judgment or opinion occurs. It is also simple in conception and relatively easily understood by non-appraisers. It is given particular emphasis and acceptance by the courts.

Direct Sales Comparison analysis requires that there be an active market of similar, competing properties. If needed market data are not readily available in sufficient volume to support the analysis, its application becomes an exercise in judgment and opinion by the appraiser. The result can then hardly be defended as truly representing Market Value. In addition, it is sometimes difficult in a dynamic market environment to accept the proposition that current values based on estimates of the future can best be measured by historic data and past actions of market participants.

## Illustrative Direct Sales Comparison Data

To illustrate the use and application of Direct Sales Comparison analysis in income-property appraising, it is necessary to work with a set of data about an assumed subject property and a few comparable sales properties. From this information, the derivation of the several components of Direct Sales Comparison analysis can be demonstrated. It should not be assumed that four comparable sales transactions are adequate to establish a market pattern in most instances. However, they will be sufficient to illustrate the technique of Direct Sales Comparison analysis, which is the objective in this case. These data are used subsequently to illustrate the application of Direct Sales Comparison analysis.

A second important point is that not every type of adjustment (for time or market conditions, location, physical characteristics, and terms of sale or financing) is necessary or applicable in every appraisal. Indeed, the fewer the adjustments required in comparable sales data, the more reliable the final results are likely to be. The mechanical techniques for each category of adjustment are the same. This is demonstrated in Exhibit 16-1. Moreover, the *measure* of each adjustment is the observed difference that the presence or absence of the given characteristic can be demonstrated to represent in the sales prices of similar, competing properties. In the examples given here, it is assumed that the appraiser has already completed his background market investigations and reached supportable conclusions about the amount of each adjustment.

**Exhibit 16-1**

**Sales Comparison Adjustment Analysis of Industrial Warehouse Properties**

| Characteristic | Subject Property | Comparable No. 1 | Comparable No. 2 | Comparable No. 3 | Comparable No. 4 |
|---|---|---|---|---|---|
| Sales Price | — | $80,000 | $96,000 | $112,500 | $130,000 |
| Date of Sale | Current | 1 yr. ago | 2 yrs. ago | Current | 1 yr. ago |
| | — | +5% | +10% | 0 | +5% |
| Location | Primary | Poorer | Same | Same | Same |
| | — | +10% | 0 | 0 | 0 |
| Ceiling Height | 18' | 18' | 18' | 18' | 22' |
| | — | 0 | 0 | 0 | −10% |
| Clear Span | Yes | No | Yes | Yes | Yes |
| | — | +10% | 0 | 0 | 0 |
| Net Adjustment | — | +25% | +10% | 0 | −5% |
| | | +$20,000 | +$9,600 | 0 | −$6,500 |
| Adjusted Sales Price | — | $100,000 | $105,600 | $112,500 | $123,500 |
| Adjusted Sales Price per Square Foot Building | — | $8.33 | $7.54 | $8.33 | $8.23 |

Assume that a five-year-old industrial warehouse property is being appraised. It is located in a district of similar warehouses, distribution facilities, and light assembly plants. There is no rail service, but access to major through highways is excellent. All necessary utilities are available in the required capacities and at acceptable rates.

The subject warehouse building is a 100' X 150' steel frame and brick structure on a 30,000 square foot site. Approximately 20% of the building area is finished as office space, with all standard required amenities. Parking, docking, and loading facilities are adequate for the type of users most likely to be attracted to the property. The building has been well maintained and is in good physical condition. It is a clear-span structure with an 18-foot ceiling. The property is currently rented on a long-term lease at $1.50 per square foot of building floor area per year.

Investigation of the market has identified four recent sales of similar, competitive properties that can provide comparable sales data for the valuation of the subject property. The market investigation also revealed that warehouse space with 22-foot ceilings generally rents and sells at a 10% premium over similar 18-foot-ceiling space, while similar warehouse space with columns (not clear-span) typically rents and sells at a 10% discount. The secondary industrial area in the market region has less good highway access, and space in that area rents and sells at a 10% discount. Finally, the level of market prices in this market has been increasing at approximately 5% per year over the past few years.

The four comparable sales properties are highly competitive with, and closely similar to, the subject property in age, construction, physical condition, and all other respects except those specifically mentioned in the following descriptions.

*Comparable Sales Property No. 1* is an 18-foot ceiling structure with columns (no clear span) with dimensions of 80' X 150'. It has office space comprising 20% of total floor area, and covers 55% of its site. It is located in the secondary industrial area in the market region. It sold one year ago for $80,000. At the time of sale, it was rented at $1.20 per square foot of floor area per year.

*Comparable Sales Property No. 2* sold two years ago for $96,000. It contained 14,000 square feet of floor area, with 2,500 square feet of office space. The site was 26,500 square feet in area. The structure had an 18-foot ceiling with no columns. The annual rental at the time of sale was $17,500. It is in the same area as the subject.

*Comparable Sales Property No. 3* was renting for $20,500 per year when it sold one month ago for $112,500. The building was a clear-span structure with an 18-foot ceiling. The 13,500 square foot building had 20% of floor area in office space, and covered 50% of the site. It is located in the same area as the subject.

*Comparable Sales Property No. 4* was a clear-span structure with a 22-foot ceiling. It sold one year ago for $130,000. The building measured 100' by 150', with 3,300 square feet of office space. At the time of sale, it was renting for $1.55 per square foot per year. It is in the same area as the subject property. The site area is 25,000 square feet.

## Special Features of Direct Sales Comparison
## Analysis for Income Properties

Within the framework of analysis reviewed above, the appraiser must pay particular attention to the specific characteristics of the property being appraised. Moreover, its *functional* as opposed to its *physical* characteristics should be given special emphasis. The use of the property and its units of use are major determinants of value.

## Problems of Comparability

Income properties are more likely to be specialized in function or specifically adapted for a particular use or user. The "market" for some types of income properties, at least, is likely to be quite thin at any given time. As a result, it may not be feasible to attempt to apply Comparative Sales analysis in such cases.

The appraiser must take special care to identify the basis for competitiveness and hence comparability among properties, in terms of the property being appraised. Moreover, market comparability is at least as important in judging whether Sales Comparison analysis can be applied meaningfully as is physical comparability among properties.

In the illustrative example provided in the preceding section, the elements of market and physical comparability among the industrial warehouse properties being compared include:

1. age, condition, and type of construction;
2. ceiling height;
3. clear span vs. columns;
4. percentage of building area in office space;
5. percentage of site coverage by building;
6. location; and
7. date of sale (prevailing market conditions).

## Use of Units of Comparison

Income properties tend not to be identical in physical configuration or size. The appraiser must therefore identify the appropriate unit or units in terms of which competing properties are used, rented, bought, sold—and valued. The use of units of comparison or units of analysis is essentially an effective device to adjust for differences in *size*. Care must be taken not to use units of comparison to obscure the fact that sometimes properties in the same use but of considerably different size may not be competing in the same market. A 10,000 square foot warehouse may not really be competing with one of essentially the same physical construction, age, condition, and location—but containing 100,000 square feet. They may attract quite different types of users and purchaser-investors.

Identification of the appropriate unit of comparison involves two sets of considerations. First, in what terms do market participants think and react with respect to this type of property? Second, which unit is capable of identifying a meaningful pattern of prices or rentals on a per-unit basis for similar, competing properties?

**Selection of Units of Comparison.** There may be more than one meaningful unit of comparison for a given type of income property in a given market. Using more than one can help the appraiser refine his final value estimate via the Direct Sales Comparison approach. This was done in the site valuation example in Chapter 15. The several types of units that may be used effectively in income-property valuation, and therefore should be considered in terms of the market behavior of purchaser-investors, include:

*Physical Units*: sales price per square foot of building area; sales price per cubic foot of building area; rental per square foot of building area per year; rental per square foot of building area per month; and sales price or rental per square foot of net rentable building area, per year or per month.

*Economic Units.* These have also been called "Operating Units" or "Income Production Units." Whatever term is applied, the point is that an income property is valued in terms of its capacity to generate income. The unit in terms of which income is generated is held to be more meaningful in some instances than mere physical units. Of course, in some cases, the physical unit (e.g., square foot of building area) *is* the meaningful and appropriate unit of income production.

In any event, different units may be used for different types of properties. Analysis in terms of economic units recognizes the fact that properties and structures of different sizes may be producing the same level of income, and that the number of units of income production is the more meaningful consideration.

Representative economic units of comparison include:

*Apartments*: sales price or rental per room, per dwelling unit;
*Office buildings*: sales price or rental per room, per "suite," per square foot of net rentable area;
*Hospitals, nursing homes, etc.*: sales price or rental per bed, per bed *licensed*;
*Theaters*: sales price or rental per seat; and
*Hotels, motels*: sales price or rental per room, per bed.

This list is only illustrative and suggestive, and could be expanded considerably. The point is that the appraiser must discover what the meaningful unit is for the type of income property being appraised in the appropriate market area, as of the valuation date.

*Gross Income Multiplier.* This term is preferred to "Gross Rent Multiplier" because other income in addition to rentals may be generated by the property. Gross rentals are of course included as part of gross income. This is often a meaningful unit of comparison, and is frequently used on conjunction with one or more other units of comparison to develop a pattern of indicated unit and property values for the subject property.

In the industrial warehouse properties illustrated in the preceding section, the units of comparison are sales price per square foot of building area, and the gross income multiplier.

### Gross Income Multiplier Analysis

Income properties do produce income. It is frequently possible to identify a ratio between sales price and annual gross income for given types of properties in a given market area.[4] This ratio is the Gross Income Multiplier: $SP/GI=GIM$.

**Rationale.** The rationale of GIM analysis is that both the sales price or value and the gross income of an income property are subject to the same market influences. They presumably move in the same direction and in essentially the same proportion in response to market conditions, locational and environmental influence, and amenities and functions offered by the property itself.

Tenants are considered to be as informed and rational in their response to market alternatives as are purchaser-investors. Thus, gross income is a market-determined phenomenon as much as is sales price or value. If a pattern of consistency in the ratio between sales price and gross income of competing properties can be identified, this ratio (GIM) can be applied to the gross income forecast for the subject property to derive an indication of value. Thus: $V = GI \times GIM$.

Gross income is a function of market forces. Net Operating Income is at least partially determined by management. Therefore, the ratio is based on *property* and market considerations, and is a *Gross* Income Multiplier.

**Adjusted vs. Non-Adjusted Gross Income and Sales Price.** It is frequently argued that sales prices and gross incomes of comparable sales properties must be adjusted to reflect the characteristics of the subject property in developing an appropriate GIM. However, if the comparable sales properties are truly comparable and competitive with the subject property, and if in fact the gross income and sales price of comparable sales properties are subject to the same market influences, the same percentage adjustments should be applied to both gross income and sales price. This does nothing but increase the opportunity to make a mechanical arithmetic error. Unadjusted gross income and sales price can therefore be used in calculating the indicated GIM for each comparable sales property. It is much more important for the appraiser to identify and use truly and closely similar, competitive comparable sales properties than it is to play with mechanical adjustments in an attempt to offset non-comparability.

**Market Rental vs. Contract Rental.** The GIM is a market-determined ratio between actual sales price and gross income of comparable sales properties. In applying it to the gross income of the subject property, care must be taken to use Market Rental as the basis for the gross income estimate *if* Market Value is being estimated.

If Contract Rental on the subject property is used to develop a gross income estimate, the resulting 'value" figure is the present worth of the Leased Fee interest or Investment Value. The appraiser may well want to estimate the present worth of the Leased Fee rather than Market Value, but he should be aware of what results he gets when using different rental figures.

**Potential Gross vs. Effective Gross.** As noted in Chapter 6, there are two different gross income estimates that can be made for an income property: Potential Gross and Effective Gross. The appraiser must be very careful to use the appropriate one consistently in making his value estimate via GIM analysis.

The availability of data generally dictates which may be used. If only rent roll or rent schedule data are available, then Potential Gross must be used. If actual rent collections are available, then Effective Gross should be used. Extreme care must be taken not to mix the two from one comparable sale property to another. Consistency is essential to make the results defensible as a legitimate value estimate via Direct Sales Comparison analysis.

Whenever possible, Effective Gross should be used. This is the amount the property is actually producing. If only Potential Gross data are available, then the appraiser must study the sales data to make sure that normal or standard market occupancy ratios are being experienced by the properties included in the analysis.

**Annual vs. Monthly Multipliers.** The only difference between an annual GIM and a monthly GIM is that the latter is 12 times the former. Which is used is largely a function of the way the market responds to the type of property being appraised. For example, monthly multipliers are frequently used for small apartment and retail properties. Annual multipliers are common in industrial property appraisals. However, there may be regional differences that alter the typical pattern. The appraiser should use what the pertinent market uses for the type of property being appraised.

**Calculation of a Gross Income Multiplier.** Information is provided in the comparable sales data on industrial warehouses given earlier in this chapter that enable the appraiser to calculate an applicable Gross Income Multiplier. These calculations must be based on rental income at the time of sale. This rental income is both Potential and Effective Gross, since no allowance for vacancy and income loss is included. The calculated GIM for each of the comparable sales properties is as follows:

*Comparable Sale No. 1:* $80,000/$14,400 = 5.56 Annual GIM
*Comparable Sale No. 2:* $96,000/$17,500 = 5.49 Annual GIM
*Comparable Sale No. 3:* $112,500/$20,500 = 5.49 Annual GIM
*Comparable Sale No. 4:* $130,000/$23,250 = 5.59 Annual GIM

The indicated annual GIM for the subject property is 5.50.

The results would be exactly the same if the percentage adjustments for location, time, ceiling height, and clear-span space were applied to both sales price and gross (rental) income. For Comparable Sales Properties 1 and 4, the annual gross income is obtained by multiplying the annual rental per square foot of building floor area by the number of square feet of floor area in the building.

## Data Required and Data Sources

The data required and the sources of those data in income-property appraisal via Direct Sales Comparison analysis are practically the same as the data and sources cited earlier for Direct Sales Comparison analysis in general. The only real distinction is the degree of specificity required for particular types of income properties.

Rental and other income information is certainly required when GIM analysis is to be applied. Property managers are frequently good sources of such information, in addition to the other sources noted earlier.

Because of the particular influence of terms of financing and conditions of sale on the value of income properties, special care must be taken to gather this information for comparable sales properties. Buyer motivations (e.g., tax loss sales) must be probed to make sure the transactions are actually representative of the market, and not special cases which are not truly comparable.

## Adjustment Processes

It has already been noted in Chapter 15 and earlier in this chapter that adjustments are made in the comparable sales data to account for differences between comparables and the subject property. The comparables are adjusted to the subject to derive an adjusted sales price for each. Each adjustment must be substantiated as fully as possible from market evidence. How much difference in sales price does the observed difference in the properties make? The amount of adjustment is the impact of the difference on sales price, and not necessarily (indeed, rarely) the *cost* of adding the item. This is a reflection of the fact that cost is not value, although on occasion it may be an appropriate measure of value.

To develop a per unit adjusted sales price, it is preferable to make adjustments in the entire property first, and then to divide the adjusted sales price by the number of units each property contains. Whenever possible, dollar adjustments should be used. They must be based on market evidence. When percentage adjustments, also based on market evidence, are made, they are translated into dollar amounts.

Cumulative percentage adjustments are rarely defensible. They carry the implication that there is a sequential and causal relationship among the several factors for which adjustments are made—that there is intercorrelation among them. The sequence of adjustments, especially when successive (but not cumulative) adjustments are to be made, is rather important. The first adjustment should be for time (i.e., different market conditions), followed by locational adjustments. The result is what the properties would have sold for if they had been subject to the same market influences and environmental influences as the subject property as of the valuation date. Then specific adjustments for *property* and *transaction* differences should be made.

Time and locational differences are most difficult to measure and justify. To the extent possible, comparable sales data should not require such adjustments. Adjustments for differences in financing terms and conditions of sale are also often difficult to justify and measure convincingly. These should be avoided if possible.

The easiest differences to measure and adjustments to justify are those involving physical differences between properties. Of course, size differences are in effect adjusted for through the use of units of comparison.

The result of the adjustment process is a series of adjusted sales prices for each of the comparable sales properties, on either a total property or a per-unit basis, or both.

## Correlation of Results

Within the adjustment process, several adjusted sales prices are typically developed—one for each comparable sale property used. These indicators typically fall into a relatively narrow range. They are processed into a single unit or total property indication of value through a technique called Correlation.

Correlation, which is discussed in detail in Chapter 20, is a procedure in which the appraiser uses logic and market evidence developed in the appraisal to select the indication of value most representative of the data processed and analyzed. It is *not* averaging. Neither a simple mean, a weighted mean, nor the median figure is taken. The indicated unit or property value figure is frequently taken as a close approximation of the comparable sale property requiring the least adjustment. This implies that the comparable sale is closest to the subject property, and should be given greatest weight.

If more than one unit of comparison is used in developing an indication of value for the subject property, the several indicators must also be correlated into a single value estimate, either per unit or for the entire property. The same general rules apply here as do for correlation in developing each per-unit value indicator.

When large numbers of sales data can be developed and processed through statistical techniques, with or without the use of electronic data processing equipment, then an "average" is an acceptable value indicator. This requires truly large numbers of observations, however, and the ability to apply statistical regression or correlation analysis within the limits prescribed by statistical theory.

It is occasionally acceptable to develop an indication of the *range* of values within which the value estimate being sought most probably falls. This is particularly helpful in investment analysis. However, most appraisal assignments require the appraiser to develop a single, most probable value figure. Under these circumstances, some variant of Correlation is necessary.

*Direct Sales Comparison Analysis Illustrated*

The information provided earlier in this chapter on an industrial warehouse property and four comparable sales can be used to derive a Market Value estimate for the subject property. The units of comparison have already been identified, the Gross Income Multiplier calculated, and the salient characteristics of comparison listed. With verified data already gathered, the appraiser would proceed first to list the characteristics of all five properties in one table and confirm the comparability of the properties with one another. This tabulation is shown in Exhibit 16-2.

In addition to the previously stated similarity among the five properties in age, condition and construction, the tabulation of characteristics in Exhibit 16-2 shows clearly that the properties are competitively similar and therefore good comparables for use in Direct Sales Comparison analysis.

**Exhibit 16-2**

**Itemization of Elements of Comparability Among Industrial Warehouse Properties**

| Characteristic | Subject Property | Compa-rable No. 1 | Compa-rable No. 2 | Compa-rable No. 3 | Compa-rable No. 4 |
|---|---|---|---|---|---|
| Building Area (Sq. Ft.) | 15,000 | 12,000 | 14,000 | 13,500 | 15,000 |
| Office Area | 20% | 20% | 18% | 20% | 22% |
| Site Coverage | 50% | 55% | 53% | 50% | 60% |
| Ceiling Height (Feet) | 18 | 18 | 18 | 18 | 22 |
| Clear Span | Yes | No | Yes | Yes | Yes |
| Date of Sale | Current | 1 year ago | 2 yrs. ago | Current | 1 year ago |
| Location | Primary | Secondary | Primary | Primary | Primary |

The adjustments were given previously for time, location, ceiling height, and lack of clear-span space. The adjustment process is illustrated in Exhibit 16-1.

The end result is a series of adjusted sales prices for each comparable sale property and an indication of adjusted sales price per square foot of building area. The figures also show that the current rental of $1.50 per square foot of building area per year being received on the subject property is the Market Rental for space of this type in the current market. Thus, the GIM of 5.50 derived from the comparable sales can be applied directly to the annual gross of $22,500 being produced by the subject property to estimate Market Value.

The two units of comparison used in this analysis are the GIM and the sales price per square foot of building area. The indication of value from the use of these two units of comparison are based on a GIM of 5.50, and an indicated value per square foot of $8.33. The results are:

GIM 5.50 X Annual Gross $22,500 = $123,750
$8.33 per Square Foot X 15,000 Square Feet = $124,950

These two indications of value are quite close and clearly substantiate each other. By rounding to an appropriate level, a Market Value estimate of $125,000 appears justified.

As a final observation, it should be noted that the $123,750 indication of value based on Gross Income Multiplier analysis also represents a value per square foot of building area of $8.25.

## Review Exercise

1. An apartment property to be appraised contains 32 3-room living units and 16 4-room living units. Annual gross income collections are $49,600. Market investigation provides data on recent sales of four similar apartment properties in the same market, all of which furnish the same services as the subject property. All are subject to the same locational influences.

   Sale No. 1 contains 48 4-room apartment units. It sold for $400,000 and was producing an annual gross of $56,640 at the time of sale.

   Sale No. 2 contains 60 3-room apartment units. It sold for $375,000 and was producing an annual gross of $55,760 at the time of sale.

   Sale No. 3 contains 40 4-room apartment units. It sold for $340,000 and was producing an annual gross of $49,200 at the time of sale.

   Sale No. 4 contains 28 4-room and 14 3-room apartment units. It sold for $326,000 and was producing an annual gross of $47,260 at the time of sale.

   a. What units of comparison may be used to estimate the value of the subject property, given the sales information provided here?

   b. Is the gross income of the subject property in line with the market, as evidenced by the comparable sales data provided? What measure may be used to answer this question?

   c. What are the indicated unit values for the subject property for each of the possible units of comparison?

   d. What is the estimated Market Value of the subject property?

## Supplementary Readings

American Institute of Real Estate Appraisers, *The Appraisal of Real Estate*, fifth edition (Chicago: American Institute of Real Estate Appraisers, 1967), Chapter 21.

Gene Dilmore, "Market Data Adjustments," *Appraisal Institute Magazine*, Volume 9, Number 4, December 1965.

Gene Dilmore, "Reasonable Time to Find a Purchaser," *Appraisal Institute Magazine*, Volume 10, Number 3, September 1966.

Howard W. Dunham, Jr., "The Adjustment Process Demonstrated," *The Real Estate Appraiser*, Volume 34, Number 6, November-December 1968.

Lloyd D. Hanford, Jr., "The Market Data Approach and Investment Property Appraisal," *The Real Estate Appraiser*, Volume 32, Number 12, December 1966.

Sanders A. Kahn, Frederick E. Case, and Alfred Schimmel, *Real Estate Appraisal and Investment* (New York: Ronald Press, 1963), Chapters 8 and 32.

William N. Kinnard, Jr., *A Guide to Appraising Apartments*, third edition (Chicago: Society of Real Estate Appraisers, 1973), pp. 20-25.

William N. Kinnard, Jr., *An Introduction to Appraising Real Property* (Chicago: Society of Real Estate Appraisers, 1968), Chapters 13 and 14.

Y.T. Lum, "Applying the Market Data (Comparative) Method," *The Real Estate Appraiser*, Volume 35, Number 2, March-April 1969.

Richard U. Ratcliff, "Don't Underrate the Gross Income Multiplier," *Appraisal Institute Magazine*, Volume 13, Number 4, Winter 1969-1970.

Alfred A. Ring, *The Valuation of Real Estate*, second edition (Englewood Cliffs, N.J.: Prentice-Hall, 1970, Chapter 10.

William M. Shenkel, *A Guide to Appraising Industrial Property* (Chicago: Society of Real Estate Appraisers, 1967), pp. 80-93.

William M. Shenkel, "Characteristics of Gross Income Multipliers," *The Real Estate Appraiser*, Volume 34, Number 2, January-February 1968.

William M. Shenkel, "Modernizing the Market Data Approach," *The Appraisal Journal*, Volume 35, Number 2, April 1967.

## Notes

1. See, for example, American Institute of Real Estate Appraisers, *The Appraisal of Real Estate*, fifth edition (Chicago: American Institute of Real Estate Appraisers, 1967), Chapters 20 and 21; S.A. Kahn, F.E. Case, and A. Schimmel, *Real Estate Appraisal and Investment* (New York: Ronald Press, 1963), Chapter 8; W.N. Kinnard, Jr., *An Introduction to Appraising Real Property* (Chicago: Society of Real Estate Appraisers, 1968), Chapter 13; and A.A. Ring, *The Valuation of Real Estate*, second edition (Englewood Cliffs, N.J.: Prentice-Hall, 1970), Chapter 10.

2. A more detailed introduction to and explanation of these principles is contained in Kinnard, *Appraising Real Property*, Chapter 13.

3. Further details on data sources for specific types of properties are provided in Kinnard, *Appraising Real Property*, Chapter 13; W.N. Kinnard, Jr., *A Guide to Appraising Apartments*, third edition (Chicago: Society of Real Estate Appraisers, 1973), pp. 22-25; and W.M. Shenkel, *A Guide to Appraising Industrial Property* (Chicago: Society of Real Estate Appraisers, 1967), pp. 81-85 and 90-92.

4. Further discussion of Gross Income Multiplier analysis, including its treatment as the "Income Approach" in residential property valuation, may be found in Kinnard, *Appraising Real Property*, Chapter 11; Kinnard, *Appraising Apartments*, pp. 25-26; and Ring, *Valuation of Real Estate*, Chapter 13.

5. Examples of the adjustment process in Direct Sales Comparison analysis for different types of income properties are provided in AIREA, *Appraisal of Real Estate*, Chapter 21; Ring, *Valuation of Real Estate*, Chapter 10; and Shenkel, *Appraising Industrial Property*, pp. 86-90.

# 17 Improvements Analysis and Cost Analysis for Income Properties

Probably no other aspect of appraising receives more time and attention in introductory appraisal courses and texts than the so-called Cost Approach.[1] As a result, nearly all readers will have a thorough grounding in the components of general improvements and cost analysis.

The major task in this chapter, therefore, is to indicate the peculiarities of improvements analysis for income-property appraisal, and to show how cost considerations enter into the appraisal of income properties. Particular attention is directed to the use of discriminating improvements analysis in developing the diminished utility (accured depreciation) estimate for the improvements. This is the key estimate in measuring the present worth or contribution of the improvements to total property value.

## Rationale of Cost Analysis and the "Cost Approach"

The discussions in Part I of this book included a consideration of the alternative courses of action potentially available to the would-be purchaser of rights in an investment property that can provide a basis for estimating their value: buy an alternative competing existing property, acquire a competitive investment producing a similar income stream, or have a similar property built that has the same utility.[2] In much of appraisal literature and teaching, these three alternatives form the basis for the so-called three approaches.[3] They are termed, respectively, the Direct Sales Comparison (Market Data) Approach, the Income (Capitilization) Approach, and the Cost Approach. To estimate Market Value, of course, each uses market data. In addition, each employs comparative analysis in one form or another to develop guides and measures for estimating the present worth or value of the property being appraised.

Whether there are or are not three "Approaches" (or more) to real property value estimation, or whether different techniques of measurement are all part of one general "Approach," is really irrelevant. The important point is that the different techniques that reflect alternative potential courses of action for the purchaser-investor are responsive to the needs and data available to approach problems confronting different types of investors in different types of properties.

Simply for purposes of presentation and distinction, the term "Cost Approach" is given its traditional meaning in this discussion. That is, it provides an estimate of property value as the sum of site value plus the present worth of the improvements. This present worth is measured by the Depreciated

347

Reproduction Cost New of the improvements: reproduction cost new minus estimated diminished utility (accrued depreciation). On the other hand, "Cost Analysis" is used here to denote the estimation of Reproduction Cost or Replacement Cost without accompanying efforts to measure diminished utility.

## Underlying Concepts and Principles

In the Cost Approach to value estimation, the purchaser-investor is assumed to consider *producing* (or having produced) through new construction a substitute, competing property with the same utility as the property being appraised. The net cost to the rational, informed purchaser-investor is the measure of the value of the subject property. This net cost includes construction costs (to the purchaser, not the contractor or builder), financing costs, holding costs, and all other costs incurred during the period of construction. The approach treats the property as a physical entity, separable for valuation purposes into site and improvements, and adds both site value and the present worth (contribution) of the improvements to derive an estimate of property value.

**Cost as a Measure of Value.** A basic underlying premise of both Cost Analysis and the Cost Approach is that cost of production is an appropriate measure of value. Cost is *not* value. They are not synonymous concepts, and they are not necessarily equal in amount. However, if cost of production of improvements is properly defined and can be measured with reliable market evidence and data, then cost can be an appropriate measure of the value being sought.

**Substitution (Opportunity Cost).** The informed and rational purchaser-investor will pay no more for an existing improved income property than the cost to him of producing a substitute property with the same utility. Since it is impossible to increase utility directly, dollar costs are taken as the proxy measure *provided* the conditions of Highest and Best Use of site are met.

**Contribution (Marginal Productivity).** In the Cost Approach, the present worth of the improvements as of the valuation date is a measure of their contribution to total property value, in addition to the independently estimated value of the site. Since improvements may or may not represent the Highest and Best Use of the site, representing either an underimprovement or an overimprovement or an improper use, they may detract from the property value that would exist if they did represent Highest and Best Use. The appraiser must therefore measure or estimate the diminished utility (accrued depreciation) experienced by the improvements in order to arrive at an estimate of the net contribution of the improvements in their present condition and status to total property value, as of the valuation date.

**Highest and Best Use.** Site is always valued as if vacant and available to be put to its Highest and Best Use, as of the valuation date. From among the several site valuation techniques discussed in Chapter 15, the only one realistically applicable in Cost Approach valuation is Direct Sales Comparison. Moreover, Highest and Best Use is the standard in terms of which diminished utility (accrued depreciation) of the improvements is measured, especially but not only functional obsolescence.

## Steps in the Cost Approach

**Site Valuation.** The first step in any Cost Approach[4] to valuation is to identify the Highest and Best Use of the site, based on an analytical evaluation of the characteristics of the site, and of the market forces at work influencing values of the type of site being appraised. The procedures followed are those described in Chapter 15.

Next, the appraiser estimates the Market Value of the site as if vacant and available to be put to that Highest and Best Use under market conditions prevailing on the valuation date. This value estimate is the foundation to which the estimated present worth or contribution of the improvements is ultimately added to produce the estimated value of the property.

**Improvements Analysis.** Since the Cost Approach requires both separation of the property into its physical components of site and improvements for purposes of analysis and the independent valuation of site (usually through Direct Sales Comparison analysis), the present worth of the improvements is really a residual similar to that in the Building Residual technique of income capitalization. That present worth is measured by the contribution of the improvements, just as it is in the Building Residual technique—except that the mechanics of measurement are different. In the Cost Approach, the contribution of the improvements to total property value is estimated from evidence of the past as opposed to a projection of future benefits.

To estimate the present worth of the improvements, it is necessary to identify carefully the size, condition, effective age (and remaining economic life), quality, and functional utility or adequacy of the building(s). This process of identification constitutes improvements analysis, which is a necessary precondition to the estimate of cost new and the estimate of diminished utility (accured depreciation).

**Cost New.** After the dimensions and characteristics of the improvements have been identified through field inspection and analysis, the appraiser next estimates the cost new of the improvements. This figure is an estimate of what it would most probably cost a purchaser-investor to have the structure(s) built new, as of the valuation date.

*Replacement Cost vs. Reproduction Cost.* The estimate of the present worth of the improvements measures their contribution to property value "as is." The objective is to derive a proxy measure of their utility. Since all existing buildings except brand-new ones were built in the past, they are usually not entirely representative of current construction methods and materials, or responsive to current market standards of functional adequacy in their present use(s).

The appraiser has two theoretical alternative ways to measure the utility of the existing improvements through cost analysis. The first, and by far the more difficult to apply, is to estimate the Replacement Cost New of the improvements. This would be the measure of what it would cost (and presumably be worth) to replace the *utility* provided by the existing structure(s). Defensible as this is as a concept, it fails in practice because what is "equal utility" cannot be measured directly, and utility ends up by being defined in terms of itself. To the extent that a building performing the same function at the same levels of market acceptability can be identified, Replacement Cost can be used by the appraiser.

Replacement Cost New is defined as:

The cost of construction new of a building (or an improvement to land) having utility equivalent to the unit under appraisal, but built with modern materials and according to current standards, design and layout.[5]

Because of the practical difficulties inherent in estimating Replacement Cost New, the Cost Approach and cost analysis almost always start measuring the present worth of improvements with an estimate of Reproduction Cost New. This is

The cost of construction new of an exact duplicate or replica [of the improvements being valued] using the same materials construction standards, design, layout, and quality of workmanship.[6]

The essence of Reproduction Cost New is that a *replica* of the subject building(s) is reproduced at current prices or costs. Reproduction cost is used as the base from which all diminished utility (accrued depreciation) is deducted. It represents the total utility that the existing improvements would have if they were brand new. All of the observed functional inutility and resulting functional obsolescence of the existing structure(s) is "built in" the cost estimate first before diminished utility can be estimated and measured properly. Thus, both reproduction cost new and all charges for diminished utility are measured at current prices under current market conditions.

*Unit Costs.* Cost new estimates are usually made on a per-unit basis. These may be per square foot of floor area, less frequently per cubic foot of building space, or some other structural unit. The unit of measurement or comparison used depends on the degree of detail required in the cost analysis to be undertaken, the method of estimating diminished utility to be employed, the amount of reliance to be placed on the Cost Approach estimate of property value, and the availability of needed data. It is also determined in part by the units in terms of which builders and investors think and behave in the current market with respect to the type of structure(s) being appraised. The use of unit costs to produce a cost new estimate for improvements places a special burden on the appraiser to identify building components carefully and to measure building dimensions, area and/or volume as accurately as possible.

*Methods of Estimating Cost New.* There are several alternative methods of estimating the Reproduction Cost New[7] of improvements potentially available to the income-property appraiser. They vary in the degree of detail and presumed accuracy they provide. Which one is selected in a given appraisal is a function of the degree of detail required in the analysis, the method of estimating diminished utility to be employed, and the availability of data in the form needed. The method of estimating cost new is a determinant of which unit of cost is to be used. The more detailed the cost estimate, the more expensive in time and money it is likely to be.

*Quantity survey method.* This is the most detailed, complicated, time-consuming, and expensive method of cost estimation. It is not usually used in appraising, and should be attempted only by an expert. Following the same procedure that an informed contractor would presumably follow in preparing a detailed construction bid, the Quantity Survey Method involves a calculation of all the quantities of labor, materials, subcontractors' fees, and equipment required for reproduction of the subject structure(s) at current prices. Each unit is estimated separately, and the cost estimate derived by multiplying each unit price by the number of units and summing the results. Overhead, profit, and other indirect costs are added at the end as a lump-sum or an appropriate percentage of total direct costs.

The degree of added precision provided by the Quantity Survey Method only infrequently justifies the extra time and expense required. Quantity Survey estimates are not necessary to produce an appropriate cost new estimate on which to base the detailed breakdown method of measuring diminished utility (accrued depreciation) recommended by professional appraisal organizations.

*Unit-in-place method.* This method of cost estimation involves calculating the unit cost of materials or component sections of a structure installed "in place." It separates the structure into its physical components (e.g., exterior walls, foundation, roof) and develops installed or "in place" unit costs for labor and materials for each of these physical components. Lump-sum additions are made for equipment and fixtures, and then indirect costs are added—usually as a percentage of total direct costs.

This method, though still relatively expensive and time-consuming, does have the advantage of being compatible with the detailed breakdown method of measuring diminished utility. Accurate measurement and description are essential in applying this method. The required data may be derived either from knowledgeable and experienced contractors in the market area, or from one of the several cost services published for this purpose.

*Trade breakdown, segregated, or builder's method.* However it is labeled, this method involves estimating the current unit costs of the major functional parts of the structure, and multiplying each by the accurately measured number of such units. Installed unit costs may or may not include pro rata indirect costs; if not, they must be added as a lump sum or percentage of total direct costs at the end. The units may be expressed for excavation, foundation, frame, exterior walls, roof, heating and cooling system, electrical system, plumbing, interior walls, floors, interior finish, and the like. The installed costs of fixtures and equipment are added at so much per element.

This method usually is a close representation of the thinking of both builders and purchaser-investors. It also provides a cost estimate to which detailed breakdown measurement of diminished utility can be applied. It is generally less detailed and complicated, and therefore less expensive and time-consuming, than either the Quantity Survey or the Unit-in-Place method. A Trade Breakdown estimate of cost new can be developed with data from most cost services, as well as from contractors' bids or estimates and data on recently constructed buildings. Accurate measurement and description are still required to apply this method effectively.

*Comparative unit method.* This method is applied by lumping or adding together all direct and indirect costs of construction of comparable or "base" structures, and dividing by the number of units in the comparable structures (square foot, square foot of foundation area, cubic foot) to derive a unit cost figure to use for the subject building(s). In this simpler and less precisely detailed method, careful and accurate measurement is still quite important.

Bench mark or base structure figures may be obtained from local contractors and/or from costs of recently completed competitive buildings similar to the subject. Cost services may also be used to derive unit costs. Adjustments from base or bench mark structures to the subject, for differences in contents, materials or equipment, may be made on a per-unit or a lump-sum basis.

Although the Comparative Unit method of cost estimating is the least accurate of the several alternatives available to the appraiser, it will usually be adequate *provided* the detailed breakdown method of measuring diminished utility is not required in Cost Approach analysis. The unit employed in making the cost estimate (square foot of floor area, square foot of foundation area, cubic foot of building volume) depends primarily on the standards of the market, as well as on the form in which cost data are made available to the appraiser.

**Elements of Cost.** Cost new to the purchaser is divided into two categories for analytical purposes: direct and indirect. These are not necessarily identified separately in the unit cost figures. However, they do represent a convenient mental checklist for the appraiser, so that he can assure himself that all necessary and appropriate elements of cost are included in the estimate of total Reproduction Cost New for the subject improvements.

*Direct costs.* These include all expenses borne directly by the contractor-builder, and usually represent out-of-pocket expenses paid by him. They can be classified as:

1. labor;
2. materials;
3. equipment; and
4. subcontractors' fees and charges.

*Indirect costs.* These include all general overhead cost borne by the contractor-builder, and passed on to the purchaser-investor in the price of the completed building, whether they actually involve out-of-pocket expenditures or not.

1. contractor-builder's overhead;
2. contractor-builder's profit on construction;
3. architect's, surveyor's, engineer's, and lawyers' fees;
4. permit and license fees;
5. insurance premiums and taxes incurred during construction;
6. financing charges during construction;
7. selling expenses: advertising promotion, sales commissions; and
8. vacancy carrying charges until first occupancy or sale.

**Remaining Economic Life of Improvements.** In order to apply the Cost Approach properly, as well as to apply physical residual techniques of income capitalization, it is necessary to estimate the remaining economic life of the improvements. As indicated earlier in Chapter 6, the economic life of improvements is the time period over which they are forecast to be capable of producing income at a competitive rate of return on the portion of total property investment represented by the investment in the improvements. Their remaining economic life is the time period over which they are forecast to be capable of producing a competitive net rate of return as of the valuation date.

This remaining economic life is the capital recovery or income projection period in physical residual techniques of income capitalization analysis. At the end of this time period, the improvements are forecast to make zero contribution to total property value over and above the value of the (residual) site. Remaining economic life is therefore also the period over which diminished utility or accrued depreciation is forecast to be experienced by the improvements.

The appraiser estimates the remaining economic life in part from the observed condition of the improvements identified through careful inspection and improvements analysis, and in part from the verified experience of similar competitive properties in the same market. In making this estimate, he is once again looking at the property through the eyes of the typically informed, prudent and rational purchaser-investor, and identifying the time period over which that most probable purchaser-investor is most likely to anticipate receiving income at a competitive rate of return. For income properties in particular, the remaining economic life of the improvements can be a critically important estimate, because it influences both capital recovery rates and hence value in Income Capitalization analysis, and the measurement of diminished utility as of the valuation date in Cost Approach analysis.

**Diminished Utility (Accrued Depreciation).** The estimate of Reproduction Cost New is a dollar measure of the total utility that a brand-new replica of the building(s) in the property being appraised would have if it were constructed as of the valuation date. Existing structures have already used up some of their total economic lives, and hence some of their total utility, however, as of the valuation date. To measure the contribution of the improvements to total property value, therefore, it is necessary to estimate the amount of total utility represented by Reproduction Cost New that has already been used up in producing past income by the valuation date, and assign a dollar figure to it. This amount of utility in the improvements that has been "used up" as of the valuation date is called Diminished Utility or Accrued Depreciation.[8]

Diminished utility is a loss or decrease in the present worth of improvements, in their observed condition as of the valuation date, from Reproduction Cost New. Diminished utility can result from a combination of physical deterioration, functional obsolescence, and/or environmental obsolescence. After the separate elements of diminished utility have been identified and measured in dollars, the total amount of diminished utility in dollars is deducted from Reproduction Cost New of the improvements. The resulting difference is the estimated present worth or contribution of the improvements to total property value.

*Measurement by Abstraction.* The simplest and most accurate way to measure the total amount of diminished utility experienced by the improvements as of the valuation date is to deduct the present worth or value of the property from the sum of site value and Reproduction Cost New of the improvements. Since site value remains the same, any difference is experienced entirely by the improvements. That difference is the amount of diminished utility.

Although this method is accurate and supportable, it is not particularly helpful in Cost Approach analysis. If the objective of the analysis is to estimate property value, then property value cannot be taken as a given. Only when the objective is to estimate some or all of unknown diminished utility is this abstraction method useful to the appraiser. Otherwise, he is forced to approach the present worth estimate of improvements by indirection, by estimating the elements of diminished utility directly.

*Direct Measurement of Diminished Utility.* Diminished utility[9] can be experienced by buildings or other improvements through one or more of three sources. The existence of diminished utility from one or more of these causes is identified through improvements analysis and the market's reaction to the observed conditions of the improvements. The *measure* of diminished utility to be charged as a deduction from Reproduction Cost New is provided by the difference the presence or absence of an item of observed condition makes on the market in the sales prices or values of otherwise similar, competitive properties. Cost is *not* the measure unless it can be demonstrated convincingly that the condition is "curable."

The *test of curability* of any observed condition in the subject improvements is whether the expenditure of the probable dollar amount required to cure it would result in an increase in sales price or value of the property of *at least* as much as the cost to cure. Curability has nothing to do with technological capability to correct the observed condition; nearly every defect, deficiency, or superadequacy in a structure can be corrected as far as construction technology is concerned. The test of curability is a market test of feasibility: Will it pay to make the expenditure?

*Physical deterioration* is the result of the physical wearing out of the structure, deferred or inadequate maintenance, action of the elements, or insect infestation. It is reduction in utility resulting from impairment of physical condition. Although the cause is physical, the effect is economic: diminished utility and hence reduced economic life or reduced net income, or both. Depending on the reactions of the market, physical deterioration may be either curable or incurable, or both. Incurable elements of physical deterioration can be further divided into short-lived items which will most probably have to be replaced before the expiration of the remaining economic life of the improvements in order to maintain its marketability and income-producing capacity; and long-lived items whose remaining economic life is the same as that of the basic structure.

*Functional obsolescence* is a reduction in the capacity of the improvements to perform the function(s) for which it is intended in accordance with current market standards of acceptability, and hence a decline in their functional utility. This decrease in utility is termed "Functional Obsolescence" because the structural component or element involved is outmoded or inefficient according to current market standards of performance for the type of space provided. Functional obsolescence is intrinsic to the structure and the property, and may be either curable or incurable, or both.

*Environmental obsolescence* is a "Loss from cost new as of date of appraisal, due to causes external to the property."[10] It is also widely termed "Economic Obsolescence,"[11] and sometimes "Locational Obsolescence."[12] Since real estate is fixed in location, it is a creature of its environment. This point has been demonstrated in Chapters 2 and 14. Any change in that surrounding environment that has a negative impact on the value of the property is shared by the components of that property: site and improvements. The impact on site value is reflected in the independently derived value estimate, usually based on Direct Sales Comparison analysis. A proportionate share of property value loss attributable to external environmental influences is charged against the Reproduction Cost New of the improvements as Environmental Obsolescence. It is always incurable, since it is not feasible or practical for the property owner to buy up the neighborhood and remove the negative influences on the value of the subject property—except in extremely rare and unusual cases of massive private investments.

All elements of diminished utility must be strong enough to be *measurable* on the market. The mere presence of an apparently negative item is not significant unless it can be demonstrated to make a measurable difference between the Reproduction Cost New of the improvements and their present worth or contribution to property value.

**Present Worth (Contribution) of Improvements.** The present worth of the improvements is obtained by subtracting the total of estimated diminished utility from all causes, from the Reproduction Cost New of the improvements.

**Property Value Estimate.** The indicated property value, as defined in the appraisal problem, is produced in Cost Approach analysis by adding the independently derived estimate of site value to the estimated present worth of the improvements. This sum is rounded appropriately, and the resulting figure is the estimate of value of the subject property via the Cost Approach.

## Improvements Analysis

Before Reproduction Cost New and diminished utility experienced by the improvements as of the valuation date can be estimated convincingly, it is necessary for the appraiser to inspect and measure the improvements carefully. The contents, quality, equipment, and condition of the several components of the structure(s) must be identified and noted for future reference in Cost Approach analysis.

### Review of General Principles

Improvements analysis identifies unequivocally the *physical* components and attributes of the property being appraised, in the same manner that site inspection and analysis do.

**Role in the Cost Approach.** The appraiser must identify, measure, describe, and analyze the pertinent features of the structure(s) in the property being appraised, in order to establish the standards for comparison with other competitive properties that have sold or rented recently in the same market. This process is necessary to establish the units and unit costs used in the estimate of Reproduction Cost New. It is also essential to provide the basis for the identification and measurement of elements of diminished utility needed to derive an estimate of present worth of the improvements. Only if detailed, accurate information about the subject building(s) is available can appropriate adjustments be made for deviations from the standards of acceptability provided by the market. Both physical condition and functional adequacy must be judged from the evidence of improvements analysis.

**Elements of Improvements Analysis.** For income properties, improvements analysis focuses particularly on the specific characteristics and functional utility that establish the basis for estimating diminished utility.

*Inspection and Physical Description.* The first step in any analysis of improvements is a field inspection and detailed description of the dimensions, contents, quality, equipment, condition, and function(s) of the improvements. This provides the data base on which the remainder of the analysis proceeds.

*Standards Set by the Market.* The physical ingredients of the improvements, their condition, and their character all combine to serve as a guide to the market acceptability and hence the marketability of the property. Marketability is a basic determinant of value. It is identified and measured in terms of standards set by the market, which means that the appraiser must discover what is being sought and accepted by other purchaser-investors and users of similar, competitive space currently and locally. Standards vary over both time and space as tastes, customs, and technology change.

There are at least three groups whose standards of acceptability and use must be incorporated into the evaluation of "market" acceptability: purchaser-investors, users, and lenders.

*Evaluation of Functional Utility.* For income properties in particular, the functional adequacy and hence functional utility of the improvements are major considerations in improvements analysis, to provide the basis for identifying and measuring functional (and environmental) obsolescence later in the Cost Approach analysis. Functional utility is the sum of the attractiveness and usefulness of the property, in terms of the use(s) for which it is intended and in accordance with market standards of acceptability. The standards are set by participants in the market and reflected in their behavior; they are not set by the appraiser.

Functional utility is also considered in relation to the identified Highest and Best Use of the site. If either the type or the intensity of current use with existing improvements is different from the Highest and Best Use of the site, the improvements will exhibit some functional inutility and functional obsolescence must be measured. The Highest and Best Use of any existing improved property is that use incorporating the existing structure(s) that is most profitable to the owner-investor; it may or may not be the Highest and Best Use of the site. Any disparity between the two is an indication of functional obsolescence, most probably incurable.

Functional utility (or inutility) may be indicated not only by the type or intensity of use in relation to the Highest and Best Use of the site, but also in the architecture, design and layout, space arrangements and room sizes, and equipment provided in the building(s).

*Estimate of Remaining Economic Life.* The character, condition, and functional adequacy of the improvements, together with the neighborhood and other environmental influences at work on them, are determinants of the remaining economic life forecast for them. This estimate must be based on evidence of market behavior of purchaser-investors in reaction to similar, competing properties with similar types of improvements. The essential question is: What remaining economic life would the most probable type of informed, rational purchaser-investor in property of this type forecast for improvements of the character and in the condition of those in the subject property? The difference between the total economic life of the improvements if they were brand-new as of the valuation date, and their remaining economic life estimated as of the valuation date, is the *effective age* of the improvements. In some aspects of detailed breakdown analysis to measure diminished utility, effective age is an important determination.

Remaining economic life, and its complement effective age, are dependent on tastes, standards, custom, and effective competition in the market; they also depend in part on observed condition of the improvements.

**Uses of Improvements Analysis.** Income-property improvements analysis is used for two basic purposes:

*Basis for Comparisons.* Not only in Cost Approach analysis, but also in both Direct Sales Comparisons and Income Capitalization, improvements analysis provides an important basis for comparisons between the subject property and similar, competing properties. Only when the salient features and characteristics of the subject improvements have been identified can an effective comparative analysis in terms of market standards be undertaken.

*Basis for Estimating Diminished Utility.* The identification and measurement of diminished utility must be based on the observed condition and characteristics of the improvements. This includes both physical condition and functional adequacy.

*Special Features for Income Properties*

As is the case with market area, neighborhood and site analysis, income-property improvements analysis consists of more than mere listing of the type, number, and condition of the several components of structure(s) and equipment. Detailed and accurate measurement are a necessary starting point, but the appraiser must then evaluate observed condition and functional utility in terms of their measurable impact on property value.

In large part, the analysis culminates in the estimate of remaining economic life of the improvements. This estimate is a forecast of the remaining time period over which the entire improved property is expected, in accordance with market standards and investor-purchaser behavior, to be a competitive economic entity. In part, the analysis of improvements in income properties is also an estimate of the extent to which the improvements meet the standards of acceptability and space requirements of the most probable type of user(s). This latter estimate requires the appraiser to match user standards and requirements with the facilities and services actually provided by the improvements being appraised, as of the valuation date.

**Detailed and Accurate Measurement.** Income-property improvements analysis requires more accurate measurement and more detailed itemization of structural components and equipment than is generally necessary in residential appraisals. This is partly because the components tend to be more expensive. The appraiser must discover the unit(s) in terms of which the market regards the type of structure(s) being appraised, and then measure or count those units accurately. This is often done with the aid of plans, blueprints and specifications.

**Detailed Itemization of Equipment and Building Condition.** Inspection checklists are almost a necessity in improvements analysis for income properties.[13] They help the appraiser avoid omissions and mistakes. They also help provide the basis for estimating overall structural condition, identifying potentially curable items of diminished utility, identifying short-lived component items and their effectve ages, and estimating Reproduction Cost New. The itemization of items of equipment is also particularly helpful in identifying elements of functional obsolescence.

For investment properties, this detailed description and division of equipment items can also have a significant impact on the after-tax cash flow of the purchaser-investor. Under the 1969 Tax Reform Act, equipment is still depreciable at accelerated rates without the hazard of recovery at full ordinary tax rates at a later date, while non-residential "real estate" is not.[14] The appraiser can perform an important service to his investor-client by carefully making these distinctions while inspecting and analyzing the improvements.

**Identification of Current Standards of Functional Adequacy.** Much income property is designed for a specific use or a narrow range of uses. The current standards of functional adequacy and space requirements set by the most probable types of users of the type of improvements being appraised, as of the valuation date, represent important determinants of the appraiser's estimate of functional obsolescence. This evidence must come from the market, and may be based on both personal investigation and published materials on user standards.

Because of the necessity to match user standards and requirements with the facilities actually provided by the property being appraised, improvements analysis for income properties is much more specific than is residential improvements analysis.

**Estimation of Remaining Economic Life.** Since physical residual techniques of income capitalization rely heavily on the forecast of remaining economic life of the improvements as the income projection period, as demonstrated in Chapter 12, the appraiser has a dual responsibility in developing this estimate as part of his income-property improvements analysis. There must be consistency between Income Capitalization and Cost Approach analysis is using the same remaining economic life.

**Evaluation of Siting and Floor Area Ratio.** Whatever "approach(es)" to income-property valuation are used, the value estimate is influenced strongly by the forecast capacity of the property to produce a competitive net return. The siting of the improvements (their positioning on the site) can have a significant impact on their market attractiveness to both users (tenants) and purchaser-investors. Siting must be consistent with the standards of acceptability established by the type(s) of user anticipated. A sketch or plot plan is extremely helpful in supporting the appraiser's conclusions on this point.

One indication of siting is the floor area ratio, which indicates how intensively a site is being used. For example, a two-story commercial building with 20,000 square feet of area on each floor on a 60,000-square-foot site has a floor area ratio of 2:3 (40,000/60,000), and a site coverage ratio of 1:3 (20,000/60,000). Siting is one basis for estimating the functional adequacy of the improvements, and therefore for identifying potential charges against cost new for functional obsolescence.

**Highest and Best Use Analysis Includes Consideration of Alternative Uses.** The appraiser must estimate the Highest and Best Use of the property with its existing improvements, or at least its most probable use, as well as that of the site. Unless supersession of uses and/or demolition of existing improvements appears called for, the existing use pattern is the one in terms of which income will be forecast for capitalization analysis.

Moreover, if a renovation or alternative use program is considered, cost is a critical ingredient in estimating the feasibility of carrying out the proposed renovation or conversion. The present ingredients and condition of the improvements are important determinants of the estimated cost of any renovation or conversion program.

### Estimation of Cost New

Although Replacement Cost New can have some uses in the valuation and analysis of income properties, particularly in evaluating alternative investment programs, the sole emphasis in Cost Approach analysis is on Reproduction Cost New.

*Reproduction Cost*

Reproduction cost estimates involve calculations of the most probable cost of having a replica of the existing improvements produced new at costs and prices prevailing as of the valuation date. This is why the description of the income-property improvements developed through improvements analysis must be detailed and accurate.

Replacement cost new, on the other hand, is an estimate of the cost of having produced a structure that will provide the same function as the structure being appraised. However, it is functionally adequate in terms of current market standards of use and performance. In some income-property investment decisions, replacement with a new structure is a realistic or possible alternative to renovation or conversion of an existing structure. In such cases, replacement cost new is compared with renovation or conversion cost, and with forecast income receipts, in making the investment decision.

The estimate of reproduction cost new may be quite detailed or relatively simple, depending on the method of measuring diminished utility to be used later in the analysis, and on the availability of data. In any event, unit costs are usually estimated, and then multiplied by the number of observed units in the structure to develop a total cost new estimate.

The Comparative Unit method can be applied on a square-foot basis for the basic structure, with specific additions and adjustments for particular items of equipment. For example, a small steel-frame industrial warehouse containing 11,600 square feet of floor area might have its reproduction cost new estimated as illustrated in Exhibit 17-1. The total reproduction cost new estimate of $80,780 could then be divided by 11,600 to obtain the total reproduction cost per square foot of building area: $6.96. This latter figure could be used as a bench mark for subsequent cost estimates of identical warehouse structures.

If all the appraiser needs is a simple cost new estimate to which gross or lump-sum estimates of diminished utility (accrued depreciation) are to be applied, an estimate similar to that illustrated in Exhibit 17-1 will usually suffice. However, if the Cost Approach analysis is to involve a detailed breakdown estimate or diminished utility by category (physical deterioration, functional obsolescence, environmental obsolescence), then a much more detailed cost estimate is required. Most commonly, the Trade Breakdown method of estimating cost new represents the best compromise between required detail, and available time and data. One such cost estimate is illustrated in Exhibit 17-2 for a 54-unit, 202-room apartment building. It is 12 years old, and is estimated to have a remaining economic life of 40 years. The effective age has been estimated as 10 years, which means that the effective age is 20% of estimated total economic life of the structure (10/50 = .20).

The appraiser has been able to obtain reproduction cost new estimates for the several functional parts of the structure. These cost figures include all indirect

**Exhibit 17-1**

**Reproduction Cost New Estimate of Industrial Warehouse Using Square Foot Unit Costs, Plus Lump-Sum Adjustments**

| Item | Area (Sq. Ft.) | Cost per Sq. Ft. | Total Cost New |
|---|---|---|---|
| Office Area | 1,890 | $10.00 | $18,900 |
| Building Shell | 11,600 | 2.11 | 24,480 |
| | | | $43,380 |

| | |
|---|---|
| Add Adjustments for: | |
| Foundations, Concrete Slab | $ 3,600 |
| Miscellaneous Items | 1,500 |
| Temporary Construction | 1,370 |
| Plumbing | 500 |
| Septic Tank, Sewage | 3,700 |
| Electrical | 11,000 |
| Manifold Slab | 230 |
| Cranes | 13,000 |
| Land Improvements | 2,500 |
| Total Adjustments | $37,400 |
| Total Estimated Reproduction Cost New | $80,780 |

Total Cost per Square Foot: $\dfrac{\$80,780}{11,600} = \$6.96$

*Source*: W.N. Kinnard, Jr., *Industrial Real Estate* (Washington, D.C.: Society of Industrial Realtors, 1967), p. 415.

costs such as builder's overhead and profit. The itemized cost estimates, together with the appraiser's best judgment of remaining economic life of each of the major components, are presented in Exhibit 17-2.

*Sources of Data*

Data of two general categories are required in making defensible cost new estimates in appraisal analysis, whether to serve as a starting point in the Cost Approach or to provide a direct basis for investment decision-making. In either

**Exhibit 17-2**

**Reproduction Cost New Estimate for Apartment: Building Trade Breakdown Method**

| Component | Reproduction Cost New | Remaining Economic Life |
|---|---|---|
| Excavation | $   9,550 | 40 years |
| Foundation | 11,860 | 40 years |
| Basement Walls | 8,320 | 40 years |
| Frame | 93,020 | 40 years |
| Floors | 62,720 | 35 years |
| Floor Covering | 30,340 | 25 years |
| Ceiling | 19,830 | 40 years |
| Roof Structure | 9,319 | 40 years |
| Roof Covering | 2,272 | 20 years |
| Exterior Walls | 108,263 | 40 years |
| Interior Construction | 47,936 | 40 years |
| Lighting and Electrical | 31,842 | 25 years |
| Plumbing | 42,234 | 40 years |
| Heating | 62,468 | 30 years |
| Elevators | 48,680 | 25 years |
| Outside Construction | 12,025 | 40 years |
| Architect's Fees, etc. (6%) | 36,040 | 40 years |
| Total Reproduction Cost New | $636,719 | |

case, the appraiser may look to local sources for current or recently past data on buildings actually built, or to standardized (usually published) sources of base structure unit costs.[15] The latter require adjustments for both geographic location and time to reflect variations in costs and prices from one market area to another, as well as changes over time. These adjustments are most commonly made with the aid of cost index figures published as supplements to the several major construction cost services.[16]

The sources utilized in any given appraisal problem will depend on the degree of detail required, plus the appraiser's experience in judging the probable responsiveness of the data from the source(s) selected to the type of cost estimate needed.

Since all cost data used in developing cost new estimates are market data, the data sources utilized must permit a cost estimate for the replica of the subject improvements under current, local market conditions.

**Local Contractors and Builders.** These represent a very significant source of cost data for the income-property appraiser, since they are constantly in touch with the market. They can provide data on unit construction costs, costs of completed structures, wage rates, materials and equipment prices, and categories of indirect costs. In particular, they are important sources of cost *differentials* for different types of structures and building components.

In some instances, appraisers may request (usually for a fee) bids or estimates for specific structures from contractors. For more common or usual types of improvements, periodic data from contractors can also provide the appraiser with bench mark cost estimates, from which minor adjustments for specific differences or items of equipment can then be made as the occasion demands.

**Cost Estimators.** Cost estimating is a highly specialized technical skill. When the nature of the appraisal problem warrants the expenditure of the required time and money, the income-property appraiser should retain the services of a professional cost estimator. This is most often necessary when highly specialized structures are to be costed, or when renovation or conversion of an existing structure is part of the client-investor's plan of alternative actions.

**Cost Studies and Surveys.** In many large metropolitan regions, construction cost studies are often available on a continuing, periodic basis. They usually provide bench mark data, but also occasionally concentrate on specific types of construction. Continuing studies frequently provide time factor adjustments through a cost index in order to enable the appraiser (as well as other users) to keep the bench mark figures current with costs and prices in the local market area. Such studies are most often available from (1) FHA regional offices; (2) builders' associations; (3) local chapters of professional appraisal associations; and (4) university research groups.

**Appraiser's Own Files.** The active income-property appraiser will necessarily develop a back-file of cost data from previous appraisal assignments and studies. To be effectively useful, they must be properly cross-indexed and kept current.

**Cost Services.** Several national cost services are available for income and investment-type properties. They offer bench mark data on standardized building types, as well as detailed unit costs for structural components and items of equipment, usually on an "installed" or "in place" basis. Three such national services of considerable use to the income-property appraiser have already been cited earlier in this section: the Boeckh, Dow, and Marshall services. These and others also publish monthly or quarterly supplements to bring specific types of property cost studies up to date with new construction methods and materials, and to provide area and time adjustment factors in index form so that the appraiser may utilize the base figures in the local market area as of the valuation date.

Cost services also provide site improvements cost data in both lump-sum and unit-cost form. They enable the appraiser to develop cost estimates for a building with any specifications and contents. Comparative Unit, Trade Breakdown, and Unit-in-Place cost estimates can be developed with any of the major cost services cited here. The selection of the specific cost service to use is largely a matter of professional experience and preference on the part of the appraiser.

While currently available cost services are generally quite flexible and responsive to the needs of income-property appraisers, they must be used with care. The relative ease of application of cost service data can obscure difficulties in comparison between the units or bench mark structures provided by the service, and the subject structure(s) being appraised. In particular, detailed comparison of construction and contents specifications is essential. Every deviation from the "norm" provided in the cost service must be identified and adjusted for before a defensible estimate of cost new for the improvements being appraised can be developed.

*Selection of Cost Estimation Method*

In selecting the method to be used in estimating the Reproduction Cost New of the improvements being appraised, the income-property appraiser must be governed by two sets of considerations.

First, what method of measuring diminished utility is to be employed in the Cost Approach analysis? The more detailed this method, the more detailed the cost new estimate must be. If the measure of diminished utility is acceptable as a lump sum with little detail, usually on an age-life basis, then a cost new estimate based on Comparative Units will usually suffice. If the detailed breakdown method is to be used to measure diminished utility, however, then a more detailed cost new estimate is essential. This requirement can usually be met by using the Trade Breakdown method illustrated in Exhibit 17-2.

Second, what data are available to the appraiser? This will influence strongly the method of cost estimation employed. A detailed analysis on questionable or incomplete data is simply not acceptable. Fortunately, most cost services (especially those cited in this chapter) provide sufficient opportunity for the appraiser to develop a supportable cost new estimate for virtually every type of income-property structure encountered in professional appraisal practice. In the few unusual cases when cost service data are not responsive to the needs of the problem, the appraiser will most likely have to retain a professional cost estimator.

## Measurement of Diminished Utility and
## Contribution of Improvements

Once the Reproduction Cost New of the improvements has been estimated as of the valuation date, the appraiser must then measure the amount of total utility provided by such new improvements that has been expended or "used up." This is a reflection of the condition, functional adequacy, and forecast remaining economic life of those improvements already provided through improvements analysis. Particularly in the case of income properties, remaining economic life is inextricably connected with the forecast income projection period. When the property is primarily an investment most probably attractive to a tax-liable private investor, the "useful life" of that type of structure over which accounting depreciation deductions may be charged under U.S. Internal Revenue Service regulations will have some impact on the estimated remaining economic life.[17]

### Categories of Diminished Utility

As noted earlier in this chapter, elements of diminished utility or accrued depreciation may be categorized under three major headings for purposes of analysis: Physical Deterioration, Functional Obsolescence, and Environmental Obsolescence. The first two are inherent to the structure or improvements itself, and may be either curable or incurable, or both. "Curability" is related to financial or investment feasibility, rather than to technological possibility. Physical Deterioration and Functional Obsolescence are experienced by and chargeable to the improvements only.

Environmental Obsolescence, on the other hand, causes a loss in total property value as a result of developments or changes outside the property itself, and therefore beyond the power or capacity of the owner-investor to do anything to correct the condition. It is thus always "incurable." Since it affects the entire property, both site and improvements, the appraiser must prorate the appropriate proportion of total Environmental Obsolescence deductions chargeable against the cost new of the improvements. Otherwise, there will be double counting in deducting for Environmental Obsolescence, since the site value estimate developed through Direct Sales Comparison analysis presumably already reflects the market's reaction to the negative influence(s) identified as Environmental Obsolescence.

Whenever the detailed breakdown method of measuring diminished utility is to be employed, the following categories of diminished utility must be *considered* by the appraiser as sources of potential deductions:

1. Physical Deterioration
   a. Curable
   b. Incurable

(1) Short-lived Items
(2) Long-lived Items
2. Functional Obsolescence
  a. Curable
  b. Incurable
3. Environmental Obsolescence — Incurable

*Special Importance of Functional*
*Obsolescence Estimate*

Estimating diminished utility for income-property improvements follows the same pattern and employs the same basic techniques applicable in Cost Approach analysis for all types of properties, including residential amenity properties.[18] The significant difference lies in the importance of functional utility or functional adequacy of the improvements in their intended use, especially since user tastes, standards, and requirements are subject to such rapid change in many types of income properties. As indicated in previous chapters, the impact of volatile market standards is accentuated by the fact that so many income-property users are likely to be tenants with greater opportunities for mobility than owner-occupants generally have.

Functional obsolescence is internal to the improvements. It stems from market-perceived inadequacies in layout, space configurations, equipment, occupancy costs, and the capacity of the space in question to support the intended use both operationally and physically. For example, the load-bearing capacity of floors can have a significant impact on the uses and users feasible for the improvements being appraised. As noted earlier, functional obsolescence can also derive from less-than-standard siting of the building on its site. The intensity of land use and the judgment of whether the building is an overimprovement or an underimprovement of the site influence the conclusion as to whether it represents the Highest and Best Use of the site.

*Degree of Detail Required and Possible*

If any Cost Approach estimate of value for an income property is to be used as a significant indicator of property value, rather than merely a check against value estimates developed through alternative forms of analysis, the cost new estimates and the indications of diminished utility must be relatively detailed. This is because of the specificity of user standards and requirements usually encountered in income properties. While many different techniques of estimating diminished utility are potentially available to the appraiser, some variant of the detailed breakdown method that analyzes and measures each of the categories of diminished utility is strongly recommended. A simple age-life or lump-sum deduction is not usually responsive to the needs of income-property appraising.

**Dependence on Improvements Analysis.** To apply detailed breakdown measurement of diminished utility, the appraiser must have a detailed, itemized description of the improvements, including indications of the condition and functional adequacy of their components. Otherwise, the required diminished utility analysis format cannot be followed. This underscores the critical importance of good, detailed improvements analysis. Every item of diminished utility charged must be supported in two ways: from the evidence of condition and character of the components of the structure being appraised, and from market evidence of the difference the presence or absence of a given component or condition makes in the market prices of otherwise similar, competing properties.

**Dependence on Detail of Cost New Estimate.** No matter how carefully the appraiser itemizes and details the components and characteristics of the improvements, and how much justification he can bring to bear to defend the estimates of market impact of those conditions and characteristics observed in the structure, the required detailed breakdown analysis cannot be applied to measure diminished utility unless the cost new estimate is presented in sufficient detail. This usually means that the Trade Breakdown method of estimating cost new illustrated in Exhibit 17-2 or an even more detailed Unit-in-Place or Quantity Survey estimate, is necessary. If the cost new estimate is based on the Comparative Unit method, it is rarely feasible to apply detailed breakdown analysis to measure diminished utility.

## *Mechanics of Estimating Diminished Utility*[19]

Once the method of estimating and measuring diminished utility has been selected, the appraiser applies the mechanical processes of measurement to the elements of diminished utility observed and identified in the analysis of the improvements.

**Curable Items.** Items of Physical Deterioration and Functional Obsolescence that have been identified as "curable" in terms of market feasibility are measured by the *cost to cure*. This means that correcting the condition will add at least as much as the cost of correcting it to market value. The informed and rational investor will therefore proceed to correct the "curable" items so identified. Curable items are usually deducted first, so as to avoid double counting. The rationale is that the remaining utility represented by the reproduction cost new, *less* the cost to cure the curable items, is the base against which incurable elements of diminished utility are measured. In effect, the appraiser is saying: "Even after correcting these curable items, the improvements will have deficiencies by current market standards that require further deductions from cost new before the present worth or contribution of these improvements can be identified."

**Incurable Physical Deterioration.** Incurable Physical Deterioration is usually subdivided between short-lived items which will most probably have to be replaced before the expiration of the remaining economic life of the entire structure, and long-lived items whose remaining economic life is the same as that of the entire structure. In the former case, the items are partially "used up" and are forecast to be replaceable at some time in the future, but the prudent purchaser-investor would not be justified in replacing them as of the valuation date. The long-lived items are simply partially "used up" in proportion to the relationship between effective age observed as of the valuation date and the remaining economic life of the improvements.

Both elements of Incurable Physical Deterioration are typically measured through some form of age-life ratio or percentage. The simple or bulk age-life approach treats the entire structure as a single entity, and applies the percentage of total economic life represented by effective age to reproduction cost new *less* the charges for curable items already made. In detailed breakdown analysis, the same basic procedure is used, except that the effective age and total economic life are estimated for each major category of structural components or equipment. The appropriate percentage deduction is then made for each of the components or items individually, and the sum of these deductions then represent the estimate of Incurable Physical Deterioration for the entire structure.

**Incurable Functional and Environmental Obsolescence.** Incurable Functional Obsolescence, and Environmental Obsolescence as well, are measured by the impact of the observed element of diminished utility on the income-producing capacity of the property. These are, after all, income properties, whose value is the present worth of the anticipated future income stream they are forecast to be capable of producing. Both Incurable Functional Obsolescence and Environmental Obsolescence result in either a diminution of gross income or an increase in operating expenses, or both. In either case, the net effect is to reduce Net Operating Income.

The decline in annual income or increase in annual operating expenses attributable to the element of obsolescence identified by the appraiser can be converted to a lump-sum estimate of decreased capital value (diminished utility) by multiplying the annual figure by the appropriate Gross Income Multiplier. The derivation and uses of the GIM were explained in Chapter 16. If the net effect of the element of obsolescence on NOI can be identified accurately, then the decrease in NOI can be capitalized at the appropriate level annuity capitalization rate or factor. This will also result in a measure of the capital loss attributable to the functional and/or environmental inadequacies found in the subject improvements. The capitalization of income loss or operating expense increase is most commonly accomplished through the GIM, however.

The measurement of Environmental Obsolescence poses one final problem. As already noted in this chapter, Environmental Obsolescence is experienced by the entire property: site and improvements alike. The impact on site value is presumably already measured by estimating site value through Direct Sales Comparison analysis. Only a part of total diminished utility experienced by the property as the result of the elements of Environmental Obsolescence observed is attributable to the improvements. The total amount obtained by capitalizing income loss or operating expense increase must somehow be apportioned between site and improvements. The most common method, which still has some operational difficulties attached to it, is to identify the percentage of total property value represented by the present worth of the improvements in closely similar, highly competitive properties. This percentage is then applied to total diminished utility from Environmental Obsolescence to obtain the amount assignable to the improvements as a deduction from reproduction cost new.

**Illustrative Example**. Starting with the Reproduction Cost New estimate and the indicated remaining economic lives of the major structural components of the apartment building illustrated in Exhibit 17-2, it is possible to demonstrate the detailed breakdown method of measuring diminished utility, and hence of estimating value via the Cost Approach. The total economic life of the structure new has been identified as 50 years. The effective ages of the structural components, expressed as percentages based upon the remaining economic lives indicated in Exhibit 17-2, are provided in Exhibit 17-3. This exhibit also indicates the amount of deferred maintenance (Curable Physical Deterioration) for each structural component.

It should be noted that the Incurable Physical Deterioration charges are levied against reproduction cost new of each major component of the structure *after* the indicated charges for Curable Physical Deterioration and Curable Functional Obsolescence have been deducted.

Because of age, outmoded materials, and changing standards, certain functional deficiencies are observed in the structure. Those which can and should be corrected immediately by a prudent purchaser-investor are as follows:

| | |
|---|---:|
| Floors | $ 300 |
| Interior Construction | 6,000 |
| Lighting | 7,000 |
| Plumbing | 1,000 |
| Heating | 800 |
| Elevators | 2,000 |
| Outside Construction | 300 |
| Total | $17,400 |

This $17,400 represents the total amount of Curable Functional Obsolescence estimated for the building. The deferred maintenance of $34,500 is the amount of Curable Physical Deterioration observed. Any Curable Physical Deterioration or Curable Functional Obsolescence is deducted from the cost new of the individual items, and the percentage of effective age to total economic life is then applied to the remainder.

**Exhibit 17-3**

## Calculation of Incurable Physical Deterioration, Detailed Breakdown Method

| Item | Cost New | Deferred Maintenance | Curable Functional | Effective Age | Incurable Physical |
|------|---------|---------------------|-------------------|--------------|-------------------|
| Excavation | $ 9,550 | $ 0 | $ 0 | 20% | $ 1,910 |
| Foundation | 11,860 | 0 | 0 | 20% | 2,372 |
| Basement Walls | 8,320 | 0 | 0 | 20% | 1,664 |
| Frame | 93,020 | 0 | 0 | 20% | 18,604 |
| Floors | 62,720 | 4,000 | 300 | 30% | 17,526 |
| Floor Covering | 30,340 | 2,000 | 0 | 35% | 9,919 |
| Ceiling | 19,830 | 4,300 | 0 | 20% | 3,066 |
| Roof Structure | 9,319 | 500 | 0 | 20% | 1,764 |
| Roof Covering | 2,272 | 500 | 0 | 35% | 620 |
| Exterior Walls | 108,263 | 4,000 | 0 | 20% | 20,853 |
| Interior Construction | 47,936 | 2,500 | 6,000 | 20% | 7,887 |
| Lighting and Electrical | 31,842 | 3,000 | 7,000 | 30% | 6,553 |
| Plumbing | 42,234 | 5,000 | 1,000 | 20% | 7,247 |
| Heating | 62,468 | 4,000 | 800 | 40% | 23,067 |
| Elevators | 48,680 | 1,700 | 2,000 | 35% | 15,743 |
| Outside Construction | 12,025 | 3,000 | 300 | 20% | 1,745 |
| Architect's Fees, etc. | 36,040 | 0 | 0 | 20% | 7,208 |
| Totals | $636,719 | $34,500 | $17,400 | | $147,748 |

After all curable items have been corrected, the property would still have functional deficiencies that result in an estimated rental income loss of $1,525 per month. The indicated annual Gross Income Multiplier for apartment properties of this type in the current local market is found to be 6.10. Finally, even after accounting for functional and physical deficiencies, it is found that the property suffers an estimated annual rental income loss of $18,000 because of deleterious influences in the local neighborhood, as compared with rental income that could be anticipated in a neighborhood competitively attractive for apartment properties of the type being appraised.

In this instance, the annual GIM of 6.10 is applied first to annual rental income loss attributable to elements of Incurable Functional Obsolescence. Annual income loss is $18,300 (12 × $1,525); and the measure of diminished utility from Incurable Functional Obsolescence is $111,630 (6.10 × $18,300).

Total diminished utility attributable to Environmental Obsolescence for the entire property is $109,800 (6.10 × $18,000). However, only part of this amount is chargeable against the reproduction cost new of the improvements. If it is found that site value typically represents 20% of total property value for similar, competing apartment properties in the current local market, then the charge against the reproduction cost new of the improvements for Environmental Obsolescence is $87,840 (0.80 × $109,800).

The estimate of the present worth or contribution of the improvements in this example can then be derived as indicated in Exhibit 17-4. It should be noted that the order of presenting the deductions for elements of diminished utility in the summary tabulation is not necessarily the order in which the individual elements are estimated and measured. This estimate would not have been possible without a detailed Trade Breakdown estimate of Reproduction Cost New, and a detailed breakdown analysis of diminished utility based on a detailed itemization of structural components and condition provided through careful improvements analysis.

## Uses and Limitations of Cost Analysis and the Cost Approach[20]

### Cost as a Measure of Value

Estimating value or present worth with cost figures is always hazardous. It must be remembered that costs used in this analysis are *production costs*. They are used to measure the contribution of improvements to total property value, and must include *all* costs of production incurred by the most probable type of informed, prudent, and rational purchaser-investor. They therefore include contractor's profit and overhead, financing, and other "waiting" costs during the construction process, as well as direct outlays for labor and materials.

Even when production costs are fully identified and accurately measured, cost and value are not synonymous terms. Cost does not create value, as is

**Exhibit 17-4**

## Summary Estimate of Present Worth (Contribution) of Improvements

| | | | |
|---|---|---|---|
| Reproduction Cost New of Improvements | | | $636,719 |
| *Less* Charges for Diminished Utility | | | |
| Physical Deterioration | | | |
| Curable | $ 34,500 | | |
| Incurable | 147,748 | | |
| Total Physical | | | |
| Deterioration | | 182,248 | |
| | | | |
| Functional Obsolescence | | | |
| Curable | $ 17,400 | | |
| Incurable | 111,630 | | |
| Total Functional | | | |
| Obsolescence | | 129,030 | |
| Environmental Obsolescence | | 87,840 | |
| Total Diminished Utility | | | −$399,118 |
| Indicated Present Worth of Improvements | | | $237,601 |

evidenced by the many instances of inappropriate improvements whose costs of production exceed their present worth or market value. Under the proper conditions, cost new may be a legitimate *measure* of value: when new improvements represent the Highest and Best Use of the site.

**The "Upper Limit" Argument.** It has been argued in past appraisal literature that cost tends to set the upper limit to value. This is predicated on the position that the informed and rational purchaser-investor would pay no more for an improved property than the cost to him of having a replica or substitute property with the same utility produced. This argument has basic validity when it is applied to cost new, and the cost figure includes *all* costs, as indicated above.

However, a logical jump is sometimes made to conclude that the Cost *Approach* estimate of value tends to set the upper limit to value. This is simply not true. Since the estimate of value in the Cost Approach is highly dependent on the estimation of the present worth of the improvements through the measurement of diminished utility, there is absolutely no guarantee that the appraiser will never overestimate the amount to be charged against cost new for diminished utility. The income property appraiser must guard carefully against this error.

*Uses of Cost New Estimates*

In many instances, the income-property appraiser requires an estimate of cost new (especially but not necessarily Reproduction Cost New) to carry out a necessary part of his valuation analysis. When this requirement is encountered, the estimate of cost new should be developed with one of the methods described in this chapter. The sources of data used should be entirely reliable, and the data supported with market evidence as much as possible.

**Build vs. Buy Decisions.** In investment analysis for purchaser-investors, one realistic alternative for the client in many instances is to build (or have built) a new structure on a vacant site, rather than buying an existing improved property. The basis for making a comparative judgment on which to base the decision will be the estimated cost new of the new structure. It is frequently more useful in such cases to hypothesize a replacement structure rather than a replica of the existing one, which means that the appraiser must estimate Replacement Cost New rather than Reproduction Cost New. Whichever is most appropriate, however, the estimate must be based on detailed description and itemized specifications of the structure to make sure that all items of cost are included in their proper amounts.

**Land Residual Technique of Income Capitalization.** The Land Residual Technique of Income Capitalization discussed in Chapter 12 requires the appraiser to develop an estimate of cost new of improvements that represent the Highest and Best Use of the site. Here, too, detailed specifications are required so that a cost estimate reflecting current local costs can be developed.

**Feasibility of Renovation or Conversion.** When an investment decision concerning proposed renovation or conversion of existing improvements is to be made, one essential ingredient in the information required to make a comparative analysis and evaluation is the cost of carrying out the renovation or conversion program. This must also be based on detailed specifications, using current local unit costs and prices.

**Cost Approach Analysis.** It has been demonstrated clearly and forcibly in this chapter that any Cost Approach analysis seeking to estimate the value of an existing improved property must start with a fully justified and supportable estimate of Reproduction Cost New of the improvements. Without such an estimate in the degree of detail necessary to carry out the measurement of diminished utility, an estimate of property value using the Cost Approach cannot be defended.

*Uses of Cost Approach Analysis*

Despite its limitations and restrictions, Cost Approach analysis does have a role in the total arsenal of tools available to the income-property appraiser for potential use in solving a particular appraisal problem.

**Special-Purpose, No-Market Properties.** It is frequently maintained that Cost Approach analysis is the only way to approach the valuation of special-purpose improved properties, especially those so specialized that they may be regarded as no-market properties. This argument is certainly applicable to the estimation of cost new, and its use as the indicator of the probable upper limit to value. However, an estimate of value using Cost Approach analysis requires market support and justification for the several elements of diminished utility charged against Reproduction Cost New. If there is truly no competitive market for the type of property being appraised, then the estimate of diminished utility is based on the appraiser's own judgment rather than that of the market. Certainly such an estimate cannot be defended as representing Market Value. And if the property is producing net income, its present worth can be estimated as readily with income capitalization analysis as it can be with Cost Approach analysis.

**New or Proposed Construction.** When an income property is to be appraised from plans or blueprints and specifications, cost analysis provides one indicator of probable Market Value, provided the appraiser can support and defend the proposition that the improvements when completed would represent the Highest and Best Use of the site. In such a situation, of course, the appraiser would be using cost new without the necessity to identify and measure elements of diminished utility.

**Ad Valorem Tax Valuation.** Real property taxation in most jurisdictions in the United States is based on the "value" of the property, from which the assessment for tax purposes is derived. It is common (and indeed required by many state legislatures and assessing officers) to separate site (land) and improvements (buildings) in valuing the property for tax purposes. Although similar results might well be achieved through income capitalization analysis with the building residual technique, Cost Approach analysis is useful when it is absolutely necessary to develop separate estimates of site and improvements. This same requirement is often present in the application of income taxes, when the point at issue is the amount of capital gain realized by an investor (or a decedent) at the time of disposition of his property.

**Basis for Depreciation Charges.** It has been noted earlier in Chapters 12 and 13, and is mentioned again in Chapter 18, that accounting depreciation charges for income-tax purposes may be levied by an owner-investor against only that portion of his property investment represented by the improvements. Land or site investment is not recoverable under income tax regulations, and is therefore not depreciable. As a result, a purchaser-investor in income-producing real estate needs an indication of the present worth of the improvements in his total property investment in order to establish a legally defensible pattern of depreciation charges that is as attractive to him as possible. Cost Approach analysis offers one alternative means for identifying the present worth of the improvements.

**Eminent Domain and Condemnation.** When public bodies, including some private organizations "affected with the public interest" such as public utilities, seek to acquire private property rights through the exercise of the right of eminent domain, the private property owner frequently resists. The matter then goes to court under condemnation proceedings. In most jurisdictions (federal and state), the courts have consistently held that it is both necessary and proper to separate site and improvements in identifying the value of the rights being acquired by the condemning authority. Whatever the merits of this position, it remains a part of the environment within which income-property appraisers making appraisals in eminent domain cases must operate. In this area of appraisal activity, Cost Approach analysis is frequently necessary to provide one basis for assigning separate values or present worth figures to site and improvements, even when greater reliance is placed on some other framework of analysis to develop the estimate of property value.

*Limitations of Cost Approach Analysis*

**Market Data Requirements: Redundancy.** The essence of Cost Approach analysis is the identification and measurement of diminished utility to estimate the present worth or contribution of the improvements to total property value, over and above the value of the site. To measure diminished utility properly and convincingly, the appraiser must have evidence from the market that indicates what differences in sales prices or rentals (or both) of similar, competitive properties in the same current market can be attributed to the presence or absence of the characteristic or condition being measured. This information is precisely what is used in Direct Sales Comparison analysis, and frequently in Income Capitalization analysis as well. In other words, the appraiser has the needed data to carry out at least Direct Sales Comparison analysis before he can legitimately undertake a Cost Approach analysis. To this extent, an attempt to estimate property value through Cost Approach analysis is redundant, and adds little or nothing to the credibility of the appraiser's estimate of property value.

If the necessary market evidence is not available, then a value estimate based on Cost Approach analysis cannot legitimately be regarded as Market Value. In such cases, present worth can also be derived through Income Capitalization analysis.

**Orientation to the Past.** Income-producing real estate has value because it is anticipated or forecast to be capable of producing a net income stream over some future period. Purchaser-investors in income properties are future-oriented. The valuation of income properties is directed primarily toward estimating the present worth of the forecast future net income stream of the property. Yet with all this future orientation, Cost Approach analysis is essentially oriented toward the past.

It does estimate site value in terms of its indicated present worth if vacant and available to be put to its Highest and Best Use, but the derivation of the indicated present worth or contribution of the improvements is almost entirely past-oriented. Once remaining economic life of the improvements is identified through careful and detailed improvements analysis, its only real use in Cost Approach analysis is to subtract it from estimated total economic life to derive the effective age of the several functional components of the structure. This effective age is used essentially to estimate the amount of utility represented by total economic life that has already been "used up" as of the valuation date. Indeed, the Cost Approach can almost be regarded as a form of Building Residual in reverse: the present worth of the improvements is the difference between the total utility they would have if they were brand new and appropriate improvements as of the valuation date, and the amount of utility that must be deducted because they are not brand new and do not (often) represent the Highest and Best Use of the site.

**Indirect Measurement of Contribution of Improvements.** The contribution or present worth of improvements in Cost Approach analysis is measured indirectly. By direct estimation of the dollar amount of diminished utility represented by the improvements in their present condition, their present worth is the residual after deducting diminished utility from Reproduction Cost New. It was noted earlier in this chapter that the present worth or contribution of the improvements is better estimated by deducting site value from total property value. This is usually a sterile exercise, however, since the typical objective of income-property appraisal analysis is to estimate property value, and not to measure either the present worth of the improvements or the amount of diminished utility they have experienced as of the valuation date.

## Review Exercises

1. A 10-story office building has a foundation area of 8,250 square feet. The site contains 25,100 square feet.
   a. What is the floor area ratio?
   b. What is the site coverage ratio?
2. A one-story industrial warehouse contains 12,000 square feet of total floor area. Office space occupies 1,200 square feet of floor area. Exterior walls are 20 feet high. The building dimensions are 80' by 150'. Interior ceiling heights are 18 feet, clear span. There are two loading docks. The roof is flat, of built-up construction.

Unit costs of construction now are identified on an installed basis as follows:

| | |
|---|---|
| Foundation: | $1.10 per square foot of foundation area |
| Exterior Walls: | $2.40 per square foot of wall area |
| Roof and Roofing: | $4.35 per square foot of roof area |
| Electrical System and Wiring: | $10,000 |
| Electrical Outlets: | 40 at $12.50 each |
| Plumbing and Sewage: | $6,000 |
| Heating System: | $7,500 |
| Cooling and Ventilation System: | $5,000 |
| Interior Finish of Office Space: | $7.20 per square foot of office area |
| Painting and Decorating: | $2,500 |
| Plumbing Fixtures: | 6 at $250 each |
| Loading Docks, Bays, and Doors: | 2 at $8,000 each |

Total indirect costs, including contractor's overhead and profits, are estimated at 22% of total direct costs.

a. What are total direct costs of construction new?
b. What are total indirect costs?
c. What is the total Reproduction Cost New of this structure?
d. What is the indicated cost new per square foot for this warehouse?

3. The warehouse in Problem 2 has an effective age of 15 years. The remaining economic life of the structure is estimated at 35 years. The electrical system will have to be replaced in 15 years, and the entire structure will most probably have to be redecorated in 5 years. The plumbing fixtures have a remaining economic life of 10 years.

There is observed deferred maintenance in the roof of $500, in the office area amounting to $600, and some painting costing $300 should be done immediately. The electrical outlets are outmoded and should be replaced immediately.

a. Indicate the amount of Curable Physical Deterioration in the structure.
b. Indicate the amount of Curable Functional Obsolescence in the structure.
c. Set up a detailed table showing the amount of Incurable Physical Deterioration experienced by each major component part of the structure.
d. Indicate total Incurable Physical Deterioration observed in the structure.

4. Because of problems in interior design, and the positioning and size of loading and docking facilities, it is estimated from market evidence that the subject warehouse in Problems 2 and 3 rents for 10¢ per square foot per year *less* than do similar, competing warehouses with more acceptable design and loading facilities. Moreover, heating and ventilating expenses in this structure are 2¢ per square foot per year *more* than in standard buildings in the same market area. Warehouse properties of this type have been selling for approximately 5.75 times gross annual rentals.

a. What is the amount of observed Incurable Functional Obsolescence in this structure?

5. a. For the warehouse building analyzed in Problems 2, 3, and 4, show a summary tabulation of total diminished utility by major category.
   b. Indicate the present worth or contribution to total property value of this warehouse building, as of the valuation date.

## Supplementary Readings

American Institute of Real Estate Appraisers, *The Appraisal of Real Estate*, fifth edition (Chicago: American Institute of Real Estate Appraisers, 1967), Chapters 10-14.

Byron M. Church, "What Cost Approach?" *The Real Estate Appraiser*, Volume 34, Number 4, July-August 1968.

Max J. Derbes, Jr., "Accrued Depreciation: Classical Method," *The Real Estate Appraiser*, Volume 31, Number 8, August 1965.

Max J. Derbes, Jr., "Accrued Depreciation: Practical Considerations," *The Real Estate Appraiser*, Volume 32, Number 4, April 1966.

Lloyd D. Hanford, Jr., "Depreciation: Fact or Fiction?" *The Real Estate Appraiser*, Volume 31, Number 11, November 1965.

Sanders A. Kahn, Frederick E. Case, and Alfred Schimmel, *Real Estate Appraisal and Investment* (New York: Ronald Press, 1963), Chapters 13, 14, 21, and 31; Appendixes A, C, and N.

William N. Kinnard, Jr., *A Guide to Appraising Apartments,* third edition (Chicago: Society of Real Estate Appraisers, 1973), pp. 26-30.

William N. Kinnard, Jr. and Stephen D. Messner, *Industrial Real Estate,* second edition (Washington, D.C.: Society of Industrial Realtors, 1971), Chapters 3 and 4; pp. 411-420 and 461-463

William N. Kinnard, Jr., *An Introduction to Appraising Real Property* (Chicago: Society of Real Estate Appraisers, 1968), Chapters 12, 15-17.

John D. O'Flaherty, "An Appraiser's Dilemma: The Cost Approach to Value," *The Real Estate Appraiser*, Volume 35, Number 1, January-December 1969.

Joseph B. Prussiano, "Blueprint Reading," *The Real Estate Appraiser*, Volume 34, Number 3, March 1968.

Alfred A. Ring, *The Valuation of Real Estate*, second edition (Englewood Cliffs, N.J.: Prentice-Hall, 1970), Chapters 11-13.

William M. Shenkel, *A Guide to Appraising Industrial Property* (Chicago: Society of Real Estate Appraisers, 1967), pp. 45-78.

William M. Shenkel, "The Depreciation Estimate: A Reconsideration," *The Real Estate Appraiser*, Volume 34, Number 7, July-August 1968.

S.M. Schwarz, "Analysis of Economic Life," *The Real Estate Appraiser*, Volume 34, Number 4, April 1968.

Carl R. Trowbridge, "The Fallacies of Depreciation," *The Real Estate Appraiser*, Volume 31, Number 12, December 1965.

Edward L. White, "Appraising from Plans and Specifications," *The Real Estate Appraiser*, Volume 32, Number 6, June 1966.

## Notes

1. See, for example, American Institute of Real Estate Appraisers, *The Appraisal of Real Estate*, fifth edition (Chicago: American Institute of Real Estate Appraisers, 1967), Chapters 10-14; Sanders A. Kahn, Frederick E. Case, and Alfred Schimmel, *Real Estate Appraisal and Investment* (New York: Ronald Press, 1963), Chapters 13, 14, 21, and 31, Appendixes A, C, and N; William N. Kinnard, Jr., *An Introduction to Appraising Real Property* (Chicago: Society of Real Estate Appraisers, 1968), Chapters 12, 15-17; and Alfred A. Ring, *The Valuation of Real Estate*, second edition (Englewood Cliffs, N.J.: Prentice-Hall, 1970), Chapters 11-13.

2. More background details are provided in Kinnard, *Appraising Real Property*, Chapter 15.

3. Examples are provided in AIREA, *Appraisal of Real Estate*; Kahn, Case, and Schimmel, *Real Estate Appraisal and Investment*; and Ring, *Valuation of Real Estate*.

4. Because the presentation in this section is essentially a review, readers may wish to seek a fuller discussion of the process. See, for example, AIREA, *Appraisal of Real Estate*, Chapter 14; or Kinnard, *Appraising Real Property*, Chapters 15 and 17.

5. Society of Real Estate Appraisers, *Real Estate Appraisal Principles and Terminology* (Chicago: Society of Real Estate Appraisers, 1960), p. 48.

6. *Ibid.*, p. 48.

7. For more details, consult AIREA, *Appraisal of Real Estate*, Chapter 12; Kinnard, *Appraising Real Property*, Chapter 15; and Ring, *Valuation of Real Estate*, Chapter 12.

8. The term "Diminished Utility" is preferred to the more widely used and traditional "Accrued Depreciation" because the latter can cause confusion with

the "Depreciation" allowable as an accounting charge in the calculation of Taxable Net Income (Chapters 6 and 18), and with the "Depreciation" representing forecast capital loss on resale of the property in Ellwood analysis (Chapters 13 and 18). For a fuller explanation of the concept of Diminished Utility and its meaning, see Kinnard, *Appraising Real Property*, Chapter 16.

9. For more details on the elements of diminished utility (accrued depreciation) and the alternative methods available for measuring them, see AIREA, *Appraisal of Real Estate*, Chapter 13; and Kinnard, *Appraising Real Property*, Chapter 16.

10. SREA, *Principles and Terminology*, p. 72.

11. See, for example, AIREA, *Appraisal of Real Estate*, Chapter 13.

12. Kinnard, *Appraising Real Property*, Chapter 16.

13. Examples may be found in Shenkel, *Appraising Industrial Property*, pp. 63-66; and William N. Kinnard, Jr. and Stephen D. Messner, *Industrial Real Estate*, second edition (Washington, D.C.: Society of Industrial Realtors, 1971), pp. 180-182 and 254-256.

14. For further details, see J. Warren Higgins, *Impact of Federal Taxation on Real Estate Decisions* (Storrs, Connecticut: Center for Real Estate and Urban Economic Studies, University of Connecticut; 1971).

15. More details and examples are provided in Kinnard, *Appraising Real Property*, Chapter 15; and Shenkel, *Appraising Industrial Property*, pp. 52-54.

16. The three leading published cost services for income properties, all of which provide monthly cost index supplements to enable the appraiser to adjust currently for local market conditions, are: *Boeckh Building Cost Manual* (Milwaukee: Boeckh Division, American Appraisal Co.; 1967), Volume I: "Residential and Agricultural," Volume II: "Commercial," and Volume III: "Industrial and Institutional"; *Dow Building Cost Calculator and Valuation Guide* (New York: McGraw-Hill Information Systems Co., quarterly); and *Marshall Valuation Service* (Los Angeles: Marshall and Swift Publication Co., monthly). The Boeckh *Manual* has a supplementary monthly *Building Cost Modifier*.

17. The IRS Guidelines, amended slightly in terms of the Revenue Act of 1969, may be found in *Prentice-Hall 1971 Federal Tax Course* (Englewood Cliffs, N.J.: Prentice-Hall, 1970), pp. 2026-2030.

18. See, for example, AIREA, *Appraisal of Real Estate*, Chapter 13; and Kinnard, *Appraising Real Property*, Chapter 16.

19. Additional examples of estimating diminished utility (accrued depreciation) with both detailed breakdown analysis and simpler age-life methods may be found in AIREA, *Appraisal of Real Estate*, pp. 207-218; Ring, *Valuation of Real Estate*, pp. 187-194; and Shenkel, *Appraising Industrial Property*, pp. 47-50, 54-60, and 71-76.

20. See also AIREA, *Appraisal of Real Estate*, Chapter 14; Kinnard, *Appraising Real Property*, Chapter 17; and Shenkel, *Appraising Industrial Property*, pp. 45-78.

# 18 Income Capitalization Analysis for Income and Investment Property Valuation

Income-producing real estate has value to potential purchasers and owners because it is forecast to be capable of producing a future flow of net income for the benefit of the owner. This is its distinguishing characteristic from amenity or public-use properties. While it is possible and frequently feasible to estimate the value of income properties through Direct Sales Comparison analysis, and sometimes useful and proper to use Cost Approach analysis in making value estimates as well, the fact remains that the typical purchaser of income property is an investor. He looks to the property to generate net income to support his investment in the property rights he has acquired, and to provide him with at least a competitive rate of return on that investment over his projected investment holding period. Therefore, the emphasis in valuing those future income receipts rests with the capitalization process as the analytical approach that most nearly corresponds to the thinking and behavior of purchaser-investors in the market for the type of property being appraised.

### Review of the Income Capitalization Process
### Applied to Market Value Estimation

The bulk of this book has been concerned with explaining and demonstrating the tools of analysis that together comprise income capitalization for income-producing real estate. The elements of the Income Capitalization process were introduced and outlined in Chapter 4. Each of the several components was developed in detail in Chapters 5-11, and the applications of the techniques based on these components were demonstrated in Chapters 12 and 13. Throughout that presentation, the focus has been on the estimation of Market Value as defined and used in real property appraising.

It has been shown that when verified, reliable market data are obtained by the appraiser and applied in Income Capitalization analysis, the resulting value estimate is a representation of what a typically informed, prudent and rational purchaser-investor of the type most likely to be attracted to the type of property being appraised would pay for the rights in question, under the current local market conditions prevailing as of the valuation date. This is Market Value. Whether Income Capitalization is considered to be a separate "approach" to Market Value estimation, or simply one variant of a single general "market approach," is irrelevant. The important point is that in forecasting future income receipts most likely to be produced by the property under absentee ownership with typically competent management, and discounting those future income receipts to a present worth estimate with rates of discount reflecting typical

383

384

investor expectations and requirements, the appraiser is simulating the thought processes and market behavior of representative purchaser-investors in the market. Buying the right to receive an income stream of specified characteristics does indeed represent one realistic alternative course of action for the purchaser-investor, and it does depict the way purchasers of income properties think and act.

*Present Worth of Forecast*
*Future Income Receipts*

However defined, whether as Market Value or Investment Value, the value of income property is always the present worth of the anticipated future net income receipts forecast to be produced by the property over a specified period of time. The essence of the Income Capitalization process, which is applicable in the valuation of *any* income property, is to identify the several components of forecast future income receipts and to discount them at the appropriate rates using the proper discounting procedures to a present worth estimate.

**What is Valued.** The owner of an interest in real estate possesses certain enforceable rights in the realty. Any such claim that carries with it the right to receive some or all of the forecast future income to be produced by an income property can be valued by income capitalization. The amount and character of the future income receivable by the owner of the rights specified are the benefits to be derived from owning those rights. The present worth estimate is the capitalized value of the forecast future income receipts, but it is a measure of the value of those ownership rights, whatever their origin, duration or character.

**Value to Whom.** The present worth or value of a given forecast future income stream is its value to the holder of the rights to the receipt of that income. The holder of the rights may be the owner of the fee simple estate, a lessor, a lessee, a mortgagee, or the holder of an easement or a lien. Moreover, his rights may be those of a representative market participant (in which case the Market Value of the rights can usually be estimated legitimately), or he may be a specific market participant with specific standards and objectives (in which case the present worth figure is the Investment Value of those rights). The point is that different values of many different types or degrees of interests in income-producing real estate may be derived from the identical mechanical process known as Income Capitalization. It is a highly flexible and adaptable analytical process for income property valuation. Only the data inputs change as the interests and the nature of the value to be estimated change.

*Tools of Analysis*

However complicated or involved Income Capitalization may become as the requirements of the specific appraisal assignment dictate, the basic valuation formula which the appraiser ultimately applies is the same. It is the simple formulation: $V = I/R$. The bulk of the appraiser's data-gathering and analysis in applying the Income Capitalization process is to identify the appropriate quantities to insert as $I$ and $R$ in the equation.

**Income Forecasting.** Probably the most demanding and time-consuming part of Income Capitalization analysis is to derive the forecast of future net income receipts. The appraiser must ascertain *how much* is to be received, *in what form, when,* and *by whom.* This has been expressed in Chapter 6 in particular as the identification (and justification of that identification) of the amount of net income receivable, the timing of the income receipts, the duration of the time period over which the income is forecast to be received, the probable stability or variability of the income stream, and finally the degree of certainty or risk associated with the forecasts of the other characteristics of the net income receipts.

Separating income forecasts into these analytical components helps to reinforce the appreciation of Income Capitalization analysis as a flexible and highly adaptable tool for the income-property appraiser. *Any* type of income flow of any size and character, receivable by any claimant, can be identified and evaluated for capitalization or discounting to a present worth estimate. The many illustrative examples provided in Chapters 5 through 13 clearly support this important point.

**Rates of Capitalization and Discount.** The purchaser-investor must be compensated for giving up the use of his funds, for foregoing alternative investment opportunities, for undertaking the burdens of investment management, and for assuming the risk(s) that actual income receipts will not materialize as favorably as the forecasts would indicate. This necessary compensation is reflected in rates of capitalization or discounting determined largely by market competition. Because income receipts are normally forecast to be generated over finite time periods only by income-producing real estate, the purchaser-investor typically seeks rates of return that offer both a competitive or specified return *on* the investment in the property (representing the required compensations enumerated above) and a return *of* any forecast capital loss over the income projection period, so that his original investment capital is recovered intact at the end of that income projection period.

Rates of capitalization and discount used in Income Capitalization analysis for income-producing real estate incorporate both types of return. This has been extensively demonstrated in Chapter 5 and Chapters 8 through 13. The many illustrative examples provided in those chapters have indicated that the capitalization or discounting process is equipped to deal with any time period of income projection, any foreseeable degree of perceived risk, any known competitive rate of return, and any method of providing for recovery of forecast capital loss. Once again, the analytical framework is identical whatever the problem; only the data inputs in the formulas need vary as the requirements of the problem dictate.

*Selection of Method(s) to Apply*

In brief, the tools of analysis available to the appraiser for applying the Income Capitalization process to the valuation of interests in income-producing real estate cover every known possibility of income forecast and purchaser-investor requirement. Indeed, as the discussions in Chapters 12 and 13 in particular have shown, the income-property appraiser really has more tools at his disposal than are necessary—and possibly than are desirable. As a result, he must select the particular "package" of analytical tools that is peculiarly applicable and responsive to the specific appraisal problem confronting him. Each method or technique has its particular applications and limitations, which the appraiser must recognize. Some are more widely adaptable than others, however, and this must also be recognized.

**Income Streams as a Series of Reversions.** Future income receipts are discounted to present worth estimates at rates reflecting compensation for time and liquidity preference, investment management expense, and assumption of risk. The *process* of discounting is based on the strict mathematical rules of compound interest and discounting, as explained in Chapter 5. The most useful single tool in the income-property appraiser's kit is the Present Worth of One factor. Given the market-determined *rate* of discount, income projection period, and periodicity of income receipts (or those specified by the investor-client), *any* future income stream of whatever character or variability can be treated mechanically as a series of individual reversions. This has been demonstrated in Chapters 5 and 11 in particular, but it bears repeating here because it is most important.

Once the dollar amount and timing of each income payment have been identified, the present worth of each can be calculated readily by simply multiplying the dollar amount by the Present Worth of One factor at the rate of discount specified, over the time period in question, with discounting in terms of the length of income periods specified. As a review, assume that an income payment in the amount of $4,000 is receivable monthly for five years, and that the appropriate Discount Rate has been identified as 11.5%. The Present Worth of One factor applicable to each monthly payment of $4,000 is the monthly factor at 11.5% for the number of months in the future that the individual $4,000 payment is receivable. The payment receivable seven months hence has a Present Worth of One factor of 0.935415, while that receivable three years (36 months) hence has a Present Worth of One factor of 0.709834, and so forth (Ellwood, page 137, column 4).

The present worth of each $4,000 monthly payment would be calculated ($3,741.66 for the payment seven months hence; $2,839.34 for the payment 36 months hence; and so forth), and the 60 present worth figures for the five-year income stream summed to derive the present worth of the entire income stream.

Of course, the appraiser need not go through this lengthy mechanical process when a level income stream is forecast. Instead, he may apply the monthly Present Worth of One per Annum factor at 11.5% for five years of 45.469824 (Ellwood, page 137, column 5) to the $4,000 monthly payment to derive the present worth of the five-year income stream: $4,000 × 45.469824 = $181,879.30. It has already been demonstrated in Chapter 5 that a Present Worth of One per Annum factor is the sum of the Present Worth of One factors over the specified time period at the specified rate of discount.

The point here is that *any* income stream of whatever character or variability can be valued by treating it as a series of reversions and applying the appropriate Present Worth of One factors to each of the individual forecast payments. The present worth of the income stream is then the sum of the present worths of the individual payments. Whenever the income-property appraiser has any doubt about the propriety of using any other form of income capitalization method, he can and should treat the forecast future income receipts as a series of reversions.

**Level Annuity Capitalization.** While it is mechanically possible to treat future income streams as declining annuities of a special type by using Straight-Line Capital Recovery, or as special types of sinking funds by using Sinking Fund Capital Recovery, neither of these methods of capitalization is usually supportable from the evidence of market behavior of purchaser-investors. The only form of income stream capitalization that has the weight of market evidence and mathematical acceptability behind it is Level Annuity Capitalization, using the Present Worth of One per Annum factor at the indicated Discount Rate.

Whenever it appears that the future income stream cannot be forecast as a level annuity, even with compensation for additional risk of non-achievement built into the Discount Rate, then the only realistic alternative for the appraiser is to handle the income stream as a series of individual reversions.

However, it is frequently both possible and appropriate to "stabilize" forecast NOI to a level annuity amount. It is important in any event for the appraiser to confine his analysis and evaluation of forecast income flows to the estimate of $I$ in the valuation equation, and not compensate for uncertainty on his (the appraiser's) part by adjusting $R$. If the level and character of future net income are forecast effectively, it is rarely necessary or appropriate to use any method other than Level Annuity Capitalization.

**Identification of Residuals.** Every method of income capitalization except Direct Capitalization with an Overall Rate requires the appraiser to identify some "residual" portion of the property or the investment, and to proceed to capitalize the "residual" income attributable or assignable to that portion in order to develop an estimate of property value. If the appraiser is to reflect the thinking and behavior of typical or most probable purchaser-investors in the market, he must be extremely cautious about using physical residual techniques of income capitalization. Income properties are single economic entities that produce the forecast income stream only with the components of the property in their particular combination and relationship to one another. Separating the physical components of the real estate and valuing each separately, even if "for purposes of analysis only," runs the risk of developing value estimates that neither reflect nor respond to the actions of market participants.

It is often necessary for the appraiser to separate the property into analytical components because the nature of the appraisal problem requires it. Otherwise, however, physical residual techniques are dangerous and potentially misleading. This is particularly true of the Land Residual Technique, in which the residual value of the land or site is subject to wide variations as minor changes in data inputs occur.

Whenever possible, therefore (and it usually is), the appraiser should employ property residual analysis if the physical or legal components of the property are the primary focus of the analysis, and mortgage-equity analysis if the financial or investment components are perceived as most important. If the techniques are applied properly and the same data inputs are used, the results should be virtually identical. This is hardly surprising, and indeed is one test of the validity of the techniques in the first place.

Property Residual and Mortgage-Equity techniques have the further advantage of forcing the appraiser to make an explicit judgment about the amount, character, and timing of any lump-sum reversion forecast. It is easy to fall into the trap of assuming no change in site value at the end of the remaining economic life of the improvements, as is implicit in the other physical residual techniques. Historical evidence and apparently continuing expectations of income-property investors indicate that this assumption is rarely supportable.

**Overall Rates and Direct Capitalization.** Whenever market data and evidence permit him to do so, the appraiser is best advised to avoid complex and involved methods of income capitalization, and use instead Direct Capitalization with an Overall Rate. The simple Overall Rate development method demonstrated in Chapter 9 is probably most justifiable to others, provided the relatively stringent data requirements can be met. Failing this, the appraiser can and should investigate the possibilities of applying Mortgage-Equity analysis to develop an appropriate Overall Rate of Capitalization. This can be done with or without the Ellwood formula, as has been shown in Chapter 13.

Because of the potential complexities of Income Capitalization analysis as a mechanical process, it is sometimes possible to lose sight of the fact that the basic valuation formula is both simple and straightforward: $V = I/R$. All of the complications arise from the frequent necessity to derive $R$ indirectly and in parts. If it is possible to develop $R$ directly through market evidence or through Mortgage-Equity analysis, the appraiser should do so. Aside from producing a value estimate much more readily explained to others, he also minimizes the risks of technical or mechanical errors in his calculations.

**Market Responsiveness.** Income capitalization is not undertaken as an interesting intellectual exercise, stimulating and challenging though it may be to the appraiser. The ultimate objective is to develop a defensible and convincing estimate of value, as defined, measured by the present worth of the forecast future income stream. That estimate must be responsive to the requirements, objectives, and behavior of purchaser-investors observed in the market. Many income capitalization techniques developed and used in the past are proxies for reliable and verified information about investor market behavior. If the analysis and the value estimate based on it are to be responsive to the actions and needs of the market, they must reflect such actions and needs through the best possible market data obtainable by the appraiser. The manipulation of figures or the insertion of simplifying assumptions is no substitute for such data.

The simplest, most direct, and most descriptive techniques of income capitalization are therefore the best. Other, more abstract methods such as the physical residual techniques may be necessary in some instances, but they must always be used with caution and sensitivity to the implications of their underlying assumptions.

## Investment Value and Investment Analysis

The point has been made many times throughout this book, and especially in the Chapters dealing with Income Capitalization analysis, that precisely the same methods and techniques useful in estimating Market Value with market data can be used to estimate Investment Value. The only real difference is that Investment Value is based on data specific to a particular investor and/or property. It is the present worth to a specific investor of specific rights in a specific property, given the requirements and expectations of that investor.

In addition, however, there are tools and techniques of analysis applicable only to the estimation of Investment Value, and of use only in making investment decisions.

### Value to the Investor

Investment Value is the present worth of a specified income stream to a specific investor. The estimate is used to assist the investor in deciding whether or not to make a particular investment.

**Forecast Income Stream.** The income stream forecast for use in deriving an Investment Value estimate is the one anticipated, or most likely to be anticipated, by the particular investor through whose eyes the appraiser is viewing and judging the property. The Net Operating Income and the reversion may be the same as those used in estimating Market Value, or they may be specific to the particular investor. Either Market Rentals, Contract Rentals, or some other rental figure may be used. Specific management skills rather than typically competent management may be assumed. Vacancy and income loss allowances may or may not be based on market experience and standards; the same applies to Operating Expenses. The point is that the appraiser must identify carefully, usually in consultation with the investor-client, precisely what income forecasts are to be used. Indeed, investment analysis may well involve estimating the present worth of several alternative possible income streams, with some assignment of probabilities to the achievement of each.

Whatever the income stream forecast, the same process of estimating the quantities involved and the same categories of income and expenses must be used by the appraiser. The difference lies in the actual dollar figures assigned to the individual items.

Most purchaser-investors are particularly interested in cash flows rather than Net Operating Income. As a result, Investment Value estimation nearly always requires the appraiser to forecast Cash Throw-Off to Equity (Before-Tax Cash Flow). In most instances, the investor is also deeply interested in how much cash he will ultimately be able to keep. This means that After-Tax Cash Flow, which is not a part of Market Value estimation, is often included as part of the income forecasting process for estimating Investment Value.

**Specific Terms of Financing.** It has been pointed out in Chapters 4 and 7, and throughout the discussion of income capitalization thereafter, that the package of mortgage (debt) financing terms can and does have a considerable influence on the present worth estimate. When Market Value is to be estimated, the pattern of mortgage financing terms must be that which the most probable type of purchaser-investor in the type of property being appraised would most probably obtain, under prevailing market conditions as of the valuation date. These constraints do not apply in investment analysis and the estimation of Investment Value.

Instead, the appraiser should use the pattern of financing terms most likely to be obtainable on the current market by the specific investor who is the focus of the analysis. Once again, an important aspect of the appraiser's contribution to his investor-client's decision-making process is to indicate the implications for present worth or Investment Value of alternative possible financing patterns.

**Income Projection Period.** The income projection period, and hence the period of capital recovery, used in Investment Value analysis is the one specified by the investor-client. It may be the remaining economic life of improvements or the remaining term of a lease, but it is equally likely to be one influenced by income-tax turnover period considerations. Depending on the degree of tax sophistication of the investor and the certainty of his own thinking and expectations, the investment analysis may well incorporate different investment holding (income projection) periods. The appraiser can then indicate the cash flow implications of each to help the investor-client make his final investment decision.

**Required Rate(s) of Return.** Rates of return and rates of discount used in Investment Value estimation are based on specific requirements or expectations provided by the investor-client. A Discount Rate can be developed, and Capitalization Rates based on it can be employed, using the mortgage constant and the equity yield rate specified. Here, too, alternative patterns and combinations can be calculated to indicate to the investor what the implications and probabilities of achieving varying sets of results might be.

By far the most important rate of return used in Investment Value analysis is the equity yield rate specified by the investor as required or sought. Investors are really interested in property value only incidentally to discovering the value, rate of return on, and probable future value of the required or anticipated equity investment. Once the equity yield rate is specified, any of the several alternative techniques and methods of estimating the present worth of the equity position can then be employed. This is the focus of the investor's interest, because it indicates how much he can or should pay in cash or equity down-payment for the property. It is therefore also the focus of investment analysis and the estimation of Investment Value.

**Illustrative Example.** The possible variations in data inputs, and hence in present worth or Investment Value estimates, are virtually limitless. With electronic data processing and computing equipment available, the investment analysis alternatives that the appraiser can consider for his investor-client are limited only by the time, money, and technical skills at their disposal. As a practical matter, the range of realistic alternatives is usually relatively small, and the entire set of comparisons can be calculated in hours or even minutes with only an electronic desk calculator and a good set of compound interest factor tables such as are provided in Part II of the third edition of the *Ellwood Tables*.

Simply to illustrate some of the ways in which data inputs can be varied throughout the framework of income capitalization analysis to reflect a specific investor's expectations or requirements, or to evaluate realistically possible alternatives, consider the income and financial aspects of the investment property that was used as a continuing example throughout Chapters 9–13. It will be recalled the property investment had the following characteristics:

Net Operating Income ($I$ or $d$): $15,000
Income Projection Period ($n$): 15 years
Equity Yield Rate ($y$): 10%
Mortgage Interest Rate ($i$): 8.5%
Mortgage Loan-to-Value Ratio ($m$): 70%
Mortgage Amortization Period: Monthly
Mortgage Maturity: 20 years
Mortgage Constant ($F$): 10.41%
Level Annuity Factor (10%, 15 years, annual): 7.6061
Reversion in 15 Years: 70% of present property value
Present Worth of One Factor (10%, 15 years): 0.2394

Sinking Fund Factor (10%, 15 years): 0.0315
Installment to Amortize One Factor (10%, 15 years): 0.1315
Discount Rate ($r$): 9% (rounded from 8.95%)
Level Annuity Factor (9%, 15 years, annual): 8.0607

All of this information is market-derived and market-based, so that the indicated present worth of the annual income stream plus reversion represents Market Value. The calculated Overall Rate based on mortgage-equity analysis with equity build-up and allowance of capital recovery was shown in Chapter 13 to be 9.97%. The identical Composite Overall Rate was developed through the Ellwood formula. The Market Value of the property, based on the application of the Overall Rate to NOI, was estimated to be $150,000 ($15,000/.0997 = $150,451.35).

The valuation of this investment property through the Property Residual technique was also illustrated in Chapter 13. In this case, the indicated Market Value was found to be $148,000.

The identical techniques and procedures can be used to indicate the Investment Value of this same property to a specific investor, in terms of his standards and expectations. Suppose that an investor considering the purchase of this property is looking for an 11% return on his equity investment. Moreover, he can obtain an 80% mortgage loan at 9% interest, with monthly amortization over a 25-year maturity. He firmly believes that through better management of the property he can increase annual Net Operating Income by 10% to $16,500. He accepts the judgment that the property will most likely sell for 70% of its present value at the end of the 15-year investment holding period.

The calculation of the Investment Value of the property to him, and hence the price he would be justified in paying for the property, would require first the development of an Overall Rate with an allowance for equity build-up and provision for capital recovery over the 15-year income projection period. The appraiser would need information about the mortgage constant, the 15-year 11% annual sinking fund factor, the Present Worth of One factor for 15 years at 11%, and the percentage of mortgage loan paid off (representing equity build-up) in 15 years.

The mortgage constant for 25 years at 9% with monthly amortization is 10.07% (Ellwood, page 97, column 6: 12 × 0.008391 = 0.100692).

The 11% annual sinking fund factor for 15 years is 0.0291 (Ellwood, page 132, column 3).

The Present Worth of One factor with annual discounting at 11% for 15 years is 0.2090 (Ellwood, page 132, column 4).

The percentage of mortgage loan paid off is calculated by taking the complement of the ratio of the Present Worth of One per Annum factor for 10 years with monthly amortization at 9%, to the factor for 25 years (Ellwood, page 97, column 5):

$$1 - (78.941692/119.161622) = 1 - 0.6625 = 0.3375 \text{ or } 33.75\%.$$

With this information, the development of the Overall Rate would be:

| | | |
|---|---|---|
| Mortgage | .80 X .1007 | = 0.0806 |
| Equity | .20 X .1100 | = 0.0220 |
| Weighted Average | | 0.1026 |
| *less* Equity Build-Up | .3375 X .80 X .0291 | = 0.0079 |
| Basic Rate | | 0.0947 |
| *plus* Capital Recovery | .30 X .0291 | = 0.0087 |
| Overall Rate | | 0.1034 |

Then:

$$V = I/R = \$16,500/0.1034 = \$159,574.47 \text{ or } \$160,000.$$

The calculation of Investment Value could also be based on a mortgage-equity variant of Property Residual analysis. The only additional information required is the 15-year 11% capitalization rate (Installment to Amortize One, Ellwood, page 132, column 6), which is 0.1391.

The mortgage-equity "capitalization rate" would be:

| | | |
|---|---|---|
| Mortgage | .80 X .1007 | = 0.0806 |
| Equity | .20 X .1391 | = 0.0278 |
| Capitalization Rate | | 0.1084 |

Then:

$$V = \frac{\$16,500}{.1084} + (.17V \times .2090)$$
$$V = \$152,214.02 + .0355V$$
$$0.9645V = \$152,214.02$$
$$V = \$152,214.02/.9645 = \$157,816.51 \text{ or } \$158,000.$$

The conclusion to be reached from this analysis is that the investor would be justified in paying as much as $160,000 for this property even though its indicated Market Value is only $150,000. This conclusion is valid only to the extent that his expectations about the terms of financing he can obtain and his ability to increase NOI by 10% through improved management of the property are supportable. They are *his* expectations, however, and not those of the market. He can therefore afford to pay more than Market Value and still expect to achieve a higher-than-market rate of return on his equity investment.

## After-Tax Cash Flow

Particularly in investment analysis, After-Tax Cash Flow is frequently calculated and used to identify the annual net cash receipts forecast to be available to the investor. It is necessarily specific to a particular investor because it is based on his own specific tax status and tax rate bracket. Many investors are especially interested in identifying how much cash they may anticipate receiving each year during the investment holding period. For valuation purposes, the present worth of After-Tax Cash Flow should be exactly the same as the present worth of Before-Tax Cash Flow (Cash Throw-Off) to any individual investor. This is because the appropriate equity yield rate applied to Cash Throw-Off should have built into it the investor's expectations of tax liability. Thus, the calculation of the present worth of After-Tax Cash Flow adds little to investment or appraisal analysis. The important calculations are those that provide the investor with indications of how much net cash flow he can anticipate in each of the individual years of the projected investment holding period.

**Meaning and Importance to the Investor.** Since the investor is presumed to be attempting to maximize his net cash position and its present worth, he therefore seeks to maximize his After-Tax Cash Flow annually, as well as the net proceeds of the reversion after taxes. There are two ways to accomplish this objective. The first and most obvious is to maximize Before-Tax Cash Flows through judicious use of leverage and good management that maximizes Net Operating Income. These efforts and their implications have been discussed and illustrated in Chapters 6 through 13.

In addition, however, the investor can legally minimize the impact of income taxes on his cash flows by planning his program of financing and depreciation carefully. In this discussion, "depreciation" refers to allowable charges against depreciable assets (the improvements) under Internal Revenue Regulations.[1] There are essentially three ways in which the investor can arrange his financing and investment income to reduce the impact of taxes on the present worth of his After-Tax Cash Flow. This is tax avoidance, which is legal and represents rational investor behavior. Tax evasion is illegal and is not considered further.

**Minimizing Income Tax Liability: Tax Shelter and Tax Deferral.** The base against which tax liability is calculated is Net Operating Income. All legitimate Operating Expenses are deductible items because they represent expenditures or accruals that are necessary in the production of income. In addition, two further items may be deducted from NOI before taxable net income is reached: mortgage interest charges and depreciation. Mortgage interest payments represent actual cash outlays by the investor. These are treated as necessary business expenses. Amortization payments included in debt service constitute equity build-up for the investor, however, and are not deductible from NOI in calculating taxable net income. The appraiser must therefore segregate annual interest payments from amortization of principal to determine the amount that can be deducted from NOI.

Depreciation is not a cash outlay, but is rather a charge to provide for recovery of anticipated capital loss. Improvements are held to be wasting assets whose loss in value can be recovered as a cost of producing income. The amount of depreciation charged is determined by set formula, and may or may not be the same as the capital recovery included in value estimation by the appraiser.[2]

To the extent that annual depreciation charges and interest charges are increased, the base of taxable income and therefore tax liability will be decreased. To this extent, the investor receives "tax sheltered" cash receipts. It is in the investor's interest, therefore, to have depreciation and interest charges as large as possible, all other considerations remaining the same. The lower the amount of taxes, the larger the amount of After-Tax Cash Flow available to the investor.

This consideration is closely related to the second: it is in the investor's advantage to *defer* income tax liability as far into the future as possible. A fundamental premise of all income capitalization is that present dollars are worth more than future dollars. If tax liability is deferred to the future and present or near-term After-Tax Cash Flows increased, then the present worth of the after-tax income stream is increased as well. This can be accomplished through the use of accelerated depreciation, in which larger amounts of depreciation may be charged in early years than would be the case with straight-line depreciation.[3] In addition, reducing the time period over which depreciation is charged, based on the "useful life" of the improvements, can also increase depreciation charges during the early years of the investment holding period.[4] Finally, careful segregation of the components of the improvements between short-lived and long-lived categories can result in substantial increases in depreciation charges in the early years of the investment holding period.[5] All of these actions reduce income tax liability in the early years and thereby increase After-Tax Cash Flow. Tax liability is deferred to later years, so that the present worth of the after-tax income stream is increased.

Arranging for partially amortized mortgages with a "balloon" payment at maturity also increases cash flows to the investor in the early years of the investment holding period in two ways. First, it reduces total annual debt service over the maturity of the loan, and thereby increases Cash Throw-Off. More importantly for tax reduction purposes, a larger proportion of annual debt service is a tax-deductible interest payment.

The third method of avoiding tax liability is to convert as much of the net proceeds of the reversion as possible to treatment as long-term capital gain rather than ordinary income. Long-term capital gains are taxed at greatly reduced effective rates as compared with ordinary income. To the extent that future income receipts can receive capital gains treatment rather than ordinary income treatment, the investor will realize a net saving in taxes. As a result, he will have more net cash proceeds that he can retain.[6]

The combination of maximizing tax-deductible charges allowable, minimizing taxable income in the early years of the investment holding period, and obtaining capital gains treatment for as much of the reversion as possible will greatly enhance the present worth of a given income stream to a tax-liable and tax-conscious investor. It will maximize his after-tax income receipts, and concentrate them in the early years when their present worth is higher.

**Characteristics and Components.** The derivation of annual income tax liability involves the following steps:

|  | Net Operating Income |
|---|---|
| *less* | Mortgage Interest |
| *less* | Depreciation Charges |
| *equals* | Taxable Income |

Taxable Income *times* Tax Rate *equals* Income Tax Liability

The appropriate and applicable rate of income taxation is the marginal rate for the investor. When Income Tax Liability for the year is deducted from Taxable Income, the result is Net Income after Taxes. This is not the same as After-Tax Cash Flow, however. The former is an accounting concept, while the latter is the point of interest for the real estate investor and the appraiser.

After-Tax Cash Flow is obtained by simply subtracting Income Tax Liability from Cash Throw-Off. The only use of the Taxable Income calculation is to provide the base for deriving the amount of Tax Liability. The steps from Net Operating Income to After-Tax Cash Flow for the appraiser are:

|  | Net Operating Income |
|---|---|
| *less* | Annual Debt Service |
| *equals* | Cash Throw-Off (Before-Tax Cash Flow) |
| *less* | Income Tax Liability |
| *equals* | After-Tax Cash Flow |

*Annual Variation.* After-Tax Cash Flow will be a different figure each year. This is because the amount of debt service represented by interest payments varies with each payment of interest and principal. Thus, the annual amount of interest paid varies; in a level-payment amortized mortgage, it declines annually. In addition, if accelerated depreciation methods are employed to calculate annual depreciation charges, the annual amount also declines. The combined charges for interest and depreciation are thus highest in the first year and decline systematically thereafter. If straight-line depreciation is used, of course, the annual depreciation charge remains constant over the capital recovery or depreciation period (usually the "useful life" allowed under Internal Revenue Service regulations).

**Calculation of After-Tax Cash Flow.** To illustrate the calculation of After-Tax Cash Flow without going into the many ramifications and possibilities inherent in any given case, assume a simple set of circumstances. These are presented for purposes of illustration only, and do not necessarily reflect what would be done in actual practice. To show the relationship among NOI, Cash Throw-Off, and After-Tax Cash Flow, consider the property income and financing characteristics of the investment property used in the examples in Chapters 9 through 13, as well as earlier in this chapter. Net Operating Income of $15,000 is forecast to be receivable as a level annuity for a 15-year period, and annual debt service is based on a mortgage constant of 10.41%. Since the estimated value of the property was concluded to be $150,000 and the mortgage loan-value ratio was 70%, assume that a 20-year, 8.5% mortgage in the amount of $105,000 has been obtained. Annual debt service is therefore .1041 X $105,000, or $10,930.50. Simply for purposes of illustration, assume that this amount is $10,930. Cash Throw-Off is then:

| | |
|---|---|
| Net Operating Income | $15,000 |
| *less* Annual Debt Service | –10,930 |
| *equals* Cash Throw-Off | $ 4,070 |

To derive After-Tax Cash Flow, it is necessary first to calculate Taxable Net Income and Tax Liability for each year. This requires indications of the amount of annual interest payments on the mortgage, the amount of annual depreciation charges, and the investor's effective tax rate. The amount of the interest payments in each year can be calculated laboriously by hand if necessary, but by calculating the percentage of mortgage principal paid off each year the appraiser can reduce his work considerably. This percentage figure is derived by using one of the methods illustrated in Chapter 13. In this instance, Ellwood's formula for *P* was applied to the first three years of mortgage payments:

$$P = (f/i - 1)(Sp - 1)$$

The resulting percentages and dollar amounts of mortgage amortization were:

Year 1: .0198 X $105,000 = $2,079
Year 2: .0216 X $105,000 = $2,268
Year 3: .0234 X $105,000 = $2,457

Subtracting each of these annual amounts of principal amortization from annual debt service yields the following total interest payments for each of the first three years. The same procedure could be followed throughout the entire income projection period or the mortgage maturity, whichever is pertinent to the analysis.

| | Year 1 | Year 2 | Year 3 |
|---|---|---|---|
| Debt Service | $10,930 | $10,930 | $10,930 |
| *less* Amortization | – 2,079 | – 2,268 | – 2,457 |
| Interest | $ 8,851 | $ 8,662 | $ 8,473 |

To derive annual depreciation charges, assume that the improvements are worth $120,000, that their "useful life" for tax depreciation purposes is 40 years, and that the 150% Declining Balance method is used to calculate annual depreciation charges. For the first three years, these depreciation charges would be:

Year 1: $4,500
Year 2: $4,331
Year 3: $4,169

The forecast of Taxable Net Income for the first three years then becomes:

|  | Year 1 | Year 2 | Year 3 |
|---|---|---|---|
| Net Operating Income | $15,000 | $15,000 | $15,000 |
| less Interest | − 8,851 | − 8,662 | − 8,473 |
|  | 6,149 | 6,338 | 6,527 |
| less Depreciation | − 4,500 | − 4,331 | − 4,169 |
| Taxable Net Income | $ 1,649 | $ 2,007 | $ 2,358 |

If the effective tax rate of the investor is 40%, then his Tax Liability in each of the first three years of the income projection period is:

Year 1: $1,649 × .40 = $659.60 or $660
Year 2: $2,007 × .40 = $802.80 or $803
Year 3: $2,358 × .40 = $943.20 or $943

With Cash Throw-Off and Tax Liability estimated for each of the first three years, After-Tax Cash Flow in each year can then be calculated as follows:

|  | Year 1 | Year 2 | Year 3 |
|---|---|---|---|
| Net Operating Income | $15,000 | $15,000 | $15,000 |
| less Debt Service | −10,930 | −10,930 | −10,930 |
| Cash Throw-Off | $ 4,070 | $ 4,070 | $ 4,070 |
| less Tax Liability | − 660 | − 803 | − 943 |
| After-Tax Cash Flow | $ 3,410 | $ 3,267 | $ 3,027 |

These figures illustrate the annual variation necessarily built into After-Tax Cash Flow. Even with constant depreciation changes on a straight-line basis, the declining interest payments each year would increase tax liability and reduce After-Tax Cash Flow. With electronic desk calculators and a systematic format for tabulating the results, a 15-year projection (or longer) can be calculated in a few minutes—most probably less time than its takes to read this demonstration of the steps involved in developing the forecasts for three years.

**Present Worth of After-Tax Cash Flows.** While it is technically possible to develop a present worth estimate for an After-Tax Cash Flow series, the figure has little meaning or independent usefulness. As noted earlier in this chapter, the present worth of the After-Tax Cash Flow logically should be equal to the present worth of the Cash Throw-Off. Both figures represent the present worth or Investment Value of the *equity* investment position.

The rate of return at which After-Tax Cash Flow is discounted to a present worth estimate is necessarily lower than the equity yield rate (or equity dividend rate) which is applied to Cash Throw-Off, and which is used to derive an Overall Rate. It is frequently difficult to obtain an appropriate after-tax yield rate to apply in any given investment analysis. Only the most sophisticated investors have a supportable basis for setting such a rate for themselves. Whatever comparable investment or "market" evidence is available is generally expressed in terms of the equity yield (or equity dividend) rate applicable to before-tax cash flows.

If the present worth of After-Tax Cash Flow is to be estimated, it must be treated as a series of separate annual reversions each discounted by the appropriate Present Worth of One factor. It is a variable annuity that must be discounted with the technique demonstrated in Chapters 5 and 11. The present worth estimates for each individual annual payment are added together to produce the estimated present worth of the entire After-Tax Cash Flow stream.

Because the calculation and use of After-Tax Cash Flow (sometimes called "Spendable Cash") in Investment Value analysis require careful and systematic step-by-step treatment, it is extremely helpful to have data analysis forms available. One set of such forms is illustrated in Exhibits 18-1 through 18-6.[a] They can be applied in both Before-Tax and After-Tax Cash Flow estimates and analyses. They are designed to be especially useful with the Ellwood formula or mortgage-equity analysis.

Exhibits 18-1 and 18-2 cover Before-Tax Cash Flow and equity yields. The data required and yields developed in After-Tax Cash Flow calculations are represented in Exhibits 18-3 and 18-4. The "proof" and use of after-tax equity yields to estimate present worth of the equity investment position are covered in Exhibits 18-5 and 18-6. Form F-2 shows the necessary treatment of After-Tax Cash Flows as a series of individual annual reversions to develop the final present worth estimate.

*Uses and Applications of Investment Value Estimates*

Investment Value is calculated and estimated to help an investor make a decision. It tells him what a particular interest in a given income property is worth to him under specified conditions. As an aid in the investment decision-making process, Investment Value is rarely used alone. Rather, it is

---

[a]The forms shown in these Exhibits are part of a larger group developed by M.B. Hodges, Jr., SREA, MAI, of McLean, Virginia; and copyrighted by the Society of Real Estate Appraisers. The author wishes to thank Mr. Hodges and SREA for their permission to reproduce the forms here. Sets of these forms may be obtained from the Society of Real Estate Appraisers, Chicago, Illinois.

## Exhibit 18-1

INVESTMENT MARKET VALUATION BY EQUITY YIELD BEFORE TAXES

Ownership Projection Term: _____ Yrs; Avg. Ann. Net Income (d): $ _____

Exist. 1st Mtge. Bal: $ _____ ; I = _____ ; Mo. Pmts.: $ _____

   Annual Debt Service: $ _____ ; f = _____

Exist. 2nd Mtge. Bal: $ _____ ; I = _____ ; Mo. Pmts.: $ _____

   Annual Debt Service: $ _____ ; f = _____

Exist. 3rd Mtge. Bal: $ _____ ; I = _____ ; Mo. Pmts.: $ _____

   Annual Debt Service: $ _____ ; f = _____

Exist. 4th Mtge. Bal: $ _____ ; I = _____ ; Mo. Pmts.: $ _____

   Annual Debt Service: $ _____ ; f = _____

New 1st Mtge. Ratio, M, = _____ ; I = _____ ; f = _____

New 2nd Mtge. Ratio, M, = _____ ; I = _____ ; f = _____

Mortgage Ratio, M, for existing or proposed mortgages in known amounts:

$$M_1 = \frac{(\$ \text{ Amount) (R)}}{d} = \frac{\$ \qquad \qquad R}{\$} = \underline{\qquad\qquad} R$$

$$M_2 = \frac{(\$ \text{ Amount) (R)}}{d} = \frac{\$ \qquad \qquad R}{\$} = \underline{\qquad\qquad} R$$

$$M_3 = \frac{(\$ \text{ Amount) (R)}}{d} = \frac{\$ \qquad \qquad R}{\$} = \underline{\qquad\qquad} R$$

$$M_4 = \frac{(\$ \text{ Amount) (R)}}{d} = \frac{\$ \qquad \qquad R}{\$} = \underline{\qquad\qquad} R$$

But if new junior Mtge., in dollars, is to be the difference between the IMV and the sum of known amounts for equity cash and the other mortgages, then,

$$M_j = 1 - \frac{(\$ \text{ Amounts) (R)}}{d} = 1 - \frac{\$ \qquad \qquad R}{\$} = 1 - \underline{\qquad\qquad} R$$

Depreciation, in %, = _____ ; or, in dollars = $\dfrac{\$ \qquad\qquad R}{d}$ = _____ R

   But if measured as the property reversion, Dep. $= 1 - \dfrac{(\text{Reversion) (R)}}{d}$

$$= 1 - \frac{\$ \qquad\qquad R}{\$} = 1 - \underline{\qquad\qquad} R$$

Equity Yield, Y, = _____ ; $1/_{S}\overline{n]}$ for Ownership Proj. Term = _____

Basic Capitalization Rate, Y-MC: If not selected from ELLWOOD TABLES, the mortgage coefficient, C, must be computed by the formula:

$C = Y + P \, 1/_{S}\overline{n]} - f$, wherein $P = (\frac{f}{I} - 1)(s^n - 1)$ for the projection term

   ∂ mortgage rate; $P_1 = (\underline{\qquad\qquad} - 1)(\underline{\qquad\qquad}) = \underline{\qquad\qquad}$

   and $C_1 = \underline{\qquad\qquad} + (\underline{\qquad\qquad})(\underline{\qquad\qquad}) - \underline{\qquad\qquad} = \underline{\qquad\qquad}$

FORM C1

**Exhibit 18-2**

$$P_2 = (\underline{\hspace{3cm}} - 1)(\underline{\hspace{3cm}}) = \underline{\hspace{3cm}}$$

and $C_2 = \underline{\hspace{3cm}} \div (\underline{\hspace{3cm}})(\underline{\hspace{3cm}}) - \underline{\hspace{2cm}} = \underline{\hspace{2cm}}$

$$P_3 = (\underline{\hspace{3cm}} - 1)(\underline{\hspace{3cm}}) = \underline{\hspace{3cm}}$$

and $C_3 = \underline{\hspace{3cm}} + (\underline{\hspace{3cm}})(\underline{\hspace{3cm}}) - \underline{\hspace{2cm}} = \underline{\hspace{2cm}}$

$$P_4 = (\underline{\hspace{3cm}} - 1)(\underline{\hspace{3cm}}) = \underline{\hspace{3cm}}$$

and $C_4 = \underline{\hspace{3cm}} + (\underline{\hspace{3cm}})(\underline{\hspace{3cm}}) - \underline{\hspace{2cm}} = \underline{\hspace{2cm}}$

<u>Overall Cap. Rate, R</u> = $Y-MC+Dep^{1}/_{Sn}$; <u>or,</u> $Y-M_1C_1-M_2C_2+Dep^{1}/_{Sn}$ (2 Mtges.); etc.

R = _____

$IMV = \dfrac{d}{R} = \dfrac{\$}{\underline{\hspace{4cm}}}$ = \$_____ Rounded to: \$_____

PROOF OF EQUITY YIELD BEFORE TAXES

<u>Annual cash flow</u> = avg. annual net income less mtge. pmts:

1)\$_____ - _____ - _____ - _____ - _____ = \$\_\_\_

2)\$_____ - _____ - _____ - _____ = \$\_\_\_

3)\$_____ - _____ - _____ = \$\_\_\_

<u>Cash Reversion upon future resale of the property:</u>

Resale price = IMV - Dep. = \$_____ - \$_____ = \$\_\_\_

Less Mtge. Bal., $b_1 = B_1(1-P_1)$, (\$_____)(1 - _____) = \$\_\_\_

Less Mtge. Bal., $b_2 = B_2(1-P_2)$, (\$_____)(1 - _____) = \$\_\_\_

Less Mtge. Bal., $b_3 = B_3(1-P_3)$, (\$_____)(1 - _____) = \$\_\_\_

Less Mtge. Bal., $b_4 = B_4(1-P_4)$, (\$_____)(1 - _____) = \$\_\_\_

Cash Reversion Before Capital Gains Taxes: \$\_\_\_

<u>Equity Cash Invested</u> = IMV less mtges. placed and/or assumed,

\$_____ - _____ - _____ - _____ - _____ = \$\_\_\_

(Target)

The sinking fund factor is from **annual** compound interest tables; thus, discount factors are from same tables, at annual rate, Y:

1) PW annual cash flow = (\$_____)(Factor _____) = \$\_\_\_

2) PW annual cash flow = (\$_____)(Factor _____) = \$\_\_\_

3) PW annual cash flow = (\$_____)(Factor _____) = \$\_\_\_

PW cash reversion = (\$_____)(Factor _____) = \$\_\_\_

1) First _____ of ownership period

2) Next _____ of ownership period Total: \$\_\_\_

3) Last _____ of ownership period (Rev. 9/70) **FORM C2**

**Exhibit 18-3**

DATA USED IN AFTER TAX YIELD VALUATION

| Year: | (1) | (2) | (3) | (4) | (5) |
|---|---|---|---|---|---|
| 1st Mtge. Bal. Begin Year | | | | | |
| $\frac{f}{I} - 1 =$ _____ $- 1$ | | | | | |
| $\times\ S^n - 1$ (from tables) | | | | | |
| $= P$ (% Mtge. Amortized) | | | | | |
| Accumulative Amortization | | | | | |
| Amortization in Year | | | | | |
| INTEREST PAID IN YEAR | | | | | |
| 2nd Mtge. Bal. Begin Year | | | | | |
| $\frac{f}{I} - 1 =$ _____ $- 1$ | | | | | |
| $\times\ S^n - 1$ (from tables) | | | | | |
| $= P$ (% Mtge. Amortized) | | | | | |
| Accumulative Amortization | | | | | |
| Amortization in Year | | | | | |
| INTEREST PAID IN YEAR | | | | | |
| 3rd Mtge. Bal. Begin Year | | | | | |
| $\frac{f}{I} - 1 =$ _____ $- 1$ | | | | | |
| $\times\ S^n - 1$ (from tables) | | | | | |
| $= P$ (% Mtge. Amortized) | | | | | |
| Accumulative Amortization | | | | | |
| Amortization in Year | | | | | |
| INTEREST PAID IN YEAR | | | | | |
| 4th Mtge. Bal. Begin Year | | | | | |
| $\frac{f}{I} - 1 =$ _____ $- 1$ | | | | | |
| $\times\ S^n - 1$ (from tables) | | | | | |
| $= P$ (% Mtge. Amortized) | | | | | |
| Accumulative Amortization | | | | | |
| Amortization in Year | | | | | |
| INTEREST PAID IN YEAR | | | | | |
| INTEREST ON ALL MTGES: | | | | | |

**FORM D1**

**Exhibit 18-4**

AFTER TAX EQUITY YIELD ANALYSIS

IMV or Purchase Price: $ ____  ____ % of Total

Land Value, Unimproved: ____  ____ Depreciation Method

Cap. Assets, ___ Yr. Life: $ ____  ____  _____

Cap. Assets, ___ Yr. Life: $ ____  ____  _____

Cap. Assets, ___ Yr. Life: $ ____  ____  _____

Cap. Assets, ___ Yr. Life: $ ____  ____  _____

| Year | (1) | (2) | (3) | (4) | (5) |
|---|---|---|---|---|---|
| NET OPERATING INCOME(*) | | | | | |
| Annual Debt Service | | | | | |
| Cash Flow Before Taxes | | | | | |
| Bal. All Mtges. Begin Yr | | | | | |
| INTEREST PAID IN YEAR | | | | | |
| ___ Yr. Assets Begin Yr | | | | | |
| x Dep. Rate @ ____ | | | | | |
| ___ Yr. Assets Begin Yr | | | | | |
| x Dep. Rate @ ____ | | | | | |
| ___ Yr. Assets Begin Yr | | | | | |
| x Dep. Rate @ ____ | | | | | |
| ___ Yr. Assets Begin Yr | | | | | |
| x Dep. Rate @ ____ | | | | | |
| TOTAL DEPRECIATION IN YR | | | | | |
| Dep. Exceeding S/L in Yr | | | | | |
| Accumulative Excess Dep | | | | | |
| Taxable Income | | | | | |
| Tax Loss Used in Year | | | | | |
| Accumulative Tax Loss to carry forward | | | | | |
| Excess Dep. Recapture Upon Resale (See FormB) | | | | | |
| State Inc. Taxes @ ___% | | | | | |
| Fed. Inc. Taxes @ ___% | | | | | |
| Taxes on Tax Preference Items if applicable | | | | | |
| SPENDABLE CASH IN YEAR | | | | | |

Note (*) If mortgagee participates in gross or net income, it is reflected in these figures.

Rev. 7/70 **FORM E1**

**Exhibit 18-5**

PROOF OF EQUITY YIELD AFTER TAXES

Cash Reversion Before Taxes:

Resale Price = V $-\frac{App}{Dep}$ = \$_____ $\overset{+}{-}$ \$_____ = \$

Less $b_1 = B_1(1 - P_1) = ($\$_____$)(1-$_____$) = $\$

Less $b_2 = B_2(1 - P_2) = ($\$_____$)(1-$_____$) = $\$

Less $b_3 = B_3(1 - P_3) = ($\$_____$)(1-$_____$) = $\$

Less $b_4 = B_4(1 - P_4) = ($\$_____$)(1-$_____$) = $\$

Less Sales Commission on Resale @ _____% = \$

CASH REVERSION BEFORE TAXES: \$

Cash Reversion After Taxes:

Book Depreciation Taken Less Amount Recaptured at Ordinary Tax Rates = \$

Actual Property Dep. or App. = $\overset{+}{-}$ \$

Capital Gain = \$

(Net Gain for Non-Corporate Taxpayers) = \$

Regular Method:

State Taxes on Capital Gain @ _____% & _____% = \$

Federal Taxes on Capital Gain @ _____% & _____% = \$

Federal Taxes on Recaptured Depreciation @ _____% & _____% = \$

Alternative Tax Method:

State Taxes, Alternative Method, @ _____% = \$

Federal Taxes, Alternative Method, @ _____% = \$

Subtotal All Taxes Except Tax Preference Taxes: \$

Add Federal Taxes on Tax Preferences: = \$

(Tax Preference is \$_____)   Total All Taxes : \$

(Deductions are  - \$_____)

and  - \$_____)   CASH REVERSION AFTER TAXES = \$

Equity Cash = \$_____ - $\frac{\text{\$_____}}{\text{all mortgages}}$ = \$

(Rev. 12/1/70)

FORM F1

# Exhibit 18-6

PROOF OF EQUITY YIELD AFTER TAXES

After Tax Equity Yield to nearest 1/8th of 1% = _____

(Unless specified, monthly compound interest factors, premised upon the receipt of 1/12th the annual spendable cash at the beginning of each month, are used in discounting future money receipts to present worth. The spendable cash receipts shown below are taken from Form E):

PW Spendable Cash, Year ____, $ _____ x _____ = $ _____

PW Spendable Cash, Year ____, $ _____ x _____ = $ _____

PW Spendable Cash, Year ____, $ _____ x _____ = $ _____

PW Spendable Cash, Year ____, $ _____ x _____ = $ _____

PW Spendable Cash, Year ____, $ _____ x _____ = $ _____

PW Spendable Cash, Year ____, $ _____ x _____ = $ _____

PW Spendable Cash, Year ____, $ _____ x _____ = $ _____

PW Spendable Cash, Year ____, $ _____ x _____ = $ _____

PW Spendable Cash, Year ____, $ _____ x _____ = $ _____

PW Spendable Cash, Year ____, $ _____ x _____ = $ _____

PW Spendable Cash, Year ____, $ _____ x _____ = $ _____

PW Spendable Cash, Year ____, $ _____ x _____ = $ _____

PW Spendable Cash, Year ____, $ _____ x _____ = $ _____

PW Spendable Cash, Year ____, $ _____ x _____ = $ _____

PW Spendable Cash, Year ____, $ _____ x _____ = $ _____

PW Spendable Cash, Year ____, $ _____ x _____ = $ _____

PW Spendable Cash, Year ____, $ _____ x _____ = $ _____

PW Spendable Cash, Year ____, $ _____ x _____ = $ _____

PW Spendable Cash, Year ____, $ _____ x _____ = $ _____

PW After Tax Cash Reversion, $ _____ x _____ = $ _____

Total (Compare to Equity Cash Investment) $ _____

FORM F2

part of comparative analysis that identifies the appropriate course of action for the investor.

**Purchase Decisions.** The basic investment decision is whether or not to proceed with a planned or proposed acquisition of an investment property. The fundamental rule is that the rational investor will not acquire a property unless its value to him (Investment Value) is greater than its Market Value. The measure of what he will most probably pay is Market Value; the reason he will pay it is that he anticipates a greater return, will accept a lower rate of return, or expects less capital loss. The tax shelter or tax advantages offered by the investment to the particular investor also influence its attractions specifically to him. The use of Investment Value, then, is to compare it with estimated Market Value to help the investor decide whether to proceed with the purchase.

In addition, a comparison of Investment Values and rates of return on equity anticipated for alternative investment opportunities helps the investor select the one that best meets his particular investment objectives.

**Proposed Development.** When proposed development alternatives, or a single development plan, is being considered, a comparison between estimated cost of development and Investment Value helps the investor decide whether to proceed at all, and if so which alternative is best in terms of his standards and objectives. Unless Investment Value exceeds estimated development cost, the investor will most probably abandon the project.

**Renovation and Conversion.** The decision whether to renovate or convert the use of an existing income property or not is simply a special case of proposed development.[7] The cost of effecting the change or improvement is compared with the present worth of the anticipated increase in net income or net cash flow stream. The expected increase in net income and its present worth may come from increased rentals, decreased vacancy, decreased operating expenses, an extension of the economic life of the improvements—or a combination of some or all of these results.

Renovation may take one or more of three forms:

1. *Rehabilitation*: "the restoration of a property to satisfactory condition without changing the plan, form or style of a structure."[8]
2. *Modernization*: "taking corrective measures to bring a property into conformity with changes in style, whether exterior or interior. It requires replacing parts of the structure or mechanical equipment with modern replacements of the same kind but not introducing capital additions."[9]
3. *Remodeling*: "changing the plan, form, or style of a structure to correct functional or economic deficiencies."[10]

In addition, conversion is changing the use or function of a structure. All but rehabilitation have the effect or intent of extending the remaining economic life of the structure(s). In all cases, the objective is to increase the present worth of the investment position in the property by more than the cost to make the renovation or the conversion. That cost includes income loss during the period of construction, waiting costs, and financing costs; as well as direct outlays by the investor for labor, materials, and the contractor's overhead and profit. The excess of increased present worth over all these costs must be sufficient to provide an attractive rate of return to the investor for his investment and for the entrepreneurial risk he is assuming. Because renovation and conversion are employed only when the structure is seriously deteriorated or obsolescent, or both, the uncertainties and risks involved are usually greater than those associated with new developments. Rates of return expected and actually received are therefore usually higher than going market rates on equity investments in similar properties without a program of renovation or conversion. It is not uncommon for anticipated rates of return to be 150% or more of comparable equity yield rates.[11]

To illustrate this comparative valuation process, assume an income property with the investment and financing characteristics used in the continuing example presented throughout Chapters 9-13 and earlier in this chapter. It will be recalled that it is forecast to be capable of producing an annual Net Operating Income of $15,000 for 15 years; Gross Income is $25,000 with an Operating Expense Ratio of 40%. The equity yield rate is 10%, and the mortgage constant is 10.41% based on a 20-year 70% loan with monthly amortization at 8.5%. It is forecast that the property will resell in 15 years at 70% of its present value, representing an overall capital loss of 30%. The value of the property in its present condition is estimated to be $150,000, based on an Overall Rate of 9.97%.

It is proposed that a $35,000 renovation program be undertaken. Ignoring income loss encountered during the construction period for purposes of simplification, a 10% increase in rentals and a 10% decrease in operating expenses are forecast as a result of the renovation. The remaining economic life of the improvements, and hence the income projection period, is anticipated to be extended to 25 years, at the end of which period it is forecast that the property will resell at 75% of its present value.

The investor-owner can obtain 70% financing of the renovation costs, but only if he refinances the entire property at 9% with monthly amortization for 25 years. The new mortgage will be based on 70% of $185,000. Because of the risks involved in the renovation program, the investor is looking for a 15% return on the additional equity he must put into the property, as well as a continued 10% on his existing equity in the property "as is."

The estimated Market Value of the property after the renovation program is completed can be calculated by using a mortgage-equity Overall Rate applied to the new NOI forecast. This NOI is $18,500, derived as follows:

| | |
|---|---|
| Gross Income | $27,500 ($25,000 plus 10%) |
| *less* Operating Expenses | − 9,000 ($10,000 less 10%) |
| Net Operating Income | $18,500 |

To develop the mortgage-equity Overall Rate, the following information is required:

Mortgage Constant: .1007 (Ellwood, page 97, column 6: 12 X .008391)
Sinking Fund Factor, 25 years, 10%: .0102 (Ellwood, page 116, column 3)
Equity Yield Rate: .1000
Mortgage-Loan-Value Ratio: .7000
Capital Loss Forecast: .2500

With this information in hand, the mortgage-equity Overall Rate with allowance for equity build-up (100% of mortgage principal in this case) and provision for capital recovery is derived according to the method shown in Chapter 13 and used earlier in this chapter.

| | | |
|---|---|---|
| Mortgage | .70 X .1007 | = .0705 |
| Equity | .30 X .1000 | = .0300 |
| Weighted Average | | .1005 |
| less Equity Build-Up | 1.00 X .70 X .0102 | = .0071 |
| Basic Rate | | .0934 |
| plus Capital Recovery | .25 X .0102 | = .0026 |
| Overall Rate | | .0960 |

Applying this Overall Rate to NOI ($18,500/.0960) results in an estimated present worth of the property representing its Market Value after the renovation program is completed of $192,708.33. This would probably be rounded to $193,000 or even $195,000 in a Market Value estimate, but the unrounded figure must be retained to test whether the investor's yield objectives for the additional equity investment have been met.

The total investment in the property is now $185,000: the original value of $150,000 plus the renovation cost of $35,000. The equity investment has increased from $45,000 (30% of $150,000) to $55,500, which is 30% of $185,000. Thus, the additional cash outlay by the investor-owner, on which he is seeking a 15% return over the 25-year income projection period, is $10,500.

The calculated present worth of the property after renovation is $192,708.33, based on a 10% equity yield rate. This exceeds the total investment in the property by $7,708.33, and is assignable entirely to the equity investment position. This excess of calculated present worth over investment cost indicates that the proposed renovation program is certainly feasible. The question remains, however: "Is the investor's objective of a 15% return on the additional equity investment while maintaining a 10% yield on the original equity position, realized in this case?"

The incremental annual income over and above that necessary to provide a 10% equity yield is $740. This is obtained by first identifying the annual NOI that would be required to support an investment of $185,000 at an Overall Rate of 9.60%. That NOI is $17,760 (.0960 X $185,000 = $17,760). Subtracting

$17,760 from the forecast $18,500 gives $740, which is 7.04% of $10,500. This 7.04% is the 25-year capitalization rate for the incremental income. A check of annual compound interest factor tables reveals that the annual Installment to Amortize One factor for 25 years at 5% is .0709 (Ellwood, page 36, column 6). This is close enough to suggest that the 15% equity yield rate on the additional $10,500 of equity investment required will probably be realized.

This conclusion can be checked by developing a mortgage-equity Overall Rate with the equity investment segregated into 10% and 15% yield segments, each weighted by its proportionate share of total equity investment. The appropriate 15% compound interest and discount factors are provided on page 151 in Ellwood.

| | | | |
|---|---|---|---|
| Mortgage | .7000 × .1007 | = .0705 | |
| Equity "A" | .2432 × .1000 | = .0243 | |
| Equity "B" | .0568 × .1500 | = .0085 | |
| Weighted Average | | | .1033 |
| less Equity Build-Up | | | |
| Equity "A" | .8108 × .70 × .0102 | = .0058 | |
| Equity "B" | .1892 × .70 × .0047 | = .0006 | |
| | | | −.0064 |
| Basic Rate | | | .0969 |
| plus Capital Recovery | | | |
| Equity "A" | .8108 × .25 × .0102 | = .0021 | |
| Equity "B" | .1892 × .25 × .0047 | = .0002 | |
| | | | +.0023 |
| Overall Rate | | | .0992 |

Applying this Overall Rate to forecast NOI ($18,500/.0992) results in a present worth estimate of $186,491.94. This is slightly in excess of $185,000, and indicates that the $35,000 renovation expenditure can proceed under the conditions and expectations specified with a resulting 15% yield rate on the additional equity investment. The investor's objectives are therefore forecast to be met, and the conclusion is "GO."

## Review Exercises

1. A property is forecast to produce NOI of $15,500 per year. An 80% mortgage in the amount of $100,000 can be obtained at 9.25% for a 15-year term, with semiannual amortization on a level-payment basis. The improvements are estimated to have a present worth of $100,000, and a 20-year straight-line depreciation schedule has been approved. The investor is in a 50% tax bracket.
   a. What is the indicated annual Cash Throw-Off?
   b. What is the indicated rate of return on equity investment?

   c. What is the amount of taxable income in each of the first five years?

   d. What is the amount of After-Tax Cash Flow in each of the first five years?

2. a. What is the indicated Overall Rate for the property in Problem 1?

   b. If an investor is seeking a 15% before-tax equity yield rate and can obtain a 9% 15-year, monthly payment mortgage of $100,000, what is the present worth of the investment in this property to him? Assume a 10-year income projection period and a forecast decline in property value of 15% at the end of 10 years.

   c. Should the investor proceed with the purchase of the property? Why or why not?

3. In the renovation example provided in the body of Chapter 18, would the owner-investor proceed if his objective was to obtain a 16% rate of return on his additional equity cash outlay? Explain your answer.

**Supplementary Readings**

American Institute of Real Estate Appraisers, *The Appraisal of Real Estate*, fifth edition, (Chicago: American Institute of Real Estate Appraisers, 1967), pp. 325-326, Chapter 22.

Frederick E. Case, "New Decision Tools for Appraisers," *The Appraisal Journal*, Volume 35, Number 1, January 1967.

Gene Dilmore, "Elements of Network Analysis," *The Real Estate Appraiser*, Volume 35, Number 2, March-April 1969.

P.B. Farrell, Jr., "Computer-Aided Financial Risk Simulation," *The Appraisal Journal*, Volume 35, Number 1, January 1969.

James E. Gibbons, "Mortgage-Equity Capitalization and After-Tax Equity Yield," *The Appraisal Journal*, Volume 34, Number 2, January 1969.

James E. Graaskamp, "A Practical Computer Service for the Income Approach," *The Appraisal Journal*, Voiume 37, Number 1, January 1969.

J. Warren Higgins, *Impact of Federal Taxation on Real Estate Decisions* (Storrs, Connecticut: Center for Real Estate and Urban Economic Studies, University of Connecticut, 1971).

M.B. Hodges, Jr., "Ellwood Plus (Or Equity Yield After Taxes)," *The Real Estate Appraiser*, Volume 35, Number 5, September-October 1969.

M.B. Hodges, Jr., "Income Capitalization for Investor Clients," *The Appraisal Journal*, Volume 36, Number 2, April 1968.

Sanders A. Kahn, Frederick E. Case, and Alfred Schimmel, *Real Estate Appraisal and Investment* (New York: Ronald Press, 1963), Chapters 18, 19, 24, 25, 26, 28, and 29.

William N. Kinnard, Jr. and Stephen D. Messner, *Industrial Real Estate,* second edition (Washington, D.C.: Society of Industrial Realtors, 1971), Chapters 5, 8, and 9.

D.S. Moss, "Equity Yields on Real Estate Investments," *The Appraisal Journal*, Volume 37, Number 3, July 1969.

*Prentice-Hall 1971 Tax Course* (Englewood Cliffs, N.J.: Prentice-Hall, 1970), Chapters 2-15.

J.R. Recht and L.K. Loewenstein, "Variations in Rates of Return," *The Appraisal Journal*, Volume 33, Number 2, April 1965.

R. Bruce Ricks, "Tax Shelter and Annual Cash Flow in Investment Real Estate," *The Appraisal Journal*, Volume 34, Number 2, April 1966.

Alfred E. Ring, *The Valuation of Real Estate*, second edition (Englewood Cliffs, N.J.: Prentice-Hall, 1970), Chapter 21.

John F. Rowlson, "Investment Property: An Analysis of Motivation," *The Real Estate Appraiser*, Volume 33, Number 5, May 1967.

William M. Shenkel, *A Guide to Appraising Industrial Property* (Chicago: Society of Real Estate Appraisers, 1967), pp. 112-122.

George Stauss, "The Effect of Tax on Yield and Value," *The Appraisal Journal*, Volume 37, Number 3, July 1969.

## Notes

1. For details, see J. Warren Higgins, *Impact of Federal Taxation on Real Estate Decisions* (Storrs, Connecticut: Center for Real Estate and Urban Economic Studies, University of Connecticut, 1971).

2. Only the principles of calculating depreciation changes and measuring their impact on After-Tax Cash Flow are considered in this book. The regulations and standards governing their application in practice require careful and detailed analysis, such as is presented in Higgins, *Federal Taxation and Real Estate Decisions*.

3. For illustrations of the implications of the several types of accelerated depreciation potentially available to investors in different types of income-producing real estate, see Higgins, *Federal Taxation and Real Estate Decisions*;

and W.N. Kinnard, Jr. and S.D. Messner, *Industrial Real Estate,* second edition (Washington, D.C.: Society of Industrial Realtors, 1971), Chapter 5.

4. Internal Revenue Service "Guidelines of Useful Lines" for different types of buildings are summarized in *Prentice-Hall 1971 Tax Course* (Englewood Cliffs, N.J.: Prentice-Hall, 1970), pp. 2026-2028.

5. *Ibid.*

6. For a detailed discussion of capital gains treatment and its impact on net cash proceeds, with illustrative examples, see Higgins, *Federal Taxation and Real Estate Decisions.*

7. The characteristics of different types of renovation and their handling in appraisal or feasibility analysis are explained in further detail in American Institute of Real Estate Appraisers, *The Appraisal of Real Estate*, fifth edition (Chicago: American Institute of Real Estate Appraisers, 1967), Chapter 22. Examples of the results of renovation and conversion programs may be found in Kinnard and Messner, *Industrial Real Estate,* Chapter 11.

8. AIREA, *Appraisal of Real Estate*, p. 363.

9. *Ibid.*

10. *Ibid.*

11. For some illustrative examples, see Kinnard and Messner, *Industrial Real Estate,* pp. 385–387.

# 19 Leased Fee, Leasehold, and Other Partial Interests in Income Properties

## Nature of Partial Interests

Real property consists of enforceable rights in real estate. The "fullest" form of private property ownership in real estate is the unencumbered Fee Simple estate. The several rights of ownership (use, exclusion, and disposition) are both separable and divisible, which means that there may be more than one legitimate claimant against a given property at any one time.[1] Since rights in realty are what are actually owned and transferred, appraisal consists of valuing those rights. Although there are occasional vestiges of the argument that Market Value is applicable to an unencumbered Fee Simple estate only,[2] it is now generally recognized that mortgage financing is an integral fact of the real estate market, and that a fee interest "encumbered" by a mortgage (existing or proposed) may indeed have measurable Market Value.[3]

Beyond this, less-than-fee interests in income-producing real estate can have both Market Value and Investment Value to specific holders of those interests. To the extent that *any* interest in real estate is transferable and there is a market for it, it is marketable. If it is marketable, then there can be a Market Value for it, although there does not necessarily have to be an identifiable and measurable Market Value in every instance.

### Types of Partial Interests

The three most commonly encountered partial interests in income properties are the Leased Fee and Leasehold estates created under a lease contract, and the mortgagee's (lender's) interest, especially under a lender-participation mortgage loan arrangement. There are other partial interests that may be created and have to be valued as well, but these three are most significant for the income-property appraiser. Moreover, the techniques for valuing other types of partial interests closely parallel those identified here for Leasehold and mortgagee's interest valuation.

**Terminology for Partial Interests.** There are technical terms for the holders of partial interests in real estate. Throughout the remainder of the discussion in this chapter, these technical terms will be employed. They have been alluded to in earlier chapters, but are specifically identified here.

The property owner who pledges his property interest as collateral for a mortgage loan is known as the *mortgagor*. The lender on a mortgage loan is the *mortgagee*.

413

Under a lease contract, the property owner or landlord who leases his property for use by another is called the *lessor*. The tenant under the lease contract is the *lessee*. Since it is frequently possible for a lessee to sub-lease some or all of the premises to another tenant, he is the *prime lessee* and *sub-lessor* simultaneously, while the party renting the property under a sub-lease is called a *sub-lessee*.

**"Encumbered" Fee.** Any circumstance beyond the limitations imposed by society that further limits the free exercise of the rights contained in a Fee Simple estate represents an "encumbrance" on that fee. As long as the property is pledged as collateral for a mortgage loan, the mortgagor is somewhat restricted in his enjoyment of the benefits from the use of the property, and he is also restricted in his free right of disposition. Similarly, when a property owner leases some or all of the real estate to a tenant, he gives up most of his right of use, much of his right of exclusion, and possibly part of his ability to dispose of the property during the term of the lease. Whether as mortgagor or as lessor, therefore, the fee holder has a less-than-full Fee Simple interest in the property as long as it is "encumbered" by a mortgage or a lease.

The term "encumbrance" can be misleading, since in general usage it usually carries negative connotations. In the strict technical legal sense, both a mortgage and a lease represent an "encumbrance" on the Fee Simple estate. Either may or may not have a negative impact on the fee holder or the value of his interest in the property, however. As pointed out in Chapters 7 and 13 in particular, a mortgage may enable the mortgagor to trade on equity successfully and enhance his equity return as a result. Similarly, a favorable lease may result in a value of the Leased Fee estate in excess of that for the "unencumbered" fee in the same property.

The important point is that the encumbered fee is an estate less than the unencumbered Fee Simple in legal terms, and that another non-fee interest in the same real estate exists. This other interest may have value as of the valuation date, and that value may be either Market Value or (more likely) Investment Value. Moreover, the valuation of the encumbered fee must take into account the existence of the other, non-fee interest as of the valuation date and include a consideration of the impact of that non-fee interest on the value (as defined) of the fee.

Finally, the valuation of the encumbered fee interest must also specify the *duration* of the non-fee interest. This is usually indicated in a contract: the mortgage note or the lease. At the end of the contract period, the encumbrance on the fee is usually extinguished, and the fee holder has an unencumbered Fee Simple interest once again. Because of this specification of a finite time period for the encumbrance, it is usually most appropriate to treat the income stream receivable by the fee holder as a form of Property Residual, as illustrated in Chapters 12 and 13.

**Leasehold.** The lessee under a lease has certain enforceable rights in the leased real estate. These rights are usually spelled out in the lease contract, and remain in existence as long as the lease is in force. Generally speaking, the lessee has the right to occupy and use the premises within the limits prescribed in the lease contract, and he also has the right to exclude others from the premises (except the lessor or his official representative on "reasonable" inspections of the property). Unless it is specifically prohibited under the terms of the lease contract, the lessee also has the common law right to sub-lease the premises for any legal use. This limited right of disposition is always subject to the terms and conditions of the lease.

The right of occupancy during the term of the lease is by far the most significant of the lessee's rights. It may have value on the market *provided* the right is actually transferable (i.e., the lessee may sub-lease the premises) *and* there is a net benefit to a lessee in occupying the premises at the Contract Rental stipulated in the lease. This net benefit occurs when the Contract Rental is less than the Market Rental for the same or competitive space. If the lessee has the right to occupy the premises for less than the going Market Rental, the present worth of this right is its Investment Value to the lessee. If the right can be transferred and is marketable, then it may have a Market Value as well.

Any value that may be ascribed to the Leasehold Estate, which is the term for the lessee's interest, is applicable for the remaining term of the lease only. The net benefit from occupancy rights at less-than-market rentals is a finite "income" stream that expires when the lease expires.

**Mortgagee's Interest.** Any mortgagee has a valuable interest in real estate: the right to receive the interest and principal amortization payments in accordance with the terms of the mortgage note. At the time that a mortgage loan is made, the present worth of the mortgagee's interest is equal to the principal amount of the loan, on the assumption that a rational determination of mortgage loan terms has been made. Subsequently, the present worth of the remaining income stream receivable under the mortgage note may be greater than or less than (as well as equal to) the outstanding balance of the loan, depending on whether the contract interest rate on the loan is greater than or less than the going market rate for loans of the same type and risk, as of the valuation date.

Special attention must be directed to the particular interests of the mortgagee under a lender-participation mortgage loan, however. The characteristics and implications of a mortgagee's participation interests are considered at some length later in this chapter.[4] The essence of this arrangement is that the mortgagee receives the right to a portion of property income and/or a portion of the equity interest in the property, in addition to the interest and principal amortization payments stipulated in the mortgage note, as part of the price of making the loan. To this extent, the lender "participates" in the income and/or equity interest of the mortgaged real estate.

This participation interest obviously has a present worth. It is valued just as any other income stream, with appropriate allowance for risk and duration. It certainly has an Investment Value. If it is transferable and marketable under applicable market conditions, it may have a Market Value as well. The mortgagee's interest under the loan itself is also transferable and usually marketable, which means that it, too, may have both an Investment Value and a Market Value under appropriate market conditions.

### *Valuation of Partial Interests*

Investment Value can always be estimated for any partial interest in income-producing real estate. It is the present worth of the forecast future dollar benefits attributable to that interest, measured in terms of the standards of acceptability established by the particular claimant: lessor, lessee, or mortgagee. In addition, the rights involved may also have a measurable Market Value if they are indeed transferable and there is a market for such rights at the time of the appraisal.

Because the income or benefits forecast for the holder of the rights in question is always limited to a contract term, it must always be capitalized as a finite income stream with a Capitalization Rate or Capitalization Factor. Moreover, the most appropriate method of treating the stream of future benefits is usually to regard it as a level annuity unless there is specific evidence to the contrary, and to compensate for any risk or uncertainty associated with the probable receipt of the benefits as forecast through an upward adjustment in the Discount Rate employed. Leased fee interests, and mortgagees' interests in both partially amortized mortgages and equity participations, also involve a lump-sum reversion at the expiration of the lease or mortgage loan contract. In such cases, the present worth estimate is best developed in Property Residual form.

There is nothing different, new or unusual about the mechanics of capitalizing forecast future benefits from a partial interest in income-producing real estate. Precisely the same techniques are used as have previously been identified as applicable and responsive to the valuation of Fee Simple estates. The only difference lies in the specifics of the answers to the questions: *Who?*, *What?* and *When?* The appraiser must examine the contract documents carefully to ascertain which party is entitled to what or how much income, and the timing of each party's income receipts. Thereafter, the estimation of the present worth of each party's interest proceeds as any other income capitalization process.

### Valuation of Interests under a Lease

A lease is a contract between two parties: the lessor and the lessee. The lessor gives up part of his rights to use, exclusion, and disposition in exchange for the lessee's promise to pay a specified Contract Rental over the term of the lease. The lessee may have other obligations as well, which are considered in the following sections. The main obligation, however, and the basis for the valuation of the lessor's interest (the leased fee) is the payment of the contract rental. The lessee in turn receives a valuable right, that of occupancy and use. If that right is worth more on the market as of the valuation date than the contract rental he is required to pay, then he has a net benefit which can be capitalized into a present worth figure.

Logically, the sum of the present worth of the lessor's interest and the present worth of the lessee's interest should equal the Market Value of the property represented by the present worth of the unencumbered Fee Simple estate. This is not necessarily the case, however, unless the market and the parties to the contract recognize the existence of negative values in some circumstances.

### Types of Leases

Leases may be classified according to their duation, the basis of calculating the rental payments to be made, and the allocation of responsibility for bearing operating expenses of the property between lessor and lessee.[5] These are the terms of the lease contract that are usually most significant as influences on the value of the interests involved. In point of fact, every lease has a specified term *and* a contract rental based on both a stipulated method of rental calculation and specification of which party (lessor or lessee) pays which operating expenses. So every lease can be classified in at least three ways.

There are other lease provisions that can influence the value of the interests created under the contract, involving obligations of lessor and/or lessee. The appraiser must study the lease contract carefully, and identify those components and classes that do have an impact on these values.[6] The interests of each participating party are defined and protected, and their obligations specified. Because each lease contract is a reflection of individual negotiation between lessor and lessee, the terms may require explanation and interpretation by the participating broker or attorney.

**Term of Lease.** Leases are classified according to duration as *long-term* and *short-term*. The dividing line between the two is rather arbitrary. Generally speaking, a lease is long-term if its first term, without taking into account renewal options, is ten years or more. This is based on convention or tradition, however, and is not a rigidly applied rule.

The important point is that the duration of the lease and its provisions must be long enough to make a difference to potential purchasers and leaders in the way they react to the lessor's interest. Broadly speaking, the longer the lease term, the greater the stability of the income stream that is forecast for the lessor's interest, and the greater the lessor's probable ability to use the lease as a basis for obtaining financing on attractive terms.

Renewal options must be treated very carefully by the appraiser. He must estimate the probability that the lessee will exercise the option to renew. The first term of the lease is generally the income projection period used in valuing leased fee and leasehold interests, without regard for renewal options, unless there is particularly strong evidence that the options are likely to be exercised. Maturities on mortgages extended on leased properties are usually limited to the first term of the lease.

**Method of Rental Payment.** The basis for calculating the method of paying the contract rental is specified in the lease contract. The most common forms of rental payment are:

1. *Flat rentals.* These are constant payments of equal amounts over the entire duration of the lease. A 20-year lease calling for rental payments of $10,000 per year is a flat-rental lease.

2. *Step-up or step-down rentals.* Step-up leases call for periodic increases in contract rental over the term of the lease; step-down leases call for periodic decreases in contract rental. The amount and timing of the increase or decrease is specified in the lease contract. For example, a 20-year lease might call for rental payments of $10,000 per year for the first five years, $12,000 per year for the next seven years, and $13,500 per year for the remaining eight years. This is a step-up lease.

3. *Percentage rentals.* Especially in leases on retail properties, it is common for all or (usually) part of the rental payment to be a stipulated percentage of gross sales receipts of the business occupying the leased space. While the specific arrangements vary widely, a frequently employed form of percentage lease calls for a fixed base rental plus a percentage of sales above a specified annual amount. For example, a lease might provide for $10,000 per year base rental, plus 5% of all sales in excess of $200,000 per year up to $500,000, and 3% of all sales receipts thereafter. The percentage rentals in excess of the base rental are called the "overage."

4. *Reappraisal rentals.* Leases sometimes call for periodic reappraisal of rental payments at specified intervals over the term of the lease. Because of administrative and enforcement problems often encountered, frequently resulting in prolonged and expensive litigation, this method of providing for rental payments is not commonly used.

5. *Sale-leaseback.* The sale-leaseback contract is really a means of providing for 100% financing of space use and occupancy.[7] In addition to specifying the periodic rental (usually a flat rental), it also provides for reacquisition of the leased property by the lessee at a specified price at the expiration of the lease.

*Timing.* It has been emphasized especially in Chapters 5 and 6 that the timing and periodicity of payments in a forecast income stream have a major influence on its present worth. This is equally true of the stream of contract rental payable under a lease.

Rental payments may be made monthly, quarterly, semi-annually, annually— or even weekly. For purposes of developing a Net Operating Income forecast to be capitalized to a present worth estimate, these payments must be converted to an annual basis. However, the compound interest or discount factors used to capitalize that income stream may be based on periods other than a year—provided the *net* rental income is receivable monthly, quarterly, or whatever.

In addition, rentals may be payable in advance (at the beginning of the rental payment period). Since compound interest and discount factors are predicated on end-of-period payments, the relatively simple but necessary adjustment illustrated in Chapter 5 must be made whenever rentals are payable in advance.

For both timing and periodicity, the terms of the lease contract must be read carefully and adhered to by the appraiser.

*Unit Rentals.* As noted particularly in Chapter 6, rentals may be expressed on a per-unit basis. The unit of rental is most commonly the unit of use of the type of space involved. For the type of property usually subject to long-term lease (manufacturing plants, industrial and wholesale warehousing and distribution facilities, retail stores, office space, and commercial-industrial sites), the typical unit of rental is the square foot of area or of net rentable area. For example, an industrial warehouse may be rented at $1.20 per square foot per year; office space may be rented at $6.50 per square foot of net rentable area per year. The number of units identified in the analysis of improvements (Chapter 17) is the basis for calculating the total annual rental contemplated in the lease contract.

"Netness". Leases may also be classified as *gross* or *net* rented leases. A fully gross lease is one in which the lessor pays all of the usual operating expenses of the property ordinarily borne by the owner. At the other end of the scale, a completely "net" lease is one in which the lessee pays all of these expenses: property taxes, insurance, maintenance, and repairs—even the owner's income tax liability in a "net, net, net" lease. In between lies a whole range of degrees of "netness" which reflect the allocation of responsibility for paying specified operating expenses, or portions of them, between lessor and lessee. This distribution of responsibility for operating expenses is a matter of individual negotiation between lessor and lessee, and is specified in detail in the lease contract.[8] The greater the proportion of operating expenses borne by the lessee, the more "net" the lease is.

Absolutely net rental leases produce an income stream to the lessor which can be treated as Net Operating Income and capitalized directly to a present worth or value figure. To the extent that the lessor pays operating expenses, they must be deducted from rental receipts to derive the NOI to the leased fee interest. One device for stabilizing the net income receipts of the lessor over the term of the lease is to insert "escalator" clauses into the contract.[9] These require the lessee to pay some or all of the element of operating expenses beyond a specified level. A common example is the "tax escalator clause," which may call for the lessee to assume all increases in property taxes above the level prevailing at the time the lease is signed. Depending on the negotiating strength of the parties and their mutual desires, other elements of operating expenses such as insurance premiums or repairs and maintenance may also be subject to "escalator clauses."

420

In exchange for the certainty and stability of Net Operating Income offered by escalator clauses, the lessor will frequently accept a lower base rental. This will, of course, be reflected in the specific terms of the lease contract.

**"Credit" vs. "Real Estate" Leases.** Another important consideration for the appraiser valuing a leased fee interest is the ability of the lessor to use the lease on the property as a basis for arranging favorable terms of mortgage financing.[10] A high-credit, low-risk tenant on a long-term lease lends a high degree of stability to the income forecast to be produced by the property, especially if the rentals are relatively "net." This stability and certainty of net income receipts provides strong support to the probable repayment of the mortgage loan in accordance with the terms of the mortgage note. When rentals are assigned to the mortgagee and the lease subordinated to the mortgage, a long-term lease to a highly rated tenant makes the mortgage loan a "credit" transaction.

The added protection afforded the mortgagee by rental assignment and lease subordination in a "credit" lease usually results in more favorable loan terms for the mortgagor-lessor: lower mortgage interest rate, higher loan-to-value ratio, and/or longer mortgage maturity. This is reflected in a reduced debt service through lower mortgage constant and/or higher leverage, which in turn tends to produce a higher present worth of the leased fee. High-credit "national" tenants are aware of the financing advantages their presence on long-term leases provides property owners. As a result, they can usually negotiate lower rentals, so that the benefits of favorable financing terms tend to be shared by lessor and lessee in proportion to their relative bargaining strength. As a broad generalization, the longer the duration of the lease with other terms remaining the same, the greater will be the financing advantage and the present worth of the lessor's income stream.

If the lessees are not high-credit firms, then the financing of the property is based primarily on the characteristics of the real estate rather than the credit of the tenants. The appraiser must carefully evaluate the character of the leasing agreement ("credit" or "real estate") to identify the financing terms most likely to prevail, assuming the interests being valued are not already subject to an existing mortgage that is forecast to continue in force over the remaining duration of the lease.

### Valuation of Leased Fee

Estimating the present worth of the leased fee, whether as Investment Value or Market Value, involves capitalizing the forecast income stream to the lessor as a Property Residual. This is because that income stream consists of Net Operating Income derived from Contract Rental and contract operating expenses over the term of the lease, plus the forecast amount of the reversion in the form of the entire property at the expiration of the lease.

**Contract Rental.** In deriving the forecast annual NOI to be capitalized to the present worth of the leased fee, the Contract Rental is the starting point. When a percentage lease is involved, the appraiser must still forecast the amount of "overages" on the basis of the experience (if any) of the subject property, the experience of similar competing properties in the local market, and the market prospects of the type of use represented by the lessee.

**Lessor's Operating Expenses: "Netness."** The operating expenses deducted from gross contract rental income to produce the forecast NOI are those specified to be borne by the lessor under the lease contract. Actual figures from the operation of the subject property (past or anticipated) under its actual management may be used, subject to adjustments based on the experience of similarly leased competing properties (if any) on the market. The *categories* of operating expense items paid by the lessor are specified in the lease contract. The *amount* of expense to be deducted depends on whether there are escalator clauses covering any of the items. If there are, the base amount of the expense item (property taxes, insurance, repairs and maintenance, etc.) is the amount deducted; if not, the appraiser must make a reasonable forecast of the stabilized amount to deduct.

In brief, the degree of "netness" of the lease determines what items of operating expense must be deducted from contract rental income, and how much must be deducted for each applicable item.

**Income Projection Period: Term of Lease.** The income projection period over which the forecast NOI is discounted to estimate the present worth of the leased fee is the remaining term of the lease as of the valuation date. This remaining term is the first or primary term only, unless there is strong evidence of a high probability that the lessee will exercise any renewal options that may be included in the lease contract.

**Lessor's Rate of Discount.** The equity yield rate applicable to the lessor's equity investment and the Discount Rate applicable to the entire leased fee will tend to be lower than the comparable rates appropriate to discounting Market Rentals to a present worth estimate for the same type of property in the same market.[11] The NOI forecast under a long-term lease typically involves less uncertainty and risk to the purchaser-investor in an income property subject to a lease than does an income stream based on Market Rentals. A lease, after all, is a contract and the lessee has a contractual obligation to pay the contract rent. He fails to do so at the hazard of his future credit rating, the risk of legal action by the lessor to force payment, and the potential for financial disaster.

Moreover, when Contract Rental is less than Market Rental for the space in question, the lessee has an incentive to maintain his use and occupancy of the premises at less-than-market rates. Even if his need for the space evaporates, it can usually be sub-leased to another tenant to the mutual advantage of both parties. There is therefore near-certainty that the forecast income under a less-than-Market Rental lease will be received over the income projection period, which tends to be reflected in the rates of discount applicable to that income stream.

When the lessee is a "national credit," there is usually too much at stake for the tenant to jeopardize his or its credit rating by defaulting on the lease. Even if the Contract Rental exceeds the Market Rental, the lessee will often honor the lease contract unfailingly, especially after all other legal means to renegotiate or abrogate the lease have proved unsuccessful. In addition, the existence of a "national credit" on a lease can result in a lower Discount Rate or Base Rate through the more favorable terms of financing frequently available for properties with "credit leases," as has been pointed out in a preceding section.

*Differential Treatment of "Excess Rental".* When Contract Rental is greater than Market Rental as of the valuation date, the difference is often termed "excess rental." There is varying opinion among appraisal authorities concerning the appropriate treatment of "excess rental" to arrive at a supportable present worth estimate.[12] It is sometimes argued that "excess rental" should be capitalized at a higher rate of discount than that applied to the portion of Contract Rental equal to Market Rental, because it is less certain to be paid by the tenant. However, the lessee is obligated to pay the full amount of Contract Rental under the lease contract, and the likelihood of his selectively paying only a portion of that rental without prompt and successful legal action by the lessor is remote.

As with most differences of opinion representing extreme positions, the solution appears to lie somewhere between the two. The lessee obliged to pay "excess rental" will most probably resort to every legal and feasible action to have the rent reduced or the lease renegotiated without jeopardizing his credit position. The longer the remaining term of the lease and the greater the expectation that Contract Rental will continue to exceed Market Rental by a significant amount, the more vigorous his efforts to obtain relief will be. Also, the probabilities of success will depend largely on the relative bargaining strength of lessor and lessee. The conclusion, then, requires nice judgment by the appraiser to estimate the probabilities that the lessee will continue (however reluctantly) to meet his rental obligations in strict adherence to the terms of the lease, or will exert sufficient pressure on the lessor to effect a change in income realized by the leased fee interest. If no change seems probable, then the same lower rates of discount apply to the entire amount of Contract Rental. If the receipt of the "excess rental" appears less certain or likely, then it should be discounted at a higher rate to reflect this uncertainty. That higher rate may still be equal to or less than the market Discount Rate, however, depending entirely on the appraiser's perceptions and professional judgment of the situation.

A special case of "excess rental" is represented by *overages* in a percentage lease, in excess of base rental. Unless the base rental is unrealistically low, which must be ascertained by the appraiser, percentage overages reflect sufficient additional risk and uncertainty to warrant a higher rate of discount. Their dependence on gross sales receipts of the tenant business renders them potentially variable, as well as less certain. The appropriate rate of discount to apply to overages depends largely on the expectations of the lessor-investor, conditioned in part by the experience of similarly leased competing properties in the same market.

**Treatment as a Level Annuity.** Absolutely net rental income is necessarily treated as a level annuity,[13] as is NOI based on leases with escalator clauses. Other net income streams may vary, no matter how certain the rental income receipts may appear, as operating expenses are forecast to vary. When operating expenses can be stabilized, as they frequently are, then NOI can also be regarded as a level annuity. Contract Rental is not subject to the same uncertainties that may call for declining annuity treatment through straight-line capital recovery when Market Rentals are capitalized in some instances. Indeed, differences in risk or uncertainty in forecast NOI between leased fee valuation and "unencumbered" fee valuation are sometimes (erroneously) compensated for by using level annuity capitalization for the former and straight-line capitalization for the latter, at what is purportedly the same Discount Rate. The respective Capitalization Rates actually reflect different level annuity Discount Rates, but the presentation is frequently expressed as a difference in presumed methods of capital recovery.[14]

Step-Up and Step-Down leases also require level annuity capitalization, except that each segment of the income stream is treated separately, and the "deferred factor" explained and illustrated in Chapters 5 and 11 is used for all portions of the income stream scheduled to begin in future years.

**Property Residual Technique.** Because the forecast income receipts for a leased fee interest consist of a finite (usually level) income stream for the remaining term of the lease, plus a reversion of whatever is left of the entire property at the expiration of the lease, the Property Residual technique of capitalization is especially applicable. Indeed, the valuation of a leased fee is the classic example of Property Residual analysis.

The flow of NOI for the remaining term of the lease is capitalized at the appropriate level annuity Capitalization Rate or Capitalization Factor to produce an estimate of the present worth of that income stream. The forecast amount of the reversion is discounted at the appropriate Present Worth of One factor over the remaining term of the lease to produce the estimated present worth of the reversion. The two present worth estimates are then summed to derive the estimated present worth (or value as defined) of the leased fee.

Unless it is provided in the lease contract through a purchase option that the appraiser is reasonably confident will be exercised by the lessee, the amount of the reversion at the expiration of the lease must be forecast by the appraiser. The same techniques of ascertaining investor expectations and judgments are employed here as were presented in the discussion of Market Value estimation with the Property Residual technique in Chapter 12. The only difference is that more emphasis is placed on the specific expectations of the lessor.

**Mortgage-Equity Applications.** As previously noted in Chapters 13 and 18, mortgage-equity analysis is applicable to virtually any income-property appraisal problem. The valuation of a leased fee is no exception. The analysis is particularly pertinent when lessee and lease contract characteristics exert a marked influence on mortgage financing terms, and the appraiser (and lessor) seeks to measure that impact. In this instance, the income projection period is the remaining term of the lease, rather than some possibly shorter investment holding period.

**Illustrative Examples.** To illustrate the technique of estimating the present worth of a leased fee, assume the following lease, income, financing, and rate-of-return characteristics for an income property under a long-term lease. The lease calls for $10,000 per year absolutely net rental (NOI), and has a remaining term of 15 years. The appropriate rate of discount for the leased fee is 10%. The "leased fee capitalization rate" is therefore 0.131474 (Ellwood, page 116, column 6).

1. *Net income as a level annuity.* The present worth of the net rental income stream to the leased fee is:

$$\frac{\$10,000}{0.131474} = \$76,061$$

If the forecast amount of the reversion in 15 years is $50,000, then its present worth to the lessor, discounted at 10% annually for 15 years is $11,970 ($50,000 × 0.239392: Ellwood, page 116, column 4). The present worth of the leased fee interest, estimated on a Property Residual basis is therefore:

| | |
|---|---|
| Present Worth of Income Stream | $76,061 |
| Present Worth of Reversion | 11,970 |
| Present Worth of Leased Fee | $88,031 |

Suppose now that the NOI of the property based on Market Rental is $12,000, and the income projection period based on remaining economic life of the improvements is 25 years. The market-derived Discount Rate is 11%, and the forecast amount of the reversion is still $50,000 receivable in 25 years. (The 11% compound interest and discount factors are on page 132 in Ellwood.) Treating the NOI as a level annuity produces the following Market Value estimate under the Property Residual technique:

| | |
|---|---|
| Present Worth of Income Stream | |
| $12,000/.118740 = | $101,061 |
| Present Worth of Reversion | |
| $50,000 × 0.073608 = | 3,680 |
| Present Worth of Property | $104,741 |
| Indicated Market Value of Property | $105,000 |

Since the present worth of the leased fee based on NOI of $10,000 is $88,000, the difference is the present worth of the leasehold. The lessee has a valuable asset in the right to occupy the premises at a Contract Rental $2,000 per year less than Market Rental. Its value or present worth is $105,000 minus $88,000, or $17,000 (actually, $104,741 − $88,031 = $16,710). The valuation of leaseholds is considered in more detail in a subsequent section of this chapter.

An interesting point emerges if the Market Rental income from the property is expected to decline over the 25-year income projection period. Using straight-line capital recovery to reflect this declining-annuity character of NOI, the "leased fee capitalization rate" becomes 15% (.11 + .04 = .15). The present worth of the income stream is then $12,000/.15 = $80,000. The present worth of the $50,000 reversion remains $3,680, so the indicated Market Value of the property is estimated at $84,000 ($80,000 + $3,680 = $83,680, rounded to $84,000)! In this case, the leased fee is worth more than the "unencumbered" fee, even though NOI based on Contract Rental is apparently $2,000 less than NOI based on Market Rental. This is a *first-year* difference only, and Market-Rental-derived NOI is forecast to decline systematically each year thereafter. This points up once again the critical importance of identifying the most probable character of the forecast future income stream over the income projection period, and carefully selecting the capital recovery method that is most nearly descriptive of and responsive to that set of characteristics.

2. *Gross rental leases: NOI as a declining annuity.* When a flat rental lease specifies gross rentals to be paid by the lessee, the NOI generated to the lessor need not be a level annuity. It all depends on what is forecast to happen to operating expenses payable by the lessor. If there are no escalator clauses in the lease, any increases in such items as property taxes, insurance premiums, repairs and maintenance, or any other element of operating expense must be borne by the lessor. It is usual to anticipate that operating expenses will indeed increase over time, so NOI will have to be treated as a declining annuity or else as a stabilized level annuity at a level somewhat lower than first-year NOI. The technique for stabilizing NOI is that explained and illustrated in Chapters 10, 11, and 12.

Suppose, for example, that gross Contract Rental on a 15-year lease is a flat $15,000 per year. Operating expenses are estimated at $3,000 the first year, and they are forecast to increase approximately 5% each year. There are no escalator clauses in the lease. The forecast amount of NOI can be calculated for each of the 15 years of the lease term, and the income stream resulting treated as a series of 15 individual reversions. If the appropriate rate of discount is 10%, the Present Worth of One factors found in column 4 on page 116 of Ellwood would be used. The 15-year stream of NOI would be as shown in Exhibit 19-1.

The income stream (NOI) receivable by the lessor shown in Exhibit 19-1 is then discounted to a present worth estimate by applying the 10% annual Present Worth of One factor for the appropriate year to that year's forecast NOI. The 15 individual present worth estimates are then summed to produce the present worth estimate for the entire income stream. This is the technique for handling *any* forecast future income stream demonstrated in Chapters 5 and 11, and

**Exhibit 19-1**

**Declining Net Operating Incomes Forecast Under a 15-Year Gross Rental Lease**

| Year | Gross Rental | Operating Expenses | NOI |
|------|-------------|--------------------|----|
| 1 | $15,000 | $3,000 | $12,000 |
| 2 | $15,000 | $3,150 | $11,850 |
| 3 | $15,000 | $3,308 | $11,692 |
| 4 | $15,000 | $3,473 | $11,527 |
| 5 | $15,000 | $3,647 | $11,353 |
| 6 | $15,000 | $3,829 | $11,171 |
| 7 | $15,000 | $4,020 | $10,980 |
| 8 | $15,000 | $4,221 | $10,779 |
| 9 | $15,000 | $4,432 | $10,568 |
| 10 | $15,000 | $4,654 | $10,347 |
| 11 | $15,000 | $4,887 | $10,113 |
| 12 | $15,000 | $5,131 | $ 9,869 |
| 13 | $15,000 | $5,387 | $ 9,613 |
| 14 | $15,000 | $5,657 | $ 9,343 |
| 15 | $15,000 | $5,940 | $ 9,060 |

illustrated in other examples throughout this book. In this case, the present worth of the income stream is $83,951.88, or $84,000.

A similar result can be obtained by "stabilizing" NOI at $11,021 and capitalizing it at the annual 10% capitalization rate for 15 years (Ellwood, page 116, column 6). The present worth estimate is $11,021/.131474 = $83,826.46. The slight difference is entirely the result of rounding. The "stabilized" income is derived by first calculating the ratio of the 14-year annual 5% Installment to Amortize One factor to the straight-line "capitalization rate" weighted by the percentage of first-year operating expenses to rental income. This ratio is .101024/.11 = .9184. Applying it to first-year NOI produces the "stabilized" NOI for the 15-year income projection period: $12,000 × .9184 = $11,021.

3. *Handling of "excess rental".* In the property considered earlier that was producing net rental income of $10,000 on a 15-year lease with a 10% rate of discount, suppose that Market Rental is actually $9,000. Thus, $1,000 of forecast NOI is based on "excess rental." The case is even clearer if it is assumed that $9,000 per year is "base rental," and the additional NOI is derived from a percentage of gross sales of the lessee: say 5% of the excess over $200,000 per year. It is forecast that annual gross sales of the lessee will approximate $220,000 over the 15-year income projection period.

Because of the greater uncertainty that the $1,000 of "excess rental" income will be received as forecast, a higher rate of discount is applied to it. In this case, assume that the appropriate rate is 13%. The Installment to Amortize One factor for 15 years at 13% is found on page 149 in Ellwood, column 6. The present worth of the $10,000 annual net income stream is then estimated as:

Present Worth of Market Rental at 10%:
  $9,000/.131474 =         $68,455
Present Worth of "Excess Rental" at 13%:
  $1,000/.154742 =         6,462
Present Worth of Income Stream:    $74,917

The uncertainty and greater risk associated with the continued receipt of $1,000 in "excess rental" or "overages" for 15 years is reflected in the fact that this income stream has a present worth approximately $1,150 less than the $76,060 that it would have if the full $10,000 were based on net Contract Rental.

4. *Rental payments in advance.* If rentals are payable in advance, the capitalization of the income stream requires only a simple adjustment in the capitalization factor or rate employed. This procedure was explained and illustrated in Chapter 5. Since the first payment is receivable immediately, its present worth is 100% of itself, so the discount factor is 1.0000. The remaining income stream is receivable for one period less than the income projection period: in this case 14 years. Thus, the present worth of $10,000 per year, payable in advance for 15 years and discounted annually at 10%, is equal to $10,000 *plus* the present worth of $10,000 divided by the 14-year annual 10% capitalization rate, or multiplied by the 14-year annual 10% level annuity factor (Ellwood, page 116, columns 6 and 5, respectively).

Present Worth of $10,000 Payable Today:   $10,000
Present Worth of 14-year Income Stream:   73,667
  ($10,000/.135746 = $73,667)
  ($10,000 × 7.366687 = $73,667)
Present Worth of 15-year Income Stream   $83,667

If the level annuity capitalization *factor* (column 5) is used to calculate the present worth of the income stream, the mechanical process can be simplified by adding 1.0000 to the factor for one period less. In this example, the factor for the 15-year income stream with rental payments in advance would be 8.366687, which could be multiplied directly by $10,000 to develop the present worth of the 15-year level income stream.

5. *Step-up and step-down rentals.* When rental changes are specified in the lease contract, the appraiser can treat the future income stream as a series of income flows starting at different times in the future. Each can be discounted to a present worth estimate as of the valuation date by using the *deferred factor* technique explained and demonstrated in Chapter 5.

Assume that a lease with 17 years remaining calls for annual net rental payments (at the end of the year) according to the following schedule:

| | |
|---|---|
| Years 1-3 | $11,000 |
| Years 4-12 | $12,000 |
| Years 13-17 | $13,500 |

The indicated rate of discount for this income stream is 9.5%. The appropriate discount factors are found on page 108 in Ellwood. The deferred factors can be developed in two ways. The first is the level annuity factor for each income period discounted by the appropriate present worth factor:

| Years | Period (Years) | Level Annuity Factor | Years Deferred | Present Worth Factor | Deferred Factor |
|---|---|---|---|---|---|
| 1-3 | 3 | 2.5089 | 0 | 1.0000 | 2.5089 |
| 4-12 | 9 | 5.8753 | 3 | 0.7617 | 4.4752 |
| 13-17 | 5 | 3.8397 | 12 | 0.3365 | 1.2921 |

Deferred factors can also be derived by taking the difference between the level annuity factor for the end of each period and the level annuity factor at the same rate for the beginning of the period. In this example, the factor for the first three years is still the three-year factor of 2.5089, since the $11,000 income stream starts as of the valuation date. The deferred factors for years 4-12 and for years 13-17 are estimated as follows:

| | |
|---|---|
| 12-year factor: | 6.9838 |
| 3-year factor: | −2.5089 |
| 9-year factor, deferred 3 years: | 4.4749 |

| | |
|---|---|
| 17-year factor: | 8.2760 |
| 12-year factor: | −6.9838 |
| 5-year factor, deferred 12 years: | 1.2922 |

The slight differences in these two sets of deferred factor calculations are entirely the result of rounding. The present worth of the income stream is then estimated by multiplying each net income figure by the applicable factor, and summing the results.

| | |
|---|---|
| $11,000 X 2.5089 = | $27,598 |
| $12,000 X 4.4752 = | 53,702 |
| $13,500 X 1.2921 = | 17,443 |
| Present Worth of Income Stream | $98,743 |

*Leasehold Valuation*

Leasehold interests are frequently transferable, and may be marketable if there is indeed a market for them and the present worth of the leasehold estate is a positive figure. Logically, a leasehold can have a Market Value, but the estimate of present worth developed through appraisal analysis typically represents Investment Value.

When Contract Rental is in excess of Market Rental, the lessee is obligated by the lease contract to pay more for the occupancy and use of the leased premises than he presumably would have to pay if the same premises were vacant and available to be leased as of the valuation date. It would therefore be in his interest and to his financial benefit to be relieved of his rent obligation under the lease. Indeed, tenants do on occasion buy up their "rights" under an unfavorable lease, which indicates that a leasehold can and does have a negative value on occasion. Except in cases when the tenant is actually seeking to buy up his remaining obligations under a lease, however, the appraiser does not normally assign a negative value to a leasehold, even though the negative value does exist.[15] This negative present worth does make it possible to satisfy the logical judgment that the sum of the present worth of the leased fee plus the present worth of the leasehold (negative in this instance) equals the present worth of the "unencumbered" fee simple on the property.

**Treatment as a Residual.** Since the major interest in leasehold valuation is concentrated on the measurement of a positive value, the focus is on cases when Contract Rental is less than Market Rental. It has already been shown in the illustrative examples of leased fee valuation earlier in this chapter that the present worth of the leasehold can be derived as the difference between the Market Value of the property based on Market Rentals and the present worth of the leased fee. One way to separate interests in income properties for analytical and valuation purposes is to divide them between the leased fee and the leasehold. The Market Value of the entire property can be estimated by capitalizing NOI based on Market Rentals with market-derived rates of discount.[16] The present worth of the leased fee can be estimated by capitalizing NOI based on Contract Rental with rates of discount derived from the lessor and/or a specific investor. All of these required items of information can be developed by the appraiser with relative confidence from market sources, the lease contract, and the lessor-investor.

The same cannot always be said about appropriate rates of discount to apply to favorable rental differentials in the leasehold interest: Market Rental less Contract Rental. There is rarely an active market in leasehold interests from which to abstract rate data. Moreover, lessees rarely approach their leasehold positions as investors; they find themselves with a probably valuable and possibly marketable interest in the leased premises almost entirely by chance. As a result, most lessees have no idea what rate of discount is applicable in their own case, and can offer little help or guidance to the appraiser.

Thus, the treatment of the leasehold as the residual difference between Market Value of the property and present worth of the leased fee is not only logical but frequently the only realistic way to estimate its value.

For analytical or comparative purposes, the rate of discount on the leasehold can be approximated by dividing the differential annual rent advantage to the lessee by the calculated present worth of the leasehold. This provides the "leasehold capitalization rate" for the income projection period, which is usually the remaining term of the lease. Reference to tables of annual Installment to Amortize One factors (column 6 in Ellwood's compound interest factor tables) for that income projection period will reveal the *range* of rates of discount at the least.

For example, suppose a leasehold interest has been estimated by abstraction to have a present worth of $25,000. The differential rental advantage to the lessee (Market Rental less Contract Rental) is $5,000 per year. Then, the "leasehold capitalization rate" is 20% ($5,000/$25,000 = 0.20). If the remaining term of the lease (the income projection period) is 15 years, the indicated rate of discount is between 18% and 19%, most likely 18.5%. This is based on an inspection of the 15-year annual Installment to Amortize One factors in Ellwood (column 6). The factor for 18% is 0.196403 (page 154); it is 0.205092 for 19% (page 155). Since 0.20 is just about midway between these two factors, 18.5% represents a very close approximation.

**Direct Capitalization of Rental Differential.** If it is possible to obtain a rate of discount for the leasehold interest which is supported by evidence from the market and/or the lessee, the favorable rental differential receivable by the lessee can be capitalized directly at the "leasehold capitalization rate." The stream of rental differential is receivable over the remaining term of the lease, at the end of which the lessee has no further claim or rights in the realty. The present worth of the leasehold interest must therefore be fully recovered or amortized over that remaining lease term, and also provide an annual return at the appropriate rate of discount. This is the essence of the Installment to Amortize One factor, as demonstrated in Chapters 5 and 11.

For example, suppose that a favorable lease is providing the lessee with a forecast annual rental differential (Market Rental less Contract Rental) of $2,500 per year, and the remaining term of the lease is 18 years. The appraiser has concluded from evidence from the market and the lessee that the appropriate rate of discount in this case is 16%. The 18-year annual Installment to Amortize One factor at 16% is 0.171885 (Ellwood, page 152, column 6). Thus, the "leasehold capitalization rate" (rounded) is 17.19%. The present worth of the leasehold interest is therefore $14,500 ($2,500/.1719 = $14,543.34).

*High-Risk Rate of Discount.* The rental advantage enjoyed by the lessee under a lease where Contract Rental is less than Market Rental is unstable and uncertain, or "fragile." It can be significantly reduced or even eliminated by relatively small declines in Market Rental based on changing market conditions beyond the control of the lessee, in an uncertain future. The longer the income projection period, the more risk or uncertainty there is associated with the continuance of the rental advantage as forecast. At the same time, the Contract Rental is fixed or specified in amount by the terms of the lease. This high risk or "fragility" of the rental advantage is compensated for by the use of relatively high rates of discount in the valuation of leasehold interests. Such market evidence as is available supports the logic of this argument; rates of discount on leaseholds twice as high as those applicable to leased fee valuation are not uncommon.[17]

**Sandwich Lease Interests.** When one or more sub-leases exist on a property, at lease one party is simultaneously a lessor and a lessee. The middle position is commonly called a "sandwich lease interest,"[18] and the party who is simultaneously a lessor and a lessee is frequently referred to as the "sandwichman." The mechanics of valuing this interest are simple. The annual *net* income receivable by the "sandwichman" is capitalized over the income projection period at the appropriate "leasehold capitalization rate." The net income is the difference between the Contract Rental he is to receive as a sub-lessor. The income projection period is the remaining term of the sub-lease. Because he has a contractual right to receive rental under the sub-lease and the amount of rental he must pay is also fixed by lease contract, the uncertainty associated with the receipt of the differential net income is directly dependent on the credit status of the sub-lessee and the relation of the Contract Rental under the sub-lease to Market Rental. The rate of discount applied to the sandwich lease interest is therefore less than that applied to a leasehold interest, but usually slightly higher than the rate of discount for the leased fee.

For example, assume a simple case of a parcel of downtown land leased for $12,000 per year with 22 years remaining on the lease. It is sub-leased for $14,000 to a parking lot operator for 22 years. The current Market Rental on the site is estimated at $16,000. The rates of discount are concluded to be 8.5% for the leased fee, 10.5% for the sandwich interest, and 10% for the unencumbered fee. The forecast amount of the reversion in 22 years is $175,000. The estimated value or present worth of the several interests would be developed as follows:

        Market Value:
            $16,000/.114005 (Ellwood, page 116, column 6)  =  $140,344
            Plus Reversion: $175,000 X 0.122846            =    21,498
            Indicated Market Value                              $161,842
                                                               ($162,000)

        Leased Fee:
            $12,000/.101939 (Ellwood, page 92, column 6)   =  $117,717
            Plus Reversion:                                      21,498
            Present Worth of Leased Fee                         $139,215

Sandwich Interest:
$2,000/.118134 (Ellwood, page 124, column 6)   = $ 16,930

Sub-Leasehold:
    Market Value                               = $161,842
    *Less*: Leased Fee          $139,215
           Sandwich Interest      16,930        −156,145
    Present Worth of Leasehold                  $  5,697

The indicated "leasehold capitalization rate" for 22 years is 35.11% ($2,000/$5,697 = 0.351062). This is in excess of 30%, which is as high as the Ellwood compound interest factor tables go (page 166).

The present worth of the reversion is the same for a fee owner, whether there are leases on the property or not. For the leased fee, it is discounted at the Discount Rate. Only the net income based on Contract Rental is discounted at the leased fee rate of discount.

## Valuation of Mortgagee's Participation Interest

Lender or mortgagee participation loans are mortgage loans in which the mortgagee receives a stipulated share of property income and/or equity interest, under the terms of the loan contract, as part of the "price" of granting the loan.[19] This participation or sharing in income and/or equity by the mortgagee is in addition to the interest income and return of loan principal incorporated into annual debt service, according to the terms of the mortgage note. It is an enforceable contractual right in the real estate, representing a partial or less-than-fee interest, and it has value. The right may or may not be transferable and marketable. Its Investment Value or present worth can certainly be estimated; under the proper conditions it can have a Market Value as well.

Because of the increased use of participation loan agreements on income properties by institutional lenders since the mid-1960s, the valuation of mortgagee participation interests has assumed greater significance for income-property appraisers. The mortgagee's claim represents a *deduction from* the present worth of the equity investor's (mortgagor's) position, and an enhancement of the present worth of the mortgagee's investment position.

### Types of Mortgage Participations

The mortgage participation agreement is a contract whose precise terms are set as a result of negotiations between mortgagor and mortgagee. While a great variety of specific terms and conditions is encountered, for purposes of analysis and evaluation these agreements can be classified under two broad categories: *income participations* and *equity participations*. With a few sub-categories under each of these general headings, it is possible to cut through the legal complexities of loan participation agreements and identify three key points: *who* is to receive how much (or *what*), and *when*. It will be recalled that these are the basic questions to be answered in characterizing *any* future income stream receivable by any party with an interest or right in income-producing real estate. Thus, while the legal and contractual details of the loan participation agreement may be complex, lengthy and varied, the valuation of the interests created under that agreement proceeds in a straightforward fashion, using valuation techniques already at the appraiser's disposal, once the characteristics of each participating party's income stream have been identified.

**Income Participation.** An income participation is the right of the mortgagee to share in some portion of future income to be generated by the property, usually over the maturity term of the underlying mortgage loan. The claim against the specified portion of property income typically remains in force even if the mortgagor pays off the loan in advance, whether through refinancing or otherwise, or the property is sold. In some instances, there is a "lock-in" provision forbidding prepayment of the mortgage loan; in others, the mortgagor must pay the mortgagee the present worth of the remaining income participation right if the property is refinanced or sold. In either case, the mortgagee's participation position is protected over the full maturity of the loan.

Income participations are usually expressed as a fixed percentage of some part of the forecast future income stream: effective gross, net operating income, or cash throw-off. The gross income participation is most common, because lenders usually recognize the influence of management and expense allocations on both NOI and cash throw-off. As the income in which the lender participates becomes more "net," the percentage of the participation increases. Thus, while a lender might be entitled to receive 5% of annual effective gross, his share of NOI might well be 25%, and of cash throw off 40%. These are simply illustrative figures to indicate general orders of magnitude.

In many cases, the participation is in income *in excess of* the levels estimated as of the valuation date, on which the loan and its terms are based. For example, the mortgagee might be entitled to 10% of rental collections in excess of the stabilized effective gross used in estimating the property value for the mortgage loan. Then, the lender is sharing in any increased benefits accruing to the property through an improved competitive market position, or inflation.

**Equity Participation.** In an equity participation, the mortgagee's right to share in future income receipts is not restricted to a finite time period (the maturity term of the loan). The mortgagee may share in the proceeds of the reversion, realized through resale or refinancing of the property, or both. There may be participation in the tax shelter provided by the property investment. Finally, the lender may be a full equity participant, becoming in effect a partner of the equity investor (mortgagor) and sharing in income, tax shelter, and any reversionary proceeds. When full equity participation occurs, often on an equal-partner 50% basis, the mortgagee frequently purchases the land and advances what amounts to a 100% loan on the improvements. This particular arrangement is not necessary, but it is a frequent form of equity participation agreement.

### Applicability of Mortgage-Equity Analysis

There are two sets of interests or rights in the income property which is subject to a lender participation mortgage loan: those of the equity investor-mortgagor and those of the participating mortgagee. The form of income-property appraisal analysis most responsive to the problem of valuing these two interests is mortgage equity analysis. As demonstrated in Chapter 13, this approach to valuation separates the total investment in an income property into its two major financial-investment components. Each can be valued separately, and the equity position is essentially the residual. The value of the property (either Investment Value or Market Value) is the sum of the present worths of these two investment components.

Although the analysis can be used to estimate Market Value, provided the conditions of Market Value estimation are met and the present worth of *both* the mortgagee's and the equity investor's investment positions are Market Value estimates, it has much broader applicability and much greater significance in the estimation of Investment Value. Particularly in lender participation cases, each party is primarily interested in the present worth or value of *his* investment position *to him*.

The present worth of the mortgagee's position is the present worth (principal sum) of the mortgage loan plus the present worth of the mortgagee's income or equity participation interest. The latter is estimated simply by discounting the future income forecast to be receivable by the participating mortgagee at the rate of discount identified as applicable to this type of mortgagee participation. The equity position is valued in precisely the same way it would normally be, as described in Chapters 13 and 18, except that the income receipts capitalized must be carefully identified so that no duplication or double counting occurs.

**Rates of Discount.** The rate of discount for mortgage debt service is of course the mortgage interest rate. The income to the equity investor-mortgagor is discounted at the indicated equity yield rate provided either by the market or by the investor himself. The additional task confronting the appraiser in a mortgage-participation valuation problem is to identify the appropriate rate of discount for the mortgagee's participation interest. When the lender is experienced in participation loans and/or sensitive to the market, which is increasingly the case among institutional lenders, the required or anticipated rate of discount can be obtained from the mortgagee. In any event, the best available evidence is that the rate of discount will certainly be higher than the mortgage interest rate because of the greater uncertainty and risk associated with probable receipt of the participation income as forecast, and probably lower than the mortgagor's required equity yield rate because the mortgagee has little or (frequently) no additional investment in the property beyond the mortgage loan.

**Illustrative Example.** In the continuing example of income property valuation used in several chapters, it was assumed that the property was forecast to produce NOI of $15,000 over a 15-year income projection period.[20] The reversion was forecast to be 70% of present value, and a 10% equity yield rate was used. Mortgage financing was assumed to be available at 8.5% interest on 70% of value, with monthly amortization over a 20-year maturity. The mortgage constant was 10.41%. Total property value was estimated to be $150,000, divided between a $105,000 mortgage (70%) and a $45,000 equity investment. Annual debt service was $10,930 ($105,000 × .1041), and cash throw-off to equity was therefore $4,070 ($15,000 − $10,930). Finally, the forecast amount of the reversion was $105,000 (.70 × $150,000), of which the net cash proceeds to the equity investor were estimated to be $60,585 ($105,000 resale proceeds *minus* 42.3% outstanding balance on the $105,000 mortgage payable to the mortgagee).

Now suppose that the mortgagee offers the investor a $105,000 mortgage at 7.5% for 15 years (based on 70% of "value") with monthly amortization, provided the mortgagee receives 20% of Net Operating Income and 20% of the proceeds of resale 15 years hence when the mortgage is fully paid off. NOI is still $15,000, the reversion is still forecast to be $105,000, and the mortgagor's equity yield rate is 10%. The appropriate rate of discount for the mortgagee's participation income is concluded to be 9.5%.

The mortgage constant would then be 11.12% (12 × .009270: Ellwood, page 73, column 6). The annual Installment to Amortize One factor for 15 years at 9.5% is 0.1277, and the Present Worth of One factor for 15 years discounted annually at 9.5% is 0.2563 (Ellwood, page 108, columns 6 and 4, respectively). The 10% capitalization rate is still 0.1315, and the Present Worth of One factor remains at 0.2394.

The mortgagee is forecast to receive $3,000 annually (.20 × $15,000) for 15 years, plus an estimated $21,000 (.20 × $105,000) in 15 years. The present worth of this income participation is:

| | | |
|---|---|---|
| Annual Income: | $3,000/.1277 = | $23,493 |
| Reversion: | $21,000 × .2563 = | 5,832 |
| Present Worth of Participation: | | $29,325 |

The mortgagor-investor will receive an estimated NOI of $12,000 for 15 years, plus a reversion of $84,000 at the end of 15 years. His forecast annual cash throw-off is:

| | |
|---|---|
| Net Operating Income | $12,000 |
| *Less* Annual Debt Service | |
| ($105,000 × .1112) | − 11,676 |
| Cash Throw-Off to Equity | $    324 |

The present worth of the equity investor-mortgagor's investment position is then estimated as:

Present Worth of Cash Throw-Off:
$324/.1315 =                                              $ 2,464
Present Worth of Reversionary Interest:
$84,000 × .2394 =                                        20,110
Present Worth of Equity Position                       $22,564

The present worth of the mortgagee's and mortgagor's investment positions, and the indicated Investment Value of the property under these conditions, is:

Mortgagee's Position:
Principal of Mortgage          $105,000
Participation Interest           29,325
Total Present Worth                                      $134,325
Mortgagor's Position (Present Worth):                     22,564
Total Present Worth of Property                          $156,889
                                            say          $157,000

The additional $7,000 in "value" above the estimated Market Value of the property is the result of the mortgagee's assumed willingness to accept a 7.5% return on the mortgage principal in this case. Such willingness is often lacking. Whatever the particular combination of factors in the particular participation agreement, the same basic framework of analysis is applicable.


## Review Exercises

1. A 24-year lease is producing $32,000 absolutely net rental to the lessor, whose required rate of return on the investment in the property is 8.75%. The forecast amount of the reversion is $275,000.
   a. What is the present worth of the net rental income?
   b. What is the present worth of the reversion?
   c. What is the present worth of the leased fee?
2. Assume the absolutely net Market Rental for the property in Problem 1 is $36,000 and the market Discount Rate for this type of property is 9.5%. The appropriate income projection period is 24 years.
   a. What is the Market Value of the property?
   b. What is the present worth of the leasehold?
   c. What is the indicated discount rate for the leasehold?
3. A lease with 23 years remaining calls for annual net rentals of $7,500 for the next 3 years, $7,000 for the following 10 years, and $6,000 for the last 10 years. The required rate of return on this investment is 11.5%.
   a. What is the present worth of this income stream?

b. What is the present worth of the income stream if annual rentals are payable in advance?

4. A five-year lease on a 12,000 square-foot warehouse calls for gross rentals of $1.50 per square foot per year. The owner's operating epxense ratio is estimated to be 25% in the first year, and operating expenses are forecast to increase 10% per year. The owner requires a 12% rate of return on his investment. Market Rentals for this type of space are $1.60 per square foot per year. The rate of discount applicable to this leasehold estate is 25%.
   a. What is the amount of NOI forecast for the lessor each year?
   b. What is the present worth of the lessor's forecast income stream?
   c. What is the present worth of the leasehold?

5. A 12-year retail lease calls for an annual base rental of $12,000, payable in advance. Operating expenses of the owner are forecast to be $4,000 per year, deductible from base rental. The lease provides for additional rentals payable at the end of each year, based on 3% of lessee's annual gross sales in excess of $200,000. The forecast annual amount of gross sales over the next 12 years is $250,000. The rate of return on base rentals is 10%, and on "overages" 14%. The forecast amount of the reversion is $75,000.
   a. What is the present worth of this leased fee?

6. A mortgagee has agreed to make a $50,000 mortgage loan at 9% interest payable monthly over a 20-year maturity. The property has forecast level gross income receipts of $12,500 per year and a 40% operating expense ratio. The mortgagee insists on receiving 4% of gross income annually, as well as 25% of the forecast reversion of $60,000 20 years hence. The mortgagor's equity yield rate is 10.5%, and the mortgagee's rate of discount on the participation income is 10%.
   a. What is the present worth of the mortgagee's investment position?
   b. What is the present worth of the mortgagor's investment position?
   c. What is the Investment Value of the property?

## Supplementary Readings

American Institute of Real Estate Appraisers, *The Appraisal of Real Estate*, fifth edition (Chicago: American Institute of Real Estate Appraisers, 1967), Chapter 25.

William R. Beaton, "Commercial Leasehold Appraising," *Valuation*, Volume 15, Number 1, January 1967.

Jerome J. Dasso, William N. Kinnard, Jr., and Stephen D. Messner, "Lender Participation Financing: Its Nature and Significance to Appraisers," *The Real Estate Appraiser*, Volume 37, Number 2, March-April 1971.

Jerome J. Dasso, William N. Kinnard, Jr., and Stephen D. Messner, "Lender

Participation Financing: Case Applications in Appraising Participation Financed Properties," *The Real Estate Appraiser*, Volume 37, Number 3, May-June 1971.

L.W. Ellwood, *Ellwood Tables for Real Estate Appraising and Financing; Part I: Explanatory Text*, third edition (Chicago: American Institute of Real Estate Appraisers, 1970), pp. 121-134.

Sanders A. Kahn, Frederick E. Case, and Alfred Schimmel, *Real Estate Appraisal and Investment* (New York: Ronald Press, 1963), Chapters 22 and 27.

W.H. Kam, "Investment Analysis of Leased Commercial Land," *The Real Estate Appraiser*, Volume 33, Number 2, February 1967.

William N. Kinnard, Jr. and Stephen D. Messner, *Industrial Real Estate,* second edition (Washington, D.C.: Society of Industrial Realtors, 1971), pp. 306-317. Chapter 10.

R. Bruce Ricks, "Valuation of Lessor and Lessee Interests in a Physical Asset," *The Appraisal Journal*, Volume 34, Number 2, April 1966.

Alfred A. Ring, *The Valuation of Real Estate*, second edition (Englewood Cliffs, N.J.: Prentice-Hall, 1970), Chapter 20.

William M. Shenkel, "Valuation of Leased Fees and Leasehold Interests," *The Appraisal Journal*, Volume 33, Number 4, October 1965.

S.C. Warwick, "Leasehold Interest Paradox," *The Real Estate Appraiser*, Volume 32, Number 3, March 1966.

S.C. Warwick, "The Two-Property Concept," *The Real Estate Appraiser*, Volume 31, Number 3, March 1965.

E.N. Yarmon, "Net Leases," *Appraisal Institute Magazine*, Volume 12, Number 4, Winter 1968.

## Notes

1. See Chapter 2 for a more detailed presentation of the nature of rights in realty and their implications for income property valuation. The discussion here is intended merely to serve as a review to put the valuation of partial interests in its proper perspective.

2. This view is represented by the discussion in Chapter 21 of Alfred A. Ring, *The Valuation of Real Estate*, second edition (Englewood Cliffs, N.J.: Prentice-Hall, 1970), especially pp. 317-318 and 327-328.

3. See, for example, American Institute of Real Estate Appraisers, *The Appraisal of Real Estate*, fifth edition (Chicago: American Institute of Real Estate Appraisers, 1967), Chapter 2; and William N. Kinnard, Jr., *A Guide to Appraising Apartments,* third edition (Chicago: Society of Real Estate Appraisers, 1973), pp. 5-6.

4. For further details, consult the two articles on "Mortgage Participation Financing," by J.J. Dasso, W.N. Kinnard, Jr., and S.D. Messner appearing in the March-April and May-June 1971 issues of *The Real Estate Appraiser*, Volume 37, Numbers 2 and 3.

5. More details and examples are provided in William N. Kinnard, Jr., and Stephen D. Messner, *Industrial Real Estate,* second edition (Washington, D.C.: Society of Industrial Realtors, 1971), Chapter 10.

6. See *ibid.* for an analysis and evaluation of individual lease clauses.

7. A particularly useful discussion of the sale-leaseback for appraisers is provided in Irving Korb, *Real Estate Sale-Leaseback: A Basic Analysis*, revised edition (Washington, D.C.: Society of Industrial Realtors, 1970).

8. For further details and examples, see Kinnard and Messner, *Industrial Real Estate,* Chapter 10.

9. See *ibid.*, pp. 323-334.

10. Further details on this issue are provided in *ibid.*, pp. 329-330.

11. See AIREA, *Appraisal of Real Estate*, Chapter 25. Empirical evidence as well as analytical judgment supporting this position may be found in R. Bruce Ricks, "Valuation of Lessor and Lessee Interests in a Physical Asset," *The Appraisal Journal*, Volume 34, Number 2, April 1966; and William M. Shenkel, "Valuation of Leased Fees and Leasehold Interests," *The Appraisal Journal*, Volume 33, Number 4, October 1965.

12. This point is covered in AIREA, *Appraisal of Real Estate*, Chapter 25; and Ring, *Valuation of Real Estate*, pp. 302-305.

13. See AIREA, *Appraisal of Real Estate*, Chapter 25; and Ring, *Valuation of Real Estate*, Chapter 20.

14. See, for example, AIREA, *Appraisal of Real Estate*, Chapter 25; and Ring, *Valuation of Real Estate*, Chapter 20.

15. For illustrations and further discussion of this point, see Ring, *Valuation of Real Estate*, pp. 307-308.

16. See AIREA, *Appraisal of Real Estate*, pp. 407-413; Ring, *Valuation of Real Estate*, pp. 307-310; and Ricks, "Valuation of Lessor and Lessee Interests."

17. See Ricks, "Valuation of Lessor and Lessee Interests," as well as AIREA, *Appraisal of Real Estate*, pp. 407-413.

18. Additional examples of sandwich lease interest valuation are included in the discussions of this topic in AIREA, *Appraisal of Real Estate*, pp. 417-418; and Ring, *Valuation of Real Estate*, pp. 310-312.

440

19. The presentation and examples used in this section are adapted from Dasso, Kinnard, and Messner, "Lender Participation Financing" (Parts I and II).

20. Additional examples illustrating the impact of varying types of mortgagee participations on the present worth of the mortgagee's and mortgagor's investment positions are provided in Dasso, Kinnard, and Messner, "Lender Participation Financing: Case Applications in Appraising Participation Financed Properties," *The Real Estate Appraiser*, May-June 1971.

# 20 Final Value Estimation and Income Property Report Writing

**Arriving at the Final Value Estimate**

The next-to-last step in the valuation of income properties is to arrive at the final estimate of value as defined.

## Single Figure vs. Most Probable Range

Once he has gone through the several steps of each of the alternative approaches he applies to value estimation, the income property appraiser is in a position to develop his findings and indications of value from each into his final conclusion. It may be that he can and should indicate the most probable range within which value (most frequently in investment analysis) is likely to fall. In the great majority of cases, however, he will be required by the client or the nature of the assignment to indicate one figure which represents his best judgment of value: the most probable selling price of the subject property under the stipulated conditions of the appraisal problem.

In the process of selecting the final estimate of value from among the alternative and frequently varying indications developed in his analysis, the appraiser must go through two distinct, important steps. First, he must *review* all his previous work and analysis, checking and verifying his data, his logic, and his technique. Second, he must apply logic and judgment through the procedure termed *Correlation* to arrive at his final estimate of value.

**Review of the Appraiser's Work.** It is both appropriate and necessary for the appraiser to review his work and analysis before attempting to correlate his findings and reach his final value conclusion(s).[1] Review is *not* correlation. Rather, it involves preparing the findings and indications of value *for* correlation.

*Multiple Indications of Value.* Application of two or more of the alternative approaches to value estimation to any appraisal problem will usually result in preliminary indications of value which are somewhat at variance with one another. Ideally, of course, if all necessary data were available and if the techniques of analysis were applied properly, the value indications from the several approaches would be the same. This rarely occurs in practice, however.

When the answers vary, the appraiser should seek to understand why. Especially if there is wide variance among the answers or one of the indications appears "out of line" (but not only under these circumstances), the appraiser must review his work to discover if any revisions or corrections seem required.

441

The applications of logic and technique and calculations can be altered if review shows them to be improper or inadequate. Data cannot be revised by the appraiser. Even if they are inadequate, they are the facts of the market place which he has been able to develop. Review and adjustment need not narrow the range of variation. It is just as possible that the range will be widened as a result of the review.

*What Is Reviewed.* In the review process, the appraiser considers at least four aspects of his previous work.

*Check mechanics*: techniques, calculations, adjustments. Errors can be made, and they must be corrected.

*Check logic and analysis*: the thinking and steps that have gone into the value estimate in each approach employed. There is a considerable amount of decision-making and choosing throughout the framework of appraisal analysis. The appraiser should review each for its appropriateness, as well as the assumptions, estimates, and conclusions he made at each step.

*Check applicability*: the relationship of the underlying principles of each approach to the nature of the appraisal problem and of the property being appraised.

*Check data and data sources*: their reliability and adequacy. Nothing can be done to alter the data, but an evaluation of their adequacy can influence the emphasis placed on the value estimate(s) from each approach in the correlation process.

### The Correlation Process

The appraiser is seeking to estimate value as defined in the appraisal problem. The value estimate should represent the best, most probable, and most defensible estimate—given the market facts, market conditions, and analytical assumptions in terms of which the appraisal is made.

Frequently, complete reliance cannot be placed on the value estimate derived from any one approach, no matter how logical its application might appear in the abstract. Even when the greatest reliance is expected to be placed on the indication of value developed from applying one approach, and this fact is well known in advance, making an estimate of value through one or both of the other alternatives serves as a check on the appraiser's thinking and work. A necessary final step in the appraisal framework prior to writing the appraisal report is to work two or more indications of value derived through alternative approaches into one final value estimate for the property. In appraisal analysis, this process is termed *Correlation*.

As a thought process, Correlation is applied throughout the entire appraisal framework, in each of the approaches to value estimation. It is not restricted to the section of the appraisal report titled "Correlation," or the three alternative approaches. Every time the appraiser makes a selection or choice from among several alternatives anywhere in his appraisal analysis, he uses a form of correlation.

**Nature of Correlation.** Correlation is the process by which the appraiser evaluates, chooses and selects from among two or more alternative conclusions or indications to reach a single answer. Correlation is in fact an "examination of conscience" by which the appraiser evaluates his own analysis.

Final Correlation is the application of this process to the indications of value derived from each of the approaches utilized in the appraisal problem at hand, to arrive at a final estimate of value. Its essence is to develop one defensible rational conclusion which approximates the one value (as defined in the appraisal problem) whose *existence* is known, but whose *quantity* is being sought.

Correlation is applied in Direct Sales Comparison analysis in selecting a single indication of value from among the several developed through the use of two or more units of comparison. In Cost Approach analysis, it involves selecting appropriate units of reproduction cost new, and the measures of diminished utility (accrued depreciation). It is also used in estimating site value. It is applied in Income Capitalization analysis to develop appropriate income streams to be capitalized, and to select appropriate rates of capitalization.

In applying the Correlation process, the appraiser weights the relative significance, applicability and defensibility of the indication of value derived from each indicator. He then places most weight and reliance on the one(s) which, in his professional judgment, best approximates the value being sought in the appraisal. He reconciles the facts, trends and observations developed in his analysis. This is based on a review of his conclusions and their probable validity and reliability.

**Basic Considerations in Correlation Analysis.** There are two constraints on the appraiser in applying his judgment to the selection of a final value estimate via the Correlation process. First, he must consider the appropriateness and applicability of the particular approach to the appraisal problem at hand. In the case of income properties, particular attention should be paid to the estimate of value derived via Income Capitalization, since this is presumed to reflect most closely the thinking and behavior of market participants. Second, the appraiser is limited by the availability and reliability of verified market data necessary for the application of each of the approaches.

Data must be available in sufficient quantity and adequate enough in reliability to warrant basing a final judgment on them. The data requirements of each of the several alternative approaches to value estimation discussed in previous chapters must be met; otherwise, the value estimate based on that approach must be rejected.

A particular approach to value estimation must be appropriate to the appraisal problem in terms of the character of the property, the value being sought, and the underlying principles and assumptions involved. This means that the appraiser must be thoroughly familiar with the logic and rationale of each of the several approaches.

After analyzing and evaluating both the data used and the appropriateness of each approach to the problem at hand, the appraiser may minimize or even ignore the indication of value developed in one or two of the approaches. He relies most heavily on the indication of value which represents the best combination of appropriateness supported by adequate, reliable data.

**Relation to the Purpose of the Appraisal.** The appraiser is seeking a final estimate of value that most closely approximates the value being sought, as defined in the appraisal problem. This is the purpose of the appraisal. It should be the best, most probable value figure obtainable under current market conditions. Therefore, the appraiser must conduct his entire analysis with the nature and characteristics of that value in mind.

*Definition of Value Sought.* The definition of value in the appraisal problem at hand establishes the criteria for judgment and selection by the appraiser. When Market Value is being sought, the final value estimate must be consistent with the reactions and behavior of a typically informed, prudent, rational purchaser-investor who is operating on the open market in competition with other informed, prudent, rational purchaser-investors.

*Rights Appraised.* The portion of the total bundle of rights of ownership being appraised will affect the final value estimate. This estimate must be consistent with the rights to be appraised, which are identified in the definition of the appraisal problem.

*Effective Valuation Date.* Especially when Market Value is to be estimated, the valuation date establishes the market conditions in terms of which value is estimated. The final value estimate must be consistent with the market conditions prevailing as of the valuation date.

*Assumptions and Limiting Conditions.* The limiting and contingent conditions and assumptions in terms of which the value estimate is made are identified in the definition of the appraisal problem. The final value estimate derived through the Correlation process must reflect the impact of these limitations and assumptions on value, as defined.

**What Correlation is Not:**
1. *Correction of past errors in thinking and/or technique.* Before applying the Correlation process, the appraiser should review each of the steps in each of the several approaches to value estimation that he has employed. This review process is designed to identify and, if necessary, correct any errors in thinking or processing of data. It prepares the materials and conclusions developed in the appraisal framework for Correlation. While it is related to Correlation as a necessary prior step, the review process is *not* part of Correlation.
2. *Application of a formula.* Correlation requires the application of careful

judgment and analysis. No mathematical or mechanical formula is an acceptable substitute for this. "There is no judgment in a lead pencil."

3. *Averaging*. Averaging is one type of formula with particular pitfalls because it is so easy and simple to apply. The appraiser's task is to apply qualitative judgment, rather than quantitative mechanics. Neither a simple average nor a weighted average is a substitute for the appraiser's judgment and analysis at this juncture.

4. *Narrowing the range of value indications*. While the objective of Correlation is usually to arrive at a single estimate of value (as defined) which is convincing and defensible, it does not follow that the range of value indications developed in the several approaches employed will necessarily be narrowed. The indications of value from each of the several alternative approaches applied in the particular appraisal are not *changed* through the Correlation process. They simply represent the information available to the appraiser for use in making his final judgment of the most probable convincing and defensible estimate of value in the light of the data available and the techniques of analysis applied.


*The Final Value Estimate*

The final value estimate is the appraiser's professional opinion or conclusion resulting from the application of the entire framework of appraisal analysis, including Correlation, to the appraisal problem at hand. It is that value which most nearly represents what the typically informed, prudent, rational purchaser-investor would pay for the property being appraised if it were available for sale on the open market as of the valuation date, given all the data (and only those data) utilized by the appraiser in his analysis.

**Value Sought.** The final value estimate is the appraiser's conclusion of what he truly believes to be the logical, reasonable and defensible measure of the value sought, as defined in the appraisal problem.

**Analysis and Experience.** A final value estimate is an opinion. It is the appraiser's professional opinion based on his knowledge, analysis, professional judgment, and experience. That experience and judgment must be supported and justified by market facts, and by logical and convincing analysis.

**Limited Applicability.** A final value estimate is valid only under carefully stipulated assumptions and conditions prevailing as of the valuation date, which in turn reflects specified market conditions.

**An Estimate.** The final value estimate is precisely that: an estimate. As such, it must be appropriately rounded to eliminate any implication of unwarranted precision or accuracy. Rounding brings the estimate to a reasonable degree of accuracy consistent with the standards of the local market, the price level or range within which the estimate falls, and the type of property being appraised. The appraiser may also indicate the *range* within which Most Probable Sales Price is most likely to be found, depending on the nature of the appraisal assignment and the wishes of the client.

## The Appraisal Report

### *Role of the Written Appraisal Report*

An appraisal assignment is not completed when the appraiser has developed a defensible estimate of value as defined, as of the valuation date. The information must be transmitted in writing to the client. The written appraisal report is the culmination of the appraiser's work and analysis. It must state clearly and convincingly what he did and why he did it. It should be capable of standing alone. Therefore, it must be a complete and consistent presentation of the data and facts considered, and the logic followed in the appraiser's analysis. A well-written appraisal report will lead the reader inevitably and inexorably to the same conclusions as those reached by the appraiser.

### *Types of Appraisal Reports*

Written appraisal reports will vary in type and length, depending on the nature of the assignment and the client's or employer's wishes. Whatever form the appraisal report takes, however, the process the appraiser employs should be exactly the same. A brief letter or short-form report requires the same data, the same analysis, the same care, and the same substantiation as does a full narrative report. The written report is simply the external evidence to the client of the appraiser's work and conclusions; the thought processes that underlie it must always be complete. In brief, all that varies from one type of report to another is the amount of information and background material that is transmitted to the client or employer.

**Letter.** Sometimes the appraiser's "report" consists of a letter to the client transmitting the appraiser's findings and conclusions. This is not really a report, but simply a written opinion of value. Nevertheless, it should be supported by every bit as much information and analysis as a more formal, detailed report must be.

**Form Report.** Many clients and employers require form reports, especially for volume work. These usually are standardized 2-page or 4-page forms on which most of the information is provided by checking appropriate boxes or filling in blanks. While they provide standardization and ease of comparison, form reports frequently do not permit the appraiser to express his findings or analysis adequately. The appraiser should never feel embarrassed or reluctant to add narrative commentary if there is insufficient space in the form to express precisely what he wishes to communicate. Any deficiency in the report is his responsibility, and not that of the form, the client, or the printer.

**Narrative Report.** Even in "simple" income-property appraisal reporting, the narrative report is best suited to permit the appraiser to explain to the reader what he did, how he did it, and why he did it. Every professional appraiser should be thoroughly familiar with the techniques and requirements of narrative report writing.

Narrative reports can run from a few pages to hundreds of pages, with or without detailed exhibits. The one pitfall to avoid in the development and presentation of a narrative report is the tendency to overdo and to write too long a report. Completeness does not mean padding or including superfluous material. From experience, judgment and the client's wishes, the appraiser must learn how much is "enough" to do the job fully and convincingly. In this connection, a one-page "Summary of Salient Facts and Conclusions" is particularly useful for the client or the reader, especially when it is placed at the beginning of the report. This permits the client to absorb the essence of the appraiser's findings, while the full report that follows serves to explain and substantiate them.

*Elements of Written Appraisal Reports*

An appraisal report may have a variety of ingredients.[2] Some are essential in *any* report; some are required under specific circumstances, (e.g., by a client, or to satisfy admission requirements of professional appraisal organizations); some are highly desirable and recommended, but not essential; some are simply desirable when time and circumstances permit.

**Tests for the Inclusion of Items.** In deciding what information should or should not be included in any written report, the appraiser can apply several tests. The following list of questions provides a guide to the appraiser to help resolve the issue in his own mind.

1. *Is it required* by the client (or by the professional organization in the case of demonstration reports)?
2. *Is it necessary* for understanding by the reader, or for processing into the final value estimate?
3. *Will it help* the reader in understanding the presentation, or the appraiser in developing his final value estimate?
4. *Is it useful* in developing the appraiser's argument or the reader's understanding?
5. *Is it feasible* in terms of the fee and the time limitations imposed on the

assignment? This should be a consideration before the assignment is undertaken and the fee set. Once agreement is reached, the professional appraiser is obligated to exert his best effort regardless of the attractiveness of the financial or time arrangements to which he has agreed.

6. *Is it well done*? Does it really convince the reader, as well as being necessary and useful?

7. *Is it well presented and well expressed*? Can it be followed easily by the intelligent lay reader?

8. *Is it inevitable* in the nature of the appraisal framework?

Perhaps the most important question of all is: "So what?" What does the inclusion of the particular items add to the development of the appraiser's argument and to the reader's understanding? The appraiser should ask himself this about every item he might otherwise question; the alert reader certainly will ask it of the appraiser, whether the appraiser happens to be present or not.

**Essential Contents of Any Report**. Regardless of its form, any written report prepared by a professional appraiser should contain as a minimum the following:

1. *Identification of the Property*: a clear and unequivocal statement, including both a legal description and at least a brief physical description.

2. *Statement of Purpose of the Appraisal*: indication of the value being sought, preferably defined from an authoritative source.

3. *Indication of Property Rights Being Appraised*.

4. *Indication of Date as of Which Value Estimate Is Made*. This establishes the market conditions in terms of which the value estimate is valid.

5. *Statement of Assumptions and Limiting Conditions*. These must be specific to the appraisal problem. Standardized statements are hazardous, especially if they include a "free and clear of all encumbrances" assumption. This is particularly inapplicable for mortgage-equity analysis.

6. *Indication of Value Estimate* (The Appraiser's Final Conclusion).

7. *Certification by the Appraiser*: including a statement that he has no financial interest in the property, he has actually inspected the property, and he has adhered to standards of professional conduct and practice.

8. *Signature of the Appraiser*.

Even a "letter" appraisal must contain these elements as a minimum if it is to perform its function for the client, and represent minimally acceptable professional practice.

**Desirable Elements of a Narrative Appraisal Report**. In addition to the foregoing essential elements, which are required of *any* written appraisal report whatever its form, a narrative appraisal report will normally include the following:[3]

1. *Summary of salient facts and conclusions*. Especially in longer, more detailed

reports, this is a useful aid to the client, or reader. It summarizes succinctly at the outset the basic points which the client is seeking.

2. *Letter of transmittal.* This is another form of summarizing the report. It should contain all the essentials enumerated in the preceding section, and should be addressed to the client. It should also indicate that an appraisal report in narrative form is being transmitted with it.

3. *Table of contents.* This is particularly useful in longer reports, so that the reader may find specific sections without undue search.

4. *Area and neighborhood analysis.* In a narrative report, the appraiser should share with the reader his findings and conclusions about the external market influences at work on the value of the subject property. As discussed in Chapter 12, the presentation should be analytical and related to the valuation problem at hand. It should not be a mere itemization of facts and figures, nor a glowing recitation of the beauties and attractions of the area which are not pertinent to estimating the value of the subject property.

5. *Site and improvements analysis.* This presents the appraiser's findings from his inspection of site and building, including an indication of both positive and negative features that influence value. This discussion should establish succinctly the basis for the adjustments and/or deductions made by the appraiser in applying the several alternative analytical approaches to value estimation.

6. *Conclusion of Highest and Best Use.* The appraiser should define Highest and Best Use for the reader, and indicate his conclusions for the subject property, supporting those conclusions with evidence from his market, neighborhood, and property analysis. A discussion of the impact of zoning restrictions and other land-use or property-use regulations is usually included here.

7. *Application of value estimation methods.* One or more of the alternative approaches to value estimation should be discussed and described in enough detail for the reader to understand the basis for the appraiser's conclusions, as well as his handling of the data employed. Commentary on the availability and probable validity of data for each of the approaches used will help the reader to follow the appraiser's analysis and conclusions. Whenever one or more of the basic alternative approaches to value estimation is *not* utilized by the appraiser and hence not presented in the report, there should be a brief explanation why.

8. *Correlation and final value estimate.* The appraiser should indicate carefully the reasons for selecting the final value estimate chosen from among the alternative indications developed in each of the approaches utilized in his appraisal. The reader should be convinced by the logic and the manner of presentation that the figure selected is the most appropriate one under the circumstances.

9. *Exhibits.* To help the reader to follow the text presentation, as well as to visualize the physical environment of the subject property; the appraiser should include exhibits which are carefully and accurately prepared, and presented in a professional and comprehensible fashion. These exhibits would normally include:

a. *Photographs*. There should be several views of the subject property, of comparable sales and rental properties, and of the immediate neighborhood of the subject property. They should be dated.
b. *Area and Neighborhood Maps*. These will help the reader understand the relationship of the subject property to public facilities, centers of employment and trade, streets and transportation facilities, and comparable sales and rental properties. Zoning can also be noted on the maps to illustrate the pattern of permitted land uses in the vicinity of the subject property.
c. *Plot Plan and Floor Plan*. Drawn carefully and accurately to scale, these plans can help the reader understand the written description of the subject property, and visualize both positive and negative features of the property discussed in the report.
d. *Tables and Graphs*. Compilations of data utilized in the body of the report can best be presented among the exhibits. The data are available for the interested reader without interrupting the flow of the narrative by including them in the body of the report.

**Characteristics of a Professional Appraisal Report.** For any narrative appraisal report, form, appearance, and manner of presentation are important ingredients in giving the proper impression of professional effort. The appraisal report is the image of the appraiser. Form is no substitute for content, but it is a significant consideration.

*Sequence.* The order in which materials are presented in the report is not ordinarily stipulated. However, a logical sequence from the general to the particular, and from background to the specifics of the subject property, adds greatly to the impact of the report on the reader.

*Vocabulary.* Appraisals are rarely written for other appraisers. The lay reader should be able to follow the appraiser's argument without a glossary or dictionary in his hand. Highly technical terminology should be kept to a minimum and defined where it is used. The terms should be employed consistently, and should be consistent with accepted professional appraisal practice.

*Objectivity.* The manner of presentation should clearly underscore the appraiser's professional detachment from, or lack of personal interest in, the results of his analysis.

*Logical Development.* The appraiser's analysis and presentation should flow logically and convincingly to the final value estimate.

*Style.* The written report should read easily and flow well. Aside from avoiding excessive technical jargon, the report should be well organized to lead the reader through the appraiser's thought processes to his conclusion. Direct and simple prose is preferable.

*Appearance.* The report should be neat and clean. It should show care in the preparation of exhibits. It should be carefully proofread, with no obvious spelling or grammatical errors.

## Supplementary Readings

American Institute of Real Estate Appraisers, *The Appraisal of Real Estate*, fifth edition (Chicago: American Institute of Real Estate Appraisers, 1967), Chapters 23 and 24.

Bernard W. Camins, "Narrative Report Writing: Its Emerging Weaknesses," *The Real Estate Appraiser*, Volume 35, Number 3, May-June 1969.

J.B. Featherstone, "Correlation and Final Value Estimation," *The Real Estate Appraiser*, Volume 34, Number 1, January-February 1968.

M.B. Hodges, Jr., "A Reference Library for Appraisers," *The Real Estate Appraiser*, Volume 34, Number 6, November-December 1968.

Sanders A. Kahn, Frederick E. Case and Alfred Schimmel, *Real Estate Appraisal and Investment* (New York: Ronald Press, 1963), Chapter 15.

William N. Kinnard, Jr., *A Guide to Appraising Apartments*, second edition (Chicago: Society of Real Estate Appraisers, 1966), pp. 51-53.

William N. Kinnard, Jr., *An Introduction to Appraising Real Property* (Chicago: Society of Real Estate Appraisers, 1968), Chapters 17 and 18.

Richard U. Ratcliff, "The Only Road to $V_p$," *Appraisal Institute Magazine*, Volume 9, Number 2, June 1965.

Alfred A. Ring, *The Valuation of Real Estate*, second edition (Englewood Cliffs, N.J.: Prentice-Hall, 1970), Chapter 23.

H. Grady Stebbins, Jr., *A Guide to Narrative Appraisal Reporting on Income Producing Properties* (Chicago: Society of Real Estate Appraisers, 1970).

## Notes

1. Further details of the process of reviewing the appraiser's work prior to

correlation to a final value estimate are provided in American Institute of Real Estate Appraisers, *The Appraisal of Real Estate*, fifth edition (Chicago: American Institute of Real Estate Appraisers, 1967), pp. 373-377; and William N. Kinnard, Jr., *An Introduction to Appraising Real Property* (Chicago: Society of Real Estate Appraisers, 1968), Chapter 17.

2. Standards for the contents of professionally acceptable appraisal reports may be found in AIREA, *Appraisal of Real Estate*, pp. 432-433; and in H. Grady Stebbins, Jr., *A Guide to Narrative Appraisal Writing on Income Producing Properties* (Chicago: Society of Real Estate Appraisers, 1970), especially pp. 4-6.

3. See Stebbins, *Narrative Appraisal Writing on Income Producing Properties*. An illustrative example of a full narrative appraisal report on an apartment property is presented in Alfred A. Ring, *The Valuation of Real Estate*, second edition (Englewood Cliffs, N.J.: Prentice-Hall, 1970), pp. 457-482.

**Appendix A**
**Suggested Solutions**
**to Review Exercises**

# Appendix A

Appraising is a judgmental process. While the results of income-property valuation techniques, especially those of income capitalization, may be precise figures, the thought processes and the decisions about data inputs that underlie the application of these techniques necessarily require selective judgment by the appraiser. Therefore, what follows is a presentation of "Suggested Solutions" to the Review Exercises at the end of most chapters in this book, not a set of "answers." Decisions and opinion have entered into the selection of mechanical techniques to apply to the problems, and in the rounding of data inputs, intermediate figures, and final value estimates.

These are not the only possible solutions in many cases. They do reflect good appraisal analysis, professionally acceptable and supportable approaches to the problems, and sound judgment in relation to the facts of each problem. Moreover, they are arithmetically accurate to the extent that available calculating equipment can make them so.

Whenever compound interest or discount factors are used in deriving the Suggested Solutions, page and column references are given. As in the body of the text, these references are to L.W. Ellwood, *Ellwood Tables for Real Estate Appraising and Financing; Part II: Tables*, third edition (Chicago: American Institute of Real Estate Appraisers, 1970).

## Chapter 2

1. The essential components of any appraisal report and the reasons for their inclusion are:
    (1) Identification of the Real Estate being Appraised: to describe in physical and legal terms what is being appraised and to make clear to the reader of the report precisely what parcel of realty is the subject of the appraisal;
    (2) Identification and Definition of Value Estimated: to make unequivocally clear to the reader what type of value has been estimated; what its components, requirements, and limitations are; and what the purpose of the appraisal has been;
    (3) Identification of Rights Valued: to make clear to the reader what has actually been valued, and what portion (if any) of the total bundle of private property rights has been excluded;
    (4) Identification of the Valuation Date (the "As of" Date): to indicate the prevailing market conditions in terms of which the value estimate has been made; and to specify the only market conditions under which the value estimate is applicable;

(5) Indication of Final Value Estimate: to provide the reader with the results of the appraiser's analysis and professional judgment, given all the conditions and limitations under which the value estimate was made.

2. a. The $250,000 figure represents Market Value.
   b. The $235,000 figure represents Investment Value to the client.
   c. The $260,000 figure represents (historical) Market Price.

3. The price at which the investor can buy a property is its Market Price. In an informed market characterized by active competition among buyers and sellers, it probably also represents Market Value.
   What a property is "worth" to the individual investor is its Investment Value to him.

4. The fee interest in the property is worth $40,000 under the conditions specified. The mortgage and the tax lien are enforceable non-ownership rights in the realty. They are "encumbrances" on the fee simple estate of the owner.

5. In the short run, apartment rentals will most probably rise. Assuming that this results in greater profits from owning and operating apartment properties, construction of new apartment developments will be encouraged.

## Chapter 3

1. The Principle of Substitution is illustrated here.
2. The applicable valuation principles are:
   a. Contribution: to measure the net effect of each alternative development proposed;
   b. Highest and Best Use: to identify the basis for selecting the use and development program forecast to be most profitable, representing the highest present worth of the site;
   c. Substitution: to measure the probable costs, incomes, and operating expenses associated with each development program proposed;
   d. Supply and Demand: to identify the reality of the "demand" suggested by market analysis, and to relate it to existing and forecast market conditions;
   e. Variable Proportions: to identify the impact on anticipated value from varying the combination of site and building in the improved property.
3. a. *Variable Proportions.* The increases in proposed building heights (and investments) result in proportionately different property value estimates.
   b. *Contribution.* The increase in estimated value resulting from the addition of 14, 2, and 4 stories, respectively, is a measure of the contribution of each additional investment to total property value.
   c. *Highest and Best Use.* The combination of site and improvements that results in the highest anticipated rate of return on total investment, and particularly the highest value of the site, is the Highest and Best Use of the site.

d. *Anticipation.* Present worth or value estimates for the alternative development proposals are necessarily based on anticipations of future net income to be generated by the property under each use plan.

## Chapter 4

1. $V = I/R$. Therefore, the present worth is $12,000/0.14 = $85,714.29. This figure would most likely be rounded to $86,000. It represents the amount that would have to be invested to produce an annual return of $12,000 if the required rate of return is 14%.
2. $I = V \times R$. $70,000 \times 0.11 = $7,700 per year. The proof is that $7,700 represents 11% of $70,000: $7,700/0.11 = $70,000.
3. A capitalization factor is the reciprocal of any given rate $(F - 1/R)$. Therefore, $1/.085 = 11.7647$ ($11.7647 \times .085 = 1.0000$).
4. $R = I/V$. $7,500/$90,000 = 0.083333. The indicated Overall Rate is therefore 8.33%.
5. a. 8.5% is the rate of interest on the mortgage loan.
   b. The mortgage constant is annual debt service expressed as a percentage of the initial principal amount of the mortgage loan. In this case, it is
      $15,620/$150,000 = 0.104133 or 10.41%
   c. The equity dividend rate is annual cash throw-off (before-tax cash flow) expressed as a percentage of the equity investment.
      Equity investment here is property value minus mortgage principal:
      $200,000 − $150,000 = $50,000
      Cash throw-off to equity here is NOI minus annual debt service:
      $24,000 − $15,620 = $8,380
      Therefore, the indicated equity dividend rate is:
      $8,380/$50,000 = 0.1676 = 16.76%
   d. The overall rate is NOI expressed as a percentage of property value:
      $24,000/$200,000 = 0.1200 = 12.00%
   e. The equity yield rate of 18% is the prorated annual rate of return on the equity investment, taking into consideration prorated annual recovery of any forecast capital loss in the reversion at the end of the income projection period.

## Chapter 5

1. a. $V = I \times F$. $I = $8,800. $F = 3.313961$ (page 124, column 1)
      Thus, $V = $8,800 \times 3.313961 = $29,162.86 (say $29,200)
   b. $F = V/I$. $V = $26,875. $I = $8,800
      Thus, $F = $26,875/$8,800 = 3.053977
      A search of annual compound interest factor tables reveals that the

458

annual Future Worth of One Factor for 12 years at 9.75% is 3.053897 (page 112, column 1). Therefore, the indicated rate of return on the investment of $8,800 with resale 12 years later for $26,875 is *9.75% per year*.

c. This case illustrates the use of the Future Amount of One Factor.

2. This is an illustration of the use of the Future Worth of One per Annum factor.

$V = I \times F$  $I = \$1,000$  $F = 216.998138$ (page 129, column 2)

Then, $V = \$1,000 \times 216.998138 = \$216,998.14$ (say $217,000)

3. This problem involves the use of the Sinking Fund factor. It is expressed as a *rate*.

$I = V \times R$.  $V = \$75,000$.  $R = 0.096111$ (page 149, column 2)

Then, $I = \$75,000 \times 0.096111 = \$7,208.33$ per year

4. a. $V = I \times F$.  $I = \$1,500$.  $F = 36.299038$ (page 102, column 5)

$V = \$1,500 \times 36.299038 = \$54,448.56$

The present worth of the net rental income stream to the lessor is $54,500.

b. $V = I \times F$.  $I = \$50,000$.  $F = 0.170440$ (page 104, column 4)

$V = \$50,000 \times 0.170440 = \$8,522$

The present worth of the forecast $50,000 reversion to the lessor is $8,522. Note that by convention and standard practice the *annual* discount factor is used for estimating the present worth of the reversion, unless it is specifically stated that some other time period should be used.

c. The present worth of the leased fee interest is the *sum* of the present worth of the net rental income stream to the lessor *plus* the present worth of the reversion to the lessor:

| | |
|---|---|
| Present Worth of Income Stream | $54,448.56 |
| Present Worth of Reversion | 8,522.00 |
| Present Worth of Leased Fee | $62,970.56 |
| say | $63,000.00 |

d. The valuation of the forecast future income stream involves the use of the Present Worth of One per Annum factor.

The valuation of the reversion involves the use of the Present Worth of One factor.

e. To derive the Present Worth of One per Annum factor for a level annual income stream payable in advance, 1.000000 is added to the factor for one less income payment period.

In this case, the 19-year annual factor at 9.25% is 8.797778 (page 104, column 5). The 20-year factor for annual payments in advance is therefore:

1.000000
+8.797778
9.797778

$V = I \times F.\ I = \$6{,}000.\ F = 9.797778$

Thus, the present worth of \$6,000 per year, payable in advance over 20 years and discounted at 9.25% is:

$$V = \$6{,}000 \times 9.797778 = \$58{,}786.67,\ \text{or}\ \$59{,}000.$$

5. To calculate annual debt service, it is necessary first to derive the mortgage constant. Since this is a monthly-payment loan, the monthly Installment to Amortize One factor for 15 years at 8.75% (page 93, column 6) is multiplied by 12 to obtain the mortgage constant: $12 \times 0.009994 = 0.119928$ or 11.99%.

   a. $\$300{,}000 \times 0.119928 = \$35{,}978.40$ annual debt service.

   An alternative approach is to calculate the monthly payment, and multiply that figure by 12:

   $$\$300{,}000 \times 0.009994 = \$2{,}998.20 \times 12 = \$35{,}978.40$$

   b. The mortgage constant can be derived in two ways with the information provided in this problem. As shown above, it is $12 \times 0.009994 = 0.119928$ or 11.99%.

   It can also be calculated by taking the percentage ratio of annual debt service to initial mortgage principal:

   $$\$35{,}978.40/\$300{,}000 = 0.119928.$$

   c. The discount factor used is the Installment to Amortize One.

   d. With the information provided in this problem, two variants of essentially the same technique may be applied to estimate the outstanding balance of the mortgage loan 10 years hence. Both use the Present Worth of One per Annum factor to estimate the present worth of the remaining income stream receivable by the lender (mortgagee).

   With dollar figures of monthly mortgage payments available, the simpler method is to calculate the present worth of a 5-year remaining stream of monthly payments of \$2,998.20, discounted at an annual rate of 8.75%. The appropriate Present Worth of One per Annum factor is 48.456109 (page 93, column 5). The calculated outstanding balance of the 15-year mortgage 10 years hence (the present worth of the remaining 5-year income stream) is:

   $$\$2{,}998.20 \times 48.456109 = \$145{,}281.11$$

   Alternatively, it is possible to obtain the *percentage* of original mortgage loan still outstanding by calculating the ratio of the Present Worth of One per Annum factor for the remaining term of the mortgage, to the Present Worth of One per Annum factor for the original mortgage maturity. In this case, the factors (page 93, column 5) and their percentage ratio are:

$$5 \text{ years: } \frac{48.456109}{100.055165} = 0.484294 \text{ or } 48.43\%.$$

Applying the ratio to the original principal of the mortgage loan yields the unpaid outstanding balance 10 years hence:

$$\$300,000 \times 0.484294 = \$145,288.17$$

6. In estimating the present worth of this income stream, the annual Present Worth of One factor with discounting at 14% (page 150, column 4) is applied to each of the first four payments separately. Since payment is in advance, the factor for one year less is used in each case. This means that the first-year payment factor is 1.000000.

   For the indefinite income stream starting at the beginning of year 5 (end of year 4), the first step is to capitalize the income stream in perpetuity at the rate of discount. This indicates its present worth or value four years hence. It is then discounted to the present with the 4-year Present Worth of One factor at 14%.

   The present worth four years hence of the indefinite income stream starting at the beginning of the fifth year is:

$$\$5,500/0.14 = \$39,285.71$$

The present worth of the lessor's income stream is then:

| Year | Rental | | Present Worth of One Factor | | Present Worth |
|------|--------|---|---------------------------|---|---------------|
| 1 | $ 2,000 | X | 1.000000 | = | $ 2,000 |
| 2 | $ 3,000 | X | 0.877193 | = | $ 2,632 |
| 3 | $ 4,000 | X | 0.769468 | = | $ 3,078 |
| 4 | $ 5,000 | X | 0.674971 | = | $ 3,375 |
| 5+ | $39,286* | X | 0.592080 | = | $23,260 |

Total Present Worth                                      $34,345
*Present Worth 4 Years Hence

7. The estimation of the present worth of this income stream requires the use of deferred factors. The Present Worth of One per Annum factors applicable here are provided on page 139, column 5 in Ellwood.
The factor for years 1-6 is 8.499956.
The deferred factor for years 7-12 is:

|  | 12-year factor: | 12.845580 |
|---|---|---|
| *less* | 6-year factor: | 8.499956 |
|  |  | 4.345624 |

The deferred factor for years 13-17 is:

|  | 17-year factor: | 14.792346 |
|---|---|---|
| *less* | 12-year factor: | 12.845580 |
|  |  | 1.946766 |

The present worth of the step-down semi-annual income stream is then calculated as:

| Years | Semi-Annual Income | | P.W. One per Annum Factor | Present Worth |
|---|---|---|---|---|
| 1-6 | $2,100 | X | 8.499956 | =$17,850 |
| 7-12 | $2,000 | X | 4.345624 | =$ 8,691 |
| 13-17 | $1,875 | X | 1.946766 | =$ 3,650 |
| | Present Worth of Income Stream | | | $30,191 |

## Chapter 6

1. a. First floor rentable space = .80 X 12,000 = 9,600 square feet
Top floor rentable space = .80 X 12,000 = 9,600 square feet
Floors 2-9 rentable space = .80 X 96,000 = 76,800 square feet
Total Rentable Space = 96,000 square feet

Potential gross first floor = 9,600 X $8.00 = $ 76,800
Potential gross top floor = 9,600 X $7.50 = $ 72,000
Potential gross floors 2-9 = 76,800 X $6.00 = $460,800
Total Potential Gross = $609,600

Rental collections first floor = .98 X $ 76,800 = $ 75,264
Rental collections top floor = .97 X $ 72,000 = $ 69,840
Rental collections floors 2-9 = .95 X $460,800 = $437,760
Total Rental Collections = $582,864

Concession ("Other") Income   = $1.00 × 91,680 sq. ft.   = $ 91,680

| Total Effective Gross | Rental Collections | $582,864 |
| | Concession Income | 91,680 |
| | | $674,544 |

b. Management Fee: .03 × $582,864 = $17,486

c. Rental Collections at Full Occupancy (Potential Gross)   = $609,600
Concession Income ($1.00 × 96,000)   = $ 96,000
Total Effective Gross at Full Occupancy   = $705,600

2. a. 73/1,200 = .0608 = 6.08% Vacancy and Rent Loss Allowance
   b. 17/200 = .0850 = 8.5% vacancy and rent loss. The subject property appears to be less well managed, or less attractive on the market, than presumably similar competing properties.

3. 
| Potential Gross Rentals | $609,600 |
| Less Vacancy and Rental Loss | − 26,736 |
| Rental Collections | $582,864 |
| Plus Concessions Income | + 91,680 |
| Effective Gross Income | $674,544 |

Less Operating Expenses

| Management (.03 × $582,864) | $17,486 | |
| Personnel ($200 × 120) | 24,000 | |
| Maintenance (25¢ × 120,000) | 30,000 | |
| Insurance ($24,000/3) | 8,000 | |
| Taxes (.04 × $2,133,600) | 85,344 | |
| Utilities (.015 × $674,544) | 10,118 | |
| Replacements (.02 × $674,544) | 13,491 | |
| Other | 6,000 | |
| | | −194,439 |
| Net Operating Income | | $480,105 |

4. a. The mortgage constant is 12 times the monthly Installment to Amortize One for 25 years at 8.75%.
   12 × .008221 (page 93, column 6) = 0.098652 or 9.87%
   b. Annual debt service is the principal amount of the mortgage times the mortgage constant.
   $120,000 × 0.098652 = $11,838.24

c. 
| Effective Gross Income | $28,000 |
| Less Operating Expenses | − 12,000 |
| Net Operating Income | $16,000 |

d. Net Operating Income            $16,000
   *Less* Annual Debt Service       − 11,838
   Cash Throw-Off              $ 4,162

e. Equity is 25% of total investment. Total investment is $120,000/.75 = $160,000. Equity investment thus = $40,000.

$$\text{Equity Dividend Rate} = \frac{\text{Cash Throw-Off}}{\text{Equity Investment}} = \frac{\$4,162}{\$40,000} = .10405$$

Equity Dividend Rate = 10.41%

## Chapter 7

1. Leverage Factor = 1.00/.20 = 5.0
2. 525 Basis Points
   5.25 Points
3. a. Loan-to-value ratio = $75,000/$125,000 = .60 = 60%
   b. Mortgage constant = 12 × 0.007902 (page 77, column 6) = 0.094824
   c. Annual Debt Service = 0.094824 × $75,000 = $7,111.80
   d. Balloon payment = Outstanding balance 15 years hence. This is equal to the present worth of $592.65 per month at 7.75% for 7 years. The Present Worth of One per Annum factor is 64.674883 (page 77, column 5). Then $592.65 × 64.674883 = $38,329.57 outstanding balance ("balloon").
   e. The amount of loan paid off in 15 years is $36,670.43
      ($75,000 − $38,329.57 = $36,670.43).
      The percentage of loan paid off in 15 years is $36,670.43/$75,000 = 48.89%.
4. If the loan is fully amortized in 15 years, the mortgage constant is 12 × 0.009412 (page 77, column 6) = 0.112944.
   Annual debt service is then $75,000 × 0.112944 = $8,470.80
5. Monthly mortgage payments on an 8% 17-year loan of $75,000 would be $75,000 × 0.008983 (page 81, column 6) = $673.73. Annual debt service is therefore 12 × $673.73 = $8,084.76. Total dollar payments of mortgage and principal are 17 × $8,084.76 = $137,440.92.
   Total interest payments are total amortization payments minus mortgage principal: $137,440.92 − $75,000.00 = $62,440.92.
   a. The 14-year 8% monthly Installment to Amortize One is 0.009914 (page 81, column 6). Monthly payments are then $75,000 × 0.009914 = $743.55. Annual debt service is 12 × $743.55 = $8,922.60. Total amortization payments are 14 × $8,922.60 = $124,916.40. Total interest payments are therefore $124,916.40 − $75,000.00 = $49,916.40.
      Annual debt service would increase by $837.84 over that for 17-year amortization ($8,922.60 − $8,084.76).

b. With a loan-to-value ratio of 80%, the principal amount of the mortgage would be $80,000.
Monthly payments are then $80,000 × 0.008983 = $718.64.
Annual debt service is 12 × $718.64 = $8,623.68.
Total amortization payments are 17 × $8,623.68 = $146,602.56.
Total interest payments are then $146,602.56 − $80,000.00 = $66,602.56.

6.    Discount Rate:                                              1.00 × 0.1100 = 0.1100
     *Less* Mortgage:                                     .70 × 0.0800 = 0.0560
     Equity Return (30%):                                   0.0540
Rate of Return on Equity = 0.0540/.30 = .18 = 18.00%

     Discount Rate:                                              1.00 × 0.1100 = 0.1100
     *Less* Mortgage:                                     .75 × 0.0825 = 0.0619
     Equity Return (25%):                                   0.0481
Rate of Return on Equity = 0.0481/.25 = .1924 = 19.24%

     Discount Rate:                                              1.00 × 0.1100 = 0.1100
     *Less* Mortgage:                                     .80 × 0.0900 = 0.0720
     Equity Return (20%)                                    0.0380
Rate of Return on Equity = 0.0380/.20 = .19 = 19.00%

He would choose the 75% loan at 8.25% because it offers the prospect of the highest rate of return on equity investment.

## Chapter 8

1. a. Overall Rate = NOI/Total property investment.
NOI = Effective Gross Income minus Operating Expenses = $50,000 − $20,000 = $30,000.
Overall Rate = $30,000/$200,000 = 0.15 = 15.00%
  b. The Operating Expense Ratio is the percentage ratio of Operating Expenses to Effective Gross Income: $20,000/$50,000 = .40 = 40%.
  c. Cash Throw-Off is NOI minus Annual Debt Service.
Mortgage constant = 12 × 0.008052 (page 89, column 6) = 0.096624.
Annual Debt Service = $160,000 × 0.096624 = $15,460 (rounded).
Cash Throw-Off = $30,000 − $15,460 = $14,540.
  d. Equity Dividend Rate is the ratio of Cash Throw-Off to Equity Investment, expressed as an annual percentage rate:

     $14,540/$40,000 = 0.3635 = 36.35%.

  e. Capital Recovery is original investment less forecast resale price (reversion):

$200,000 - (.70 \times \$200,000) = \$60,000$.

f. The level annuity capitalization rate for the income stream is 0.15. This is a close approximation to the 12% 15-year Installment to Amortize One of 0.146824 (page 148, column 6). The capital recovery rate (sinking fund factor, page 148, column 3) is therefore approximately 0.026824.

g. The indicated discount rate from $f$ above is 12%. As a check, the weighted average of the mortgage interest rate and the equity yield rate can be taken. The equity yield rate is Cash Throw-Off minus first-year capital recovery ($14,540 - $4,000) divided by equity investment: $10,540/\$40,000 = .2635$. The discount rate then becomes:

| | |
|---|---|
| Mortgage: | $80 \times .0850 = 0.0680$ |
| Equity: | $.20 \times .2635 = \underline{0.0527}$ |
| Discount Rate | $0.1207$ |

h. Annual capital recovery is the total amount of capital recovery ($60,000) divided by the number of years in the capital recovery period (15): $60,000/15 = \$4,000$. The straight-line capital recovery rate is then $4,000/\$60,000 = 0.0667$. The indicated discount rate is $0.15 - 0.0667 = 0.0833$.

2. a. The annual Present Worth of One per Annum factor for 35 years at 13% must be calculated. It is the 5-year factor discounted by the 30-year Present Worth of One factor, plus the 30-year factor. These are found on page 149, columns 5 and 4.

5-year Present Worth of One per Annum factor times 30-year Present Worth of One factor, at 13% annually = $3.517232 \times 0.025565 = 0.089918$.

30-year Present Worth of One per Annum factor at 13% = 7.495653.

35-year Present Worth of One per Annum factor at 13% - 7.495653 + 0.089918 = 7.585571.

Present worth of income stream = $7.585571 \times \$10,000 = \$75,855.71$.

b. The indicated capitalization rate is the reciprocal of the level annuity capitalization factor. $R = 1/F; R = 1/7.585571 = 0.131829$.

The sinking fund factor (annuity capital recovery rate) at 13% for 35 years can be derived by using the formula: $s_n = i/S^n - 1$. Since $i = 0.13$, the only needed item is $S^n$. This Future Worth of One factor for 35 years at 13% is found by multiplying the 30-year factor by the 5-year factor (page 149, column 1):

$1.842436 \times 39.115924 = 72.068587$

Then, $s_n = 0.13/(72.068587 - 1) = 0.001829$.

Since the calculated level annuity capitalization rate is 0.131829, and the discount rate is 0.13, the difference is the level annuity capital recovery rate: $0.131829 - 0.13 = 0.001829$.

3. The present worth of this income stream is $24,000 × 3.604776 (page 148, column 5) = $86,515 (rounded to the nearest dollar).
The total amount of capital recovery is the full present worth: $86,515.
The return *on* the investment in the first year is 0.12 × $86,515 = $10,382.
The difference is first-year capital recovery: $24,000 − $10,382 = $13,618.

The return on the outstanding balance of the investment in the second year is 0.12 × ($86,515 − $13,618) = 0.12 × $72,897 = $8,748. The remainder of the $24,000 income is capital recovery: $24,000 − $8,748 = $15,252.

The 5-year income stream is divided between return on investment and capital recovery as follows:

| Year | Income | Return on Balance | Capital Recovery |
|------|--------|-------------------|------------------|
| 1 | $24,000 | $10,382 | $13,618 |
| 2 | $24,000 | $ 8,748 | $15,252 |
| 3 | $24,000 | $ 6,917 | $17,083 |
| 4 | $24,000 | $ 4,867 | $19,133 |
| 5 | $24,000 | $ 2,571 | $21,429 |
| | | | $86,515 |

**Chapter 9**

1. a. Overall Rate = NOI/Total property investment
   O.R. = $15,600/$130,000 = 0.12
   b. The straight-line capital recovery rate = $1/n = 1/25 = 0.04$.
   c. The effective straight-line capital recovery rate = .04 × .7692 = 0.0308. This is the straight-line capital recovery rate weighted by the proportion of total property investment represented by the improvements.
   d. The discount rate is the overall rate minus the effective capital recovery rate: 0.12 − 0.0308 = 0.0892.
2. The mortgage constant is 12 × 0.008678 = 0.104136.
   The indicated overall rate is the weighted average of the mortgage constant and the equity yield rate:

| Mortgage: | .65 × .1041 = 0.0677 |
|-----------|----------------------|
| Equity: | .35 × .1150 = 0.0403 |
| Overall Rate | 0.1080 |

3. GIM = 4.5. Its reciprocal, as a "gross capitalization rate" is 1/4.5 = 0.2222. Then, by abstraction, the overall rate and discount rate are:

GIM "capitalization rate"     0.2222
*Less* operating expense rate (.35 × .2222)   −0.0778
Indicated Overall Rate     0.1444
*Less* effective capital recovery rate
   (.75 × .025)     −0.0188
Indicated Discount Rate     0.1256

4. a. First Mortgage:    $.0775 \times \$80,000 = \$6,200$
    Second Mortgage:    $.1150 \times \$12,000 = \$1,380$
    Equity:    $.1500 \times \$\,8,000 = \$1,200$
    Total Income Required    $\$8,780$

  b. First Mortgage:    $.80 \times .0775 = 0.0620$
    Second Mortgage:    $.12 \times .1150 = 0.0138$
    Equity:    $.08 \times .1500 = \underline{0.0120}$
    Indicated Discount Rate    $0.0878$

    Also, $\$8,780/\$100,000 = 0.0878$

  c. Trading on equity; the use of leverage. With an 8.78% rate of return on the investment, the equity is able to generate a 15% rate of return on his equity investment by using debt financing.

## Chapter 10

1. a. Mortgage:    $.60 \times .0750 = 0.0450$
    Equity:    $.40 \times .1250 = \underline{0.0500}$
    Indicated Discount Rate    $0.0950$

  b. Straight-line capital recovery rate $= 1/n = 1/20 = 0.0500$
  c. Effective straight-line capital recovery rate $= .80 \times .05 = 0.0400$
  d. The Overall Rate equals the Discount Rate plus the effective capital recovery rate: $.095 + .04 = 0.1350.$
  e. The present worth of the property, based on Direct Capitalization using the Overall Rate is: $V = I/R$; $V = \$27,000/.135 = \$200,000.$
  f. The capital loss is 80% of value: $.80 \times \$200,000 = \$160,000.$
  g. Annual straight-line capital recovery in dollars is $\$160,000/20 = \$8,000.$

2.

| Year | Return on Investment | Capital Recovery | NOI | End-of-Year Investment |
|---|---|---|---|---|
| 1 | $19,000 | $8,000 | $27,000 | $192,000 |
| 2 | $18,240 | $8,000 | $26,240 | $184,000 |
| 3 | $17,480 | $8,000 | $25,480 | $176,000 |
| 4 | $16,720 | $8,000 | $24,720 | $168,000 |
| 5 | $15,960 | $8,000 | $23,960 | $160,000 |

3. a. Total capital loss to be recovered is the initial investment minus the forecast amount of the reversion: $200,000 − $40,000 = $160,000.
   b. The level annuity capital recovery rate is the annual sinking fund factor for 20 years at 9.5% (page 108, column 3): 0.018477.
   c. The level annual amount of capital recovery, compounded at the discount rate of 9.5% for 20 years, is found by multiplying the total amount of forecast capital loss to be recovered by the level annuity capital recovery rate: $160,000 × 0.018477 = $2,956.32.
4. a. The sinking fund capital recovery rate at 5% for 20 years (page 36, column 3) is 0.030243.
   b. $160,000 × 0.030243 = $4,838.88.
5. a. The monthly Installment to Amortize One factor for 25 years at 7.5% (page 73, column 6) is 0.007390.
   The level monthly amortization payment (principal and interest) is $120,000 × 0.007390 = $886.80.

| Month | Interest | Principal | Total Payment | Outstanding Balance |
|---|---|---|---|---|
| 1 | $750.00 | $136.80 | $886.80 | $119,863.20 |
| 2 | $749.14 | $137.66 | $886.80 | $119,725.44 |
| 3 | $748.28 | $138.52 | $886.80 | $119,586.92 |
| 4 | $747.42 | $139.38 | $886.80 | $119,447.54 |
| 5 | $746.55 | $140.25 | $886.80 | $119,307.29 |

## Chapter 11

1. a. Gross Rental Income (40,000 × $1.25)    $50,000
   Less Operating Expenses                    − 15,000
   Net Operating Income                        $35,000

   b. Mortgage constant is 0.103876 (page 104, column 6).
   Amount of mortgage is .80 × $300,000 = $24,000.
   Annual debt service is therefore .103876 × 240,000 = $24,930.
   Cash Throw-Off to equity is equal to NOI minus annual debt service:

   $35,000 − $24,930 = $10,070.

   c. The indicated discount rate is:

   Mortgage:         .80 × .0925 = 0.0740
   Equity:           .20 × .0130 = 0.0260
   Discount Rate                   0.1000

d. The indicated equity dividend rate, based on Cash Throw-Off of $10,070 and a presumed equity investment of $60,000 is:

$10,070/$60,000 = 0.167833.

e. The Present Worth of One per Annum (level annuity) factor for 18 years at 10% is 8.201412 (page 116, column 5).
The present worth of the income stream under the lease is:

$35,000 × 8.201412 = $287,049.

f. The Present Worth of One factor for 18 years at 10% is 0.179859 (page 116, column 4).
The present worth of the reversion is: $235,000 × 0.179859 = $42,267.

g. The present worth of the leased fee interest is:

| | |
|---|---|
| Present Worth of Income Stream | $287,049 |
| Present Worth of Reversion | 42,267 |
| Present Worth of Leased Fee | $329,316 |
| | ($330,000) |

h. If $300,000 is used as present worth, the forecast amount of capital loss is $300,000 − $235,000 = $65,000.
Based on the present worth of the leased fee (which is more appropriate to the equity investor's viewpoint), forecast capital loss is $330,000 − $235,000 = $95,000.

i. The mortgage constant is 10.39% (.103876: page 104, column 6).

j. Annual debt service is .103876 × $240,000 = $24,930.

k. The amount of capital loss forecast over years 19-40 is $235,000 − $55,000 = $180,000.

l.
| | | |
|---|---|---|
| Gross Rental Income (40,000 × $1.10) | $44,000 | |
| Less Operating Expenses | − 15,000 | |
| Net Operating Income | $29,000 | |

m. The level annuity capitalization rate for 22 years at 10% is 0.114005 (page 116, column 6).
The straight-line capitalization rate for 22 years at a 10% discount rate is the sum of the discount rate and the straight-line capital recovery rate (1/22 = 0.045455):

| | |
|---|---|
| Discount Rate | 0.100000 |
| Straight-Line Capital Recovery Rate | 0.045455 |
| Straight-Line Capitalization Rate | 0.145455 |

n. The Present Worth of One factor for 18 years at 10% is 0.179859 (page 116, column 4).

The Installment to Amortize One factor for 22 years at 10% is 0.114005 (page 116, column 6).

The straight-line capital recovery rate for 22 years is 1/22 = 0.045455

(1) The present worth of $29,000 per year for 22 years, beginning 18 years hence, and treated as a level annuity with discounting at 10% is:

$$\$29,000/.114005 = \$254,375 \times .179859 = \$45,752.$$

(2) The present worth of $29,000 per year for 22 years, beginning 18 years hence, with straight-line capital recovery and a 10% discount rate is:

$$\$29,000/.145455 = \$199,374 \times .179859 = \$35,859.$$

o. Present Worth of Income Stream in 18 years      $254,375
Present Worth of Reversion in 18 years
    ($55,000 × .122846*)                             6,577
Present Worth of Property                         $261,952
                                    say    $262,000
*Present Worth of One for 22 years at 10% (page 116, column 4)

2. The Present Worth of One factors with annual discounting at 11.5% are found on page 140, column 4 in Ellwood. The 5-year Present Worth of One per Annum (level annuity) factor at 11.5% is 3.649878 (page 140, column 5). The Present worth of the income stream is then estimated as:

| Years | NOI | Discount Factor | Present Worth |
|-------|-----|-----------------|---------------|
| 1-5 | $23,000 | 3.649878 | $83,947 |
| 6 | $22,000 | 0.520416 | $11,449 |
| 7 | $21,000 | 0.466741 | $ 9,802 |
| 8 | $20,000 | 0.418602 | $ 8,372 |
| 9 | $19,000 | 0.375428 | $ 7,133 |
| 10 | $17,500 | 0.336706 | $ 5,892 |
| Present Worth of Income Stream | | | $126,595 |

## Chapter 12

1. a. Gross receipts of the business are $20 × 120 × 365 × .82, or $718,320.

Annual gross rental is therefore .35 × $718,320 = $251,412.
Operating expenses are .45 × $251,412 = $113,135.
Net Operating Income in the first year is thus:

$$\$251,412 - \$113,135 = \$138,277.$$

b. The discount rate is:

| | |
|---|---|
| Mortgage: | .50 × .0950 = 0.0475 |
| Equity: | .50 × .1850 = $\underline{0.0925}$ |
| Discount Rate | 0.1400 |

c. NOI can be stabilized by calculating the percentage ratio of the level annuity capitalization rate to the straight-line capitalization rate, and multiplying first-year NOI by that percentage.
The level annuity capitalization rate for 25 years at 14% is 0.145498 (page 150, column 6).
The straight-line capitalization rate for 25 years at a 14% discount rate is the sum of the discount rate (.14) and the 25-year straight-line capital recovery rate (1/25 = .04): 0.18.
The stabilizing percentage is then:

$$\frac{.145498}{.180000} = .8083 \text{ or } 80.83\%$$

Stabilized NOI is: $138,277 × .8083 = $111,769.
d. Income necessary to support the investment in the site is 0.14 × $200,000 = $28,000.
e. "Stabilized" income available to support the investment in the improvements is $111,769 − $28,000 = $83,769.
f. The level annuity capitalization rate for 25 years at 14% is 0.145498 (page 150, column 6).
g. The present worth of the improvements is $83,769/.145498 = $575,740.
h. The indicated value of the property, using the building residual technique is:

| | |
|---|---|
| Net Operating Income (stabilized) | $111,769 |
| *Less* Income to Support Site Investment | − 28,000 |
| Income Available to Improvements | $ 83,769 |
| | |
| Present Worth of Improvements | $575,740 |
| *Plus* Site Value | 200,000 |
| Indicated Value of Property | $775,740 |
| | ($775,000) |

i. The mortgage constant is 12 × 0.009321 (page 105, column 6) = 0.111852.

j. Annual debt service is equal to mortgage constant (0.111852) times mortgage principal (.50 × $775,000):

$$0.111852 \times \$387,500 = \$43,343.$$

k. Cash throw-off to equity is:

| | |
|---|---|
| Net Operating Income (stabilized) | $111,769 |
| *Less* Annual Debt Service | − 43,343 |
| Cash Throw-Off | $ 68,426 |

l. The indicated equity dividend rate is "stabilized" cash throw-off to equity divided by equity investment:

$$\$68,426/\$387,500 = 0.1766 = 17.66\%.$$

2. The level annuity capitalization rate for 40 years at 11% is 0.111719 (page 132, column 6).

| | |
|---|---|
| Net Operating Income | $475,000 |
| *Less* Income Necessary to Support Investment in Improvements ($2,800,000 × .111719) | − 312,813 |
| Income Available to Support Site Investment | $162,187 |
| | |
| Present Worth of Site ($162,187/.11) | $1,474,427 |
| *Plus* Present Worth of Improvements | 2,800,000 |
| Indicated Value of Property | $4,274,427 |
| | ($4,300,000) |

3. a. Discount Rate  0.1050
   Effective Capital Recovery Rate
   (.85 × .045455 = .0386)  0.0386
   Overall Rate  0.1436

   b. $V = I/R$.
   $V = \$80,000/.1436 = \$557,103$ (say $557,000)

   c. The straight-line capitalization rate over 22 years with a 10.50% discount rate is: .1050 + .0455 = .1505.
   The Present Worth of One factor for 22 years with annual discounting at 10.5% is 0.111181 (page 124, column 4).
   The present worth of the property, using the property residual technique, is then estimated as:

| | |
|---|---|
| Present Worth of Income Stream ($80,000/.1505) | $531,561 |
| Present Worth of Reversion ($225,000 × .111181) | 25,016 |
| Indicated Value of Property | $556,557 |
| | ($557,000) |

4. The level annuity capitalization rate for 17 years at 9.75% is 0.122741 (page 112, column 6).
   The Present Worth of One factor for 17 years with annual discounting at 9.75% is 0.205647 (page 112, column 4).

|  |  |
|---|---|
| Gross Rental Income | $72,000 |
| Less Operating Expenses (.35 × $72,000) | − 25,200 |
| Net Operating Income | $46,800 |
|  |  |
| Present Worth of Income Stream | |
| ($46,800/.122741) | $381,291 |
| Present Worth of Reversion | |
| ($200,000 × .205647) | 41,129 |
| Present Worth of Leased Fee | $422,420 |

5. a. The indicated Overall Rates for the comparable sales properties are:

| Sale A: | $48,500/$350,000 = 0.1386 |
|---|---|
| Sale B: | $58,000/$405,000 = 0.1432 |
| Sale C: | $40,250/$287,500 = 0.1400 |

   The indicated Overall Rate applicable to the subject property is 0.1400.
   b. $V = I/R$.
   $V = \$44,500/.14 = \$317,857$ (say $318,000)

## Chapter 13

1. a. The mortgage constant is 12 × 0.009897 (page 105, column 6) = 0.118764.
   The "simple" mortgage-equity Overall Rate is:

| Mortgage: | .65 × .1188 = 0.0772 |
|---|---|
| Equity: | .35 × .1400 = 0.0490 |
| Overall Rate | 0.1262 |

   b. The equity build-up credit is based on the 12-year sinking fund factor at 14%: 0.036669 (page 150, column 3).
   It is also necessary to calculate the percentage of the 17-year mortgage loan paid off in 12 years. This is the *complement* of the ratio of the 5-year Present Worth of One per Annum factor for monthly payments at 9.5%, to the 17-year factor (page 105, column 5):

   $$1 - (47.614827/101.032486) = 1 - 0.4713 = 0.5287$$

The Basic Rate with credit for equity build-up is:

| Mortgage: | .65 X .1188 | = .0772 |
|---|---|---|
| Equity: | .35 X .1400 | = .0490 |
| Weighted Average: | | .1262 |
| *Less* Credit for | | |
| Equity Build-up: | .5287 X .65 X .0367 = | −.0126 |
| Basic Rate | | 0.1136 |

c. The Overall Rate includes a credit for capital recovery as well. This is the sinking fund factor for the equity rate, weighted by the percentage of total investment represented by capital loss. It is added to the Basic Rate to develop the Overall Rate:

| Basic Rate | | 0.1136 |
|---|---|---|
| *Plus* Allowance for Capital Recovery: | .15 X .0367 = | 0.0055 |
| Overall Rate | | 0.1191 |

d. $V = I/R$
$V = \$50,000/.1191 = \$419,815$ (say \$420,000)

e.

| Basic Rate | | 0.1136 |
|---|---|---|
| *Minus* Allowance for Capital Gain: | .10 X .0367 | −0.0037 |
| Overall Rate | | 0.1099 |

$V = I/R$
$V = \$50,000/.1099 = \$454,959$ (say \$455,000)

2. a. The percentage of mortgage loan outstanding at the end of 12 years is: $47.614827/101.032486 = 0.471282 = 47.13\%$.
  b. The mortgage-equity "capitalization rate" for the income stream is:

| Mortgage: | .65 X .1188 = 0.0772 |
|---|---|
| Equity: | .35 X .1767 = 0.0618 |
| "Capitalization Rate" | 0.1390 |

The present worth of the income stream is: $\$50,000/.1390 = \$359,712$. The reversion is forecast to be 85% of present value $(.85V)$. The net cash reversion to the equity investor is $.85V$ *less* the outstanding balance of the mortgage $(.4713 \times .65V = .3063V)$. The net cash reversion is thus $.85V - .3063V = .5437V$. This is discounted to a present worth estimate by the Present Worth of One factor: 0.2076 (page 150, column 4).

Thus,
$V = \$359,712 + (.5437V \times .2076)$
$V = \$359,712 + .1129V$

$$V - .1129V = \$359,712$$
$$.8871V = \$359,712$$
$$V = \$359,712/.8871 = \$405,492 \text{ (say } \$405,000)$$

c. If the reversion is $1.10V$, then the net cash reversion is $1.10V - 0.3063V = 0.7937V$.

The present worth of the net cash reversion is $.2076 \times .7937V = 0.1648V$.

The present worth of the income stream remains the same.

Then,
$$V = \$359,712 + .1648V$$
$$.8352V = \$359,712$$
$$V = \$359,712/.8352 = \$430,690 \text{ (say } \$431,000)$$

3. a. Mortgage constant remains at 0.118764.

Annual debt service is $.118764 \times \$250,000 = \$29,691$

b.
| | |
|---|---|
| Net Operating Income | $50,000 |
| *Less* Annual Debt Service | − 29,691 |
| Cash Throw-Off | $20,309 |

c. The present worth of the equity investment is the *sum* of the present worth of the 12-year Cash Throw-Off of $20,309 capitalized at the 12-year level annuity capitalization rate at 14%, *plus* the present worth of the net cash reversion.

The present worth of the income stream is $20,309/.176669 = $114,955.

The amount of the net cash reversion is 85% of the total investment *minus* the outstanding balance of the mortgage.

Total investment is $250,000/.65 = $384,615.

The amount of the reversion is $.85 \times \$384,615 = \$326,923$.

The outstanding balance of the mortgage is $.4713 \times \$250,000 = \$117,825$.

Thus, the net cash reversion is $326,923 − $117,825 = $209,098.

The present worth of the net cash reversion is thus $.2076 \times \$209,098 = \$43,408$.

The present worth of the equity investment then is estimated as:

| | |
|---|---|
| Present Worth of Income Stream | $114,955 |
| Present Worth of Net Cash Reversion | 43,408 |
| Present Worth of Equity Position | $158,363 |

d. The equity dividend rate is the ratio of CTO to the present worth of the equity investment position, expressed as an annual percentage:

$$e = \$20,309/\$158,363 = 0.128243 = 12.82\%$$

4. The Ellwood formula for the Overall Rate is $R = y - mc - app. \ 1/s_n$.

   a. To estimate the percentage of loan paid off in 12 years $(P)$, the formula is:

$$P = (f/i - 1)(Sp - 1)$$

In this problem,

      $f = 0.118764$ (page 105, column 6: 12 × 0.009897)
      $i = 0.095$
      $Sp = 3.112764$ (page 105, column 1: 12-year factor)

Then:
      $P = (.118764/.095 - 1)(3.112764 - 1)$
      $P = (1.250147 - 1)(2.112764)$
      $P = 0.528502$ or 52.85%

   b. The formula for $c$ is: $c - y + P \ 1/s_n - f$

      $y = 0.14$
      $1/s_n = 0.036669$ (page 150, column 3)

Then:
      $C = .14 + (.528502 \times .036669) - .118764$
      $C = .14 + \ 019380 - .118764 = .159380 - .118764$
      $C = 0.040616$

   c. The formula for $r$ is: $r = y - mc$
      $m = 0.65$

Then:
      $r = .14 - (.65 \times .040616) = .14 - .026400$
      $r = 0.1136$ or 11.36%

   d. $R = r - app. \ 1/s_n$
      $app. = .10$

Then:
      $R = .1136 - (.10 \times .036669)$
      $R = .1136 - .003667$
      $R = .109933$ or 10.99%

   e. $V = I/R. \ I = \$50,000. \ R = .109933$
      $V = \$50,000/.109933 = \$454,822$ (say \$455,000)

5. $V = I/R$. $V = \$350,000$. $I = \$50,000$.

$R = \$50,000/\$350,000 = .0142857$

$R = y - mc + dep. \, 1/s_n$

$y \quad = .17$

$m \quad = .65$

$1/s_n = .030466$ (page 153, column 3)

$P \quad = .528502$

$f \quad = .118764$

$C \quad = y + P \, 1/s_n - f$

$C \quad = .17 + (.528502 \times .030466) - .118764$

$C \quad = .067338$

To solve for *dep.*:

$.142857 \qquad = .17 - (.65 \times .067338) + .030466 \, dep.$

$.030466 \, dep. = .142857 - .17 + .043770$

$dep. \qquad\quad = .016627/.030466 = 54.58\%$

## Chapter 15

1. a. Net Income per square foot per year is $20\cancel{c} - 2\cancel{c} = 18\cancel{c}$.

Annual NOI is 10,000 square feet times $18\cancel{c} = \$1,800$.

The level annuity capitalization rate for 15 years at 12% is 0.146824 (page 148, column 6).

The Present Worth of One factor for 15 years at 12% is 0.182696 (page 148, column 4).

The site is forecast to be worth $1.50 per square foot in 15 years. ($15,000/10,000).

The present worth of the site per square foot is:

| | |
|---|---|
| Present Worth of Income Stream: | |
| $\$0.18/.146824 =$ | $1.23 |
| Present Worth of Reversion: | |
| $\$1.50 \times .182696 =$ | 0.27 |
| Site Value per Square Foot | $1.50 |

b. The value of the site is: $10,000 \times \$1.50 = \$15,000$.

As a check:

| | |
|---|---|
| Present Worth of Income Stream: | |
| $\$1,800/.46824 =$ | $12,260 |
| Present Worth of Reversion: | |
| $\$15,000 \times .182696 =$ | 2,740 |
| Indicated Site Value | $15,000 |

c. NOI per square foot = 17¢ − 2¢ = 15¢.
With no lease, capitalization in perpetuity is employed.

$$\$0.15/.12 = \$1.25 \text{ per square foot}$$

10,000 × $1.25 = $12,500 Indicated Site Value

2. a. Level annuity capitalization rate for 40 years at 10% is 0.102259 (page 116, column 6).

| | |
|---|---:|
| Net Operating Income | $20,000 |
| *Less* Income Necessary to Support Investment | |
| in Improvements ($100,000 × .102259) | 10,226 |
| Income Available to Support Site Improvement | $ 9,774 |

| | |
|---|---:|
| Present Worth of Site ($9,774/.10) | $ 97,740 |
| *Plus* Present Worth of Improvements | 100,000 |
| Indicated Value of Property | $197,740 |
| | ($198,000) |

b. Straight-line capital recovery rate is 1/40 = 0.025.
Straight-line capitalization rate is .10 + 0.25 = 0.1250.

| | |
|---|---:|
| Net Operating Income | $20,000 |
| *Less* Income Necessary to Support Investment | |
| in Improvements ($100,000 × .1250) | 12,500 |
| Income Available to Support Site Investment | $ 7,500 |

| | |
|---|---:|
| Present Worth of Site ($7,500/.10) | $ 75,000 |
| *Plus* Present Worth of Improvements | 100,000 |
| Indicated Value of Property | $175,000 |

3. a. Total site development costs are 50 × $2,000 = $100,000. Site development costs are $25,000 per year in each of the first four years.
Total developed site area is 40 acres (.80 × 50).
Total sales receipts are 40 × $10,000 = $400,000.
Sales receipts are $80,000 per year for each of five years.
Total sales expenses are 40 × $2,000 = $80,000.
Sales expenses are $16,000 per year for each of five years.
The forecast net income receipts per year are:

| Year | Sales Receipts | Sales Expenses | Development Costs | Net Receipts |
|---|---|---|---|---|
| 1 | $80,000 | $16,000 | $25,000 | $39,000 |
| 2 | $80,000 | $16,000 | $25,000 | $39,000 |
| 3 | $80,000 | $16,000 | $25,000 | $39,000 |
| 4 | $80,000 | $16,000 | $25,000 | $39,000 |
| 5 | $80,000 | $16,000 | 0 | $64,000 |

The present worth of this income stream is estimated by treating it as a four-year level annuity capitalized at 14%, plus a reversion in 5 years discounted at 14%.

The level annuity capitalization rate for 4 years at 14% is 0.343205 (page 150, column 6).

The Present Worth of One factor for 5 years with annual discounting at 14% is 0.519368 (page 150, column 4).

The present worth of the tract of land to the potential investor is:

| | |
|---|---|
| Present Worth of 4-year Income Stream: | |
| ($39,000/.343205) | $113,635 |
| Present Worth of Reversion: | |
| ($64,000 × .519368) | 33,230 |
| Indicated Value of Land | $146,865 |

This income stream could also be treated as a series of 5 separate reversions, each discounted by the 14% Present Worth of One factor for the applicable year. If it were a variable income stream, it would have to be valued that way.

4. Using the land residual technique and level annuity capitalization under both use alternatives, the indicated land values would be calculated as follows:

The level annuity capitalization rate for 5 years at 11% is 0.270570; for 35 years it is 0.112927; and for 50 years it is 0.110599 (page 132, column 6).

The Present Worth of One factor at 11% for 5 years is 0.593451; for 40 years, it is 0.015384; and for 50 years, it is 0.005418 (page 132, column 4).

The present worth of the property under apartment use would be:

| | |
|---|---|
| Present Worth of Income Stream: | |
| ($100,00/.110599) | $904,167 |
| Present Worth of Reversion: | |
| ($1,000,000 × .005418) | 5,418 |
| Indicated Value of Property | $909,585 |
| | ($910,000) |

The present worth of the property under office building use would be:

| | |
|---|---|
| Present Worth of 5-year Income Stream: | |
| ($60,000/.27570) | $221,754 |
| Present Worth of Deferred 35-Year Income | |
| Stream: ($140,000/.112927 × 593451) | 735,724 |
| Present Worth of Reversion: | |
| ($1,500,000 × .015384) | 23,076 |
| Indicated Value of Property | $980,554 |
| | ($980,000) |

Based on the evidence provided, the use of the site for an office building appears preferable.


## Chapter 16

1. The subject property contains 48 units and 160 rooms. Annual rental per room per year is: $49,600/160 = $310

   a. The most probable units of comparison that can be derived from the sales evidence provided are:
      Sales Price per Living Unit (S.P./Unit)
      Sales Price per Room (S.P./Room)
      Gross Income Multiplier (GIM)
   b. The best basis for evaluating rentals in the subject property is to reduce the annual gross rental figures for the comparable sales properties to annual rental per room. Because of the different "mix" of 3-room and 4-room units among the several properties, annual rental per apartment unit does not appear to be appropriate. The annual rental per room figures are:

   > Sale No. 1: $56,640/192 = $295.00
   > Sale No. 2: $55,760/180 = $309.78
   > Sale No. 3: $49,200/160 = $307.50
   > Sale No. 4: $47,260/154 = $306.88

   The annual $310 rental per room being received by the subject property is at the upper end of the range indicated by the experience of the comparable sales properties, but it is still apparently competitive. No downward adjustment appears necessary to bring the subject property's rentals in line with the market.
   c. The best way to indicate the unit values and measures reflected by the four comparable sales properties is to present them in a tabular analysis grid, as follows:

|  | Sale No. 1 | Sale No. 2 | Sale No. 3 | Sale No. 4 |
|---|---|---|---|---|
| Sales Price | $400,000 | $375,000 | $340,000 | $326,000 |
| Gross Income | $56,640 | $55,760 | $49,200 | $47,260 |
| GIM | 7.06 | 6.73 | 6.91 | 6.90 |
| No. Units | 48 | 60 | 40 | 42 |
| S.P./Unit | $8,333 | $6,250 | $8,500 | $7,762 |
| No. Rooms | 192 | 180 | 160 | 154 |
| S.P./Room | $2,083 | $2,083 | $2,125 | $2,117 |

The indicated Gross Income Multiplier is 6.90.

The indicated Sales Price per Room is $2,100.

No real pattern emerges for Sales Price per Living Unit. However, a possible measure might be $8,000.

d. The value of the subject property, using the units of comparison, developed above, is indicated to be:

| | | |
|---|---|---|
| GIM: | 6.9 X $49,600 | = $342,240 |
| S.P./Unit: | 48 X $8,000 | = $384,000 |
| S.P./Room: | 160 X $2,100 | = $336,000 |

No weight can be placed on the "per unit" value indicators because of the lack of market comparability among properties with respect to the size and "mix" of living units.

The indicated value based on the GIM is probably a little high, reflecting the fact that annual rental per room in the subject property is at the top of the indicated range for the market.

Taking these factors into consideration, and recognizing that these are income properties, the most probable estimate of Market Value developed from this Direct Sales Comparison analysis is $340,000.

## Chapter 17

1. a. The floor area ratio is the ratio of total building area to site area.

    Total building area is 82,500 square feet (10 X 8,250). Therefore, the floor area ratio is $82,500/25,100 = 3.29:1$.

   b. The site coverage ratio is $8,250/25,100 = 0.33:1$.

2. Foundation area is 80 X 150 = 12,000 square feet.

   Wall area is (2 X 80 X 20) + (2 X 150 X 20) = 9,200 square feet

   a. Total direct costs of construction new are:

| | |
|---|---|
| Foundation ($1.10 X 12,000) | $ 13,200 |
| Exterior Walls ($2.40 X 9,200) | 22,080 |
| Roof and Roofing ($4.35 X 12,000) | 52,200 |
| Electrical System | 10,000 |
| Electrical Outlets (40 X $12.50) | 500 |
| Plumbing and Sewage | 6,000 |
| Heating System | 7,500 |
| Cooling and Ventilating System | 5,000 |
| Interior Finish, Office (1,200 X $7.20) | 8,640 |
| Painting and Decorating | 2,500 |
| Plumbing Fixtures (6 X $250) | 1,500 |
| Loading Docks, etc. (2 X $8,000) | 16,000 |
| Total Direct Costs | $145,120 |

b. Total Indirect Costs are .22 × $145,120 = $31,926.40.
c. Total Reproduction Cost New is:

| Direct Costs | $145,120 |
|---|---|
| Indirect Costs | 31,926 |
| Total Cost New | $177,046 |

d. The indicated cost per square foot is:

$$\$177,046/12,000 = \$14.75$$

3. a. Curable Physical Deterioration:

| Roof | $ 500 |
|---|---|
| Office area | 600 |
| Painting | 300 |
| Total | $1,400 |

b. Curable Functional Obsolescence:
Electrical Outlets $500

c. The 15-year effective age of basic structural components represents 30% of total estimated economic life. This is applied to indirect costs as well. The electrical system has an effective age of 50% (15/30).
Decoration has an effective age of 75% (15/20).
Curable items must be deducted from cost new before applying the percentage of effective age to estimate Incurable Physical Deterioration.
The items of Incurable Physical Deterioration are:

| Item | Cost New | Curable Deduction | Adjusted Cost New | Percent Incurable Physical | Incurable Physical |
|---|---|---|---|---|---|
| Foundation | $13,200 | $ 0 | $ 13,200 | 30 | $ 3,960 |
| Ext. Walls | 22,080 | 0 | 22,080 | 30 | 6,624 |
| Roof | 52,200 | 500 | 51,700 | 30 | 15,510 |
| Elec. System | 10,000 | 0 | 10,000 | 50 | 5,000 |
| Elec. Outlets | 500 | 500 | 0 | — | 0 |
| Plumbing | 6,000 | 0 | 6,000 | 30 | 1,800 |
| Heating | 7,500 | 0 | 7,500 | 30 | 2,250 |
| Cooling | 5,000 | 0 | 5,000 | 30 | 1,500 |
| Office | 8,640 | 600 | 8,040 | 30 | 2,412 |
| Decorating | 2,500 | 300 | 2,200 | 75 | 1,650 |
| Fixtures | 1,500 | 0 | 1,500 | 30 | 450 |
| Docks | 16,000 | 0 | 16,000 | 30 | 4,800 |
| Indirect | 31,296 | 0 | 31,926 | 30 | 9,578 |
| Total | $177,046 | $1,900 | $175,146 | | $55,534 |

d. Total observed Incurable Physical Deterioration is $55,534.
4. a. Total income loss is 12¢ per square foot per year (10¢ + 2¢).
   This is an annual income loss of $0.12 × 12,000 = $1,440.
   The capitalized value of this annual income loss is 5.75 × $1,440 = $8,280.
   Incurable Functional Obsolescence is $8,280.
5. a. Physical Deterioration

| | | |
|---|---|---|
| Curable | $ 1,400 | |
| Incurable | 55,534 | |
| Total | | $56,934 |

Functional Obsolescence

| | | |
|---|---|---|
| Curable | $ 500 | |
| Incurable | 8,280 | |
| Total | | 8,780 |
| Total Estimated Diminished Utility | | $65,714 |

b. | | |
|---|---|
| Reproduction Cost New of Improvements | $177,046 |
| Less Diminished Utility | − 65,714 |
| Present Worth (Contribution) of Improvements | $111,332 |

## Chapter 18

1. a. Cash Throw-off is NOI minus Annual Debt Service.
   The mortgage constant is 2 × .062297 (page 103, column 6) = 0.124594.
   Annual Debt Service = .124594 × $100,000 = $12,459 (rounded).

   Then: :
   | | |
   |---|---|
   | NOI | $15,500 |
   | Less Annual Debt Service | − 12,459 |
   | Cash Throw-Off | $ 3,041 |

   b. Total property investment is $100,000/.80 = $125,000.
   Equity investment is .20 × $125,000 = $25,000.
   Rate of return on equity investment is $3,041/$25,000 = 0.12164.
   c. Taxable Income is equal to NOI *minus* mortgage interest payments *minus* depreciation charges.
   Annual depreciation charges are $100,000/20 = $5,000.
   Annual interest charges, based on semi-annual amortization payments of $6229.70, are:

Year 1: $4,625.00 + $4,550.78 = $9,175.78
Year 2: $4,473.13 + $4,391.89 = $8,865.02
Year 3: $4,306.89 + $4,217.96 = $8,524.85
Year 4: $4,124.92 + $4,027.57 = $8,152.49
Year 5: $3,925.72 + $3,819.17 = $7,744.89

Taxable Income in each of the first five years then becomes:

| Year | NOI | | Interest | | Depreciation | | Taxable Income |
|------|-----|---|----------|---|--------------|---|----------------|
| 1 | $15,500 | − | $9,176 | − | $5,000 | = | $1,324 |
| 2 | $15,500 | − | $8,865 | − | $5,000 | = | $1,635 |
| 3 | $15,500 | − | $8,525 | − | $5,000 | = | $1,975 |
| 4 | $15,500 | − | $8,152 | − | $5,000 | = | $2,348 |
| 5 | $15,500 | − | $7,745 | − | $5,000 | = | $2,755 |

d. After-Tax Cash Flow is equal to Cash Throw-Off *minus* Income Tax Liability. Income Tax Liability is 50% of Taxable Income each year.

| Year | Cash Throw-Off | | Income Tax Liability | | After-Tax Cash Flow |
|------|----------------|---|----------------------|---|---------------------|
| 1 | $3,041 | − | $ 662 | = | $2,379 |
| 2 | $3,041 | − | $ 818 | = | $2,223 |
| 3 | $3,041 | − | $ 988 | = | $2,053 |
| 4 | $3,041 | − | $1,174 | = | $1,867 |
| 5 | $3,041 | − | $1,378 | = | $1,663 |

2. a. $R = I/V$. $I = \$15,500$. $V = \$125,000$.
$R = \$15,000/\$125,000 = 0.1240 = 12.40\%$.

b. Mortgage Constant is $12 \times 0.010142$ (page 97, column 6) = 0.121704.
Level annuity capital recovery rate for 10 years at 15% is 0.049252 (page 151, column 3).
Capital loss to be recovered in 10 years is 0.15.
Percentage of mortgage paid off in 10 years (factors from page 97, column 5) is:

$$1 - (48.173373/98.593409) = 1 - .4886 = .5114$$

The mortgage-equity Overall Rate with credit for equity build-up and allowance for capital recovery is then developed as follows:

| | | |
|---|---|---|
| Mortgage: | .80 × .121704 | = .0974 |
| Equity: | .20 × .15 | = .0300 |
| Weighted Average: | | .1274 |
| *Less* Credit for Equity Build-Up: | | |
| | .5114 × .80 × .049252 | = .0202 |
| Basic Rate: | | .1072 |
| *Plus* Allowance for Capital Recovery: | | |
| | .15 × .049252 | = .0074 |
| Overall Rate: | | .1146 |

Then, $V = I/R = \$15,500/.1146 = \$135,253$
The present worth of the property is $135,253.
The amount of the mortgage is $100,000.
The difference or *residual* of $35,253 is the present worth of the equity investment position.
  c. Since the amount of equity investment required is $25,000 and its present worth is $35,253, the investor should proceed.
3. In this example:

NOI = $18,500
First Mortgage = 70% of investment with .1007 constant
Equity Yield on 24.32% of investment = .10
Yield on incremental equity of 5.68% of investment = .16
Income projection period = 25 years
Mortgage maturity = 25 years
Capital loss forecast = 25%
Sinking Fund Factor for 25 years at 10% = .0102 (page 116, column 3)
Sinking Fund Factor for 25 years at 16% = .0040 (page 152, column 3)

The total proposed investment is $185,000, of which $35,000 is the anticipated cost of renovation.
The mortgage-equity Overall Rate with credit for equity build-up and allowance for capital recovery then becomes:

| | |
|---|---|
| Mortgage: | .7000 × .1007 = .0705 |
| Equity A: | .2432 × .1000 = .0243 |
| Equity B: | .0568 × .1600 = .0091 |
| Weighted Average | .1039 |

| | | |
|---|---|---|
| *Less* Credit for Equity Build-Up: | | |
| Equity A: | .8108 × .70 × .0102 = .0058 | |
| Equity B: | .1892 × .70 × .0040 = .0005 | |
| | | −.0063 |
| Basic Rate | | .0976 |

*Plus* Allowance for Capital Recovery:
Equity A:           .8108 × .25 × .0102 = .0021
Equity B:           .1892 × .25 × .0040 = .0002
                                              +.0023
Overall Rate                                   .0999

Then,
$V = I/R$.
$V = \$18,500/.0999 = \$185,185$.

Yes, the owner-investor would proceed. The estimated present worth of the property after renovation (\$185,185) is greater than the estimated total investment required (\$185,000).

## Chapter 19

1. a. The level annuity capitalization rate for 24 years at 8.75% is 0.100989 (page 96, column 6).
The present worth of the net rental income is therefore:

$$\$32,000/.100989 = \$316,866$$

b. The Present Worth of One factor for 24 years with annual discounting at 8.75% is 0.133567 (page 96, column 4).
The present worth of the reversion is therefore:

$$\$275,000 × .133567 = \$36,731$$

c. The present worth of the leased fee is the *sum* of the present worth of the net rental income stream *plus* the present worth of the reversion:

| | |
|---|---|
| Present Worth of Income Stream | \$316,866 |
| Present Worth of Reversion | 36,731 |
| Present Worth of Leased Fee | \$353,597 |
| | (\$354,000) |

2. a. Market Value is the sum of the present worth of the income stream based on net Market Rental, plus the present worth of the reversion, both capitalized at the market rate of discount.
The level annuity capitalization rate for 24 years at 9.5% is 0.107134 (page 108, column 6).
The Present Worth of One factor for 24 years with annual discounting at 9.5% is 0.113256 (page 108, column 4).
The Market Value of the leased property is estimated as:

Present Worth of Income Stream:
| | |
|---|---|
| $36,000/.107134) | $336,028 |
| Present Worth of Reversion: | |
| $275,000 × .113256) | 31,145 |
| Indicated Market Value of Property | $367,173 |
| | ($367,000) |

b. The present worth of the leasehold is the *difference* between the Market Value of the property and the present worth of the leased fee:

| | |
|---|---|
| Market Value | $367,000 |
| Present Worth of Leased Fee | − 354,000 |
| Present Worth of Leasehold | $ 13,000 |

By *calculation*, the present worth of the leasehold is $13,576 ($367,173 − $353,597).

c. The rental advantage enjoyed by the leaseholder is $4,000 per year ($36,000 − $32,000) for 24 years.
The indicated capitalization rate on the leasehold is:

$$\$4,000/\$13,576 = 0.294638$$

Inspection of Installment to Amortize One factors (shown as column 6 in Ellwood) for 24 years reveals the following:

29% factor (page 165): 0.290644
30% factor (page 166): 0.300554

The indicated rate of discount applicable to the leasehold is therefore approximately 29.4%
If $13,000 were used as the present worth of the leasehold, the capitalization rate would be $4,000/$13,000 = 0.307692. This indicates a rate of discount of approximately 30.6% (page 166, column 6).

3. a. The level annuity capitalization factors at 11.5% (page 140, column 5) applicable in this problem are:

23 years: 7.984471
13 years: 6.583482 (difference 1.400989)
 3 years: 2.422619 (difference 4.160963)

The *deferred factor* for years 4-13 is 4.160863, the difference between the 13-year factor and the 3-year factor.
The *deferred factor* for years 14-23 is 1.400989, the difference between the 23-year factor and the 13-year factor.
The present worth of the income stream then becomes:

| Year | Annual Net Rental | | Factor | Present Worth |
|---|---|---|---|---|
| 1-3 | $7,500 | X | 2.422619 | $18,170 |
| 4-13 | $7,000 | X | 4.160863 | $29,126 |
| 14-23 | $6,000 | X | 1.400989 | $ 8,406 |
| Total Present Worth | | | | $55,702 |

b. If annual rentals are payable in advance, the pertinent capitalization factors (page 140, column 5) become:

22 years: 7.902685
12 years: 6.340583 (difference 1.562102)
 2 years: 1.701221 (difference 4.639362)

The capitalization factor for the first 3 years is 1.000000 *plus* 1.701221, or 2.701221.
The *deferred factor* for years 4-13 is then 4.639362.
The *deferred factor* for years 14-23 is then 1.562102.

The present worth of the income stream with payments in advance is:

| Years | Annual Net Rental | | Factor | | Present Worth |
|---|---|---|---|---|---|
| 1-3 | $7,500 | X | 2.701221 | = | $20,259 |
| 4-13 | $7,000 | X | 4.639362 | = | $32,476 |
| 14-23 | $6,000 | X | 1.562102 | = | $ 9,373 |
| Total Present Worth | | | | | $62,108 |

4. a. Gross rental income is 12,000 X $1.50 = $18,000 per year. NOI forecasts for the 5-year term are:

| Year | Gross Rental | | Operating Expenses | | NOI |
|---|---|---|---|---|---|
| 1 | $18,000 | — | $4,500 | = | $13,500 |
| 2 | $18,000 | — | $4,950 | = | $13,050 |
| 3 | $18,000 | — | $5,445 | = | $12,555 |
| 4 | $18,000 | — | $5,990 | = | $12,010 |
| 5 | $18,000 | — | $6,589 | = | $11,411 |

b. Each annual NOI must be discounted by the appropriate 12% Present Worth of One factor (page 148, column 4) to derive its present worth. The sum of these individual present worth figures is the estimated present worth of the 5-year income stream:

| Year | NOI | | Present Worth of One Factor | | Present Worth |
|---|---|---|---|---|---|
| 1 | $13,500 | X | 0.892857 | = | $12,054 |
| 2 | $13,050 | X | 0.797194 | = | $10,403 |
| 3 | $12,555 | X | 0.711780 | = | $ 8,936 |
| 4 | $12,010 | X | 0.635518 | = | $ 7,633 |
| 5 | $11,411 | X | 0.567427 | = | $ 6,475 |

Total Present Worth of Income Stream $45,501

c. The lessee's annual rental advantage is 12,000 X $0.10 = $1,200.
The annual capitalization factor for 5 years at 25% is 2.689280 (page 161, column 5).
The present worth of the leasehold is:

$$\$1,200 \times 2.689280 = \$3,227$$

5. a. The base rental income stream is $8,000 per year net, payable in advance. The annual capitalization factor for 12 years at 10% (page 116, column 5) with payments in advance is 1.000000 + 6.495061 = 7.495061.
"Overage" percentage rentals are .03 X $50,000 = $1,500 annually.
The annual capitalization factor for 12 years at 14% with end-of-year payments is 5.660291 (page 150, column 5).
The reversion is most probably discounted to a present worth figure at the base-rental discount rate. The Present Worth of One factor for 12 years with annual discounting at 10% is 0.318631 (page 116, column 4).
The present worth of the leased fee is estimated as:

| | |
|---|---|
| Present Worth of Base Rental Income Stream: ($8,000 X 7.495061) | $59,960 |
| Present Worth of "Overage" Income Stream: ($1,500 X 5.660291) | 8,490 |
| Present Worth of Reversion: ($75,000 X .318631) | 23,897 |
| Present Worth of Leased Fee | $92,347 |
| | ($92,500) |

6. a. The present worth of the mortgagee's investment position is the *sum* of the present worth of the mortgage amortization stream *plus* the present worth of the mortgagee's participation position.

Since the mortgage loan is current, its principal amount is taken as its present worth to the mortgagee: $50,000.

The mortgagee's participation in gross income is .04 × $12,500 = $500 per year.

The annual capitalization factor for 20 years at 10% is 8.513564 (page 116, column 5).

The mortgagee's participation interest in the forecast reversion is .25 × $60,000 = $15,000.

The Present Worth of One factor for 20 years with annual discounting at 10% is 0.148644 (page 116, column 4).

The present worth of the mortgagee's investment position is:

| | |
|---|---|
| Mortgage Principal | $50,000 |
| Present Worth of Gross Income Participation ($500 × 8.513564) | 4,257 |
| Present Worth of Participation in Reversion ($15,000 × .148644) | 2,230 |
| Present Worth of Mortgagee's Investment Position | $56,487 |

b. The NOI receivable by the mortgagor is forecast to be:

| | |
|---|---|
| Gross Income | $12,500 |
| *Less* 4% Participation | − 500 |
| Gross Receipts | $12,000 |
| *Less* Operating Expenses (.40 × $12,500) | − 5,000 |
| NOI to Mortgagor | $ 7,000 |

Annual debt service is $50,000 times the mortgage constant of 0.107964 (12 × 0.008997: page 97, column 6). Cash Throw-Off to Equity is:

| | |
|---|---|
| NOI to Mortgagor | $7,000.00 |
| *Less* Annual Debt Service | − 5,398.20 |
| Cash Throw-Off | $1,601.80 |

The annual capitalization factor for 20 years at 10.5% is 8.230909 (page 124, column 5).

The mortgagor's share of the forecast amount of the reversion is $45,000 (.75 × $60,000).

The Present Worth of One factor for 20 years with annual discounting at 10.5% is 0.135755 (page 124, column 4).

The present worth of the mortgagor's investment position is estimated as:

Present Worth of Cash Flow:
($1,601.80 × 8.230909)     $13,184
Present Worth of Reversionary Interest:
($45,000 × 0.135755)     6,109
Present Worth of Mortgagor's
Investment Position     $19,293

c. The Investment Value of the property is the *sum* of the present worth of the mortgagor's investment position *plus* the present worth of the mortgagor's investment position:

| | |
|---|---|
| Present Worth of Mortgagee's Position | $56,487 |
| Present Worth of Mortgagor's Position | 19,293 |
| Indicated Investment Value of Property | $75,780 |
| | ($76,000) |

# About the Author

William N. Kinnard, Jr. is currently Professor of Finance and Real Estate in the School of Business Administration, the University of Connecticut. He formerly served as Associate Dean, Head of the Finance Department and Director of the Center for Real Estate and Urban Economic Studies at Connecticut.

In addition to his academic responsibilities, Dr. Kinnard has been active in the field of real estate valuation and counseling for nearly 20 years. He was Director of Urban Redevelopment for the City of Middletown, Connecticut for two years, and has been a consultant in urban renewal and economic development for many communities throughout the United States. He is a member of several professional real estate organizations, and holds the following professional designations: SRPA (Society of Real Estate Appraisers); MAI (American Institute of Real Estate Appraisers); ASA (American Society of Appraisers); CRE (American Society of Real Estate Counselors).

Dr. Kinnard is also a member of Lambda Alpha, the honorary real estate fraternity, and is a past president of the American Real Estate and Urban Economics Association. He has been educational consultant to the Society of Real Estate Appraisers, the Society of Industrial Realtors, the National Institute of Real Estate Brokers, and the American Right of Way Association. He has lectured internationally on appraisal and urban economics topics, and has been a visiting professor at the University of Florida, UCLA, and Brown University.

In addition to scores of articles on valuation and related real estate topics, his publication activity has included service as an advisory editor to both the *Encyclopedia Americana* and the *American Heritage Dictionary of the English Language*. Among his several books are: *A Guide to Appraising Apartments* (Society of Real Estate Appraisers, 1966); *Industrial Real Estate* (Society of Industrial Realtors, 1967); *An Introduction to Appraising Real Property* (Society of Real Estate Appraisers, 1968); *Effective Business Relocation*, with S.D. Messner (D.C. Heath, 1970).

The 1967 first edition of *Industrial Real Estate* received the Arthur A. May Award of the American Institute of Real Estate Appraisers. The revised 1971 second edition of this book was prepared in collaboration with Dr. Stephen D. Messner.

# Index

# Index